Emerging Theologies
from the Global South

EDITORIAL ADVISORY BOARD

Stephen B. Bevans *(Catholic Theological Union)*
Alexander Chow *(University of Edinburgh)*
Rosalee Velloso Ewell *(United Bible Societies, UK)*
Oscar García-Johnson *(Fuller Theological Seminary)*
Emmanuel Katongole *(University of Notre Dame)*
Jenny Te Paa-Daniel *(University of Otago)*
Fernando F. Segovia *(Vanderbilt University)*
Katalina Tahaafe-Williams *(Uniting Church, Australia)*

Senior Editorial Consultant

Joshua Erb

Emerging Theologies
from the Global South

Edited by
MITRI RAHEB & MARK A. LAMPORT

Introduction by Theo Sundermeier

Afterword by Chloë Starr

CASCADE *Books* • Eugene, Oregon

EMERGING THEOLOGIES FROM THE GLOBAL SOUTH

Copyright © 2023 Wipf and Stock Publishers. All rights reserved. Except for brief quotations in critical publications or reviews, no part of this book may be reproduced in any manner without prior written permission from the publisher. Write: Permissions, Wipf and Stock Publishers, 199 W. 8th Ave., Suite 3, Eugene, OR 97401.

Cascade Books
An Imprint of Wipf and Stock Publishers
199 W. 8th Ave., Suite 3
Eugene, OR 97401

www.wipfandstock.com

PAPERBACK ISBN: 978-1-6667-1183-7
HARDCOVER ISBN: 978-1-6667-1184-4
EBOOK ISBN: 978-1-6667-1185-1

Cataloguing-in-Publication data:

Names: Raheb, Mitri, editor. | Lamport, Mark A., editor. | Sundermeier, Theo, foreword. | Starr, Chloë, afterword.

Title: Emerging theologies from the global south / edited by Mitri Raheb and Mark A. Lamport; foreword by Theo Sundermeier; afterword by Chloë Starr.

Description: Eugene, OR: Cascade Books, 2023 | Includes bibliographical references and index.

Identifiers: ISBN 978-1-6667-1183-7 (paperback) | ISBN 978-1-6667-1184-4 (hardcover) | ISBN 978-1-6667-1185-1 (ebook)

Subjects: LCSH: Theology. | Globalization—Religious aspects—Christianity

Classification: BR118 E4 2023 (paperback) | BR118 (ebook)

03/26/23

For *Mitri*—To the theological pioneers in the Global South; to Archbishop Desmond Tutu, his life, work and leadership in the Global South; and to all those who work hard to keep the gospel relevant for their communities

For *Mark*—To eight of my favorite people—Lennox, Lydia, Hawkins, Wyatt, Makenna, Addison, Alayna, and Gweneth

Contents

About the Editors and Editorial Advisory Board   xi
Acknowledgments   xiii
Preface   xv

Introduction: The Emergence of Contextual Theology in the Global South   1
   THEO SUNDERMEIER

SECTION 1 | ORIENTATION ESSAYS

Chapter 1: The Interpretative Challenge for Grace and Peace in the Global South: A Hermeneutical Perspective   7
   MITRI RAHEB AND MARK A. LAMPORT

Chapter 2: Theologizing from the Global South: A Critical Reflection   19
   FERNANDO F. SEGOVIA

SECTION 2 | MAJOR PARADIGMATIC THEMES FROM EMERGING THEOLOGIES

Chapter 3: The Postcolonial/Decolonial Option in Theology   37
   OSCAR GARCÍA-JOHNSON

Chapter 4: Intercultural Theology   52
   VOLKER KÜSTER

Chapter 5: Migration Theology   66
   GEMMA TULUD CRUZ

Chapter 6: Pentecostal Theo-Praxis   79
   CONNIE AU

Chapter 7: Diaspora Mission Theology   93
   HARVEY C. KWIYANI

Contents

SECTION 3 | EMERGING THEOLOGIES FROM LATIN AMERICA

Chapter 8: Catholic Liberation Theology　　　　　　　　　　　　　　　111
ANA MARÍA BIDEGAIN

Chapter 9: Protestant Liberation Theologies　　　　　　　　　　　　　123
RAIMUNDO C. BARRETO JR.

Chapter 10: Latina Feminist Theology　　　　　　　　　　　　　　　　136
MICHELLE A. GONZALEZ

Chapter 11: Popular Bible Reading and Popular Theology: An Experience from Northeast Brazil　　　　　　　　　　　　　　　　149
ODJA BARROS

Chapter 12: Teología India: A Context Theology　　　　　　　　　　　162
SYLVIA MARCOS

SECTION 4 | EMERGING THEOLOGIES FROM ASIA

Chapter 13: Indian Theologies　　　　　　　　　　　　　　　　　　　177
MUTHURAJ SWAMY

Chapter 14: Filipino Theology　　　　　　　　　　　　　　　　　　　193
ELEAZAR S. FERNANDEZ

Chapter 15: Chinese Theologies　　　　　　　　　　　　　　　　　　205
ALEXANDER CHOW

Chapter 16: Sri Lankan Theology　　　　　　　　　　　　　　　　　　217
JUDE LAL FERNANDO

Chapter 17: Korean Theologies　　　　　　　　　　　　　　　　　　　231
SEBASTIAN KIM

Chapter 18: Palestinian Contextual Theology　　　　　　　　　　　　246
PETER LODBERG

Chapter 19: Middle Eastern Theologies　　　　　　　　　　　　　　　259
VIOLA RAHEB

SECTION 5 | EMERGING THEOLOGIES FROM AFRICA

Chapter 20: Theological Ethics in a Time of Crisis　　　　　　　　　　273
AGBONKHIANMEGHE E. OROBATOR

Chapter 21: An Egyptian Theology　　　　　　　　　　　　　　　　　287
SAFWAT MARZOUK

Chapter 22: African Liberation Theology　　　　　　　　　　　　　　302
DAVID TONGHOU NGONG

Chapter 23: African Women's Theologies 314
LÉOCADIE LUSHOMBO

SECTION 6 | EMERGING THEOLOGIES FROM OCEANIA

Chapter 24: Coconut Theology 331
SEFOROSA CARROLL

Chapter 25: Oceania Theology 344
RANDALL PRIOR

Chapter 26: Māori Theology 357
WAYNE TEKAAWA

Chapter 27: Moana Theology 370
TE AROHA ROUNTREE

Chapter 28: Australia's First Nations Theology 384
ANNE PATTEL-GRAY

SECTION 7 | EMERGING THEOLOGIES FROM DIASPORIC AND INDIGENOUS VOICES

Chapter 29: North American Indigenous Theology 397
CARMEN LANSDOWNE

Chapter 30: African American Theology 411
FREDERICK L. WARE

Chapter 31: Latinx Theologies 425
RUDOLPH REYES II

Chapter 32: Asian American Theologies 436
PETER C. PHAN

SECTION 8 | REFLECTIVE ESSAYS FROM THE GLOBAL SOUTH: STORIES OF STRUGGLE, PERSPECTIVE, AND THE FUTURE

Chapter 33: Latin American Reflective Essay 453
LUIS N. RIVERA-PAGÁN

Chapter 34: Asian Reflective Essay: Pathways for Building God's Household in Asia 464
JOSE MARIO C. FRANCISCO

Chapter 35: African Reflective Essay: Theology as Critical Discourse 475
ELIAS KIFONBONGMBA

Chapter 36: Oceania Reflective Essay: Theology of Prophetic Anger 486
KATALINA TAHAAFE-WILLIAMS

Contents

Chapter 37: Diasporic Reflective Essay: A Theological Reflection on Diaspora
   Consciousness   495
   KEUN-JOO CHRISTINE PAE

Afterword   505
   CHLOË STARR

About the Contributors   511

Index of Names and Subjects   517

About the Editors and Editorial Advisory Board

EDITORS

MITRI RAHEB (Dr. theol., Philipps-Universität, Marburg, Germany) is the founder and president of Dar al-Kalima University College in Bethlehem, Palestine. The most widely published Palestinian theologian to date, he is the author or editor of twenty-four books that deal with modern Middle Eastern church history, contextual theology, and the Israeli-Palestinian conflict, including *Surviving Jewel: An Enduring Story of Christianity in the Middle East* (2022); *Christianity in the Middle East: Historical Sketches and Contemporary Practices* (2020); *Faith in the Face of Empire: The Bible through Palestinian Eyes* (2014); and *The Invention of History: A Century of Interplay between Theology and Politics in Palestine* (2011).

MARK A. LAMPORT (PhD, Michigan State) has been a professor for thirty-five years at universities in the United States and Europe. He is editor of *Surviving Jewel: An Enduring Story of Christianity in the Middle East* (2022); *Theological Foundations of Worship* (2021); *Christianity in the Middle East: Historical Sketches and Contemporary Practices* (2020); *Hymns and Hymnody: Historical and Theological Introductions* (2019); *Encyclopedia of Christianity in the Global South* (2018); *Encyclopedia of Martin Luther and the Reformation* (2017); *Encyclopedia of Christianity in the United States* (2016); and *Encyclopedia of Christian Education* (2015). He works from Grand Rapids and Fort Myers.

EDITORIAL ADVISORY BOARD

STEPHEN BEVANS (PhD, University of Notre Dame) is a priest in the Roman Catholic missionary congregation of the Society of the Divine Word and Professor of Mission and Culture, emeritus at Catholic Theological Union, Chicago. Bevans is author of

Essays in Contextual Theology (2016) and, with Clemens Sedmak, *Does God Love the Coronavirus?* (2021). He is perhaps most known for his *Models of Contextual Theology* (2002).

Alexander Chow (PhD, University of Birmingham) is senior lecturer in theology and world Christianity in the School of Divinity, University of Edinburgh, and is co-director of the Centre for the Study of World Christianity. His recent books include *Chinese Public Theology* (2018) and *Ecclesial Diversity in Chinese Christianity* (2021).

C. Rosalee Velloso Ewell (PhD, Duke University) is a Brazilian theologian and serves as principal of Redcliffe College in the United Kingdom. She is the New Testament editor of the Comentário Bíblico Contemporáneo and has written and edited various books and articles.

Oscar García-Johnson (PhD, Fuller Theological Seminary) is associate professor of theology and Latinx studies and author of *Spirit Outside the Gate: Decolonial Pneumatologies of the American Global South* (2019) and co-author of *Theology without Borders: Introduction to Global Conversations* (2015).

Emmanuel Katongole (PhD, Katholic University, Leuven, Belgium) is professor of theology and international peace studies, University of Notre Dame. His recent publications include *Who Are My People? Love, Violence and Christianity in Sub-Saharan Africa* (2022) and *Born from Lament: The Theology and Politics of Hope in Africa* (2017).

Jenny Te Paa Daniel (PhD, Graduate Theological Union) is esteemed indigenous professor at the National Centre for Peace and Conflict Studies, Otago University, New Zealand, and co-chair of the National Centre for Religious Diversity. Recent publications include "EsseQuamVideri: To Be and Not to Seem" in *Vulnerability and Resilience: Body and Liberating Theologies* (2020).

Fernando F. Segovia (PhD, University of Notre Dame) is professor of New Testament and early Christianity at Vanderbilt University. His research encompasses early Christian origins, theological studies, and cultural studies. He is author of *Decolonizing Biblical Studies: A View from the Margins* (2000) and co-editor of *Latino/a Biblical Hermeneutics: Problematics, Objectives, Strategies* (2014).

Katalina Tahaafe-Williams (PhD, University of Birmingham, UK) is an Oceanian missiologist and contextual theologian currently serving the Uniting Church in the Northern Territory of Australia. Her recent publications include *The Edinburgh Companion to Global Christianity—Oceania* (2021).

Acknowledgments

WHAT SEEMED OBVIOUS TO us on the many publishers' catalog listings was a dearth of recognized theological expression from scholars residing in the Global South. After releasing our two-volume, 1,100-page *Encyclopedia of Christianity in the Global South* (2018) it dawned on us that more than merely historical recounting and contemporary practices seemed necessary in telling the story of the church in the Global South. As we encountered the contributions of those 250 authors representing several dozen countries, primarily from the Global South, that the operating theological assumptions we found emerging from the pieces should be explored more deeply.

So, we explored our initial inklings for this project with a range of scholars. Academicians such as Robert Gallagher, Chloë Starr, Brian Stanley, Emma Wild-Wood, and Adriaan van Klinken offered depth. Their responses were both encouraging and challenging. The task would be to dig around the fringes of numerous global regions to identify and narrow down the most critical themes, movements, and theological expressions. Then, to secure commitments from the most articulate voices representing these voices.

The editorial advisory board we recruited, a stellar group of scholars and practitioners, produced extensive and creative ideas for content and prospective authors. A huge thanks to the following for embracing and endorsing our book concept: Stephen B. Bevans (Catholic Theological Union, Chicago), Alexander Chow (University of Edinburgh), Rosalee Velloso Ewell (United Bible Societies, UK), Oscar García-Johnson (Fuller Theological Seminary, California), Emmanuel Katongole (University of Notre Dame), Jenny Te Paa-Daniel (University of Otago, New Zealand), Fernando F. Segovia (Vanderbilt University, Nashville), and Katalina Tahaafe-Williams (Australia). The sections, which organize the content, and chapters which broaden these eight major themes, represent our best attempts at naming theologies emerging from the Global South. Perhaps soon an additional set of chapter-themes will need to be amended.

The value of the book has been enhanced, in our view, by an expert who has written an insightful afterword—Chloë Starr (Yale Divinity School, Yale University, Connecticut).

Acknowledgments

We are further grateful to Michael Thomson, acquisitions and development editor at Wipf and Stock/Cascade Books, for seeing our vision and shepherding this project through the editorial process. Having worked with Michael on other projects, his keen global insights and breadth of knowledge in the theological world made sense for us to pitch this to him. Your support, Michael, is inspiring. Chris Spinks, the internal editor, likewise was discerning and accommodating as was the rest of the Cascade production team.

Finally, we are beholden to Philip Bustrum and Mel Wilhoit for their keen attention to the indexing, and Joshua Erb, senior editorial consultant, for superb work in reading and herding all our content into shape for publication. Thanks to all!

Preface

THIS IS A BOOK *about* Christian theology, but not confessional in nature. That is, this volume does not promote a particular Christian viewpoint; nevertheless, many of the contributors claim Christianity as their own. These forty chapter-authors are largely from the Global South, although a number of them have studied theology in the Global North. *And maybe that's why.* Perhaps crossing national boundaries freed them up to think how Western thinking did not quite fit the cultural situations from which they had come. Voyaging beyond one's experience is a proven educational experience.

They are Roman Catholic, Anglican, and various strands of Protestant and Pentecostal; they are brown, black, and white; as a group, they speak dozens of languages and scatter across the socio-economic spectrum. The contributors write as scholars who are experts in sociology, history, theology, and anthropology; they write as pragmatists and reforming leaders; they also write as those who have become dissatisfied with the theological *status quo*, long dominated by Western theologians, yet love the church and wish to stir change, consider contextualization, and be recognized as peers in the academy and church.

We suspect that professors and students who encounter this book as a companion for theological courses in colleges and universities, or those interested laypersons who take on the contents of this volume, will also be a diverse group.

And while these authors may have their own religious commitments, it would ultimately be our desire for readers to encounter opinions and religious beliefs with which they do not agree. This, we argue, is the happy consequence of academic engagement in a diverse society and for a faith which is grace-filled and mission-focused. Not for a moment are we arguing that equally valid truth exists in all ideologies—we will save that discussion for another venue—however critique and reflection and even emotion is central to an honest reevaluation of what a person believes, how one has come to understand such positions, and an assessment if there are new bits to supplement one's most closely held Christian commitments.

Preface

MISSION AND ORGANIZATION

Emerging Theologies from the Global South is a one-volume examination of providing a comprehensive study of the rise of theologies from the Global South on five continents (Asia, Africa, Latin America, the Pacific, in addition to subaltern voices from North America). This handbook offers a first of its kind—a comprehensive study of new theological voices and approaches that has emerged with an emphasis in recent decades in response to contextual and global challenges. Take heed, newness can evoke defensiveness and postures of self-preservation. This provocative-leaning book also fosters a profound dialogue among scholars, leaders of Christian theological schools and ministry organizations, as well as students and laypersons preparing for ministry in a postmodern environment.

While Christianity has been a sustaining force and dominant story line of the historical foundations of Christianity worldwide, obvious social, political, and scientific inroads have lessened its influence and altered the issues considered. *ETGS* will explore the strengths and weaknesses of the Christian faith and traditions as well as its rich and textured history with a discernable eye toward how the message, strategies, and initiatives of Christianity has adapted to contemporary life.

The book is organized into eight major sections—*orientation essays* (to frame the issues at stake); a synthesis of *major paradigmatic themes* which lie at the heart of emerging theologies; a sampling of emerging theologies from world regions—*Latin America and the Caribbean, Asia, Africa, and Oceania*; theological voices from *diaspora and indigenous* groups; and finally, essays from those who are reflected on *stories of struggle, perspective, and the future* of theology in the Global South. This volume, then, is intended to engender gracious dialogue between the most visible themes in Christianity with fresh theological voices in culture today.

BUT BEFORE LAUNCHING INTO THESE EMERGING THEOLOGIES . . .

This book is very timely and expansive. It invites the reader to embark on a journey to the Global South, to visit five different continents, to explore diverse contexts, and to map some of the most interesting Christian movements. Through this reference book, readers can meet and be inspired by some of the most brilliant theologians and scholars across the Global South. These contributors represent different schools of thought and come from diverse denominational backgrounds, yet they all share a common goal to develop a theology that is relevant to their people. They struggle to give meaning to a context shaped by suffering, exploitation, and resilience, and to maintain the notion of holistic liberation.

Readers beware—in this multivoiced volume, authors present and propose more than a few unconventional claims on Christianity and exercise variant slants in the name of hermeneutics. One must discern which of these theologies speak with orthodoxy to propel the mission of God, and which, if any, may be highjacked as cultural accommodation and slipshod interpretative nuance.

Two truths remain stalwart in the story of the church: *first,* the church survives by the mercy of God, not because of the wisdom, purity, or consistent faithfulness of Christians; and *second,* authentic Christian faith has taken many shapes and can be expected to assume still other shapes in the future. Creative orthodoxy. Maintain and adapt!

INTRODUCTION

The Emergence of Contextual Theology in the Global South

THEO SUNDERMEIER

"You are the salt of the earth; you are the light of the world" (Matt 5:13, 14). With these sayings, Jesus founded the church and, at the same time, defined its nature and its mission in the world. The church is characterized in the *first* declaration, by a simple, unspectacular, diaconal way of life. This means love of the neighbor, standing by the other, and not leaving them alone. And where there is hardship, the church is naturally present with its assistance.

The *second* saying of Jesus makes mission the essential characteristic. Diaconal engagement is not limited to the narrow context; it knows no ethnic, social, or political boundaries. The same applies to the gospel, which seeks to be proclaimed worldwide.

The church is characterized by passing on the gospel and practicing diakonia. How do they become reality? Love of the neighbor, compassion, has always found its way—at the local level and in distant countries, among friends and enemies, in practical, charitable ministry and in diaconal institutions. That has never been in dispute. But how does proclaiming the gospel come about?

There are two replies to this. Matt 28:18–20 says: The gospel must be passed on worldwide in the power of the risen Christ. The Pentecostal event (Acts 2:1–13) goes further and specifies that everyone is meant to hear the gospel in *their own language*. Aramaic, Greek, or Latin are not the "right" languages of proclamation and should not be the actual and final language of the liturgical form in which it is proclaimed. Language is the framework of our lives. The gospel seeks to enter people's hearts in their own language and "fill them with the spirit." But that also means that everyone hears the gospel differently. The content changes with the language. The message sounds different in every language, strikes new chords with the hearers, brings out the new undertones and creates new spaces of understanding. For a long time that was not understood. Instead—amongst other things due to the Latin translation, the Vulgate—the language of Rome won the day in theology and liturgy. It set the tone worldwide, well into the modern age. Theology in Catholic seminaries in Africa was taught in Latin as late as the twentieth century.

If we want to retrace the long path of "intercultural theology" we can distinguish three stages: indigenous theology/indigenization, inculturation, and contextual theology. Luther's translation of the Bible opened doors, so that the Bible was soon translated into different languages in Europe. Protestant missions in the nineteenth century continued on this path. The missionaries learned the local languages and, in some cases, saved them from extinction by transforming them into written languages. Building schools was the necessary consequence, for everyone was meant to be able to read the Bible themselves. An unintended yet largely accepted outcome was that building schools also paved the way for the dissemination of colonial languages. Without the concept of "indigenization" becoming the theme running through proclamation, this still happened, since the gospel spread more through indigenous preachers than through the missionaries. It was only following the World Mission Conference of Edinburgh in 1910 that this subliminal concept began to underlie missionary proclamation, as a late fulfilment of the first Pentecostal event.

Let me illustrate, with two examples, how translation can also change the content of the biblical text. My students at the Lutheran Theological Seminary in Namibia insisted that Leah had blue eyes. It was in the Bible, they said. The Finnish missionaries, it quickly became clear, had wanted to find the right way of saying that Leah (Gen 29:17) was not good-looking. Blue eyes in the Ovambo culture were regarded as ugly.

It did not surprise me to hear from the Herero that Abraham wanted to sacrifice his son Isaac on the "ancestral fire" (Gen 22). As there was no term for altar in Otjiherero, the early missionaries introduced the new concept of "altari." After 1910, the World Mission Conference inspired a progressive missionary to introduce the indigenous term "okuruuo," the name for the traditional place where they called on the ancestors and sacrificed to them. The early missionaries found the name inappropriate and rejected it as "heathen."

The Second Vatican Council attached greater value to the concept of dialogue for the missionary encounter with other religions and hence also to the significance of civilizations. Consequently, the notion of "inculturation" (used in *Catechesi tradendae* in 1979 and in *Redemptoris missio* in 1990) gave remarkable impetus to independent creativity in local churches the world over. Vatican II sparked a flurry of conferences and publications on the theologies of what was still called the Third World. Liturgies were rewritten and new forms of theological language developed, particularly in Latin

America. The mission encyclical, however, then erected barriers against the upcoming diversity. Inculturation was now regarded as a sensitive area that could only be fostered in consensus with the "communion of the whole church."

In Protestant mission theology the dominant concept is "contextual theology." The church does not inculturate—instead, the gospel looks for people in their social relations and lifeworlds, seeking to take root and to flourish credibly in this environment. It addresses sociological interpretations seriously and has no fear of getting close to Marxist analyses. Rather, it takes up the social dialogue so that the theological statements are relevant and speak to people in their various situations.

A host of contextual theologies have been conceptualized. While the concept of culture prevailing in inculturation theology is too narrow (cultures are not closed systems but have always existed in exchange with other cultures when it comes to receiving and rejecting strangers) and it manifests a latent ethnocentrism, contextual theology runs the risk of becoming too narrowly focused and of no longer doing justice to the present global situation. This is not only characterized by international capital flows but also through our being connected worldwide through television and internet access for everyone. Hence the most remote area of the world becomes our own immediate neighborhood. Nor may we overlook the surges of refugee movement, or the slums in the megacities.

Intercultural theology, by contrast, recognizes the plurality of theologies, since the gospel seeks to speak to people in other languages, but also links them up. It promotes exchange and supports the freedom to consider cultures from both an internal and an external perspective. Its umbilical cord is threefold: the word of God, our own words, and those of the outsider. It practices changing perspective, while also being open to—and encouraging—new ways of interpreting the biblical words. At the same time, intercultural theology weaves diversity without having to reach a consensus at all costs, albeit striving for one. It does not say "anything goes," however, since it looks for orientation to a biblically founded ethic. As has occasionally been remarked, intercultural theology develops an *intercultural hospitality*. Which, in turn, is sustained by a hermeneutic of trust.

SECTION 1

Orientation Essays

CHAPTER 1

The Interpretative Challenge for Grace and Peace in the Global South

A Hermeneutical Perspective

MITRI RAHEB AND MARK A. LAMPORT

Christianity is a West Asian phenomenon. It was in Palestine that Jesus lived and was crucified; it was in Jerusalem that the church was born; and it was in Asia Minor where the followers of Jesus were called Christians. From there, Christianity spread north and east and south to the Horn of Africa. It was along the Silk Road that West Asian Christians propagated their faith in peaceful manner, establishing churches in China as early as the first quarter of the seventh century. In that sense, Christianity crossed North Africa and reached East Asia before it crossed to northern Europe. And yet, Christianity has been perceived as a Western or European phenomenon. This is mainly due to four factors: the Constantinian conversion and the adaptation of Christianity as the religion of the Roman Empire; the rise of Islam in West Asia and North Africa which resulted in pushing the Christian empire northwards; the expansion of Europe westwards to the Americas; and the nineteenth-to-twentieth-century European and North American world missions that spread a Western blend of Christianity into Central and Southern Africa, East and South Asia, and Oceania.

While Christianity was formerly perceived as a Caucasian Euro-American phenomenon, the center of gravity has shifted geographically southwards. It is, therefore, imperative to look south to where Christianity started and where it is spreading. The term Global South was introduced to replace two earlier terms: "Third World" and "developing countries." At the end of the Cold War and the fall of the Iron Curtain, the term Third World was used to distinguish it from "First World" for Western countries and "Second World" for the countries of the obsolete Soviet Bloc. Meanwhile, as the center of global economic growth has shifted, the dichotomy of "developed" versus "developing" countries no longer proved helpful. The term *Global South* became the dominant term used in social sciences, humanities, and science in the twenty-first century. Global South is not so much a geographic reference, nor is it limited to geographical areas outside Europe and the US. Rather, the Global South is "everywhere, but always somewhere."[1] The Global South refers mainly to those parts of the world that suffered under the legacy of European colonialism, as well as "those parts of the world that have experienced the most political, social, and economic upheaval, and which have suffered the brunt of the greatest challenges facing the world under globalization."[2]

SHIFTING EPISTEMOLOGY AND CONTEXTUAL THEOLOGY OF THE CHURCH

A focus on the Global South is imperative as it corresponds with the demographic shifts of the past few decades. In 1910, eighty percent of Christians were living in Europe (66 percent) and North America (15 percent), while the remaining Christians lived mainly in Latin America (12 percent) and Africa (4 percent). A century later in 2010, there has been a seismic shift in world Christianity with less than forty percent of Christians residing in Europe (26 percent) and North America (12 percent), and a growing number of Christians living in Latin America (24 percent), Africa (22 percent), and Asia (15 percent).[3] Very soon, Africa and Latin America will make up over half of the two billion Christians worldwide. The emergence of local and independent churches has accelerated this process. The face of Christianity is changing rapidly, and this trend is not confined to one denomination but is felt across the denominations.

The 2013 election of Pope Francis as the first pope from the Global South is symptomatic of this shift. Today, almost three-quarters of Catholics are found in Latin America, Africa, and Asia. The largest Lutheran church today is no longer located in the land of Luther, Germany, but in Ethiopia. The largest Anglican church today is in Nigeria rather than in England, and the largest Pentecostal churches are found in the Global South.

With this demographic shift southwards, new Christian theological voices inevitably emerged. Until the 1960s, Western theological tradition dominated. Seminaries and theological faculties in Rome, Cambridge, Heidelberg, Geneva, Amsterdam, and Princeton were the locations that set the tone. Classical neoscholastic Roman Catholic, German-oriented Lutheran, Anglo-American Reformed and Pentecostal theologies, and mainly conservative forms of these theologies were exported from the north to the south without taking into account the changing context and settings. The

---

1. Sparke, "Everywhere But Always Somewhere."
2. López, "Preface & Acknowledgments," v.
3. Johnson and Ross, *Atlas of Global Christianity*, 8.

major libraries, the available funding, and the high-caliber people were all located in the north. Seminaries in the south, if they existed at all, were ill-equipped and were intended to train local priests and ministers who would pastor the local congregations, and thus expand the influence of that denomination. In fact, many of the promising theologians from the Global South were sent north for their theological education and returned with a Western mindset and a striving to be a good copy of the theologians in the north. In many countries in the south, the big names to look and translate were Tillich, Moltmann, and Cragg, to name a few.

The impression was, and to some extent still is, that seminaries in the north develop real theology while theologians in the south develop exotic ideas called "contextual" or "liberation" theologies. For a long time, the north has been under the illusion that there is something like a contextless theology, or that this is an ideal to strive for. The north has long had a form of theological hubris, while in the south a theological inferiority complex prevailed. In other words, Western theology was part and parcel of European colonial thinking and practice. Over the course of the years, there has been strenuous debate about the role of Christian missions in the context of European colonialism. Christian missionaries were often portrayed as "cultural imperialists" or as "agents of the empire." It is not possible to conclude that the European Christian mission to the Global South was unambiguously a colonialist enterprise, nor is it possible clearly to distinguish between the two.

What the two had in common was a desire for the expansion of Western Christian and European influence beyond national or geographic borders. The case can surely be made that both phenomena, "mission" and "colonialism," stem from a common European expansionist culture that felt itself superior and powerful enough to bring others who were at a great distance under their military or religious control. Both groups were convinced that they had (European) "products" to offer, and that there were "markets" abroad awaiting fulfillment. Western theology was thereby offered to the churches in the south and cemented their dependency.

While diverse articulations of native theologies always existed in the south, it took a long time to establish indigenous, contextual, and independent theologies in the Global South. The classical Eurocentric theologies were seen as irrelevant to the fundamental questions facing the people in the global south. It was time for these people to drink from their own wells and to develop theologies rooted in their context, their culture, and their indigenous experiences. An important milestone in this development was, without doubt, the establishment of the Ecumenical Association of Third World Theologians (EATWOT) in 1976 in Dar es Salaam, Tanzania. New contextual theological trends emerged: water buffalo theology in Japan,[4] *minjung* theology in Korea, coconut theology in the Pacific Islands, and olive tree theology in Palestine, to name a few.

---

4. While the author of the book by that name was Japanese—Kosuke Koyama—he was writing in Thailand and for that context.

In the mid-1970s, and within the larger framework of biblical criticism, theological academia began to experience a fundamental change in orientation and direction. The emergence of postcolonialism in the seventies as a critical academic study of north-south relations and the ideological, socio-economic, and political consequences on the colonized, gave many Global South theologians the academic tools to critique Eurocentric theologies that were instrumental in holding churches in the south hostage to northern theology. These new models of contextual theologies proved that the subaltern could speak; that indigenous theologians could raise their voices to articulate the fate of their people who are still paying the price of colonial history and failed states, resulting in poverty, social injustice, and political upheaval. The 1970s also saw the rise of concepts such as ideological criticism and racial/ethnic criticism which left their imprint on theological developments in both north and south, and led to the rise of feminist theology, Black theology in South Africa, Dalit theology, Latinx theology, Palestinian theology, etc.

Interestingly, many of these theologies were developed by theologians from the Global South who studied abroad. Their experience in crossing borders and being immersed in a different environment resulted in them becoming more critically aware of their native context. Thus, many of the theologies from the Global South are very much connected to the biography of the theologians themselves. Their encounter with a new context was the trigger for questions of identity. In that sense, contextual theologies are often intercultural theologies. This trend was intensified by the pattern of intercontinental migration from the Global South to the north that weaved migration studies into theologies of migration. The result was that the north lost its monopoly over theology, or at least it diminished. Christianity today has become a multicentered, multifocal, multifaceted, and increasingly diverse religion globally. As evident in this book, there is no corner of the world today without a blend of contextual theology. This is true for the north itself which houses a good number of Global South theologians.

With this shift southwards, another major theological shift took place. The monoreligious Christian context of Europe meant that Eurocentric theologies were concerned with intra-Christian polemics (Catholic versus Protestant) and denominational identities (Lutheranism, Anglicanism, Calvinism, etc.). In contrast, theologies from the Global South tend to be ecumenical in nature and focus more on the suffering of local people due to the socio-economic and political context rather than on denominational doctrinal differences. Theologies from the Global South had to relate to the multireligious context in which they existed. Many Christian theologians live in contexts dominated by Islam such as in West Asia and North Africa, or with Hinduism like in South Asia, or Buddhism and Shintoism like in East Asia. In other contexts, such as Africa and Latin America, the influence of primal and indigenous forms of religion cannot be ignored by contextual theologies. This existing religious plurality influenced many of the theologies of the Global South to be interreligious in nature.

The Interpretative Challenge for Grace and Peace in the Global South

The domination of Western epistemology is slowly coming to an end. With a gradually secularizing north, a decline in the number of theological seminaries in the West is evident. Simultaneously, new theological centers are opening in Asia, Africa, Oceania, and Latin America. The era of German theologians setting the tone for the global church is gradually ending. Today, some of the loudest and most creative voices in theology speak from the emerging marginality of the Global South, and their impact influences the conversation in the United States and Europe. The bottom line is that contemporary Christianity today looks significantly different than it did a century ago.

Without question, the world in which contemporary Christianity exists and negotiates has circumnavigated quite a journey. Let us be reminded.

THE ENCHANTED WORLD OF CHRISTIANITY

As late as 1900 over 80 percent of the world Christian population was Caucasian, and over 70 percent resided in Europe.[5] But while the *World Christian Encyclopedia* assesses the percentage of Christians worldwide to have been 33 to 34 percent for the last several generations, and projects the same proportion in the coming half-century,[6] the European-Caucasian majority is not *the case* at the start of the twenty-first century.

A generation ago, and for centuries before that across much of the Western world, many could have recounted rather homogeneous stories of their Christian-oriented childhoods and described them, as social philosopher Charles Taylor has in *A Secular Age*, as an "enchanted world," a phrase he employs to describe conditions of cultures that favor religious belief.[7]

---

5. Barrett et al., "Status of Global Mission, Presence, and Activities, AD 1800–2025," 30.
6. Barrett et al., *World Christian Encyclopedia*.
7. Taylor, *Secular Age*.

As is quite clear, *this* is not a Christian-leaning "enchanted world" any longer. While some lament this shift and pine for "a Christian world," others feel unshackled from the tyranny of a monolithic ethos that seems as a restriction of personal and social and even theological freedoms.[8] As is evident in the twenty-first century, broad socializing undercurrents dominate the global village and challenge the foundations of Christianity.

One of the more intriguing stories, and as it has evolved through the centuries of Christianity as it has existed in the world, is the ebb and flow of various movements, denominations, and groups within Christianity. At this point, traditional mainline denominations are in retreat while Evangelical and Pentecostal groups realize growth. Another facet to this story is the degree to which social issues, e.g., immigration, poverty, and injustice, percolate throughout society and bump up against the response(s) of the global church. Of course, there is no monolithic "response" to these issues, but rather varying responses about, for example, abortion, euthanasia, and sexual identity, to name but a few.

This book attempts to cull out various theologies mounting from a range of Christian perspectives on thorny topics from today's headlines in a descriptively transparent way. Furthermore, this volume is an attempt to contribute to an ongoing dialogue about changing the power dynamics and lingering dominance of northern theology. Over the two millennia of the history of Christianity, how the church has tended to respond in the face of cultural pressure has often emerged in predictable patterns: *first*, to withdraw into itself and hunker down to withstand the heat of the day; and/or *second*, to capitulate to cultural values and thereby become closely identified with popular sentiment. In the first case, Christianity then loses its audience and credibility by disappearing from the scene, losing an opportunity to speak its theological perspective into a culture awash in pluralism; and in the second case, Christianity loses its distinctive message by merely assimilating to groupthink.

Neither of these strategies, whether intentional or not, is desirable for having a conspicuous effect in the public square. Perhaps a third tack has a greater likelihood for consequential outcomes—a posture of gracious humility and civil engagement,[9] despite an increasing atmosphere that seems to have given up on these qualities—more favorably prods toward gaining a more receptive hearing in a postmodern culture that has embraced outrage, offense, and entitlement as its default predispositions.[10]

---

8. Contemplate a theoretical case study—how might the world be different if Christianity did not exist in it? Yes, some would wish for the disappearance of Christianity and lambast its deeds and lingering influence in contemporary culture—an outdated, contemptuous element that has made ruin of social practices and personal freedoms. In Christianity's absence, what would the global agenda be, what would the moral fiber reflect, what would communities embrace as a shared value if the Christian faith could be extracted from the lives of individuals and the communities across the land?

9. James Davison Hunter's *To Change the World: The Irony, Tragedy, and Possibility of Christianity in the Late Modern World* (Oxford, 2010) is pulling in the same direction here.

10. Of course, not all global southerners would agree nor even some of the contributors to this

The question, then, as the church encounters issues as societies move through the course of human experience is, *what response(s) does the Christian religion offer to contemporary issues based on its understanding of the revealed words of God through Scripture, tradition, reason, and experience?* To be sure, various versions of Christianity has gotten it horribly wrong on various issues through the centuries and must repent of its narrow vision and insensitivity to the innate value of humans as well as turning a deaf ear to the guidance of the Holy Spirit. Christianity is littered with egregious interpretations and practices that have been flat-out inexplicably sinful and distasteful. The penalty for this has been a growing reputation of distrust by the culture at large toward Christianity, from which it may never fully recover, and righteous indignation from some within the church.

CONTEXTUAL FACTORS IN CONSTRUCTING THEOLOGICAL DISCOURSE

It is most timely, as theologian Fernando Segovia, one of our editorial advisory board members, points out (in a personal email), that the release of this book coincides with the fiftieth anniversary of the launching of "liberation theology," a fermentation process borne of religious-theological reflection from the Global South.

That being one of many examples of upstart reform movements brewing theologies from the Global South, we observe three macro-factors which play a role in remaking the Christian faith in the twenty-first-century, postmodern world scene:[11]

First, Christianity is related to the social conditions among the culture in which it exists. Certainly, the heuristic circumstances of a given culture and the experiences of Christians within it are bound to interact with the content of what is taught in faith communities—acting as a sort of countermeasure in dealing with hostile or dangerous or distracting or theologically charged life situations.

Second, Christianity tends to be mingled into some measure of relationship with the national consciousness of the culture in which it exists. While it may seem obvious, the governmental authorities of any given country may have varying relational degrees with Christianity ranging from congenial to hostile. In some countries on the global front, detrimental conditions for Christianity exist. America has had a rather intertwined destiny with Christianity from the nation's earliest days. In days gone by, a "home field advantage" undergirded a Christian culture and message; whereas, in the

---

book. See, for example, our respected colleague Katalina Tahaafe-Williams in her chapter 38. Her argument for *a theology of prophetic anger* is that the marginalized seem forever to be silenced by so-called postures of gracious humility and civility (often proposed by privileged voices) so that their righteous outrage is to be suppressed lest they be shown up to be the typecast angry-and-lacking in civil discipline (or self-control) creatures their 'superiors' have already assumed them to be! We appreciate her points.

11. Some material from this subsection is adapted from the Section One "Preview" in Lamport and Edie, *Nurturing Faith*.

current postmodern world, Christianity has lost its favored status. Christianity is being repositioned as one of many competing stories in the marketplace of ideas and truths. This is the age of pluralism and a shift in the national relationship to Christianity is fueled, among other factors, by media outlets, popular opinion, and court rulings.

Third, Christianity adapts and responds to contemporary issues when a society experiences rapid change. The pace of Western cultural change is frenetic and driven largely by cultural developments, technological inventions, and medical advancements. With such change, society is confronted with an array of new, often avant-garde topics, and the teachings of the church must respond by assisting believers in the task of theological reflection upon this rapid change, rather than naïvely capitulating to cultural drift.

What do you think—*is this first third of the twenty-first century the most challenging time in the history of Christianity for a reasonable hearing in the square of public opinion? Are fresh, emerging expressions of Christianity necessary to gain a more vigorous dialogue with other worldviews and the contextual issues that arise? Can theologies from the Global South exist compatibly with those from the Global North?*

If "yes" to any of the above questions, then a well-intended plan to engage a Christian worldview with contemporary culture must be considered. We propose three tent poles to guide the dialogue—theology with *peaceful resolve,* with *graceful interpretation,* and with *meaningful engagement.*

A PURPOSE AND METHOD FOR PRODUCTIVE THEOLOGICAL-CULTURAL DIALOGUE

To augment perspective toward this desirous engagement of gracious dialogue both *between* Christianity and the secularizing forces, and *within* the various traditions of the Christian faith, we offer these preliminary observations which affect the facilitation of graceful, meaningful interaction:[12]

- *Theology with peaceful resolve*—Christian teaching seeks to identify a viable consensus on what Christians have always believed. This is hardly the case in our postmodern world. This consensus is based on sacred texts known to have continuous authority for worshiping communities. Scripture remains the primary source and credible criterion of Christian teaching. This consensus, derived from authoritative councils of the early church, sees essential doctrines as unifying

---

12. I am particularly indebted in this section to insightful and ecumenical perspective from the late Thomas Oden included in the Epilogue to his masterful tome, offering a synthetic argument for embracing the wisdom of foundational theologians from centuries ago. See his *Classic Christianity,* 842–59. We realize the principles of engagement, as articulated in this section, may come across as theological without context, i.e., without immediate connection to the consequences of the shift. They do address the context of a world turned aggressive—the crisis of social breakdown. What they may not accurately reflect is to show how they grow out of the shift in general and the Global South in particular. We ask for feet-on-the-ground practical theologians and churches and parachurch organizations to contextualize these principles. Thanks to Fernando Segovia (Vanderbilt University) for pointing this out.

factors, such as statements regarding the nature of Jesus, and Scripture, and humanity. Indeed, the great "doctors" of the church—Athanasius, Basil, Gregory of Nazianzus, John Chrysostom, Ambrose, Augustine, Jerome, and Gregory the Great—agree on the core beliefs of Christianity. Clearly, many issues that confront Christianity in the present time do not have the clear advantage of councils and do not rise to the level of fixed ecclesiastical dogma but rather fall into the category of either important doctrine or personal preference. Because contemporary Christianity has no great doctors, and due to the issues which confront the church in these times, a profound lack of consensus reigns. Some view these opportunities for dialogue as a welcome prospect to confront social issues and apply reasonable theological application for living. Others see these dialogues as inevitably deepening a rift in the unity of church thereby lessening its influence within the unbelieving world of skeptics and antagonists.

But Christian teaching should have as its objective the peacemaking intent of uniting the body of Christ—the goal being conciliatory. Bringing consensus is humbling work, where opinions and preferences belong in the background. The aim is to state the widest possible agreement that works interdenominationally, intergenerationally, and interculturally. This precarious task is best achieved by realistic, calm, reasoned critical effort—marked by a discerning spirit, a careful vigilance for recognizing points which have misshapen the faith, and where false teachings abound. Given the persistence of human self-deception (including that which is manifest in institutional and organizational contexts), one may not be surprised to find heresy mixed inconspicuously with orthodoxy. Regrettably, the steady preoccupation of modern theology has focused more often on how Christian teaching has been modifying, shifting, retracting, and has chosen less to emphasize centrist orthodoxy and the long, stable history of belief.

A problem which has emerged (and continues still) is "how can one speak of the Bible as having any authority when it is so clearly at the mercy of its interpreters?"[13] The fundamental problem of Protestant theological identity, as Alister McGrath extrapolates, as other branches within Christianity perceived, was primarily about a certain way of doing theology that could lead to an uncontrollable diversity of outcomes. And who would have the definitive prerogative to decide what is orthodox and what is heretical? This was "a dangerous idea" McGrath argues that opened the floodgates to "a torrent of distortion, misunderstanding, and confusion."[14]

- *Theology with graceful interpretation.* The Holy Spirit is the Teacher and enables Christians with insight to see how the truth of Scripture is to be rightly interpreted and acted upon. Yet other competing interpretations creep in, i.e., nationalistic,

---

13. McGrath, *Christianity's Dangerous Idea*, 93.
14. McGrath, *Christianity's Dangerous Idea*, 208–9.

paternalistic, imperialistic, and so on. An antitype case study merely to illustrate this point from the Global North. Nowhere are these shameful interpretations more pronounced than in the four-hundred-year history of Christianity in the United States. How else would one explain scriptural justifications for war, slavery, church splits, bigamy, racism, bombing abortion clinics, and a virtually never-ending multitude of cultural, political, and ethical conflicts? It is no wonder theologian Stanley Hauerwas resorts to hyperbole: "No task is more important than for the church to take the Bible out of the hands of individual Christians in North America. North American Christians are trained to believe that they are capable of reading the Bible without spiritual and moral transformation. They read the Bible not as Christians, not as a people set apart, but as democratic citizens who think their common sense is sufficient for the understanding of scripture."[15]

No wonder Global South theologians find it time for distancing itself in its hermeneutics. Who "owns" Scripture? The Bible is not simply a repository of true information about God, Jesus, and the hope of the world. But it is, as Tom Wright posits, part of *the means by which*, in the power of the Spirit, the living God rescues people and the world, and takes them forward on the journey toward God's new creation, and makes them agents of that new creation even as they travel.[16] However, as Harvard Divinity School professor Harvey Cox warns,[17] the cultural influence of the Bible today fosters a wary suspicion of current scholarship, and it makes readers fall back on a literalistic understanding of its contents. Another dangerous distortion.

Scripture is authoritative: it has the power to change lives and cultures and deserves to be proclaimed with confidence but not with arrogance. In *Scripture and the Authority of God: How to Read the Bible Today*, Wright reminds us that living with the authority of Scripture means living in that story that Scripture tells. It means soaking ourselves in that story, as a community and as individuals. It means Christian leaders and teachers must themselves become part of the process, part of the way in which God is at work not only *in* the Bible-reading community but *through* that community in and for the wider world. The revelation of God through Scripture is the wellspring from which faith is nurtured. Spirit-given wisdom is required, however, to discern the intention of Scripture and sound hermeneutical practices, and to identify duplicitous agendas proffered by those who wish to manipulate theological truth to serve narrowly held positions.

The Bible has both authority and relevance, and the secret to both is Jesus Christ. Scripture ought to be read (and rightly interpreted) through the "key" of Jesus's ministry, life, death, and resurrection. Proper readings of Scripture cannot be

---

15. Hauerwas, *Unleashing the Scriptures*, 15.
16. Wright, *Simply Christian*, 191.
17. Cox, *How to Read the Bible*, 207ff.

opposed to God's self-revelation in Jesus. Secondarily, Christians look to the witness of persons and communities, past and present, who offer exemplary performances of Scripture as keys to faithful interpretations of it.

- *Theology with meaningful engagement.* The Bible is not a weapon but an instrument of healing and reconciliation, a divine instrument that sits above cultures and religions and individuals for evaluation of them and not the reverse. A pronounced and cautious humility should be observed when attempting to speak for God. Because our love remains frail and partial—subject to our own hopes and fears—our hearing of God's voice as we read Scripture always needs testing by reference to other fellow Christians, past as well as present, and indeed other Scripture passages themselves. Listening to God's voice in Scripture does not put us in the position of having infallible opinions.

It is because humanity is a paradox that the human study of God (i.e., theology) remains a continuing irony strewn with both blood and flowers. The healthier the study of God, the more candid it is about its own limitations, the stubborn limits of its own knowing, its own charades, masks and broken mirrors. That is why the disciplined study of God is best experienced from within a lighthearted, caring community that laughs as its own undertakings.

But we find ourselves in a culture that leads with demand, offense, thin-skinned entitlement, and elaborately claimed personal freedom and liberation from any force that may oppress, and a vitriolic disdain for authority—teachers and schools, police and government, institutions and churches. And so, one wonders: *how will people discuss and resolve the many issues raised in these chapters?* We hope productive, humble, gracious discussions may occur. Perhaps, we offer in humility, this is a good starting point for the establishment of rules for civil theological engagement between and within the Global North and Global South. A hermeneutic of Scripture and a hermeneutic of culture, and perhaps also prophetic, bold, and honest.

BIBLIOGRAPHY

Barrett, David B., et al. "Status of Global Mission, Presence, and Activities, AD 1800-2025," *International Bulletin of Missionary Research* 32 (2008) 30.
———. *World Christian Encyclopedia: A Comparative Survey of Churches and Religions in the Modern World.* 2 vols. Oxford: Oxford University Press, 2001.
Cox, Harvey. *How to Read the Bible.* New York: HarperOne, 2015.
Hauerwas, Stanley. *Unleashing the Scriptures: Freeing the Bible from Captivity to America.* Nashville: Abingdon, 1993.
Johnson, Todd M., and Kenneth R. Ross, eds. *Atlas of Global Christianity.* Edinburgh: Edinburgh University Press, 2009.

Lamport, Mark A., and Fred P. Edie. *Nurturing Faith: A Practical Theology for the Educational Mission of the Church*. Grand Rapids: Eerdmans, 2021.

López, Alfred J. "Preface & Acknowledgments." *The Global South* 1 (2007) v–vi.

McGrath, Alister. *Christianity's Dangerous Idea: The Protestant Revolution—A History from the Sixteenth Century to the Twenty-First Century*. San Francisco: HarperOne, 2007.

Oden, Thomas. *Classic Christianity: A Systematic Theology*. San Francisco: HarperOne, 1987–1992.

Sparke, Matthew. "Everywhere But Always Somewhere: Critical Geographies of the Global South." *The Global South* 1 (January 2007) 117–26.

Taylor, Charles. *A Secular Age*. Cambridge: Harvard University Press, 2007.

Wright, N. T. *Simply Christian: Why Christianity Makes Sense*. New York: HarperOne, 2006.

CHAPTER 2

Theologizing from the Global South

A Critical Reflection

FERNANDO F. SEGOVIA

The present volume constitutes a handbook or compendium of Christian religious-theological production—arising from and addressed to contextual realities and experiences—from outside the parameters of its traditional domain across the North Atlantic world of Western Europe and northern America. Fifty years ago, any such compilation lay beyond the realm of imagination. This compendium reveals, therefore, the remarkable transformation that has taken place in the world of the Christian tradition as well as in the realm of Christian studies over the space of five decades. I take the 1970s as point of comparison because it is at this time that such production outside the borders of the North Atlantic finds its beginnings. I am referring here to the irruption of liberation theology in Latin America and the Caribbean, subsequently embraced in Africa and the Middle East as well as Asia and Oceania, duly adapted to their own historical-political and social-cultural circumstances. The handbook represents both a tribute to and an heir of that liberationist project, providing an overview of the many paths flowing from that moment of creation, while also contemplating appropriate channels for future pursual.

This transformation the compendium unfolds in three interrelated ways: key themes; range of expressions; foundational forces. Chapter 1, authored by Mitri Raheb and Mark A. Lamport, weighs and conveys such multidimensional representation of the transformation by reviewing the ways of the past, assessing the tensions of the present, and discerning the options for the future. In so doing, they cast the exercise in terms of a dialectical opposition between a Global North and a Global South. To begin with, such nomenclature is presented as replacing previous renditions of this opposition dating back to the Cold War (1945–1989): a spatial-geopolitical configuration in terms of three "worlds" (First, Second, Third) and a spatial-economic differentiation in terms of two "worlds" (developed and developing). Further, this nomenclature is filtered through the work of Alfred J. López on marks of the Global South[1]: the long imprint of colonialism, the deep scars of endless social upheavals, and the severe burden of globalization.[2] Lastly, the opposition conveyed by such nomenclature is described as a process of radical transformation underway for some time now: steep decline of a dominant Global North alongside robust ascendancy of a subordinate Global South.

My goal in this critical reflection is to examine the notion of the Global South, used to name this religious-theological production from outside the North Atlantic. It is a category that I find in need of theorization. Toward this end, I shall have recourse to the field of Global South studies. First, in adopting such nomenclature for Christian studies, it is imperative to have a well-informed sense of signification in the host field of studies. Second, in deploying it within Christian studies, it is helpful to situate such application within the overall discursive framework of the host field. Such a venture on my part is but incipient in nature. I begin with a critical analysis of terminology and signification, continue by examining the transformation as constructed by the editorial introduction and then situating it within the framework of Global South studies, and conclude with a comment on the challenges ahead.

CONSTRUCTING THE GLOBAL SOUTH

The term "the Global South" is neither self-evident nor determinate. There is a trajectory of critical discussion regarding signification, within which a variety of major positions can be readily identified. An excellent point of entry into this theoretical discussion, highly complex as well as highly conflicted, is provided by a collection of essays that appeared as a special issue of the journal *The Global South*, "The Global South as Subversive Practice."[3] Its editor was Dr. Sinah Theres Kloß, a social anthropologist, presently affiliated as a research group leader with the Bonn Center for Dependency and Slavery Studies at the University of Bonn. In her contribution, which also functions as an introduction to the volume, she explains the origins of the project.[4] In 2015, while at the University of Cologne, she was called upon to organize a workshop on the idea of the Global South. It is out of this venture, then, that emerges

---

1. López, "Introduction."

2. López is the founding editor of the journal *The Global South*, a position that he held for its first two volumes (2007–2008). This essay serves as the editorial introduction to the launching of the journal.

3. Kloß, *Global South as Subversive Practice*.

4. Kloß, "Global South as Subversive Practice."

this collection of studies, six in all, in 2017,[5] though not as a volume of proceedings; in fact, its contents are a mixture of original presentations and later contributions.

Two essays prove particularly relevant for my purposes, insofar as they provide a delineation of the various meanings attached to the concept of "the Global South." The first of these is the piece by Kloß, "The Global South as Subversive Practice: Challenges and Potentials of a Heuristic Concept" (2017). She names three semantic categories in all: metaphorical; structural; and epistemic. The second is a contribution by Nina Schneider, a historian, presently a Research Group Leader in the Käte Hamburger Kolleg/Centre for Global Cooperation Research (KHK/GCR21) at the University of Duisburg-Essen. It is titled "Between Promise and Skepticism: The Global South and Our Role as Engaged Intellectuals" (2017). She too mentions three semantic strands: geographical, subaltern, and flexible.

A number of comments are in order. With regard to the delineations, there is considerable agreement between the two mappings, although differences in content and emphasis are also present. In both cases, moreover, the descriptions of the various categories are not as keenly drawn and discussed as one might wish, due in part to the flowing nature of these discursive strands. With respect to their objectives, both pieces advance a position and project of their own. Given its introductory dimension, the essay by Kloß includes a critical appraisal of the proposal by Schneider. In what follows, I begin with a combined exposition of the spectrum of significations and then go on to examine and compare the constructive projects underlying each delineation.

Range of Significations

In setting forth the overall semantic spectrum of the term, I proceed by way of degree of agreement and mode of presentation. I begin with a category that is directly analyzed by both, which I would characterize as "geographical"—bringing together the "metaphorical" of Kloß and the "geographical" of Schneider. I continue with two categories that are also common to both, but addressed in differing ways. One of these I would classify as "structural"—comprising the "structural" of Kloß and the "geographical" of Schneider. While foregrounded by Kloß, it is approached indirectly by Schneider as a dimension of a historical process. The other I would present as "subaltern"—combining the "geographical" of Kloß and the "subaltern" of Schneider. While advanced as such by Schneider, it is broached indirectly by Kloß within the context of the "structural" category. I conclude with two categories that are developed in detail by only one. The first I would call "flexible"—unique to Schneider, from whom I borrow the term. While acknowledged by Kloß, it is left unaddressed. The second I would call "epistemic"—unique to Kloß, from whom I take the term. While mentioned by Schneider, in indirect fashion, it is left untouched.

---

5. The workshop took place in June of 2016 at the Global South Studies Center, bearing the title of "Conceptual (Re)Locations of the 'Global South.'"

Geographical. This first category involves the use of the term as a synonym for the spatial-geopolitical designation of "the Third World," which emerges in the 1950s and 1960s within the context of the Cold War. Such usage inherits and conveys the geographical and primarily pejorative connotations of the earlier designation: the conditions of widespread poverty and structural underdevelopment associated with the nations of Africa, Asia, and Latin America. This meaning both Kloß and Schneider identify as the most common, right through our own times. Indeed, this is the meaning adopted by a new journal on the Global South launched in 2015, *Bandung: Journal of the Global South*.[6]

A critique along not dissimilar lines is lodged. For Kloß, given its metaphorical character, the term loses its heuristic value in the course of the 1990s, following the breaking apart of the Second World constituted by the Soviet Union and the Eastern Bloc. Without the opposition between a First World and a Second World, a reference to a Third World—a nonaligned and noninvolved bloc of nations—loses its capacity for describing the existing world order. Consequently, a recourse to the "Global South" as substitute represents but a futile exercise in political correctness: an attempt to preserve the geographical signification via a cleaner term, yet one that skirts the change in political realities and that maintains the focus on economic development. For Schneider, given its geographical foundation, the term continues the various shortcomings inherent in the "Third World": bypassing the diversity present in such a spatial-geographical delimitation; ignoring the divisions hidden by the primary focus on nation-states and interstate relations; and overlooking the hybridity present outside and between the spatial-geographical divisions.

Structural. This has to do with the use of the term along the lines marked by the notion of "the South," a designation that Kloß traces back to important historical references of the 1930s[7] and that both see as becoming common in the 1970s, in the light of the process of decolonization. This usage can preserve in some instances the primary connotations of economic disparity. By and large, however, it is described as a deliberate attempt to move beyond the limitations embodied in "the Third World"—not only reflecting the growing presence of the previously colonized but also moving away from its East-West conceptual framework. This it does by emphasizing the question of whence: the dynamics of inclusion and exclusion in the governance and direction of the global structural system, wherein the North assumes the role of agent and assigns the role of object to the South. A critique of this turn is offered mainly by Kloß.

---

6. Wong, "Inaugural Editorial." As the editorial explains, the journal has its origins in an international conference on the Global South held at the City University of Hong Kong in May of 2014.

7. These references are important not only for a sense of historical trajectory but also as a resource for future theorization. One is a product of Latin America: the use of "the South" as the title for a literary magazine, *Sur*, published in Buenos Aires from 1931 through 1992, which brought together a highly distinguished group of intellectuals as contributors. The other is a product of Europe: a reference to "the South" (Gramsci, *Southern Question*, 19, 30).

She points out how this meaning is challenged from a variety of sides with the advent of the 2000s. First, semantically, the term is viewed as a simple substitute for "Third World," adding no nuance whatever. Second, economically, the rise of a number of "transition economies,"[8] represented by a group of nations known by the acronym BRICS (Brazil, Russia, India, China, South Africa), shatters the adoption of the North-South distinction. These nations cannot be classified in either bloc, occupying instead a hybrid position between them. Lastly, politically, the use of "the South" is challenged as bypassing the question of origins: while such usage does address the dynamics behind the international system, it tends to bypass the processes that led to such a global state of affairs. Schneider limits herself to affirming the first challenge above: any appeal to "the South" fails to break away from the model of a "geographic, nation-based" system, even if reconfigured in terms of a broader structural framework.

Subaltern. This category involves the use of the term along the lines of Alfred J. López to refer to all those throughout the world severely impacted by the neoliberal project of globalization—economically, politically, culturally. Such usage expands the meaning of "the Global South" beyond the connotations attached to both "the Third World" and "the South." It moves the discussion beyond both the geographical dimension (focus on the triad of Africa, Asia, and Latin America) and the political-economic framework (focus on nation-states and interstate relations). It denotes instead a common formation across regions and nations, along the lines of a transnational class of the excluded and the marginalized. It also conveys a sense of conscientization: these come to realize their own predicament as well as the fate that they share with so many others around the world.

A critique is offered by both, from different perspectives. That of Schneider, from a geopolitical angle, is more substantial. It could be argued that the focus on the detritus of globalization only serves to deflect or blunt the critique mounted against the richer nations of the world—whether North America or Europe, Japan or Australia. It could also be argued that such a reading only serves to mask the structural differential structures of power at work in the world and their ramifications for the underside—the aftereffects of consumer and business practices. Thus, it could be argued that a signification bearing a geographical foundation would be to the advantage of the triad formed by Asia, Africa, and Latin America. That of Kloß, from a semantic angle, is pointed. If Global South is to stand for all subalterns, she asks, what need is there to invoke a substitute category that adds nothing by way of nuance?

Flexible. This refers to a line of thought that moves beyond a set geographical or social foundation to present the term as a fluid metaphor designed to convey a relationship of inequality. As a result, the distinction between a dominant "North" and a subordinate "South" may be applied to any number of particular situations involving "Norths" and "Souths," whether within nations or between nations. Schneider offers no critique of such usage, on the grounds of its inherent flexibility. What she

---

8. Kloß, "Global South as Subversive Practice," 4.

does do is explain its raison d'être. From a narrower geopolitical angle, such flexibility makes it possible to set aside any global geographical framework of domination. From a broader social angle, such flexibility allows for casting aside distinct gradations of economic development, analyzing differential relations within individual nations, and integrating factors other than economics into the picture.

Epistemic. This category marks a line of thought that does preserve a basic spatial-geographical foundation, while foregrounding an epistemic abyss that separates the knowledges of the Global North from the knowledges of the Global South, whereby the former are advanced as superior, valid, and universal, while the latter are regarded as inferior, defective, and provincial. In so doing, the category aims to dismantle the abyssal line by displacing the universalist impulses of the dominant knowledges and integrating the local impulses of subordinated knowledges, both by themselves and in conversation with one another. No critique of this line of interpretation is brought forward; to the contrary, it is this category that provides the discursive matrix for Kloß's constructive proposal.

CONSTRUCTIVE PROPOSALS

In laying out their respective delineations of meaning, both Kloß and Schneider offer a pointed critique of the various options, as noted above in the exposition of the semantic spectrum. In effect, such mappings are advanced in both cases as discursive platforms for moving beyond and charting new paths. Both are searching, therefore, for new visions of and projects for the future regarding the idea of the Global South. This endeavor they pursue along different paths. While Kloß moves to redirect an existing strand of meaning, Schneider argues for a novel orientation altogether. At the same time, a common impulse is also at work: utopian thinking. I turn first to the project envisioned by Schneider, since it is subjected to critique by Kloß in the formulation of her own project. Schneider does comment on the road taken by Kloß, but not directly.

Nina Schneider

Behind the various definitions of the Global South, Schneider points to the enthusiastic reception accorded to this term among intellectuals. Her critique, with respect to both the categories at work and the nomenclature as such, is trenchant. Regarding the latter, the different strands of meaning are described as existing side by side in the field, mixed together in largely indiscriminate fashion and without appropriate critical comparison. Regarding the former, such categories are described as troublingly vague, unable to capture properly the parameters of the signified by each designation in question. Such imprecision, she adds, is actually celebrated by its manifold proponents as creating a "promising site of struggle," through which the "Global South" can be effectively deployed as a polyvalent tool toward global transformation. Any such sense of strategic fluidity she rejects, however.

Beyond the ever-present need for conceptual clarity, she counters, the term itself can just as easily continue to replicate untoward connotations of the past and thus prove counterproductive to any such transformation. In effect, it can readily affirm, rather than deconstruct, the traditional and problematic dichotomy between North and South as well as solidify, rather than dismantle, long-standing differential relations of power. In the face of such "sunshiny utopian potential" on the one hand and such a "shadowy side" on the other hand, Schneider poses a fundamental question for "engaged intellectuals." They must consider "whether multiple definitions of the Global South necessarily *give voice* to the unprivileged and *damnés* of this world or perpetuate their silencing . . ."[9] Her own response is to opt for caution.

To be sure, there is no question that such an ardent quest for transformation on the part of intellectuals is to be welcomed and promoted, for behind the overall embrace of the "Global South" as a banner and behind the multiple strands of signification adopted lie utopian projects with corresponding calls for new modes of political activism. Such projects Schneider ties directly to the critical state of global affairs, especially in terms of social-economic developments: erosion of the welfare state; implantation of austerity ideology; and spread of the neoliberal project at all levels of human life. Given such devastating forces, the turn to the "Global South" as a "potential tool for social, political, and cognitive change" is readily understandable.[10] Such an undertaking, Schneider argues, is imperative, but not at the expense of semantic imprecision or counterproductive frameworks. The role of "engaged intellectuals" must be to guard against any usage that may embody "an unjust and violent world order" and to adopt instead a meaning that sets aside "a utopian ideal that is never realized" and that is able to "catalyze *real change*."[11]

In the face of such starkly critical times, the term "Global South" cannot be salvaged. In the urgent search for a more egalitarian global state of affairs, none of the significations in use is acceptable and no new definition is possible. The term inherently conveys geographical connotations, oppositional and discriminatory, that are grounded in and derived from the "Western-centric episteme" and that prove singularly ineffective for any utopian project. Its continued usage would only entrench in the field a "geographical imaginary" that would address "certain social realities" but not others, thus "over-determining and generalizing other aspects of our world."[12] To

---

9. Schneider, "Between Promise and Skepticism," 19.
10. Schneider, "Between Promise and Skepticism," 20.
11. Schneider, "Between Promise and Skepticism," 20.
12. Schneider, "Between Promise and Skepticism," 33–34. Here, she notes, the work of Escobar (*Encountering Development*) has been influential, in particular his notion of "colonization of reality." This is a process whereby discursive constructs become emplaced in theorization, bearing a meaning that is imagined yet framing the overall conception of reality. That precisely is the danger of "Global South"—structuring reality in social theory, yet built on imaginary geographical foundations

catalyze real transformation, a different rallying cry is essential. This has happened before, as with Franz Fanon's recourse to "the wretched of the earth"—a term characterized as "unambiguous and capable of triggering important changes."[13] It needs to happen again, and toward this end Schneider suggests a designation that is less Western-centric and already in use: "the majority of the world" or "Majority World"—a term whose demographic character does capture global reality, insofar as the great majority of the urban population lives in the Global South.[14]

In opting for such nomenclature, Schneider appeals, not by way of grounding but by way of support, to the epistemic signification, to which she refers as "Southern Theory"[15] and which Kloß follows.[16] In seeking to affirm the subordinated knowledges of the Global South and to develop new knowledges, it is necessary to avoid any omission or silencing of excluded realities and voices. Yet, that is precisely what happens with any continued usage of "Global South," given its insurmountable inaccuracies and pejorative divisions. New knowledges demand new formulations. Here her distinction between "radical decolonial" and "imperialist" approaches is to the point. In the pursuit of egalitarianism, the former marks those that do so without regard to the axes of personal identity, while the latter marks those that privilege a dominant group along any axis.[17] Adherence to the "Global South" can only be described, therefore, as imperialist—irretrievably beholden to the interests of Western-centrism.

Sinah Theres Kloß

For Kloß, in direct response to Schneider, the use of "Global South" should not be discarded. While its semantic and ideological weaknesses have to be acknowledged, crafting a new term provides no way out of the quandary. From the perspective of historical-political trajectory, no novel nomenclature can bypass a reference to the traditional opposition in theorization—whether between First World and Third World of the metaphorical signification or between North and South from the geographical signification. From the perspective of social-cultural analysis, no novel nomenclature can avoid the heavy burden brought by this trajectory upon the subaltern—hierarchical structures, modes of domination, material-discursive ruination. At this point,

---

produced by the Western episteme.

13. Schneider, "Between Promise and Skepticism," 35.

14. For the first term, Schneider draws the work of Collin Butler ("North and South, the (Global)"); for the second, on that of McEwan (*Postcolonialism and Development*).

15. The term is taken from Connell (*Southern Theory*), who uses in contradistinction to Northern Theory.

16. At the same time, Schneider point outs that the production of new knowledges from the South has not gone unchallenged, but ultimately takes no stance in this regard (Schneider, "Between Promise and Skepticism," 35n2).

17. Schneider, "Between Promise and Skepticism," 36n3.

moreover, any evasion of this trajectory and this burden proves quite dangerous, given the backlash against the struggles and the claims of the subaltern.[18]

The use of "Global South" should be preserved, therefore, but only, Kloß specifies, in revised fashion. Such reconfiguration brings together the subaltern and the flexible significations: the subaltern of the world stand at the forefront of attention, not as a homogenous, unchanging category but as a diverse, variable one. The category is advanced thereby as expansive enough to serve as a material and discursive terrain that subaltern formations everywhere can claim as theirs, in their own respective ways, and can marshal toward transformation, through joint empowerment and mutual relations. As a result, the Global South emerges as "a process that reflects, highlights, and potentially transforms dominant and subalternized positionalities."[19] It is a process, therefore, that can be joined, defined, and activated from any number of vantage points, all of which perceive themselves as subalternized, but always with awareness of and in collaboration with the other vantage points.

This sense of a process Kloß brings to bear on the academic-scholarly world by way of the epistemic signification: a strategic program toward transforming the abyssal line that separates the dominant knowledges of the Global North and the subordinated knowledges of the Global South. To this end, the academic-scholarly world, she argues, could function as a "liminal space of transition": embodying a "phase of antistructure" wherein power relations are restructured and creating a "new model of social, economic, and political interactions"—with egalitarianism as foundation.[20] Such a program entails a set of major as well as minor interventions, given the wide range of practices in question and the hold of epistemic inequality throughout. Indeed, the dynamics and mechanics in question involve, among others, geographical locations, academic institutions, linguistic usages, scholarly networks, publication ventures, and conference participation. All of this calls for critical reflection and action from the "political consciousness" of the Global South.[21]

THEOLOGIZING FROM THE GLOBAL SOUTH

In invoking the designation "the Global South" as a marker for the volume, Raheb and Lamport activate a field of studies that, as the preceding exposition has shown, is convoluted and controverted. Such a designation can convey a variety of different meanings and inspire a variety of utopian projects. At the same time, such a designation can be better emplaced and construed in the light of the historical trajectory

---

18. It is worth pointing out that the demographic rationale used by Schneider on behalf of the new term proposed recurs to the idea of the "Global South" (Schneider, "Between Promise and Skepticism," 35).
19. Kloß, "Global South as Subversive Practice," 8.
20. Kloß, "Global South as Subversive Practice," 8.
21. Kloß, "Global South as Subversive Practice," 14.

outlined and the constructive proposals advanced by two scholars of Global South studies. This is what I should like to develop in this reflection on the handbook. My aim is not to determine the valid path to follow but to understand and weigh whatever path is selected against the range of the critical repertoire. Thereby fruitful comparative analysis can be undertaken regarding matters of method and theory as well as questions of visions and models in the pursuit for transformation. I shall proceed by examining the representation of the process behind the remarkable transformation of Christian studies highlighted by the editors.

Looking Back: Awakening and Deconstruction

With regard to the past, the analysis is expansive and optimistic. It approaches the shift in the world of global Christianity in both material and discursive fashion. The material dimension is developed in terms of demographics. Over the course of the twentieth century, a process traced from 1910 to 2010, the location of Christians worldwide undergoes a drastic change: the percentage of those residing in the Global South doubles, while the percentage of those living in the Global North decreases by half. Furthermore, this change affects the entire spectrum of ecclesial formations. This spatial-geographical inversion of Christians in the world could not but have far-reaching repercussions for the discursive dimension of Christianity. This is pursued in terms of theological production. Since the latter part of the twentieth century, a period extending from the 1970s through today, such production flourishes throughout the Global South, yielding a Christianity characterized as a "multi-centered, multi-focal, multi-faceted, and increasingly diverse religion globally." It is this plurality of Christian theology, arising from all corners of contemporary Christianity, that the volume gathers together and brings across.

Such proliferation of theological visions is marked by a variety of key moves and traits. First, the emerging theologies begin to see their roots and callings as contextual in nature, tied to and directed at their historical-political circumstances and social-cultural settings—leaving behind the predominant universalist stance displayed by theologies crafted in the Global North. Second, these theologies regard it as incumbent upon them to analyze such circumstances and settings as an integral part of the theological endeavor, appealing to other fields of study toward this end and hence adopting an extensive interdisciplinary lens—turning away from the primarily idealist and disciplinary moorings of dominant theologies from the Global North.

Third, the new theologies foreground new areas of attention as a result of their focus on context, incorporating such facets of everyday life as exploitation and poverty, oppression and injustice, at both the local and the global level—breaking with the pervasive silences and omissions regarding such realities and experiences on the part of the dominant theologies of the Global North. Fourth, these theologies turn to novel currents of analysis in the human and social sciences with a focus on inequality, examining thereby all formations and relations of human identity through the lens of differential power and opting for a stance of engagement on behalf of the other—moving away from the positions of distantiation and neutrality assumed by the theologies of the Global North. Lastly, the emerging theologies embark on new directions of religious-theological discussions in the light of their attention to context, moving more along ecumenical as well as interreligious lines—leaving behind the traditional intra-Christian and inter-ecclesial modes and disputes followed by the theologies fashioned in the Global North.

Taking together this list of ruptures, what one witnesses at work over the last fifty years is a process of deconstruction and reconstruction regarding the state of affairs of Christian theology up to the 1970s. The discursive framework in place until then the editors characterize as a fundamental component of the North Atlantic imperial-colonial enterprise. At the heart of the project lay an expansionist agenda, intent on establishing presence and control, material and discursive alike, beyond its spatial-geographical boundaries across the Global South. This was grounded in a sense of superiority, carried out by way of overt and raw power, and driven by self-benefit. The result was the subordination of all global others, anchored in the erasure of native contexts and dependency on foreign forces. For the editors, the spread of the Christian tradition and the shape of global theology formed a foundational part of this crusade and its program of dialectical opposition. It is this construction that begins to be dismantled and replaced by the contextual theologies of the Global South, feeding on such critical movements as postcolonial studies and ideological studies. The result is "that the north lost its monopoly over theology" and contextual theologies left "no corner of the world unoccupied," including the Global North itself.

Looking Around: Under Duress and toward A Voice

With respect to the present, the handbook proves more pointed and pessimistic. In the wake of the radical shift in the provenance and tenor of Christian theology, the diversity of theologies from the Global South are said to face a very different and highly problematic historical-political and social-cultural context. This state of affairs is described from a twofold perspective. From a religious-theological angle, gone are the days of a pervasive Christian environment. Such foundations have given way to an inversion of ecclesial formations, with the liberal churches losing much ground to conservative churches, and the irruption of social crises into the agendas of the churches, such as poverty and migration. Second, from a social-cultural perspective, vanished as well are the days in which a sense of civility would still command a place in the public arena. Such a disposition the postmodern era has been replaced with a triad of outrage, offense, and entitlement as its default presuppositions, driving demands for personal freedom from all forces deemed oppressive and displaying a disdain for all authority, whether embodied in social groups or in social institutions.

As a result, the world of Christian theology finds itself under duress. With respect to internal ecclesial transitions and external social pressures, what emerges is decidedly varied and conflictive. With respect to mode of engagement, the result is a lack of hearing and a sense of distrust. In such times of crisis, various paths are possible, but not all are appropriate. The spectrum is clear. At one end, there is the option of withdrawing from the world and turning in upon itself, seeking to survive under trying circumstances—isolationism, however, deprives Christianity of having a voice in the world of postmodernity. At the other end, there is the option of subscribing to the values of the world and following the winds of the moment, attempting to endure by accommodating to the circumstances—submission, however, deprives Christianity of offering a message to the world. In the center, a third option is postulated, beyond silence or immersion. It would begin by acknowledging that Christianity bears much guilt for its present quandary, given the disastrous paths forged by so many of its teachings and its practices. It would continue by speaking openly in and to the world, but with a different tone and a different attitude—the way of gracious humility and civil engagement. Only then, perhaps, will Christian theology get a more receptive hearing in the world.

Looking Forward: Opting for Peace, Grace, and Engagement

With regard to the future, the handbook again turns expansive and optimistic. Given the disregard for and disrepute of Christian theology in the era of postmodernism, a situation largely brought upon itself by any number of untoward social and cultural choices, the handbook ventures a program for gracious humility and civil engagement. This program seeks a reconstruction of Christian theology for today. For this task, three key factors must be kept in mind. To begin with, the Christian religion should be seen as related to all social and cultural dimensions of any context. Moreover, it should be approached as related to the political-national framework of any context. Lastly, it should be viewed as responsive to all manifestations of rapid change in any context. Thus, the program envisioned for our times is grounded on three foundations: peaceful resolve, graceful interpretation, and meaningful engagement.

The first principle has Christian theology in mind. In view of its diverse and conflicted constitution, the program calls for forging as broad a consensus as possible—across formations, generations, and cultures—in order to further unify in the "body of Christ." Toward this end, it is essential to proceed in reasoned and discerning fashion. An obstacle in this process is the multiplicity of interpretations regarding the Bible and the effects thereof on its authority. The second principle also has Christian theology in sight. Given the many distortions to which the Bible has been subjected, the program calls for an approach to the biblical texts as a story within which individuals and communities place themselves, out of which they convey God's revelation, and from which they craft the vision of a new creation. For this purpose, the reading of the Bible must be filtered through the figure and the message of Jesus as well as through the witness past and present alike of exemplary individuals and communities. The third principle has the world primarily in mind. In view of the problematic trajectory of Christian theology, the program calls for a spirit of healing and reconciliation when speaking of God in order to avoid any sense of infallibility and to fashion instead a lighthearted, caring community. Imperative in this regard is the use of the Bible not as a weapon but as a means for mending that overarches cultures, religions, and individuals.

GLOBAL SOUTH THEOLOGIZING

What I should like to do by way of conclusion is to highlight various dimensions of the handbook in the light of the field of studies as outlined by Kloß and Schneider. I begin with a foundational observation. I find the handbook to be much closer to the constructive proposal of Kloß. Not only is the category Global South invoked as a distinctive marker for the project, but also flexibility is placed at the core of its usage, given the multiple regions and voices that it encompasses. In so doing, the collection represents enormous diversity and ready ownership. Many voices and faces, from many regions and nations, were willing to embrace the project as characterized, as involving the Global South, and to offer their respective religious-theological reflections from and for their own respective historical-political and social-cultural circumstances within the Global South.

A primary direction adopted by the project has to do with the epistemic signification, following the path of Kloß in this regard as well. The latter seeks to advance the project of the Global South within the academic-scholarly world, as part of the entire horizon of global networks of inequality. The collection focuses on one component of this world, the religious-theological production of Christian studies in general and Christian theological studies in particular. Such production is presented in oppositional terms: the liberation of the subordinated knowledges of the Global South from the dominant knowledges of the Global North, yielding the collapse of the imperial-colonial enterprise of the North Atlantic and its replacement by way of multicentricity.

Another direction evident in the project involves the crucial importance of spatial context, both by way of continued reference to the geographical signification and the espousal of the subaltern signification, again siding with Kloß. The connection to the historical trajectories and ramifications represented by the designations the Third World and the South is without question. In documenting the voices and regions engaged in theologizing from the Global South, the collection follows the traditional mention of Africa, Asia, and Latin America. With this historical framework in mind, the use of Global South cannot be divorced from the paths and consequences of imperial-colonial domination. The connection to the presence of subalterns throughout the world, including the Global North, is likewise without question. In presenting voices and regions active in theologizing from the Global South, the collection includes the contributions of indigenous formations as well as ethnic-racial minoritized groups in the Global North. With this historical amplification in mind, the use of the Global South is expanded to include the enduring traditions of native peoples and the exploding diasporas of the South.

A further direction also touches upon the subaltern signification, this time by way of the conditions rather than the presence of subalternity. This social perspective is present from the start, as the editors define the Global South through the eyes of Alfred López: colonialism, upheaval, and globalization. Then, it becomes explicit in the representations of the past and the present of the transformation. Regarding the former, they point out how, in turning to the contextual, these theologies foreground inequality—exploitation and oppression. Regarding the latter, they note how, in the process of theologizing, social crises take center stage—poverty and migration. The collection is thus keenly mindful of the paths and consequences of imperial-colonial domination. On this point, the project connects directly not only with Kloß but also with Schneider. On the one hand, Kloß works with a sense of the subalternized everywhere as objects of hierarchy, domination, and ruin. On the other hand, Schneider points to the critical state of the world in socio-economic terms and hence the need for a term that can address the fate of the unpriviliged and the wretched, the great majority of people by far.

I conclude with a second foundational observation. Both Kloß and Schneider offer constructive proposals that are utopian in vision, given the deplorable state of global affairs and the radical transformation in order. For the former, the utopian ideal focuses on a reconceptualization of the academic-scholarly world by way of eliminating the epistemic opposition between Global North and Global South—a call for new practices and new models grounded in egalitarianism. For the latter, the utopian ideal is present in all significations of the Global South, and her own search for a new formulation is no different—a call for a radical decolonial approach grounded in egalitarianism for all. The handbook follows suit. What the editors see in this project is a repositioning of Christian theology for postmodern times—a new global presence marked by peace, grace, and engagement, grounded in a sense of egalitarian mending before and toward all.

CONCLUSION

This project on emerging theologies from the Global South signifies a major contribution to the field of Global South studies. It shows how relevant, indeed necessary, a consideration of religious-theological production is for this field. Such inclusion proves as appropriate, and as indispensable, as that of any other strand of cultural production, whether in the human sciences, such as literature and historiography, or in the social sciences, such as sociology and economics. Such relevance does, to be sure, place weighty demands on religious-theological thinkers and critics, given the need for expertise in Global South studies. The project also signifies a major contribution to the field of Christian studies. It shows how important, in fact essential, it is for such studies to proceed, in this day and age, on a global key. It demonstrates the need to move away from the dialectical opposition of yesteryear, wherein the Global North dictates to the Global South and the Global South bows to the Global North, and toward dialogical engagement for all and in all directions. Again, to be sure, such multidirectionality does place enormous demands on the part of Christian thinkers and critics.

It is with such demands that I conclude. First, the task of reading such production from throughout, accompanied by critical engagement and comparative analysis. Second, given the orientation of all such production, the task of acquiring the knowledge and sophistication necessary, in terms of historical-political and social-cultural contextualization, to read any production in situ. Lastly, given the long-range trajectories and overarching scenarios behind such production, the task of deploying models of the world system, to see how different contexts fit into and related to their respective structures and ideologies. What the handbook has done in this regard is commendable. What remains to be done, nonetheless, is forbidding, yet inevitable—such is the gift and the burden of this remarkable transformation.

BIBLIOGRAPHY

Butler, Colin D. "North and South, the (Global)." In *The International Encyclopeida of the Social Sciences,* edited by Raewyn Connell, 542–44. Farmington Hills, MI: Gale, 2008.
Connell, Raewyn. *Southern Theory: The Global Dynamics of Knowledge in Social Theory.* Malden, MA: Palgrave, 2007.
Escobar, Arturo. *Encountering Development: The Making and Unmaking of the Third World.* Princeton: Princeton University Press, 1995.
Gramsci, Antonio. *The Southern Question.* Translated by Pasquale Verdicchio. New York: Bordighera, 2015.
Kloß, Sinah Theres. "The Global South as Subversive Practice: Challenges and Potentials of a Heuristic Concept." *The Global South* 11 (2017) 1–17.
———, ed. *The Global South as Subversive Practice.* Special issue of *The Global South,* 11 (2017).
López, Alfred J. "Introduction: The (Post) Global South." *The Global South* 1 (2007) 1–11.
McEwan, Cheryl. *Postcolonialism and Development.* New York: Routledge, 2009.
Schneider, Nina. "Between Promise and Skepticism: The Global South and Our Role as Engaged Intellectuals." *The Global South* 11 (2017) 18–37.
Wong, Pak Nung. "Inaugural Editorial: Envisioning South-South Relations and Development: Past, Present and Futures." *Bandung: Journal of the Global South* 2 (2015) 19.

SECTION 2

Major Paradigmatic Themes from Emerging Theologies

CHAPTER 3

The Postcolonial/Decolonial Option in Theology

OSCAR GARCÍA-JOHNSON

Not long ago, a host of an Australian podcast who was interviewing me about one of my books opened his program by saying:

> You write, "in truth, every theology bears the marks of a narrative of its theologian, who is the teller." As a way of helping us wade into this conversation can you talk to us a little about yourself and how this autobiography shapes both the style and hopes for the book?[1]

The undergirding presupposition here is that positionality, epistemic and otherwise, is the starting point of the decolonial option in Christian theology, in a postcolonial setting. Let me begin with a quote that summarizes my experience in the context of the Western Christian academy during my formational stage as a scholar and teacher:

> Originally, I came to seminary because of a Latinx and ministry question. But this question gradually morphed into a different set of questions subsumed under a more universal, significant, and overarching body of knowledge, which arguably is to give an account of the classical questions of Christianity, the church, and the Christian witness....This subalternization of my particular quest for knowledge made me realize that I had become indeed an impostor to my own self and my own people: my teaching, preaching, evangelizing, counseling, and healing gifts were all conduits by which my students were

---

1. Miller, "Episode 64: Spirit Outside the Gate."

also barbarically civilized, by virtue of my own mimicking of the subversion I was exposed to during my educational process. I had become an expert on civilizing my own people, with a doctoral degree to prove it . . . . I could only teach them the subject of Western theology and its applicability to their context, however translated into their "barbaric" environments. Borrowing from Homi Bhabha, I had been participating in the barbaric transmission of culture with the rhetoric of civilization. I had been an impostor. I needed to migrate. I needed exodus in the midst of exile.[2]

The podcaster was intrigued by the transformation of character and metaphor in my autobiography: from a place of colonial privilege as a Chiquita banana kid, raised in Honduras in the precincts of the Chiquita company, formerly known as The United Fruit Company, to a place of decolonial vocation as a diasporic Latinx activist scholar in Los Angeles, California. I told him that it was not my own choosing. In real life, in contrast to theological monographs, one rarely chooses a whole trajectory or even the orienting categories that come to define one's intellectual agenda. One discovers it along the way, by choosing her/his own steps mindful of the epistemic horizons surrounding oneself.

Postcolonialism is usually referred to as an "intellectual and political pursuit . . . not too preoccupied with detachment and neutrality" and emerging from "indigenous and diasporic contexts."[3] I have come to appreciate my exilic/diasporic human condition, noticing that space is more determinative than time and geography, more compelling than history. That is, the *where* comes to be more insightful than the *when* because it gives shape to the *who* and the *what* of one's life and living. Thus, the paradox I use to represent this conundrum is "exodus in the midst of exile." Biblically speaking, the former points to a journey of faith that seeks self-identity and relative stability after slavery and oppression. The latter points to displacement, "a place for losing identity and social stability . . . where one learns to live in interstitial angst after one has been deprived" of one's true home and true self. But let us make no mistake here, for exilic/diasporic self-consciousness and embodiment render not merely "ambiguity and disorientation but also imaginaries and decolonial tropes with the potential to reframe world captivities that are not usually available to those living at the center of wealth, intellectual privilege, and racial hegemony."[4]

The way I have come to understand myself and articulate my story in the context of the academy, the city, and the church seems to coincide with the unsettling tenors of postcolonialism, as a form of enunciation. To say it with Graham Huggan:

---

2. García-Johnson, *Spirit Outside the Gate*, x–xi.
3. Sugirtharajah, *Exploring Postcolonial Biblical Criticism*, 13.
4. García-Johnson, *Spirit Outside the Gate*, 10.

> This much is clear: 'postcolonial' is a troubled term in an embattled set of social and historical circumstances . . . To some extent, postcolonial studies amount to the sum of its own internal differences.[5]

WHY CHOOSE POSTCOLONIALISM/DECOLONIALISM IN CHRISTIAN THEOLOGY TODAY?

Although the reader may infer my answer to this question from previous paragraphs, Sri Lankan biblical scholar R. S. Sugirtharajah speaks clearly on this matter:

> For those of us who were from the former colonies and taught by missionary scholars, and who were tired of interacting with Western agendas, the arrival of postcolonial criticism came as an act of emancipation from the tyranny of Western biblical scholarship. These Western reading strategies grew out of nineteenth-century Europe's rationalism and pietism and were not of the remotest interest to us in any of our hermeneutical quests . . . Postcolonial criticism enabled us for the first time to frame our own questions rather than battling with somebody else's. It provided us with a new set of conceptual tools to investigate the text and interpretation.[6]

I concur with Sugirtharajah in principle, but in my case, I should register that a number of independent intellectual traditions preceding postcolonial theory—ranging from the Latin American literary boom, liberation philosophy and theologies, integral mission, and US Latino/a (diaspora) theologies—had begun to help me relocate elsewhere when thinking theologically as the Western agendas continue to dominate the theological fields.

Adding to Sugirtharajah on matters of global pertinence when doing scholarship, the notable Argentinian decolonial thinker and semiotician, Walter Mignolo, affirms that "[i]n the last few decades no global-political, epistemic and aesthetic phenomenon can be explained without the concept of coloniality."[7] His statement is a global scholarly manifesto, for in the past five hundred years in the history of colonial modernity[8] westernized scholarship has been oblivious to coloniality in spite of the fact that there is a registry of decolonizing (anti-colonial and anti-hegemonic) efforts in the struggle for holistic liberation and postcoloniality in most colonial, ex-colonial,

---

5. Huggan, "Introduction," 22.
6. Sugirtharajah, *Exploring Postcolonial Biblical Criticism*, 2.
7. Mignolo, "Decolonizing Western Epistemology/Building Decolonial Epistemology," 20.
8. The concept of colonial modernity is a decolonial concept arguing that colonial logic (different types of colonialities) is from the start a constitutive part (the hidden side) of Western modernity and has evolved with it in sophisticated ways. In cases such as Latin America, the Caribbean, South East Asia, and Africa, historical colonialism has been overcome through political independence, a colonial logic hidden and nurturing modernity continues to shape global space, time, matter, human imagination, and performance within the so-called West and its global neocolonial relationships.

and neocolonial settings of the world. In other words, postcolonialism/decolonialism has been present as a practice from below since the first day that colonialism was established as a global system. Anti-colonial and alter-colonial resistance have taken multiple shapes in order to give meaning to the oppressive conditions of human life under the colonial regime and to struggle for liberation aided by different types of tricontinental tactics (anti-colonial writings, Marxism, religious liberationism, feminism, psychoanalysis, poststructuralism, Abya Yala indigenism, etc.).

That different forms of colonial order have occupied and shaped the global space up to today is a shared understanding among postcolonial/decolonial thinkers. What is not a consensus is to what degree we can affirm that the Christian itinerary has not only played a role in supporting but also in resisting this global order in different geographies. To say it differently, in the eyes of the most adamant postcolonial/decolonial critics, the Christian witness is suspected of being complicit with (a component of) the colonial order until today and cannot be decolonized.

In *Decolonizing Christianity: Becoming Badass Believers* (2021), the Cuban-American ethicist Miguel De La Torre takes to heart the postcolonial/decolonial challenge on Christianity by calling for the rise of "badass believers:"

> *Decolonizing Christianity* is not an attempt to teach white people how to relate to those on their margins so that they can feel peace and serenity. Instead, these pages seek to demonstrate how dispossessed communities have believed the lie of white supremacy, which has relegated them to be among the least of these for our time. To an extent, this is an evangelical book reaching out to and seeking the salvation of people of color who carry the weight of indignity, whose very humanity has been denied by whiteness. This book is a call to those who are weary of racism and heavily burdened by ethnic discrimination.[9]

Building on previous works and continuing his uncompromising critique on white Evangelicalism in America in the backdrop of the Trump administration, De La Torre adopts a postcolonial self-critical attitude by focusing on his own religious social location, the Evangelical leaders of color (and most particularly Latinos/as) who are implicated with Trumpism and seem oblivious to white male normativity in church life and politics. His self-critical stance functions as a tactic of double critique that uses soteriological language and disruptive ethics. He is known, among other things, for his ethics from the margins or "ética para joder" (ethics to f**k the system), which arguably continues the survival ethics of the oppressed since colonial times. Refueling James Cone's polemic statement "all white Christianity is satanic,"[10] De La Torre suggests a prophetic soteriology that unsettles the *status quo* of white male normativity in American Evangelicalism by calling for "badass believers" with a badass praxis and an agenda of: radical solidarity with the oppressed, celebration of culturally diverse

---

9. De La Torre, *Decolonizing Christianity*, 7–8.
10.. De La Torre, *Decolonizing Christianity*, 8. See also Cone, *Black Theology of Liberation*, 10.

belief, rejection of patriarchal laws, survival ethics, liberation of all, rejection of Eurocentric theological thought, disruptive/revolutionary temple [worship] cleansing, calling "bull**it" on religious and political hypocrisy, and costly sacrificing of all for the sake of Christianity otherwise.[11]

De La Torre is not the only Christian theologian, or the most elaborate, to adopt a postcolonial/decolonial prophetic stance to meet some of the challenges presented by postcolonial/decolonial critics on the case of Christianity.[12] Yet his voice speaks without filters on the tasks ahead for Christian theologians and religionists to make a postcolonial/decolonial mark in the public sphere.

In conclusion, the theological and missiological task today is faced with the duty of developing a non-westernized epistemology (as an indispensable component of its discourse) and a decolonizing agenda (as a Christian witness to the world). The inability or unwillingness for a given Christian expression or tradition to comply with this decolonizing demand in a time of global coloniality can only help support the claim that such a Christian expression or tradition is essentially a westernized and colonizing form of world Christianity—a component of the current global (neo)colonial order.

So far we have done three things as a way of introducing postcolonialism/decolonialism within the context of Christian discourse: (1) positioned the author of this chapter in the story of colonial modernity within the Western Christian academy; (2) argued that we live in a world where global coloniality is a governing reality lived painfully by subaltern communities, sharing colonial-modern-imperial subjugations in the world (within and outside the west) and inaptly by uncommitted westernized populations with racial-gender-economic privilege; and (3) claimed coloniality is an indispensable theological theme requiring a postcolonial/decolonial approach informing Christian theology. Readers not familiar with the tenets of postcolonial discourse and decoloniality as a praxis may wonder about the difference between postcoloniality and decoloniality and how theological discourse may be affected by these differentiated perspectives. We will briefly attend to this matter, locating both perspectives accordingly; but there is no way to decouple them and have a fair understanding of their historical trajectory and potential contributions. Since day one of the conquest and the establishment of different colonial projects around the world, we will see decolonizing efforts from the oppressed and the *añoranza* (nostalgic dream) of a postcolonial *bien vivir* (good living).

---

11. De La Torre, *Decolonizing Christianity*, 159–218.

12. Major postcolonial/ decolonial theological works include: Liew and Segovia, *Colonialism and the Bible*; Segovia, *Decolonizing Biblical Studies*; Jennings, *Christian Imagination*; Carter, *Race*; Medina, *Christianity, Empire and the Spirit*; Barreto and Sirvent, *Decolonial Christianities*; Smith, Lalitha, and Hawk, *Postcolonial Conversations*; Pui-lan, *Postcolonial Imagination and Feminist Theology* and *Postcolonial Politics and Theology*.

POSTCOLONIALISM AND ITS THEORETICAL INTERVENTIONISM

For full disclosure, I do not consider myself to be a postcolonial or a decolonial theologian. I think such and identifier commands evidence of a decolonial praxis I cannot provide with confidence at the moment and a situated theorization I am only beginning to produce. Nevertheless, I am in a decolonial route, in the search for postcolonial futures. And I am taking this journey as a Christian theologian. I first encountered the so-called postcolonial theory and its holy trinity (Edward Said, Homi Bhabha, and Gayatri Spivak) by way of engaging with philosophy of liberation and the epistemic decolonial shift led by Enrique Dussel, Walter Mignolo, Catherine Walsh, and a select number of Americano/a/x philosophers, literary critics, political theorists, ethnic study scholars, and so on. When reading what postcolonial theorists like Said, Bhabha, Spivak, Young, and others articulate, I found myself more in line with the practices they analyze than with their theoretical apparatus. Interestingly, when it comes to decoloniality and its analytics, I find myself attracted to its theoretical production.

The concept "postcolonial" serves the purpose of marking the intended theoretical disruption and rejection of the colonial regime and its rhetorical ramifications on all aspects of experiencing, knowing, acting, and imagining human life, social contract, and our relationship to the cosmos. On the other hand, the enunciation of this shift takes different shapes depending on the geopolitics of knowledge evoked by particular communal histories sharing common colonial-modern-imperial subjugations. It is important to notice that while postcolonialism may be used as a "tricontinental theoretical and political position which embodies an active concept of intervention within such oppressive circumstances," as notable postcolonial theorist Robert Young argues, *postcoloniality* "by contrast, puts the emphasis on the economic, material and cultural conditions that determine the global system in which the postcolonial nation is required to operate."[13] To what degree we can assure that these different concepts are matters of postcolonial semantics rather than modern ones is up for debate.

Decoloniality was merely emerging as a theoretical discourse during the 1990s, when a group of colonial and literary critics gathered to find a space for situated theorization from the American Global South. Postcolonial theory, by contrast, entered a second stage and gained recognition in different intellectual forums within and outside the west. Such recognition was built up with the seminal works of the Palestinian-American Edward Said (*Orientalism*, 1978; *Culture and Imperialism*, 1993) and his critique on Western discourses as political acts with material effects. The work of Homi K. Bhabha, a British educated and Indian literary critic (*The Location of Culture*, 1994) added critical content by demonstrating the instability and ambivalence of colonial discourses and offered hybridity as the space for resistance and existence.

---

13. Young, *Postcolonialism*, 57.

The influential voice of Gayatri C. Spivak, Indian literary critic and deconstructivist feminist ("Can the Subaltern Speak?," 1988), concurrently offered a stunning criticism on the commodification of the subaltern, who historically lacked a platform for self-expression in the social and political forum, in cultural and scholarly production, hence, she advocated for their agency.

After the 1990s Pramod K. Nayar suggests postcolonialism experienced two major shifts:

> The first is the shift toward a transnationalization of European histories, the second, extending the first shift to the contemporary age, an increased attention to locating politics, problems, and processes of the postcolony within the context of globalization, neocolonialism, and decolonization. Both these shifts may be subsumed under a new, or emergent, methodological rubric of postcolonial studies: an emphasis on exchanges, links, hybridities of racial, national, and cultural relations of "West versus East" of early postcolonial studies.[14]

In this transition, as Nayar observes, postcolonialism developed self-criticism (theoretical) by challenging its own binarism and essentialisms but at the same time its "strident colonial discourse" was replaced by "the sense of an uncertain colonial."[15]

DECOLONIALISM AND ITS RELATIONAL PRAXIS

"Decoloniality has a history, *herstory,* and praxis of more than 500 years," assert Walsh and Mignolo, two of the foremost decolonial thinkers in the Global South.[16] They present decoloniality as a relational praxis operationalized by "two types of activities at once: the thinking-doing and the doing-thinking."[17] I refer to these activities as situated theorization or praxis-grounded theorization.

Decoloniality's praxiological emphasis grounds historiography, semiotics, philology, epistemology, ethics, etc., in activities of resisting communities sharing colonial/modern/imperial subjugations whose identities and practices precede, transverse, and transcend modern Western archives. In Walsh and Mignolo's words: "decoloniality has been a component part of (trans)local struggles, movements, and actions to resist and refuse the legacies and ongoing relations and patterns of power established by external and internal colonialism."[18]

Decolonialists like Dussel, Mignolo, Walsh, and Boaventura de Sousa Santos help me think of decoloniality as a tactic of epistemic disobedience that emerges at the borders of multiple disciplines (the abyssal line to use de Sousa Santos nomenclature) and

---

14. Nayar, "Introduction," 2.
15. Nayar, "Introduction," 2.
16. Mignolo and Walsh, *On Decoloniality*, 16.
17. Mignolo and Walsh, *On Decoloniality*, 9.
18. Mignolo and Walsh, *On Decoloniality*, 16.

practices with the intended consequence of delinking from the logic of coloniality, the rhetoric of modernity, and the grammar of Occidentalism, which I think inform the DNA of Western monoculturalism. In the practice of decolonial delinking, I have come to do a lot of *unlearning* of westernized canonical knowledge and *relearning* of denied diasporic and indigenous canons of knowledge from the past and the present. In a sense, this is what *the thinking-doing* and *the doing-thinking* is about. Decolonialism, as a framing devise for decolonial praxis, "implies the recognition and undoing of the hierarchical structures of race, gender, heteropatriarchy, and class that continue to control life, knowledge, spirituality, and thought, structures that are clearly intertwined with and constitutive of global capitalism and Western modernity."[19] Decoloniality is about the whole life of the whole peoples of the whole world of all histories.

What is often said of postcolonialism can also be said of decolonialism: it is susceptible to the charge of conceptual inadequacy due to the immensity of its subject. Paraphrasing Dussel when referring to the task of Latin American critical intellectuals: *we have to [re]do it all (disciplinarily) in our continent*. Indeed, this is what informs the origination of decolonialism as an original and situated intellectual project in the 1990s.

Preceded by the historic continental conversations of philosophy of liberation, dependency theory, subaltern studies, and Chicano border studies, the Modernity/Coloniality/Decoloniality project (MCD) represents a collaborative framing approach emerging in the late 1990s from within a group of more than a dozen Latin American and Latinx intellectuals gathered to address the shortcomings in the social theories of modernity and postmodernity as articulated by "First World" countries.[20] MCD concluded that the modernity/postmodernity debates of the time represented a "narrow and euro-centered framework of analysis signaled by a declamation of the end of history, the naturalization of the inexorable victory of capitalism, and the lack of a critique on power in theories of modernity/postmodernity."[21]

Again, decolonialism is a situated and praxis-oriented intellectual project that creates the environment for decoloniality. This explains why the 1990s became an amniotic environment conducive for the emergence of MCD and decolonialism. In the global context of the Americas, there were several significant indigenous uprisings:[22]

- Indigenous peoples in Ecuador and Bolivia in 1990.

---

19. Mignolo and Walsh, *On Decoloniality*, 17.

20. This group was constituted by a diverse group of critical thinkers and social scientists: Aníbal Quijano (Perú), Enrique Dussel (Argentina-México), Edgardo Lander (Venezuela), Arturo Escobar (Colombia), Catherine Walsh (Ecuador), Nelson Maldonado-Torres (Puerto Rico), Zulma Palermo (Argentina), Santiago Castro-Gómez (Colombia), Fernando Coronil (Venezuela), and Walter Mignolo (Argentina-EEUU). See Grupo de Estudio Sobre Colonialidad (GESCO), "Modernidad/Colonialidad/Descolonialidad."

21. Mignolo and Walsh, *On Decoloniality*, 17.

22. Mignolo and Walsh, *On Decoloniality*, 25.

- The Zapatistas in Mexico in 1994 along with the continental organization against the colonial celebrations of 1992.
- The massive uprising of 1990 organized by the Confederation of Indigenous Nationalities of Ecuador (CONAJE).

Walsh and Mignolo note that "because of the character and nature of this period of Indigenous-led resurgence and struggle . . . They gave substance and form to what Arturo Arias, Luis Cárcamo-Huechante, and Emilio del Valle Escalante call the 'territory of indigenous agency' . . . new spheres of mobilization, subjectivity, and decolonizing production."[23]

Judging as inadequate the forerunning and emerging analytical frameworks (including postmodernism, poststructuralism, and the Southeast Asian postcolonial model), MCD's analytical framework sought to change the terms of the conversation by focusing on power analysis in theories of modernity with the following postulates:[24]

1. The origins of modernity are dated to the end of the fifteenth and the beginning of the sixteenth centuries and are directly connected with the conquest of America and the European control of the Atlantic.
2. It follows that colonial power has built world-systems aided by experimenting with different local forms of capitalism in colonial territories and Europe correspondingly as part of the agenda of modernity, resulting in global exploitation.
3. Modernity, as a planetary phenomenon, is then a function of European asymmetric relationships of power with other contexts, particularly but not exclusively with the colonial subjects, which has resulted in the process of subalternization of colonial subjects and peripherization of noncapitalist European and non-European economies. Explaining the necessity of race, ethnicity, gender, and class as subaltern categories all related to labor, productivity, and power.
4. Finally, Eurocentrism/Occidentalism provides the grammar and metaphysics necessary for modernity to produce specific forms of knowledge and subjectivities.

One of the main goals of decoloniality is to provide decolonial futures as its discursive praxis, which accompany decolonizing movements beyond merely articulating deconstructive analytics. In this sense, decoloniality is "for the creation, and cultivation of modes of life, existence, being, and thought *otherwise*; that is, modes that confront, transgress, and undo modernity/coloniality's hold . . . It is the for that takes us beyond the *anti* stance."[25] It is with this positive note that I want to move to the next section to explore what kind of dangers, resources, and tactics postcolonialism

23. Mignolo and Walsh, *On Decoloniality*, 26.
24. See García-Johnson, *Spirit Outside the Gate*, 64–65. These postulates are adapted from GESCO, "Modernidad/Colonialidad/Descolonialidad."
25. Mignolo and Walsh, *On Decoloniality*, 18.

and decolonialism may offer to the Christian theologian as s/he goes ahead discerning her/his decolonial task in our time of (neo)colonial global order.

DISCERNING THE DECOLONIAL TASK IN CHRISTIAN THEOLOGY

As an immigrant from the South, bilingual writer and speaker, and Latinx diaspora theologian native from one of the most impoverished-Americanized-displaced counties of the American continent, I have come to appreciate what postcolonial/decolonial perspectives have to offer in terms of praxiological commitments, situated epistemologies, intercultural analytics, and ethics of globalization. My concerns for their blind spots (dangerous essentialisms and reductions) in their interpretation, for instance, of the Christian phenomenon as manifestly colonial are always present. These theoretical liabilities come with the package and do not prevent me from taking advantage of the great assets these perspectives offer to the theological task in terms of imagining and crafting decolonial futures.

Evidently not all resistance qualifies as decolonizing or even postcolonial. Postcolonialism, as an interventionist discourse with the agenda to disrupt the multifaceted colonial order in the world, comes with certain fixations, obsessions, and flaws that are important to be aware of. Sugirtharajah finds that postcolonialism, in its most representative literary form, is:[26]

- Obsessed with diaspora, migrancy, border crossing, and yet there are massive segments of colonized humanity that do not fit these thematizations for they never migrated.

- Fixated with the west (model, content, and form of knowledge production) at the expense of other regions that require disciplinary attention in an interest of reconstructive proposals. An example of a different approach would be Kuan-Hsing Chen's self-referential model, which is the view of Asian societies (instead of Western societies) from each other's points of reference.[27] The same goes for the American continent and its diverse societies (as opposed to the United States of America, Canada, and Europe) and the original concept of "Our America" (Nuestra America) by the Cuban philosopher, poet, and liberator José Martí with an epistemic and geopolitical history dating from 1890.

- Guilty of canonical insularity that favors certain theoreticians engaged with Western criticism at the expense of newer voices emerging in different parts of the world and not necessarily engaged with the canonical West.

- Yet to become more praxis-oriented, with a track record that demonstrates societal "re-existence"—to use an indigenous decolonial term. Here the indigenous (re)emergence as (re)existence and (re)viving as making visible what is working

26. Sugirtharajah, *Exploring Postcolonial Biblical Criticism*, 24–27.
27. See Chen, *Asia as Method*.

in the social conditions of traditionally muted societies can be a complementary resource for postcolonialism.[28]

In terms of decolonialism's "dangers" Walsh dedicates a full chapter in *On Decoloniality* to offer some helpful self-criticism. As a situated postcolonial approach, decolonialism may be said to suffer from similar pathologies as postcolonialism, but, as we have shown, its locality, analytics, and praxis are not rooted exclusively in diaspora communities or migratory narratives but more so on border communities (not all related to migration but more about invasion and displacing acquisitions of the land) and indigeneity. Walsh is clear that the following dangers are present and recurrent in the decolonial option:

- Thinking and offering decoloniality as a model where coloniality is no longer present. Decoloniality aims at creating the conditions to re-exist in the backdrop of coloniality without any illusion that coloniality will come to an end rather soon and easily. Likewise, one needs to be aware of the danger of thinking that decoloniality cannot happen within the womb of imperial/occidental structures and geographies. The "outside or exteriority" is a nourishing notion, but many live, Walsh acknowledges, in the cracks of empire and coloniality—"the place of our location, agency, and everyday struggle."[29]

- Thinking of decoloniality as a "condition of illumination or enlightenment that some possess and others do not."[30] In the same breath, the danger of commodifying decoloniality is a great risk, notices Walsh, as if one could silo such an option and assigned it to a selected guild such as the MCD.

- The constant presence of "simplifications, generalizations, essentializations, and over-subjectivations . . . (particularly by well-intended and conscientious whites)."[31]

SO, WHAT'S CHRISTIAN THEOLOGY GOT TO DO WITH IT?

Postcolonial, and more recently, decolonial theologies have become a popular marriage of terms in monographs and university courses around the world. Several Christian thinkers have adopted different aspects of de/postcolonialism. That much we know. I only provide a preliminary and narrow view of these perspectives as I have come to experience them. I have no intention, interest, or capacity to qualify, as if one could have the expected neutrality, objectivity, and universality, what is *truly* postcolonial or decolonial in a given articulation by other theologians. To do that would be a modern/colonial/occidental act, a dishonest act of treason to the very subject and communities we are addressing in this chapter. All I can offer to the readers, acknowledging my

---

28. See Albán Achinte, "Pedagogías de La Re-Exitencia," 443–68.
29. Mignolo and Walsh, *On Decoloniality*, 82.
30. Mignolo and Walsh, *On Decoloniality*, 81.
31. Mignolo and Walsh, *On Decoloniality*, 81.

incompetence, is my imagination and how I have used de/postcolonialism. This does not mean, of course, I would not debate with other postcolonialists/decolonialists where they are positioning themselves when opting for de/postcolonialism in their discourses, and specially, to whose benefit they are using this option: production for promotion or delinking for re-existence?

I am asked by doctoral students exploring postcolonial/decolonial horizons, *ex-vangelicals* craving decolonizing spiritualities, and non-Christian activists aware of the role of faith in social emancipation, how do I tie what seems like a mutually excluding composite (Christian theology and postcolonialism/decoloniality) together? I truly believe Christian theology needs decoloniality as much as decoloniality needs Christian theology *otherwise*. Since day one of the conquest, and at the beginning of most colonial orders around the world, a westernized-hyperlocal form of Christian theology was presently fueling the eschatological imagination that gave substance to the conquering ethics of the west in its various colonial projects: be it the reconquest of Jerusalem, through massacres, in Iberian colonialism, or a genocidal supersessionism encrypted in a Manifest Destiny in British-American settler colonialism and the Protestant missions. Simultaneously, as witnessing *from another place* to the Galilean crucified messiah of the Gospels, resistance has built up through faith from the margins and interstitial spaces of oppressed communities sharing colonial/modern/imperial subjugations. There is more to Christianity than coloniality and complicity with empire. And there is more to postcolonialism/decoloniality than anti-westernism and anti-Christianism. The decolonial task in Christian theology stands right in between and beyond this tension.

It is not uncommon for me to express to my students and colleagues that my theological method is transoccidentality, my tactic is decoloniality, my agenda is liberationism, and my positionality is postcolonial. Elsewhere I have said:

> Transoccidentality claims that the theological process is a vital part of the decolonial imaginary—interstitially present and utopically proposing . . . This would require Christian theology . . . losing . . . its colonial/modern/Occidental pretention of truth, goodness, and beauty . . . The grand intellectual project for us Christians today ought to be building Christian theologies and missions at the service of the global population rather than using the population at the service of theology and mission.[32]

I hope the reader can grasp by now the clear message that postcolonialism/decolonialism will not do the theological work for us. As a theologian I have to respond theologically to the challenges and opportunities presented by these perspectives. As illustrated at the beginning of this chapter, the place of enunciation is critical as we learn to build global awareness, engagement, resistance, and re-existence. Thinking

---

32. García-Johnson, *Spirit Outside the Gate*, 66–67.

about the decolonial task in Christian theology, postcolonialism/decolonialism may help me commit to:

1. Realize that I am *where* I theologize.[33] This simply and radically relocates my theological imaginary, informs my theological trajectory, and transforms my vocation by way of situated praxis and committed theorization. This becomes a counter-Cartesian tactic of decolonial delinking from the modern/colonial/Western mind-body dualism (I am therefore I think) informing theological education, modern science, and Western geopolitics globally.

2. Identify and commit to the real issues making up the conditions of the most vulnerable communities of the world while excavating and deactivating the archives giving power knowledge to power structures and individuals with the capacity to shape the peoples, lands, and memories of entire populations that are literally dying before their time because they are valued less than the rest. Here, the work of the epistemologist of the South, de Sousa Santos, may help me move beyond monocultural scientific (linear) models of knowledge through the model of ecology of knowledges and the "principle of incompleteness of all knowledges." This is "the precondition for epistemological dialogues and debates among different knowledges" and peoples around the world. Such principle helps me develop academically but always grounded in existing communities, in contrast to grounding my knowledge exclusively in archival communities studied in books and curated as artifacts in a museum. "What each knowledge contributes to such a dialogue is the way in which it leads a certain practice to overcome a certain ignorance."[34]

3. Elaborate my theological projects for the sake of holistic people's transformation not merely for institutional promotion or guild recognition. If anything, engaging in postcolonial/decolonial scholarship attracts more criticism than compliment in academic spaces where white Western normativity informs academic excellence. I recently made the decision to write theologically in Spanish, my native language—a decision I had postponed for a least ten years. It has taken me that long to find my theological voice in my own native language. A visionary Spanish publisher (Editorial CLIE, Barcelona, Spain) is publishing a seven-volume series in the field of systematic theology from the Global South, intriguingly entitled *Teología del Nuevo Mundo* (*Theology of the New World*)—New World is a bad word in the Americas. Undoubtedly, I use it intentionally to demonstrate the underside of the European project during colonial times and how, after five centuries of colonial modernity, a new world, indeed a new self-creation, has emerged against the aftermath of the colonial wound (genocides, epistemides,

---

33. Based on Mignolo's "I am where I think," see Mignolo, *Local Histories/Global Designs*, Part 2.
34. Santos, *Epistemologies of the South*, 189.

ecocides, deicides, matricides, etc.). The first volume serves as the introduction, where I offer five theses for the making of theology of the New World.

- A theology of the New World ought to begin with faith and seek for faith in all peoples and lands of the Americas (and elsewhere), past, present, and future—before and beyond Western modernity.
- A theology of the New World ought to begin with *Docta Ignorantia* (learned ignorance) as a form of basic knowledge in the fostering of an ecology of knowledges, as we learn to re-cognize the knowledge of God in creation (Mother Earth/Pachamama and the other).
- A theology of the New World ought to begin with the *pro-biotic* principle (abundant life for all) of the Gospel of Jesus of Nazareth as we abandon the *anti-biotic* principle of Western civilizing missions and world evangelization (abundant life for the chosen ones).
- A theology of the New World ought to begin with the praxis of the Spirit as *Decolonial Healer*, the first word of the theological discourse.
- A theology of the New World ought to begin with theology as *biography* as we learn to co-read the Bible through narratives under the principle of theological abundance and generosity rather than theological exclusivity and exceptionalism.

Regardless of how far these theses go or how relevant they become to the intended audience (educated Christian millennials from the Spanish-speaking world), I confess I could not have thought of the theological task in these terms without the influence of de/postcolonialism.[35]

BIBLIOGRAPHY

Albán Achinte, Adolfo. "Pedagogías de La Re-Exitencia: Artistas Indigenas y Afrocolombianos." In *Pedagogías Descoloniales: Prácticas Insurgentes de Resistir (Re)Existir y (Re)Vivir*, edited by Catherine E. Walsh, 1:443–68. Quito, Ecuador: Ediciones Abya-Yala, 2013.

Barreto, Raimundo, and Roberto Sirvent. *Decolonial Christianities: Latinx and Latin American Perspectives*. Cham: Palgrave Macmillan, 2019.

Carter, J. Kameron. *Race: A Theological Account*. Oxford: Oxford University Press, 2008.

Chen, Kuan-Hsing. *Asia as Method: Toward Deimperialization*. Durham, NC: Duke University Press, 2010.

Cone, James H. *A Black Theology of Liberation*. Maryknoll, NY: Orbis, 2010.

De La Torre, Miguel. *Decolonizing Christianity: Becoming Badass Believers*. Grand Rapids: Eerdmans, 2021.

---

35. Other theological examples, in English, of the decolonial theological task can be found in some of my recent works: "Politics of the *Espíritu*:"; "Faith Seeking for Land"; *Spirit Outside the Gate*.

García-Johnson, Oscar. "Faith Seeking for Land: A Theology of the Landless." In *Theologies of Land: Contested Land, Spatial Justice, and Identity*, edited by K. K. Yeo and Gene L. Green, 38–68. Eugene, OR: Wipf & Stock, 2020.

———. "The Politics of the Espíritu: Ethics as Recognition–Assemblage–Decolonial Healing." In *T&T Clark Handbook of Political Theology*, edited by Rubén Rosario Rodríguez, 355–71. New York: T. & T. Clark, 2019.

———. *Spirit Outside the Gate: Decolonial Pneumatologies of the American Global South*. Downers Grove, IL: IVP Academic, 2019.

Grupo de Estudio Sobre Colonialidad (GESCO). "Modernidad/Colonialidad/Descolonialidad: Aclaraciones y Réplicas Desde un Proyecto Espitémico en el Horizonte del Bicentenario." *Pacarina del Sur: Revista del Pensamiento Crítico Latinoamericano* (November 20, 2016). http://www.pacarinadelsur.com/home/abordajes-y-contiendas/108-modernidad—colonialidad—descolonialidad-aclaraciones-y-replicas-desde-un-proyecto-epistemico-en-el-horizonte-del-bicentenario.

Huggan, Graham. "Introduction." In *The Oxford Handbook of Postcolonial Studies*, edited by Graham Huggan, 28–38. New York: Oxford University Press, 2016.

Jennings, Willie James. *The Christian Imagination: Theology and the Origins of Race*. New Haven: Yale University Press, 2010.

Kwok, Pui Lan. *Postcolonial Imagination and Feminist Theology*. Louisville: Westminster John Knox, 2005.

———. *Postcolonial Politics and Theology: Unraveling Empire for a Global World*. Louisville: Westminster John Knox, 2021.

Liew, Tat-siong Benny, and Fernando F. Segovia. *Colonialism and the Bible: Contemporary Reflections from the Global South*. Washington, DC: Lexington, 2018.

Medina, Néstor. *Christianity, Empire, and the Spirit: (Re)Configuring Faith and the Cultural*. Leiden: Brill, 2018.

Mignolo, Walter D. "Decolonizing Western Epistemology/Building Decolonial Epistemology." In *Decolonizing Epistemologies: Latino/a Theology and Philosophy*, edited by Ada María Isasi-Díaz and Eduardo Mendieta, 19–43. New York: Fordham University Press, 2012.

———. *Local Histories/Global Designs: Coloniality, Subaltern Knowledges, and Border Thinking*. Princeton: Princeton University Press, 2000.

Mignolo, Walter D., and Catherine E. Walsh. *On Decoloniality: Concepts, Analytics, Praxis*. Durham, NC: Duke University Press, 2018.

Miller, Liam. *Love, Rinse, Repeat*. "Episode 64: Spirit Outside the Gate." November 27, 2020. http://www.loverinserepeat.com/podcast/garciajohnson.

Nayar, Pramod K. "Introduction." In *Postcolonial Studies: An Anthology*, edited by Pramod K. Nayar, 1–12. Malden, MA: Wiley-Blackwell, 2015.

Smith, Kay Higuera, et al., eds. *Evangelical Postcolonial Conversations: Global Awakenings in Theology and Praxis*. Downers Grove, IL: InterVarsity, 2014.

Santos, Boaventura de Sousa. *The End of the Cognitive Empire: The Coming of Age of Epistemologies of the South*. Durham, NC: Duke University Press Books, 2018.

———. *Epistemologies of the South: Justice Against Epistemicide*. Boulder: Routledge, 2014.

Sugirtharajah, R. S. *Exploring Postcolonial Biblical Criticism: History, Method, Practice*. Hoboken, UK: John Wiley & Sons, 2011.

Young, Robert J. C. *Postcolonialism: An Historical Introduction*. Anniversary edition. Chichester, West Sussex: Wiley-Blackwell, 2016.

CHAPTER 4

Intercultural Theology

VOLKER KÜSTER

FOUNDATIONS

Terminology

The neologism intercultural theology specifies a particular way of doing theology, namely interculturally. The prefix inter- competes with a number of other fashionable wordings such as multi-, cross-, or trans-cultural. Instead of using them synonymously, I opt for a clear differentiation. *Multi*-cultural was probably the first word creation in this semantic field. It describes the existence of many different cultures in one given society. Since little attention was paid to the inner cohesion of the society, but the idea was that everyone could live out his or her own cultural identity, conflicts were inevitable. Today we are experiencing a crisis of the major European multicultural societies like Great Britain, France, or the Netherlands that have large immigrant diasporas due to their colonial past. Even though 20 percent of Germany's population are of migrant background and its cities are multicultural as well, it never officially accepted being an immigrant country. Work migrants who have been invited since the "economic miracle (*Wirtschaftswunder*)" in the 1950s were euphemistically called "guest worker (*Gastarbeiter*)." Hate of immigrants and open racism have led to the rise of right-wing parties and fascism in many European countries. The failure of EU refugee politics has caused a restrictive border regime that further escalates the crisis.

Cross-cultural is a term coined in American social anthropology for the comparison of mainly primal cultures but also resonates with music and fashion discourses on crossover. Proponents of the prefix *trans*- claim that it expresses the fluidity and intermingling of cultures while they suspect the term *inter*-cultural of essentialism. Yet at least in theological discourse that never has been the case. Intercultural theology is focusing on the space in between cultures and their interactions. It is aware of phenomena such as syncretism, double or multiple religious belonging, hybridity, etc. Trans- on the other hand has the strong connotation of "beyond," and therefore is endangered of not taking seriously cultural differences. Transnational corporations (TNC), *Cocacolonization,* and *McDonaldization* are the trailblazers of neoliberal consumer capitalism that slip national taxation, exploit cheap labor, and destabilize local cultures. Here we are already in the middle of the discussion about the term culture itself, which has probably become one of the most contested terms in times of identity politics. Clifford Geertz's semiotic definition of culture as a man-made web of meanings that has to be hermeneutically approached is still helpful due to its openness. A close reading of any given culture allows to disclose hybridizations and point out identity markers taking seriously the inevitable glocalization, without neglecting cultural peculiarities and diversity.

Emergence

Werner Ustorf has characterized intercultural theology as "theological repentance of the north." When his teacher Hans Jochen Margull, his predecessor on the chair of "Theology of Mission" in Birmingham Walter Hollenweger and the catholic theologian Richard Friedli founded the series *Studies in the Intercultural History of Christianity* their agenda was to create a platform to observe the theological developments in the Global South. They can be considered as the founding fathers of intercultural theology as a continental project in the west, which emerged from the pluri-discipline missiology, religious studies, and ecumenics taught in different combinations at European theological faculties.

The turn from the 1960s to the 1970s has seen contextual theologies sprouting in the Global South and its diaspora. These were theological identity reconstructions in the aftermath of decolonization, secular emancipation movements, and the formation of a new world order after World War II. Its coordinate system was defined by the East-West conflict between the two ideological blocks of capitalism and liberal democracy versus communism as well as the North-South conflict between the affluent industrial countries and the, in terms of infrastructure, underdeveloped Third World. Neocolonialism often by the former colonial nations or the newly emerged superpowers was trying to secure natural resources, accompanied by export of cheap labor to countries with totalitarian governments that suppressed unions and proxy wars between the superpowers on other peoples' territory. The two major schools of contextualization, liberation theologies as well as inculturation and dialogue theologies are still recognizable today. Since the military dictatorships in Latin America or South Korea have been replaced by young democracies or populist regimes, as has been the apartheid regime in South Africa, while the gap between rich and poor still widens in the era of globalization and neoliberal consumer capitalism, liberation theologies have to be reshaped. Conceptions of culture have become much more fluent and ambiguous and with it also the contextual theological project. Proponents of interreligious dialogue have become aware that there is no perpetual advancement in interreligious relations but that dialogue has its purpose in itself as a continuing conversation. Also, there is no dialogue without addressing the other side of the coin which is interreligious conflict. New generative themes on the agenda of the second and following generations of contextual theologians are gender, ethnicity, and ecology.

Around the 1980s a number of projects in some way or the other claimed the heritage of mission studies to negotiate religious pluralism. John Hick and Paul Knitter tried to deconstruct *The Myth of Christian Uniqueness* and propagated a pluralist theology of religions, which turns out to be a disguised form of inclusivism distorting the distinctive identities of lived religions. Hans Küng promoted *Global Ethics*, ascribing religions the role of peacekeepers. In the US the Jesuit Francis Clooney revived Christian apologetics in the form of comparative theology. Yet religions are distinct entities with their particular identities and inner pluralisms which have to be taken seriously. Intercultural theology makes this diversity and "otherness" its starting point counteracting destructive strategies like "othering."

Meanwhile Lamin Sanneh pointed out that world Christianity was no longer a Western religion but is flourishing in the Global South free from the self-doubts of enlightenment Christianity. Contextual theologies are however a form of enlightenment of the enlightenment, a critical discourse with the Western academic theological heritage, colonialism, and Eurocentrism at large. The foundation of the Ecumenical Association of Third World Theologians (EATWOT) let to a successful South-South dialogue and became a model for doing intercultural theology.

Dilemmas

Intercultural theology is aware of the fluidity and ambiguity of all theology. It negotiates at least four dilemmas:

- The relevance-identity dilemma negotiates the quest for relevance of Christian faith in a particular context and the preservation of its identity.
- The particularity-universality dilemma negotiates between local forms of Christianity and its claims to universality.
- The exclusivism-inclusivism dilemma negotiates between claims to absoluteness and inclusion.
- The unity-plurality dilemma negotiates between tendencies to reduce diversity and those to embrace and celebrate it.

While pluralist theology of religions tries to open up to other religions by parenthesizing in Christian teaching what does not seem to be compatible, I try to carve out and emphasize that even those generative themes that function as identity markers in Christian tradition are compatible with our pluralistic lifeworld. The renaissance of trinitarian teaching in the works of Karl Rahner, Jürgen Moltmann, and Leonardo Boff fostered a communicative and relational image of God. "God is God in community." With Boff this got liberation theological overtones. Moltmann portrait the crucified God as being vulnerable. Liberation theologies identified the suffering Christ with the suffering of the most vulnerable, the poor and oppressed. Kenotic Christology also furthers the image of God exposing him/herself to the world and becoming vulnerable. The Holy Spirit blows where she likes, as is often colloquially stated, allowing to search for God's presence through the christological lens in cultures and religions. If God created the world the latter are part and parcel of this act. Therefore, we neither have to give up trinitarian teaching nor Christology in order to do theology interculturally. Different from comparative theology the driving force behind all this is not Christian apologetics but ethical to contribute to human flourishing. Intercultural theology is not about creating a new meta-system but providing a platform for dialogue and a habitus of respect, recognition and empathy for the "other."

Imperatives

Intercultural theology is intrinsically driven by three imperatives:

Hermeneutic imperative: Intercultural theology is a hermeneutical endeavor. In order to understand the other, we have to communicate and vice versa. Contextual theology is also based on hermeneutics evolving in the circle between text and context. From the context emerges the criterion of relevance: what does Christian faith have to contribute to a particular lifeworld? The theology formulated in response to this question has to be tested against the text which provides the criterion of identity. There is not only a single meaning to a text but on the other hand not everything goes. The text contains a universe of meanings that at the same time sets the boundaries of its interpretation. The hermeneutical circle has to be paced time and again. The context constantly changes, in the hermeneutical process one never returns to the same context.

While the context is the variable in the hermeneutical process the text is the relational constant. Every change in one's social location offers new perspectives on the text and brings other aspects of the universe of meanings to the fore. The hermeneutical circle thus already generates its checks and balances. Yet every contextual theology has to stand the test in the ecumenical forum of the community of storytelling and interpretation of glocal Christianities. The criterion of dialogue necessitates an intercultural platform.

Contextual theology is committed to a hermeneutics of suspicion. Liberation theologies debunked the use of the bible as justification of colonialism, yet they stopped in front of the text. Feminist theology however also exposed the patriarchal elements in the text itself not only in its interpretation. As did postcolonial theology. By pointing out that the land was not empty Musa Dube implicitly also criticized the earlier focus of liberation theology on the Exodus. Musimbi Kanyoro finally turned the hermeneutics of suspicion against the culture as well. When African patriarchal culture reinforces patriarchal traditions in the text one has to intervene. With her dictum "*we are the text*, and the Bible and tradition of the Christian church are the context of our theology,"[1] Chung Hyun-Kyung once and for all made clear that the hermeneutical circle can be equally entered through both poles, text and context. Human experience with God and live stories become sources of our doing theology. This matches in Western tradition with the homiletics of Ernst Lange who wants to intertwine (*versprechen*) our lifeworld with the world of the text or the philosophy of Wilhelm Schapp who envisions a narrative anthropology, "we are enmeshed in stories."[2]

Identificatory imperative: The initial basic formular of the World Council of Churches focused on the acknowledgment of Jesus Christ as common denominator. Jesus himself asked his disciples "Who do you say I am?" (Mark 8:27–29). Each believer, belonging to a Christian community in a particular culture has to answer this question anew. Latin American liberation theology discovered Jesus Christ in the poor and oppressed, for Black theologians he became the Black messiah, for *minjung* theology he was present among the *minjung*, in India he became a *Dalit* and in Japan a *burakumin*. Second-wave feminist theologians questioned a God who sacrificed his son on the cross and whether a male savior could save women, but saw Jesus in solidarity with the women around him and discovered his female side. Women theologians from the Global South and its diaspora criticized Western feminist theologians for not reflecting on their social location in terms of oppressive structures that exploit women of color. They discovered Jesus in the face of their grandmothers, mothers, and sisters. In the context of African traditional religion Jesus was seen as an ancestor, in a Hindu context as religious teacher (*guru*) or incarnation of a God (*avatar*) in the context of Buddhism as enlightened one (*bodhisattva*). The discovery of the presence of Christ among the wretched of the earth, encountering him as a familiar religious figure, seeing his face mirrored in the face of a suffering or joyful fellow human being contributes to identity reconstructions in traumatic and posttraumatic circumstances, caused by (neo)colonialism, dictatorships, populist regimes, and the destructive forces of neoliberal capitalism.[3]

Dialogical imperative—The criterion of dialogue involves contextual theologies in a perpetual intercultural discourse. Like Islam and Buddhism Christianity is

1. Chung, *Struggle*, 11.
2. Schapp, *Entanglement in Stories*, 56.
3. Cf. Küster, *Many Faces*.

a missionary religion. In conjunction with colonialism, imperialism, and Cold War ideology it has contributed to a lot of suffering and conflict in the Global South. At the same time, it often brought medical service and education especially also for the poor and underprivileged, women and children. In spite of being the religion of the oppressors, it was embraced by the colonized as a liberating message against all odds. Today mission should only take place as a dialogical endeavor showing respect for the cultural-religious identity of the other. Yet mission and interreligious dialogue are two pair of shoes. Mission is about converting the other to one's own faith, dialogue is about understanding each other's faith and creating a peaceful living together. Representatives of other religions are suspicious that Christians have a hidden missionary agenda, even when they claim to come for dialogue. They criticize that already the language game of interreligious dialogue is dominated by Christian terminology and concepts. On the other hand, there is no dialogue without witness of one's own faith, otherwise it is a religious studies seminar. Theologically the triune God is God in relation and therefore per se dialogical. As God is in constant internal dialogue and with creation so should be human beings.

DIMENSIONS

Since intercultural theology emerged from the pluri-discipline missiology, religious studies, and ecumenics it is carrying with it questions of intercultural, interreligious and interconfessional exchange. My vision is that we can learn from interreligious encounters how to negotiate commonalities, difference, and chances of learning from each other in intercultural and interconfessional dialogues.

The interreligious dimension

I differentiate between a theology of religions that operates in the frame of reference of one's own faith system and asks for the place of other religions in it and a theology of dialogue. While the former is bound to the exclusivism-inclusivism dilemma the latter transcends this boundary and makes itself vulnerable to the position of the other (Hans Jochen Margull). In mutually recognizing ones claims to absoluteness strategies to negotiate pluralism can develop. In interreligious dialogue we at least differentiate between three strands: the dialogue of hands is preconceptual and ethical oriented it brings together adherents of different religions in times of crisis and catastrophe to work for the survival and sustenance of the community. In the dialogue of the heart the mystics of different religious traditions meet, it is postconceptual and spiritually oriented. The dialogue of the mind brings together the learned of the different religions, it is conceptual and intellectually oriented. It is prone to conflict because we almost inevitably reach a point where we can at best agree to disagree.

Jewish-Christian dialogue is the mother of the modern dialogue movement. It was initiated out of Christian guilt complexes after the Holocaust and has therefore an ethical foundation. Attempts to broaden it to a trialogue with Muslim attendance in the late twentieth century have not been very successful, not in the least due to the political circumstances. Yet even in dialogues between two of the Abrahamic religions—as they are often referred to today, to express their kinship—the third party should be kept in mind as sitting at the table. Jews and Christians share parts of their sacred texts, and the Hebrew Bible and the Qur'an know the major biblical personas, from Abraham to Mary and Jesus. Christians believe that Jesus is the Messiah, Muslims revere Jesus as a Prophet. Jews do neither, nor do Christians and Jews accept Mohammed as a Prophet. While the younger religion accepts the older as predecessors, the older religions regard the younger as a heresy. Even though they believe in the same God their traditions are so diverse that they are distinct religions, with diverting images of God. In dialogue with Hinduism and Buddhism which are kindred religions as well the mystical dimension is predominant. Christian ashrams and Zen retreats or Zen monks reading Master Eckart are good examples. In Buddhist-Christian dialogue commonalities and differences between the concepts of God and Absolute Nothingness are explored. Dialogue with traditional religions is often rather an inner dialogue of Christian theologians with their own heritage. In China there is also dialogue with the religions of Chinese origin Confucianism and Daoism. Finally, there have been initiatives for dialogues with new religious movements and atheists as well.

The intercultural dimension

Intercultural theology started as a project to monitor the developments of Christianity in the Third World. EATWOT is a good theological example of the empire writing back. It had its inaugural meeting in Dar es Salaam, Tanzania in 1976, only five years after the publication of Gustavo Gutiérrez's groundbreaking *Theology of Liberation*. EATWOT is an initiative from the Global South that brought together theologians from Africa, Asia, and Latin America to discuss their theological agendas. The heuristic question of "commonalities, differences and cross fertilization" formulated at the second General Assembly in Mexico City (1986) defines the discourse well. When Engelbert Mveng speaks of "anthropological poverty"[4] and Aloysius Pieris states "the common denominator linking Asia with the rest of the Third World is its overwhelming poverty. The specific character defining Asia within the other poor countries is its multifaceted religiousness."[5] They build bridges between the two big schools: inculturation and dialogue theologies originating from Africa and Asia, and liberation theology with its strong hold in Latin America. EATWOT's first president, Sergio Torres, characterized Latin America as the most westernized continent of the Third

---

4. Fabella and Torres, *Irruption of the Third World*, 220.
5. Pieris, *Asian Theology of Liberation*, 69.

World.[6] While it gained independence already in the nineteenth century, Africa and Asia were in the middle of their postcolonial identity reconstructions. With South Korean minjung theology and Black theology in South Africa emerged liberation theologies early on also in these continents which were sensitive to the cultural-religious dimension of their respective contexts. Latin American liberation theology on the other hand had to come to terms with folk Catholicism, the indigenous traditions, and the Afro-Latin American minority. In the second generation, people like EATWOT president Diego Irarrázaval merged liberation with inculturation theology. James Cone early on claimed his "double identity" as American with African roots. Yet even though Cone and Virgil Elizondo have been founding members EATWOT kept an ambivalent stance over against these representatives of the diaspora. Mercy Amba Oduyoye proclaimed the "Irruption within the irruption"[7] creating space for women theologians within EATWOT. Her intervention resulted in the inception of EATWOT's women's commission and the election of Oduyoye as its first female president. With its continental conferences, local initiatives, and the quinquennial general assembly, EATWOT was the most successful intercultural platform so far. Currently there are still very active local chapters and their journal *Voices* still appears, but the central organization is in lack of funds and seems to be in a phase of reorientation.[8]

The interconfessional dimension

The ecumenical movement is committed to the idea of unity of the Christian traditions. It originates from the confluence of three major movements—mission, life and work, as well as faith and order, which all organized international conferences and are still major fields of the work of the WCC. Already the World Mission Conference at Edinburgh 1910 conceded that the competition among Christian confessions and denominations on the mission field is an obstacle because it highly irritates the locals and the converts. The World Conference of Life and Work in Stockholm 1925 focused on the ethical responsibility of churches, while the first World Conference on Faith and Order in Lausanne 1927 was called to negotiate differences in faith convictions and church organization to pave the way for growing consensus and towards unity. After more than a centenary of multilateral and bilateral meetings between Christian confessions, denominations, and groups we have reached a certain impasse. Many divisions have been overcome but others remained separative, where we only can agree to disagree.

A major obstacle are the differing visions on Christian ministry, apostolic succession, and papal supremacy, which do not block intercommunion in the least. The visions of unity differ in the three major confessional families. The Orthodox churches

---

6. Torres, *Third World Theologies*, 121.
7. Oduyoye, "Reflections," 246.
8. https://eatwotglobal.com/index.html.

strive for one church on the basis of the first seven councils, the Catholic church expects that the other churches return under the supremacy of the pope, while the mainline Protestant churches talk about "unity in reconciled diversity" or in certain Evangelical, fundamentalist, and Pentecostal strands are not interested in unity at all. Here we could learn from interreligious dialogue, where it is clear from the outset that the goal cannot be one single religion but one has to learn from each other's differences and join a common search for truth. The plurality of global Christianities can then become enriching instead of being a threat. The ecumenical movement would become a laboratory of intercultural theology.

TOOLS

The toolbox of intercultural theology contains a variety of theories and methods that allow a multiaxial approach integrating different perspectives. At the same time, it has to be noted that contextual theologies and intercultural theology are not only avant-garde within theology but have also anticipated broader critical discourses. Contextual theology for instance was postcolonial criticism *avant la lettre* reflecting on the distortion's colonialism did to local cultures and reconstructing identities that were aware of their hybrid nature.

STORY THEOLOGY

Doing theology with Asian resources, ordinary readers or even the Bible closed are catch phrases that point to new hermeneutical approaches. The rich universe of stories people live by, myths, fables, fairy tales, literature, films, or songs are drawn into a dialogical process of doing theology. C. S. Song, Kosuke Koyama, and South Korean *minjung* theology are pioneers of story theology. Ernesto Cardenal's *The Gospel in Solentiname* reading the biblical text in the lifeworld of the farmers and fishermen of lake Nicaragua has become proverbial for the ordinary reader approach that takes into account the voices from the margins, the poor or subaltern, as they are referred to in postcolonial theory. New Testament scholar Musa Dube opens up a dialogue with the African-initiated churches whose prophets claim that they get their inspiration directly from God with the Bible closed and whose members are inspired by the spirit in their Bible reading (*semoia* reading). "Can the subaltern speak?" (Gayatri Spivak)—yes, but their voices are hardly heard of. How to give the voiceless an audience without speaking on behalf of and patronizing them is one of the core research ethical questions in contextual and intercultural theology. Local agency and local knowledge have to be respected in their own right and approached in a dialogical way. The interconnectedness of different forms of oppression triggered by classicism, racism, sexism, etc. is debunked.

Aesthetics and Hermeneutics

Art is an important source of intercultural theology and a way of doing contextual theology. There are Christian artworks from all phases of the missionary expansion of Christianity. These are visual expressions of a contextual theology and intercultural exchange long before the spoken or written word. It started with symbolic representations rather than with figurative images. The cross and the fish in the Roman catacombs have their correspondents in the cross on the lotus flower depicted on top of the stele of Sianfu or the St. Thomas Cross in Chennai. These are depictions of the Syrian cross that is not so much a symbol of suffering and death than a cosmic tree of life or the axis of the world. The cross is not superimposed on the lotus flower but elevated by it like the Buddha or Hindu gods sitting or standing on the lotus. The rites controversy put an end to these early forms of accommodation. The missionary awakening of the nineteenth century was driven by Eurocentrism, everything local was neglected. Only after the devastating experiences on the killing fields of the Great War, the Vatican changed its mission strategy again. The apostolic letter *Maximum illud* (1919) by Benedict XV was intended not the least to push back French colonial nationalism in China. Eurocentric overtones remained yet it called for a Chinese clergy. As a consequence, it came to a Catholic renaissance that wanted to revive traditional cultures in a Christian key. Neo-accommodation produced in Catholic art schools became fashionable in China, Japan, Vietnam, India, and elsewhere. The post-World War Two era saw a rich production of contextual Christian art in Africa, Asia, and Latin America. Today art inspired by Christian faith and generative themes moves out of the contextualization framework and the churches and becomes part of the glocal art world. At the same time theologians are seeking dialogue with the secular art world. What can we learn from art for our doing theology, where can we find traces of God's presence beyond the churches?

I understand aesthetics as perception of the senses beyond the predominant visual orientation, further it is not limited to beauty alone but also comprises the ugly and evil. The earlier presupposed relationship between ethics and aesthetics has to be reconstructed in any given concrete case. Aesthetics is based on sensual experience and emotion, any attempt to verbalize it leads inevitably to loss. This is where hermeneutics come into play to negotiate this loss. Yet any fixation of meaning is only temporary and has to open up to the universe of meaning of the text or work of art respectively.

Ethics

Intercultural theology is not about creating a new meta-system but about generating a platform for dialogue. It therefore has a strong ethical orientation, creating a habitus of respect, recognition, and empathy over against the cultural-religious other.

It develops strategies to empower the poor and oppressed to regain their subjecthood through conscientization. The interconnectedness of different forms of oppression like classicism, sexism, racism, ageism, etc. calls for *deep solidarity* between the different identity discourses. Intercultural theology anticipated intersectionality in theology.

RISKS

The fall of the Berlin Wall became iconic for the new epoch of globalization. Even though it might seem a Western perspective on first sight, the deterioration of the former Soviet Union destabilized the power alliances of the Cold War era. In looking back the question may well be asked whether the proclaimed end of the Second World is not indeed a Western perspective. Communism survived in China in combination with state capitalism and the Cold War never really ended in countries like South Korea or Taiwan. The "end of history" (Francis Fukuyama) and the "clash of civilizations" (Samuel Huntington) which was seen as a follow-up to the Cold War world order were proclaimed by the augurs of the American empire wet dreams of white supremacy. Robert Schreiter saw the expansion of neoliberal consumer capitalism and the compression through new communication technologies as signature of the end of the bipolar world order. Today China is claiming its position as empire metaphorizing the ancient Silk Road for its neocolonial aspirations. Russia regained strength under the former KGB officer Wladimir Puttin. The US and the EU are meanwhile torn apart by populist politicians and a weakness in reforming nation-states and financial markets in times of globalized capitalism steered by transnational corporations.

We are moving from contextualization to glocalization, over the years interculturality and contextuality of theology have become increasingly intertwined. German sociologist Ulrich Beck has characterized our globalized world as a risk society that is vulnerable and torn by crises, a few of which we are going to look into by way of concluding:

- *Economic crisis*—The Asian financial crisis of 1997/1998 showed the weakness of the so-called tiger and panther states and caused economic hardship for the common people. The gap between the rich and the poor is unaltered widening. This was reinforced by the global financial crisis of 2007/2008 that we are still suffering from. In their manifesto *Occupy Religion* Kwok Pui-lan and Joerg Rieger have revisited liberation theologies in light of the 99 percent against the 1 percent. They emphasize that "there is no safe place in the middle" left and point out that identity politics can be played against its proponents by stoking up conflicts between the different interest groups. The authors call instead for "deep solidarity" that negotiates and recognizes difference.[9] Religions should free themselves from their neoliberal captivity and become spaces of care and resistance.

9. Pui-lan and Rieger, *Occupy Religion*, 217–29.

- *Terrorism*—The 9/11 terrorist attacks of 2001 were regarded by Westerners as the beginning of a new era. The terrorists were however the offspring of the Arab middle and upper class, well-integrated into the capitalist system. Tinyiko Maluleke has raised the issue of the equality of life regarding the thousands of human beings dying every day of illness and starvation in Africa and elsewhere in the Global South. The threat of terrorism has impacted our lifeworlds from security checks at airports and train and bus stations to antitank barriers at Christmas markets. At the same time the war on terror has destabilized the Middle East and tormented its peoples. This is one of the root causes of the current migration crisis. The dialogue of the hands may be a way of bridging the gap even to fundamentalist groups within the different religious tradition. By experiencing the religious other, whom they do not know much about but are full of prejudices against as the one who is reaching out a helping hand in a situation of despair may make a difference and open up a chance to change hostile attitudes. Intra-religious dialogue is also an important strategy, we have to address the fundamentalists in our respective traditions and confront them with their distortions of our shared religion. Women have often been pioneers of reclaiming their religious traditions with little support by the silent majority.

- *Migration*—The European refugee crisis of 2015 was the culmination of developments that were triggered by the war on terror and inner Arabian/Islamic power struggles as well as Russia's and China's ambitions in global politics. Ruthless criminal organization made human trafficking a flourishing branch of neoliberal capitalism. Despots like Erdogan or Lukaschenko instrumentalize it for their political ends. The migration issue is a laboratory of intercultural theology; poverty, exploitation, various forms of oppression, terror, rape, and ecological disasters are the intersecting generative themes of the context. Classism, racism, sexism, and cultural-religious identities are high on the agenda. The rights of the refugees, the rights of the population of the receiving country, and, lest we forget, the rights of those majorities who stayed behind have to be negotiated.

- *Pandemic*—The COVID-19 crisis overlaps in many ways with the aforementioned other crises. It is not only us who are trying to interpret the virus, the virus is also interpreting us. It lay open the social and economic inequalities and various forms of oppression. While populists like Trump, Johnson, or Bolsonaro but also the Swedish government put individual freedom and economic interest first, most Western countries prioritized the protection of life in fighting the pandemic. Ethical issues at stake were *triage*, herd immunity, and vaccination. The mask became emblematic for an alternative pandemethics. Initially when masks were not available on a broad scale and experts were still questioning their effectiveness people started to sew masks and distribute them among family and friends. Wearing such a mask was meant to protect the other, not oneself, not knowing whether others would do the same to protect me. This mask-ethics marks a shift in Western neoliberal capitalist behavioral habits. The complete opposite was the latter FPP-2 mask with filter that allowed me to breath better but also spread my germs freely. The Western hygiene strategies wear a mask, wash your hands, watch your distance (3W) and the 3G-rule—vaccinated, recovered, or tested—are not feasible in the Global South. Whole families live in one room, hundreds share one water tab, and neither masks nor tests or even vaccines are available in sufficient numbers. Some Western countries contributed to the international vaccination fund COVAX but at the same time reserved the available vaccines for themselves. Intercultural ethics raises questions about the equality of life, solidarity, and the fair sharing of resources. What the virus has revealed may not be covered up again. Intercultural theology imagines Pantopia—the wordplay is a contraction of pandemic and utopia and at the same time a reference to the Greek *pan*—utopia for all as an alternative vision to the "new normal" of neoliberal capitalism.

BIBLIOGRAPHY

Abraham, K. C., ed. *Third World Theologies*. Maryknoll, NY: Orbis, 1990.

Beck, Ulrich. *World Risk Society*. Cambridge: Polity, 1999.

Chung, Hyun Kyung. *Struggle to Be the Sun Again: Introducing Asian Women's Theology*. Maryknoll, NY: Orbis, 1990.

Clooney, Francis X. *Comparative Theology. Deep Learning Across Religious Borders*. Chichester, UK: Wiley-Blackwell, 2010.

Dube, Musa W. *Postcolonial Feminist Interpretation of the Bible*. St. Louis: Chalice, 2000.

Geertz, Clifford. *The Interpretation of Cultures: Selected Essays*. New York: Basic Books, 1973.

Hyun-Kyung, Chung. *Struggle to be the Sun Again. Introducing Asian Women's Theology*. Maryknoll, NY: Orbis, 1990.

Irarrázaval, Diego. *Inculturation: New Dawn of the Church in Latin America*. Maryknoll, NY: Orbis, 2000.

Kanyoro, Musimbi R. A. *Introducing Feminist Cultural Hermeneutics: An African Perspective*. London: Pilgrim, 2002.

Knitter, Paul, and John Hick. *The Myth of Christian Uniqueness. Toward a Pluralistic Theology of Religions*. Maryknoll, NY: Orbis, 1988.

Küng, Hans. *Global Responsibility. In Search of a New World Ethics*. London: SCM, 1991.

Küster, Volker. *The Many Faces of Jesus Christ: Intercultural Christology*. Maryknoll, NY: Orbis, 2001.

Küster, Volker, with Dorothea Erbele-Küster, eds. *Between Pandemonium and Pandemethics. Responses to Covid-19 from Theology and Religions*. Leipzig: EVA, 2022.

———. *Einführung in die Interkulturelle Theologie*. Göttingen: Vandenhoeck & Ruprecht, 2011.

———. *God/Terror. Ethics and Aesthetics in Contexts of Conflict and Reconciliation*. Sheffield: Equinox, 2021.

———. *A Protestant Theology of Passion. Korean Minjung Theology Revisited*. Leiden: Brill, 2010.

———. "Visual Arts in World Christianity." In *Wiley-Blackwell Companion to World Christianity*, 368–85. London: Wiley-Blackwell, 2016.

Küster, Volker, with Dorothea Erbele-Küster and Michael Roth. *Many Faces/Theologieinfiziert. Religiöse Rede im Kontext der Pandemie*. Stuttgart: Kohlhammer, 2021.

Maluleke, Tinyiko. "Of Collapsible Coffins and Ways of Dying: The Search for a Catholic Contextuality in African Perspective." *The Ecumenical Review* 54 (2002) 313–32.

Oduyoye, Amba Mercy. "Reflections from a Third World Woman's Experience and Liberation Theologies." In *The Irruption of the Third World: Challenge to Theology*, edited by Virginia Fabella and Sergio Torres, 246–55. Maryknoll, NY: Orbis, 1983.

Pieris, Aloysius. *An Asian Theology of Liberation*. Maryknoll, NY: Orbis, 1988.

Pui-lan, Kwok, and Joerg Rieger. *Occupy Religion: Theology of the Multitude*. Lanham, MD: Rowman & Littlefield, 2013.

Sanneh, Lamin. *Whose Religion is Christianity?: The Gospel beyond the West*. Grand Rapids: Eerdmans, 2003.

Schapp, Wilhelm. *Entanglement in Stories*. Albany: University of New York, 2018.

Schreiter, Robert J. *The New Catholicity: Theology between the Global and the Local*. Maryknoll, NY: Orbis, 1997.

Ustorf, Werner. "The Cultural Origins of 'Intercultural Theology.'" *Mission Studies* 25 (2008) 229–51.

CHAPTER 5

Migration Theology

GEMMA TULUD CRUZ

THE MIGRATION OF VULNERABLE POPULATIONS

Scholars say that at no other point in history has the number of people on the move at such a large scale that the current historical period is being referred to as the age of migration.[1] The 2020 UN Department of Economic and Social Affairs' International Migration Report notes that prior to the disruptions to migration flows caused by the COVID-19 pandemic, the number of international migrants had grown robustly over the past two decades. It is estimated that the number of persons living outside of their country of origin reached 281 million in 2020, roughly equal to the size of the entire population of Indonesia, the world's fourth most populous country. The same report states that disruptions caused by the COVID-19 pandemic may have reduced the number of international migrants by around 2 million globally.[2] However, as the 2021 migration crisis on the Belarus border with Poland shows,[3] the mass migration of people, particularly vulnerable populations, is an issue that is not going away, especially when global economic and political insecurities persist and there are people smugglers who profit from peoples' misery and desperation or, perhaps worse, when there are politicians and state authorities who weaponize migrants.

---

1. See Castles and Miller, *Age of Migration*; Solimano, *International Migration in the Age of Crisis and Globalization*; and Haywood, *Great Migrations*, 244–49.
2. UNDESA, "International Migration 2020 Highlights."
3. See *BBC News*, "Belarus Border Crisis."

It is common knowledge that a great number of people who move today are forced to do so in one way or another. This is buttressed by the fact that the most prevalent root of contemporary migration is underlying disparity in access to safety and livelihood opportunities. For many people, especially those from the Global South, migration is the best, if not the only, way out of poverty and death-dealing conditions. To be sure, there is real obligation to protect persons fleeing from disastrous environmental conditions as well as extreme poverty and economic conditions that generate and drive conflict.[4] Unfortunately, some transit and destination countries are making it increasingly difficult, if not impossible, to cross borders for people who need to move. A work visa with (the possibility for) permanent residency is usually dangled for the highly skilled worker, and permanent residency (in some cases a passport or outright citizenship) is blatantly offered for the rich,[5] but the door is firmly shut for the poor, who desperately need to move.

Vulnerable populations on the move are increasingly labeled and treated as "undesirable aliens"—potential burdens on society, threats to cultural identity, and dangers to national security. These "undesirable" migrants are then forced to take clandestine and dangerous journeys, either on their own or with the help of unscrupulous human smugglers. Problems occur for these migrants in the way they are perceived, treated, and received in transit and destination countries. In the words of a Latinx migrant:

> I have stowed away in baggage compartments of buses and almost suffocated in a boxcar; I almost froze to death in the mountains and baked to death in the deserts; I have gone without food and water for days, and nearly died on various occasions. As difficult as these are, these are not the hardest parts of being a migrant. The worst is when people treat you like you are a dog, like you are the lowest form of life on earth.[6]

In Hungary, Black people especially bore the brunt of the legacy of the 2015 migrant crisis in Europe.[7] Prior to the crisis, the word "migrant" ("migráns" in Hungarian) had a neutral connotation. It was only in the wake of the crisis that migrants started to be largely depicted as a threat to public security, creating a strong anti-immigrant sentiment. It is a shift that has created a surge in xenophobic rhetoric and "fear of the other," with African migrants primarily on the receiving end. Tobi Ojo was spat on at a train station while Maveens Okwudiri Okwunwa stopped going to IKEA after consistently being followed around the store by security guards.[8] Indeed, these migrants are subjected to various indignities that pose questions about what it means to be Christian. Pope Francis's speech to the US Congress in 2015 during the migrant

---

4. DeLorey, "Economic and Environmental Displacement," 231–48.
5. See, for example, *BBC News*, "Malta's Golden Passports."
6. As quoted in Groody, "Passing Over," 49.
7. I have written on this elsewhere. See Cruz, "When the Poor Knock on Our Door," 195–211.
8. Kovacs, "Hungary's African Immigrants Hope for #BLM Reckoning."

and refugee crisis in Europe draws attention to the problems and possibilities for a Christian response to vulnerable people on the move such as those from the Global South. The pope pointed out that "we must not be taken aback by their numbers, but rather view them as persons, seeing their faces and listening to their stories, trying to respond as best we can to their situation" in a "humane, just, and fraternal" way and not to give in to the common temptation nowadays "to discard whatever proves troublesome."[9]

This chapter considers the migration of people from the Global South as *locus theologicus*. More specifically, it reflects on the features of a theology of migration that takes seriously the search for *bare life*, which fuels human mobility from the Global South. The chapter argues that doing justice to the experiences of migrants from the Global South means taking into account what is at the heart of their journeys, that is, the struggle for survival and well-being individually and collectively.

LIBERATION THEOLOGY AS HERMENEUTICAL FRAMEWORK

Many migrants from the Global South in contemporary times are increasingly not the usual migrants who move in search of a *better* life; a good number move in search of *bare* life.[10] Data of countries of origin of irregular border crossings from January to October 2021 on the European Union's eastern land border, for instance, shows the overwhelming majority of migrants come from war-torn Iraq followed by other countries persistently plagued by economic and political insecurity such as Afghanistan, Syria, and Congo.[11] Indeed, because it is the world's poor that is mainly on the move, or desperate to move, migration is rooted in the search for survival and/or the bare necessities of life.

One can argue that liberation theology is in a good position to serve as a hermeneutical framework in reflecting on migration from the Global South from a theological perspective. Such an argument could be made based on a number of reasons. First, liberation theology is concerned with the critical reflection on praxis in the light of the word.[12] Second, liberation theology's methodology involves socio-analytic mediation,[13] which entails an interdisciplinary approach in setting the context for the theological reflection. It engages praxis in a dialogue not only with theory but also with the social sciences in view of envisioning and articulating emancipatory Christian praxis. It brings the gospel into a fuller and more fruitful dialogue with a broader range of disciplines and with civil society, making transnational studies in other disciplines, such as sociology, anthropology, economics, and political science, valuable.

9. Roberts and Kirchgaessner, "Pope Francis urges Congress."
10. Sassen, "Making of Migrations," 11.
11. *BBC News*, "Belarus Border Crisis."
12. Praxis refers to reflective action or action that arises from a critical reflection on God's word.
13. Boff, *Introducing Liberation Theology*, 24–31.

Liberation theology's contextual approach also suits the need for interrogating the spatial dimension of transnational politics, which is necessary to develop a more nuanced understanding of power relations, including the ways in which migrants constitute meaningful forms of political membership.

Third, liberation theology privileges the experiences and perspectives of the poor and oppressed.[14] This method fits well in reflecting on migration from the Global South since the majority of Southern migrants are poor. Gustavo Gutierrez, a pioneer of liberation theology, regards migrants as icons of the poor in the modern globalized world.[15] Gioacchino Campese echoes this perspective in his reference to irregular migrants as "crucified people."[16] Migrants who may not be economically poor still experience marginalization as migrants from undesirable ("shithole")[17] countries. Such marginalization is an illustration of poverty and symptom of global social injustice from a liberationist perspective.

Fourth, liberation theology engages in a critique of systems and structures. To be sure, migration from the Global South cannot be viewed in isolation but must be understood within the context of broader global processes, systems, and structures. Raúl Sánchez Molina, for example, notes how, on the one hand, Salvadorans in the US have highly contributed to relieving poverty in El Salvador, particularly by providing housing and education to their children left in the homeland and subsidizing health care and pensions to their elderly. On the other hand, Molina points out how structural conditions in their homeland still push them to migrate to meet labor needs in the US.[18] A critique of such problematic systems and structures can be seen in the works of theologians of migration who, in one way or another, employ a liberationist approach.[19]

> Fifth, liberation theology is oriented towards social justice. It can meaningfully contribute to the debate on migration with its two basic requirements: the human person must remain the priority at all times and those who are poor deserve special care. Daniel Groody, for instance, contends that to limit one's compassion to the borders of one's nationality, one's family, or even one's self is a migration toward disintegration.[20] Pope Francis himself reminds people of faith and goodwill that "each of us is responsible for his or her neighbor: we are our brothers' and sisters' keepers, wherever they live" and that "bibli-

---

14. See Gutierrez and Müller, *On The Side of the Poor*.
15. Gutierrez, "Poverty, Migration, and the Option for the Poor," 76–86.
16. Campese, "¿Cuantos Mas?," 271–98.
17. Former US president Donald Trump demonstrated this discriminatory attitude in his reference to African countries, Haiti, and El Salvador as "shithole" nations. See Vitali et al., "Trump referred to Haiti and African nations."
18. Molina, "Modes of Incorporation," 274.
19. Cruz, *Toward a Theology of Migration*; Ahn, *Theology and Migration*; De La Torre, *U.S. Immigration Crisis*; Snyder, *Asylum-Seeking, Migration, and Church*; Groody, *Border of Death, Valley of Life*.
20. Groody, "A Mission of Reconciliation," 80.

cal revelation urges us to welcome the stranger."[21] Francis, whose father was an Italian immigrant to Argentina, eloquently articulates the aptness of a liberationist approach in making sense of unwanted migration:

"Migrants and refugees . . . are an occasion that Providence gives us to help build a more just society, a more perfect democracy, a more united country, a more fraternal world and a more open and evangelical Christian community. Migration can offer possibilities for a new evangelization, open vistas for the growth of a new humanity foreshadowed in the paschal mystery: a humanity for which every foreign country is a homeland and every homeland is a foreign country."[22]

By articulating a vision of community that supersedes national boundaries within which religious transnational civil society agents take center stage, Francis also encourages peoples' sense of belonging in multiple settings. If the term "alien" is to be used at all it should be for those who have so disconnected themselves from God and others that they are incapable of seeing in the vulnerable stranger a mirror of themselves, a reflection of Christ, and a challenge to human solidarity.[23]

MIGRATION THEOLOGY AND THE GLOBAL SOUTH

What might a Christian theology of migration from the Global South that is informed by liberationist perspectives look like? What resources and insights from the Christian tradition might be vital for such a theology? Taking cue from Pope Paul VI's point that "The first means of evangelization is the witness of an authentically Christian life,"[24] and the World Council of Churches' call to mission from the margins characterized by struggle and resistance toward justice and inclusivity,[25] I explore here two key features of a theology of contemporary migration from the Global South.

Anamnestic Hospitality

Historically, with the exception of the indigenous population, the dominant group in the "local" population in many destination countries such as the United States, Canada, Australia, and New Zealand, were former migrants or descendants of migrants. The dominant group, in other words, trace their citizenship or residency to the journey they made, or the journey made by members of their family, many years or generations ago. French couple Linda and Yves adopted Sayid, a Syrian refugee, in recognition of the migrant background they share with him. Yves's Polish grandmother

---

21. Pope Francis, "Message for World Day of Migrants and Refugees 2016."
22. Pope Francis, "Message for World Day of Migrants and Refugees 2014."
23. Groody, "'Mission of Reconciliation,'" 80.
24. Pope Paul VI, *Evangelii Nuntiandi*, 41.
25. See World Council of Churches, "Together Towards Life," 355–80.

was sent to Auschwitz while Linda's Italian grandparents arrived penniless in Paris in the 1930s.[26] Vietnamese American theologian Peter Phan, a former refugee, reflects on this responsibility of those with migrant backgrounds to always remember "where they came from." Being a migrant, Phan insists, is a permanent identity and not a phase of life that can eventually be shed as one acquires better social status. Phan identifies three ethical reasons why migrants ought to remember where they came from:

1. being a migrant enables one to know "the heart of a migrant";
2. knowledge of the migrant's heart is cultivated by remembering one's own personal experience of being a migrant; and
3. remembering one's past as a migrant provides the ethical grounding for one's just and loving treatment of migrants.[27]

Hospitality within a liberationist theology of migration also takes on an anamnestic dimension because migration and care for the stranger and itinerant are deeply woven into the Bible and the Christian tradition.[28] Remembering the migrant roots of Christianity "enables humanization and promotes the common quest for justice and global solidarity; it liberates individuals and society to learn from one another."[29] In criticizing the response of some Czech Republic politicians, who used Christian values as a reason for excluding the other (especially the Muslim other) during the 2015 crisis, Tim Noble points to the need to assert the fundamental Christian belief on loving our neighbor as ourselves. Noble insists that we cannot live up to this fundamentally Christian practice by excluding from the list of possible neighbors all those whom we have decided that we do not and cannot love.[30] Churches play a critical role in transforming the "ecology of fear" that permeates local communities into an "ecology of faith" since the various forms and levels of encounters they facilitate make them ideal places for newcomers as well as bridge builders between asylum seekers and a hostile public.[31] To recall the Christian tradition of the works of mercy is to come to understand dialogue and charity as the "art of encounter," "art of relationship," and "art of living," that evoke a sense of human solidarity, which does not allow cynicism, barbarism, and indifference to prevail.[32] Indeed, a Christian approach from the perspective of anamnestic hospitality includes overcoming fear, so often associated with the presence of a stranger (or different culture) among us.[33] Fear may stem

---

26. Topping, "It was the natural thing to do."
27. Phan, "Always Remember Where You Came From," 177.
28. See Senior, "Beloved Aliens and Exiles," 20–34.
29. Polak, "Migration as a Sign of the Times," 60.
30. Noble, "Mission as Hospitality Towards 'The Other,'" 196–97.
31. Snyder, "Un/settling Angels," 576.
32. Parolin, "Responsibility and Solution Sharing," 131–32.
33. Naish, "Mission, Migration, and the Stranger in our Midst," 7–30.

from ignorance, from not knowing how to behave in the presence of diversity, or from convictions that are based on stereotypes, even after getting to know each other better. Many cling to their distinctive cultures but the fear that fuels such an attitude may be based on a false defense of one's own culture or way of life.[34] It is a fear of the loss of one's own familiar ways of doing things when encountering new people and communities and foreign practices of worship.

I am aware that hospitality as a virtue does not receive universal acceptance among theologians. In addressing the US immigration crisis under Donald Trump, for example, Miguel De La Torre explicitly rejects hospitality by arguing how it masks complicity.[35] Most theologians who work on migration are cognizant of the loopholes of an uncritical approach to hospitality that they sharpen their argument by using terms such as "countercultural," "radical," "mutual," and "prophetic."[36] I posit that taking a critical approach means not getting stuck in our theological reflection with the use of the metaphor of the stranger, or the practice of "welcoming the stranger." The problem with a simplistic focus on, or spiritual elevation of, Matt 25:35 (I was a stranger and you welcomed me) is that the gravity and complexity of the ethical challenge could be, at best, missed, and at worst, downplayed. It runs the risk of giving the impression of a well-intentioned benevolence that, while laudable, provides half-baked solutions. Acts or practices of welcome should be a phase or a stage, and not the only means, in witnessing to hospitality. Churches, in other words, need to be careful in exalting the stranger in a manner that runs the risk of keeping migrants perpetual foreigners. This is illustrated in the often superficial celebration of diversity in churches through the use of ethnic feasts or cultural festivals that, at best, simplistically showcase and, at worst, exoticize migrants' cultures. The *oikonomia*, the household of God, must be all-embracing and draw everyone into a committed communion, transcending geographical and human-made barriers so that none of us is any longer "a stranger or an alien, but [we] are citizens with the saints and also members of the household of God" (Eph 2:19).

Prophetic and Strategic Solidarity

Regina Polak speaks of migration as a sign of the times insofar as it highlights the inhumanity and injustice of economic, political, and social systems and frameworks, as well as the incapacity of people to coexist in diversity and difference without any solidarity.[37] Polak criticizes how in Europe the word "migrant" has become an ex-

---

34. Veglio, "Challenges of Mercy," 130.

35. De La Torre argues instead for the responsibility of restitution or making reparation in *U.S. Immigration Crisis*, 63–66.

36. See Pohl, *Making Room*; Myers, "Our God is Undocumented," 53–72; and Snyder, "Dangers of 'Doing Our Duty,'" 353–55.

37. Polak, "Migration as a Sign of the Times," 60.

tremely stigmatized term in the manner the discourse of the "other," the "alien," the immigrated other, the socio-economically disadvantaged other, and the national or cultural other are mingled with catchwords like "migration" and "Islam." Polak writes

> Migrants, and especially Muslim migrants, are turned into paradigmatic others and even into "aliens" so to speak, into those who do not belong here. Xenophobia, nativism, a restorative authoritarian defense of Christian values (suddenly rediscovered by people who actually do not have any church connection), secularist and anti-religious prejudices, liberal, and feminist critique of Muslim patriarchy and fundamentalism, the fear of terrorist networks, all these arguments mingle with anti-Muslim discourse.[38]

The entanglement of "refugee," "violence/conflict/terror," and "religion" contributes to the production of narrow policy responses, exclusionary politics, and a growing trend towards "securitizing" forced migration rather than treating the refugee crisis primarily as a question of humanitarianism, or solidarity with fellow human beings.[39] There is a need for an ecclesiology that bridges the gap between the conceptual (the church that people preach) and the concrete (the church that people practice), particularly a coalitional church that aims at overcoming the contrast between refugees and receivers in order to make a church a church for all.[40] The tragic and unjust nature and character of contemporary migration in/from the Global South means that the churches cannot remain spiritual ghettos, nor mere agents or providers of charitable services. It does not suffice, in other words, for the churches to simply facilitate and nurture encounters between migrants and the local population, or be contented with acts of hospitality that do not have durable long-term solutions in mind. There is a need to reach out with "radical hospitality, compassion, and justice," with the churches "proclaiming the gospel in a context of relationships of mutuality and engagement."[41] There is a need, too, for an approach and perspective that goes beyond "assistentialism," "helper syndrome,"[42] or the simple rhetoric of emergency and works, towards awakening the conscience of society and raising awareness on both personal and political levels. Christians need "to balance a concern for responding to pressing presenting needs and problems . . . with attention to deeper structural analysis and the tackling of root causes . . . . developing other sensitivities and skills . . . from cross-cultural facility and interfaith awareness to understanding the ways in which immigration intersects with broader webs of oppression."[43] There is need, in other words, for solidarity that is prophetic.

38. Polak, "Migration as a Sign of the Times," 65.

39. An astute treatment of this perspective is offered in Mavelli and Wilson, eds., *Refugee Crisis and Religion*.

40. Schmeidel, "Coalitional Church," 151–66.

41. Howell, "Multiculturalism, Immigration and the North American Church," 82.

42. Campese, "Responses of the Church to the Challenge of Immigration," 232.

43. Snyder, "Faces of Migration," 236–37.

Solidarity is about building relationships, identifying and working together toward common goals, providing mutual support rather than unilateral charity, and engaging in shared struggle with people who are different. Christian theologians argue, and rightly so, that realistically speaking no one can be in solidarity with all the world's people, or all the world's unwanted migrants, at once. First, there is no generic universal relationship of solidarity but only concrete particular instances.[44] Second, solidarity can be quite demanding. Tisha Rajendra argues that solidarity as a universal practice "cannot make much sense in contexts where the subjects of solidarity do not have the resources to make much of an impact on those outside of their communities" and that, in reality, "only citizens of developed countries, with their billions in surplus wealth . . . [and] outsized political influence could even imagine being in solidarity with everyone."[45] Indeed, solidarity itself may be easier said than done when one comes face-to-face with unwanted migration. At the height of the Rohingya crisis in 2015, for example, Muslim-majority Malaysia was highly critical of Myanmar's treatment of the predominantly Muslim Rohingyas, seemingly in solidarity with fellow Muslims. When push came to shove, however, and the Rohingyas were at the border asking to be allowed to enter, the Malaysian authorities rejected and turned them back both in 2015 and 2020.[46] Thus, "to raise a voice in prophetic announcement that God is doing something new again is not a vocation for the weak and the fearful, the unconscious and the uncommitted. It is not a vocation that dodges criticism by being sure to do nothing, say nothing, and be nothing."[47] Prophetic solidarity involves risks.

The argument for realism, the effectiveness of particular forms of solidarity, and the risky as well as fraught judgments and involvements that solidarity demands, means that prophetic solidarity may be possible by prioritizing those most in need. The WCC document Cape Town Commitment, for instance, identifies those who are most vulnerable as "economic migrants seeking work; internally-displaced peoples because of war or natural disaster; refugees and asylum seekers; victims of ethnic cleansing; people fleeing religious violence and persecution; famine sufferers—whether caused by drought, floods, or war; victims of rural poverty moving to cities" (no. 22). This priority for the most vulnerable is desirable from a liberationist perspective because it has clearer potential to save lives and make a real difference.

Acts of solidarity become prophetic and strategic, too, when they involve attention to the causes of hostility, or anti-immigrant sentiments, among the local population and develop a more complex compassion.[48] Indeed, we cannot afford to neglect

---

44. Steck, "Solidarity, Citizenship, and Globalization," 163.

45. Rajendra, "Burdened Solidarity," 97–98.

46. During the 2015 crisis many Rohingyas died at sea after Southeast Asian nations, including Malaysia, turned the Rohingyas' boats back. See *The Jakarta Post*, "Malaysia turns back Rohingya boat over virus fears."

47. Chittister, "Prophet in You," 37.

48. Snyder, "Dangers of 'Doing Our Duty,'" 357.

the anti-immigrant sentiments that fester in the local population, especially in small towns and cities, where migrants and refugees are increasingly being funneled by states to the point of offering incentives, such as Australia's and Canada's regional migration schemes. Complex compassion entails addressing the economic factors that fuel anti-immigrant sentiments among the local population who are disenfranchised. Right-wing political party Golden Dawn's phenomenal ascent in Greek politics was directly linked to the Greek financial crisis while Brexit's success is regarded as a working-class revolt. Any meaningful and effective Christian response to unwanted migration cannot ignore or leave these people behind because they and the economic morass they are in are not going away. An expansive view of neighbor love is vital in this regard so as not to create gaps or missing links in the response.

Solidarity becomes prophetic and strategic, as well, when it is collaborative. It works with all peoples, groups, and institutions regardless of religion or ideological persuasion. As a leader of the successful Australian campaign Let Them Stay opines, "when you have people like the churches and the doctors and other standing up—everybody from all walks of life—the Government really does have no choice but to listen to that overwhelming sentiment."[49] Solidarity as response to the suffering of the poor is an ethical demand but it is also a practice that is salvific for those who enter into solidarity with the poor,[50] not just for those who serve on the front line but for policy makers and decision makers, too.

CONCLUSION

This chapter shows that a theology of migration from the Global South must recognize two needs. The first is that of an unconditional response: wherever there is suffering, there should be intelligent, tangible acts of charity. The second is unity that draws from faith and from the passion for the dignity of every human person. It is a unity that, given the plurality and complexity of circumstances, builds up just and inclusive communities. It is an ecclesial response anchored in *koinonia* (church in communion), *leitourgia* (church in service), and *martyria* (church in witness).

The chapter also points to a church of/for all peoples as an embodiment of a Christian theology of migration of vulnerable populations. A church of/for all peoples is a church without borders. It is a faith community where migrants don't just survive but also thrive irrespective of their identity and the reasons and circumstances surrounding their migration. A church of/for all peoples, in other words, is inclusive. It is a church not confined to religious rituals or piety nor the boundaries of parochial walls or divisions of ideological differences. In a globalized world wracked by poverty, violence, tensions, and division a church of/for all peoples serves as a counterforce for harmony, an institution for transformation, and a home for all.

49. Oriti, "Let Them Stay labeled a success."
50. Sobrino, *Bearing with One Another in Faith*, 10–11.

BIBLIOGRAPHY

Ahn, Ilsup. *Theology and Migration*. Boston: Brill, 2019.

BBC News. "Belarus Border Crisis: How Are Migrants Getting There?" November 26, 2021. https://www.bbc.com/news/59233244.

———. "Malta's Golden Passports: 'Loopholes' Found in Citizenship Scheme." April 22, 2021. https://www.bbc.com/news/world-europe-56843409.

Boff, Leonardo. *Introducing Liberation Theology*. New York: Orbis, 1987.

Campese, Gioacchino. "¿*Cuantos Mas*?: The Crucified Peoples at the U.S. Mexico Border." In *A Promised Land, A Perilous Journey*, edited by Daniel G. Groody and Gioacchino Campese, 271–98. Notre Dame: University of Notre Dame Press, 2021.

———. "The Responses of the Church to the Challenge of Immigration." In *Flight and Migration: Between Homelessness and Hospitality*, edited by Klaus Krämer and Klaus Vellguth, 111–32. Quezon City: Claretian, 2020.

Castles, Stephen, and Mark J. Miller. *The Age of Migration: International Population Movements in the Modern World*. 4th ed. New York: Guilford, 2009.

Chittister, Joan. "The Prophet in You: Answering Christ's Call Requires Courage." *U.S. Catholic* 35 (2019) 37.

Cruz, Gemma Tulud. *Toward a Theology of Migration: Social Justice and Religious Experience*. New York: Palgrave Macmillan, 2014

———. "When the Poor Knock on Our Door: A Theological Response to Unwanted Migration." In *Christianity and the Law of Migration*, edited by Silas Allard et al., 195–211. London: Routledge, 2021. .

De La Torre, Miguel. *The U.S. Immigration Crisis: Towards an Ethic of Place*. Eugene, OR: Cascade, 2016.

DeLorey, Mary. "Economic and Environmental Displacement: Implications for Durable Solutions." In *Driven from Home: Protecting the Rights of Forced Migrants*, edited by David Hollenbach, 231–48. Washington, DC: Georgetown University, 2010.

Francis (Pope). "Message for World Day of Migrants and Refugees 2016." https://www.vatican.va/content/francesco/en/messages/migration/documents/papa-francesco_20150912_world-migrants-day-2016.html, accessed December 1, 2021.

———. "Message for World Day of Migrants and Refugees 2014." https://www.vatican.va/content/francesco/en/messages/migration/documents/papa-francesco_20130805_world-migrants-day.html.

Groody, Daniel. *Border of Death, Valley of Life: An Immigrant Journey of Heart and Spirit*. Lanham, MD: Rowman & Littlefield, 2007.

———. "Migrants and Refugees: Christian Faith and the Globalization of Solidarity." *International Review of Mission* 104 (2015) 314–23.

———. "A Mission of Reconciliation: Theological Perspectives of Pilgrim People." In *On "Strangers No Longer": Perspectives on the Historic U.S.-Mexican Catholic Bishops' Pastoral Letter on Migration*, edited by Todd Scribner and J. Kevin Appleby, 63–83. Mahwah, NJ: Paulist, 2013.

———. "Passing Over: Migration as Conversion." *International Review of Mission* 104 (2015) 49.

Gutierrez, Gustavo. "Poverty, Migration, and the Option for the Poor." In *A Promised Land, A Perilous Journey: Theological Perspectives on Migration*, edited by Daniel Groody and Gioacchino Campese, 76–88. Notre Dame: University of Notre Dame Press, 2008.

Gutierrez, Gustavo, and Cardinal Gerhard Ludwig Müller. *On The Side of the Poor: The Theology of Liberation*. New York: Orbis, 2015.

Haywood, John. *The Great Migrations: From the Earliest Humans to the Age of Globalization*. London: Quercus, 2009.

Howell, Brian. "Multiculturalism, Immigration and the North American Church: Rethinking Contextualization." *Missiology: An International Review* 39 (2011) 82.

The Jakarta Post. "Malaysia turns back Rohingya boat over virus fears." April 17, 2020. https://www.thejakartapost.com/seasia/2020/04/17/malaysia-turns-back-rohingya-boat-over-virus-fears.html.

Kovacs, Kasia. "Hungary's African Immigrants Hope for #BLM Reckoning." *Politico*, August 5, 2020. https://www.politico.com/news/2020/08/05/hungary-african-immigrants-392116.

Mavelli, Luca, and Erin Wilson, eds. *The Refugee Crisis and Religion—Secularism, Security and Hospitality*. Lanham, MD: Rowman and Littlefield, 2016.

Molina, Raúl Sánchez. "Modes of Incorporation, Social Exclusion, and Transnationalism: Salvadorans' Adaptation to the Washington, DC Metropolitan Area." *Human Organization* 67 (2008) 274.

Myers, Ched. "Our God is Undocumented: Sanctuary and Prophetic Hospitality." In *Our God is Undocumented: Biblical Faith and Immigrant Justice*, edited by Ched Myers and Matthew Colwell, 53–72. New York: Orbis, 2012.

Naish, Tim. "Mission, Migration, and the Stranger in our Midst." In *Mission and Migration*, edited by Stephen Spencer, 7–30. Calver: Cliff College Publishing, 2008.

Noble, Tim. "Mission as Hospitality Towards 'The Other.'" In *Reforming Theology, Migrating Church, and Transforming Society: A Compendium for Ecumenical Education*, edited by Uta Andree et al., 196–97. Hamburg: Missionshilfe, 2017.

Oriti, Thomas. "Let Them Stay labeled a success, more than half of 267 asylum seekers in community detention." *ABC News*, April 2, 2016. https://www.abc.net.au/news/2016-04-02/let-them-stay-labelled-success-asylum-seeker-community-detention/7294456.

Parolin, Pietro. "Responsibility and Solution Sharing: The Role of Religious Organizations Responding to Large Movements of Refugees and Migrants." *People on the Move* 46 (2016) 131–32.

Paul VI (Pope). *Evangelii Nuntiandi*. http://www.vatican.va/content/paul-vi/en/apost_exhortations/documents/hf_p-vi_exh_19751208_evangelii-nuntiandi.html.

Phan, Peter. "Always Remember Where You Came From: An Ethics of Migrant Memory." In *Living (With)out Borders*, edited by Leo D. Lefebure, 173–86. Washington, DC: Georgetown University Press, 2022.

Pohl, Christine. *Making Room: Recovering Hospitality as a Christian Tradition*. Grand Rapids: Eerdmans, 1999

Polak, Regina. "Migration as a Sign of the Times: Questions and Remarks from a Practical Theological Perspective." In *Migration as a Sign of the Times,* edited by Judith Gruber and Sigrid Rettenbacher, 60. Leiden: Brill, 2015.

Rajendra, Tisha. "Burdened Solidarity: The Virtue of Solidarity in Diaspora." *Journal of the Society of Christian Ethics* 39 (2009) 97–98.

Roberts, Dan, and Stephanie Kirchgaessner. "Pope Francis Urges Congress to treat immigrants in 'humane and just' way." *The Guardian*, September 25, 2015. http://www.theguardian.com/world/2015/sep/24/pope-francis-congress-speech-immigration-climate-change-abortion.

Sassen, Saskia. "The Making of Migrations." In *Living With(out) Borders: Catholic Theological Ethics on the Migrations of Peoples*, edited by Agnes Brazal and Maria Teresa Davila, 11–22. New York: Orbis, 2016.

Schmeidel, Ulrich. "Coalitional Church: Ecclesiology in the Age of Migration." In *Christian Theology in the Age of Migration: Implications for World Christianity*, edited by Peter Phan, 151–66. Lanham: Rowman and Littlefield, 2020.

Senior, Donald. "Beloved Aliens and Exiles: New Testament Perspectives on Migration." In *A Promised Land, A Perilous Journey*, 20–34. Notre Dame: University of Notre Dame Press: 2008.

Snyder, Susanna. *Asylum-Seeking, Migration, and Church*. Surrey: Ashgate, 2012.

———. "The Dangers of 'Doing Our Duty': Reflections on Churches Engaging with People Seeking Asylum in the UK." *Theology* 110 (2007) 353–55.

———. "Faces of Migration: U.S. Christianity in the Twenty-First Century." In *Christianities in Migration: The Global Perspective*, edited by Elaine Padilla and Peter Phan, 236–37. New York: Palgrave Macmillan, 2016.

———. "Un/settling Angels: Faith-Based Organizations and Asylum-Seeking in the UK." *Journal of Refugee Studies* 24 (2011) 565–85.

Sobrino, Jon. *Bearing with One Another in Faith: Theology of Christian Solidarity*. Edited by Jon Sobrino and Juan Hernandez Pico. Translated by Phillip Berryman. New York: Orbis, 1994.

Solimano, Andrés. *International Migration in the Age of Crisis and Globalization: Historical and Recent Experiences*. Cambridge: Cambridge University Press, 2010.

Steck, Christopher. "Solidarity, Citizenship, and Globalization: Developing a New Framework for Theological Reflections on U.S.-Mexico Immigration." *Journal of Peace and Justice Studies* 14 (2004) 153–78.

Topping, Alexandra. "It was the natural thing to do: Family who took Calais migrant into their home." *The Guardian*, August 22, 2015. https://www.theguardian.com/uk-news/2015/aug/21/calais-migrant-family-syria-refugee-help.

UNDESA. "International Migration 2020 Highlights." https://www.un.org/development/desa/pd/sites/www.un.org.development.desa.pd/files/undesa_pd_2020_international_migration_highlights.pdf.

Veglio, Antonio Maria. "The Challenges of Mercy: The Welcome and Integration of Migrants and Refugees, Dialogue and Charity." *People on the Move* 46 (2016) 129–32.

Vitali, Ali, et al. "Trump referred to Haiti and African nations as 'shithole countries.'" *NBC News*, January 12, 2018. https://www.nbcnews.com/politics/white-house/trump-referred-haiti-african-countries-shithole-nations-n836946.

World Council of Churches. "Together Towards Life." In *Ecumenical Missiology: Changing Landscapes and New Conceptions of Mission*, edited by Kenneth Ross et al., 355–80. Oxford: Regnum, 2016.

CHAPTER 6

Pentecostal Theo-Praxis

CONNIE AU

Is there such a thing as Pentecostal theology in the Global South (GS)? Most Pentecostals in that region are more concerned about praxis: how to lead worship and practice spiritual gifts; how to receive God's blessings according to the "prosperity gospel." They focus more on theo-praxis (practices relating to God) than theo-logy (understandings relating God). If St. Anselm defines theology as "faith seeking understanding," then for most GS Pentecostals, faith is about seeking doing. If there are any theologies in GS Pentecostalism, most of them are borrowed from western Pentecostalism and are translated into local languages, adapted to suit their contexts, then practiced out. When GS Pentecostals trace back the historical roots of Pentecostalism in seminaries, they tend to first study the roots of western Pentecostalism, then how the missionaries spread it to their own countries in the twentieth century. GS Pentecostals tend to prioritize finding spiritual strategies, human and financial resources, and architectural buildings for the sake of church growth instead of constructing indigenous theologies. This tendency generally matches the pragmatic nature of people in that region and explains why they have had significant growth since the second half of the twentieth century.

Considering the western influence on GS Pentecostalism, this article firstly illustrates the classifications and doctrines of western Pentecostalism; secondly, three guiding principles behind GS Pentecostal praxis: cosmology, the kingdom of God, and the prosperity gospel; thirdly, the practices of healing and exorcism with examples from some GS areas.

CLASSIFICATIONS AND DOCTRINES OF WESTERN PENTECOSTALISM

Pentecostalism is a conglomeration of Classical Pentecostalism, Charismatics in the mainline Protestant churches and the Roman Catholic Church, and independent Charismatic churches. Classical Pentecostalism includes Holiness Pentecostals, "Finished-Work" Pentecostals, and Oneness Pentecostals, which developed in the United States. They all emphasize the experience of Spirit baptism proved by the initial physical experience of speaking in tongues. Holiness Pentecostalism inherits John Wesley's teaching on sanctification which happens after conversion and before Spirit baptism. The "Finished-Work" Pentecostals reject sanctification as the requirement of Spirit baptism as Jesus' sacrifice on the cross cleanses all sins away. Oneness Pentecostalism does not believe in the Trinity but God as one person with different names. In this article, the word "Pentecostal" refers to followers and churches belonging to this conglomeration.

Classical Pentecostalism inherits the "fourfold gospel" from the Holiness movement in the nineteenth century in North America and some parts of Europe, which stressed Christ as Savior, Sanctifier, Healer, and the soon coming King. Pentecostals add one more character of Christ—baptizer of the Holy Spirit. This character opens the gateway for Christians to experience the infilling power of the Holy Spirit as Christ has promised (Luke 3:16; John 14:16). When Christians are baptized by the Spirit, they are prone to surrender their self-will to the Spirit and are led to an uncertain and uncontrollable mystical and ecstatic state. Classical Pentecostals insist that this experience is evidenced with speaking in tongues, but most Charismatics reject this teaching because no gift or other gifts can be granted to those who are baptized by the Spirit. According to Paul, other "more extraordinary gifts" include healing and prophecy (Rom 12:6–8; 1 Cor 12:8–10) and there are some ordinary gifts like service, teaching, exhortation, mercy, etc. All the gifts are given to all believers, including laity and clergy, for evangelization and edification of the church (1 Cor 12:7, 11; 14:12; Eph 4:8–12).

Pentecostalism arose during the decline of western Christendom in the twentieth century. The two world wars caused disenchantment with Christianity in western society while capitalism seemed to be a reliable engine to redevelop the society and its economy. Secularism therefore had the opportunity to breed in this western soil. In the 1960s, the Harvard religion scholar Harvey Cox proposed a theory for the "postreligious" age where secularism would dominate the spirit of the society in his *The Secular City*.[1] However, he withdrew his theory when he witnessed the growth of Pentecostalism in Latin America, Africa, and Asia where Christianity and other religions like Islam, Hinduism, and Buddhism had been adhered to and secularization had never taken root. He claims, "Today it is secularity, not spirituality, that may be headed for extinction."[2] Before the Second World War, it was primarily western

---

1. Cox, *Secular City*.
2. Cox, *Fire from Heaven*.

Pentecostals who spread revival and renewal to many parts of the world fervently, based on their claim of a call from God. After the war, through leveraging the fruits of globalization, including easy travel, internet communication, and capitalism, Pentecostals worldwide swiftly broke through geographical and cultural barriers to spread the gospel of Christ's salvation and the experiences in the Holy Spirit. This movement is known for its capability of organically contextualizing the gospel in different cultures and traditions, which make Pentecostal churches vary greatly from one another. As Jelle Creemers puts it, Pentecostalism is a "non-institutional and diverse ecclesial movement."[3] This is one of the reasons why it can "win many souls for Christ" and its growth has been significant in the GS where cultures are so diverse.

GUIDING PRINCIPLES

- *Global South Cosmology: A Spirit-Filled World*—"Global South" is not only a geographical concept, but also relates to political, economic, and cultural aspects. Geographically this terms refers to Asia, Africa, Latin America, the Pacific, and the Caribbean. Politically these regions are less democratic or even autocratic with a republic whose genuineness is questionable. Some of them have a military government. Moreover, many GS countries are former colonies of countries in the Global North (GN). Economically, these regions are industrializing and rely on manufacture and export to support their economies. Culturally, aboriginal rites, customs, and religions can still be found in these regions and are exported to other countries through migration caused by political, economic, and educational push-and-pull factors in this globalized world. Most GS people struggle with unfavorable political and economic circumstances and a traditional cosmological view.

  The GS is not only the birthplace of major religions but is also a seedbed for the cultivation of shamanism, animism, spiritism, and ancestral worship.[4] Paul G. Hiebert uses the term the "excluded middle" to depict "beings and forces that cannot be directly perceived but are thought to exist on this earth. These include spirits, ghosts, ancestors, demons, and earthly gods and goddesses who live in trees, rivers, hills, and villages."[5] They cohabit with humans and other natural entities on earth. The Chinese popular religion combining Confucianism, Buddhism, and Taoism has had a legion of gods and spirits throughout several thousand years of mythology, which constitutes part of the real world in Chinese mentality. Samuel Hio-Kee Ooi rightly names this cosmic view as "pantheistic

---

3. Creemers, "Intertwined Problems," 1.
4. Ma, "Pentecostalism," 30.
5. Hiebert, "Flaw," 183.

cosmology."⁶ Most GS people are no strangers to this excluded middle through their personal encounters with spirits, mythology, hearsay from acquaintances, and even the widespread physical and breathing exercises like *qigong* developed from Taoism, and *yoga* from Hinduism. Some Christians guard against these exercises as they are the means to open a door for evil spirits to enter human souls.

While much of mainline Protestantism disregards such cosmology, namely, the operation of witchcraft and spirits in the human world, the Catholic Church recognizes its genuine existence especially ancestral worship due to the tradition of the veneration of saints. To counter the assaults on human bodies and souls by evil forces, it provides tools like the Rite of Major Exorcism which can only be performed by the priests who are trained to be exorcists with the permission of the bishop. Pentecostals go even further by believing that all Christians, both clergy and laity, can be endowed with the gifts of healing and exorcism to daily counter the spirit-filled world, according to their readings of certain Scriptures, particularly Joel 2:28, the Gospels, Acts, and some of Paul's epistles. Such belief in the democratization of gifts also empowers them to face political, socio-economic, and religious challenges in their societies. As J. Kwabena Asamoah-Gyadu comments, "Pentecostal religion is popular because it takes indigenous worldviews of mystical causalities seriously, democratizes access to the sacred, and purveys an interventionist piety that helps ordinary people to cope with the fears and insecurities of life."⁷ For example, the Chin people in Myanmar had for generations strongly believed that spirits and demons operated in every aspect of their lives, including births, marriages, deaths, etc. They offered animal sacrifices and conducted rituals to seek protection. But when a group of Christians evangelized this tribe and performed healing and other miracles in the early 1970s, many Chins were converted and nowadays 90 percent of them are Christians. They are delivered from the threats of evil spirits and they worship in churches to replace their animistic rituals.⁸

The spirit-filled cosmology engraved in the mind of the GS people does not only operate where they are, but travels to other parts of the world through migration. Migrants carry this cosmology to other countries and believe that evil spirits are not only working in their home countries, but also in their new domiciles. Claudia Währisch-Oblau studied the West African Pentecostals in Germany and one of her interviewees commented, "There are as many demons in Europe as there are in Africa, only you don't want to realise it."⁹ She conducted a case study in the Christ-for-All Evangelistic Ministries, an African-majority church

---

6. Ooi, "Study," 150.
7. Aechtner, *Health, Wealth, and Power*, 15.
8. Cole, "Historiographic Approaches," 74.
9. Währisch-Oblau, *Missionary Self-Perception*, 279.

in Dortmund, and discovered that their evangelism is almost synonymous with "spiritual warfare," which can only be confronted by the clergy and laypeople who are anointed with spiritual power. Their evangelists proclaimed, "We break every stronghold of the enemy"; "we bind all powers of the enemy in the name of Jesus."[10] Hence, the targets of their evangelism are not primarily human beings, but the evil powers behind them. They aim to break the bondage in their lives with the Holy Spirit so that they can be holistically saved by and reconciled with God. She concludes that "if nothing happens in the spiritual realm, no conversion can be achieved. Salvation is holistic: it has a spiritual and a material side."[11] To ensure their successful evangelism, Pentecostal migrant churches train their members to focus on prayer to "prepare the spiritual atmosphere" instead of the evangelistic tools and methods to convey the gospel message by words.[12] They are prepared to evangelize fellow Africans and to engage in reverse mission—to bring back the gospel to the westerners.

Although GS Pentecostals believe that evil spirits operate everywhere in this world, they also adhere to the belief that the Creator Spirit is an ultimate force which overpowers them, so they no longer fear demons. They also acknowledge the dominant role of the Holy Spirit in their lives and ministries and surrender to his guidance. Simon Chan describes the Holy Spirit in Pentecostalism as an "active personal agent" who inspires, guides, speaks, and empowers individuals in supernatural events.[13] In this sense, Pentecostal ministers cannot be paralleled with the shamans who interact with spirits for healing and communication with the other world in north Asia, nor the diviners who diagnose, prescribe, and perform healings in Africa, nor other kinds of spiritual agents, because Pentecostals are guided by the Holy Spirit to perform miracles while those agents initiate invocation of the targeted spirit(s).

- *The Kingdom of God*—The last aspect of the "full gospel," Jesus as the soon-coming King, implies his ownership of a kingdom. Pentecostals believe that they are the means of bringing this kingdom on earth through spiritual gifts. They reject cessationism, which argues that all spiritual gifts were limited to the apostolic community and have ceased since the completion of the Bible because it substantially endows Christian with full divine revelation. They adhere to the belief that spiritual gifts have been used from the early church, through the medieval period, to modern times until now by men and women, clergy and laypeople to glorify God, edify the church, and spread the gospel unto the ends of the earth. They perceive that the performances of tangible gifts enable Christians to

---

10. Währisch-Oblau, *Missionary Self-Perception*, 273–74.
11. Währisch-Oblau, *Missionary Self-Perception*, 284.
12. Währisch-Oblau, *Missionary Self-Perception*, 286.
13. Chan, *Grassroots Asian Theology*, 146.

foretaste the kingdom of God and to "live out the life of the future in the present age." Gordon Fee, a former Assemblies of God biblical theologian, even suggests that for Paul, the Holy Spirit is "an experienced end-time reality who serves both as evidence that the future is already at hand and as the guarantee of its final consummation."[14] Pentecostals interpret the eschatological paradox of "already but not yet" from the perspective of spiritual gifts. The manifestations of gifts bringing the presence of God's kingdom, his care and salvation on earth ("already"), but his complete salvation and sovereignty will only occur when Jesus returns ("not yet"). Particularly for the GS Pentecostals who attribute calamities to the attack of evil spirits and human agents, the continuity of spiritual gifts and their eschatological expectation are messages of hope, which affirm to them that God's kingdom is right here and now. Opoku Onyinah specifically reckons that the exorcism of demons is one of the convincing means to demonstrate the visible sign of God's kingdom which defeats the dominion and power of Satan.[15]

Some GS Pentecostals have gone further to perceive the kingdom of God as a lifestyle, instead of solely the performances of spiritual gifts which can only be experienced during the Sunday services and revival meetings. This phenomenon can be found in a transnational Pentecostal network called Asia for Jesus, which was founded by Taiwanese and Indonesian pastors. Its "Kingdom Culture Online School" provides the "Kingdom Culture Equip Course" to equip Chinese Christians around the world to spread the kingdom culture in Asia and bring innovation to their own environments with apostolic and prophetic visions. It specifically trains full-time church leaders and helps laypeople initiate a ministry in their workplaces. This school generally adopts the ideas of the kingdom of God formulated by American Pentecostals like Bill Johnson, Kris Vallotton, and Jack and Trisha Frost; and students are recommended to read their books, some of which are translated into Chinese. The syllabus contains three sections. The first one is entitled "Daily Life: Interacting with Others," which introduces how to preach the gospel and use the supernatural power in daily life as a leader of the kingdom of God. The second one is called "Relationship with God: Building up Relationship with Jesus, God the Father, and the Holy Spirit," which discusses how to be "hospitable" to God's presence, the Spirit's wisdom, creation, and gifts; and how to listen to and receive God's voice as a prophet. The third section is called "Belief: Destroy Lies and the Fake Lens Filter," which emphasizes that Christians are the royal and blessed people, and they should restore this self-image through overcoming shame, fear, and lies. The graduates of this course are awarded a certificate and are qualified to be instructors of the course.[16]

14. Fee, *Paul*, 176.
15. Onyinah, "Spiritual Warfare," 326.
16. https://www.asiaforjesus.net/web/onlineschool/#. The titles of the three sections are translated by the author.

Besides traditional Pentecostal teachings on apostolic and prophetic ministries, this course also teaches self-identity, self-recognition, and self-empowerment, as being the heirs of the kingdom of God. Although it is produced by Pentecostal leaders in Taiwan and Indonesia, it mirrors some of the latest American Pentecostal understandings of the kingdom of God, which have gone beyond Classical Pentecostalism. It does not emphasize so much the component of "not yet" in the traditional eschatological teaching, but more on the "already." Since the kingdom of God is "already" partially fulfilled on earth and Christians as God's children are "already" granted the royal identity, what they should do is to live this life on earth with this positive self-image and to engage in apostolic and prophetic ministries in every area of their daily lives.

- *Prosperity Gospel*—The "prosperity gospel" is about naming and claiming God's blessings, especially health and wealth. It can be traced back to American preachers and televangelists like Kenneth E. Hagin, Oral Roberts, and Benny Hinn.[17] Considering that former colonies in the GS gained independence one after the other in the post-Second World War era and the locals faced the restructuring of their political, social, and economic settings, prosperity gospel is "a potential gatekeeper to social transformation in postcolonial global Christianity" as Andreas Heuser reckons.[18] The GS version of the prosperity gospel also advocates engaging in spiritual battles against the evil forces behind sicknesses and poverty and has become a distinct Pentecostal interpretation and demonstration of Christian salvation. Gradually prosperity preachers in the West, Latin America, Asia, and Africa have influenced one another through physical and virtual evangelistic networking.[19] Heuser states, "Prosperity theology has become synonymous with global Pentecostalism. Prosperity gospel seems to represent an ideal-type of 'transnational transcendence' or a specific religious economy that 'travels well.'"[20] Whether the prosperity preacher is a celebrity or unknown, whether s/he preaches in a megachurch, a stadium with thousands of seats, on television, radio, online, or in a mini-church with a handful of members, the prosperity gospel which conveys the belief of and key to a successful and painless life aptly draws people's attention and enhances church growth.

Prosperity gospel is based on a "contractual understanding of faith," meaning being obedient to God and offering him divine giving in exchange for his blessings in finance, employments, health, psychological well-being, and relationships. Heuser defines the aim of prosperity gospel as "to reinstate the contractual

---

17. Maltese, "Prosperity Gospel," 530.
18. Heuser, "Prosperity Theology," 417.
19. Heuser, "Prosperity Theology," 531.
20. Heuser, "Prosperity Theology," 410.

relationship with God that opens the way to divine blessings again."[21] Besides the metaphor of contract, "sowing and reaping" is also commonly used in the prosperity circles, as found in 2 Cor 9:6. Faith is analogized as "seed" which can multiply divine grace "at least tenfold."[22] In 2016 I interviewed a group of ten Filipina domestic helpers working for families in Hong Kong. They belonged to a Catholic Charismatic Renewal (CCR) community called the Loved Flock, which is the second largest CCR group in the Philippines and its branches are found in many countries. One of them reckons the holistic feature of the prosperity gospel by saying, "The more we give, the more God blesses us, the more we receive the blessing of God. Not only in material things, in good health, good relationship with our family, employers. That's why we are always generous to give in this community because we see the blessing that God gives."[23]

This exchange of material blessings with the immaterial faith has become a "law of faith." In this sense, illnesses, poverty, unemployment, domestic abuse, and all other adversities are considered as spiritual problems rather than the injustices in political, social, and economic institutions; inequality in the realms of gender, race, and class; and personal moral issues. To follow the same logic, prosperity in those areas is a spiritual matter, which is defined with biblical references relating to material blessings (e.g. Mal 3:10–12; Matt 25:14–30; John 10:10; Phil 4:19; 3 John 1:2). Since poverty is a spiritual issue, the sole effective way to terminate the destiny of poverty and to unlock the treasure box of divine blessings is to repent from sins. Pentecostals do not consider solving these burning issues progressively—through years of human endeavor and toil to transform the socio-economic structure advocated in postmillennialism, rather a radical rupture implied in premillennialism by the power of the Holy Spirit, so that God's kingdom can be realized here and now.

Asian Pentecostal leaders of megachurches share their visions and teachings on the prosperity gospel through transnational networks, international conferences, church visits, and theological education. The late Rev. Yonggi Cho's (1936–2021) prosperity teaching has influenced many Asian and Western Pentecostal leaders since the 1970s. His "Theology of Blessings" was developed out of his impoverishment after Japanese colonialism and the Korean War in the 1950s. Cho sees the kingdom in two perspectives: "the future aspect of the kingdom" and "the present reality of the kingdom of God." He believes that the world can experience the eschatological kingdom through Christ and the Spirit, which means that the gospel is not just about hope for eternal life and salvation of the soul, but also brings about "prosperity in life and physical health and wellness that would keep

---

21. Heuser, "Prosperity Theology," 412.
22. Heuser, "Prosperity Theology," 413.
23. Interview with Filipino domestic helpers, July 10, 2016, Hong Kong.

the balance between spirituality and reality." He particularly sees healing as "a sign of the coming of the kingdom of God to the earth."[24]

Although the prosperity gospel has been criticized for cultivating greed and avarice, it has given hope to millions of the impoverished who struggle with daily poverty in most of the GS countries.[25] It is put into practice through exorcism and healing with the power of the Holy Spirit to instantaneously tackle life's problems and most importantly, the alleged spiritual powers behind them. It is a guiding principle of the practices of healing and exorcism in GS Pentecostalism to counter the indigenous cosmic view of a spirit-filled world. The following explains the practices of exorcism and healing in the GS.

THEO-PRAXIS IN GLOBAL SOUTH PENTECOSTALISM

- *Healing*—The practice of healing in Pentecostalism can be traced back to the Holiness movement in the nineteenth century in Europe and North America. Holiness preachers spread the belief of "faith cure" and "shorter way" to be healed from illnesses. In other words, instant healing would not happen without faith. The sick should abstain from using medication to demonstrate their absolute faith in Christ's healing power. Both Holiness and "Finished-Work" Pentecostals comfortably adopted the Holiness teachings of healing.[26] They staunchly believed and practiced the doctrine of Jesus as healer found in the full gospel in the early twentieth century. Numerous incidents of healing and even raising of the dead around the world were recorded in their periodicals. Charismatics emphasize healing more frequently than the other full gospel doctrines. Some healing preachers teach that since sicknesses are the consequences of sin, entire sanctification must include physical perfection, not only inner purification. They believe that Christ's sacrifice achieved dual salvation, delivering humanity from spiritual sinfulness and physical illnesses. Isa 53:5 was frequently quoted to prove that Christ's suffering released the power of physical healing for sinners. Healing as a vivid salvific experience particularly attracts the poverty-stricken people in the GS to convert to Christianity and has contributed to the rapid growth of the Pentecostal and Charismatic movements since the early twentieth century.

Besides Spirit baptism, healing is a common denominator of Classical Pentecostals and Protestant and Catholic Charismatics and constructs their shared identity as the Christians who are open to any experiences in the Holy Spirit. The Christians who do not belong to this kind consider praying for the sick as an intercession for the sufferers and their families so that they may feel more

24. Lee, "Kingdom," 151.
25. Ma, "David Yonggi Cho," 146.
26. Alexander, "Divine Healing," 258, 260.

comfortable and peaceful, but Pentecostals take this prayer as forcing God's hand to bring the sick back to health. They do not pray quietly, but loudly with authority; they not only pray with voice, but also lay their hands on the sick; use materials like oil, water, and handkerchiefs (Acts 19:12); blow onto the face of the sick to transmit the breath and power of the Spirit; or speak out the words of knowledge to declare to the congregation what the Holy Spirit has revealed to them about the sickness of certain individuals.[27]

The use of physical gestures and materials convey a sacramental meaning to the act of healing—using visible objects to channel God's grace to individuals, as the Catholic Church has advocated. Thomas J. Csordas even notes that the use of symbols in Pentecostalism is parallel to certain practices in Hinduism. For examples, blowing on the face of the supplicants is akin to the Hindu practice of *duha*; the repetitive calling on Jesus' name is like a Hindu mantra.[28] This is one of the reasons for the indigenous Indians to accept Christianity. Moreover, with the assistance of modern technology, evangelists have used television, radio, and the internet to perform healing. For example, Derek Prince hosted a radio program, and Edir Marcedo, who founded the Universal Church of the Kingdom of God (UCKG), has a television station. Furthermore, healing conventions are held in many countries, be they rich or poor, medically developed or undeveloped, Christian or Muslim-dominated countries like Indonesia and Malaysia. Pentecostals dare to try out any available physical and virtual means to preach the gospel and perform miracles within the legal boundaries.

Healing is a means for migrants from the GS to the GN to evangelize the local people who are more abundant in material, economic, educational, medical, and technological dimensions but are more suspicious about Christianity. This phenomenon has been happening in the West even though Christianity has played a significant role in its advanced civilization for centuries. The wealth in the GN cannot satiate people's desire for inner healing, including memories, emotions, and relationships. Reginald Alva illustrates how the Catholic Charismatic communities infill the spiritual vacuum of the Japanese. More than half of the Catholic population in Japan is formed by migrants from South America and the Philippines who are active in the CCR.[29] Their regular prayer meetings, retreats, and conventions led by international Catholic Charismatic leaders across the country attract the reserved Japanese who have sought spiritual therapists, shamans, and new religious movements to release their life pressures. They not only experience relief from physical and psychological illnesses through divine

27. I once attended a healing service conducted by a male evangelist who revealed a woman in the congregation suffering from a gynaecological sickness. He asked her to come forward for prayer and so she did. As a woman I can imagine how embarrassing it was to admit personal sickness in public.

28. Csordas, "Catholic Charismatic Healing," 335.

29. Alva, "Catholic Charismatic Renewal," 43.

healing, but are advised to practice repentance, forgiveness, and reconciliation to receive inner healing. Catholics are particularly encouraged to receive the sacrament of reconciliation.[30]

- *Exorcism*—The rising awareness of the power of the devil and the corresponding exorcism methods were frequently emphasized in the second part of the charismatic renewal in the 1980s and early 1990s.[31] An American Pentecostal preacher, Cindy Jacobs, names seven kinds of stronghold: (1) personal stronghold, (2) stronghold of mind and thoughts, (3) stronghold of ideas and concepts, (4) stronghold of occultism, (5) stronghold in society, (6) stronghold in a city and a church, and (7) stronghold where Satan is.[32] Moreover, Pentecostals have modernized the terms of exorcism techniques like "spiritual mapping, ground-level warfare, cosmic-level warfare, and evicting the ruler of the city."[33] Exorcists pray out loud to proclaim their victory over the devil through Jesus' power. Such prayer is called "authority prayer" or "prayer of command."[34] Other spiritual methods such as fasting, declaring Scriptures, intensive prayer, and confession of sins are also implemented. The most important of all is to be anointed by the Holy Spirit for empowerment like the kings in the Old Testament.[35] In West Africa, some Pentecostal churches set up "prayer camps" to pray for deliverance for the victims of witchcraft by a team of people led by a prophet.[36] In everyday life, Pentecostals are taught to be alert and well-prepared for any unexpected spiritual attacks by the devil who is like a "roaring lion" (1 Pet 5:8) through putting on the whole amour of Christ (Eph 6:10–13), reading Scriptures, prayer, and fasting.[37] For example, Jashil Choi, the mother-in-law of the late Rev. Yonggi Cho who was the former senior pastor of the Yoido Full Gospel Church in South Korea, wrote a book called *Korean Miracles* to record testimonies on how Pentecostals engaged in deliverances, power encounters, and healing through fasting and prayer.[38]

Onyinah coins the term "witchdemonology" to recount the cooperation between the demonic forces and the human agents (witches) in West Africa.[39] In Ghana, "witchcraft" and "demons" are almost synonymous.[40] In this globalized world where individuals are connected together through internet, telephone, and

30. Alva, "Catholic Charismatic Renewal," 44.
31. Onyinah, "Spiritual Warfare," 322.
32. Ooi, "Study," 147.
33. Ooi, "Study," 324.
34. Währisch-Oblau, *Missionary*, 281.
35. Ooi, "Study," 280.
36. Anderson, *Spirit-filled World*, 184.
37. Onyinah, "Spiritual Warfare," 326.
38. Cole, "Historiographic Approaches," 69.
39. Onyinah, "Spiritual Warfare," 323.
40. Anderson, *Spirit-filled World*, 184.

television, if transcontinental healing is feasible between the healers and the supplicants who are thousands of miles away, then curses cast on individuals through witchcraft are possible too. A missionary from West Africa who was sent to Hong Kong to minister to African students and migrants told me that a member of his church was shouting fiercely during a service. He noticed that this person might have been possessed by demons and conducted exorcist prayer with other leaders. Eventually he found out that it was caused by a spell cast by a witch from Africa.[41]

The UCKG which was established in Brazil has spread inside and outside the country. The one in South Africa was founded in a small white Lusophone community in Johannesburg in 1992. It began to target the black South Africans in the following year and the number of followers increased dramatically. It has become one of the fastest growing churches in South Africa and has opened 320 branches there.[42] UCKG in South Africa follows its mother church's teaching in Brazil regarding the penetration of the devil's work in all dimensions of the society and personal lives. It does not only consider that indigenous witchcraft and sorcery are the evil means to attack individuals, but also denounces the Catholic Church, the mainstream Protestant churches, the African independent/initiated churches, and even the Pentecostal and charismatic churches which are insensitive to the spiritual warfare as the "creations of demonic powers and as major facilitators of evil in the world."[43] Moreover, its mother church in Brazil encourages its members to be "politicians for Christ" since it conceives the political realm as a spiritual domain which needs "spiritual reform" and where God should be the center. The UCKG aspires to turn Brazil into a theocratic state.[44]

Similar demonization of other religions and Christian denominations can be found in Indian Pentecostalism. Pentecostal evangelists tend to condemn Hindu gods as idols. Some also name Vishnu the Indian God as "the personification of the devil."[45] These condemnations aggravate hatred from the followers of other religions against the Pentecostals and lead to vandalism and the burning of church buildings and even murders in Pentecostal churches.

CONCLUSION

Human beings keep looking for ways to cope with current life problems and avoid future calamities through religion and science. Shamanism, the occult, magic, and

41. WhatsApp conversation, November 27, 2021.
42. Van Wyk, "All Answers," 138.
43. Van Wyk, "All Answers," 146.
44. Van Wyk, "All Answers," 146.
45. Bauman, "Pentecostals," 18–19 (8–34).

indigenous medicine have been used for this purpose for centuries and even new religious practices have arisen in recent decades. Pentecostalism which manifests the kingdom of God through tangible spiritual gifts and gives people a hope for material blessings through the prosperity gospel seems to fulfill this human desire. The significant growth of Pentecostalism in the GS suggests that people there still believe in a mystical operation in this world that cannot be fully explained by western rationalism, no matter how much it has advanced human civilization. Having said that, it is superstitious to believe that Pentecostalism can give answers to all life problems. Human beings still need to be open to both religion and science, experiences and rationalism, theories and praxis which may offer us explanations and solutions regarding unpredictable contingencies and crises.

BIBLIOGRAPHY

Aechtner, Thomas. *Health, Wealth, and Power in an African Diaspora Church in Canada.* New York: Palgrave Macmillan, 2015.

Alexander, Kimberly Ervin. "Divine Healing: Sacramental Signs of Salvation." In *The Routledge Handbook of Pentecostal Theology*, edited by Wolfgang Vondey, 257–67. London: Routledge, 2020.

Alva, Reginald. "Catholic Charismatic Renewal Movement and Healing in Japan's Religious Culture." *Claritas: Journal of Dialogue and Culture* 5 (2016) 41–51.

Anderson, Allan Heaton. *Spirit-filled World: Religious Dis/Continuity in African Pentecostalism.* Cham: Palgrave Macmillan, 2018

Bauman, Chad M. "Pentecostals and Interreligious Conflict in India: Proselytization, Marginalization and Anti-Christian Violence." *PentecoStudies* 16 (2017) 8–34.

Chan, Simon. *Grassroots Asian Theology: Thinking the Faith from the Ground Up.* London: IVP Academic, 2014.

Cole, Deborah Kaye. "Historiographic Approaches to Asian Pentecostalism." *Asian Journal for Pentecostal Studies* 9 (2006) 59–82.

Cox, Harvey. *Fire from Heaven: The Rise of Pentecostal Spirituality and the Reshaping of Religion in the Twenty-first Century.* New York: Addison-Wesley, 1996.

———. *The Secular City: Secularization and Urbanization in Theological Perspective.* New York: MacMillan, 1965.

Creemers, Jelle. "The Intertwined Problems of Representation and Reception in Pentecostal Ecumenical Involvement: A Case Study." *One in Christ* 46 (2011) 142–61.

Csordas, Thomas J. "Catholic Charismatic Healing in Global Perspective: The Case of India, Brazil, and Nigeria." In *Global Pentecostal and Charismatic Healing*, edited by Candy Gunther Brown, 331–50. Oxford: Oxford University Press, 2011.

Fee, Gordon D. *Paul, the Spirit, and the People of God.* Grand Rapids: Baker Academic, 1996.

Heuser, Andreas. "Prosperity Theology: Material Abundance and Praxis of Transformation." In *The Routledge Handbook of Pentecostal Theology*, edited by Wolfgang Vondey, 410–20. London: Routledge, 2020.

Hiebert, Paul G. "The Flaw of the Excluded Middle." In *Landmark Essays in Mission and World Christianity*, edited by Robert L. Gallagher and Paul Hertig, 179–80. Maryknoll, NY: Orbis, 2009.

Lee, Sang Yun. "The Kingdom of God in Korean Pentecostal Perspective." In *Global Renewal Christianity: Asia and Oceania Spirit-Empowered Movements—Past, Present, and Future*, edited by Vinson Synan and Amos Yong, 143–57. Lake Mary, FL: Charisma House, 2016.

Ma, Julie. "Pentecostalism and Asian Mission." *Missiology: An International Review* 35 (2007) 23–37.

Ma, Wonsuk. "David Yonggi Cho's Theology of Blessing: Basis, Legitimacy, and Limitations." *Evangelical Review of Theology* 35 (2011) 140–59.

Maltese, Giovanni. "Prosperity Gospel." In *Brill's Encyclopedia of Global Pentecostalism*, edited by Michael Wilkinson et al., 530–33. Leiden: Brill, 2021.

Onyinah, Opoku. "Spiritual Warfare: The Cosmic Conflict between Good and Evil." In *The Routledge Handbook of Pentecostal Theology*, edited by Wolfgang Vondey, 321–33. London: Routledge, 2020.

Ooi, Samuel Hio-Kee. "A Study of Strategic Level Spiritual Warfare from a Chinese Perspective." *Asian Journal for Pentecostal Studies* 9 (2006) 143–61.

Van Wyk, Ilana. "All Answers: On the Phenomenal Success of a Brazilian Pentecostal Charismatic Church in South Africa." In *Pentecostalism in Africa: Presence and Impact of Pneumatic Christianity in Postcolonial Societies*, edited by Martin Lindhardt, 136–62. Leiden: Brill, 2015.

Währisch-Oblau, Claudia. *The Missionary Self-Perception of Pentecostal/Charismatic Church Leaders from the Global South in Europe: Bringing Back the Gospel*. Leiden: Brill, 2012.

CHAPTER 7

Diaspora Mission Theology

HARVEY C. KWIYANI

NON-WESTERN MISSION IN THE WEST

This essay focuses on the missiological discourse that have emerged in Europe and North America in the first two decades of the twenty-first when non-Western Christians have come to the West and attempted to engage in mission among Westerners. The general term used to describe these non-Western missionary movements in the West include "diaspora mission" (among some Asian scholars) and "reverse mission" among some African scholars. In this essay, I discuss the implications of these terms on our missiology, suggesting that while they are good social descriptors, they both do not faithfully describe God's mission in the world of the twenty-first century. Moving on from these two terms, I will go on to discuss the missiological implications of the rising presence of African, Asian, and Latin American Christians and missionaries in the (Western) world. I will highlight the non-Western missionary movements that have emerged in the world in the past five decades. In the end, I will propose three theological warrants for making space for and engaging these new missionary movements.

Diaspora Christianity

The word "diaspora" originates from the Greek word *diaspeirein*, which comes from the combination of *dia-* (meaning "across") and *speirein* (meaning "scatter"). It is, thus, generally translated "scatter across" or "disperse" and, as a noun, *dispersion*, *dissemination,* or *diffusion.* The anglicized word *diaspora* connotes, for instance, the scattering or dispersion of people for whatever reason from a particular piece of land to one or other parts of the world. Historically, it has been almost exclusively used to describe the dispersion of Jewish people from the promised land to the wider world around and beyond the Mediterranean region that took place beginning in the eighth century BCE. As a technical term, *diaspora* was originally, and most generally, used in reference to the community of the Jews outside Palestine from about 100 BCE to 100 CE.[1] Following the emergence of the Septuagint in the third century BCE, the term *diaspora* grew into a notion with three aspects; the land where Jews were dispersed, the situation of being dispersed, and the people being dispersed.[2]

The dispersion of the Jews, first to Assyria and later to Babylon, is often viewed negatively in the Scriptures—they were to always long to return to Palestine. Ps 137 epitomizes this longing for a return to Jerusalem: "If I forget you, O Jerusalem, let my right hand wither! Let my tongue cling to the roof of my mouth, if I do not remember you, if I do not set Jerusalem above my highest joy." "Diaspora" was, thus, originally connected, to a large extent, with negative notions stressing the painful disconnect that comes from the scattering of a community and breakdown of society exiled from their promised land, heading towards destruction at the hands of otherworldly kingdoms. Naturally, these negative connotations of the term "diaspora" made the concept acquire soteriological implications making the dispersion a punishment for disobedience against the Law with the possibilities of subsequent regathering and returning to the promised land and following repentance and renewed obedience.[3] This promise of a return home to Jerusalem shapes a great deal of postexilic literature for Old Testament Jews and, for New Testament Christians, the heavenly Jerusalem serves as a beacon of hope where they, as sojourners will return to be "home" in the presence of God.

It is in the context of this dispersion that the New Testament takes place—the narrative of the New Testament is shaped to a considerable extent by the diaspora. Jesus was taken to Egypt as an infant, to a country that was home to hundreds of thousands of Jews at the time. Philo, a Jewish philosopher of Alexandria once commented that "Jews in Alexandria and Egypt from the Libyan slope to the borders of Aethiopia do not fall short of a million" and "that no single country can contain the Jews because of their multitude."[4] Strabo, a Greek geographer of the first century CE said, "you can't go anywhere in the civilised world without encountering a Jew."[5] John Mark, Barnabas, Paul, Timothy, Priscilla, and Aquila, to name a few, were Jews of the diaspora. Later on, we find that some epistles (like Hebrews, 1 Peter, and James) were written to those of the diaspora. Paul and Peter focused their mission strategy on Rome as it was both

---

1. "Diaspora," in Douglas and Cairns, *New International Dictionary.*
2. Hock, "Religion on the Move," 236. Also see Haar, *Halfway to Paradise,* 77.
3. Hock, "Religion on the Move," 236.
4. Philo, *In Flaccum,* cited Collins, *Between Athens and Jerusalem,* 5.
5. Strabo, *Geography,* 16, also cited in Collins, *Between Athens and Jerusalem.*

the heart of the empire as well as home to an influential community of Jews. As much as we understand the Bible to be a book about migrations, we must also appreciate it as a book about life in the diaspora. It is migration that creates the diaspora.

In the twenty-first century, we live in the "age of migration"[6] and, as a result, life in the diaspora is normative for many. The United Nations statistics suggest that almost 300 million people of the world's population are international migrants—living in countries other than where they were born or have their roots—in the diaspora.[7] Approximately 3–5 percent of the world population are migrants. As a result, the term "diaspora" has become applicable to peoples of all ethnicities and not only the Jews. We talk of the African diaspora,[8] the Indian diaspora (or, as Sam George has called it, the Desi diaspora[9]), the Asian diaspora,[10] as well as the Latin American diaspora.[11] Of course, we could also bring it down to talk of national diasporas, for instance, the Nigerian diaspora, the Filipino diaspora, or the Brazilian diaspora. Generally, people migrate with their religions. Migration of Christians from Christian communities in various parts of the world has resulted in the creation of diaspora churches, especially in the Western world of Europe, North America, Australia, and New Zealand.

Getting Our Language Right

The term "diaspora missiology" has come into common use in the years following Wan's *Diaspora Missiology: Theory, Methodology, and Practice*.[12] Herein, Wan defines diaspora missions as "Christians' participation in God's redemptive mission to evangelize their kinsmen (sic) on the move, and through them to reach out to the natives in their homelands and beyond."[13] The concept itself developed from a presentation that Wan made at the 2004 consultation of the Filipino International Network in Seoul, South Korea as a response to the increased diasporization of people groups and the shifting of Christianity's center of gravity to the Global South. In *Diaspora Missiology*, Wan identifies three types of diaspora missions. The first is *missions to the diaspora* in which mission involves reaching the diaspora groups themselves. Second, we have *missions through the diaspora*. In this model, diaspora Christians reach out to their kinsmen wherever they are. Third, there is *missions by and beyond the diaspora* and it involves "motivating and mobilizing diaspora Christians for cross-cultural

---

6. Castles and Miller, *Age of Migration*.
7. International Organization for Migration, *World Migration Report 2020*, 2.
8. Adogame, *African Christian Diaspora*.
9. George, *Desi Diaspora*.
10. Raj and Jacobsen, *South Asian Christian Diaspora*.
11. Espinosa, *Latino Pentecostals in America*.
12. Wan, *Diaspora Missiology*.
13. Wan, *Diaspora Missiology*, 5.

missions."[14] He suggests diaspora missiology to be an alternative to traditional missiology as it draws from various interdisciplinary subjects such as biblical studies, theology, mission, migration, and diaspora studies to form a complementary but distinct discipline.[15]

Even though the term "diaspora missiology" has enjoyed extensive usage, it remains generally problematic and is, thus, often used with some explanation.[16] The most significant limitation of the language of "diaspora missiology," for the sake of the argument of this essay, is that it creates an unnecessary distinction between "non-diasporic" or what Wan calls "traditional" missiology (supposedly of Western missionaries working in the rest of the world) and diasporic mission that involves missionaries from the rest of the world (especially those working in the West but may also include those serving in mission elsewhere). "Diaspora missiology" does not attend to the five centuries of the dispersion of Western Christians and, thus, the creation of a Western diaspora, that had a huge impact on Christian mission in the world. Indeed, the current phenomenon of world Christianity is a result of this diasporization of Europe that took place for 450 years, starting around 1500 CE and reaching a crescendo in the nineteenth century and the first half of the twentieth century. Baines has suggested that higher than 25 percent of Europe's population migrated from Europe between 1814 and 1930, yet nowhere is their missiology called a diaspora missiology even though they were Christian migrants. Looking back at the nineteenth century, we could say that the Scottish missionaries who worked in Malawi or Kenya, the Moravian missionaries who worked in South Africa, as well as the British missionaries who worked in China and India were diaspora missionaries. While Asians, Africans and Latin Americans may proudly call themselves diaspora missionaries (and there are many who refuse to use the term for themselves), in most Western countries, "diaspora" implies "the other," "an outsider," and, generally speaking, unwelcome guests who are to be tolerated or encouraged to move elsewhere. To be a diaspora person in the current migrant-weary context of Europe means being an *inferior* and exotic "other" who demands pity and is best left to exist at a distance.

An equivalent term to diaspora mission is "reverse mission." Matthew Ojo popularized it in his 2007 essay, defining it as "the sending of missionaries to Europe and North America by churches and Christians from the non-Western world, particularly Africa, Asia and Latin America, which were at the receiving end of Catholic and Protestant missions as mission fields from the sixteenth to the later twentieth century."[17] In 2011, a Korean missionary in Europe, Hun Kim, defined "reverse mission" as when non-Western churches return with the gospel to societies that initially brought the

---

14. Wan, *Diaspora Missiology*, 5.
15. Wan, *Diaspora Missiology*, 5.
16. For example, see Krabill and Norton, "New Wine in Old Wineskins."
17. Ojo, "Reverse Mission," 380–82.

gospel to them.[18] Some African scholars, prominent among them a Nigerian Baptist pastor in London, Israel Olofinjana, have preferred to use "reverse mission" (and "reverse missiology") instead of "diaspora mission" and "diaspora missiology."[19] Olofinjana says "African Christians ministering in the UK now are directly or indirectly a harvest of seeds sown by the early missionaries to Africa."[20] A small circle of African theologians have followed Olofinjana to write about the significance of "reverse mission" in Europe.[21] Olofinjana himself has led the charge by publishing several blog posts and speaking in seminars about how "there is indeed such a thing as reverse mission and reverse missiology."[22] By "reverse mission," Olofinjana and his colleagues mean the missionary work of African Christians in the West—and this is really an *African* conversation. They have sometimes included Asian and Latin American Christians in "reverse mission" but, to a large extent, they focus on African Christians in Europe or North America in their definition. For Olofinjana, the justification for keeping "reverse mission" is that European mission in Africa in the nineteenth and twentieth centuries was actually mission going forward.[23] Now that African Christians have come to Europe and are attempting to engage in mission among the people who sent missionaries to African a century or two ago, this is mission in reverse.

The terms "reverse mission" and "reverse missiology" are usually used with a descriptor—they are generally controversial. Of course, "reverse mission" is not the most appropriate term for the rising presence of African Christians and missionaries in Europe and North America. Many of them are simply Christian migrants and even though they may call themselves missionaries, they are not the modern equivalent of the European missionaries who went to Africa two hundred years ago. Calling them "reverse missionaries" is quite insensitive and theologically unjustifiable. Admittedly, it is evident that some aspects of global migration trends have changed, as seen in the rise of non-Western populations in the postcolonial West. However, mission has not reversed even though missionaries are now able to move from African to the West.

Essentially, then, both "diaspora missiology" and "reverse missiology" are not as helpful as they seem. They may be easy to use but they do not do justice to the mission of God that involves all followers of Christ in the world as brothers and sisters, equal before God. What missionary movement has not involved a dispersion of some kind—intentional or otherwise? What international mission is not diaspora mission? After all, God's mission is God's mission, no matter where it originates or where it flows. Migration trends have reversed, but there is no such thing as reverse mission. In the twenty-first century, we have many people from the Majority World migrating

18. Kim, "Migrant Workers and 'Reverse Mission,'" 148.
19. Olofinjana, "Reverse Mission."
20. Olofinjana, *Reverse in Mission and Ministry*, 2.
21. Adedibu, "Origin, Migration."
22. Olofinjana, "Theology of Reverse Mission."
23. Olofinjana, "Theology of Reverse Mission."

to the West, contrary to what happened between 1500 and 1950. Yet, God's mission continues to move forward. God continues to scatter God's people around the world and even if it is not God doing the scattering, God still uses the scattering for good. Many Christians have come from around the world to the West and, yes, they will have missionary impact on Western culture, but this is not reversal of mission. It is mission just being itself, no matter where it originates.

NON-WESTERN MISSIONARY MOVEMENTS

All in all, we need be bold enough to shift the language from both diaspora missiology and reverse missiology to simply talk about non-Western missionary work in the West. We may as well talk about African, Asian, and Latin American missionary presence and work in Europe and North America. The mission of God in the twenty-first century involves the people of God from all around the world. This is what should happen when Christianity has effectively reached every country in the world—mission ceases being a Western endeavor as non-Western Christians respond to God's call to engage in mission. Whoever responds to the work of the Spirit on the lives and converts to Christianity, regardless of where they are in the world, are called to participate in God's mission. Some of them will serve in mission in their own countries and continents while many others will find their way to other continents including Europe and North America, but they must all partake of God's mission in the world.

This emergence of non-Western missionary movements is good news. The undoing of Europe's Christendom, evident in the marginalization and slow disappearance of Christianity in Europe due to the ongoing secularization of Europeans mean that Europe will struggle to keep recruiting and sending missionaries to the world.[24] Europe itself needs to be re-evangelized. It needs missionaries sent to Europe from around the world. While the United States has its "functional Christendom"[25] that continues to uphold Christianity's influence on society, yet, the growing numbers of the spiritual-but-not-religious part of the populations reveals that there is also secularization happening there.[26] In addition, its Christianity is deeply entangled in politics and shaped, to a large extent, by capitalism, and it finds an increasingly suspicious audience as it tries to engage a world less enthusiastic about US imperialism. The other mission-sending countries of Australia and New Zealand face similar issues, but their contribution to world mission has always been smaller than that of Europe and North America. They also both need a fresh missional engagement and evangelization.

Given this new reality, it is needful and, therefore, hopeful that world Christians pick up the baton and engage in mission not only in their own continents but also in other continents. One hundred years ago, a typical missionary would most definitely

---

24. To read more on secularization of Europe, see Davie, *Europe*.
25. Guder, *Missional Church*, chapter 3.
26. Kenneson, "What's in a Name?."

be white, most likely a European or an American, and they would be working in some remote place in Africa, Asia, or Latin America. Today, people of all races from all continents engage in God's mission. A typical missionary in the twenty-first century will possibly be a Nigerian woman teaching in Northern Ghana, a Korean teenager leading a choreography team in London, a Brazilian pastor leading a church in Portugal or Mozambique, an Eritrean refugee taxi driver in Minneapolis, a Belgian priest in charge of a parish in India, or indeed, a Malawian scholar teaching in Britain. Mission is slowly becoming a truly from-everywhere-to everywhere phenomenon. Todd Johnson observes that "of the ten countries sending the most missionaries in 2010, three were in the global South: Brazil, South Korea, and India."[27] In addition, the second top ten countries include six from the global South such as South Africa, the Philippines, Mexico, China, Colombia, and Nigeria. Thus, nine out of twenty countries sending the most missionaries are in the Majority World. While the US still sends the highest absolute number of missionaries, it is now Palestine that sends the most missionaries per million church members (followed by Ireland, Malta, Samoa, and South Korea).[28] Overall, I believe it is now possible to talk about at least three main tracks of non-Western mission movements observable in the world today: the African, Asian, and Latin American mission movements at work in the West.

African Missionary Work

African Christians in Africa rarely use the term "missionary" to identify themselves.[29] They use "missionary" for foreigners, usually white Western missionaries. However, in the West, it is common for them to say that they are actually the missionaries that God has sent to re-evangelize their new host nations. Just like the Great European migration of the nineteenth century, most African migrants are simply Christians caught up in migration and bringing their Christianity with them. This makes it rather difficult to count how many missionaries have been sent from Africa. For instance, the thousands of Redeemed Christian Church of God (RCCG) pastors leading congregations in Britain would be counted among missionaries from Nigeria.[30] In the same way, the hundreds of Church of Pentecost (COP-UK) pastors in Britain would be counted among Ghanaian missionaries serving in Britain.[31] The largest church in Europe, The Blessed Embassy of the Kingdom of God, located in Kiev, Ukraine, is

27. Centre for the Study of Global Christianity, *Christianity*, 76.
28. Centre for the Study of Global Christianity, *Christianity*, 76.
29. They identify as pastors, prophets, apostles, and other titles. In the West where they talk of Europe and North America as a mission field, African pastors speak of themselves as missionaries even though very few of them are trained in cross-cultural mission or registered with a mission agency.
30. The RCCG is the most visible of Nigerian denominations in Britain, but they form only a small portion of African Christians around the country. It can be found in more than 175 countries (including almost every country in Africa).
31. The Church of Pentecost is a Ghanaian denomination currently found in ninety-two countries.

led by a Nigerian known as Sunday Adelaja. In Britain, the largest congregation is the Kingsway International Christian Centre and it is led by another Nigerian called Matthew Ashimolowo. *Christian migration* from Africa has, since the 1970s, made Africa a contender for the continent with the most missionaries. Hollenweger says "Christians in Britain prayed for many years for revival, and when it came they did not recognize it because it was black."[32]

Another key aspect of the African missionary that must be acknowledged is that of the Afro-Caribbean Christians who have been present in Europe and in North America for much longer than the African migrants. The connection between the Black West Indies and Europe and North America has existed for centuries, going back to the times of the transatlantic slave trade. However, it has increased in the aftermaths of the Second World War when Britain needed to import labor from the West Indies and the United States changed its immigration laws to allow people from places like the West Indies to migrate to the United States.[33] West Indian migration from "The Islands" to Britain was accelerated in the 1950s when many Caribbean families responded to an invitation from the British government to come and help rebuild the "mother country" after the devastation of the Second World War. In Britain today, their presence is seen in Afro-Caribbean denominations like the Church of God of Prophecy and the New Testament Church of God. Both these denominations are in their second or third generation of existence in Britain. The flagship church for the Afro-Caribbean community in Britain today in the Ruach City Church in Brixton, London.

Asian Missionary Movements

From Asia, there is a strong mission movement arising largely from India, China, South Korea, and the Philippines. Just like all other mission movements taking place now, the Asian missionaries are focusing on reaching not only their fellow nationals scattered in the diaspora but also the entire world for Christ. For instance, in 2020, it was estimated that there were about 27,000 South Korean missionaries serving in more than 160 countries,[34] up from 20,000 in 2010.

Until 2015, South Korea was known to send more missionaries around the world than any other country except the United States.[35] This led Rebecca Kim in 2015 to argue, contrary to Todd Johnson's Centre for the Study of Global Christianity report (cited above), that "on a per capita basis, South Korea sends out the most missionaries

---

32. Hollenweger, "Foreword" to Roswith Gerloff's *Plea for British Black Theologies*, ix.

33. For more, see Chin and Villazor, *Immigration and Nationality Act*. One consequence of this act is that it made possible the migration of non-Western people to America, many of whom are Christians.

34. Lee, "South Korea's Missionary Movement."

35. It is now fifth, with Brazil, Italy, and France sending more missionaries than South Korea.

in the world."³⁶ South Korean missionaries come imbued with the fervor common to Pentecostal and Charismatic Christians and a desire to reach some of the hardest places for the gospel like China. Media reports suggest that in 2017 that the Chinese government is expelling hundreds of South Korean missionaries from China, however, this did not seem to deter many more of them from seeking to enter China.³⁷ Today, as Rebecca Kim shows us, hundreds of Korean missionaries live and work in North America, both providing pastoral care to fellow Koreans living there and attempting to reach out to US and Canadian peoples in the process. The Korean Christian Association in the UK is quite vibrant, with about twenty congregations scattered around the country under their care. In addition, every year, a group of around fifty young South Korean missionaries visit Britain to pray for the country—as a token of appreciation for the many British missionaries that served in Korea for almost two hundred years ago. In Africa, the presence of South Korean missionaries is quite pronounced in countries like Kenya, Zambia, and Ghana.

This case of South Korean missionary work in the world is significant because it was the first non-Western nation to send a large numbers of missionaries in this postcolonial era. In addition, as a non-Western nation, they model for many what mission without imperialism would look like. They evangelize not in their language but in English or a local one. They do not build churches that look like the churches in Korea. Instead, they let locals shape what they believe their church ought to look like. Most importantly, they do not impose their culture as they work in the world. They try to bring only the gospel and nothing else. As Kim puts it, Korean missionaries launched their work from a position of economic and political weakness.³⁸

Latin American Missionary Movements

Latin American missionaries have also made their impact around the world. Among Evangelicals, Brazil currently sends the second highest number of missionaries around the world.³⁹ Many of them are in Portuguese-speaking countries such as Portugal, Angola, and Mozambique. However, there are also quite a few Brazilian missionaries in Britain, Germany, and North America. For the Roman Catholic Christianity, Latin American Christians have helped to sustain the church in parts of the world where Roman Catholics are not very strong in numbers. For instance, in North America, Christians of Latin American heritage now account for one-third of all Catholics, largely due

---

36. Kim, *Spirit Moves West*, 28. Johnson's data, in this case, are more credible.

37. For instance, Reuters reported in March 2017 that China had expelled thirty-two South Korean missionaries.

38. Kim, *Spirit Moves West*, 28.

39. Brazil had registered 34,000 missionaries sent around the world in 2010. Centre for the Study of Global Christianity, *Christianity*, 76.

to massive Hispanic immigration from Latin America.[40] Indeed, a 2007 Pew Trust Research established that 68 percent of all Latin Americans identified as Catholics.[41] More than 50 percent of all Catholics in the US under age twenty-five are of Hispanic descent.[42] If it were not for the presence of these Hispanic Christians, the Catholic church would not be as strong in the United States today. In addition, as long as current trends hold, Latin American Christian presence in the Catholic Church in North America will continue to rise for the foreseeable future. As Father Virgilio Elizondo suggested in his widely acclaimed book, *The Future is Mestizo*, to survive this generation, the Roman Catholic Church in the United States must embrace the cultural diversity that has come about through the presence of Hispanic Catholics in the country.[43] Indeed, the future of the Roman Catholic church in North America looks very Hispanic.

In addition, Latin American Pentecostal and Charismatic denominations have spread across the Spanish- and Portuguese-speaking worlds. Pentecostal Christianity in the United States has also been greatly invigorated by the presence of Hispanic Pentecostal Christians, mainly from Mexico and Brazil. According to Gastón Espinosa, Hispanic Pentecostals form the second largest group of Latin American Christians in the United States and their population is growing from the many defections from the Roman Catholic church.[44] Their numbers are growing rapidly and they are increasingly becoming a powerful block.[45] In England, some of the largest migrant congregations comprise of members from Latin America. Olivia Sheringham suggested in 2013 that the Brazilian consulate has a list of more than fifty Brazilian religious denominations in London, while the Evangelical Alliance—an alliance of Evangelical movements in London—estimates more than eighty Brazilian Evangelical churches in the city ranging from the internationally established *Igreja Universal do Reino de Deus* (known in English as the Universal Church of the Kingdom of God)—which now has a total of sixteen temples in London—to the *Assembleia de Deus*, and to much smaller sects and independent denominations—many of which have been set up in London by Brazilians in response to growing demand.[46]

---

40. Population Reference Bureau, "Immigration Gives Catholicism a Boost in the United States," 2008.
41. Pew Research Center, "Changing Faiths." Also Pew Research Center, "Between Two Worlds," 2009.
42. U.S. Conference of Catholic Bishops, *Hispanic Catholics in the United States*.
43. Elizondo, *Future is Mestizo*.
44. Espinosa, *Latino Pentecostals in America*.
45. For instance, the largest Assemblies of God church in the US is New Life Covenant Church, Chicago. Its eleven thousand members are largely Hispanic and pastored by a Latino pastor, Wilfredo De Jesús. For more on this, see http://mynewlife.org. The Assemblies of God is the largest Latino Protestant, Evangelical, and Pentecostal denomination in the US.
46. Sheringham, *Transnational Religious Spaces*, 69.

THINKING THEOLOGICALLY ABOUT NON-WESTERN MISSION

Christianity has followers in every country in the world. Much of Christianity has come out of the missionary work of Europeans (and their descendants in the wider Western world) and, therefore, bears some marks of the European civilization, but there is also a de-Westernization of Christianity. Of course, with a third of Christians being white Westerners, Christianity has moved far away from its old identity as a "white man's" religion. This growing presence of non-Western Christians, their languages, and their cultures continues to shape the way we understand the faith and how we engage in mission. Christ not only has followers in every major people group; he also has witness-bearers among all peoples in the world for to follow Christ is to respond to his calling to partake of God's mission. This new reality that the mission of God includes all Christ-followers of the world has serious implications on how we theologize about mission. Below are three key themes that need careful consideration in twenty-first-century missiological discourse.

The Missionary Calling of All Believers

That all Christians are invited to be witness-bearers for Christ in the world is beyond dispute. However, this is not how mission has always been understood. During the era of the Western missionary movement, mission generally occurred in the non-evangelized lands of the Latin America, Africa, and Asia. It would be carried out by trained people who left the West to serve God. Thus, mission and the church were separate and, therefore, there was a gap between ecclesiology and missiology. The church was in Christendom—which was Europe—and mission happened outside it. Missionaries were the chosen few who went to Africa, or Asia, or Latin America. That work of mission involved those Christians who supported the missionaries but, for the most part, the majority of Christians had little to nothing to do with mission. Mission in the twenty-first century, where there are more Christians in Africa and Latin America than in Europe, requires us to change the way we think about mission. Theologically, we understand that all followers are witness-bearers, and socially, all witness-bearers must serve where God wants them to, be it in their own communities or across borders to other lands. Mission is from anywhere to anywhere. In addition, we understand as well that there is no wall of separation between the church and mission. Wherever the church is, there must it engage in mission. It is for this reason that the church exists. Wherever there are followers of Christ, there must they engage in mission. It is for this reason that God has called and placed them where they are.

The Theology of the Body

The question that usually comes as a response to the proposals made above asks whether it is still appropriate for Western Christians to go to Africa and Latin America to serve in mission when, realistically speaking, these continents have more Christians than Europe or North America. The answer lies in the missionary call to make disciples that does not stop when people convert to Christianity. Conversion is only step one of a long journey of discipleship where God uses people to shape one another into the image of the Son of God. Paul argues that God has given the body of Christ gifts "for the equipping of the saints for the work of ministry, for the edifying of the body of Christ, till we all come to the unity of the faith and of the knowledge of the Son of God, to a perfect man, to the measure of the stature of the fullness of Christ" (Eph 4:12–13).[47] He goes on to add that this body is "joined and knit together by what every joint supplies, according to the effective working by which every part does its share, causes growth of the body for the edifying of itself in love" (Eph 4:16). Essentially, Paul is suggesting here that the livelihood of the body depends on the mutual exchange between its members. God has given the members gifts for one another. In a sense, then, all Christians have gifts for one another, and they are called to give and receive of each other. While African, Asian, and Latin American Christians have gifts for one another, they also bring numerous gifts when they migrate to the West. The same applies to Western Christians who continue to bring their gifts to world Christianity, they must receive from the rest of the world as well. Mission itself often depends on the gift of hospitality, especially to the stranger whose eyes can see in a culture what those inside it may not.

The Migrant as a Theologian

The theme of migration should inform our missiology. The Bible has been rightly called a Book of Migrations.[48] If we took migration out of the Bible, there would be no story to tell. God revealed to the patriarchs in the context of migration. Abraham's friendship with God took shape in the context of migration. Jacob's dream at Bethel happened in the context of migration. God would eventually require that Israel always remembers that they are descendants of migrants. Each year, they would recite "My father was a wandering Aramean" at Passover and, six months later, get out of their houses to live in tents at the Feast of Tabernacles. Indeed, as followers of Christ, and spiritual descendants of Abraham, we too must always remember that our father in the faith was an immigrant. To understand that this Christian faith makes us all descendants of an immigrant could change the way we treat one another; it could help us realize that we are all *diaspora* people.

---

47. All scriptural references from the NRSV.
48. Carroll, *Bible and Borders*.

Mission itself is directly connected to migration—not only of Christian missionaries but also of Christians in general. Christian traders, farmers, diplomats, and migrants in general have been crucial to mission. For instance, Hanciles has shown the significant role played by migrants in the spread of Christianity over the centuries.[49] The process of migration is itself a theologizing experience[50]—it often draws people closer to God, causing them to reflect on God's sustaining power in a foreign land. In addition, migration not only needs to be thought of theologically—as in, we need a robust theology of migration—it also moves theologies around, mixing theological thoughts from different parts of the world to help the body—and there is *only* one body—to understand God better. A robust understanding of the migration of theology is needed and migrants themselves—the people of the diaspora—will be our leading theologians.

CONCLUSION

By connecting mission to migration, we connect mission to the diaspora. Of course, both "migration" and "diaspora" are terms loaded with extensive political connotations. In contemporary Western parlance, migrants—diaspora people—are those who have come from other parts of the world to the West. Westerners rarely think of themselves as migrants even after they have migrated—the term "diaspora" hardly applies to them. Case in point—Howles, a British missionary living in Uganda recently tweeted, "It always fascinates me that I, a British man living in Uganda for 10 years, have *never* been called an immigrant in my whole life."[51] For the sake of God's mission in the world, we will do well to move away from these terms to begin to talk about and, therefore, accept the missionary movements that have emerged in Africa, Asia, and Latin America. That way, we will help prepare the body of Christ around the world to be able to receive from one another. The body needs this exchange.

BIBLIOGRAPHY

Adedibu, Babatunde. "Origin, Migration, Globalisation and the Missionary Encounter of Britain's Black Majority Churches." *Studies in World Christianity* 19 (2013) 93–113.

Adogame, Afeosemime U. *The African Christian Diaspora: New Currents and Emerging Trends in World Christianity*. London: Bloomsbury Academic, 2013.

Carroll R., M. Daniel. *The Bible and Borders: Hearing God's Word on Immigration*. Grand Rapids: Brazos, 2020.

Castles, Stephen, and Mark J. Miller. *The Age of Migration: International Population Movements in the Modern World*. New York: Guilford, 2009.

---

49. Hanciles, *Migration and the Making of Global Christianity*.

50. Smith, "Religion and Ethnicity in America," 1155.

51. Twitter, @ChrisHowles, 5/12/21, 18:47. https://twitter.com/chrishowles/status/1467566194660188161?s=21 (emphasis mine).

Centre for the Study of Global Christianity. *Christianity in Its Global Context, 1970–2020: Society, Religion, and Mission.* South Hamilton, MA: Gordon-Conwell Theological Seminary, 2013.

Chin, Gabriel J., and Rose Cuison Villazor. *The Immigration and Nationality Act of 1965: Legislating a New America.* Cambridge: Cambridge University Press, 2015.

Collins, John J. *Between Athens and Jerusalem: Jewish Identity in the Hellenistic Diaspora.* Grand Rapids: Eerdmans, 2000.

Davie, Grace. *Europe—the Exceptional Case: Parameters of Faith in the Modern World.* London: Darton Longman & Todd, 2002.

Douglas, James Dixon, and Earle E. Cairns. *The New International Dictionary of the Christian Church.* Grand Rapids: Zondervan, 1974.

Elizondo, Virgilio P. *The Future is Mestizo: Life Where Cultures Meet.* Oak Park, IL: Meyer-Stone, 1988.

Espinosa, Gastón. *Latino Pentecostals in America: Faith and Politics in Action.* Cambridge: Harvard University Press, 2014.

George, Sam. *Desi Diaspora: Ministry among Scattered Global Indian Christians.* Bangalore: SAIACS, 2019.

Gerloff, Roswith. *A Plea for British Black Theologies: The Black Church Movement in Britain in Its Transatlantic Cultural and Theological Interaction with Special References to the Pentecostal Oneness (Apostolic) and Sabbatarian Movements.* Frankfurt am Main: P. Lang, 1992.

Guder, Darrell L., ed. *Missional Church: A Vision for the Sending of the Church in North America.* The Gospel and Our Culture Series. Grand Rapids: Eerdmans, 1998.

Haar, Gerrie ter. *Halfway to Paradise: African Christians in Europe.* Cardiff: Cardiff Academic, 1998.

Hanciles, Jehu J. *Migration and the Making of Global Christianity.* Grand Rapids: Eerdmans, 2021.

Hock, Klaus. "Religion on the Move: Transcultural Perspectives. Discourses on Diaspora Religion between Category Formation and the Quest for Religious Identity." In *Christianity in Africa and the African Diaspora: The Appropriation of a Scattered Heritage*, edited by Afe Adogame et al., 235–47. London: Continuum, 2008.

Hollenweger, Walter. "Foreword" to *A Plea for British Black Theologies: The Black Church Movement in Britain in Its Transatlantic Cultural and Theological Interaction with Special References to the Pentecostal Oneness (Apostolic) and Sabbatarian Movements* by Roswith Gerloff, ix–x. Frankfurt am Main: P. Lang, 1992.

International Organization for Migration. *World Migration Report 2020.* United Nations Migration (Geneva).

Kenneson, Philip D. "What's in a Name? A Brief Introduction to the 'Spiritual but Not Religious.'" *Liturgy* 30 (2015) 3–13.

Kim, Rebecca Y. *The Spirit Moves West: Korean Missionaries in America.* Oxford: Oxford University, 2015.

Kim, Sŏng-hun. "Migrant Workers and 'Reverse Mission' in the West." In *Korean Diaspora and Christian Mission*, edited by Sŏng-hun Kim and Wonsuk Ma, 146–52. Oxford: Regnum, 2011.

Kim, Sŏng-hun, and Wonsuk Ma, eds. *Korean Diaspora and Christian Mission.* Oxford: Regnum, 2011.

Krabill, Matthew, and Allison Norton. "New Wine in Old Wineskins: A Critical Appraisal of Diaspora Missiology." *Missiology* 43 (2015) 442–55.

Lee, Jae Kyeong. "South Korea's Missionary Movement." *Biblical Recorder. Baptist Press*, 2018. https://www.brnow.org/opinions/voices-opinion/South-Korea-s-missionary-movement/.

Ojo, Matthew. "Reverse Mission." In *Encyclopedia of Mission and Missionaries*, edited by Jonathan J. Bonk, 380–82. London: Routledge, 2007.

Olofinjana, Israel O. *Reverse in Mission and Ministry: Africans in the Dark Continent of Europe*. Milton Keynes: AuthorHouse, 2010.

———. "Reverse Mission: African Presence and Mission within Baptists Together in the United Kingdom." *Journal of European Baptist Studies* 19 (2019).

———. "Theology of Reverse Mission." https://www.baptist.org.uk/Articles/372473/Theology_of_Reverse.aspx.

Pew Research Center. "Between Two Worlds: How Young Latinos Come of Age in America." https://www.pewresearch.org/hispanic/2009/12/11/between-two-worlds-how-young-latinos-come-of-age-in-america/.

———. "Changing Faiths: Latinos and the Transformation of American Religion." https://www.pewresearch.org/hispanic/2007/04/25/changing-faiths-latinos-and-the-transformation-of-american-religion/.

Population Reference Bureau. "Immigration Gives Catholicism a Boost in the United States." http://www.prb.org/Publications/Articles/2008/uscatholicsandimmigration.aspx.

Raj, Selva J., and Knut A. Jacobsen. *South Asian Christian Diaspora: Invisible Diaspora in Europe and North America*. Farnham: Ashgate, 2008.

Sheringham, Olivia. *Transnational Religious Spaces: Faith and the Brazilian Migration Experience*. New York: Palgrave Macmillan, 2013.

Smith, Timothy L. "Religion and Ethnicity in America." *The American Historical Review* 83 (1978) 1155–85.

U.S. Conference of Catholic Bishops. *Hispanic Catholics in the United States*. Washington, DC: U.S. Conference of Catholic Bishops, 2007.

Wan, Enoch. *Diaspora Missiology: Theory, Methodology, and Practice*. Portland: Institute of Diaspora Studies, 2011.

SECTION 3

Emerging Theologies from Latin America

CHAPTER 8

Catholic Liberation Theology

ANA MARÍA BIDEGAIN

In the second half of the twentieth century, sectors of Latin American Catholicism wondered how to be faithful to the message of Jesus that calls for justice in a reality marked by enormous economic, social, racial, political, and cultural inequalities. Among them, the majority were young men and women who knew themselves to be sons and daughters of God, created in his image. United in this brotherhood, they knew that they had to reach out to the most impoverished and lacking in education, health, housing, and work, who were also their brothers and sisters. They knew that, together with them, they had to change a reality that could not be willed by God. These groups of Christians, strengthened in community prayer, found Jesus alive in the daily life of their neighborhoods and families, and discovered the need for the emergence of a new theology.

Gathered in small communities of equals, and advised by some priests, they used a method, a spiritual path,[1] that allowed them first of all to analyze the reality that surrounded them and to understand the challenges that following Jesus implied in the historical circumstances in which they had to live and give witness with their actions, participating in the political, social, economic, and cultural life. They were urged to clarify the deep motivations, the spiritual reasons that gave meaning to their life

---

1. I would like to thank one of my PhD students Gremaud Angee for assistance with the final editing. We refer to the communities of specialized Catholic Action movements, such as the Young Catholic Workers (YCW), JEC Students; JUC, University; JIC independent workers; and JAC agricultural workers, teaching teams, Pax Romana in its branches of students, professionals, and intellectuals. Movements of childhood and lay movements organized by congregations and religious orders. The spiritual path is the revision of life that I will explain later.

choices. It was a matter of reflecting critically on their actions, the ways of approaching Christian practice and being capable of allowing themselves to be challenged by the need for coherence between Jesus's proposal and the life of each person. This provoked changes in attitudes and mentalities, a real individual and overall conversion, a cultural change, a new lifestyle.

The challenges, to strengthen spiritual motivations and to deepen the validity of the commitments assumed, demanded a different and renewed theological depth and responses. "A theology marked out by reality because faith has become incarnate."[2] With this vision and liberating experience of different communities in the region, young theologians, who advised them, began to write and present the parameters of a new theology, which would be recognized by different groups, but also persecuted even within the same church: liberation theology.

Liberation theology dialogues with reality as a place where God reveals himself, inviting people to take personal and community action against the unjust situations that surround them and to reflect on those practices.[3] It is a reflection on the historical reality lived by these Christians, their spirituality and their "ecclesiality." That is, their experience of being church, of walking together living the faith in community, centered on love for the most vulnerable and impoverished in many ways.

The explanation of the genesis of the emergence of this theology does not lie in the publication of a book or books, or in the theological influences from other latitudes, nor in the theoretical debates that it has generated a posteriori, but in the spiritual and socio-ecclesial transformations of Latin American and Caribbean Christianity in the twentieth century, which is the focus of this chapter.

FERTILIZING THE TERRAIN: SOCIAL ACTION AND ORGANIZATION OF THE LAITY

Towards the middle of the twentieth century, after a strong period of confrontation with the liberals, the church achieved a readjustment and in many cases a reintegration into the state, facilitated by the establishment of the welfare states of the 1940s–1950s. These looked to the local churches to assist them with the provision of human and organizational resources to meet social needs. While the state provided financial resources, it gained the legitimacy of the church, and broadened the electoral social base to achieve social and political stability. Religious orders and congregations, particularly those of women, played an essential role in this process by attending to social works, especially health and education, especially for women. In doing so, they helped them prepare for the conquest of civil and political rights around the middle of the century and full access to university for those who achieved this privilege. In almost all countries, new dioceses were created, and seminaries were strengthened with the

---

2. Urán, *La Iglesia de Medellín y el Movimiento Estudiantil de América Latina*, 67.
3. Gutiérrez, *Teología de la liberación: perspectivas*.

presence of foreign religious. Thus, by 1950 the church enjoyed a comfortable position in most Latin American and Caribbean states, consolidating itself as a strong and growing institution with great social influence.

Since 1930, at the behest of Rome, an elite of male and female laity had been organized into associations known as Catholic Action. Linked to the bishops, by a mandate, they were participants in the evangelization process and gradually became aware of and took concrete actions in the face of great social disparities. Within this framework, they broke with the ties to the old conservative parties and opting for the advantages of the democratic model, and inspired by the social doctrine of the church, founded Christian Democratic Parties, following the European experience.

Several transformations and concerns had been manifesting themselves in the heart of the church since the fifties and were preparing the way for the Second Vatican Council and influenced the bishops. This is the case of the liturgical and biblical movements and all the activities developed by Catholic Action. Within these apostolic movements, particularly the youth movements received much attention and support from the bishops. Given their methodology (revision of life: See-Judge-Act), they influenced other sectors of the church, which began to use it and, decades later, it was recognized as the basis of the Latin American theological method.

The essence of this method called life review is that the faithful gathered in small communities of equals (students, workers, farmers, teachers, professionals) analyze how the presence of God is found in what they are living, with the joys, daily challenges, and conflicts. How the message of Jesus helps to deepen this encounter, and to motivate actions that allow the transformation of situations that are ethically unacceptable. This method requires clarifying the deep motivations and spiritual reasons that give meaning to life choices and motivate us to act in a certain way. It is a matter of reflecting critically on the ways in which one's personal Christian practice, the group and the ecclesial community have been carried out. To be able to allow oneself to be challenged by the need for coherence between the proposal of Jesus and the life of each person and of the community. This provokes changes in attitudes and mentalities, a real individual conversion and on the whole, a cultural change, a new style of life. That is why it is a revision of life. Reviewing life to project action. This pedagogical effort allows the formation of people who, living Christian values and being aware of the social injustices of the reality in which they live, become subjects of their own history and can help transform that reality, so that God's love can be lived in fullness. Central themes and spiritual experiences systematized shortly after, by liberation theology.

Along with this path of the laity, we must mention other transformations in the life of the church in Europe that had an impact on Latin America and opened avenues for the changes that will be proposed by the council and allowed new pastoral and theological proposals to flourish. For example, to confront the process of secularization and based on studies of the sociology of religion, pastoral work was rethought in

France. There and in Belgium the specialized movements to which we have referred had been initiated. University centers such as Louvain, the Institut Catholique de Paris, and seminaries run by Jesuits and Dominicans in Brussels, Paris, and Lyon were spaces that facilitated the theological development of the current known as "Nouvelle Theologie." But they also received many young Latin American priests to complete their theological formation and education in sociology of religion. Until then, many Latin American priest mainly had been formed in Pio Latin American Seminar, the Gregorian and other universities in Rome. Now, in addition to Italy, they also went to Germany, Switzerland, Spain, Holland, Canada, and the United States, mostly to France and Belgium. Upon their return, their pastoral work was strengthened and many of these young theologians,[4] were teaching in the seminaries, advising Catholic Action movements, and/or attending parishes.

At the request of the bishops, they developed sociological studies in various dioceses that allowed the creation of joint pastoral care for a greater and coordinated attention to the parishioners. In addition, the arrival in Latin America of new contingents of religious men and women from Canada, the United States, Spain, Italy, Belgium, Germany, and Holland allowed the advancement of many pastoral projects in the cities as well as in rural areas.

The French Dominicans had a great influence because they created research centers in many Latin American countries in the fifties, dedicated to the problems of development in the then-called Third World countries. They made Catholics understand the reasons for the poverty of two-thirds of the world and the concentration of wealth in the other third, due to the new colonial ties established after World War II and the way in which the processes of decolonization had taken shape. The Jesuits also created research, social action, and popular education centers for the human promotion of marginalized social sectors.

Together with the international ecclesial changes, there were political changes that influenced Latin America and the emergence of liberation theology. The echoes of the social and civil movements that shook American society were facts that showed the difficulties of a society that was projected as a model. Europe, another beacon of modernity, was shaken by workers' and students' mobilizations. They were rethinking the parties' traditional way of doing politics with their backs turned to social diversity. They began to criticize the impact of the technological industrial process on nature and proposed a new interpretation of Marxism, which was articulated outside the canons of Soviet communism. The advance of the Russian tanks on Prague showed with crudeness the Soviet authoritarianism and turned eyes to other revolutionary experiences, such as the Chinese revolution, which proposed that the revolutionary

---

4. For example, Gustavo Gutiérrez of Peru, Lucio Gera of Argentina, Pablo Dabezies of Uruguay, Gilberto Gimenez of Paraguay, Louis de Senna and Almery Becerra of Brazil, the Jesuit Juan Luis Segundo of Uruguay, and Henrique de Lima Vaz were advisors to the university students' movements and pioneers of liberation theology.

vanguard could be peasant. The emergence of the decolonized countries of Africa and Asia which, together with Latin America, sought a different, nonaligned path, forming the bloc of Third World countries.

Among sectors of European Christians, a dialogue between Marxism and Christianity was seen as possible and even necessary, and the birth of a Christian or at least progressive left, open to dialogue with the proposals of Mounier's[5] personalism. The breaking of molds also involved the growing presence of women in the universities and the reading of Simone de Beauvoir (*The Second Sex*, 1947); although they had little impact on the large public, her ideas were read by Christian students such as Rose M. Muraro, laying the foundations for the feminism that emerged later.

The dialogue between Christian and Marxist became a tragedy in Latin American Catholicism. On the one hand, the Cuban Revolution showed the armed struggle to seek political change, which together with the corruption of traditional political leaders, the closing of political options for free democratic play, or the establishment of dictatorships, led to the emergence of a disparity of internationally connected and influential armed organizations. It is worth mentioning that, although these never managed to be the only, nor the preferred option for most Catholics, the armed organizations had a great impact, especially in the media due to the entry into the guerrilla ranks of Camilo Torres, sociologist, university chaplain, and linked to Pax Romana, who died two months after joining the guerrillas in 1966.

The pastoral and educational programs, carried out in rural areas and marginalized urban neighborhoods in defense of working and impoverished populations, necessarily led to encounters with Marxist organizations, with whom they sometimes disputed and sometimes collaborated. All these circumstances were the reasons for tensions within the church that became more acute and manifested themselves before, during, and after the council.

THE RECEPTION OF THE COUNCIL AND THE LATIN AMERICAN CHURCH'S OPTIONS

The Second Vatican Ecumenical Council (1961–1965), by defining the church as the people of God and recognizing the divine presence in human history, legitimized and at the same time opened new perspectives. John XXIII's emphasis on the need to build a poor church, especially in Third World countries, impacted the Latin American faithful and theologians. By calling twenty-three women to participate as auditors and in the council's own commissions and the insistence on attending to the poor and the young in a preferential way, he strengthened the path already taken by important sectors of Catholicism.

---

5. Emmanuel Mounier was a French Christian philosopher who was attentive to social and political issues. Among his works are *Manifesto in the Service of Personalism* (1936), *What is Personalism?* (1947), and *Personalism* (1949).

At the same time as the council sessions, an informal group of bishops and theologians from different regions of the world, including Latin America, continued to debate the "church of the poor."[6] These meetings allowed them to discuss new theological currents and innovative pastoral options with leading authors. Many of these bishops signed a document in which they pledged that upon returning to their dioceses they would adopt a simple life stripped of possessions, and a new pastoral attitude oriented to the poor and workers.[7]

After the council, several meetings were held in Latin America on topics of vital importance for the continent, such as the economic and political situation and integration of Latin America. Of special interest was the role of Catholic universities, considering that student movements were the social movements with the greatest political impact. In addition, they were the ones who received with greater force the impact of the accumulation of events, which at the end of the sixties shook the world and especially the youth. The bishops also carried out a profound revision of the missionary work. They focused the mission on the promotion of the people, in the Afro and indigenous communities, so that they could become the subjects of their own projects and destinies.

At the same time, they saw the need to hold diocesan synods calling priests, but also religious men and women and the laity to rethink, in the light of the conciliar documents, the mission of the church in the historical conditions of each place. These bishops, inspired by the experiences of specialized Catholic action, worked so that the small communities were constituted by all sectors of the people of God, and the diocesan assembly meetings, propitiated unique experiences of *synodality*, which allowed the growth and maturity of the laity in communion and participation.[8]

These pastoral innovations were strengthened by the documents emanating from the Second Conference of the Latin American Episcopate in Medellin, Colombia, in 1968, organized by the Latin American Episcopal Council (CELAM) where the reception of the Council in Latin America and the Caribbean was delineated. Among other issues, institutionalized violence was denounced as a generator of more violence and the need to change the bonds of injustice and oppression experienced by the most defenseless in society. Although it was a conference of bishops, it was attended by theologians, pastoralists, and some lay leaders, who contributed the experiences of local churches and the various Catholic movements.

---

6. In the discussion on the church of the poor, there are always two related aspects: on the one hand, there is the theme of the poverty that the church should practice and, on the other hand, the attention and service that the church should give to the poor. Numbers 8 of *Lumen Gentium* and 5 of *Ad Gentes* are usually cited as the texts that refer to the Church of the poor, but in the whole of the documents there is a very nourished reference to the theme as has been highlighted by Planellas (*La iglesia de los pobres en el Concilio Vaticano II*).

7. Because of the place where they met, it is known as the "Pact of the Catacombs" see Beozzo, *El Pacto de las catacumbas*.

8. Dabezies et al., *Hacia el sínodo panamazónico*.

The church of the poor as a theological concept was taken up again in Latin America, but the reception was not only theoretical, but also experiential. The exaggerated growth of rural-urban migration, which, although it had begun decades before, in the 1960s exposed huge slums not only of poor but also of miserable populations, without even a minimum literacy. They had to go from an almost Paleolithic agrarian world to live in modern cities that required them to be moderately literate for any work. They barely survived in a society where opulent neighborhoods were growing, and they were increasingly marginalized. As we have already mentioned, various ecclesiastical sectors were already working there. That is why this proposal to build a church of the poor was so widely accepted in Latin America and encouraged the work that was being developed with the new proposals and reflections emanating from the council to be deepened.

Couples of laypeople, priests, and religious chose to go and live in the slums and rural areas and were integrated into forms of work that allowed them a daily contact and an experiential knowledge of these populations. Many bishops decided to live simply and sold their episcopal palaces to finance projects of various kinds for the benefit of the poor and went to live in humble houses in marginalized neighborhoods on the peripheries. Others decided to live in total simplicity in a room in the houses where the bishopric also functioned. They gave up their clothes and the use of ostentatious ornaments, but above all, they gave a great turn to the pastoral projects.[9]

The idea and spirit were to support and empower citizens to organize and fight for fundamental rights that were being denied to them, such as work, housing, education, health, transportation, and all kinds of public services. They chose to live among the poor, in neighborhoods lacking public services, not out of love for poverty or because it would help them to sanctify themselves, but as a way of standing in solidarity with the poor, protesting against social injustice, and, above all, because being close to them, they could know how and when to bring them the good news of the gospel, tell them about God's love, and help them to organize themselves to get out of the social, political, cultural, and religious marginalization in which they lived.[10] Along with the decision to become involved in the life of the poor was the decision to support the pastoral work and mission of the church as requested by the bishops at the council and Medellin.

At the end of the sixties, the Catholic students had the Latin American Secretariat of MIEC-JECI (International Movement of Catholic Students—International Young Catholic Students) SLA MIEC-JECI established in Montevideo. They had the financial and institutional backing of the church and were accompanied in each country

---

9. Beozzo, *El Pacto de las catacumbas*.

10. We could cite many cases and experiences that we knew personally, but I think it is important to review the first paragraph of the Introduction of the book by G. Gutiérrez (*Teología de la liberación: perspectivas*, 1), when he says: "This work attempts a reflection, based on the Gospel and the experiences of men and women committed to the liberation process, in this subcontinent of oppression and dispossession that is Latin America."

by those theologians educated in Europe, who had assisted as advisors to the Latin American bishops at the council and at the Medellin conference in 1968, or by European and North American priests and religious installed in Latin America and who facilitated the deepening of the methodology of the life review we have mentioned. Their documentation and information service prepared publications, distributed throughout the continent and elaborated by themselves or by ecclesiastical advisors, which informed and analyzed the different national university, social, and political contexts, disseminated reports with methodological proposals and theological reflections, which allowed them to continue deepening their faith and understanding the context in which they lived. In addition to the profusion of publications by and for students, but which reached many other sectors of the Latin American Christian environment, there was also the articulation with the team of professionals and intellectuals gathered around the *Revista Víspera*. Through the network of movements, these publications had a presence in the whole region with a great impact on the ecclesial group. The dialogue with students and intellectuals from historic Protestant churches strengthened ecumenism, especially with the Christian Students Movement (MEC), the group Church and Society in Latin America (ISAL), and the magazine *Cristianismo y Sociedad (Christianity and Society)*.

However, the context in which they had to act was not favorable. In many countries they were experiencing the authoritarianism of civil-military dictatorships based on national security doctrines and sponsored economic models that tended to increase the marked differences between rich and poor in the region. It is within this framework of realities that those who, on a personal and community level, had committed themselves to this new understanding of the message of Jesus, knew that they lived in eminent danger of going to prison, exile, or even death.

In people with economic power and political influence, the fear to the spirit of Kennedy's proposal of the Alliance for Progress was alive, which showed that the best way to prevent the advance of communism was to carry out a green revolution. It consisted, first, in a fiscal reform, so that the states would have the necessary resources to establish the great social reforms that were essential and second, to put an end to the latifundia property, by means of agrarian reforms, which would allow access to land to medium and small landowners. These would be the consumer base for the industrial products that Latin America could produce. Both aspects, fiscal and land division, irritated Latin American landowners, who showed themselves to be their great opponents and began to look, also with bad eyes, at the development proposals that were beginning to be discussed within the church, especially the actions of several bishops, who decided to put church lands in the hands of peasants by developing agrarian cooperatives, as was the case of Monsignor Proaño in Ecuador or Monsignor Larraín in Chile.[11]

After Kennedy's assassination, the Alliance for Progress was disfigured. From fiscal and agrarian reform, it went on to distribute financial aid to buy armaments

11. Bidegain, *Obispos de la Patria Grande, Pastores, Profetas y Mártires*.

and contraceptives, together with the promotion of antinatalist campaigns. Because of this new policy, financial aid to Latin American governments and the strengthening of the armament of the military and police forces increased, with the purpose of stopping the feared communist advance and militarily empowering the states that were inspired by national security, establishing dictatorships as Brazil did in 1964, followed by Argentina in 1968, then Chile and Uruguay in 1973.

Student mobilizations and street demonstrations were repressed with excessive military violence, provoking massacres such as those in the Plaza de las Tres Culturas—Tlatelolco—in Mexico, as well as in Rio de Janeiro, Montevideo, and other cities in South America. The assassination of student leaders, the imprisonment, torture, disappearance, and exile of student youth, as well as other traditionally repressed sectors such as urban and rural workers, became normalized events. In this context of pain and dispossession, a theology marked by the experience of God lived by men and women in Latin America became more urgent every day.

In October 1971, Gustavo Gutiérrez published in Lima *Theology of Liberation: Perspectives*. This book in its pages systematizes and reflects theologically on those forms of Christian life of women and men in Latin America sustained by the spirituality and commitment demanded by the gospel with liberation, as he himself announces in his introduction. Gutiérrez's book had an enormous resonance and has been a publishing success translated into fifteen languages by nineteen publishing houses around the world, which continue to reprint it and therefore he is recognized as the initiator of this current that led to the change of perspective and the development of the most important theological movement in Latin America and internationally in the twentieth century.

It was not a solitary path but tied to a socio-ecclesial process that sustained and generated space for many reflections throughout the continent and at a universal level, accompanied and followed by other theologians. Among them, it is worth mentioning a young Colombian lay theologian, Rafael Ávila Penagos, who in 1970 had published *La Liberación*, a text designed for the teaching of religion. Between 1968 and 1986 the Uruguayan Juan Luis Segundo, SJ, published in five volumes *An Open Theology for an Adult Laity*. In 1972 the Brazilian Leonardo Boff published *Jesus Christ the Liberator* and Lucio Gera his *Argentine Theology of the People*.

However, difficulties and tensions quickly manifested themselves both outside and within the church itself in the face of the new theological discourse, but above all in the face of the socio-ecclesial movement that accompanied it, which we have just explained. Although part of the church authorities in Latin America and in Rome appreciated these pastoral and theological transformations, other bishops, priests and religious, nuns and laity preferred to continue with the project of the church of Christianity, proposed before the council, which seemed to them a better option and it was difficult for them to appropriate the council's discourse.

The pastoral and educational programs, carried out in rural areas and marginalized urban neighborhoods in defense of working and impoverished populations, as we have already said, led to encounters with Marxist organizations, with whom they sometimes disputed and sometimes collaborated. This generated much confusion, simplifications, and misunderstandings. Given the Cold War context, these political dialogues were overstated. Although there was dialogue and a rapprochement in the way of analyzing, understanding, and naming reality, the motivations and sense of orientation of the work were very different. However, as many of those Christians were pushed to leave all these works among the poor, church authorities didn't perceive that the opportunity was lost to be where the pastoral presence was most needed. This space was later occupied by other Christian churches.

Nelson Rockefeller, in his Rockefeller Report of August 1969, in addition to backing dictatorial governments in Latin America, and recommending the strengthening of the armed forces through training and the sale of weapons to Latin American states, pointed out the youth and the church as vulnerable to subversive penetration. Until now it was considered that, because of Rockefeller's comment, he was the one who had first called the attention of the North American leadership and raised the international alarm about the supposed Marxist infiltration in the church and among the youth. However, the documentation we handle shows us that regardless of the information and attention with which the US authorities carried out their intelligence work, it was Latin Americans who set off the alarms and created the imaginary that the entire Latin American church was infiltrated by Marxism.[12]

The North American and then the Latin American press, without much investigation, did not delay in launching headlines accusing the "Red Bishops" in each of the countries, generating great confusion and conflicts in society and in the church. In this way, they brought the church into disrepute and generated contradictions and annoyances among sectors of the same dioceses, while the bishops, alarmed, did not always manage to be clear about what had happened.

Latin American elites, accustomed to hearing the message of a church that used to support the status quo, were dismayed to see that the religious institution was defending the rights of all, particularly the rights of the poor. There were, then, many tensions as accusers from the left and the right sought to take advantage of the situation. They all used half-truths and defamation campaigns were continuous against members of the church. In one way or another, many bishops became the target of accusations and persecutions that often ended in their banishment, imprisonment, torture, and martyrdom, as well as that of many clergy, and laypeople.

12. The president of Colombia, Carlos Lleras Restrepo, who received Paul VI in Bogota on August 22, 1968, visited president Richard Nixon at the White House on June 13, 1969. On this state visit, Lleras Restrepo denounced the Latin American Church. "President Lleras said that many of the bishops and priests in various countries had become involved in university, labor and student affairs, using the same slogans and concepts as the Marxists." President Nixon said he would like the Rockefeller mission to report on the church and its role in Latin America ("Rockefeller Report," 1–2).

In the ecclesiastical sphere, different tendencies were manifested, positions were radicalized, and without much internal debate and tensions were created that lasted for many years. Since 1972, there was a drastic change of orientation in the leadership of CELAM, which was later strengthened by the accession of John Paul II to the pontificate (1978). This new trend was initially critical of the pastoral experience proposed by the bishops who had led CELAM until then, and of the theological maturity that had taken place in Latin America. From Rome, and headed by Cardinal Joseph Ratzinger, head of the Secretariat for Doctrine and Faith, there were several calls for attention to Latin American theological production, which were again used politically. At the same time, liberation theology began a new phase with the theology produced by women, indigenous, and Afro-descendant populations, which also suffered the onslaught of the new ecclesiastical and political authorities. However, later in 1986 John Paul II himself wrote: "We are convinced that liberation theology is not only opportune, but useful and necessary."

The controversy over the "church of the poor" extended to the concept itself which, although widely accepted in the 1960s and 1970s, was displaced from theological, historical, and social science literature from the 1980s onwards, despite being a concept present in the message of Jesus and the beginning of the history of the church. It was identified with a criticism of the churches of the rich countries, or of rich sectors of the Latin American church for remaining installed and defending, above all, a church of power. However, the "church of the poor" has been a resilient church, which remains alive in the sufferings and hopes of women and men throughout the continent and has been expressed in the Pan Amazonian Synod (2019) and in the Latin American Ecclesial Assembly (2021) convened by CELAM.

The "church of the poor" that comes from the gospel, and that in recent times John XXIII, Paul VI, and now Pope Francis, son of the Latin American church, recalled again, today continues to question us, encouraging us, uniting us. There was no lack of condemnations about the option for the poor, however, the most painful thing has been the martyrdom of the Latin American and Caribbean people of God for bringing to life "the church of the poor" and making possible the emergence of liberation theology.

REFERENCES

Beozzo, Oscar. *El Pacto de las catacumbas/The Pact of the Catacombs. Una Iglesia Servidora y pobre*. Sao Paulo: Paulinas, 2015.

Bidegain, Ana María. *Obispos de la Patria Grande, Pastores, Profetas y Mártires/Bishops of the Patria Grande, Pastors, Prophets and Martyrs*. Bogotá: CELAM, 2018.

———. *Why Did The Catholic Hierarchy 'Not Understand' Camilo?* San José: Pasos, 2016. San Francisco: Ignatius, 1984.

Congregation for the Doctrine of the Faith. *Instruction on Some Aspects of Liberation Theology (August 6, 1984): Instruction on Christian Freedom and Liberation.* San Francisco: Ignatius, 1984.

Dabezies, Pablo, et al. *Hacia el sínodo panamazónico/Towards the Pan-Amazonian Synod: Challenges and Contributions From Latin America and the Caribbean.* Salamanca: Ediciones Sígueme, 2022.

Gutiérrez, Gustavo. *Teología de la liberación: perspectivas.* Lima: Sígueme, 1971.

Planellas, Joan. *La iglesia de los pobres en el Concilio Vaticano II.* Barcelona: Herder, 2014.

"Rockefeller Report." Report presented to president Richard Nixon by the Mission to Latin America headed by Mr. Nelson A. Rockefeller on August 30, 1969.

Segundo, Juan Luis. *Teología Abierta para el laico adulto.* Buenos Aires: Lohlé, 1972.

Tamez, Elsa. *Through Her Eyes: Women's Theology from Latin America*, New York: Orbis, 1989.

Urán, Carlos H. *La Iglesia de Medellín y el Movimiento estudiantil de América Latina.* Montevideo: Spes, MIEC-JECI, 1970.

CHAPTER 9

Protestant Liberation Theologies

RAIMUNDO C. BARRETO JR.

Most of the existing literature on Latin American liberation theology (LALT) tell the story of liberation theology from a Catholic perspective. At the time the first writings of an emergent theology of liberation in Latin America surfaced, most of its authors were Catholic. Catholicism was then the largest expression of Latin American Christianity.

Protestant churches, at the time, represented a tiny minority of Latin American Christians. Furthermore, liberationist trends were at the fringe of that Protestant minority, not enjoying the institutional support that Catholic liberation theologians received in their church. Although a movement that faced significant resistance within the Catholic Church, the emerging liberation theology was backed by the mobilization of many Latin American bishops who wanted to implement the new openness advanced during Vatican II in the life of the Latin American Church. Building on Pope John XXIII's pre-Vatican II call for the Catholic Church to become a church of the poor and on the council's emphasis on *aggiornamento* to respond to the problem of mass poverty, socio-economic inequalities, and political oppression, some of the Latin American bishops who participated in the meetings of Vatican II in 1962–1965 began to reflect on how the language of Vatican II could be received and interpreted in the Latin American context.

A group of them participated in the "church of the poor" group during the council. Many were among those who signed the *Pact of the Catacombs*, a lifelong commitment to live in poverty and dedicate their lives to the evangelization of the poor. As they championed the cause of the poor in Vatican II, these bishops sowed the seeds of the liberation turn in Latin America and beyond. Those efforts led to the CELAM conference in Medellin, Colombia, in 1968, which became the first major regional forum where the issue of poverty and social justice occupied the center of the church's life and mission.

Medellin is considered the bedrock of Latin American liberation theology. It resulted from a decades-long development of what Michael Löwy coined liberationist Christianity—a series of grassroots movements that prepared the way for the development of LALT, including the base education movement, rural unions, the Catholic Agrarian Youth (JAC), and the liturgical renewal movement.[1] All of these developments created the conditions for the boom of the base ecclesial communities in the 1970s. Brazil alone is said to have had as many as eighty thousand base communities at the peak of the movement.

EARLY PROTESTANT ROOTS OF LATIN AMERICAN LIBERATION THEOLOGY[2]

Liberationist developments in Latin American Protestant churches faced different challenges. They belonged to much smaller ecclesiastical structures which were also highly fragmented. There was nothing to compared to the Latin American Episcopal Council (CELAM) to support or coordinate with them. The national ecumenical structures of the time were small and fragile. In the case of Brazil, despite multiple attempts to create ecumenical structures following the Panama Conference of 1916, only in 1934 was the Brazilian Protestant Confederation formed with only five member churches. Those incipient and fragile ecumenical forums, though, became incubators of a Protestant social theology—which took a variety of forms.

This chapter presents an overview of the rise and development of this less visible liberation theology stream that emerged in Latin American Protestant circles in the 1950s and 1960s. It shows the roots of a Protestant Latin American liberation theology which began to take shape with the rise of the Church and Society movement in the mid-1950s, leading to the formation of the Commission on Church and Society (ISAL—*Iglesia y Sociedad*) in 1961, and lists some key Protestant contributions to LALT.

At the same time that important developments were preparing the Latin American Catholic Church for Vatican II and the post-council surge of liberation theology in Medellin (1968), unrelated events were happening in a minority sector of Latin American Protestantism, prompting them to make a distinct contribution to the rise of liberation theology, one of the most influential theological movements of the last quarter of the twentieth century.

---

1. Löwy, *War of Gods*, 1996, 32–33.
2. A lengthier version of this story can be found in Barreto, *Protesting Poverty*.

In setting the context for the rise of Latin American liberation theology (LALT), Gustavo Gutiérrez stated:

> In Latin America the world in which the Christian community must live and celebrate its eschatological hope is the world of social revolution; the Church's task must be defined in relation to this. Its fidelity to the Gospel leaves it no alternative: the Church must be the visible sign of the presence of the Lord within the aspiration for liberation and the struggle for a more human and just society. Only in this way will the message of love which the Church bears be made credible and efficacious.[3]

One of the main issues that both Catholic and Protestant theologians had to deal with in the 1950s and 1960s was the question about the meaning of the gospel in a revolutionary situation. What is the role of the church in such a context? In Catholic circles, the sacramental nature of the church, as one can see in the quote from Gutiérrez, was one of the symbols used in emergent theology. The church must be a visible sign of God's presence in the struggle of the poor and oppressed for liberation. In the case of Protestants, the answers to similar questions were articulated through the symbols of the responsibility and mission of the church in a revolutionary context.

Using different symbols and approaches, Catholic and Protestant theologians gave birth to a theology that not only drew attention to "the poor's human dignity," attributing to them a "historical and religious mission," but which also identified the poor—in their multifaceted concrete existence—as "the agents of their own liberation and the subject of their own history."[4] As Löwy explains, the various liberationist theologies that emerged in Latin America in the last quarter of the twentieth century advanced some basic tenets:

1. An emphasis on idolatry, not atheism, "as the main enemy of religion;"
2. A call for the church to work for "historical human liberation as the anticipation of the final salvation in Christ, the Kingdom of God;"
3. A critique of the dualistic historical view that distinguished between human history and divine history;
4. A new reading of the Bible based on the perspective of the oppressed;
5. A sharp denunciation of dependent capitalism as structural sin;
6. The adoption of Marxist social analytical tools "to understand the causes of poverty;"
7. The embracing of a "preferential option for the poor and solidarity with their struggle for self-liberation;" and

---

3. Gutiérrez, *Theology of Liberation*, 148.
4. Löwy, *War of Gods*, 34.

8. The formation "of Christian base communities among the poor as a new form of Church."[5]

While not all forms of liberation theology paid the same attention to each of these tenets, all of them to some extent engaged with them. What was innovative in liberation theology was its function as critical reflection on historical praxis.

Argentine theologian José Miguez Bonino once stated that Latin American Protestantism was characterized by "an ethic of withdrawal from the world accompanied by legalistic rigidity."[6] Likewise, Brazilian theologian Rubem Alves concluded that the type of Protestantism that predominated in Brazil was characterized by a pietist spirituality, combined with a literalistic understanding of the Bible and an intrinsic individualism.[7]

How could a liberation theology emerge in such a context? The origins of the liberationist Christianity that gave birth to the Protestant stream of LALT can be traced back to the rise of the ecumenical efforts in the early twentieth century for the evangelization of the continent. The dissatisfaction of US missionary agencies invested in the evangelization of Latin America with its neglect in the official agenda of the World Missionary Conference that met in Edinburgh in 1910 led them to intensify the coordination of the missionary efforts in the region. Robert E. Speer, the secretary of the Board of Foreign Missions of the Presbyterian Church at the time, organized two luncheon meetings during the Edinburgh conference "to present his concerns about the recognition of Latin America as a legitimate field for missionary endeavor," and worked behind the scenes with John R. Mott, the head of the Edinburgh Continuation Committee, to make "sure that the follow-up regional conferences after Edinburgh included a conference on Latin America."[8] Those meetings led to the organization of the Committee on Cooperation in Latin America and its first conference in Latin America, the Panama Conference of 1916, which Speer hoped to be a Latin American equivalent of the Edinburgh Conference. The agenda of the Panama Conference was controlled by North American missionaries who wanted to expand the North American Protestant influence in the region.

Evangelism was the chief goal of the conference. In particular, its organizers were concerned with strategies to evangelize the Latin American intellectual elites so Protestantism could make a deeper impact on Latin American culture and society. Some of the Latin American Protestant leaders participating in that conference, though, noted the tight missionary control of its agenda, setting off an irreversible search for autonomy.

---

5. Löwy, *War of Gods*, 35.
6. Bonino, *Faces of Latin American Protestantism*, 41.
7. Alves, *Protestantismo e Repressão*, 35ff.
8. Sinclair and Solano, "Dawn of Ecumenism in Latin America," 3–4.

The Panama Conference was the first of a series of meetings, which set in motion a growing concern with the social dimension of the gospel. Erasmo Braga (1877–1932), a young Brazilian Presbyterian who attended the Panama Conference and translated its ideals into the Brazilian context, dreamed of a Protestantism capable of becoming a vital agent of social transformation and a channel of moral and political progress in the region. To achieve that ideal, he promoted a concerted emphasis on education. While still mimicking the US liberal Protestant ideal that saw its own success as the pathway for real freedom and progress, Braga and other Latin American Protestant leaders made important contributions to the quest for a Latin American Protestant identity. As part of that quest, he urged Latin American Protestants to overcome the individualism and the sectarianism he saw as prevalent in most Protestant churches. He challenged the Protestant churches to move beyond what he identified as "church-centeredness" to relate with Latin American society in all its dimensions, advocating a non-sectarian Protestant attitude, which nurtured some of the later developments in the Latin American Protestant understanding of its Christian public witness.[9] Braga's response to Protestant provincialism included the creation of opportunities and structures to enable collaboration among the churches for the evangelization of society.

A number of events followed the Panama Conference. Two of the most important continental follow-ups took place in Montevideo (1925) and Havana (1929). As Jean Pierre Bastian explains, these two conferences occurred during the critical times leading to the depression of 1929. Consequently, its participants "were concerned with this awareness in relation to the necessity of articulating an evangelical Latin American response to the crisis."[10] Braga chaired the Montevideo Conference in 1925, the first to adopt Spanish as its official language. That conference underscored Jesus's call for universal fellowship and the need to pay attention to the "growth of social idealism among university students in Latin America," taking notice of rising social movements such as the temperance leagues, feminist movements, workers' movements, and students' movement, of which a growing number of Protestants were becoming a part.[11]

The conference in Havana (1929), chaired by Mexican poet, writer, and journalist Gonzalo Báez-Camargo, highlighted the themes of Evangelical solidarity, education, social action, and literature. The need for the "Latin Americanization" of Protestantism on the continent was debated along with the danger of North American control of the churches.[12] In emphasizing the autonomy of the national churches, the Havana Conference set the tone for the rise of a Latin American Protestant theology.

---

9. Braga and Grubb, *Republic of Brazil*, 130.
10. Bastian, *Breve História do Protestantismo*, 11.
11. Bullon, *Protestant Social Thought*, 78.
12. Neto, *O Novo Rosto da Missão*, 104.

Section 3 | Emerging Theologies from Latin America

THE CHURCH AND SOCIETY MOVEMENT

However, it was the rise of what became broadly known as the Church and Society movement in the 1950s that caused a drastic turn towards the elaboration of a Protestant theology attentive to the important social issues of the time.

The rise of the Student Christian Movement was particularly important for the formulation of an ecumenical theology that tackled the social problems and drastic economic disparities found in Latin America. The many local groups of the Student Christian Movement "acted as ideological incubators for the production of young Protestant Christians who were sensitive to the social and political implications of the Christian Gospel and who subsequently became the foremost spokesmen for the ISAL movement in the 1960s."[13]

Students related to this movement were exposed to key political and social ideas in formation on campuses across the Latin American nations. As they became increasingly aware of the Christian's responsibility to address political and economic problems, they were encouraged to take part in the resolution of those problems. Given its locally based organization and national and continental networks, the Student Christian Movement embodied the Latin American ecumenical movement's ability to connect the demands of local, national, and regional realities with "socio-political perspectives, perceptions, and concepts" mediated through a global context.[14]

While student Christian organizations had existed in Latin America since the 1920s, the Latin American Student Conference that met in São Paulo in 1952 made a unique contribution for the Latin American Protestant students to engage the social reality of the continent through new lenses. Key for that shift was the encounter of its participants with North American Presbyterian missionary Richard Shaull. After spending a decade in Colombia, Shaull had returned to the US where he spent a couple of years participating in a group studying the relationship between Christianity and socialism in New York, under the leadership of Reinhold Niebuhr, John Bennett, and Searle Bates. While influenced by those thinkers, Shaull realized that the context where their reflection on Marxism took place was much different from that he had encountered in Colombia, where "crowds [were] condemned to live in extreme poverty, completely marginalized."[15] Shaull's perception of the reigning injustice of the societal structures of the modern world, particularly in the so-called dependent societies, led him to imagine a Christian faith capable of producing a passionate relationship with the poor. Considering his background and previous experience in the region, Shaull became an ideal conversation partner for a group of students interested in understanding their role as Christians in the revolutionary situation in Latin America.

---

13. Neely, "Protestant Antecedents of the Latin American Liberation Theology," 185.
14. Neely, "Protestant Antecedents of the Latin American Liberation Theology," 185.
15. Shaull, *Surpreendido Pela Graça*, 79.

The main topic of the 1952 student conference in Brazil was "The Christian Vocation." Shaull was its main speaker.[16] The reflections he provided resonated with the concern of those Latin American Protestant students who were in search of theological language to interpret their role in the reality of rapidly changing societies—particularly in the Latin American booming urban centers. In the 1950s, the anti-imperialist sentiment spreading in the Third World had turned Marxism into an attractive response to the social injustices plaguing the region. For those interested in understanding their Christian vocation in such a context, examining the Marxist responses and engaging the secular views on social revolution theologically was of critical importance.

The WSCF Latin American conference provided a unique opportunity for serious reflection on that topic. The conference offered the opportunity for Shaull to share his thoughts on the topic of the relationship between Christianity and Marxism. But this was far from a one-way conversation. In the course of the conference, Shaull became deeply impressed by the intellectual questions that group of students posed to him. In the following year, he moved to Brazil, where he would serve as a theological mentor for a number of those students in the following years.

Shaull later published his lectures in a booklet that would become a theological guide for many in the Student Christian Movement (SCM). In that brief collection of essays, he interrogated "the revolutionary situation" in which the Latin American Christian students found themselves, emphasizing Christ's call for them to respond to the needs of their neighbors, especially those who were hungry, marginalized, destitute, and in intolerable poverty.[17]

Shaull's use of the word "revolution" in those reflections provided a new foundation for a spirituality that could contribute to the transformation of society in Latin America and beyond and offer a linguistic common ground for the SCM and its non-Christian dialogical partners.[18] Shaull saw the SCM and its small local groups as a new form of the modern church. For him, one of the greatest contributions of the movement was that:

> as small teams of lay persons and trained theologians worked together on the issues facing them in a revolutionary situation, they found themselves dealing with new questions and seeking new approaches. And they began to articulate theological and ethical positions that went beyond what they found in the books and study materials they were using.[19]

Those groups succeeded in equipping themselves to engage secular ideologies as they sought to offer a Christian perspective to the struggle for a more just society. In

---

16. Faria, *Fé e Compromisso*, 109.
17. Shaull, *O Cristianismo e a Revolução Social*.
18. Faria, *Fé e Compromisso*, 110.
19. Shaull, "Theological Developments," 8.

that process, they learned to approach the Bible in a new way, no longer "as a source of abstract, sterile doctrines, but as the story of God's presence and action in human life and in concrete historical events in the world across the centuries," which helped them to approach their historical situation through the lenses of God's action in the world.[20]

Interacting with Shaull, the Christian Student Movement launched the foundations for a theological approach, which, although not yet a full-fledged liberation theology, was at the cusp of formulating a theology that emphasized God's presence and action in the world, calling upon all Christians (lay and clergy) to join God in the struggle for life and justice wherever they were.

During the difficult years that followed the military dictatorships that emerged throughout Latin America in the 1960s and 1970s, many of those who had been part of the ranks of that movement found a home in nonreligious movements to continue resisting the abuses of the authoritarian regimes that emerged in Latin America in the following decades. Others contributed to the rise of new ecumenical organizations in the region. Some of those Protestant revolutionaries were forced into exile, while others ended up imprisoned or even killed. Paulo S. Wright, an American citizen born in Brazil, and one of Shaull's students, was elected to a state legislative house in Santa Catarina. After the military decree known as AI-5 (Institutional Act number five), which closed the Brazilian congress in 1968, Wright joined *Ação Popular*, a Catholic left-wing organization that, in the 1960s, had become a broad left-wing umbrella for multiple revolutionary fronts. He ended up imprisoned, tortured, and killed by the military. His political trajectory was deeply influenced by the theological insights he learned at the SCM, as one can see in a letter he wrote in 1959:

> Our commitment is to discern the work God is doing, testifying God's redemptive action, experiencing complete freedom to take sides, suffering with those who are suffering, crying with those who are crying . . . feeding those who are hungry . . . Our attitude for sure cannot conserve the enormous and scary imbalances that exist in our society. Our missionary and political witness is to be always on the side of the disinherited, spiritually or materially so, because God loved the world to the point of sending God's son, who became the most impoverished of all human beings so that we could find in him the meaning of life, which is abundance.[21]

Inspired by the prophetic Protestant theologies of Richard Shaull, Paul Lehman, and Dietrich Bonhoeffer, Wright made an option for a radical immersion into the revolutionary struggle, compelled to take the side of the disinherited and destitute and work in solidarity with them no matter how risky it was.

The Student Christian Movement was just one face of a broader Church and Society movement whose origins can be traced back to the formation of a committee

---

20. Shaull, "Theological Developments," 9–10.
21. Wright, *O Coronel Tem um Segredo*, 27–28.

in the Brazilian Evangelical Confederation known as the Church's Sector of Social Responsibility, in 1955. Between 1955 and 1962, that committee sponsored four national consultations, which progressively contributed to the development of a Protestant liberationist stream in Latin America. In 1955, the committee focused on the ecumenical concern the "Social Responsibility of the Church," as a program of study and action for the Protestant churches.[22] In 1957, it sought to understand the impact of "rapid social changes" upon the mission of the church. In 1960, it emphasized "the presence of the Church in the evolution of nationality."[23] Finally, in 1962, it adopted the more radical theme "Christ and the Brazilian Revolutionary Process."[24] Despite the theological evolution of these conversations, the encouragement of individual participation in those struggles was balanced with the reluctance to identify the reign of God with a particular political movement.[25]

The fourth consultation was the most consequential. On the one hand, it signaled that the optimism of the "development era" had passed, since millions continued to wrestle with underdevelopment and poverty.[26] On the other hand, it reminded the participants that while many oppressed groups and other sectors of society articulated possible alternatives to achieve social changes, the *Evangélico* (or Protestant) churches were missing in action. The topic chosen for this consultation was an invitation to reflect on concrete encounter of the Christian message with the critical situation of the Brazilian society at that time.

This consultation, known as *Conferência do Nordeste*, laid the groundwork for the development of a Protestant liberation theology. Some of its organizers had also played a role in the creation of the Latin American Committee on Church and Society (*Iglesia y Sociedad en América Latina*, ISAL), an organization on the vanguard of the development of a Protestant liberationist Christian theology.

After the 1964 military coup in Brazil and the authoritarian regime that followed, the Church's Sector of Social Responsibility was shut down. Those among its leaders who were not forced to hide or leave the country joined their Catholic counterparts to create ecumenical initiatives such as *Paz e Terra*, the *Centro of Estudos Biblicos* (CEBI), which popularized the method known as popular reading of the Bible, and the *Centro Ecumênico de Informações* (CEI). CEI's work focused on popular pastoral action, the accompaniment of the struggles of popular sectors of society, the mobilization of ecumenical solidarity, providing services to vulnerable groups, and supporting their struggle for social and political emancipation.

Many of the participants of ISAL (the continental face of the Church and Society movement) became theologians in their own right, contributing to the theoretical and

22. César, "Church and Society," 135.
23. César, "Church and Society," 136.
24. César, "Church and Society," 136.
25. Shaull, *O Cristianismo e a Revolução Social*, 86.
26. César, *Conferência do Nordeste*, 42.

practical development of LALT. The most significant of them was Rubem Alves. His dissertation at Princeton Theological Seminary in 1968 (published in 1969) was the first book-length treatise on liberation theology.[27]

Alves had been a student of Richard Shaull in Brazil in the 1950s. In the mid-1960s, forced to leave Brazil when he learned that the military regime was after him, he moved to Princeton for his PhD work, reencountering his old friend and mentor. Alves's contribution to liberation theology was unique. While not in disagreement with the liberationist activist political orientation, Alves, as Daniel Migliore underscores, intended "on going deeper, probing the sources of creativity, imagination, and hope in human life, examining the use and abuse of language, marking the difference between humanistic messianism and messianic humanism, exploring the importance of the body, play, the gift of nature, the experience of beauty."[28]

While understanding the need for political action, Alves feared that the wrong motivation to act could lead to bitterness instead of liberation. Thus, he increasingly shifted his emphasis towards theopoetics, proposing "that we begin to operate with the aesthetics of beauty."[29] He envisioned a praxis in which the ability to dream feeds the desire to transform reality from within the broken bodies and hearts which only beauty can move. Alves challenged LALT to be more than a theology of subsistence, but one that acknowledges that our broken bodies are also the center or our desires.

Another Protestant theologian to make an important contribution to liberation theology was Methodist theologian José Miguez Bonino. Bonino was the only Latin American Protestant observer in Vatican II. In his reflections on the reception of the council in Latin America, he highlighted both its ecumenical nature and its concern with understanding the mission of the church in light of the "social question."[30] In addition to his own theological contributions to the task of building a liberation theology in a Protestant key,[31] Bonino was an active ecumenist whose dialogical praxis can be seen in his ongoing dialogue with the Catholic concerns with the social question and interaction with the emerging Evangelical theology of integral mission in the *Tercer Congreso Latinoamericano de Evangelización*, an Evangelical gathering, bringing it into conversation with liberationist developments in the region. Among other things, Bonino, a Methodist, highlighted the significance of developments in the Catholic understanding of evangelization (the new evangelization), calling for Latin American Evangelicals to move beyond apologetic discourse and seek a more understanding approach which emphasized encounter and mutual respect. Bonino saw himself as an *Evangélico*,[32] a hybrid term used in Latin American to include a plurality of meanings.

27. Alves, "Towards a Theology of Liberation."
28. Personal correspondence on August 8, 2019.
29. Alves, "From Liberation Theologian to Poet," 20–24.
30. Bonino, "Reception of Vatican II," 267.
31. Bonino, *Doing Theology*.
32. Bonino, *Faces of Latin American Protestantism*, vii.

While affirming the need for theology to take sides,[33] Bonino was also concerned with the problem of a fragmented witness and the need to rethink the understanding of the *ecumenical* to embrace the broader dimension of the human, challenging the totalizing nature of global capitalism and revealing the need to expose its ambition to coopt the *oikumene*.

Sergio Arce Martinez, Adolf Ham Reyes, Beatriz Melano Couch, Julio de Santa Ana, Zwinglio Mota Dias, Jether Ramalho, and Orlando Costas, among others, are other Protestant liberationist thinkers whose contributions stem from the Protestant liberation Christianity this chapter highlights. Each of them offered a particular contribution, building upon those liberationist Protestant roots. Martinez and Reyes developed a theology in revolution out of the Cuban context.[34] Melano, the first Latin American Protestant woman to receive a PhD in theology, inspired a generation of women to offer a gender critique of liberation theology, making their own contributions to expand this theological genre. She was also an active participant in the Ecumenical Association of Third World Theologians (EATWOT).

Santa Ana brought the influence of liberation theology to the global stage through his work on the ecumenical group on the church and the poor in the World Council of Churches.[35] In addition to being theologians in their own right, Dias and Ramalho modeled a liberationist pastoral praxis, not only through their work as pastors but also as creators of important ecumenical liberationist projects in Brazil and beyond. And Baptist theologian Orlando Costas was one of the founding members of an Evangelical movement, which, while not affiliated with liberation theology, has been in dialogue with it. Costas's work on the above-mentioned *misión integral* theology makes numerous references to Rubem Alves and Richard Shaull. For him, liberation theology has posed a tremendous challenge to contemporary theology, which Evangelicals should take seriously, especially because of its biblical contents. He saw liberation theology's insistence on engaging the concrete historical situation as a key challenge for an Evangelical theology of mission, affirming that the biblical Christian faith has a historical character, firmly rooted in concrete historical situations.[36]

A new generation of Protestant pastors and scholars who see themselves in continuation with that legacy include Presbyterian theologian Claudio Carvalhaes (Union Theological Seminary), Baptist theologian Ronilso Pacheco (a doctoral student working on a Brazilian Black liberation theology), and Baptist biblical scholar Odja Barros (whose work advances a popular feminist hermeneutics), among others. It is possible to say these days that if Catholic liberation theology has lost adepts in the past few decades, the number of Latin American Protestants embracing it in creative ways has significantly grown, confirming what David Tombs once stated:

33. Bonino, "For Life and Against Death," 1154–58.
34. See Fernández-Albán, *Decolonizing Theology*.
35. de Santa Ana, *Towards A Church*.
36. Costas, *Church and Its Mission*, 241.

Whether a recognizable movement called liberation theology persists or not, the issues that it dealt with will continue to remain just as pressing as before. The terminology may vary but Christian theology will need to keep faith with and build upon the ethical, methodological and epistemological principles of liberation theology if it is adequately to engage with these issues in the new millennium.[37]

In other words, while the liberationist language of the sixties and seventies may have changed, new forms of liberating theologies continue to emerge in response to the persistence of injustice and oppression. As this chapter has shown, not only have multiple Protestant Christians in Latin America tackled these issues, but a new generation is moving their work ahead.

BIBLIOGRAPHY

Alves, Rubem. "From Liberation Theologian to Poet: A Plea that the Church Move from Ethics to Aesthetics, from Doing to Beauty." *Church and Society* (May-June 1993) 13–37.

———. *Protestantismo e Repressão*. São Paulo: Editora Ática, 1979.

———. "Towards a Theology of Liberation: an Exploration of the Encounter between the Languages of Humanistic Messianism and Messianic Humanism." Washington, DC: Corpus, 1969.

Barreto, Raimundo C. *Protesting Poverty: Protestants, Social Ethics and the Poor in Brazil*. Waco, TX: Baylor University Press, 2023.

Bastian, Jean-Pierre. *Breve História do Protestantismo en America Latina*. Mexico City: Casa Unida de Publicaciones, 1986.

Bonino, José Miguez. *Doing Theology in a Revolutionary Situation*. Minneapolis: Fortress, 2007.

———. *Faces of Latin American Protestantism*. Grand Rapids: Eerdmans, 1997.

———. "For Life and Against Death: A Theology that Takes Sides." *The Christian Century*, November 26, 1980, 1154–58.

———. "The Reception of Vatican II in Latin America." *Ecumenical Review* 73 (1985). http://doi.org/10.1177/004056391207300403.

Braga, Erasmo, and Kenneth Grubb. *The Republic of Brazil: A Survey of the Religious Situation*. London: World Dominion, 1932.

Bullon, H. Fernando. *Protestant Social Thought in Latin America*. Eugene, OR: Wipf & Stock, 2015.

César, Waldo. "Church and Society—or Society and Church?" In *Revolution of Spirit: Ecumenical Theology in Global Context: Essays in Honor of Richard Shaull*, edited by Nantawan Boonprasat Lewis, 133–48. Grand Rapids: Eerdmans, 1998.

———, ed. *A Conferência do Nordeste: Cristo e o Processo Revolucionário Brasileiro, Volume 1*. Recife: CEB, 1962.

Costas, Orlando. *The Church and Its Mission: A Shattering Critique from the Third World*. Wheaton, IL: Tyndale, 1976.

---

37. Tombs, "Latin American Liberation Theology," 58.

de Santa Ana, Julio, ed. *Towards A Church of The Poor: The Work of an Ecumenical Group on the Church and the Poor*. Geneva: World Council of Churches, 1982.

Faria, Eduardo Galasso. *Fé e Compromisso: Richard Shaull e a Teologia no Brasil*. São Paulo: ASTE, 2002.

Fernández-Albán, Ary. *Decolonizing Theology in Revolution: A Critical Retrieval of Sergio Arce's Theological Thought*. New Approaches to Religion and Power. Basingstoke, Hampshire: Palgrave MacMillan, 2018.

Gutiérrez, Gustavo. *A Theology of Liberation*. Maryknoll, NY: Orbis. 2019.

Löwy, Michael, *The War of Gods: Religion and Politics in Latin America*. New York: Verso, 1996.

Neely, Alan. "Protestant Antecedents of the Latin American Liberation Theology." PhD diss., The American University, 1977.

Neto, Luiz Longuini. *O Novo Rosto da Missão*. São Paulo: Ultimato, 2002.

Plou, Dafne S. *Caminos de Unidad: Itinerario del Diálogo Ecumenico en América Latina 1916-1991*. Quito: CLAI, 1994.

Shaull, Richard. *O Cristianismo e a Revolução Social*. São Paulo: UCEB, 1953.

———. *Surpreendido Pela Graça*. Rio de Janeiro: Record, 2003.

———. "Theological Developments in the Brazilian SCM, 1952-1964." Unpublished manuscript, The Richard Shaull archives, Luce Library, Princeton Theological Seminary.

Sinclair, John H., and Arturo Piedra Solano. "The Dawn of Ecumenism in Latin America: Robert E. Speer, Presbyterians, and the Panama Conference of 1916." *The Journal of Presbyterian History* 77 (1999) 1-11.

Tombs, David. "Latin American Liberation Theology Faces the Future." In *Faith in the Millennium*, edited by Stanley E. Porter et al., 85-101. Sheffield: Sheffield Academic, 2001.

Wright, Delora Jan. *O Coronel Tem um Segredo: Paulo Wright Não Está em Cuba*. Petrópolis, Brazil: Vozes, 1993.

CHAPTER 10

Latina Feminist Theology

MICHELLE A. GONZALEZ

The academic voices grouped under the category of Latina feminist theology represent a collective of authors in the United States that both claim a Latina heritage and also focus their scholarship on the faith experiences of Latinas in the United States. While not a self-professed theological movement, these scholars all have training in the academic discipline of theology and also self-identify as Latinas. They also overwhelmingly claim that the insights of their scholarship represent the religious life of Latinas. However, as one of the most diverse and largest racial-ethnic groups in the United States, it can be increasingly difficult for scholars to make broad generalizations about Latinas and Latinos as a whole. This tension is one of several that is found in the work of Latina feminist theologians which will be addressed in this overview of Latina feminist theology. I begin by discussing the category of Latino/a broadly. I then move to a synopsis of the development of Latina feminist theology and key figures in the field. The third and final section highlights shared themes among Latina theologians, with concluding comments on challenges to the future of the field.

Latina feminist theology must be contextualized in light of the broader discipline of Latino/a-Hispanic-Latinx theology within the United States. Since their earliest writings, the lived religious practices of Latino/a Christian communities have been and remain a definitive starting point for Hispanic-Latino/a-Latinx theologian. As defined by Orlando O. Espín, "Latino/a theology was born as a methodological approach to the study of Latino/a religious reality, as much as a contributor to the overall study of Latino/a communities and realities that also interpret themselves through inescapably religious lenses."[1] These religious practices are often centered around ecclesial life, though Latino/a theologians also incorporate popular religious practices—those Latino/a religious practices that exist on the border of Christian churches and can incorporate and be influenced by non-Christian elements. Latino/a theologians, as trained scholars in the field of theology, at times struggle to employ the language and historical insights of their field, which has developed exclusively without the consideration of the religious life of Latinos and Latinas. This struggle is a result of the absence of Latin American and Latino/a intellectual and religious traditions within the history of academic theology. While recognizing that the limits of the theological paradigm impact other minoritized populations in the United States and the Global South, it remains a core intellectual dilemma for Latino/a theologians, who often struggle for appropriate language to name and describe the populations and religious practices they claim to represent in their writings while remaining loyal to academic theology.

LATINO/A THEOLOGY[2]

As a theology that claims to be written by and represent a racial-ethnic group in the United States, the task of naming and identifying this population is a central concern for Latino/a theologians. Their insights on Latino/a identity tend to fall into two categories: defining what is particularly Latino/a about Latino/a theological discourse and offering a nuanced description of the Latino/a community generally while also acknowledging its internal diversity. Latino/a theologians have overwhelmingly grounded the authenticity of their writings based on them writing about Latino/as *as* Latino/as. In this paradigm I as a Cuban-American theologian write Latina theology as a Latina, and the authenticity of my theological claims are based on my Cuban-American identity. The claim that I as a Cuban-American can speak for all Latino/as however, was much easier for me to make ten to fifteen years ago. In a moment marked by debates on the role of race and the study of racial inequality in the history and life of the United States, the Latino/a population remains a complex, growing group that both confirms and challenges simplistic reductions of identity today. One only has to look at the 2020 presidential election, which revealed to us that it is extremely difficult, if not impossible, to make broad generalizations about the Latino/a community as a whole.[3]

---

1. Espín, "Introduction," 3.
2. I use the terms Latinx, Latino/a, and Hispanic interchangeably. In South Florida, where I am from, the term Hispanic is often used. However, I quickly learned during my years in California that this was unacceptable there, since it was interpreted as embracing our Spanish heritage and rejecting the influences of African and Indigenous peoples on our culture, history, and identity. The term Latinx is one that has risen to prominence in the academy, and frankly, is less cumbersome in speech than Latino/a; however, I find the term highly problematic. It is not only counterintuitive to both the English, and frankly for me, the Spanish language, but it is also a term that is not used by the majority of Latino/as in the USA.
3. Cadava, *Hispanic Republican*; Morales, *Latinx*.

The internal diversity masked by the broad category of Latino/a, whether based on geography, nation of origin, economic class, gender identity, and race, to name a few, reveals a population that at times seems to have very little that it shares collectively across the board. This is seen in our history. As noted by Daisy L. Machado, "The history of Latina/os in the United States is a history about the micro and the macro of the Latino reality; it is about a specific and unique Latino group, but it is also about how that one group, whether Mexican or Cuban or Peruvian or Dominican, becomes a part of that larger bundle of relationships that *is* the Latino community in the United States."[4] We cannot even agree on what to call ourselves, with Hispanic, Latino/a, and Latinx being used by different age groups and generations in different parts of the United States. This is the case, in spite of the fact that Latino/as would overwhelmingly rather be categorized by their nation of origin, Cuban-American in my case, than describe themselves in these pan-ethnic terms.

This claim is further problematized by the fact that there are many non-Latino/a theological scholars who have substantial commitments to Latino/a communities and are writing about them, yet these scholars are not allowed to claim their work as Latino/a theology. They may be writing about Latino/a religious experiences, however since they are not Latino/a they cannot claim to be writing Latino/a theology. In their creation and promotion of a notion of a "theological birthright," Latino/a theologians have limited the scope and nature of their theological contributions. On the one hand, they have created an "us" and "them" regarding who has an "authentic" theological voice. Second, the contention that a Latino/a has the most authentic voice about Latino/as automatically leads to the claim that their writings on non-Latino/a topics do not have the same theological weight. This limits their work to Latino/a communities. There is something unsettling about an academic discourse being reduced to the author's birthplace, heritage, and/or native language.

Because Latino/a theologians have remained so concerned with describing authentic Latino/a identity and remaining engaged in the publics of academic theology, Latino/a theologians often write in an intellectual isolation that limits the nature and scope of their writings and prevents substantial interdisciplinary dialogue. As noted by R. J. Hernández-Diaz, "Hispanic theologians, who have been by and large too fixated on disciplinary boundaries, have emphasized cultural and social context to such an extent that it reduces the applicability of their work to broader discussions."[5] One field that has been a clear conversation partner for Latino/a theologians has been liberation theologies, particularly in the United States and Latin America.

Connected to their substantial work on identity, the importance of difference and hybridity has been a theme within Latino/a theology. This began with a heavy emphasis on the category of *mestizaje*. The importance of *mestizaje* is one way for Latino/a theologians to speak of racial and cultural hybridity within their communities. *Mestizaje*

---

4. Machado, "History and Latino/a Identity," 35.
5. Hernández-Diaz, "Hispanic Liberative Theologies," 101.

names the ambiguity and in-betweenness of Latino/a identity. *Mestizaje/mulatez* designates the mixed reality of Latino/a peoples: the former refers to the mixture of Indigenous and Spanish cultures, the latter to the mixture of Indigenous and African cultures. *Mestizaje/mulatez* not only portrays the Latino/a context; these terms also reflect the worldview in which Latino/as exist as hybrid people. This mixture and ambiguity are also the hermeneutical lens through which Latino/as see the world and has ontological implications for the methodology of Latino/a theology. In embracing *mestizaje-mulatez*, Latino/as are expressing solidarity with other marginalized people of color and attempting to dismantle dualistic constructions of race that plague identity politics.

Latino/a theology shares a close connection to Latin American liberation theology, even though not all Latino/a theologians claim a liberationist hermeneutic. There are some Latino/a theologians who explicitly claim a liberationist identity, while others distance themselves from this categorization, though they may utilize liberationist sources in their scholarship. We will see a parallel in how Latina theologians specifically accept or reject feminism in our next section. Whether they self-identify as liberation theologians or not, Latino/a theologians often privilege the poor and oppressed in a manner that mirrors the hermeneutics of liberation theologians and also adopt methodological elements of liberation theologies in their writings. Liberationist methodological patterns in Latino/a theology include: a critical reading of the contemporary context of Latino/as through the lens of power; the incorporation of the concrete voices of Latino/as in their theology; the role of autobiography; and its utopian vision. While there exist liberationist strands within the writings of some Latino/a theologians, Latino/a theology as a whole is not a self-proclaimed liberation theology.

Does Latino/a theology offer a counterpoint to Latin American and other liberation theologies? Not at all. And here we find another methodological dilemma in assessing Latino/a theology. While Latino/a theologians do present Latino/a communities, as they should, as overwhelmingly marginalized and oppressed communities here in the United States, that does not translate into the theological vision of Latino/a churches. Liberationist theologies only represent a small percentage of Latino/a churches. Current trends in Latino/a Christianity demonstrate that these populations are becoming increasingly *evangélico* (Evangelical), characterized by a more conservative theology that does not emphasize the socially transformative action so fundamental to the work of liberation theologians. Being a member of a marginalized community does not automatically lead one to have a theologically progressive vision.

The first Latino/a theologians began writing at a time when Black liberation theologians had risen to prominence in the United States and had made race the primary lens through which to understand oppression and liberation. In a similar vein, liberation theologians in Latin America defined oppression and liberation through the lens of poverty and economic class. Latino/a theology arose at the crossroads of these two definitive impulses. US-based Latino/a theologians, rightfully wanting to distinguish themselves from and avoid being eclipsed by their Latin American counterparts, did not engage in class analysis and privileged the category of culture and ethnicity through a language centered on race.

LATINA FEMINIST THEOLOGY

The question of how to categorize Latino/a theology as liberationist or not serves as an appropriate transition to our focus on Latina feminist theology. The role of feminism within Latina theology remains contested, and while this chapter focuses on Latina feminist theologians, debates over the role of feminism within Latina theology merits discussion. Latina feminist theologians are those scholars who situate themselves within the broader networks of liberation theologies and feminist theologies globally. Latina feminist theologians privilege Latina experiences of poverty and oppression through a feminist hermeneutic. This emphasis on marginalization is also the case for Latina theologians who are not explicitly feminist. Latina theologian Ana María Pineda, for example, does not categorize her scholarship as explicitly feminist. Pineda can be categorized as a pastoral theologian.[6] And while many continue to refer to the groundbreaking work of Ada María Isasi-Díaz and María Pilar Aquino, the most recognized Latina theologians historically, who quite explicitly understand their work as feminist and liberationist, not all Latina theologians are feminist.

Unlike their feminist colleagues, pastorally focused Latina theologians emphasize ministry within the Latino/a community. These pastoral Latina theologians do not outright reject the label of feminist or liberationist, yet they also clearly do not self-identify as feminist or liberation theologians. They also worry that an emphasis on feminism will lead to a theology that does not engage the Latino/a community as a whole. As noted by Nancy Pineda-Madrid, "Because they interpret *feminism* to be a narrow issue, an explicitly 'feminist' theology does not bear priority for them."[7] There exists a third group of Latina theologians, Evangelical Latinas. This group of Latina theologians rejects any sort of feminist hermeneutic. Loida Martell-Ortero, in her theology of *mujeres evangélicas*, expresses reservations about both Latina feminist and *mujerista* theologies because of their Roman Catholic emphasis and what she sees as their secular origins.[8] Martell-Ortero articulates, as an alternative, her theology *evangélica*, whose sources are found in the faith and practices of Protestant Latina women. She is critical of the blind categorization of all Latina voices as "feminist." In a similar vein Elizabeth Conde-Frazier grounds her liberationist work in a Christocentric theology: "For *evangelicas* the power to *luchar*, to fight the good fight, comes from the Jesus who came to give life more abundantly."[9]

---

6. The distinction between Latina feminist and pastoral theologians is highlighted by Nancy Pineda-Madrid in "Latina Roman Catholic Theologians."
7. Pineda-Madrid, "Latina Roman Catholic Theologians," 1194.
8. Martell-Ortero, "Women Doing Theology."
9. Conde-Frazier, *Latina Evangélicas*, 66.

As a liberation theology, Latina feminist theology understands its scholarship as a reflection on the divine emerging from the context of a marginalized people. Its theological influences and sources can be traced to four major developments in the latter half of the twentieth century: Latin American liberation theology, feminist theology, feminist critical theory, and US Latino/a theology. The sources of Latina feminist theology are not reduced to these three. However, it is from these theologies that Latina feminist theologians derive their analysis of the economic, patriarchal, and ethnocentric structures and constructs that oppress Latinas. As noted by Miguel de la Torre and Edwin Aponte, "U.S. Latina feminist theologies enable Latina women to understand multiple oppressive structures, identify their preferred future, and confront internalized oppression. Furthermore, Latina feminist theologies identify the importance of female leadership, even in the midst of oppression, in maintaining the health and life of the *comunidad*."[10] This connection between theology and community is fundamental in their work.

Within Latina feminist theology there is a distinction between *mujerista* and Latina feminist theology, embodied particularly in the works of Ada María Isasi-Díaz and María Pilar Aquino. As the edited volume entitled *Religion, Feminism, and Justice: A Reader in Latina Feminist Theology* demonstrates, there is a clear line between those who embrace the term *mujerista* and those who describe their theology as "Latina feminist." As the editors of the volume state in the introduction, "We acknowledge the important work and contributions of Ada María Isasi-Díaz in developing what she has defined as *mujerista* theology. However, we have opted to name ourselves Latina feminists."[11] The exclusion of Ada María Isasi-Díaz's voice from this project affirms the distinctions among Latina theologians that claim a feminist hermeneutic.

In her groundbreaking text, *En la Lucha/In the Struggle: Elaborating a Mujerista Theology*, Isasi-Díaz elaborates an early definition of *mujerista*. "A *mujerista* is a Latina who makes a preferential option for herself and her Hispanic sisters, understanding that our struggle for liberation has to take into consideration how racism/ethnic prejudice, economic oppression, and sexism work together and reinforce each other."[12] Rejecting the term *feminist hispana*, she argues that for many Latinas, feminism is viewed as an Anglo creation which marginalizes Latino/a concerns. Isasi-Díaz also highlights the painful history and marginalization of Latinas within the white, Euro-American feminist community. These factors contribute to her rejection of "feminist" as an appropriate term to designate Latinas concerned about sexist oppression. Throughout her scholarship Isasi-Díaz takes seriously the work of grassroots Latinas and highlights the significance of daily life (*lo cotidiano*), *mestizaje/mulatez*, and *la lucha* (the struggle) as fundamental to her theology.

---

10. Aponte and De La Torre, *Introducing Latinx Theologies*, 138.
11. Aquino et al., "Introduction," xiv.
12. Isasi-Díaz, *En la Lucha/In the Struggle*, 4.

Whether it is her analysis of the ethical, epistemic, and hermeneutic value of *mestizaje/mulatez*, difference, or her understanding of these terms as revelatory of identity, a clear emphasis on hybridity is a hallmark of Isasi-Díaz's work. Underlying these writings as what she describes as "a fluid social ontology, which is based on the hybridity and diversity that are key realities/understandings we need to deal with in this twenty-first century."[13] *Mestizaje/mulatez* refers to the Latino/a condition as racially and culturally mixed people attempting to negotiate their identity within the dominant culture of the United States. It is a fundamental theological theme within Latino/a theology as a whole. And while Isasi-Díaz and others argue that *mestizaje/mulatez* functions ethically within their corpus as a condemnation of racism and ethnic prejudice, there have been substantial critiques of how these concepts are used to whiten Latino/a populations and eclipse the presence of Black and Indigenous Latino/as.[14] A fundamental aspect of Isasi-Díaz's emphasis on difference is a reconceptualization of this notion as relational. As she thoughtfully points out, difference is traditionally understood as exclusionary, as that which divides. Instead, Isasi-Díaz constructs difference in terms of relationships, showing that differences are relative. A foundational insight within her corpus is that the traditional, oppositional, and static categories of identity that have been imposed on Latino/as do not speak to their lived realities. For Isasi-Díaz, theoretical concepts must ring to people's daily lives or they are of little value.

Isasi-Díaz's writings on *lo cotidiano* (daily life) are the foundation of many of the concepts and terminology that saturate her *mujerista* theology. For Isasi-Díaz, the incorporation of daily life into her *mujerista* theology transforms the very nature of the theoretical foundation of theology as a whole. "Hispanic/Latino theology's insistence on the importance of our people's lived experience and *lo cotidiano* is not indicative of any lack of theoretical depth but rather contributes to the reformulation of what constitutes a theory."[15] Daily life is not only material, but also cultural. It is something that is conscious, not merely repeated mechanically. It does not refer exclusively to the private or domestic sphere. Epistemologically, it is linked to what is known as "common sense." Due to its material and epistemological value, for Isasi-Díaz *lo cotidiano* exemplifies the unity of action and reflection. This interest in *lo cotidiano* began early in her corpus with her use of ethnography and the inclusion of the voices of everyday Latinas in her academic publications. *Lo cotidiano* has in turn developed into a sophisticated concept that is fundamental to understanding her research project. As Isasi-Díaz has repeatedly pointed out, *lo cotidiano* has been traditionally deemed irrelevant and insignificant for academic reflection. Within liberation theologies, daily life has been subsumed under the structural. This is perhaps one of its greatest errors. Instead, Isasi-Díaz proposes, structural change must be grounded in *lo cotidiano*, and if it is not, structural transformation will at worst fail and at best be fleeting.

13. Isasi-Díaz, "Burlando al Opresor," ch. 9 in *La Lucha Continues*.
14. Gonzalez, "More than Christian and Mestizo."
15.. Isasi-Díaz, "Preface" to *Mujerista Theology*, xiii.

María Pilar Aquino has contributed pioneering scholarship in the area of Latina feminist theology. In her work Aquino highlights the historical exclusion of women from theology as well as the institutional silencing that denies the life and subjectivity of women. The entry of women into the theological arena is an epistemological revolution that challenges the very nature of theological scholarship. A hermeneutics of suspicion leads Aquino's analysis of the ideologies informing the dominant theological discourse. One also finds in her work a privileging of daily life as a theological category. Aquino argues that feminism is indigenous to Latin Americans and cautions that ignoring this reality erases the concrete, historical struggles of women against sexism and patriarchy. To those who call themselves *mujeristas*, Aquino writes, "With these views, not only do they show their ignorance regarding the feminist tradition within Latin American communities, but they also attempt to remove from us our authority to name ourselves according to our own historical roots."[16] Aquino rejects the term *mujerista* because in her view it erases the history of feminism within Latin America.

For Aquino, daily life is also the foundation of the structural. "Daily relationships become the basis and image of all social relations. This is why analysts stress that daily life permeates the public as well as the private spheres."[17] The category of *lo cotidiano* is not without contention. As noted by Aquino, "Although daily life has been a space controlled by dominant ideologies and religions, twentieth-century currents in liberation though underestimated *lo cotidiano's* critical weight, the analytic magnitude of daily living, and its counter-hegemonic political value."[18] In her excellent introduction to the theological method of Roman Catholic Latino/a systematic theology, Aquino names *lo cotidiano* as a key analytic category within Latino/a theology. Citing the contribution of feminist theory's emphasis on the category of daily life, Aquino also highlights the particular significance of this category for women. For, as everyone in this room knows well, in the polarization of the public and the private it is the woman that is reduced to the private sphere. Contrarily, within Latino/a cultures daily life is understood in a holistic manner, encompassing the totality of one's life. The dichotomy of the public and the private is rejected.

The category of *lo cotidiano* expands the topics of theoretical reflection, including in particular those excluded by androcentric theories. Daily life is the site of humanity's encounter with the divine and thus God's salvific presence. Therefore the lived faith and its daily expression must be a central dimension of theological elaboration, its point of departure. In Latino/a theologies, this emphasis on concrete life also appears in the centrality of popular religion within this theology. For it is the everyday rituals that transcend the boundaries of public and private that embody the holistic nature of daily life. The emphasis on *lo cotidiano* is a hallmark of Latina feminist theologies. As noted by Matina ethicist M. T. Dávila, "*Lo cotidiano* reflects Latinas' way of knowing

16. Aquino, "Latin American Feminist Theology," 94.
17. Aquino, *Our Cry for Life*, 40.
18. Aquino, "Theological Method in U.S. Latino/a Theology," 38.

that privileges their lived realities and that of the other marginalized: realities of class, racial, and gender oppression, of political invisibility or persecution, or lack of access to those tools of life that the dominant group has come to take for granted such as education, housing, food, adequate medical care, or political influence."[19]

While groundbreaking figures, the work of Latina feminist theology has moved beyond these earlier debates on naming and is expanding its subjects. Robyn Henderson-Espinoza challenges Latina feminist theology to emerge from its heteronormativity and engage the lives and struggles of queer persons.[20] Nichole Flores examines the Latino/a notion of extended communal family as an avenue for extending our understandings of community, connecting familial solidarity with the common good.[21] Nancy Pineda-Madrid challenges Latino/a theologians to be aware of their publics and the manners in which they self-limit their work, calling Latina theologians to contextualize the preferential option for Latina women as one that empowers all, not just Latinas.[22] Pineda-Madrid's own work on women on the border also examines sex trafficking and femicide on the border, describing the "disposable women" on the border as a commodity with no human worth within global capitalism. For Pineda-Madrid, they embody a crucified people, "a particular group who suffer based on their shared historical reality, their collective vulnerability."[23] I appreciate the concrete starting point of Pineda-Madrid's starting point. Both scholars encourage us to look beyond the academic rhetorical implications of our identity constructions and engage how they impact Latinas in their everyday lives.

The literary writings of Latina authors is the subject matter in the essay by Teresa Delgado, where she explores the contributions of Puerto Rican women to Latina theology as prophets for the Puerto Rican people, arguing they are a critical source for Latina feminist theology.[24] These authors, Delgado contends, present an understanding of what it means to be human through the use of narrative and story. In her work Delgado gives theological value to literature. Delgado is not the only Latina scholar working on the intersection of Latina religious experience and literature. Though not a theologian, Laura Pérez's work examines the visual, performative, and literary work of Latinas as an expression of Latina folk religion.[25] Within the work of Chicana artists in particular, Pérez finds a rejection of the reduction to the lived everyday religion of Latinas as mere superstition. In my own work I have explored the poetry, plays, and essays of colonial Mexican nun Sor Juana Inés de la Cruz as a historical church mother

---

19. Dávila, "Latino/a Ethics," 252.
20. Henderson-Espinoza, "Queer Theory and Latino/a Theologizing," 330.
21. Flores, "Latino/a Families."
22. Pineda-Madrid, "Feminist Theory and Latina Feminist/Mujerista Theologizing," 356.
23. Pineda-Madrid, "Sex Trafficking and Femicide Along the Border," 88.
24. Delgado, *Puerto Rican Decolonial Theology*.
25. Pérez, "Spirit Glyphs."

for the Latin American church.[26] Attention to Afro-Cuban religious experience and non-Christian religious expressions as sources for theology is also a prominent theme in my corpus.

Jeanette Rodríguez's scholarship emphasizes Our Lady of Guadalupe as a source of empowerment for Mexican-American women and the importance of oral tradition and cultural memory for Latina spirituality. Again we find Latinas' everyday faith is fundamental within Latina theology. The faith lives of our mothers and grandmothers are not found in the theological canons studied in universities and seminaries. They are instead remembered and lived in our spiritual lives. This is also why Latina scholars include the voices of everyday grassroots Latinas. Their stories and struggles are cited along with the other greats of the Christian theological tradition, a methodology used by both Rodríguez and Isasi-Díaz. Rodríguez also connects her own research to the arts, emphasizing the Aztec tradition of *flor y canto* (flower and song). "According to this worldview, the deepest recesses of being human can only be expressed in the metaphor of poetry and beauty. While it recognizes the significance of reason and logic, this particular world view takes seriously the affect, the intuitive, and the aesthetic."[27] This connection to the aesthetic is a theme that is found in many works by Latina theologians, for example Ana María Pineda's writings on murals.[28]

CHALLENGES

Latina feminist theology must be contextualized in light of the broader theological production of Latinas as a whole and the diversity of theological approaches. Protestant Latina theologians are becoming more and more prominent voices in the theological arena. Mayra Rivera's work presents not only a new horizon in terms of this, but more significantly in her incorporation of postcolonial writings within the discourse of Latina theology. As Nancy Pienda thoughtfully describes, "Mayra Rivera (Puerto Rican, Methodist), well-versed in post-colonial theory, 'radical orthodoxy' and liberation theologies, developed the first sustained constructive work on the doctrine of God by any Latina theologian. In her first monograph, she offers a reformulation of divine transcendence in which relationality and intimacy play a preeminent role."[29] Rivera's research focuses on how power functions in the Latino/a construction of the doctrine of God.

Both Elizabeth Conde-Frazier and Arlene Sánchez Walsh center their theological scholarship on Pentecostals and Evangelicals. Conde-Frazier focuses her work on theological education and missiology. Her scholarship reminds us of the significance of theological education within the discipline of theology and the broader ecclesiological

---

26. Gonzalez, *Sor Juana*.
27. Rodríguez, "*Tripuenteando*," 75.
28. Pineda, "*Imagenes de Dios en el Camino*."
29. Pineda-Madrid, "Latina Theology," 82.

context.³⁰ Situating her work in Southern California, "Sánchez Walsh focused on the ambivalent relationship that Mexican-American Pentecostals have with their ethnic identity as it relates to their religious identity."³¹ Her work offers a much-needed contribution to a growing geographic and religious demographic in the United States, providing a space for their distinctive theological voice.

Like their Latino colleagues, Latina theologians must be attentive of the dangers found in essentializing Latina experience and become more nuanced in their elaboration of Latino/a identity. A more generalized description of Latina identity as a whole always risks erasing and marginalizing portions of our population that do not fall neatly into broader categories. This emphasis on maintaining the particularity within our communities is both theological and ethical. Latino/a theologians must embrace a principle of unity amidst diversity as a central feature of their theology. While it is important to maintain the coalitions that exist between different Latino/a groups, it is equally important not to subsume certain sectors of our population at the expense of others.

Another concern is feminism. It is imperative that Latina feminist theologians begin to explore the convergences and differences among their theological projects. This process must also include the voices of those Latina theologians who do not employ a feminist hermeneutic. The goal of this exploration is not to find some sort of resolution or to homogenize Latina theological expressions. Instead, Latina theologians must find avenues for collaboration and support in spite of their different theological standpoints. What hangs in the balance is the role of feminism within Latino/a theology in general. We must bring the gender critique to bear on our own scholarship and examine how feminist critiques impact Latina and Latino theology as a whole.

Linked to this is the relationship between feminism and broader Latino theological discourse. Orlando O. Espín indicates that, "There is no question in my mind but that one significant dynamic within Latino/a theology, over the last three decades, has been the ever-increasing reception and incorporation of methodological concerns and issues raised by feminist critical theory."³² While I agree that feminist critical theory is more visible within Latino/a theology as a whole, the role of feminism within Latino/a theological expressions remains a contested site, even among Latinas themselves.

In this same chapter Espín raises a very important point regarding a challenge that all Latino/a theologians face, "*The question for Latino/a theologians is whether our work in fact furthers the goals of our people—their struggles for equality and dignity, for decent housing, education, and health care.* An equally necessary question is whether our theology prophetically challenges our people to grow beyond our biases, our idols, and our sins."³³ I could not agree more. As an academic discipline whose very life depends on the validation and the parameters of the academy, the impact of

---

30. Conde-Frazier, "Religious Education in an Immigrant Community."
31. Pineda-Madrid, "Latina Theology," 82.
32. Espín, "Introduction," 6.
33. Espín, "Introduction," 7.

our work and how we define that impact must be critically examined and constantly interrogated. This is especially urgent given the self-professed concrete advocacy for Latino/a communities and their concrete realities.

Latina feminist theology is a liberation theology with a multilayered analysis of US Latina existence. It reflects on the divine emerging from the context of a marginalized people. Latina feminist theologians often work on related topics, but they are not a homogeneous, self-proclaimed group of scholars. Their commonalties include feminist critical analysis, contextual accent, and a liberationist emphasis in their work. Informed by these analyses, these theologians destabilize androcentric and hierarchical theologies, offering an emancipatory vision that promotes the full humanity of all.

BIBLIOGRAPHY

Aponte, Edwin David, and Miguel A. De La Torre. *Introducing Latinx Theologies*. Maryknoll, NY: Orbis, 2020

Aquino, María Pilar. "Latin American Feminist Theology." *Journal of Feminist Studies in Religion* 14 (1998) 89–107.

———.*Our Cry for Life: Feminist Theology from Latin America*. New York: Orbis, 1993.

———."Theological Method in U.S. Latino/a Theology: Toward an Intercultural Theology for the Third Millennium." In *From the Heart of Our People: Latino/a Explorations in Catholic Systematic Theology*, edited by Orlando Espín and Miguel Díaz, 6–48. Maryknoll, NY: Orbis, 1999.

Aquino, María Pilar, et al. "Introduction" to *A Reader in Latina Feminist Theology: Religion and Justice*, edited by María Pilar Aquino et al., xiii–xx. Austin: University of Texas Press, 2002.

Cadava, Geraldo. *The Hispanic Republican: The Shaping of an American Political Identity, from Nixon to Trump*. New York: Ecco, 2020.

Conde-Frazier, Elizabeth. "Latina Evangélicas: A New Voice in Hispanic/Latina Theology." *Latin American Theology* 10 (2015) 63–84.

———. "Religious Education in an Immigrant Community: A Case Study." In *Hispanic Christian Thought at the Dawn of the 21st Century: Essays in Honor of Justo L. González*, edited by Alvin Padilla et al., 187–200. Nashville: Abingdon, 2005.

Dávila, M. T. "Latino/a Ethics." In *The Wiley Blackwell Companion to Latino/a Theology*, edited by Orlando O. Espín, 249–66. Chichester: Wiley Blackwell, 2015.

Delgado, Teresa. *A Puerto Rican Decolonial Theology: Prophesy Freedom*. New York: Palgrave Macmillan, 2017.

Espín, Orlando O. "Introduction." In *The Wiley Blackwell Companion to Latino/a Theology*, edited by Orlando O. Espín, 1–11. Chichester: Wiley Blackwell, 2015.

Flores, Nichole. "Latino/a Families: Solidarity and the Common Good." *Journal of the Society of Christian Ethics* 33 (2013) 57—72.

Gonzalez, Michelle A. *A Critical Introduction to Religion in the Americas: Bridging the Liberation Theology and Religious Studies Divide*. New York: New York University Press, 2014.

———. "More than Christian and Mestizo: Race, Culture, and Identity within Latino/a Theology and Religious Studies." In *Critical Dialogues in Latinx Studies: A Reader*, edited by Ana Y. Ramos-Zayas and Mérida M. Rúa, 94–103. New York: New York University Press, 2021.

———. *Sor Juana Beauty and Justice in the Americas*. Maryknoll, NY: Orbis, 2003.

Henderson-Espinoza, Robyn. "Queer Theory and Latino/a Theologizing." In *The Wiley Blackwell Companion to Latino/a Theology*, edited by Orlando O. Espín, 329–46. Chichester: Wiley Blackwell, 2015.

Hernández-Diaz, R. J. "Hispanic Liberative Theologies." In *Introducing Liberative Theologies*, edited by Miguel de la Torre, 89–111. Maryknoll, NY: Orbis, 2015.

Herrera, Marina. "Who Do You Say Jesus Is?: Christological Reflections from A Hispanic Woman's Perspective." In *Reconstructing the Christ Symbol: Essays in Feminist Theology*, edited by Maryanne Stevens, 72–93. New York: Paulist, 1993.

Isasi-Díaz, Ada María. *En la Lucha/In the Struggle: A Hispanic Women's Liberation Theology*. English and Spanish ed. 10th anniversary ed. Minneapolis: Fortress, 2004.

———. *La Lucha Continues: Mujerista Theology*. Maryknoll, NY: Orbis, 2004.

———. *Mujerista Theology: A Theology for the Twenty-First Century*. Maryknoll, NY: Orbis, 1996.

Machado, Daisy L. "History and Latino/a Identity: Mapping a Past that Leads to Our Future." In *The Wiley Blackwell Companion to Latino/a Theology*, edited by Orlando O. Espín, 35–52. Chichester: Wiley Blackwell, 2015.

Martell-Ortero, Loida. "Women Doing Theology: Una Perspectiva Evangélica." *Apuntes* 14 (1994) 67–85.

Morales, Ed. *Latinx: The New Force in American Politics and Culture*. New York: Verso, 2018.

Pérez, Laura E. "Spirit Glyphs: Reimagining Art and Artist in the Work of Chicana Literature." In *Rethinking Latino(a) Religion and Identity*, edited by Miguel A. De La Torre and Gastón Espinosa, 267–85. Cleveland: Pilgrim, 2006.

Pineda, Ana María "*Imagenes de Dios en el Camino*: Retablos, Ex-Votos, Milagritos, and Murals." *Theological Studies* 65 (2004) 364–79.

Pineda-Madrid, Nancy. "Feminist Theory and Latina Feminist/Mujerista Theologizing." In *The Wiley Blackwell Companion to Latino/a Theology*, edited by Orlando O. Espín, 347—363. Chichester: Wiley Blackwell, 2015.

———. "Latina Roman Catholic Theologians." In *Encyclopedia of Women and Religion in North America*, edited by Rosemary Skinner Keller and Rosemary Radford Ruether, 1193–200. Bloomington: Indiana University Press, 2006

———. "Latina Theology." In *Liberation Theologies in the United States*, edited by Stacey Floyd-Thomas and Anthony Pinn, 61–85. New York: New York University Press, 2010.

———. "Sex Trafficking and Femicide Along the Border." In *Living With(out) Borders: Catholic Theological Ethics on the Migration of Peoples*, edited by Agnes M. Brazal and María Teresa Dávila, 81–90. Maryknoll, NY: Orbis, 2016.

———. *Suffering and Salvation in Ciudad Juárez*. Minneapolis: Fortress, 2011

Rodríguez, Jeanette. *Stories We Live/Cuentos Que Vivimos: Hispanic Women's Spirituality*. New York: Paulist, 1996.

———. "*Tripuenteando*: Journey toward Identity, the Academy, and Solidarity." In *Feminist Intercultural Theology: Latina Explorations for a Just World*, edited by María Pilar Aquino and Maria José Rosado-Nunes, 70–88. Maryknoll, NY: Orbis, 2007.

CHAPTER 11

Popular Bible Reading and Popular Theology

An Experience from Northeast Brazil

ODJA BARROS

It is incontestable that the Bible occupies a key place in the life of Protestant communities in Latin America, and specifically Brazil. However, despite the principle of free interpretation of Scripture, it can be affirmed that appropriation of the Bible is repeatedly done in an individualistic way, and by static, imposing, vertical, and non-participatory pedagogies. Otherwise, the Bible is often associated with merely spiritual problems, so it cannot relate its teachings to the broader reality and its different contexts.

The pedagogical practice of community reading of the Bible, of a wide portion of the Brazilian Baptist churches has been marked by the systematic reproduction and repetition of contents, without any articulation with the great social, political, and cultural dilemmas, and that touch the respective contexts. The use of the Bible to reinforce ancient doctrinal positions, as well as to refute religious theologies and practices different from those officially assumed by the institutions. In the Pinheiro Baptist Church, located in northeastern Brazil, it was the community practice of popular Bible reading, developed since the mid-2000s, that led to the breaking and interrupting of this pattern.

The city of Maceió, capital of Alagoas, one of the nine states of the Northeast Region of Brazil where the Pinheiro Baptist Church is located, is a kind of "synthesis city" of the Brazilian reality where it finds all the problems faced in national and even global reality: from prostitution to the environmental threat, from street children to institutional violence. Maceió hosts all the complexity of the struggles that take on many parts of the world today. In line with the reality of the Latin American popular majorities, Maceió and Alagoas may serve as an example as micro images of what has been the micro image of Latin America over the last five centuries.[1]

Alagoas currently has one of the worst rates of human development in the country, and Maceió is where most violent deaths occur annually among the young population of Brazil, in proportional terms. The natural beauty of its beaches, as well as the diversity of cultural expressions present in this capital, has to live side by side with a social reality very present in the metropolises of Latin America. Urban violence, the sexual exploitation of children and adolescents, political corruption, deficiencies in the education and health system, structural unemployment, and informality in economic activities are some of the social wounds strongly present in the life of the city of Maceió. The city currently has about three hundred favelas, the living conditions of its inhabitants reaching unbearable levels. Historically, political power in Alagoas and Maceió has always been marked by omission in relation to the demands of popular majorities, and by the option opened by local elites. The explanation of this lies in the fact that, also historically, political power and economic power in Alagoas coincide, which is characterized as a chronic dilemma for the majority of the poor and unassisted population.

However, despite the scenario pointed out above, in the same way as we have seen emerging in Latin America, from the 1960s on, a new form of theological reflection, born from the imperative of a transformative and liberating praxis, the Alagoas and Maceió context call for the emergence of a new posture of protestant mother churches and Baptist tradition. It is in this context that it would situate the experience of popular reading of the Bible in Northeast Brazil.[2]

Northeast Brazil has been a region from which very interesting ecclesial works come from, few though, being articulated with the dilemmas of popular majorities, and with a notion of "Christian mission" whose agenda is part of society. These churches perform "creative ministry," characterized by centrality of the poor and the search for social justice. The Pinheiro Baptist Church, although not located in the needy community, has its member formed by plurality. The social strata of the city of Maceió should also be included in this list of Christian community, marked by the "creative diaconal ministry" field, especially sociopolitical action and active participation in the most pressing issues in the state of Alagoas and in the capital Maceió. The IBP has been marked by a differentiated attitude from what could be considered an average performance of the Baptist churches in this context.[3]

The formation of Pinheiro Baptist Church, in Maceió, should be situated in the larger context of the history of mission Protestantism in the state of Alagoas, the one represented mainly by the Baptists, follows the same logic as the history of Protestant mission in Brazil. Arriving in this country in the second half of the century, coming

1. Monteiro, *Um Jumentinho na Avenida*, 1–15.
2. Gutierrez, *Teologia da Libertação*, 133–64.
3. Monteiro, "A igreja evangélica e o nordeste brasileiro," 42–70.

from the largest of the missions from the United States, the historical Protestants.[4] Inserted in this context marked by the presence and influence of the fundamentalist currents of the American Baptists, the walk and historical praxis of this Baptist community is even more interesting, to the model of rupture with conservative ideological perspectives, and to the face of local socio-political dilemmas. The history of the Pinheiro Baptist Church began in the 1930s, more precisely in 1936, and it was consolidated as an autonomous Baptist church in the year 1970.

While the Alagoas Baptist churches continue with a theology still attached to their fundamentalist matrices, by adopting the methodology of popular reading of the Bible, in its pedagogical practice, the Pinheiro Baptist Church inaugurated a new possibility of relationship with the Bible, marked by greater popular participation and the direct relationship with the dilemmas faced in the daily lives of people living in these communities. In place of vertical and unparticipative appropriations, this new form of biblical hermeneutics privileges the community in its role as a subject of theological reflection. What is observed is that the practice of popular reading of the Bible provoked relevant community transformations, not only related to the way of reading and interpreting the Bible, but leading to the revision of pedagogical practices and a new popular theological-pastoral praxis, committed to the transformation of unjust realities that involve or contextualize the community in which a church is inserted.

This introduction aims to situate the reflection proposed in this article in an experienced and incarnated context, because the popular reading of the Bible and popular theology is only possible to conceive from concrete communities and realities.

POPULAR BIBLE READING AND POPULAR THEOLOGY: "OUR STEPS COME FROM AFAR"

To situate the popular reading of the Bible in the Latin American and Brazilian context, it is necessary to know its "steps that come from afar." The first experience of the Latin American people with the Bible was traumatic. Christianity arrived in Latin America as a religion of oppression and its main instrument was the Bible.[5]

The Latin American biblist and theologian Pablo Richard recalls a popular saying from Guatemala: "When the Spaniards arrived, they told us indigenous to close our eyes, to pray. When we opened our eyes, we had the Bible, and they had our land." Pablo Richard also says that the historical trauma of indigenous peoples with the Bible

---

4. "Historical Protestantism" is the way in which the sociological typology in Brazil classifies churches originating from the mass movement of American missionaries that arrived to nineteenth-century Latin America. Among those that stand out are Baptist, Presbyterian, Methodist, Mennonite, and congregation churches. In addition, they can be considered as belonging to historical Protestantism as churches belonging to the immigration wave undertaken in Brazil, in the same period, whose emphasis falls on the Lutheran Church.

5. Cardoso Pereira, "Changing Seasons," 50.

is recorded in the famous open letter that several indigenous movements wrote to John Paul II when he visited Peru, five hundred years after the invasion, saying:

> We the Indigenous of the Andes and America decided to take advantage of a visit from John Paul II to return his Bible, for in five centuries she gave no love, no peace, no justice. Please take your Bible back, and return it to our oppressors, because they need your moral precepts more than we do. Because of the arrival of Christopher Columbus, America was imposed with force, culture, language, religion, and some values of Europe. The Bible came to us as part of a cultural change imposed. She was an ideology weapon of this colonialist attack. The Spanish sword, which during the day attacked and killed the body of the Indigenous people, became at night the cross that attacked the Indian soul.[6]

The Bible in Latin America is linked to a history of massacre because it is a story of colonization and devastation of the original cultures. The Bible has even been used to demonize the religious culture of the original peoples, to condemn their rituals, dances, and sacred symbols. The Bible was also used to inculcate concepts and visions of Eurocentric theology, heralded as universal and neutral. However, it brought not only a vision centered on the European world, but on the European man, that is, a racist, colonial, and patriarchal theology.

It was in the counter course to this Christian tradition that colonized the Bible, faith, as cultures and bodies, that the popular reading movement of the Bible and the popular Latin American liberation theologies spouted. In the search to develop as bases of colonial theology of domination, which legitimizes a biblical and theological hermeneutics of colonial domination-oppression. It was from the critical dialogue with the fundamental concepts of the Judeo-Christian tradition that the popular reading of the Bible and popular theology developed a biblical-theological critique of traditions from the reality of the Latin American peoples. In this perspective, the birth of a biblical hermeneutics that could bring Christian theology to the popular and community bases begins to be woven. Thus, we sought to discover the critical potential of this same Judeo-Christian tradition, so that it could counter as a critique of the traditions of domination, which developed within Western Christianity and legitimizes the process of colonization.[7]

The popular reading of the Bible was fed by the critical resistance of the popular Christian religion that takes place from a deep dialogue with the sacred texts, which could serve as the basis for a Christian theology on the periphery of the colonized world. Born in popular movements,[8] the popular reading of the Bible represents a theological systematization of the pains and groans of women, men, and groups submitted to the models of patriarchal colonial oppression of the religious structures

---

6. Richard, *Hermenéutica Biblica India*, 10.
7. Gutierrez, *Teologia da Libertação*, 53.
8. Gutierrez, *Teologia da Libertação*, 56.

that dominate Latin America. For Michel Lowy, the birth and systematization of this theology is the result of the great transformations of the foundations of the church.

> Liberation theology is only the visible "tip of the iceberg," the systematic spiritual expression of a profound change within the Church and of the Christian people long before the publication of the first works of the new theologians. ... This movement presents itself as a broad informal network, a vast and diverse current of religious, cultural, and political renewal, present both "at the base," in communities, neighborhood associations, unions, peasant leagues, as in the summit, in bishoprics, pastoral commissions, national and regional episcopal conferences.[9]

The popular reading of the Bible, therefore, is part of a broader biblical and theological movement born of the faith lived by people in communities, from the experience of the poor oppressed in Latin America. For Hugo Assmann, the central core of this movement, is the resignification of religious tradition as a critical instrument of reality, based on sensitivity to culture and popular religiosity. And, according to him, this is the great merit of these hermeneutics and liberation theologies that will be responsible for a deep internal critique of the traditions of classical Christian theology.[10]

These new possibilities of reading the nascent Bible stem from the action of organic interpreters who, from the 1980s on, participated in a process of critical emancipation, which was taking place in Latin American countries. Thus, a Latin American biblical theology was used, to assume the arduous task of promoting a historical reconstruction of popular roots, which gave rise to the Bible by affirming, from a praxis of liberation, the new paths of biblical hermeneutics, which seeks to reconstruct the experiences of the oppressed and the oppressed of the Bible. In 1979, the Bible artist Elsa Tamez released the book that can be considered another landmark of Latin American biblical hermeneutics: *A Bíblia dos Oprimidos*. Says Elsa Tamez:

> The story told by the different biblical stories is a story of oppression and struggle, as well as the history of our Latin American peoples—in our present history we can also discern the continuation of divine revelation. Therefore, I believe that reflecting on liberation exerts no pressure on the actual treatment of the biblical. It is the center of the whole historical context in which divine revelation develops; and only this center can we understand the meanings of faith, grace, love, peace, sin, and salvation.[11]

This biblical movement provoked profound change in the proposal of biblical interpretation, elaborated from the Latin American context. In 1984, the first issue of the journal *Estudios Biblicos/Biblical Studies* was published, which brought, as its thematic first issue title, the article by the Latin American theologian Pablo Richard: *The*

---

9. Lowy, "As esquerdas na ditadura militar," 310.
10. Cabral, *Bíblia e Teologia Política*, 82.
11. Tamez, *A Bíblia dos Oprimidos*, 7–8.

Bible as Memory of the Poor, thus assuming the hermeneutic axis. Richard states that "an exegesis and every scientific explanation of the Bible only makes sense when the service of this *first* reading of the Bible by the poor is placed." This article highlights the importance of a critique of fundamentalist hermeneutics, which functions as an instrument of domination that, in the name of a sacred text, "manipulates consciences and promotes a continuous action of colonization of minds, undoing all autonomy and consciousness and imagination of the reader of the Bible."[12] Richard states:

> When the biblical text is absolutized, then it becomes a law and instrument of repression of the historical conscience of a people. There is no worse domination than that exercised in the name of a "sacred" and "divine" text. The biblical text is only an instrument of liberation from religious consciousness when read from history, but a story of liberation, where man (and woman) is the subject of their own destiny. The absolutization of the biblical text as the material and direct word of God is the ultimate denial of history and of the man (and the woman) as the subject of his own history.[13]

In the face of all interpretive history of the Bible, based on colonizing and patriarchal roots and, from the hermeneutic criterion of oppression-liberation, responsible for the hermeneutic turn produced by liberation theology, it is born as biblical hermeneutics of Latin American liberation. These hermeneutics seek to break with a long-term tradition, which determined the hermeneutic locus of Bible reading in Latin American, which subjected an entire continent and culture to an oppressive hermeneutic-theological project of colonial-patriarchal roots, instrumentalized by political-ecclesiastical objectives, which ended in a tragic and irreversible massacre of the entire Amerindian religious culture, that penetrated violently into our continent under the sign of oppression.[14]

POPULAR BIBLE READING: PURIFYING THE BIBLE FROM IDEO-THEOLOGIES OF OPPRESSION-DOMINATION

The biblical hermeneutics of Latin American liberation sought to subject the biblical tradition to "a great process of purification of its oppressive historical expressions" and enable a decolonization of the Latin American religious imaginary.[15]

> Christianity penetrated our continent under the sign of oppression. Not only by the fact that it came by force, as the conqueror's religion, but also by the fact that it functioned as a religion of oppression. If what originates biblical faith is an experience of liberation that allows us to recognize God as a "liberator,"

---

12. Richard, *Lectura Popular de la Bíblia en América Latina,* 20.
13. Richard, *Lectura Popular de la Bíblia en América Latina,* 24.
14. Croatto, *Os Deuses da Opressão e a Busca do Deus Libertador,* 65.
15. Croatto, *Os Deuses da opressão e a busca do Deus Libertador,* 65.

Latin America could not be evangelized, for in it God could not be "experienced" as a deliverer. That is the turning point. As a result, the natives of Latin America were left with their oppressive gods, but less oppressive than the god of conquerors . . . As unconscious self-defense, they accepted Christian forms for their traditional worldview. In this way, they did not free themselves, but at least proclaimed and still proclaim their misery. If evangelization did not make liberation experienced at the economic and social level, where it takes place in an archetypal and radical way, then it lost the possibility of speaking authentically of the "God of Liberation." So that the biblical faith—in its liberating kerygmatic nucleus—is believable to the Latin American man (and woman), it must go through a great process of purification of its historical expressions. And the only way to accomplish it is through a new liberation experience.[16]

It is from an interpretation of the vital reality of the peoples of the Latin American continent and their relationship with the Bible that the popular reading of the Bible proposes that the approximation with biblical texts is not with the ties present in the gaze of the inherited tradition, but from the perspective of the explored and exploited. The popular reading of the Bible is not, in this sense, simply a new interpretation of the texts of the Judeo-Christian tradition, but "supposes another process," which is the interpretation of the sacred texts, from certain practices that break with a broad process of oppression, colonization, and clericalization of Bible reading.

POPULAR BIBLE READING IN BRAZIL

The 1970s was fundamental in the gestation of the popular Bible reading and popular theology movement in Brazil for rediscovery of the Bible by the basic popular movements. It was from the movement of Basic Ecclesial Communities (CEBs) that the movement called popular reading of the Bible was born. In the popular meetings of formation and celebration in the CEBs, a correlation was sought between reading the Bible and the life suffered in the communities of the Latin American peripheries. In Brazil, the main touchstone for this relationship between the Bible and life is Carmelite friar Carlos Mesters, one of the main inspirations of the Latin American popular Bible reading movement. For Mesters:[17]

> This reading that the poor make of the Bible presents a new context that allows scientific exegesis to meet again with the mission within the church. That is, it offers the exegete a new picture within which it is possible to rediscover what should be the "service of the word" within the church, even the service (of that) whose life is summarized in the scientific study of the Bible.[18]

---

16. Croatto, *Os deuses da opressão e a busca do Deus libertador*, 66.
17. Santos, *Uma hermenêutica bíblica popular e feminista*, 1–150.
18. Mesters, "*Como se faz teologia bíblica hoje no Brasil?*," 10.

In this period, the ideas of the Brazilian educator Paulo Freire also exert profound influence, which will serve as a basis and inspiration for a generation of a Christian militancy, engaged in processes of resistance to imperialist and Eurocentric culture. The book *Behind the Words*,[19] a study on the gateway into the world of the Bible, published in 1974, marks the history of Bible reading in Latin America and is undoubtedly the first major contribution to Latin American biblical hermeneutics, laying the foundations of a popular reading that takes on as its hermeneutic locus a preferential option for the poor. In 1978, inspired by Brother Carlos Mesters, the Center for Biblical Studies (CEBI) was inaugurated, which played a significant role in the development of Latin American biblical hermeneutics, which reflected with great ownership the method of learning Paulo Freire's pedagogy.[20]

It was on this horizon that the popular reading of the Bible in Brazil and Latin America developed, and the deconstructed and sedimented interpretive tradition built in almost five hundred years of Christianity's history on the continent, which gave rise to the historical-theological project of domination and colonization, which left deep scars on the Bible that is read and lived in Latin America to this day. In this new way of reading the Bible in Latin America, we seek to identify the roots of domination and oppression that are both in the biblical texts and in the interpretative layers that overlap the text, rejecting the traditions that are at the origin of the whole process of domination, thus reconstructing an interpretative tradition identified with the longings for liberation.[21]

The popular reading of the Bible, as a popular biblical movement, has been enriched by different approaches and looks. According to Elaine Neuenfeldt, the movement of approximation to the biblical text, which is defined as popular, is based on a participatory, contextualized, and critical posture. "This posture articulates the awareness of the absence, of the loss of the Bible with the desire for presence." Popular reading faces the losses and imprisonments of the Bible that have happened and happen from literalist and fundamentalist conceptions that tear the text out of its historical context, which do not consider its social place, nor look at the conditions that produced and reselected the texts.[22]

It also faces the imprisonment of the Bible that happens in academicism, which is different from academia. Academicism is a way of doing academia, removed from the concrete life and reality of the people. The scientific devices proclaimed in academies, institutes, theses, and manuals, are pretentiously said to be objective and universal. But in proclaiming themselves in this way, they cloister the vivacity and spirituality of biblical witness. The dynamism of popular reading springs from the people's environment and explicitly articulates their choice for people excluded and marginalized

---

19. Santos, *Uma hermenêutica bíblica popular e feminista*, 14.
20. Mesters, *Por Trás das Palavras*, 1–240.
21. Richard, *Lectura Popular de la Bíblia em América Latina*, 27.
22. Santos, *Uma hermenêutica bíblica popular e feminista*, 21–25.

from the dominant system. Thus, it gives the people back the power to take the Bible into their hands, gaining the right to articulate their own reading of the Bible, reality, and their faith.[23]

The popular reading of the Bible has as one of its instrumentals the hermeneutic triangle: reality, text/Bible, and community. The method is characterized by its circularity or spirality. That is, as a circle, there is no rigid definition by which one should begin reading and, as a spiral, it is indicated that it is not a process closed, but, on the one hand, open to new perspectives, and, on the other, that allows and promotes openings of perspectives in the reading itself. Understanding that life in its concreteness is the place where the word of God is articulated and entertained is that reality is what determines the gateway to the biblical text. In this sense it can be said that popular reading of the Bible is part of reality. This gateway considers the concrete needs of daily life, but also the broader structuring of society must be on the horizon of understanding.[24]

One of the most interesting features of the popular Bible reading proposal is the call for a community practice of biblical reading and interpretation. It is part of a proposal of ecclesiology, in which the power of interpretation is not exclusive to the clergy, priests or pastors, theologians or intellectuals, but is also in the hands of the community that becomes a true subject of the process. Return the holy book to the people who wrote it in a dynamic of reappropriation. It is, concretely, a continuous reinterpretation of the Bible derived from the situations of daily life, both at the ecclesial and social level, to transform, as far as possible, this reality into a permanent journey towards the utopia expressed in the category of kingdom of God. It calls for a methodological change in relation to knowledge that is generated not by vertical transmission, but from community construction.[25]

The method of popular reading is much more than an instrument, it also becomes content, taking concrete life as a hermeneutic horizon and not increasing the amount of data about the Bible. With a hermeneutic developed from the people and community committed to the transformations of the structures of the world in which they live, it also uses the contributions of the biblical sciences, to avoid naïve, individualistic, or fundamentalist interpretations, which often consider the Bible as a book without history. The popular reading of the Bible is therefore part of the Latin American biblical movement, which breaks with the criteria and methods of European scientific exegesis and proposes a biblical hermeneutics identified with the Latin American reality in a perspective of liberation, returning interpretative authority to the community. This new way of reading the Bible contributes to the disruption of colonialist interpretive traditions and provides tools for a critique of patriarchal reading of the Bible.[26]

---

23. Neuenfeldt, "*Diálogo entre leitura popular e leitura feminista da Bíblia,*" 121.
24. Neuenfeldt, "*Diálogo entre leitura popular e leitura feminista da Bíblia,*" 125.
25. Barros, *Flores que Rompem Raízes,* 281–91.
26. Mesters, "*Como se faz teologia bíblica hoje no Brasil?,*" 7–19.

POPULAR BIBLE READING: WHAT, WHY, AND HOW TO INTERPRET IT?

From three questions, I would like to point out at least three elements that characterized community practice with LPB in the Pinheiro Baptist Church.

What to interpret? Interpreting life with the help of the Bible

In the practice of popular reading of the Bible in the IBP, community life became the first book where the revelation of God is sought. The progressive discovery that the word of God is not only in the Bible, but also in life, and that the main goal of reading the Bible is not to interpret the Bible, but to interpret life with the help of the Bible was one of the important steps. The Bible ceases to enter people's lives through the door of authoritarian imposition, instead entering through the door of personal and community experience. It is present not as a book that imposes doctrine, but as good news that reveals God's liberating presence in daily life and struggle. In the event of this profound connection between the Bible and life, it is important to have in our eyes the real questions that come from today's life and reality, and not artificial questions that have nothing to do with people's everyday life. Here appears the importance that the person who studies and facilitates the study of the Bible in the group or in the community has coexistence and pastoral experience inserted among the people, stepping on the same floor. Have a global view of the Bible, but also of the concrete life where people who will interpret the Bible live. Thus, reading the Bible produces a mutual enlightenment between the Bible and life.

Why interpret? An ethical-community interpretation

Probably, one of the most interesting characteristics of the biblical interpretation proposed by the popular reading of the Bible is the call for a new personal and community ethics that emerges from the interpretation of the Bible and life. The study and interpretation of the Bible gained meaning as it provoked the community to transform itself and the reality around it. A socio-political community commitment was being generated. The community is encouraged to transform, as far as possible, reality into a permanent journey towards the utopia expressed in the category of the kingdom of God. According to Fiorenza: "Taking the biblical reading from the individual spiritual scope of the private reader and building a forum, that is, a public space in which ekklesia, the radically democratic assembly can debate and decide the political meaning of the scriptures."[27]

The churches are a privileged space to foster a proposal for reading the Bible from a liberating and awareness-raising perspective. Groups in religious communities

---

27. Schüssler-Fiorenza, *Caminhos de sabedoria*, 42–51.

can bring together people from different experiences and realities: people who have no formal education but have rich experience, people who are politically engaged, or people who have never engaged in any movement. Ultimately a community with all kinds of differences have in common the fact that they live in a reality of oppressiveness and injustices. Through the popular groups of the Bible, one can give access to communities that are on the margins of academies and closed circles, intellectualized to the tools of critical investigation of discourses and knowledge.

How to interpret? In an environment of faith and freedom

A good interpretation takes place in an environment of safe spaces and sharing life, through chants, prayers, celebrations, and feast. The Baptist Church Pinheiro community develops not only biblical studies, but community meetings with playful, festive, and welcoming experiences that become part of the Bible- and life-reading process. Without this context we cannot discover the meaning that the text has for us today. For the meaning of the Bible is not only an idea or a message that is captured with reason and is objectives through reasoning; it is also a feeling, a consolation, a comfort that is felt with the heart, the senses, the affections. The community in this safe and celebratory space is placed in the interpretation of the biblical text with all its body, its thinking, and its affections. During the study, they speak, participate, they go out of silence. They also begin to have more freedom to ask questions about the text without fear, exercising their right to suspect, imagine, create. Conflicts are also part of the interpretive process. The interpretations and concepts learned, and the new interpretations generate conflict, tension, and even resistance, but it is in this conflict that individual growth and that of the group occur. They are also perceived, through speeches, new searches, concerns, and perceptions being constructed. The community is aware of realities that were not perceived before and always say, "I now understand things differently." And all this happens in a safe space of freedom. Popular reading of the Bible as community and political hermeneutics is important to impact religious communities by making them more committed to the transformation of unjust structures inside and outside the churches.

CONCLUSION

The Bible continues to be an important matrix that shapes religious, political, and social discourses. Biblical discourses are one of the components of the Latin American popular imaginary, in print, in society and in churches, and as models of life, relations, ethics, and political culture. In this sense, the biblical text and its interpretations collaborate theologically to broker oppressive or liberating theological discourses and practices.

The community practice of popular reading of the Bible in the IBP made great contribution to unmask the colonial schemes of oppression present in the biblical-religious discourse and to break the interpretative fixity of the text, provoking a new hermeneutic approach, leading to rethinking the methods and lenses used to read the Bible in this community. Reading the Bible as communitarian from popular reading has been a source of liberation for many people and groups within the churches. In the case of the Pinheiro Baptist Church, the redirection of community practice in terms of biblical hermeneutics caused, together with other community processes, important ruptures with patriarchal models and discourses, which resulted in a reconfiguration of its theological-pastoral praxis.

Biblical hermeneutics working the biblical text from technical places, from theoretical premises (in general) do not consider the social, cultural, or political place of the interpreting community. The critical look directed at Scripture is defined by the scientific discipline that underlies interpretation. The popular reading of the Bible, in turn, proposes a biblical reading from the life and reality where the community is located. The popular reading of the Bible is used in the field of biblical interpretation to a new place, method, and meaning that represent an important transformation in overcoming fixed or supposedly "neutral" readings and interpretations of biblical texts, emphasizing the political-transforming character of biblical hermeneutics.

The popular reading of the Bible proposes a new subject of biblical interpretation: not the academy, but the people and the community. The popular reading of the Bible allowed centuries of academic exegesis to be stripped, and set aside titters about clerical clothing and biblical science to rediscover with the people and communities. Once forgotten texts were reread, their conflicts revealed, denouncing deceptive neutrality. Class, gender, and sexual and racial identities were being articulated in the interpretive process of the biblical text, revealing the diversity of life and the Bible. The colonizing face of the Bible was unmasked, and the Bible became multicolored, multiform, disturbing the unambiguous readings of the text. Popular reading is the result of this "conversion" of subject, meaning, and method, which occurred in the field of biblical hermeneutics.

It is necessary to face normative fixity with the polysemic opening proper to the texts, subverting and displacing the authoritarian place that is no longer the text, but life and human dignity. Thus, the path of popular reading proved important in the purpose of breaking the interpretative fixity of the text, provoking a new hermeneutic approach in the interpretive practice of the Pinheiro Baptist Church. From this experience of a religious community and its engagement with hermeneutic processes of transformation, it is possible to generate new forms of knowledge in the field of biblical hermeneutics that value more the relationship of concrete practices of biblical reading experienced in religious communities and different social groups, and academic production.

BIBLIOGRAPHY

Barros, Odja. *Flores que Rompem Raízes: Leitura Popular e Feminista da Bíblia.* São Paulo: Editora Recriar, 2020.

Cabral, Jimmy Sudário. *Bíblia e Teologia Política: escrituras, tradição e emancipação.* Rio de Janeiro: Mauad X Mysterium, 2009.

Cardoso Pereira, Nancy. "Changing Seasons: About the Bible and Other Sacred Texts in Latin America." In *Feminist Interpretation of the Bible and the Hermeneutics of Liberation,* edited by Silvia Schroer and Sophia Bietenhard, 48–58. London: Sheffield, 2004.

Croatto, José Severino. *Os deuses da opressão e a busca do Deus libertador.* São Paulo: Paulinas, 1985.

Gutierrez, Gustavo. *Teologia da Libertação.* Petrópolis: Vozes, 1985.

Lowy, Michael. "As esquerdas na ditadura militar: o cristianismo de libertação." In *Revolução e Democracia (1964): As esquerdas no Brasil,* edited by João Ferreira and Daniel Araão Filho, 3:88–102. Rio de Janeiro: Civilização Brasileira, 2007.

Mesters, Carlos. "Como se faz teologia bíblica hoje no Brasil." *Estudos Bíblicos* 1 (1987) 7–19.

———. *Por Trás das Palavras.* São Paulo: Vozes, 1999.

Monteiro, Marcos. "A igreja evangélica e o nordeste brasileiro." In *Diaconia no contexto nordestino: desafios—reflexões—práxis,* 42–70. São Leopoldo: Sinodal, 2003.

———. *Um jumentinho na Avenida: A Missão da Igreja e as Cidades.* Viçosa: Ultimato Editora, 2007.

Neuenfeldt, Elaine. "Diálogo entre leitura popular e a leitura feminista da Bíblia." *Estudos Teológicos* 45 (2005). http://www3.est.edu.br/publicacoes/estudos_teologicos/vol4502_2005/et2005-2i_eneuenfeldt.pdf.

Richard, Pablo. *Bíblia: memória histórica dos pobres.* Estudos Bíblicos 1 (1987) 20–30.

———. *Hermenéutica Bíblica India: revelación de Dios em las religiones indígenas y en la Biblia (Después de 500 años de dominación).* Revista Bíblica Latinoamericana 11. San José/Costa Rica: RIBLA 1992.

———. *Lectura Popular de la Biblia en América Latina: hermenéutica de la liberación.* Revista de Interpretação Bíblica Latino-americana 1. San José/Costa Rica: Rebue, 1988.

Santos, Odja Barros. *Uma hermenêutica bíblica popular e feminista na perspectiva da mulher nordestina: um relato de experiência.* Master's thesis, Faculdades EST, São Leopoldo, 2010.

Schussler-Fiorenza, Elisabeth. *Caminhos de sabedoria: uma introdução à interpretação bíblica feminista.* São Bernardo do Campo: Nhanduti, 2009.

Tamez, Elsa. *A Bíblia dos Oprimidos: A Opressãona Teologia Bíblica.* 3rd ed. San José/Costa Rica: DEI, 1986.

CHAPTER 12

Teología India

A Context Theology

SYLVIA MARCOS

Is *Teología India* indigenous theology? What makes it different from *Teología de la Liberación*, liberation theology? Even though both "theologies" are centered on a preferential option for the poor and the indigenous peoples as subjects of faith, *Teología India*, or *Sabiduría India* (indigenous wisdom), as many of the local pastoral actors prefer to call it, goes beyond liberation theology, complementing Catholic liturgy with practices and reflections on faith emerging from Mesoamerican philosophical heritages.

This innovative theological project is grounded in a philosophical approach, a serious and respectful relationship with indigenous Mayan communities. These people's beliefs and practices within their *pueblos*[1] belong to the Catholic diocese and are included in its pastoral work in San Cristobal de las Casas, Chiapas, Mexico. Much of what I will review here springs from a long interview I did with Don Samuel Ruiz, the late bishop emeritus of the regional diocese, who worked in San Cristobal for more than forty years.[2] I will also bring forth some of my own systematizations on "embodied thought"[3] and some lessons learned from my extended ritual participation and

---

1. *Pueblo*, as a concept, is the contemporary collective subject of most justice struggles in indigenous movements of the Americas. A recent ontological perspective has proposed an epistemology of collective action (González Casanova, "Epistemología del animal politico"), so the term *pueblo*, has become the concept where collective struggles are built.

2. The late, emeritus Catholic bishop Don Samuel Ruiz was a key political defender of the Mayan indigenous populations in his dioceses in the southeast state of Chiapas, Mexico. He and his collaborators developed a "pastoral indígena" that allowed him to propose and coin the term *Teología India* during his more than forty years of tenure at the dioceses of San Cristobal de las Casas Chiapas.

3. Marcos, "Embodied Religious Thought," 371–82.

presence in the region. Since 1974, when I was first invited by Don Samuel to come to the diocese, I have been loosely but regularly connected to the grassroots projects of *Teología India* and autochthonous churches in Chiapas.

This Catholic proposal is evolving quietly, offering new insights on faith and how we can live together and sustain the earth as well as respect the plurality of the diverse religious and cultural practices and beliefs present in the area. A fresh Catholic Church, innovative and committed to social justice is emerging. Chiapas is a tiny point on earth, but it is pregnant with hope.[4]

THEOLOGY AS A CONSTELLATION OF PRACTICES: A CEREMONY IN THE FOREST OF CHIAPAS

"O You by whom we live and move, nothing we say here is real. What we say on this earth is like a dream. We only mutter like one waking from sleep..."[5]

"Ipalnemohuani is the God through whom we live"
Netzahualcoyotl (Toltec chief and thirteenth-century poet)[6]

"Tloquenahuaque" is the Lord of close vicinity, del "cerca y del junto"[7]

I arrive having been invited to the mass in celebration of an anniversary of *Universidad de la Tierra* (CIDECI) in San Cristobal de las Casas. The *ermita* (chapel) is full. I can see a crowd gathering at the altar. At the side of the bishop stand the priests that will co-celebrate and beside them, a man and his wife, elderly Tzotzil Mayan people. They are *tunnhel*: deacons. Man and woman as a unit, representing the deacon participation in unity, they incarnate the Mesoamerican concept of "duality," and will contribute as co-ministers in the ceremonial mass. Dressed in their local attire, they stand proudly by the side of the bishop.

The music we hear in this Catholic mass is the ritualistic sacred music of the surrounding indigenous hamlets. We can recognize the structure of the Eucharist, although we could easily be distracted by the splashes of color, the languid repetitious rhythm of indigenous sacred tunes, and the collectivity that ministers the mass. Several priests and ordained indigenous deacons populate the higher space of the chapel. The readers of the Scriptures are women and they read in three languages: Spanish, Tzotzil, and Tzeltal. Who leads the ritual? I would answer: the collectivity.

---

4. Hope is inscribed in the collective ritualization of *Teologia India*. It springs from hope to be respected and accepted as belonging to indigenous collectivities that have been brutally subjected, physically exploited, and discriminated as inferior and primitive due to their particular way of conceiving God, the universe, nature, and themselves.

5. Bierhost, *Cantares Mexicanos*, 170.

6. León-Portilla, *Pre-Columbian Literatures*.

7. León-Portilla, *Aztec Thought and Culture*.

In this very concrete experience, many of the tenets of *Teología India*, and of the project of "autochthonous churches" are perceptible even to an unprepared onlooker as "excerpts of practice." The pastoral work of the Diocese of Chiapas grows and develops ever more towards a respect and recognition of the values, spirituality, devotions, and ritual practices of the region's indigenous peoples. In what follows, I hope to present the epistemic context, dreams as prophecy, myths as history, and indigenous languages as conceptual systems. Not a finished analysis of a stable reality, but a study reflecting the haziness of reality and the process of permanent change.

Colonial Influences

We should be perceptive to the ways in which native peoples adapted to their colonial circumstances, accommodated the Christian hierarchy, and selected, absorbed, and synthesized new ideas and beliefs. On the basis of being a distinct people,[8] they assert a common past, which has been in part suppressed, in part fragmented, by colonialism. They participate in the emergence of a cultural revitalization that reunites the past with the present as a political and religious force. We are witnessing the transformation of indigenous religion itself, not forcedly through conversion and hybridization, and even less through "commodification," but through its own internal processes of metamorphoses and migrations.

The term religion was, according to Jonathan Smith, first ". . . extended to non-Christian examples in the literature of exploration particularly in descriptions of the complex civilizations of Mesoamerica . . ."[9] However, in contrast to the Christianity imported by the Spaniards, indigenous Mayan religious conceptual systems are formed by a complex web of epistemic particularities. Among others, we find concepts of time/place, gender, nature, and self/community embedded in particular cultural perceptions.

The Epistemic Context of Teología India

Knowledge systems pervade our thinking, influence our conceptions of causality, and guide our sensory perceptions. At all times, we are immersed in an epistemic system that organizes the way we conceptualize the material world around us to "fit" this cognitive system.[10] When we approach *Teología India* or *Sabiduría India*, we can discern the underlying cognitive structure, which is intimately bound to indigenous cosmology. Some particularities of these indigenous traditions are: concepts of nature and of the divine in which a merging of transcendence and immanence occurs, a belief in a bidirectional flow of spiritual forces between the realm of the deities and human existence, metaphors as the selected vehicles for conveying hermetic meanings, and beliefs that are *embodied*,

---

8. Warren and Jackson, "Introduction" to *Indigenous Movements*, 13.
9. Smith, "Religion, Religions, Religious," 269–85.
10. Marcos, "Cognitive Structures and Medicine," 87–96.

and thus articulated implicitly rather than explicitly. "The word comes and goes, goes and returns, the word walks... to achieve unity say the indigenous."[11]

Both Pierre Bourdieu and Michel Foucault have written about the quiet way in which an epistemic configuration can operate and express itself. It quietly takes on existence through practices, through actions. The *episteme* is embodied and thus exists. "... actions can supply moments of reinterpretation and reformulation."[12] Belief and thought enact themselves through corporeality. Without physicality, there is no sustenance and foundational reality for ideas, beliefs, thoughts, and especially for *reflections on faith*. Here we can grasp the main tenets of indigenous spirituality and thus of the intercultural project of *Teología India*. We could call it an *embodied theology*.

Its embodied character is also the reason why it is often perceived from the outside as a variable *set of practices*. Samuel Ruiz affirms that "...the indigenous people prefer the term *sabiduría* (wisdom) to theology: *sabiduría india*." He adds, "Theology is systematic, abstract...," (and I could add *disembodied*) "... this abstraction is foreign to the Indians [...], who live a communal life. They nourish themselves from contemplation and reflections on nature, myths, and dreams."[13]

Dreaming as Prophecy

Thinking about the meaning and place of dreams in indigenous Tzotzil communities, Don Samuel adds:

> ... the Acteal local inhabitants who had been displaced from their hamlet,[14] they had decided to return home. But some of them had dreams, premonitions. Actually, it was an old woman and old man and three others. The five of them agreed in interpreting those dreams as an omen. 'This is not the opportune time to return... We cannot go back now.'"[15]

For the local people, dreams are encoded messages. Dreams are communications from wise ancestral protecting spirits. Don Samuel heard the indigenous interpretations; he understood and valued them in their indigenous context. He even called the dreams "prophetic" and advised to follow them.[16] The people did not return to their hamlet at that time.[17]

---

11. "La palabra va y viene, se va y vuelve, la palabra camina... para alcanzar la unidad dicen los indígenas," Gómez, in Ruiz and Torner, *Cómo me convirtieron los indígenas*, 79.

12. Pierre Bourdieu, in Moore, *Passion for Difference*, 155.

13. Marcos, "Semillas del Verbo," 33–59.

14. He (Don Samuel) is referring to the massacre of forty-five people, members of the community of *Las Abejas,* perpetrated by paramilitaries backed by the state government.

15. Marcos, "Semillas del Verbo," 33–59.

16. Marcos, "Semillas del Verbo," 33–59.

17. Although it would be beside the point I am making here, it was the best decision possible at that time and with that situation. In Marcos, "Semillas del Verbo."

Myths Weaving History

Myths are history, a history that gets constructed and reconstructed permanently. Myths are considered facts. Don Samuel tells me about the story of a grain of coffee being given to the peoples there by "el Señor" in the origins of time, to help them in their survival. But it is well known that coffee was brought to the region in the early years of the last century. How to interpret this?

> . . . through a telling or a re-telling of their myths, indigenous people enact a reflection or and "indigenous wisdom" that has been transmitted through their elders . . . the sources from which this presence of God is perceptible spring form within the confines of indigenous culture . . . the reflection which derives from that is not as among us based in philosophy, but rather in mythology. Myth is a form of abstract reflection about things . . .[18]

Paraphrasing Diane Bell, "the body of wisdom often called 'myths' by outsiders, for the Mayans is a matter of fact."[19]

A Debt the Church Should Honor

Don Samuel looks at me challengingly and smiles: "the Gospel did not arrive to America with Christopher Columbus's three caravels. God was here before." One can never overemphasize the importance of indigenous reflection. It initiates a dialogue that never took place in the five hundred years since the first evangelization. A foreign culture was imposed over the indigenous culture in order to express the gospel. There was no reciprocal listening . . . it was not possible to recognize anything positive in a religion that was not Christian . . . . simply, that which was indigenous had no value and had to be eradicated. Only now, after Vatican II are we commencing to correct this serious error.[20]

Samuel often speaks about "how the indigenous converted me."[21] The evident irony of the power inversion implied in this expression, gives a clue into the depth of his commitment to amend the Catholic Church's presence and evangelization in Mexico.

EMBODIED THEOLOGY

I have analyzed one of the main characteristics of Mesoamerican Mayan thought: a thought that is not built on mutually exclusive categories. A thought that does not separate matter from spirit, earth from sky, death from life, a thought that is embodied

---

18. Marcos, "Seeds."
19. Bell, "Desperately," 52–53.
20. Marcos, "Seeds," 3.
21. Ruiz and Torner, *Cómo me convirtieron los indígenas.*

or incarnate.[22] One of its main characteristics is the perception of things in flux, both flowing and "fusing." This notion of a continuous flux between the material and the spiritual, of a permanent oscillation between the two poles of a duality is basic to a deep understanding of the proposals of *Teología India* which can best be perceived as a "constellation of practices."

These practices include not only the rhythms of local indigenous music, the chanting, dancing, and rituals like "el caracol"[23] but also the veneration of deities inside caves, and the rituals on the sacred space on mountain tops. These practices of *Teología India* cannot be fully comprehended by a pastoral work inspired by the conventional Christian strategies of "inculturation" defined as the missionary project of incorporating indigenous music and art into Catholic liturgy.[24] A deeper effort is now taking place. It includes joint reflection on faith, consultation of elders (women and men) considered the bearers of the indigenous religious traditions.

"*Teología India* is a way of reuniting the strength of God, the strength of the elders, and thanks to this strength, confronting conflicts and keeping hope. It is the indigenous themselves who do this work. It is they who speak with the elders."[25] Each community has a group of young indigenous theologians, who speak with the elders who tell them and explain to them the ancient words.

This commitment is far beyond the "preferential option for the poor," one of the basic tenets of liberation theology. Indigenous theology commits itself to respecting the epistemic and philosophical backgrounds of the Mayan cosmos and to building a "theological" perspective in harmony with it. The Christian philosophical religious tradition that came with the missionaries was plagued by a disdain for matter and rejection of earthly dimensions contradictory to the pristine Christian faith in the incarnation. Catholics committed to indigenous wisdom move away from these disincarnate conceptions, to accommodate a universe where earth and matter are sacred, where natural beings express divinity, and where the spiritual and the material are fused.

According to the Mayan vision of the cosmos, human life is intimately connected with its surroundings. All surroundings have life, so they become sacred. We encounter earth, mountains, valleys, caves, plants, animals, stones, water, air, moon, sun, stars, which share in sacredness.[26] In the words of Carlos Camarena, a Jesuit at the Bachajón Mission in Chiapas since 1963: "For the indigenous peoples material and

22. Marcos, "Embodied Religious Thought," 371–82.

23. In ancient Mesoamerica deep seashells were the symbol of new beginning.

24. Gifford, "Nature," 122.

25. "La Teología India es una manera de reunir la fuerza de Dios, la fuerza de los abuelos, y gracias a esta fuerza, hacer frente a los conflictos y conservar la esperanza. Son los propios indígenas los que hacen el trabajo. Son ellos los que hablan con los abuelos." Alicia Gómez, in Ruiz and Torner, *Como me convirtieron los indígenas*, 79.

26. Hunt, *Transformation*.

spiritual realities are the same."²⁷ Eugenio Maurer, a Jesuit parish priest committed to the indigenous populations, says:

> For the people of Guaquitepec all mountains are "alive" in that they are the font of life: they are the site of cornfields; firewood comes from their slopes; springs emerge from them . . . they are the dwelling place of important sacred beings . . . they have power in their own right.²⁸

For Indigenous peoples, the world is not "out there," established outside of and apart from them. It is within them and even "through" them. *Teología India* tells this explicitly. It is not an abstract reflection springing from pure spirit or pure mind. It is grounded, it is practices, actions, rituals and devotions, processions, embroidering, dancing and chanting. All these actions have to be incarnated into bodies which are themselves a vortex of emanations and inclusions from the material as well as the nonmaterial world. As such, carnal bodies are intertwined in the divine and belong to the sacred domain.²⁹

"Here you cannot distinguish between God and the world, between God and his creation."³⁰ Thus, *Teología India* has to be found in the myriad incarnated and corporeal ways by which the indigenous peoples express their beliefs. "The indigenous cultures are characterized by their unity," says Andrés Aubry, and he adds: "unity also between death and life."³¹ Here again, we find the duality and fluid oscillation between opposed and complementary poles.³²

Our Mother Earth Sacred Earth

Frequently we hear indigenous demands for their land and their territory. It seems that this demand is the central claim of all indigenous peoples all over the world. "The survival of native peoples is inextricably linked to land."³³ What do demands for earth and for land mean? For indigenous peoples, there are multiple meanings that can be read into their relationship to the earth. The symbolism of earth as mother ties women to it. They are earth's incarnations and reproducers. Indigenous Mayan Comandanta

---

27. "Para los indígenas las realidades espirituales y materiales son lo mismo," in Ruiz and Torner, *Cómo me convirtieron los indígenas*, 88.

28. Gossen and León-Portilla, *South and Meso-American Spirituality*, 232.

29. Marcos, "Embodied Religious Thought," 371–82.

30. "Aquí no se puede distinguir entre Dios y el mundo, entre Dios y su obra" (Aubry, in Ruiz and Torner, *Cómo me convirtieron los indígenas*, 63). Andres Aubry was a French historian who, since 1974, coordinated and organized the *Archivo Diocesano*/the Archives of the Dioceses of San Cristobal de las Casas.

31. "Las culturas indígenas se caracterizan por su unidad . . . Unidad también entre la muerte y la vida" (Aubry, in Ruiz and Torner, *Cómo me convirtieron los indígenas*, 67).

32. Marcos, *Taken from the Lips*.

33. Smith, "Report."

Esther, addressing Congress, expressed it in the following way: "Queremos que sea reconocida nuestra forma de respetar la tierra y de entender la vida, que es la naturaleza que somos parte de ella" (We want our way of respecting earth and understanding life to be recognized: that it is nature and we are part of her).

In her idiosyncratic Spanish, a very complex concept of earth came through. First earth is a persona. At the National Congress of Indigenous Peoples (2002) in the city of Nurio, Michoacán, an indigenous woman spoke. "Todavía nuestro rio, nuestro árbol, nuestra tierra, están como están . . . . todavía están vivas" (All our rivers, our trees, our earth are as they are, they are still alive).[34] Earth is alive, we must respect her as we respect other beings. Earth is a person.

In much of the Mesoamerican mythology the earth appears as a sacred place.[35] She is a bountiful deity. She is also a place where danger and evil could befall humans who inhabited her. Earth is also a slippery, perilous place.[36] It is conceived within the classic duality of good and evil. As a supernatural being, she could harm or benefit, depending on your deeds or other contextual situations.

The indigenous perspective on earth is an unstable moral one and the moral prescription is that one must act very carefully in all circumstances. As inheritors of ancient spirituality they have developed a vigilant spirituality, characterized more by cautious expectancy than by messianic hope.

Interconnectedness of All Beings: Mode of Being in the World

The "world" for the Mesoamericans was not "out there" established outside of and apart from them. It was within them and even "through" them. Actions and their circumstances were much more imbricated than is the case in Western thought where the "I" can be analytically extracted from its surroundings. Further, the body's porosity reflects an essential porosity of the cosmos, a permeability of the entire "material" world that defines an order of existence characterized by continuous transit between the material and the immaterial. The cosmos emerges literally, in this conceptualization as the complementarity of a permeable corporeality.

Klor de Alba writes that the Mesoamerican peoples "imagined their multidimensional being as an integral part of their body and of the physical and spiritual world around them." He adds that their conceptual being was much less limited than that of the Christians at the time of the conquest and more inclined toward forming "a physical and conceptual continuum with others, with the body and with the world beyond."[37]

---

34. Vera Herrera, "Autonomía."
35. Marcos, *Sacred Earth*.
36. Burckhart, *Slippery Earth*.
37. Klor de Alba, "Contar Vidas," 18.

Indigenous Languages

The conceptual source of *Teología India* springs from local indigenous languages. Aubry affirms that "a language is a conceptual system." As an example he mentions that in Tzotzil, there is no word for the verb *ser*. To take a Spanish "equivalent," let's consider the verb *estar* in its differences with *ser*. *Estar* means "being in relation" to someone else or to a situation or to the natural surroundings (*entorno*). There is no concept of an ontology where a being is conceived by itself, alone, individual, separate.

Teología India is greatly enhanced by the use of terms, meanings, and syntactic turns proper to indigenous Mayan languages. *Teología India* in Chiapas could not be grasped without those languages that provide it with its foundation. The pastoral work of the diocese makes permanent use of one or several of those languages, allowing for their particular conceptual meanings to inform its commitments and work.

Theología India *as an Outcome*

"Teología India is the final result of a pastoral action."[38] *Teología India* and its practices do not stem from a project started by the will of the bishop, the priests, the nuns, and the pastoral agents at the diocese of San Cristobal. They did not sit together to discuss and decide how it had to be done. It is the result of their pastoral approach with indigenous communities, and of their respect and awe for the indigenous religious universes. These indigenous universes are so elusive, so rich, and have been discarded in the past. It is the end result of many years of getting close to the indigenous peoples and communities with an attuned ear, a respectful attention, and a congenial attitude. Especially vital is the attitude of pastoral actors, listening and learning to absorb indigenous epistemic worlds and how to work with and through them. Perhaps hidden is the idea, that I venture here as my own, that the pastoral agents, nuns and priests, and the bishop himself could discover a way of feeling and conceiving God that would also enrich their own.

The Collective Way of Understanding God

Teología India is and must be a collective experience. It is practiced within the collective corporeality and embeddedness of liturgies.[39] Historically, Christianity has a strong communitarian sense, and early Christian assemblies have been a model and are always in the background of our hopes for a better Catholic community. Yet, the indigenous lived experiences of community are grounded in a concept of collectivity

---

38. Kovic, "Maya Catholics," 187–207.

39. This is why Don Samuel was adamant about not allowing me to interview him about *Teología India* on his own. This is why in his book *Cómo me convirtieron los indígenas,* he insisted that several pastoral agents be interviewed alongside him.

hard to understand for the westernized mentality. It is easy to be entranced by the ways we see them acting, living, and believing through community. It stands out as an ideal. Some of the first Catholic missionaries that arrived in the Americas agreed, describing these communitarian ties as "the Christianity of the Indians."[40]

To indigenous peoples, even today, a community is not conceived as a collectivity of individuals, according to the Western scheme exposed by Louis Dumont in his *Essays on Individualism*.[41] For the westernized mentality, a whole (Greek *holon*) is a collection of individuals (Greek *atomoi*); accordingly, Europeans, North Americans, and westernized Mexicans are trapped in an *atomistic holism* that renders notions of the person as node of a network of relations and of one's place in the world as a *topos* in a *cosmos*. For the indigenous Mesoamericans, the full person has always in her/himself parts of the collectivity: the *calpulli*, the *Junta de Buen Gobierno*, the *pueblo*. It means that a part of him/herself belongs to the collectivity of which he is a part. The person is not complete without that part. If it were missing, he or she would experience it as the loss of a "limb" or another vital entity without which he or she lacks integrality and coherence as a person.

The embeddedness of the person in the collective cannot be equated to the consideration of the *ego* as a totally separate individual being, body and soul. With our concepts of the unitary soul or unitary identity or unitary subjectivity, we are unable to approach in depth what collectivity means for the indigenous people. We can only try.

In Catholic faith-based organizations like "Las Abejas" (The Bees), we can detect the kind of communitarianism that pervades the indigenous worlds. Their cellular structure. As in the case of Acteal (municipality of Chenhalo),[42] it allows for maximum flexibility. They are one of the most visible outcomes of the outreach of pastoral work of the diocese. This cellular collective structure enables the constituent organizations to shift arenas, modifying their strategies in response to attacks by the federal and state police and paramilitary forces. It permitted the collective mode of organization to extend to regions. Indigenous peoples in the self-constituted autonomous regions of Northern Chiapas and the Lacandon rainforest as well as bordering hamlets of highland municipalities (*municipios autónomos*) are in fact engaged in the practice of collective autonomy while waiting for the government to implement the San Andrés Accords.

The diocesan pastoral work sustains and builds around these indigenous practices. Spirituality is linked to a communitarian sense in which all beings are interrelated and complement each other.

June Nash affirms, the indigenous people are seeking autonomy in daily practice through *Juntas de buen gobierno,* operating within an indigenous collectivity. Through

---

40. Some of these early colonial sources are Fray Bernardino de Sahagún, Fray Diego Durán, and Motolinía, who admired the collective cohesion and sharing of the local Indigenous peoples they were catechizing.

41. Dumont, *Essays*.

42. As noted, forty-five members of the community of *Las Abejas* were massacred.

the practices of *mandar obedeciendo* (obeying we lead), one could easily think of the early Christian communities being embodied in contemporary practices by these indigenous rebels and their supporters.

FINAL REFLECTIONS

Beyond inculturation, the diocesan pastoral work in Chiapas threads a new path to build a true intercultural dialogue that we may call *Teología India* or *Sabiduría India*. It is based on a constellation of practices, which have to be understood in the context of the interconnection between matter and spirit, of the embodied sacredness of beings, of earth, nature, and humans and on the epistemic philosophical backbone of the indigenous communities. This is the Catholic Church in Chiapas: balancing faith and politics, theology and justice, devotion and rights, mind and bodies, orthodoxy and inculturation.

BIBLIOGRAPHY

Bell, Diane. "Desperately Seeking Redemption." *Natural History* 106 (1997) 52–53.
Bierhost, John, trans. and ed. *Cantares Mexicanos: Songs of the Aztecs*. Stanford: Stanford University Press, 1985.
Burkhart, Louise M. *The Slippery Earth: Nahua-Christian Moral Dialogue in Sixteenth-Century Mexico*. Tuscon: University of Arizona Press, 1989.
Dumont, Louis. *Essays on Individualism*. Chicago: University of Chicago Press, 1992.
Gifford, Paul. "The Nature and Effects of Mission Today: A Case Study from Kenya." *Social Sciences and Missions* 20 (2007) 117–47.
González Casanova, Pablo. "Epistemología del animal político." *La Jornada*, August 2021. https://bit.ly/3ACMAQj.
Gossen, Gary, and Miguel León-Portilla. *South and Meso-American Spirituality: From the Cult of the Feathered Serpent to the Theology of Liberation*. New York: Crossroad, 1997.
Hunt, Eva. *The Transformation of the Hummingbird: Cultural Roots Of a Zinacantecan Mythical Poem*. New York: Cornell University Press, 1977.
Klor de Alva, J. Jorge. "Contar Vidas: La Autobiografía Confesional y la Reconstrucción del Ser Nahua." *Arbor* 515–516 (1988) 49–78.
Kovic, Christine. "Maya Catholics in Chiapas México: Practicing Faith on Their Own Terms." In *Resurgent Voices in Latin America Indigenous Peoples Political Mobilization and Religious Change*, edited by E. L. Cleary and T. J. Steigenga, 187–207. New Brunswick, NJ: Rutgers University Press, 2004.
León-Portilla, Miguel. *Aztec Thought and Culture*. Norman, OK: University of Oklahoma Press, 1990.
———. *Pre-Columbian Literatures of Mexico*. Norman, OK: University of Oklahoma Press, 1969.
Marcos, Sylvia. "Cognitive Structures and Medicine." *Curare* 11 (1988) 87–96.
———. "Embodied Religious Thought: Gender Categories in Mesoamerica." *Religion* 28 (1998) 371–82.

———. "Sacred Earth: Mesoamerican Perspectives." *Concilium* 5 (1995) 27–37.

———. "The Seeds of the Word in Indigenous Wisdom: Interview with D. Samuel Ruiz." English manuscript, translated by Jean Robert. Unpublished, 2001.

———. "Las Semillas del Verbo en la Sabiduría India, interview of Don Samuel Ruiz." *Revista Académica para el Estudio de las Religiones*. Tomo II: Chiapas el Factor Religioso, 33–59. México: Publicaciones para el Estudio Científico de las Religiones, 1998.

———. *Taken from the Lips: Gender and Eros in Mesoamerican Religions*. Boston: Brill Academic, 2006.

Moore, Henrietta. *A Passion for Difference: Essays in Anthropology and Gender*. Bloomington: Indiana University Press, 1994.

Nash, June. *Mayan Visions: The Quest for Autonomy in an Age of Globalization*. New York: Routledge, 2001.

Ruiz, Samuel, and Carlos Torner. *Cómo me convirtieron los indígenas*. España: Sal Terrae, 2002.

Smith, A. "Report on the Native Health and Sovereignty Symposium." *Political Environments* 6 (1998) 32.

Smith, Jonathan. "Religion, Religions, Religious." In *Critical Terms for Religious Studies*, edited by Mark Taylor, 269–85. Chicago: University of Chicago Press, 2004.

Vera Herrera, Ramón. "Autonomía no es independencia, es reconciliación." *La Jornada* March 27, 2001, 4.

Warren, Kay, and Jean E. Jackson, eds. *Indigenous Movements, Self-Representation, and the State in Latin America*. Austin: University of Texas Press, 2002.

SECTION 4

Emerging Theologies from Asia

CHAPTER 13

Indian Theologies

MUTHURAJ SWAMY

At the outset, I must admit that this chapter is on Indian theologies, but it will offer only very brief discussions of some theological approaches. Bringing the numerous and diverse Indian theological scenes into one single chapter is simply not going to be possible. Therefore, I will describe Indian theologies as I see and experience them. My colleagues in India may tell the story differently.

This chapter presents Indian theologies in three sections: theologies that are critical of the empire, questioning and replacing the frameworks and tools developed in the West; theologies that call Indian Christians to actively engage with fellow Christians, their religious neighbors, and with the wider society; and theologies that challenge oppression, and work for the liberation of those marginalized. These are not strictly separate types, and they shape and influence each other.

THEOLOGIES CRITICAL OF THE EMPIRE

Most contemporary Indian Christian theologies have their roots in Hindu and Indian Christian engagement with the West, especially since the nineteenth century. While, Christianity has been in India from first century CE—according to tradition, St. Thomas the apostle came here and was martyred—systematic theological efforts in engaging with the West arose, when modern Christianity, accompanied with Europe's imperial expansions, arrived. Indian engagement with Western theologies generally involved challenging the universalizing tendencies of the West, and its contempt for other cultures and religions. Some original efforts in this regard came from Indians who admired Jesus Christ and his ethical teachings, but were not interested in Christian doctrines or the missionary emphasis on religious conversion.[1] Later, as Indian Christian converts started to interpret the gospel to fellow Indians, they too felt the importance of its Indian interpretations: the Western cultural and philosophical frameworks were often hindrances for communicating the gospel to fellow Indians. They critiqued the "Western captivity of the gospel."

While the indigenous efforts continued into the twentieth century and have shaped and continue to shape much of what happened in the last fifty years or so in Indian theologies, in the last few decades, postcolonial perspectives questioning Western imperialism, and its violence—both physical and epistemic—have helped develop Indian postcolonial theologies challenging the empire.

Indigeneity and Theology: "Indian" Christian Theology

One of the distinctive aspects of Indian Christian theologies is the search for authentic Indian Christian experience and identity, against the totalizing worldviews of Western theologies. For Indian Christians, their identity is both Indian and Christian at the same time. "Indian-hyphenated-Christian," some prefer to call it.[2] This leads to look for theological resources from Indian heritage to make sense of Christian faith in experience, doctrine, worship, and language, among others. Indian Christian theology critiques the Western theologies for their importation of the European culture and philosophy to India, as interpreting the gospel in European frameworks does not work here. As one of the early Indian Christian theologians Sadhu Sundar Singh said, what India needed was "the Water of Life, but not in the European Cup,"[3] which some later theologians have summarized as "the water of life in an Indian cup."[4]

The efforts for theological indigeneity has taken different forms. First, finding common points and synthesis between Christianity and Indian cultural and religious traditions. Some Hindu reformers of the nineteenth century initiated these, and later more joined. They include Ram Mohan Roy, Ramakrishna, Vivekananda, M. K. Gandhi, and S. Radhkrishnan. While emphasizing synthesis of different religious traditions, nevertheless, they had the idea that Hindu systems offer better platforms for such synthesis. Among the Hindu converts to Christianity, K. M. Banerjee,[5] K. C. Sen,[6] and Brahmabandhav Upadhyaya[7] have played significant roles in indigenization

---

1. Sharma, *Neo-Hindu*.
2. Duraisingh, "Indian," 81–101; Sebastian, "Pressure," 27–41.
3. Singh, "Living Christ," 76.
4 Boyd, *Introduction*, 86–109.
5. Banerjea, *From Exclusivism to Inclusivism*; Banerjea, *Dialogues*.
6. Scott, *Keshub*.
7. Lipner, *Brahmabandhab*; Tennent, *Building*. Painadath and Parappally, *Hindu-Catholic*.

of Christianity. Through their lives and works they have argued that being culturally Hindu and religiously Christian is possible.

Second, the use of Indian philosophical and cultural frameworks to interpret Christian doctrines. Sen developed his original theological idea of Trinity as *sat-chit-ananda* (truth-consciousness-bliss). For Upadhyaya, Indian foundation of Christianity should be built on Indian systems, and he chose Advaita. Appasamy,[8] building on Ramanuja's *Vishishta Advaita*, argued that Christianity should be interpreted as *Bhakti marga*, meaning devotion to God. In the early twentieth century Chenchiah[9] and Chakkarai[10] built further on these foundations. As the leader of the Madras Rethinking Group,[11] Chenchiah challenged Hendrik Kraemer at the eve of the second World Missionary Conference in 1938 in Tambaram in current Chennai, for Kraemer's argument, built on Barthian theology, that Christianity replace other religions.[12] These theologians invited others to consider Hindu Scriptures, particularly Vedas, as the Old Testament for India.

Third, the use of local languages. *Brahman* and *Ishwar* were often used for God. Jesus's incarnation was *avatara*, the Holy Spirit *anthararyamin* (in-dweller), salvation *moksha*, *ashram* (hermitage) indigenous form of church, and several others in this direction. Many vernacular Christian traditions also emerged. For instance, Vedanayagam Sastriar's numerous lyrics in Tamil, and N. V. Tilak's poems in Marathi have contributed to indigenization of theology in India.[13]

Fourth, inculturation in church architecture and liturgical traditions. Most important was conceiving an indigenous church in the form of *ashram*. Many Roman Catholics such as Henri le Saux (Abhishiktananda)[14] and Bede Griffiths[15] were involved in this. For them this was a monastic way of life helping with meditation, prayer, and yoga. Among the Protestants, Stanley Jones's *Sattal* Christian Ashram in North India.[16] Often these were seen as places for interreligious engagement, particularly with Hinduism.

Indigenization continued to be significant in post-independent India. Particularly since the 1960s, after Vatican II's openness towards other religions, many Indian

---

8. Appasamy, *Theology*; Appasamy, *Indian*.
9. Thangasamy, *Theology of Chenchiah*.
10. Thomas, *Vengal Chakkarai*.
11. Jathanna, "Madras," 74–97.
12. Chenchiah, "Jesus."
13. Selvanayagam, "Waters," 57–58.
14. Abhishiktananda, *Saccidananda*; Abhishiktananda, *Hindu-Christian*.
15. Griffiths, *Christian Ashram*; Griffiths, *Christ in India*.
16. Jones, *Christ*.

theologians such as Amaladoss,[17] Amalorpavadass,[18] and Panikkar[19] have engaged in this. Protestant theologians such as Devanandan[20] and Samartha[21] also have worked in this direction. No wonder there is now a vast amount of Indian theological literature produced on inculturation.[22]

It is not an exaggeration to say that the Indian theological commitment to indigeneity has impacted almost all other theological developments in India in the last few decades. The criticism of and resistance to the Western frameworks has shaped many theologies, including theologies of dialogue and liberation. However, this has also faced criticisms. One is for its Sanskritic captivity: Indian theological engagements with the West were mostly by elites with Brahmanical backgrounds, mostly excluding other local traditions. Dalit theology emerging in the 1980s vehemently challenged this way of theologizing in India.

Further, some Hindus see Christian indigenization as new ways of converting Hindus. The Indian Christian argument that Christianity is Indian rarely convinces many Hindus, particularly the current extreme Hindu nationalists who continue to attack Christians for their "foreignness."

Another criticism is theologies of inculturation still imitate the Western ways of doing theology. Pointing out the limitations in searching for authentic experience solely in indigenous forms in an increasingly globalized, multicultural, and multireligious world, Sugirtharajah observes that "repeatedly, in the name of indigenization/inculturation, Christian themes such as Incarnation, Atonement and the Trinity were super-imposed on to Hebraic and Hellenistic concepts, in an attempt to force a spurious theological validation, which does not easily emerge organically."[23]

Coloniality and Theology: Postcolonial Theologies

More recently, theologies critical of the West have utilized insights from Edward Said's work *Orientalism*, and similar works challenging the empire. At the center of the criticism is Western hegemony and domination, and Western theologies shaped by imperialism and its violence.

Postcolonial mission theologies challenge many theological assumptions behind the cross-cultural missions which are scattered in the missionary writings: attitudes to mission, church, other religions and cultures. The connections between Christian

---

17. Amaladoss, *Becoming Indian*; Amaladoss, *Beyond Inculturation*.
18. Amalorpavadass, *NBCLC*, 316–29.
19. Panikkar, *Unknown Christ*.
20. Devanandan, *Gospel*.
21. Samartha, *Hindu*.
22. Collins, *Christian Inculturation*.
23. Sugirtharajah, "Postcolonialism," 231.

mission and imperialism is particularly focused.[24] Postcolonial theologies argue for looking at mission not strictly from the perspectives of the Westerners, but also from the perspectives of the recipients of mission, and how in their responses to mission they developed their own theologies.

During the last two decades, postcolonial criticisms in theology in India have been particularly developed by R. S. Sugirtharajah, from Sri Lanka, who has close association with the Indian theological scenes. His focus is specifically in relation to the Bible and its interpretations, and he has published several seminal works on postcolonial critiques of the Bible.[25] Challenging Indian Christians about the different ways colonialism is at work now, and pointing out the lack of proper engagement by Indian Christian theology with colonialism, he sees postcoloniality as being open to multiplicity: "What postcoloniality indicates is that we assume more-or-less fractured, hyphenated, double, or in some cases multiple identities."[26]

Building on his works, postcolonial frameworks have been employed in many Indian theological works, particularly in the area of biblical interpretation. These works critique the power and domination of the empire both in the ancient worlds, and by the modern Europe which continues to affect most of the world.[27]

Postcolonial frameworks are also applied in many theologies of liberation—Dalit, tribal and, womanist—which will be discussed later, which see colonialism as a hegemony and domination in any context, not only in the historical European empire. Thus postcolonialism is about challenging any power and hegemony of any oppressors. Another aspect of postcolonial theology is to identify and challenge the continuing forms of colonialism: neocolonialism found in the capitalistic structures carefully designed to profit the West by shifting resources continuously from the Global South through economic globalization.

Another important development is the colonial constructions of Hinduism as a single religion and its implications for doing theology in India. Today, particularly Hindu nationalistic forces have exploited this for political power, which has thrown challenges to minorities in India. Building on works of scholars in different fields, these theologies invite to resist Hindu nationalism and its dangerous trajectories.[28]

THEOLOGIES CALLING FOR ENGAGEMENT

Another feature of Indian theologies is their emphasis on Indian Christians engaging with their fellow Christians, people of other religions, and in the public square. India's

24. Dharmaraj, *Colonialism*.
25. Among Sugirtharajah's several works, *Bible*; *Postcolonial Criticism*.
26. Sugirtharajah, "Postcolonialism," 235.
27. Joy, *Mark*; Samuel, *Postcolonial*; Lalitha, "Postcolonial," 75–87; Lalitha, "Great Commission," 89–104.
28. Sahayadhas, *Hindu Nationalism*; Swamy, "Christian Missionary," 581–99.

multireligious context, about which the Western theologies had difficulty with generally, has been a dominant shaper of theology in India. What the Sri Lankan theologian Aloysius Pieris said about the Asian context in general—religious plurality and poverty shaping Asian theologies—has a particular significance for India.

Plurality and Theology: Theologies of Dialogue

In India, the context of plurality of religions and traditions is mostly seen as a fertile context for theologizing, rather than something to be rejected.

Ecumenical engagement and theologies are an integral part of Indian Christianity since the beginning of the twentieth century. While the Western missionary societies in India were generally divided due to their different church denominations, sections of Indian Christians worked together for united churches, leading to the formation of the Church of South India in 1947 and the Church of North India in 1970. These initiatives have inspired other churches both in India and beyond, though in the twenty-first century, more work needs to be done on ecumenism, including for the more established churches to be open to growing Pentecostal and independent churches.

Dialogical openness is already found in the efforts for indigenization discussed above. In post-independence India, dialogical theologies were articulated with more urgency for Christians to engage with their neighbors from other religious traditions. P. D. Devanandan,[29] M. M. Thomas,[30] and Stanley Samartha[31] were key figures among the Protestants, and numerous Roman Catholic theologians including Amaladoss,[32] Panikkar, and Pathil[33] have creatively developed these theologies. Particularly, Vatican II opened up new possibilities.[34] Dialogical theologies developed in India have immensely shaped the global context. Samartha set up the interreligious dialogue unit in the World Council of Churches, and was its first director. K. P. Aleaz[35] and Israel Selvanayagam[36] are among many others who have contributed by offering different models and approaches for Christian engagement with other religions.

But theologies of dialogue are not without their critics. Criticisms for indigenization apply here as well. The Hindu traditions these theologians have engaged with are mostly Brahmanical traditions which are challenged by liberation theologies for their oppression of the marginalized. The very roots of Dalit theology are found in its

---

29. Devanandan and Thomas, *Preparation*; Devanandan, *Christian Concern*.
30. Thomas, *Man*; Thomas, *Risking Christ*.
31. Among Samartha's many works are *Courage* and *One Christ*.
32. Among Amaladoss's many works, *Making Harmony*.
33. Pathil, *Religious Pluralism*.
34. Kuttianimattathil, *Practice*.
35. Among Aleaz's several works, "Pluralistic Inclusivism," 265–88.
36. Among Selvanayagam's several works are *Evangelism* and *Dialogue*.

rejection of Indian theologies' engagement with these traditions. This has sometimes led to tensions between theologians of dialogue and theologians of liberation. As part of attempts to find common grounds between these, "a liberation theology of dialogue" has been articulated.

Also, like inculturation, some Hindus suspect that interreligious dialogue is practiced to convert Hindus to Christianity. In fact such fears are justified sometimes, because in some Christian circles—ones more conservative—interreligious dialogue is sometimes used as an evangelization method. For them, if interreligious dialogue doesn't promote evangelism and conversion to Christianity, it needs to be rejected. In the global Christian context too, while many churches and Christian communities have embraced dialogical approaches to other religions in an increasing multireligious contexts, there are criticisms. A fascinating work by Ambrose Mong shows how when it comes to interreligious dialogue, the Vatican has taken a hard approach on theologians of dialogue in India.[37]

In spite of these criticisms, theologies of dialogue continue to flourish. Currently works focus on the importance of everyday religion and grassroot voices in interreligious relations rather than seeing dialogue only through the voices of elite institutions, theologians, and leaders.[38]

Theology and Society: Theologies of Participation

Christian public engagement is another key mark of Indian theologies, particularly in a context when Indian Christians are suspected of foreignness. This has roots in engaging with other religions, but also emerged particularly within the contexts of struggles for Indian independence against European colonialism. Prominent Indian Christian leaders such as K. T. Paul[39] invited Indian Christians to participate in these struggles.

In post-independence India, when the attitudes towards Indian Christians only got harder, the Christian participation in society received further emphasis. The Christian Institute for the Study of Religion and Society (CISRS) invited Christians to participate and contribute to the welfare of the nation. They, together with others, developed theologies of economic development and social justice. Christians building democratic governments and working with secularism, communism, and Marxism rather than sidelining them are key features. This is indeed significant, given the Cold War context in which the "Christian West" saw these as enemies to overcome. The works of Devanandan and M. M. Thomas[40] in CISRS, and Paulose Mar Paulose, who preferred to be called a "secular theologian," are significant.[41]

37. Mong, *Tale*.
38. See Swamy, *Problem*; David, *Beyond Boundaries*.
39. Thomas, *K. T. Paul*.
40. Thomas, *Secular Ideologies*; Devanandan and Thomas, *Christian Participation*.
41. Paulose, *Encounter*.

Theologies of public engagement are significant also because they challenged sections of Indian Christians who generally have an aversion to politics, believing that Christ's kingdom is not of this world. Against this, these theologies critique the isolationism built on the pure otherworldliness of the kingdom of God. Indian theologies of engagement have hugely shaped the contextual and liberation theologies which invite Christians to respond the crises and challenges in this world. This approach is highly important given the current challenges for Christianity in India particularly thrown by Hindu nationalism. These efforts have led to the articulations of political and public theologies in India[42] which contribute to global political theologies.

THEOLOGIES CHALLENGING EXCLUSION

The third group of Indian theologies are those that challenge exclusion. These focus on socio-economic exploitations, discrimination, and oppression experienced by marginalized groups. They challenge the power structures and domination in the contexts of the caste system, patriarchy, government policies that put marginalized groups into more suffering, state violence, and corporate greed, among many others. They invite people to reimagine theologizing and explore new perspectives and methods in doing theology.

Marginality and Theology: Liberation Theologies

Dalit theology emerged in India in the 1980s in the context of marginalization experienced by Dalit people and communities for centuries. The term *Dalit* means broken and destroyed, and is used as a self-identity of people kept outside the caste system for ages. Influenced by worldwide liberation theologies, and experiences of Dalits in India as discrimination and violence against them continued and increased, Dalit theology brought new and creative ways of thinking about God, salvation, and hermeneutics.

Working for Dalit liberation through Dalit literature and many Dalit movements goes back to many decades, with huge influence from B. R. Ambedkar in the post-independent India who worked on Dalit empowerment, and Dalit theology, utilizing these developments, emerged as a creative form of theologizing in the Indian context. It sees the inhumane experiences and violence faced by Dalits as important sources of theologizing. There has been affirmative action by the Indian government, set up in post-independence India, but this has improved Dalits' lives very little. Dalit Christians are exempted from the affirmative action, and in spite of their struggles for the last seven decades, this has not changed. Worst of all, the caste system has crept into the Indian church in many areas, and this has added only more marginalization for Dalit communities.

---

42. Patrick, *Public Theology*.

Dalit theology is based on the liberator God who is on the side of the oppressed against the oppressors. The Exodus experience of the Hebrew people, and the Nazareth manifesto are often reflected biblical texts, and during the last four decades many such texts with liberation motifs have been articulated by Dalit theologians. Dalit theology emphasizes Dalit dignity and Dalit identity. In the context of violence, Dalit bodies are at the center of theological articulations. Some prominent Dalit theologians include A. P. Nirmal,[43] M. Azariah,[44] M. E. Prabhakar,[45] James Massey,[46] V. Devasahayam[47] and Sathianathan Clarke,[48] Bama,[49] and Felix Wilfred.[50]

Dalit theology is highly critical of Indian theology's Sanskritic captivity, and has developed a hermeneutic of liberation, theologizing through oral traditions, stories, songs, dance and many other folk forms of religion. Some younger generation of Dalit theologians working currently on Dalit theology are Y. T. Vinayaraj,[51] Joseph Prabjakar Dayam,[52] Peniel Rajkumar,[53] Anderson Jeremiah,[54] Jayachitra Lalitha, and Joshua Samuel.[55]

Tribal and Adivasi theologies take place in the context of the plights of the tribal people found mainly in central India and in northeast India, and more recently Adivasi theologies have focused on people scattered in all parts of India.

Central to tribal theology is land, and tribal people's integral connection with it and the ways their identities are shaped by it: their culture, religion, spirituality, and belief in God cannot be conceived without it. But due to various actors, their community, identity, and access to land are often denied and crushed. States and corporations seek to destroy their lives and identities in the name of development. Several government laws promote violence against tribal communities, alienate them from their land, and break their identities. State violence against them in many parts of northeast India increase by keeping Indian military presence to fight insurgency.

This alienation to the land and misery surrounding the displacement form the basis of tribal theology. Community and egalitarian principles such as love, justice,

---

43. Nirmal, *Heuristic Explorations;* Nirmal, "Towards a Christian," 27–40; Nirmal, *Reader;* Nirmal, *Towards a Common.*

44. Azariah, *Pastor's Search.*

45. Prabhakar, *Towards.*

46. Massey, *Roots;* Massey, *Towards;* Massey and Fernando, *Dalit World;* Massey and Prabhakar, *Frontiers.*

47. Devasahayam, *Dalit and Women;* Devasahayam, *Frontiers.*

48. Clarke, *Dalits;* Clarke et al., *Dalit Theology.*

49. Faustina, *Karukku;* Christopher, "Between Two Worlds," 7–25.

50. Wilfred, *Dalit;* Wilfred, *Margins-Site.*

51. Vinayaraj, *Re-imagining;* Vinayaraj, *Dalit Theology.*

52. Dayam, *Re-Imagining.*

53. Rajkumar, *Dalit Theology.*

54. Jeremiah, *Community.*

55. Samuel, *Untouchable Bodies.*

peace, harmony, and care for each other which are hallmarks of the tribal societies are important for tribal theology. It questions the negative treatment of tribal indigenous religions by Christian missionaries and modernization forces, and encourage an engagement with such traditions. Recently as Hindu nationalism is enforcing Sanskritization in these communities, tribal theology articulates ways to challenge them.

Nirmal Minz[56] is a tribal theologian in India focusing on tribal communities in central and north India. In the northeast, as the tribal communities are not a homogenized community, but consists of several tribes, tribal theologizing takes place in several ways. Some tribal theologians working in this context include Wati Longchar,[57] Thanzauva,[58] S. Shimray,[59] Razouselie Lasetso,[60] and Yangkahao Vashum.[61] Many tribal womanist theologians like L. Longkumer and Chungi Hrangthan add their unique voices by specifically bringing their perspectives.[62]

Adivasi theologies focus on the brokenness of indigenous peoples scattered in all parts of India due to exploitations and displacement. Against preconceived notions that Adivasis are primitive and so need modernization, theologies focus on distinct Adivasi traditions and resources. Adivasi resistance and resilience against the alienating forces is central to Adivasi theologies. Built on the integral nature of their lives, the liberative aspects of their community lives are celebrated.

Feminist/womanist theology works in the context of the oppression and exploitation of women in patriarchal structures and systems. In India, on the one hand, owing to some Hindu and folk religious beliefs in the powerful consorts of gods—Parvathi, Saraswathi, Lakshmi—and belief in fierce and powerful goddesses such as Durga and Kali, women are revered as *Shakti*. Women contribute to family and community equally like men, more so in many circumstances. However, on the other hand, women are marginalized and face many discriminations and abuses including female infanticide, sexual abuse, trafficking, lack of education, exclusion from public lives, the dowry system, domestic violence, sexual division of labor, and lack of representation, despite government affirmative actions. Among already marginalized communities such as Dalits and tribes, women are doubly and triply marginalized on account of gender, class, and caste/tribe.

Among Christians, the situation is similar. Women contribute to church and communities immensely. They work to support the church and are involved in mission in different capacities, including fundraising, caring for the needy, visiting the sick and the bereaved, and praying with them. Yet, they are mostly excluded. Ordination

56. Minz, "Cultural Identity," 21–25.
57. Longchar, *Traditional*; Longchar, *Encounter*; Longchar and Davis, *Doing Theology*.
58. Thanzauva, *Towards*; Thanzauva, *Theology*.
59. Shimray, *Introducing*; Shimray, *Tribal Theology*.
60. Lasetso and Vashum, *Tribal*; Lasetso, *Garnering*; Lasetso et al., *In Search*; Vashum, *Christology*.
61. Vashum, *Tribal Theology*; Vashum, *Christology*.
62. Hrangthan, *Theologizing*. Longkumer, *No More*.

of women in the church, though a reality now, still has a long way to go, as women are generally excluded from leadership and decision-making.

Feminist theology challenges the exclusion and exploitation of women. Aruna Gnanadason,[63] Prasanna Kumari,[64] Gabriele Dietrich,[65] Evangeline Anderson-Rajkumar,[66] L. Hnuni,[67] Narola Imchen,[68] Elizabeth Joy,[69] Lalrinawmi Ralte,[70] and Limatulla Longkumer[71] are some working on this. As well as pointing to the continuous plight of women in India, they highlight the leadership roles in church and communities women are already offering. Some theologians employ critical insights from other liberation theologies and frameworks such as postcolonialism that challenge power.[72] Many of them emphasize womanist theology to work with other religions and women's movements, bringing together resources on liberation. The connection between the liberation of women and creation is a key feature of womanist theology. It is committed to holistic theology: working not just for women, but for the liberation of the whole of humanity—women, men, children, indigenous, local, and tribal communities, and creation: a "total liberation."[73]

Eco-theologies in India, also known as green theology, like in other parts of the world, call for the protection of environment against the onslaught of it. The predominantly rural nature of Indian society adds particular significance. They challenge multinational corporations, mostly run by the West, capitalism, and its power structures, government inaction in many contexts which are responsible for the destruction of the earth.

Central to eco-theologies are the organic relationships between the divine, humans, and nature. They offer new ways of reading the Bible to challenge its traditional interpretations about male dominion over everything else. They emphasize peace with God, with other communities, and with nature.

Eco-theologies point out the ways environmental crises particularly affect the poor, the marginalized, women and children, and tribal and indigenous people. The irony is that while these are the people who are affected most, they are also the ones who depend most on the earth, and who contribute most to safeguard it.[74] Eco-

---

63. Gnanadason, *Towards*; Gnanadason, *No Longer*.
64. Kumari, *Reader*; Kumari, *Feminist Theology*.
65. Dietrich, *New Thing*; Dietrich, *Women's Movement*.
66. Anderson-Rajkumar, "Politicising the Body," 100–102.
67. Hnuni, *Vision*.
68. Imchen, *Women in Church*; Imchen, *Women's Issues*.
69. Joy, *Lived Realities*.
70. Ralte, *Women*; Ralte and Anderson-Rajkumar, *Feminist Hermeneutics*; Ralte et al. *Envisioning*.
71. Longkumer, *No More Sorrows*; Longkumer and Longkumer, *Side by Side*.
72. Sebastian, "Implications," 82–99.
73. Gnanadason, "Women," 740–41.
74. Longchar and Vashum, *Tribal Worldview*.

theologies call for a spirituality based on earth-care. They underscore the need for garnering together the religious resources from other religious traditions and secular movements. Some working on eco-theologies include Anand Veeraraj,[75] George Matthew Nalunakkal,[76] V. J. John,[77] and George Zachariah.[78]

More recently liberation theologies focus on human health and disability. In the context of the worldwide HIV/AIDS crisis, particularly affecting people in the poorest parts of the world, theologies have highlighted the need to overcome stigma associated with these and wholeness and healing for all.[79] Theology of disability focuses on the marginalization of people with disabilities, and their voices in theologizing. Pointing to the healing in the Bible, and what Jesus did for those suffering with various sicknesses and disability, they invite everyone to contribute to wholeness for all. Samuel George[80] has offered significant theological articulation on this. Similarly, child theology calls for attention to the marginalization of children in many contexts in India, and Rohan Gideon is a key theologian working on this currently.[81] Highlighting many issues faced by children such as female infanticide, sexual abuse, child labor, child marriage, and street life, child theology calls to work against these, mainly learning from the ways Jesus dealt with the children around him.[82]

CONCLUSION

Let me conclude this chapter with three of my observations. First, most theologies discussed above are theologies by elite theologians. They do involve lived realities, nevertheless, mostly articulated by trained theologians. While these are important, and India needs more theologizing, nevertheless, the huge amount of theologizing done by ordinary Christians in their everyday lives needs a focus. From indigenization to interreligious dialogue to public engagement to liberation theologies, there are so many voices. The twenty-first-century Indian theologians and theologies need to see that these voices are heard even if in their messy and untidy forms. Second, there are already critical mutual enrichments of Indian theologies which need to continue in creative ways. Many interfaces between these theologies are identified and reflected. Each theology can offer a critique of the other, as well as learn critical insights from each other. This also means that each theology needs to be self-critical where

---

75. Veeraraj, *Green*.
76. Nalunakkal, *Green Liberation*.
77. John, *Ecological Vision*.
78. Zachariah, *Alternatives*.
79. Prabhakar and Nalunnakkal, *HIV/AIDS*; Kambodji, *HIV*; Lasetso, *Health and Life*; Kuruvilla and Longchar, *HIV/AIDS*.
80. George, "God," 454–62; "Voices," 96–103.
81. Gideon, *Child Labor*; "Migrant," 347–54.
82. Jeyaraj, *Children*.

necessary, especially in areas where the "other" is excluded. The womanist theology's commitment to total liberation of humanity and creation is a great insight here. Third, Indian theologies need to continue to seek to enlarge their boundaries, both by exploring more partners and by contributing to theologies in the global context. Critical engagement with, rather than a complete rejection of, the West, as well as exploring more avenues for engaging with theologies in the other parts of the Global South, especially East Asia, Africa, Latin America, and the Middle East, among others, is indeed a timely necessity in today's context of world Christianity.

BIBLIOGRAPHY

Abhishiktananda (Swami). *Hindu-Christian Meeting Point*. Delhi: ISPCK, 1976.
———. *Saccidananda*. London: SPCK, 1974.
Aleaz, K. P. "Pluralistic Inclusivism: A Viable Indian Theology of Religions." *Asia Journal of Theology* 12 (1998) 265–88.
Amaladoss, Michael. *Becoming Indian*. Rome: CIIS, 1992.
———. *Beyond Inculturation*. Delhi: Vidyajyoti/ISPCK, 1998.
———. *Making Harmony*. Delhi: ISPCK, 2003.
Amalorpavadass, D. S. *NBCLC Campus*. Bangalore: NBCLC, 1982.
Anderson-Rajkumar, Evangeline. "Politicising the Body." *Asia Journal of Theology* 8 (2004) 100–102.
Appasamy, A. J. *An Indian Interpretation of Christianity*. Madras: CLS, 1924.
———. *The Theology of Hindu Bhakti*. Madras: CLS, 1970.
Azariah, M. *A Pastor's Search for Dalit Theology*. Delhi: ISPCK, 2000.
Baago, K. *Pioneers of Indigenous Christianity*. Madras: CLS, 1969.
Banerjea, K. M. *Dialogues on the Hindu Philosophy*. London: CLS, 1903.
———. *From Exclusivism to Inclusivism*. 2 vols. Delhi: ISPCK, 1998.
Boyd, Robin. *An Introduction to Indian Christian Theology*. Madras: CLS, 1969.
Chenchiah, P. "Jesus and Non-Christian Faiths." In *Rethinking Christianity in India*, edited by Siga Aries. Ebook. Madras: Sudarisanam, 1938.
Christopher, K. W. "Between Two Worlds." *Journal of Commonwealth Literature* 47 (2012) 7–25.
Clarke, Sathianathan. *Dalits and Christianity*. Delhi: Oxford University Press, 1998.
———, et al. *Dalit Theology in the Twenty-first Century*. Delhi: Oxford University Press, 2010.
Collins, Paul. *Christian Inculturation in India*. London: Ashgate, 2007.
David, Maria. *Beyond Boundaries*. Delhi: ISPCK, 2009.
Dayam, J. P. *Re-Imagining an Indian Theology of the Cross Using Dalit Cultural Resources*. Ann Arbor: ProQuest, 2011.
Devanandan, P. D., and M. M. Thomas, eds. *Christian Participation in Nation-Building*. Bangalore: CISRS, 1960.
Devanandan, P. D. *Christian Concern in Hinduism*. Bangalore: CISRS, 1961.
———. *The Gospel and the Hindu Intellectual*. Bangalore: CISRS, 1959.
———. *Preparation for Dialogue*. Bangalore: CISRS, 1964.
Devasahayam, V., ed. *Dalit and Women*. Madras: Gurukul, 1992.
———. *Frontiers of Dalit Theology*. Delhi: ISPCK, 1997.

Dharmaraj, Jacob. *Colonialism and Christian Mission*. Delhi: ISPCK, 1993.
Dietrich, Gabriele. *A New Thing on Earth*. Delhi: ISPCK, 2001.
———. *Women's Movement in India*. Bangalore: Breakthrough, 1988.
Duraisingh, Christopher. "Indian Hyphenated Christians and Theological Reflections: A New Expression of Identity." *Religion and Society* 27 (1980) 81–101.
Faustina, Bama. *Karukku*. Translated by L. Holmström. New Delhi: Oxford University Press, 2012.
George, Samuel. "God of Life and Justice." *Ecumenical Review* 64 (2012) 454–62.
———. "Voices and Visions from the Margins on Mission and Unity." *International Review of Mission* 100 (2011) 96–103.
Gideon, Rohan. *Child Labor in India*. Delhi: ISPCK, 2016.
———. "Migrant and Refugee Children." *Theology* 120 (2017) 347–54.
Gnanadason, Aruna. *No Longer a Secret*. Geneva: WCC, 1993.
———, ed. *Towards a Theology of Humanhood*. Delhi: ISPCK, 1989.
———. "Women and Church in South Asia." In *Oxford Encyclopedia of South Asian Christianity*, edited by Roger Hedlund, 740. Oxford: Oxford University Press, 2012.
Griffiths, Bede. *Christian Ashram*. London: Darton, Longman & Todd, 1966.
———. *Christ in India*. Bangalore: ATC, 1986.
Hnuni, R. L. *Vision for Women in India*. Bangalore: ATC, 2009.
Hrangthan, Chungi. *Theologizing Tribal Heritage*. Delhi: ISPCK, 2008.
Imchen, Narola. *Women in Church and Society*. Jorhat: WSC, 2001.
———, ed. *Women's Issues in the 21st Century*. Jorhat: Barkataki, 2001.
Jathanna, O. V. "The Madras Rethinking Group." *Religion and Society* 44 (1997) 74–97.
Jeremiah, Anderson. *Community and Worldview Among Paraiyars of South India*. London: Bloomsbury, 2013.
Jeyaraj, Jesudason ed. *Children at Risk*. Bangalore: CFCD, 2009.
John, V. J. *The Ecological Vision of Jesus*. Tiruvalla: CSS-BTTBPSA, 2002.
Jones, E. Stanley. *The Christ of the Indian Road*. Nashville: Abingdon, 1925.
Joy, David. *Mark and Its Subalterns*. London: Equinox, 2014.
Joy, Elizabeth. *Lived Realities*. Bangalore: CISRS, 1999.
Kambodji, Alphinus, et al. *HIV and Inclusive Community*. Changmai: CCA, 2013.
Kim, Kirsteen "India." In *An Introduction to Third World Theologies*, edited by John Parratt, 44–73. Cambridge: Cambridge University Press, 2004.
Kumari, Prasanna, ed. *Feminist Theology*. Chennai: GLTC, 1999.
———, ed. *A Reader in Feminist Theology*. Madras: Gurukul, 1993.
Kuruvilla, Philip, and Wati Longchar, eds. *HIV/AIDS: Towards Inclusive Communities: A Theological Reader*. Nagpur: NCCI, 2013.
Kuttianimattathil, Jose. *Practice and Theology of Interreligious Dialogue*. Bangalore: Kristy Jyoti College, 1998.
Lalitha, Jayachitra. "The Great Commission." In *Teaching All Nations*, edited by Mitzi Smith et al., 89–104. Philadelphia: Fortress, 2014.
———. "Postcolonial Feminism, The Bible and the Native Indian Women." In *Evangelical Postcolonial Conversations*, edited by Kay Huguera Smith et al., 75–87. Downers Grove, IL: InterVarsity, 2014.
Lasetso, Razouselie, ed. *Garnering Tribal Resources for Doing Tribal Theology*. Jorhat: ETC, 2008.
———, ed. *Health and Life*. Jorhat: ETC, 2007.

Lasetso, Razouselie, et al., eds. *In Search of Peace.* Jorhat: ILEMA, 2013.
Lasetso, Razouselie, and Yangkahao Vashum, eds. *Tribal Christian Theology.* Jorhat: ETC, 2007.
Lipner, Julius. *Brahmabandhab Upadhvaya.* Delhi: Oxford University Press, 1999.
Longchar, W. A., ed. *Encounter between Gospel and Tribal Culture.* Jorhat: TSC, 1999.
———. *The Traditional Tribal World View and Modernity.* Jorhat: ETC, 1995.
Longchar, W. A., and Larry Davis, eds. *Doing Theology with Tribal Resources.* Jorhat: TSC, 1999.
Longchar, W. A., and Yangkahao Vashum, eds. *Tribal Worldview and Ecology.* Jorhat: TSC, 2008.
Longkumer, Limatula, ed. *No More Sorrows in the Garden of Justice.* Jorhat: WSD, 2007.
Longkumer, Limatula, and Talijungla Longkumer, eds. *Side by Side.* Jorhat: CCA-EGY, 2004.
Massey, James. *Roots: A Concise History of the Dalits.* Delhi: ISPCK, 1991.
———. *Towards a Dalit Hermeneutics.* Delhi: ISPCK, 1994.
Massey, James, and Leonard Fernando, eds. *Dalit World, Biblical World.* Delhi: Vidyajyoti, 2005.
Massey, James, and Samson Prabhakar, eds. *Frontiers in Dalit Hermeneutics.* Bangalore/Delhi: ISPCK, 2005.
Minz, Nirmal. "Cultural Identity of Tribals in India." *Social Action* 43 (1994) 21–25.
Mong, Ambrose. *A Tale of Two Theologians.* Cambridge: James Clarke, 2017.
Nalunnakkal, George. *Green Liberation.* Delhi: ISPCK, 1999.
Nirmal, A. P. *Heuristic Explorations.* Madras: CLS, 1990.
———, ed. *A Reader in Dalit Theology.* Madras: Gurukul, 1990.
———. "Towards a Christian Dalit Theology." In *Frontiers in Asian Christian Theology,* edited by R. S. Sugirtharajah, 27–40. Maryknoll, NY: Orbis, 1994.
———, ed. *Towards a Common Dalit Theology.* Madras: Gurukul, 1990.
Painadath, Sebastian, and Jacob Parappally, eds. *A Hindu-Catholic.* Bangalore: ATC, 2008.
Panikkar, Raimundo. *The Unknown Christ of Hinduism.* London: Darton, Longman & Todd, 1964.
Pathil, Kuncheria, ed. *Religious Pluralism.* Delhi: ISPCK, 1999.
Patrick, Gnana. *Public Theology.* Philadelphia: Fortress, 2020.
Paulose, Paulose Mar. *Encounter in Humanization.* Tiruvalla: CSS, 2000.
Prabhakar, M. E., ed. *Towards a Dalit Theology.* Bangalore: CISRS, 1988.
Prabhakar, Samson, and George Nalunnakkal, eds. *HIV/AIDS.* Bangalore: BTESSC/SATHRI, 2004.
Rajkumar, Peniel. *Dalit Theology and Dalit Liberation.* London: Ashgate, 2010.
Ralte, Lalrinawmi. *Women Re-shaping Theology.* Bangalore: UTC, 1998.
Ralte, Lalrinawmi, and Evangeline Anderson-Rajkumar, eds. *Feminist Hermeneutics.* Delhi: ISPCK, 2002.
Ralte, Lalrinawmi, et al. *Envisioning a New Heaven and a New Earth.* Delhi: NCCI, 1998.
Sahayadhas, R. *Hindu Nationalism and the Indian Church.* Delhi: CWI, 2013.
Samartha, S. J. *Courage for Dialogue.* Geneva: WCC, 1981.
———. *The Hindu Response to the Unbound Christ.* Madras: CLS, 1974.
———. *One Christ Many Religions.* Geneva: WCC, 1996.
Samuel, Joshua. *Untouchable Bodies, Resistance, and Liberation.* Leiden: Brill, 2020.
Samuel, Simon. *A Postcolonial Reading of Mark's Story of Jesus.* Edinburgh: T. & T. Clark, 2007.

Scott, David, ed. *Keshub Chunder Sen*. Madras: CLS, 1979.
Sebastian, Jayakiran. "Pressure on the Hyphen." *Religion and Society* 44 (1997) 27–41.
Sebastian, Mrinalini. "Implications of Postcolonial Thinking for Feminist Praxis in India." In *Feminist Theology*, edited by Prasanna Kumari, 82–99. Chennai: GLTS, 1999.
Selvanayagam, Israel. *A Dialogue on Dialogue*. Madras: CLS, 1995.
———. *Evangelism and Inter-faith Dialogue*. Birmingham: Selly Oak Colleges, 1993.
———. "Waters of Life and Indian Cups." In *Christian Theology in Asia*, edited by Sebastian Kim, 41–70. Cambridge: Cambridge University Press, 2008.
Sharma, Arvind. *Neo-Hindu Views of Christianity*. Leiden: Brill, 1988.
Shimray, S. *Introducing Theological Ethics*. Jorhat: PBC, 2011.
———, ed. *Tribal Theology*. Jorhat: TSC, 2003.
Singh, Sadhu Sundar. "The Living Christ." In *Readings in Indian Christian Theology*, edited by R. S. Sugirtharajah and Cecil Hargreaves, 1:73–77. Delhi: ISPCK, 1993.
Sugirtharajah, R. S., ed. *The Bible and Postcolonialism*. Sheffield: Sheffield Academic, 1998.
———. *Postcolonial Criticism and Biblical Interpretation*. Oxford: Oxford University Press, 2002.
———. "Postcolonialism and Indian Christian Theology." *Studies in World Christianity* 5 (1999) 229–40.
Sumithra, Sunand. *Christian Theology from an Indian Perspective*. Bangalore: TBT, 1990.
Swamy, Muthuraj. "Christian Missionary Constructions of Hinduism." In *The Oxford Handbook of Mission Studies*, edited by Kirsteen Kim et al., 581–599. Oxford: Oxford University Press, 2022.
———. *The Problem with Interreligious Dialogue*. London: Bloomsbury, 2016.
Tennent, T. *Building Christianity on Indian Foundations*. Delhi: ISPCK, 2000.
Thangasamy, D. A. *The Theology of Chenchiah*. Bangalore: CISRS, 1966.
Thanzauva, K. *Theology of Community*. Aizawl: AICS, 2004.
———. *Towards A Tribal Theology*. Jorhat: MTC, 1989.
Thomas, Joseph. *K. T. Paul*. Serampore: Senate of Serampore, 1976.
———. *Man and the Universe of Faiths*. Bangalore: CISRS, 1975.
———. *Risking Christ for Christ's Sake*. Geneva: WCC, 1987.
———. *Secular Ideologies of India and the Secular Meaning of Christ*. Bangalore/Madras: CISRS/CLS, 1976.
Thomas, M. M., and P. T. Thomas. *Towards an Indian Christian Theology*. Tiruvalla: New Day, 1992.
Thomas, P. T. *Vengal Chakkarai*. Madras: CLS, 1981.
Vashum, Yangkahao. *Christology in Context*. Delhi: CWI, 2017
———, ed. *Tribal Theology and the Bible*. Jorhat: TSC, 2011.
Veeraraj, Anand. *Green History of Religion*. Bangalore: Centre for Contemporary Christianity, 2006.
Vinayaraj, Y. T. *Dalit Theology After Continental Philosophy*. New York: Palgrave Macmillan, 2016.
———. *Re-imagining Dalit Theology*. Tiruvalla: CSS, 2008.
Wilfred, Felix. *Dalit Empowerment*. Delhi: 1SPCK, 2008.
———. *Margins-Site of Asian Theologies*. Delhi: ISPCK, 2008.
Zachariah, George. *Alternatives Unincorporated*. London: Equinox, 2015.

CHAPTER 14

Filipino Theology

ELEAZAR S. FERNANDEZ

Out of the depths of the Filipino people's rich and challenging life experiences have emerged theological articulations that speak of their understanding of who they are, their plight, their hopes, and their journey toward a new and better tomorrow, and various approaches or ways of doing and articulating theology. These approaches are not exclusive. Instead, they manifest varied contexts, interests, and expressions, which mutually inform and enrich each other. They come in various theological genres, such as popular religiosity or folk Christianity and liberation theology, including the theology of struggle, feminist-*babaylan* theology, theology of inculturation, and indigenous theology.

A WAY OF DOING CONTEXTUAL THEOLOGY

Filipino theology is an expression of a theological movement known as contextualization. As an explicitly contextual theology, one cannot do Filipino theology without being intentionally attentive to the Philippine context and the Filipino people's cultural idioms. Here, contextualization is understood not simply as a mode of communication (finding cultural vehicles for the universal and essential Christian gospel) but a mode of apprehending the world. This way of understanding contextualization does not simply see the context as a stage or a passive receiver of the social agent's action; instead, the context is active in informing and shaping the agent's interpretation of the world. To engage in theological construction, the theologian must not limit herself or himself to appropriating cultural media from her or his context but must discern and articulate the theological message in and through the complexities of the context. There is no theological message apart from context. This makes the discernment and articulation of the theological message fraught with danger but a necessary task for those who seek to do contextual theology.

The birth of Filipino theology cannot be separated from the nationalist struggles of the once colonized nation from imperializing powers. Following this line of thought, a Filipino way of doing theology can only be anti-imperial as well as anti-colonial in sentiment and must be committed to the liberation of the colonized, marginalized, and diasporized subalterns. Its direction is liberation not only of the Filipino people but also of the subjugated and exploited earth. Because the Filipino is not a generic whole but is composed of real flesh-and-blood people with varied gender, sexuality, and ethnic identities that intersect, it is important that this theology be attentive to the plight and voices of those minoritized by such constructed categories. These include the voices of women, children, LGBTQ+ people, and the indigenous people of the land (*Lumads*).

Caught in the vortex of imperial geopolitics, a postcolonial discourse is a critical lens for doing Filipino theology. Postcolonial criticism offers help in making the "Critical Asian Principle" be critical enough, which applies to the Philippines, being a part of Asia.[1] The post in postcolonial, which is not identical to the formal event of decolonization and independence, provides critical discursive ammunition for the critical principle. Postcolonial critique of power exposes hegemonic categories and ways of seeing, whether embodied in the Global North's discourse or by citizens of the Global South. Employing contrapuntal reading and the musical strategy of fugue, postcolonial criticism alerts us to muted voices in the text and it equips us to read simultaneously the imperial imprint and the spirit of resistance.[2] Also, the post in postcolonial subverts any easy and lousy identification of what is called "distinctively Asian" or "distinctively Filipino" within the bounded space of national boundaries.

Pursuing postcolonial criticism, the Philippines as the context for theological reflection should be viewed in a much broader sense. There is no such thing as the Philippine context apart from the wider context of which it is a part. This context cannot be properly understood apart from its connection to the wider context. The choice of the Philippine context is more a matter of focus and not a way of sealing it off from the rest of the world. A physical boundary defines the Philippines, but what makes the Philippines and what makes a Filipino are shaped by forces beyond its geographic boundaries. This means that the context that shapes Filipino theology is not confined to its geographic boundary, much more so in the era of globalization.

Furthermore, the Filipino is not only the one who is physically present in the Philippines but wherever Filipinos are and wherever discourses about the Philippines are happening, especially as we think of the ever-growing Filipino diaspora. Also, the

---

1. http://atesea.net/accreditation/doing-theologies-in-asia/.
2. Said, *Musical Elaborations*.

Philippine context must be understood in a dynamic sense. Attempts to trace the truly Filipino by rooting it in its ancient and indigenous expression do not do justice to the dynamic character of the ever-changing Filipino context and Filipino identity.

DISCERNING THE DIVINE SPIRIT IN THE PHILIPPINE CONTEXT

From a theological point of view, we cannot say that we know God if we do not know our context; conversely, we know our context if we know God. This is based on the understanding that God's presence is mediated through the world. In this case, understanding one's context is not a prolegomenon to theology but an integral part of doing theology.

Given the history and the challenges that the Filipino people have faced up to the present, some salient features that have given shape and hue to Filipino theological articulation can be identified. Depending on one's hermeneutical lens, Filipino theology is a theology that springs from the history of suffering of the Filipino people and their longings and struggles for a new and better tomorrow. Why this history of suffering and struggles for a better tomorrow?

In the wider background, the Philippines has a long history of colonization. One cannot continue theologizing without taking account of this. From the early beginnings of the formation of the Filipino nation, the narrative fabric of suffering started to take shape because of the so-called "liberation" projects of the colonial masters and their local allies. The Filipino people are among the most "liberated" people in the world, says the nationalist Filipino historian Renato Constantino. As he puts it:

> First came the Spaniards who "liberated" them from the "enslavement of the devil," next came the Americans who "liberated" them from Spanish oppression, then the Japanese who "liberated" them from American imperialism, then the Americans again who "liberated" them from the Japanese fascists. After every "liberation," they found their country occupied by foreign "benefactors."[3]

Unfortunately, the religion that carried the name of the one who was crucified by the imperial power of his time played a crucial part, wittingly or unwittingly, in the subjugation and colonization and continuing suffering of the Filipino people. The cross came along with the swords and cannons of the *conquistadores* as the Bible came along with the guns of modern imperializing nations. Mission and colonization were inseparable: to colonize was to missionize, and to missionize was to colonize.[4]

The missionaries and the Bible played an important role in the colonizing project and taming the people's minds. Christian imperial scripturism came along with the rise of Western imperial powers. The British and the Foreign Bible Society took the

---

3. Constantino, *Philippines*, 1:12.
4. Bosch, *Transforming Mission*, 303.

axiom seriously both theologically and politically: "Protestants without Bibles are soldiers without weapons, ready neither for conquest nor for defence."[5]

Peoples' native wisdom and religiosity have suffered much from the imperializing use of the Bible. Oblivious of the cultural context of the Bible and its interpreters, imperial powers and their native informants have claimed universal normativity and exclusivity of the Bible and their interpretations to oppose and denigrate indigenous wisdom and religious practices.

Succeeding imperializing forces came to colonize and exploit the nation, again parading to the world their noble intentions. When direct colonization was no longer acceptable and beneficial, the oppressive and exploitative forces came with a more benign face: neocolonialism. More recently, they are riding on the rising tide of economic globalization; underneath, however, is the specter of neoliberal capitalism or centralized capitalism.

Hoopla and euphoria are everywhere. Development projects, especially infrastructures, are sprouting here and there. Roads, bridges, ferries, and airports connect the many islands. Hydroelectric dams have been constructed to harness electricity for the growing industry. There is no doubt that the GDP has gone up, but the question is, whose income or profit has gone up? GDP is not an accurate indicator or measure of the economic well-being of the people. GDP does not expose the inequality in the system. What happens to the tribal people living in those affected areas when hydroelectric dams are constructed? The plight of the common people must be the gauge that has to be used to measure the nation's well-being.

If the economic situation is going strong and vibrant, why is it that many Filipinos leave the country every day, facing dangers and loneliness in foreign lands to have a reliable income to support their families? Many are working in what are called 3D jobs: demanding, dirty, and dangerous. In the past few years, this author has been privileged to listen to difficult and challenging stories of im/migrants, stories that are normally, when possible, kept in the im/migrant's heart. "*Every time I go to work, I kneel in front of toilet bowls to make them clean and spotless. The toilet bowl has become my altar,*" says a Filipino domestic worker in Rome.

An anecdote about a child crying because he was so hungry is a reminder of how seriously precarious the situation is. To quiet the child, the father tried to scare him: "*Huwag kang maingaydiyan, may bampira*" (Keep quiet, there's a vampire.) The hungry and irritated child responded, "*Kahit bampirakakainin ko*" (I'll eat even a vampire). The poverty and suffering of people have become so acute that not even the threat of a vampire could silence a hungry child.

Sweet and soothing words that have circulated in the time of the pandemic, like "we are in the same boat," ring hollow in the experience of the many, if not a mockery of the intelligence of the common people. Maybe a more appropriate one would be to say, "people are facing the same storm, but they are on different boats." Some are

---

5. Sugirtharajah, *Bible and the Third World*, 52.

in luxury liners, but many are in their outrigger motorboats and smaller *bancas* or *barotos*.

When global wealth soars to an enormous height but leaves many in squalor and dying in abject poverty, something is terribly amiss. There is a deep crisis when nation-states use more of their resources on policing dissent and military armaments than education and health care. When the ecosystem is sacrificed to pursue short-term economic benefits, usually for the few, such as large-scale mining, deep crisis or deep darkness is present.

The country is in a deep socio-moral crisis. Graft, corruption, and impunity have engulfed the land. A story had circulated that when Pope Francis visited Sri Lanka, he was greeted by elephants. When he arrived at the Ninoy Aquino International Airport (NAIA), he was welcomed by crocodiles (crocodile is a metaphor for power-hungry and corrupt politicians). This circulated on Facebook: "Welcome to the Philippines where the spread of corruption is faster than the speed of internet connection."

Cancer has been used as a metaphor to speak of this social crisis. We know what cancer does; it attacks the system and spreads quickly. Graft and corruption undermine the political system at the very core. The integrity of the whole body politic is at stake. People lose faith in the system when its integrity is compromised, and more corruption and criminality spread like cancer. While the entire nation suffers, the onus falls heavily on the already disempowered and impoverished population.

The COVID-19 pandemic has only exposed the fault lines in our socio-political, economic, and health care system, a system driven by the pursuit of the "bottom line"—profits. It has unveiled the destructive path we have taken for quite some time. If we continue with business as usual, worse catastrophic socio-political and ecological unraveling is to be expected. When profit becomes god, deciding what matters and who will live or die, the "essentials" will be the "sacrificials" and the "front-liners," as well as the "backliners" will be cannibalized by the vulture-like, carcass-hungry "bottom-liners." Resources earmarked for COVID-19 treatment and to help alleviate the economic misery of the people have not escaped from being devoured by the vulture-like bottom-liners. Even while in pandemic crisis, a political humor has circulated: "*Dumatingna ang Delta, hindi pa ang delata. At paanomakararating ang ayuda kung may-nakaharangna buwaya. At kung makararating man, imbis na apat nalibo apat na ligo.*" (Delta has arrived but not the government's canned goods assistance for the needy. And, how can the assistance arrive if a crocodile is blocking the way? Even as some goods have arrived, instead of P4,000.00, the people received four *Ligos* [four canned sardines].)

Compounding the misery, at the height of the pandemic, the administration of president Rodrigo Duterte has passed and executed one draconian measure after another, such as the war on drugs, anti-terror law, and book purging. Since President Duterte launched the war on drugs, bodies of victims have littered the streets, mostly the poor peddlers and users, and even as his term is about to end, drugs continue to fester throughout the land. Others who see the drug problem as social and psychological are calling to "stop the killing and start the healing." Meanwhile, the main targets of the anti-terror law have been those individuals and institutions tagged by the administration to be in cahoots with communists, the New People's Army, and political activists. Those critical of the system are red-tagged, which is tantamount to a death warrant. Reinforcing the anti-terror law is the campaign to purge or ban books from libraries considered "subversive" materials by the government.

Time and again, we have witnessed how wielders of power, both the state and powerful elites, use whatever cultural, legal, and military power at their disposal to block or silence the message they do not want to hear. If silencing the message is not enough, they go after and silence the messenger. This was the plight of the early Filipinos when they resisted the Spanish and US occupations, and this silencing has continued in the banning of books considered subversive and in the killings of *Lumad* leaders who speak up against the exploitation of extractive industries and the journalists, priests and pastors, and lawyers who defend the people's rights.

Proudly, Philippine history is not only a history of suffering and silence but of struggle. The peaceful Pacific is not that peaceful; it is also a turbulent Pacific. Despite its brutality, the pacification campaign did not completely pacify our people; it did not silence the Filipino people completely. The people had the courage to trouble the waters, and they were charged as troublemakers for doing so. Many of those who resisted paid dearly for their refusal to be silenced; they paid dearly for troubling the waters.

THEOLOGICAL ARTICULATIONS FROM THE CRUCIBLE OF SUFFERING AND HOPE

What kinds of questions are the interlocutors of Filipino theology asking in relation to the theological task? What urgent concerns are they grappling and wrestling with today? How are the Filipino theologians dealing with them in the task of theological construction?

The questions that the suffering and struggling Filipinos bring to bear on the theological task are not the result of the gradual erosion of the religious world they inhabit because of the assault of modern science and the growing secularization of society. The springboard of their questions is their empty and growling stomachs, emaciated bodies, and the continuing betrayal of their dreams by political leaders. Starting from this location where God's seeming absence calls out for divine justice (theodicy), they have raised their anguished questions: How can we believe in a just and loving God when we are suffering from terrible injustice? How can we worship the Lord of all when we must deal with those who lord over us, deciding who will live, starve, and be tortured? How can we grapple with trinitarian God-talk when we are grappling with another form of the unholy trinity—the absence of breakfast, lunch, and supper?[6]

These questions point to the pervasive and dominant pattern that runs through the narrative fabric of the lives of common Filipinos. The dominant pattern that has emerged from the warp and weft of the people's experience is the narrative fabric of suffering, struggle, and hope.

Suffering has become so pervasive that it has created a culture of suffering. Beyond the glaring and pervasive poverty, a culture of suffering can be discerned in the day-to-day conversations, songs, poems, and stories that people share. When life is perceived as a narrative of suffering with no end in sight, it is not a surprise that fatalism has been woven into the social fabric. Caught in what appears to be an inevitable cruel fate, they can only think of *kapalaran* (literally dictated by the lines on one's palm) or *gulong ng palad* (wheel of fortune), like the message of Rico Puno's song: "*Bakit kaya sabuhay ng tao/Mayr'ongmayama't may apisamundo?/Kapalaran . . . /Kung hanapi'y di matagpuan/At kung minsa'ylumalapit/Nang 'di moalam.*" (Why are there wealthy and poor in this life? Fate . . . when you look for it you seem not to find it, but there are times when it just comes to you, even without you knowing.)

It is not a surprise that the image of a suffering Christ Jesus is popular among Filipinos. The Jesus who suffers occupies a central place among the marginalized Filipinos because they see in Jesus's plight their very own plight. With suffering being a pervasive narrative in people's lives and the Crucified or the Suffering One a pervasive icon, it is not a surprise that Holy Week occupies a central place in the church's calendar. More than Christmas Eve mass, the Good Friday event draws a much larger crowd—many of whom do not go to church on regular Sundays—on an extremely hot summer day. This is generally true also of the Protestant churches.

Several Holy Week activities vividly portray the suffering and agony that the Son of God endured. The *pasyon* (reenactment of the life and death of Jesus through plays and readings) portrays the poor, lowly, and beaten Christ. This practice is more prevalent in certain parts of the Philippines, where the *sinakulo* (passion play) and *pabasa* (readings) have long histories. But the most vivid, if not gory, depiction of Jesus's suffering is the practice of self-flagellation during the Holy Week by those who have made *panata* (vow). The penitents (almost always male) walk barefoot in procession with faces veiled and lash their backs with rope or bamboo sticks until they bleed. In some places, others are commissioned to do the lashing.

But suffering woven with fatalism is not the only narrative. Though many have accepted their plight with resignation, the Filipino people have a long history of struggle. Filipino history is not only a history of suffering, exploitation, and betrayal to local and foreign powers; it is also a history of resistance and struggle. "*Ibon man may layang lumipad*" (like a caged bird that longs to fly for freedom), the Filipino people have refused to be caged forever. They have struggled to set themselves free; they have

---

6. Fernandez, *Toward a Theology of Struggle*, 7.

reclaimed the Christian faith into a "*pananampalatayang pumipiglas at nagpapalaya*" (a faith that struggles and liberates).

True, the image of the suffering and crucified Christ is prevalent and is often interpreted through the lens of passive acceptance and endurance of suffering, but a tradition *of suffering that struggles* is also present. With theologies of atonement in mind, it is easy to conclude that the penitents do this as an act of penance for their own or others' sin. Penance may not be totally absent but, as Benigno Beltran's study suggests, the penitents do the self-flagellation primarily as a form of *damay*—sympathy with or participation in Jesus's suffering.[7] Self-flagellation, for the penitents, is an act of solidarity with the suffering Jesus. Penance for sins is not the main focus of popular Christology, but *pakikiramay* or identification with the suffering of Jesus, who in the first place embodied this quality. And closely associated with *pakikiramay* (sympathy or maybe empathy) is *malasakit* (suffering with). Following Beltran's point: "To make the truth of Jesus one's own is to have *damay* and *malasakit* with him, to be his disciple and share his destiny."[8]

Pakikiramay and *malasakit* with Jesus is a fitting response of the common Filipinos to Jesus because he embodied these qualities in his very own life. They belong to the attributes of Jesus, which can be observed in his life, ministry, and death. Indeed, for the suffering and struggling common people, Jesus was a person for others. Even with all the risks involved, he pursued God's cause of bringing the reign of God amid human destruction. Because of Jesus's love for the world expressed through his *pakikiramay* and *malasakit* with the disenfranchised, like many Filipinos who have raised their prophetic voice, he earned the ire of the power wielders and suffered a violent death. While *bahalana* (what will be will be) seems to be associated with *kapalaran*, the *bahalana* intertwined with the *malasakit* of Jesus forms into a *bahalana-malasakit*, taking risks in struggling with the disenfranchised of society.[9] Moreover, as embodied in the life of Jesus and the tradition of the little ones, there is not only a *bahalana-malasakit* but also a *bahalana-sapakikibaka* (taking a risk for the people's struggle).

While the resurrection tradition is not totally absent in popular religious expressions, it is weak compared to the crucifixion tradition. We can cite some reasons: People are already exhausted from the Good Friday event, and the weather (hot summer) does not suggest the emergence of a new life from winter to spring. Nevertheless, if the Holy Week celebration has the *pasyon*, the resurrection celebration has the *salubong*. *Salubong* is the reenactment of the dawn meeting of Jesus and his mother, in which the statues of the Risen Christ and the Sorrowful Mother are unveiled by a girl in the attire of an angel, singing the *Regina Coeli*. Then the removal of the veil during the meeting is accompanied by the release of doves and *bati*, a dance of joyful

---

7. Beltran, *Christology of the Inarticulate*, 247.
8. Beltran, *Christology of the Inarticulate*, 115.
9. de Mesa, *In Solidarity with the Culture*, 147–77; de Mesa, *And God Said, "Bahala Na!,"* 81–161; also, Dagdag, "Emerging Theology in the Philippines Today," 7.

celebration.¹⁰ In a situation where the forces of death continue to reign, the *salubong* celebration is a source of inspiration, vision, and hope. It is founded on the belief that, like Jesus, the Filipino people will someday have their resurrection. The *salubong* points to the dawn that ushers in the new day for the suffering people. Or, in the idiom of the people, "*Ang araw bago sumikat nakikita muna'y banaag*" (Early dawn precedes the sunrise).

The common people's desperate situation and the Christian tradition have given birth to the *salubong*. Any faithful interpretation of the common people's resurrection tradition must be rooted in the people's desperate situation. It is out of the banality of crucifixions that the common people speak of resurrection. The notion of a grand resurrection somewhere and someday may not be totally absent in the people's common discourse understood either as hope or escape, but this grand resurrection makes sense only when we reinterpret resurrection as that which happens to people on the other side of the various kinds of deaths in the here and now.

Resurrection amidst the various kinds of deaths may be hard to find in the lives of the little people, but they are not totally absent. The story of Aling Maria gives us a glimpse of what resurrection is in the experience of those who are living at the edge. She has lived in the North Cemetery (Manila) since 1955. In the 1960s, at her son's request, who had acquired a small piece of land and house at a relocation site, she joined him. But the situation at the relocation site was so desperate that, in the words of Aling Maria, "I couldn't stand it anymore. I came back to the cemetery after a month—and have not left since. I think I might stay here—forever."¹¹ Living in the cemetery, where there was peace, was, for Aling Maria, a resurrection experience.

Indeed, it is difficult to find grand moments of resurrection. For those who are barely making it in life, survival is already a foretaste of resurrection. It is in this most banal experience of resurrection that we need to see Jesus's resurrection. With Jesus's resurrection embodying their very own resurrection, the common people have been enabled to read their history with new eyes, seeing it as a history of survival, struggle, and of not giving up whatever little ray of hope is present. With this lens of reading history, the struggling common people have liberated the past from being a prison house. They engage in the retrieval of the past because they know that it is necessary for the journey toward a new and better tomorrow. Looking back to one's past is a way of forging a new tomorrow through dedication to the present in acts of transformation. Here *kasaysayan* (history) is not only an *alaala* (memory) but also has become a *pangako* (promise).

What is this *pangako*? For Filipinas, it is liberation from the clutches of patriarchy; for the gay communities, it is liberation from the culture of heterosexism, "othering," and homophobia.¹² For the fisherfolks, it is not about the apocalyptic vision of

---

10. *People's Participation for Total Human Liberation*, 36.
11. Gerlock, "Living and the Dead," 75.
12. Orevillo-Montenegro, "Christology from a Filipino Woman's Perspective," 56–57.

sea or ocean disappearing (Rev 21:1). That would not be a *pangako*, but a *bangungot* (nightmare) for those whose daily life depends on the sea. A more appropriate image of *pangako* for the lowly ones is that of a banquet—a popular image of Jesus's eschatological vision. For those who have barely enough to survive, like those who depend on *tilapia* (a kind of fish more affordable to the common people), *daing* (dried fish), and *bagoong* (salted fish) for food, what could be the best expression of the *pangako* if not a banquet—a fiesta? The fiesta is characterized by abundant food—*lechon* (roasted pig), *embotido, hamonado, pancit, calderita,* and various kinds of desserts. In God's eschatological fiesta, everyone is welcome to the table; it is an egalitarian meal. The outcasts and marginalized from various forms of "isms" are welcome.

An abundant harvest or catch leads to a fiesta celebration, but even an ordinary meal is a sacrament. When there is little harvest or catch, they still make it enough for the family. In a Filipino idiom, "*Kung maiksi ang kumot, matutongmamaluktot*" (literal translation: If the blanket is short, one must know how to curl up). Poor families with lots of children always ensure that every member is present during mealtime and that everyone has an equal share. Maybe because they barely have enough to get by, necessity has taught them that eating, more than filling one's stomach, is a communal event. One does not eat alone. Eating is an occasion for sharing not just food but life. Eating is a mark of relationship, of connection. A true meal happens when there is a "unison of hearts."[13]

Deep connections among Filipinos are often expressed through the language of food and internal organs. The word *kapatid* (brother or sister), suggests Melanio Aoanan, is a contraction of "*patid ng bituka*" (connected by a single intestine). Other Filipino languages, such as the Cebuano *sumpaysatinai* and the Ilocano *kapugsatitibagis*, speak of this intestinal connection. Filipino theology, continues Aoanan, is truly an incarnational and, more specifically, an intestinal theology—a *bituka* (intestine) and *pagkain* (food) theology.[14] Without romanticizing poverty, it is ironic that those who have more material goods in life eat alone more often than those who have less. They may be eating more nutritious food, but not necessarily a communally and spiritually nourishing meal.

Giving birth to the *pangako* of an eschatological fiesta is not easy, and one must not give up hope amidst many challenges. There is a story of the life of Mang Juan, a poor peasant from my hometown. Like many peasants in that area, he struggles to eke out a living. On some days, he walks with a sack of rice seeds (*palay*) on his back. Looking at Mang Juan and his sack of seeds, he symbolizes the dreams of his people. Juan is a dreamer; he is a dream-keeper. More than that, he walks the dream: he is a dream-walker. His feet are grounded in the stark realities of his native place even as his head is in the clouds. Day and night Mang Juan is living by a dream that things can be different for him and others.

13. Tagle, *Easter People*, 51.
14. Aoanan, *Bituka Theology*, 26–39.

The Filipino people have carried their own sack of seeds—seeds of dreams and seeds of new life. Their feet are grounded in the realities of our globalized localities. They stay close to the ground to feel the soil's life, yet they also remain close to their dreams so they can feel the seeds longing and struggling to break forth from the ground to what they can be. Are our dreams closely connected to the ground on which we walk, they ask?

Birthing the *pangako* demands so much from the people; it calls for their transformation. The common Filipinos know that it requires a transformation of *loob* (core or center), a fundamental concept. They recognize that hardness of heart (*katigasan ng loob*), more than dullness of thought, is the greatest obstacle to transformation, which requires *pagbabalikloob* (repentance). For the lowly ones with diminished agency, transformation means the empowerment of *loob* to develop *lakas ng loob* (courage). While human effort is crucial, the common Filipinos believe that the transformation of *loob* is a *kaloob ng Dios* (gift of God) who has the attribute of *kagandahangloob* (compassionate, willing the well-being of the people).[15]

However, the development of *lakas ng loob* can come only through a long gradual work of faith development and people empowerment. Only empowered people can effect transformation. The only antidote to the power of organized money is the power of organized people. Organizing the "critical yeast" is essential to develop the "critical mass." The yeast, the tiniest ingredient, when mixed correctly with other ingredients, and when the right environment is provided, is the only ingredient that has the capacity and power to help others grow.

Moreover, birthing the *pangako*—a new and better tomorrow—requires faithful companions along the way. As the root of the word companion (Latin: *cum panis*) suggests, it means sharing the life-nourishing *tinapay* (bread) or *baon* (meal prepared for the journey) for the common journey. The common people are aware that their dreamed-for new tomorrow can only come through the help of companions. They know the essence of communal endeavor through the *bayanihan* spirit (spirit of helping one another). Beyond dreaming individual dreams and making these dreams rooted in the hard facts of our contexts, the challenge is for the Filipino people to dream and walk together toward a new and better tomorrow. Giving birth to a hopeful tomorrow requires committed and courageous people who are willing to take risks to make their hopes and dreams come true.

Filipino theology is an intentional articulation of the journey of the Filipino people—their quest for who they are, their plight and struggles, and their hopes and dreams—toward a new and better tomorrow. It seeks to illumine the faith-praxis of the people even as it continues to be informed and transformed by the same faith-praxis. As the journey of the Filipino people continues, so does its theological reflection continue to evolve and grow.

---

15. Beltran, *Christology of the Inarticulate*, 241.

BIBLIOGRAPHY

Aoanan, Melanio. *Bituka Theology: Seven Essays on Filipino Contextual Theology*. Mandaluyong, Philippines: Merryland, 2021.

Beltran, Benigno. *The Christology of the Inarticulate: An Inquiry into the Filipino Understanding of Jesus the Christ*. Manila, Philippines: Divine Word, 1987.

Bosch, David. *Transforming Mission: Paradigm Shifts in Theology of Mission*. New York: Orbis, 1991.

Constantino, Renato, in collaboration with Letizia Constantino. *The Philippines: A Past Revisited, Volume 1*. Quezon City, Philippines: Renato Constantino, 1975.

Dagdag, Theresa. "Emerging Theology in the Philippines Today." *Kalinangan* 3 (1983) 61–87.

de Mesa, José M. *And God Said, "Bahala Na!": The Them of Providence in the Lowland Filipino Context*. Quezon City, Philippines: Jose M. de Mesa, 1979.

———. *In Solidarity with the Culture: Studies in Theological Re-rooting*. Maryhill Studies 4. Quezon City, Philippines: Maryhill School of Theology, 1987.

Fernandez, Eleazar. *Toward a Theology of Struggle*. Maryknoll, NY: Orbis, 1994.

Gerlock, Ed. "The Living and the Dead." In *Signs of Hope: Stories of Hope in the Philippines*, 201–21. Quezon City, Philippines: Claretian, 1990.

Orevillo-Montenegro, Muriel. "Christology from a Filipino Woman's Perspective." In *Christologies, Cultures, and Religions: Portraits of Christ in the Philippines*. Edited by Pascal D. Bazzell and Aldrin Penamora. Metro Manila: OMF, 2016.

People's Participation for Total Human Liberation. Pasay City, Philippines: Alay Kapwa, 1982.

Said, Edward. *Musical Elaborations*. New York: Columbia University Press, 1991.

Sugirtharajah, R. S. *The Bible and the Third World: Precolonial, Colonial and Postcolonial Encounters*. London: Cambridge University Press, 2001.

Tagle, Luis Antonio. *An Easter People: Our Christian Vocation to be Messengers of Hope*. Quezon City, Philippines: Jesuit Communications Foundation, 2012.

CHAPTER 15

Chinese Theologies

ALEXANDER CHOW

Chinese theologies have existed as long as there has been the transmission and the translation of the Gospel into Chinese contexts[1]—from the 625 Church of the East (or "Nestorian") mission traveling the Silk Road, to the starts of Roman Catholic missions in the thirteenth and sixteenth centuries, and to the late-nineteenth and early twentieth century surge of Christian missions in general from every major Protestant, Roman Catholic, and Orthodox group. Scholarship on Chinese theologies has tended to start with the writings of the earliest converts to the Catholic and Protestant missions, paying particular attention to these encounters and to the debates around the development of Chinese Christian vocabulary.[2] Much attention has also been given to the heyday of Chinese theological development during the Republican era (1912–1949)

---

1. Some may contest this and hold to the view that Chinese theology arises when Chinese Christians begin to formulate unique theological reflections. However, the act of translation is fundamental to the indigenization process. See Starr, *Chinese Theology*, 15–40; Sanneh, *Translating the Message*.

2. Particular attention has been paid to Chinese Catholic literati of the seventeeth century, the most famous being Xu Guangqi (1562–1633), Li Zhizao (1565–1630), and Yang Tingyun (1557–1627), as well as early Protestant evangelists of the nineteenth and early twentieth centuries—men like Liang Fa (1789–1855) and He Jinshan (1822–1871) and women (often described as "Bible women" in English or "women evangelists" [*nu chuandao*] in Chinese) like Dora Yu (Yu Cidu, 1873–1933) and Mary Stone (Shi Meiyu, 1873–1954). For overviews of these figures and some of their thinking, see Standaert, *Handbook of Christianity in China: Volume One*, 404–20, 632–52; Tiedemann, *Handbook of Christianity in China: Volume Two*, 247–77; Lutz, "Jesus in the Early Protestant Evangelists."

Some studies also examine the theology of Hong Xiuquan (1814–1864), the founder of the Taiping Heavenly Kingdom, who is often seen as developing a heterodox version of Protestant theology. For a recent work critiquing this view, see Kilcourse, *Taiping Theology*.

and into the first decade of the People's Republic of China (1949–).[3] Following the initial reception of Christianity, Chinese theological development in the twentieth century often sought ecclesial and theological independence from their foreign missionary forebearers, coinciding with broader Chinese efforts in nation-building and modernization.

In this present volume on "emerging theologies" of recent decades, we turn to a less well understood historical period of Chinese theological development. During and immediately following the Cultural Revolution (1966–1976), Christians in mainland China were relatively cut off from the rest of the world and could not initially benefit from the theological ferment coming from the World Council of Churches, the Ecumenical Association of Third World Theologians, the Lausanne Movement, or the Second Vatican Council. This would change as Deng Xiaoping introduced his "reform and opening up" policy, when mainland Chinese Christians in the 1980s began to experience greater liberties with regard to the practice of the Christian faith. This led to what many have described as a "Christianity fever" (*Jidujiao re*)—a fantastic growth of Christianity experienced, initially in the rural countryside, but eventually in the 1990s throughout the entire country. However, with the start of Xi Jinping's administration in 2012, many Chinese Christians have experienced the curbing of previous liberties. Furthermore, Xi Jinping has promoted a campaign for the "Chinafication" or "Sinicization" of religions (*zongjiao Zhongguohua*), to adapt religions ideologically to China's socialist society.[4]

---

3. For Chinese Protestants, much work has been done on intellectuals associated with the Peking Apologetic Group in Yenching University and the Chinese YMCA, notably Wu Leichuan (1870–1944), T. C. Chao (Zhao Zichen, 1888–1979), and Wu Yaozong (1893–1979). Along with these "progressives" who wrote primarily for academic audiences, theological output was also produced in the form of published sermons and other church-based publications by evangelists such as Wang Mingdao (1900–1991), Watchman Nee (Ni Tuosheng, 1903–1972), and John Sung (Song Shangjie, 1901–1944). For general overviews, see Ng, *Jidujiao yu Zhongguo shehui bianqian*; Lam, *Chinese Theology in Construction*; Lian, *Redeemed by Fire*; Starr, *Chinese Theology*, 73–99, 128–53; Reilly, *Saving the Nation*.

Considerably less attention has been placed on Chinese Catholic theology, partly because it has tended to be found within less-recognized genres of theological output: pastoral addresses, newspaper articles, memoirs, and so forth. Major Catholic theological minds of this period tended to be statesmen, diplomats, newspaper editors, and the occasional career clergy—figures like the Ma brothers (Ma Xiangbo [1840–1939] and Ma Jianzhong [1845–1900]), Lou Tseng-tsiang (Lu Zhengxiang, 1871–1949), Joseph Zi (Xu Zongze, 1886–1947), John C. H. Wu (Wu Jingxiong, 1899–1986), and Paul Yu Pin (Yu Bin, 1901–1978). In contrast to studies on Protestant theologians, writings about Catholic theological contributions are more limited. For a few works, see Charbonnier, *Christians in China*, 410–19; Li, "Christianity and Cultural Conflict in the Life of Ma Xiangbo"; Lindblom, "John C. H. Wu and the Evangelization of China"; Lai and Li, "Chinese Catholic Response to Sino-Japanese War"; Starr, *Chinese Theology*, 100–127; Batairwa Kubuya, "Paul Yu Pin and the Challenge of Faith Identity"; Wong, "Yu Bin and Vincent Lebbe's Theology of Resistance."

Regretfully, relatively little is known and has been written about Chinese Christians associated with the Church of the East or the Russian Orthodox Church.

4. We can see some developments related to this in a meeting held by the state-sanctioned Protestant Three-Self Patriotic Movement, which in 2014 brought together church leaders and academics to discuss the Chinafication of Christianity. For English translations of many of these papers, see *Chinese*

Theologically, the pregnant discussions from 1950s around church-state relations and the creation of "patriotic" organizations were initially carried into the reform and opening up era. Many of the most well-known Chinese theological voices tended to be senior figures who lived through the earlier debates and became associated with state-sanctioned Christian organizations, the Protestant Three-Self Patriotic Movement (TSPM) or the Catholic Patriotic Association (CPA).[5] These individuals were afforded a more visible platform within mainland China and, through global networks, on the world stage. While there were also senior figures associated with unregistered house churches (Protestant) or underground churches (Catholic) in the 1980s, their theology has not been as accessible or readily studied. In the 1990s, a second generation of Chinese theologies was beginning to be produced within China's secular universities and think tanks. Ironically, many of those writing in this academic movement of Sino-Christian theology (*Han yu shenxue*) did not self-describe as Christians, but were often described as "cultural Christians" (*wenhua Jidutu*).[6] They tended to be less concerned about local Chinese churches and more interested in engaging Christian theology for the purposes of the developing Chinese society. Into the first decades of the twenty-first century, a third generation of Chinese theologies arose mainly within China's urban centers. Many of the main thinkers in this generation were involved in the Tiananmen Square democracy movement in 1989. Then, they were students or young scholars who became disillusioned by the government clampdown and, in the 1990s, converted to Christianity and eventually looked for theological means to transform society. In contrast to the cultural Christians, these intellectuals now saw themselves as "Christian scholars" (*Jidutu xueren*) who looked to develop church-based theologies, from within the local church, often reviving forms of Neo-Calvinist theology for the Chinese context. Alongside these three generations,[7] Chinese theologies during this time were also being produced by those outside mainland China, in Asia and in Western contexts like North America and the United Kingdom.[8]

Theological Review volume 26.

Note that while many sources translate *Zhongguo hua* as "Sinicization," given the statist orientation of the campaign, I tend to use "Chinafication" or "Chinization." This was also the practice of *Chinese Theological Review* in volume 26, though volume 27 shifted to "Sinicization."

5. I have not included Orthodoxy here because the current population of Chinese Orthodox is quite small and it is not a legally recognized religion in mainland China.

6. In contrast to the English phrase of "cultural Christian," meaning a person who was raised within a culture shaped by Christianity, the Chinese phrase conveys a notion of being "cultured"—that is, an elite, educated status. To be a Chinese "cultural Christian" is to be a person interested in the intellectual importance of Christianity especially for the purposes of cultivating Chinese society.

7. For an in-depth discussion of these three generations, see Chow, *Chinese Public Theology*, 48–114.

8. There is some debate as to who are "Chinese" in Hong Kong, Taiwan, and North America. In this chapter, I am using the term as a generic label as opposed to entering into debates around how it relates to other identities, like Hong Kongese or Taiwanese. See chapter 37 of this volume for a broader view of Asian American theologies.

Mindful of these points, this chapter on emerging Chinese theologies will discuss the theology produced by mainland Chinese Christians, with some reference to those writing from outside the country. To focus this discussion, this chapter will highlight the two major theological themes: Christology and ecclesiology.

CHRISTOLOGY

Chinese theologians have written much on the key theological theme of Christology. This is perhaps not surprising given that Christ, who reveals God through the Incarnation, is the central figure of the Christian religion. But the person of Jesus Christ also echoes key paradigms prevalent in the Chinese religio-philosophical context.[9] Hence, earlier Chinese Christologies have often spoken of him as an older brother, a political leader, or a wise and moral exemplar.[10]

In recent decades, perhaps one of the most important Chinese christological developments has been that of the Cosmic Christ.[11] K. H. Ting (Ding Guangxun, 1915–2012), a longtime leader of the TSPM, is the best-known proponent of the Cosmic Christ.[12] In his important speech on the topic delivered in England in 1991, Ting argues that the theme has come about through a history of struggle in China ever since the establishment of the People's Republic of China in 1949. In particular, Chinese Christians "have seen and experienced goodness, truth and holiness among followers of other paths and ways than that of the church."[13] Hence, the cosmic nature of Christ speaks of the universal extent of Christ's domain and care, which can be expressed by Christians and non-Christians alike. But secondly, the Cosmic Christ also underscores how Christlike love should be understood as the greatest of God's attributes. Ting explains, "To confess that Christ is Godlike is now seen to be not so important as to affirm that God is Christlike and that Christlike love is the way God intends for the running of the cosmos."[14] Instead of an Augustinian view that it is not possible not to sin (*non posse no peccare*), what we find in Ting is a view of theological anthropology, perhaps influenced by Mencian Confucianism, which underscores an optimism in the human potential to do good. Elsewhere, Ting argues that we need to move beyond the language of "sinner" because it divides between those who are saved from sin and those who are not saved. Rather, he prefers to speak about the solidarity found among all who are "sinned against" by the evils endured in this world.[15]

---

9. Instead of speaking about "religion" or "philosophy," both of which are Western constructions, I prefer to use the more ambiguous phrase "religio-philosophical."

10. See Malek, *Chinese Face of Jesus Christ*.

11. For a detailed discussion on these developments, see Chow, *Chinese Public Theology*, 55–62.

12. See Chow, *Theosis*, 90–100.

13. Ting, "Cosmic Christ," 415.

14. Ting, "Cosmic Christ," 417.

15. Ting, "Human Collectives as Vehicles of God's Grace," 44–46.

For Ting, these reconceptualizations of hamartiology and Christology enable Chinese Christians to see the moral goodness of others within Chinese society, especially as expressed by those who are not Christians such as Chinese communists. But, as Edmond Tang explains, "It was not so much an effort to extend a friendly arm to Marxist atheists but a reflection of the fidelity of God even in the darkest moments of personal and social despairs."[16]

The "dark moments" experienced in Chinese society in the last half century have been a source for much spiritual and theological reflection. We can see this in the writings of Wang Weifan (1927–2015), another TSPM proponent of the Cosmic Christ.[17] In an article written in 1985, Wang reflects on how the prior thirty years brought great pain and suffering to the Chinese church.[18] Referring to the Song of Solomon, Wang sees this experience as a journey of maturation from "my beloved is mine" (2:16) to "I am my beloved's" (7:10). Chinese Christians now understand that "Jesus is not only the Lord of the souls of Christian believers, but also the Lord of the cosmos and the Lord of history."[19] As the Lord of the cosmos, God must be understood as an ever-generating God (*shengsheng Shen*) who is involved in the dynamic of creation, recreation, and new creation. Therefore, the work of redemption is not simply the saving of souls, but the beckoning of Christians to participate in this ever-generating process as co-creators with God in this world wherever they may be. But secondly, as Lord of history, Christ is very much aware of the historical strife experienced in humanity. For Wang, Christ as the suffering servant is a powerful image for those in China who have experienced great suffering through social, political, and economic distress. In contrast to Ting, who is generally considered a theological liberal, Wang self-identified as an Evangelical. It is therefore interesting to see Wang pushing back on a singular focus on an individualistic understanding of Christ's lordship and embracing the implications of its universal extent—across space (the cosmos) and time (history).

As China continued to develop its socialist market economy in the 1990s, this brought about new "dark moments." Aloysius Jin Luxian (1916–2013) of the CPA put the situation bleakly:

> To tell the truth, I had no fear for our Catholics facing the challenge of persecution [during the Cultural Revolution]. But, now, facing the challenge of modernization, of pure materialism, of the idolatry of money, of individualism, I have fears. How to teach the Catholics to live the Gospel?[20]

---

16. Tang, "Cosmic Christ," 141.
17. See Chow, "Wang Weifan's Cosmic Christ."
18. The three decades prior are quite significant because they include the beginnings of the People's Republic of China, the creation of the Three-Self Patriotic Movement, and the height of the Cultural Revolution.
19. Wang, "Zhongguo jiaohui," 9, translation mine.
20. Jin quoted in Madsen, *China's Catholics*, 114.

This sentiment was echoed by others, such as Zhuo Xinping (b. 1955), a scholar in the field of Sino-Christian theology:

> The recognition of the existence of this "darker side" in human nature means that the Chinese cannot completely reject the idea of original sin.... In the present period of social mutations in China, the appearance of cases of moral bankruptcy, human corruptibility and pessimism about life have led many Chinese to understand and experience the meaning of the fallen nature of humanity.[21]

Remarkably, what we find in Zhuo's essay, as a non-Christian academic who studies Christianity, a view that differs quite significantly from Ting's optimism. The prevalence of existential challenges in Chinese society offers evidence of original sin, pointing to the reality of human depravity and the need for the salvific work of Christ. However, far from simply reiterating Augustinian-Reformed understandings of sin and salvation, Chinese theologies speak to the spiritual value in suffering. On a popular level, we find this quite prevalent among house church leaders, through sermons of the older generation of pastors such as Allen Yuan (Yuan Xiangchen, 1914–2005) and Samuel Lamb (Lin Xiangao, 1924–2013),[22] and proclaimed through the songs of the *Canaan Hymns* (*Jia'nan Shixuan*) of Ruth Lü (Lü Xiaomin, b. 1970).[23] As one observer puts it:

> Suffering is a means of remembering Christ and imitating his actions. In their own broken bodies, Christians remember Christ's body that was broken for them; in their bleeding, they remember Christ's blood that was shed for them. They suffer "in remembrance of him."[24]

Through these examples, we are reminded of the cost of discipleship and of the transformative power of suffering.

The cosmic Christologies of Ting and Wang point towards different metaphysical starting points than the Hellenistic approach of the church fathers, to speak of a two-natures Christology.[25] The Chinese American Enoch Wan argues that a more fruitful starting point can be found in the *Dao*—a fundamental notion within all Chinese religio-philosophical traditions. For Wan, a theology of the *Dao* pushes against the dialectical and paradoxical approaches found in Western theology, and offers a harmonious unity of Christ's divine and human attributes.[26] Kwok Pui-lan (b. 1952) agrees, arguing that dualistic systems have problematically subjugated both women and nature.[27] She too notes that Chinese religio-philosphical thought emphasizes "the balance of heaven and earth, yang and ying [sic], sun and moon, and father and

---

21. Zhuo, "Original Sin in the East-West Dialogue," 82.
22. Qin, "Samuel Lamb's Exhortation Regarding Eternal Rewards," 69–71.
23. Sun, "Songs of Canaan," 108–11; Starr, *Chinese Theology*, 266–68.
24. Sun, "Songs of Canaan," 110–11.
25. See Ting, "Cosmic Christ," 418.
26. Wan, "Tao," 26.
27. Kwok, "Ecology and Christology," 122.

mother. Instead of binary opposites, they are seen as complementary, mutually reinforcing and interplaying with one another."[28] From this basis, Kwok insists on an organic model of Christology which rediscovers the potential of wisdom Christology and proposes that Jesus is one epiphany of God among many others. The Taiwanese American C. S. Song (b. 1929) has likewise pushed against metaphysical discussions of Christology and instead argued that it is through flesh and blood—through suffering people—that Jesus Christ is best known, declaring, "*Jesus, in short, is the crucified people! Jesus means crucified people.* To say Jesus is to say suffering people. To know Jesus is to know crucified people."[29]

For these Chinese theologians, the preoccupation is less about a wholesale discarding of mainstream Chalcedonian Christology; rather, these are attempts at a rediscovery of Jesus in the Bible from the perspective of those steeped in Chinese religio-philosophical thinking and informed by the struggles of Chinese Christians. It also recognizes that Chinese Christians, in mainland China and elsewhere, are a religious minority. Hence, these Christologies lend themselves towards a more inclusive understanding of the work of God and of the resources available for theologizing. This leads to our next section that shifts our attention from the central figure of Christianity to the people who represent this central figure to others—namely, the church.

ECCLESIOLOGY

Perhaps the longest standing Chinese critique against Christianity has been that it is a "foreign religion" or *yangjiao*—that is, teachings (*jiao*) from the ocean (*yang*). It is of no accident that the Chinese phrase was coined in the 19th century after Western gunboats opened up China through the Opium Wars (1839–1842 and 1856–1860) and forced the signing of unequal treaties. Missionaries entered the country under the auspices of various European empires—initially, British Protestants, French Catholics, and Russian Orthodox. Protestants had the added complexity of the multiplicity of foreign denominations replicated in missions to China. Hence Protestant Christianity has been perceived as a foreign *and* divisive force. As early as 1910 Cheng Jingyi (1881–1939) declared, "[Chinese Protestants] hope to see, in the near future, a united Christian Church without any denominational distinctions . . . . Speaking generally, denominationalism has never interested the Chinese mind. He finds no delight in it, but sometimes he suffers for it!"[30]

Under the People's Republic in the 1950s and again after the Cultural Revolution in the 1980s, Chinese Christians have been asked about whether the church they are a part of could be understood as an undivided Chinese church. In the last few decades, for both Protestants and Catholics, the Chinese church is often discussed in

---

28. Kwok, *Introducing Asian Feminist Theology*, 90.
29. Song, *Jesus, the Crucified People*, 216, emphasis in original.
30. World Missionary Conference, *Report of Commission VIII*, 196.

terms of two realities—the state-sanctioned organizations (TSPM or CPA) and unregistered churches (Protestant house churches or Catholic underground churches). But in each of these existences, there have been attempts to underscore the unity that exists within. For instance, Protestant house churches have written united appeals and confessions which underscore their common theology and their resolve to not register with the TSPM; the latter, they argue, is against Christian teachings about having two heads or two masters, the government and Christ.[31] While the same can be said of Catholic underground churches, they tend to offer the additional charge that the CPA has separated from communion with the Pope and, therefore, is no longer "Catholic" or universal.[32]

However, leaders of the stated-sanctioned Christian organizations have been less willing to see themselves as separate from Christians participating in non-registered communities. K. H. Ting has celebrated the idea that the Chinese Protestant church is now in a post-denominational era. Furthermore, he argues in the *People's Daily*:

> As the TSPM, our task is to unite all the country's Christians and we must not treat house gathering Christians as disreputable. As a TSPM leader, I cannot say they are illegal. In interpreting the constitution, one must not say that those within the church have freedom of [religious] belief and that those within the homes do not have freedom of [religious] belief.[33]

In this state-run periodical, Ting defends Protestants as having the constitutional right to freely choose which Christian community to join, whether that be house gatherings (*jiating juhui*; his term for house churches) or TSPM-registered churches—both of which should be seen as legitimately part of the same Chinese church. A similar stance has been asserted by Aloysius Jin Luxian. In his most explicit statement on the subject, Jin asserts that the CPA is "a political mass organization and not a church. Its role is to help ensure that church work is well done, but it is not a church itself."[34] Referring to the ecclesiology of the Second Vatican Council, Jin insists that the CPA helps the Chinese church in the process of inculturation, in order to contribute to the Catholic or universal church made up of the local churches around the world.[35]

By the 1990s, we see the development of a new understanding of the church primarily articulated by academics involved in the field of Sino-Christian theology. Liu Xiaofeng (b. 1956), drawing on the writings of Ernst Troeltsch, argues that the Chinese church exists in three basic forms: the church-type (*da jiaohui* or German *Kirche*), the sect-type (*xiao jiaopai* or German *Sekt*), and mysticism (*shenmi zhuyi* or

---

31. See "Appendix A: United Appeal" and "Appendix B: Confession of Faith" in Aikman, *Jesus in Beijing*, 311–25.

32. For an important document on this, see "Thirteen Points" in Tang and Wiest, *Catholic Church*, 142–45.

33. Zhao and Ting, "Tan Luo shizong jiaozheng ci wenti," 3, translation mine.

34. Jin, "Role of the Patriotic Association," 113.

35. See Zhu, "Bishop Jin Luxian and the Chinese Catholic Patriotic Association," 56.

German *Mystik*). While the church-type is represented by the TSPM and the CPA, the second sect-type is represented by Protestant house churches and (possibly) Catholic underground churches. The third mystical church, which is represented by academics like himself, tends to emphasize personal spiritual experience apart from traditional ecclesial communities; but they often form their own communities of intellectuals. Furthermore, the mystical church has an inclination towards scientific and reflective theology and is able to offer important religious insights for the creation of Christian culture.[36] From Liu's perspective, this third ecclesial reality is more capable than the other two in developing Christianity to meet the challenges of contemporary Chinese society, thereby making significant contributions to the Chinese church and Chinese theology.[37]

While not all Chinese Christians have agreed with the viability of this "mystical church," we see this disposition evolving in new forms of Protestant urban intellectual churches in the early twenty-first century. Prior to this time, house churches were small gatherings of a few dozen members because they were limited to meeting in people's homes. However, in 2005, a change in the government regulations on religious affairs came into effect that offered the possibility for churches to register with the government without needing to go through the TSPM.[38] Many house church networks decided to forgo their home-based gatherings and form large churches of several hundred to a few thousand, renting their own facilities, and seeking to register directly with the government. In one prominent example, Pastor Jin Tianming (b. 1968) of the Shouwang Church in Beijing argues that this aspiration offered a potential for the church to have constructive dialogue with the government and to move beyond the deadlock within the Chinese church between the "illegal" house churches and the "adulteress" TSPM.[39] Many of these groups saw themselves as creating a "third church" or "third way" that sought to register with the government, albeit not through the TSPM, and able to contribute to the Chinese civil society. Furthermore, these churches tended to draw from Reformed theology, especially neo-Calvinist teachings on sphere sovereignty and the cultural mandate, to develop a public theology.[40]

While there are differences in each of these aforementioned formulations—in registered and unregistered Christian entities, and those who see themselves as offering a third approach—there is a general consensus that the institution of the church is a good thing. In many other parts of the world there has been a disillusionment with institutionalism. Chinese theologians have time and time again seen the value of building up and creating new understandings of the church institution—oftentimes as a means to change the broader society or the wider church. It is valuable to see

---

36. Tan, "Culture-Christians on the China Mainland," 50–52.
37. Tan, "Culture-Christians on the China Mainland," 55.
38. In practice, this policy was hardly realized.
39. Jin, "Tuidong jiaohui dengji dao jintian," 40–41.
40. See Chow, *Chinese Public Theology*, 92–114.

how this is developed outside the mainland, where Chinese Christians likewise have a tendency to emphasize the building of local communities, such as local Chinese churches, but also in the creation of national and transnational Chinese Christian networks, such as the North American Congress of Chinese Evangelicals or the international Chinese Congress of World Evangelism. The local church contributes to something larger than itself. The Chinese American theologian David Ng insists that the church can be best understood in terms of Confucian values of concentric circles of relationships of the individual, in the family, neighborhood, state, and the cosmos.[41] Chinese theologians see the importance of each local community as contributing to a greater community, whether that be the Chinese society or the national church and, ultimately, the world.

CONCLUSION

This brief discussion of emerging Chinese theologies since the 1980s must be understood as the most recent episode in a centuries-old encounter and interaction between Christianity and Chinese peoples. Much of this has been informed by long-standing Chinese religio-philosophical traditions which, for many Chinese today, are becoming less and less epistemologically relevant. Furthermore, the contingencies of Chinese sociopolitical contexts, both within mainland China and beyond, continually offer new possibilities for theological encounter and articulation. We wait and see how the emerging Chinese theologies can contribute to theological conversations around the globe, and become corrected or eclipsed by new emergent Chinese theologies as we move forward in time.

BIBLIOGRAPHY

Aikman, David. *Jesus in Beijing: How Christianity is Transforming China and Changing the Global Balance of Power*. Rev. ed. Washington, DC: Regnery, 2006.
Batairwa Kubuya, Paulin. "Paul Yu Pin and the Challenge of Faith Identity in Religious and Denominational Dialogue." *Fu Jen International Religious Studies* 7 (2013) 1–29.
Charbonnier, Jean. *Christians in China: A.D. 600–2000*. San Francisco: Ignatius, 2002.
Chow, Alexander. *Chinese Public Theology: Generational Shifts and Confucian Imagination in Chinese Christianity*. Oxford: Oxford University Press, 2018.
———. *Theosis, Sino-Christian Theology and the Second Chinese Enlightenment: Heaven and Humanity in Unity*. New York: Palgrave Macmillan, 2013.
———. "Wang Weifan's Cosmic Christ." *Modern Theology* 32 (2016) 384–96.
Jin, Aloysius Luxian. "The Role of the Patriotic Association." In *The Catholic Church in Modern China: Perspectives*, edited by Edmond Tang and Jean-Paul Wiest, 112–19. Maryknoll, NY: Orbis, 1993.

---

41. Ng, "Path of Concentric Circles," 85. See also Chow, *Chinese Public Theology*, 146–50.

Jin, Tianming. "Tuidong jiaohui dengji dao jintian." [The Promotion of Church Registration] *Xinghua* [Almond Flowers] (2008) 40–42.

Kilcourse, Carl S. *Taiping Theology: Localization of Christianity in China, 1843–64.* New York: Palgrave Macmillan, 2016.

Kwok, Pui-lan. "Ecology and Christology." *Feminist Theology* 15 (1997) 113–25.

———. *Introducing Asian Feminist Theology.* Sheffield: Sheffield Academic, 2000.

Lai, Pan-chiu, and Li Lili. "Chinese Catholic Response to Sino-Japanese War: A Study of Xu Zongze's Public Theology of War and Peace." In *Yearbook of Chinese Theology 2017*, edited by Paulos Z. Huang, 166–86. Leiden: Brill, 2017.

Lam, Wing-Hung. *Chinese Theology in Construction.* Pasadena, CA: William Carey, 1983.

Li, Tiangang. "Christianity and Cultural Conflict in the Life of Ma Xiangbo." In *Ma Xiangbo and the Mind of Modern China, 1840–1939*, edited by Ruth Hayhoe and Lu Yongling, 89–142. Armonk, NY: M. E. Sharpe, 1996.

Lian, Xi. *Redeemed by Fire: The Rise of Popular Christianity in Modern China.* New Haven: Yale University Press, 2010.

Lindblom, John A. "John C. H. Wu and the Evangelization of China." *Logos* 8 (2005) 130–64.

Lutz, Jesse G. "Jesus in the Early Protestant Evangelists." In *The Chinese Face of Jesus Christ*, edited by Roman Malek, 2:725–42. Sankt Augustin: Institut Monumenta Serica, 2003.

Madsen, Richard. *China's Catholics: Tragedy and Hope in an Emerging Civil Society.* Berkeley: University of California Press, 1998.

Malek, Roman, ed. *The Chinese Face of Jesus Christ.* 5 vols. Sankt Augustin: Monumenta Serica, 2002–.

Ng, David. "A Path of Concentric Circles." In *Journeys at the Margin: Toward an Autobiographical Theology in American-Asian Perspective*, edited by Peter C. Phan and Jung Young Lee, 81–102. Collegeville, MN: Liturgical, 1999.

Ng, Lee-ming (Wu Liming). *Jidujiaoyu Zhongguo shehui bianqian.* [Christianity and Social Change in China] 3rd ed. Hong Kong: Chinese Christian Literature Council, 1997.

Qin, Daniel. "Samuel Lamb's Exhortation Regarding Eternal Rewards: A Socio-Political Perspective." *Studies in World Christianity* 26 (2020) 63–83.

Reilly, Thomas H. *Saving the Nation: Chinese Protestant Elites and the Quest to Build a New China, 1922–1952.* New York: Oxford University Press, 2021.

Sanneh, Lamin. *Translating the Message: The Missionary Impact on Culture.* Rev. and exp. ed. Maryknoll, NY: Orbis, 2008.

Song, C. S. *Jesus, the Crucified People.* Minneapolis: Fortress, 1990.

Standaert, Nicolas, ed. *Handbook of Christianity in China: Volume One: 635–1800.* Leiden, Brill: 2001.

Starr, Chloë F. *Chinese Theology: Text and Context.* New Haven: Yale University Press, 2016.

Sun, Irene Ai-Ling. "Songs of Canaan: Hymnody of the House-Church Christians in China." *Studia Liturgica* 37 (2007) 98–116.

Tan, Xing (pseudonym of Liu Xiaofeng). "Culture-Christians on the China Mainland." *Tripod* 6 (1990) 46–55.

Tang, Edmond. "The Cosmic Christ." *Studies in World Christianity* 1 (1995) 131–42.

Tang, Edmond, and Jean-Paul Wiest, eds. *The Catholic Church in Modern China: Perspectives.* Maryknoll, NY: Orbis, 1993.

Tiedemann, R. G., ed. *Handbook of Christianity in China: Volume Two: 1800–present.* Leiden, Brill: 2010.

Ting, K. H. "The Cosmic Christ." In *Love Never Ends: Papers by K. H. Ting*, edited by Janice Wickeri, 408–18. Nanjing: Yilin, 2000.

———. "Human Collectives as Vehicles of God's Grace." In *Love Never Ends: Papers by K. H. Ting*, edited by Janice Wickeri, 43–48. Nanjing: Yilin, 2000.

Wan, Enoch. "Tao—The Chinese Theology of God-Man." *His Dominion* 11 (1985) 24–27.

Wang, Weifan. "Z hong guo jiaohui de mou zhong shenxue bianqian." [Changes in Theological Thinking in the Church in China] In *Nian zai cangmang: Wang Wei fanwen ji* (1979–1998), 3–10. Hong Kong: Christian Study Centre on Chinese Religion and Culture, 2011.

Wong, Stephanie M. "Yu Bin and Vincent Lebbe's Theology of Resistance: Catholic Participation in the Chinese War Effort Against Japan." In *Modern Chinese Theologies I: Mainland and Mainstream*, edited by Chloë F. Starr. Minneapolis: Fortress, forthcoming.

World Missionary Conference. *Report of Commission VIII: Cooperation and the Promotion of Unity*. Edinburgh: Oliphant, Anderson, and Ferrier, 1910.

Zhao, Puchu, and K. H. Ting (Ding Guangxun). "Tan Luo shizong jiaozheng ci wenti." [On the Implementation of Religious Policy] *Renmin ribao* (September 9, 1980) 3.

Zhu, Rachel Xiaohong. "Bishop Jin Luxian and the Chinese Catholic Patriotic Association of Shanghai." In *People, Communities, and the Catholic Church in China*, edited by Cindy Yik-yi Chu and Paul P. Mariani, 45–59. Singapore: Palgrave Macmillan, 2020.

Zhuo, Xinping. "Original Sin in the East-West Dialogue—A Chinese View." *Studies in World Christianity* 1 (1995) 80–86.

CHAPTER 16

Sri Lankan Theology

JUDE LAL FERNANDO

Theologies emerging from Sri Lanka (hitherto called Lankan theology) form an essential part of the Asian theological movement. Lankan theology embodies critical reflections of faith on a range of socio-political conflicts that affected diverse national groups in the country. These conflicts were formed with an increasing awareness of poverty, religious discrimination, and national oppression undergone by various communities, mainly as a result of Western colonial practice and subsequent neocolonialism. In identifying salient features of Lankan theology, it is necessary to interrogate the historical conditions that have formed the country; a theology that liberates requires critical reflection on historical praxis. Part one of this chapter probes how the island was shaped as a country through its encounter with European colonial powers and accompanying Christian missions. This is the broad context within which specific socio-political conflicts emerged. Part two demonstrates a range of Christian theological responses to these conflicts. The conclusion reflects on how Lankan theology may be enhanced by furthering an anti-imperialist and postcolonial standpoint to bring together the distinct struggles of the oppressed peoples on the island.

A CRITICAL REFLECTION OF HISTORY

The Broad Context: The Colonial

In ancient times, the island was called "Taprobane" by cartographers from overseas, but the islanders who belonged to different kingdoms identified themselves with the dynastic domains to which they belonged, some with dual allegiances. In the European colonial era, the Portuguese (1505–1658), Dutch (1658–1796), and British (1815–1948) called the island "Ceylon," derived from "Sinhala-dīpa": the island of the Sinhala ethnic group. Locally this term referred to the kingdoms of the Sinhala-speaking southern part of the island, with a predominantly Buddhist population, and not to the north's Tamil dynastic domain with a predominantly Hindu population. Muslim communities were present in all the kingdoms.

The Portuguese and Dutch maintained two administrative units for the maritime provinces in the north and the south that they conquered, and in these regions (amongst the Buddhists and Hindus respectively) most of the proselytizing Christian missions were established. British colonial rule succeeded in controlling the entire island from 1815. Politically, it was Christian rulers that dominated a non-Christian people of different faiths. Theologically, Christ was pitted against Buddhists, Hindus, and Muslims. Socially, Christianity became the only religious tradition present amongst the two ethnic/linguistic groups: Sinhalese and Tamils. Economically, British rule marginalized both Sinhala and Tamil peasantry and promoted local landlords who joined the plantation sector where thousands of laborers brought from South India were exploited.

As the geo-strategic importance of the island in the Indian Ocean region increased in containing other rival imperial powers like France, British rule amalgamated diverse regions of the island into a rigid political structure in 1833. With an Orientalist gaze, the colonial officers who translated ancient Pali texts into English portrayed the history of the island as a perennial conflict between "native" Sinhala Buddhists and "invading" Tamils (thus portraying ancient South Indian dynastic invasions in racially nationalist terms). The island that was treated by local Buddhist history as "Dhamma-dīpa" (island of *dhamma*) was territorialized as belonging to racially "superior" Aryan Sinhalese (a numerical majority), as opposed to "inferior" Dravidian Tamils (a numerical minority). The close relationship of the Sinhalese with Buddhism was racialized, erasing Tamil contributions to Buddhism. Tamils were portrayed as essentially Hindus, although Tamil language and culture are broader than Vedic Hinduism. British occupation converted the island into a strategic asset, separating it from India, and even regenerating ancient Buddhist sites.

A covert imperial theology lay beneath this liberal intervention: the British become the saviors of Sinhala Buddhists, whose land has been defiled by Hindu Tamils. The Sinhalese were made to believe that the entire island belongs to them, while the British Empire forged a state structure on the island to fit its geo-strategic complex: the white saviour returns ancient but lost glory to the island. The founder of Sinhala Buddhist nationalism, Anagarika Dharmapala, embodied this colonial mindset, declaring his enmity towards non-Sinhalese, whereas his "loyalty to the British Throne is as hard as a rock."[1] Thus were generated the historical conditions of the Sinhala-Tamil

---

1. Guruge, *Anagarika Dharmapala*, 46.

conflict, leading to the oppression of Tamils by the Sinhala-dominated neocolonial state, formed after formal independence in 1948.

For centuries, Christian missions had occupied a powerful position in different colonial periods and engaged in aggressive missionary activities against the local faith communities. The close relationship between the churches and the British state led to the formation of Christian schools that not only engaged in proselytism, but was also a service provider to the colonial state, delivering a job-oriented education to form a privileged social class, whilst also carrying the "white man's burden" of civilizing the natives. Thus, the Christian churches not only propagated theological and civilizational supremacy over Sinhala-speaking Buddhists and Tamil-speaking Hindus and Muslims, they also wielded economic and social power that alienated faith communities within the two main linguistic groups. This linguistic colonization disparaged vernacular education (limited to primary level), as being riddled with error and superstition. The emerging system of education and employment alienated a majority of Sinhalese and Tamils. The English language and Christianity together bolstered colonial social power, propagating a theology of domination and exclusion; this was carried out under a strategically engineered unitary political structure, emboldening internal Sinhala supremacy over the Tamils.

The Specific Context: Postcolonial or Neocolonial?

After formal independence, marginalized Sinhala social groups who had resisted the dominance of the English language were driven by the Sinhala racial ideology associated with the unitary political structure. Sinhala was declared the only official language in 1956, excluding Tamils from state and public sector employment. Nonviolent Tamil protests were attacked by Sinhala racist groups, with hundreds killed. In 1972, Ceylon was renamed "Sri Lanka," and declared a unitary state that accords a primary place to Buddhism. As oppression and repression heightened, the Tamil national movement evolved into an armed mode which by the 1990s had gradually formed a *de facto* state, "Tamil Eelam," in the north and east of the island. The Sri Lankan state's war against the Eelam Tamils, which officially ended in 2009, massacred thousands and totally destroyed the Tamil state; the colonially engineered unitary state was thus reconsolidated, perpetuating oppression. This war was supported mainly by Britain and the US.

Particularly after formal independence, Sinhala Christians in the south gradually identified themselves with a state-led racial ideology, in which the island was given to the Sinhalese by God. During the war (1981–2009) they prayed for the security forces. Tamil Christians became part of the secular Eelam Tamil national movement; priests, pastors, and nuns drew significantly on the themes of Exodus and exile in their reflections with a people undergoing continuous displacement.

By the end of 1960s, a Sinhala-educated generation (mostly sons and daughters of those who fought for "Sinhala Only" in the mid-1950s) faced marginalization as they could not find employment in an economic system that continued to maintain colonial conditions. The first Sinhala youth revolt took place in 1971, with nearly ten thousand massacred by state forces. The official church stood for law and order rather than for justice for the alienated. Although there were marginalized sectors of Christians, particularly the fishing communities on the Western coastal belt, they mostly followed the church hierarchy and only a small number were part of the revolt. This socio-political conflict, however, challenged many Christians. The second youth revolt (1987–89) followed further marginalization of Sinhala youth after neoliberal economic reforms. The state massacred nearly sixty thousand young men and women, including Buddhist monks. The official church distanced itself from the uprising or sided with the government, despite many more Christian communities being affected than in the first revolt. By then many Christians who had embraced a critical historical consciousness regarding the role of the church challenged state repression and demanded social justice.

A majority in the Sinhala political movement in the south (both Buddhist and Christian) which demanded social justice, failed to question the unitary state structure and its racial ideology even after they themselves had encountered brutal state repression. They opposed the 2002 peace process between the Tamil liberation movement and the Sri Lankan state, which was meant to formally reduce the power of the unitary state, and demanded a military solution invoking the global war on terror. The military victory of the Sri Lankan state, aided by the global powers, generated deep polarization between Sinhalese and Tamils. The Sinhala Church opposed the Tamil Church's demand for justice for victims of war. After this military victory, Sinhala racist groups launched an anti-Muslim campaign, which intensified after suicide attacks on churches and hotels on Easter Sunday 2019. A Sinhala Christian and Buddhist alliance has been forged against Tamils and Tamil-speaking Muslims. The Sinhala Christian hierarchy has conflated its demand for justice for the victims of the Easter attacks with Islamophobia. What liberating theological insights have emerged in this historical trajectory?

TOWARDS POSTCOLONIAL THEOLOGIES

Progression of the Theological Imagination

Lankan theology emerged from increased awareness of the collective experiences of alienation, and also from a people's collective dignity, inseparable from culture, language, and faith. A theology that liberates, opposes domination, and declares freedom in creative ways. Theologies that emerged out of the conflicts treated above, do not rely on the institutional power of the church and Christian superiority, but on Scriptures, faiths, local cultures, languages, and socio-political experiences. Theological resistance to Eurocentrism has progressed from being a theology of inculturation and dialogue to one of liberation, and has endeavoured to include all three aspects.

Tamil is Spiritual and Secular

Thani Nayagam was a Tamil Christian leader and a renowned linguist, whose mastery of Tamil culture and language earned him the title "adigalaar" (someone who is loved, respected). He studied Tamil not to proselytize Hindus, as his predecessors did, but to plunge into the lived experience of his people, whose literature captures distinctive relationships between the divine, the human, and nature. Four creative theological features emerge from his commentaries on Tamil literature, resisting not only English and Sinhala supremacy, but also Brahmin-dominated Hindu claims over Tamil culture and language. First, the Tamils upheld the transcendence of God in a specific material or cosmic way: "Nature, and their primary occupation, determine the aspect under which this Supreme God is determined."[2] Transcendence was experienced in the hills (God as "Murukan" or "Ceeyon," Lord of the Hill, the hunter), when these were the only habitable places. Murukan means beauty, youth, and godhead; ancient Tamils associated the godhead with perennial youth and beauty as reflected in nature.[3]

This idea of a youthful God has emerged from the Tamil indigeneity of Christian faith. God is called "Thirumaal" or "Mayoon." "Varunam" was the name given to God when Tamils moved to the maritime tracks.[4] These names disclose the plurality of aspects under which God is worshiped, and connect the transcendence of God with the immanence of daily life and work. Second, the relationship between the beauty of nature and God-consciousness in Tamil poetry reminds Christians of Jesus's parables of the reign of God.[5] The material spirituality evident in both express a sense of the sacredness of the cosmos and livelihood, resisting consumerist materialism. Third, Nayagam realizes that the Tamil Bhakti literature grants irreducibly self-involving possibilities for expressing praise of the divine. The words are imaginatively potent and may initiate their readers into a deep spiritual experience. Promoting Tamil entails propagating a sense of God ("Katavul") which is not exclusive to one faith and Nayagam does so with a modern secular sensibility. Tamil, therefore, is spiritual and secular, it is neither religiously exclusivist nor anti-religious, but pluralist. Fourth, Nayagam recovers the humanism and universality in the spirituality of Tamil speakers, and which is enshrined in an ancient poem: "Every locality is my locality, everybody is my relative."[6] He stated that to be a Tamil necessarily implies "the citizenship of the

---

2. Thani Nayaga Adigalaar Centenary Celebration Committee, *Complete Works*, 1:62.
3. Thani Nayaga Adigalaar Centenary Celebration Committee, *Complete Works*, 1:59.
4. Thani Nayaga Adigalaar Centenary Celebration Committee, *Complete Works*, 1:66.
5. Pillai, "Grace of Experiencing Nature," 63.
6. Velupillai, "Thani Nayagam Adikal," 55.

world."[7] The colonial racialization of Tamil as inferior is subverted by Nayagam with the eyes of faith. "I bowed with folded hands towards the Church of Jesus and to God who had given me Tamil as my mother tongue."[8] In the 1950s, he joined nonviolent protests over discrimination against the Tamil language, and founded the quarterly *Tamil Culture* (1952) and the International Association of Tamil Research (1964).

Creatureliness in the Bible and Not-Self in Buddhism

Lynn A. de Silva, a Sinhala theologian, returns to the scriptural sources of both Buddhism and Christianity, overcoming polemics against Buddhism while retrieving the core of the biblical message. His mastery of Pali, biblical Hebrew, and Greek enabled him to offer a mutually corrective view of the respective teachings of both traditions. Traditionally, Christianity has been presented as a belief in the existence of an immortal soul, and Christian missionaries dismissed the Buddhist doctrine of *anattā* (not-self or no soul). Buddhist scholars who challenged Christian polemics then argued against the existence of an indestructible soul and God. De Silva states that the Buddhist teaching of not-self accords with the biblical account, in which human beings are created out of dust and return to dust at death, while holding on to the doctrine of God. The traditional view that human beings have an indestructible, immortal soul is not biblical, but Hellenistic. The doctrine of not-self can awaken Christians to their human creatureliness. What corrective, then, can Christians offer to Buddhists? Not-self is not the fragmentation of the human person into several components or nihilism; it prompts us to seek something beyond our individuality. The biblical term *pneuma* (spirit) does not signify the existence of soul, "but a dynamic quality of being which uplifts human beings above finite existence."[9] This capacity to overcome egoistic individuality can be interpreted by the Buddhist as not-self. If we are not-self, or embody creatureliness, then the meaning of life lies in the reality beyond our individual self which is an aspect of the Ultimate Reality: Nirvana/God. No-soul does not imply a denial of God, but rather seeing God. Not-self does not lead to nihilism, but to *Nirvana*, Enlightenment.[10]

De Silva's efforts to enhance mutual understanding of both traditions was a response to the socio-political reality of the 1960s and 1970s, which was marked by an increasing awareness of the alienation of Sinhala working classes, peasants, university students, and of Tamils. He extends his dialogical approach to secular activists, engaged in Marxist social analysis in seeking justice. A Christian emphasis on creatureliness prompts human beings to enter into right relationships based on mutuality. A Buddhist doctrine of not-self leads one to selflessness. Both traditions uphold

---

7. Xavier, "Thani Nayagam," 118.
8. Xavier, "Thani Nayagam," 120.
9. De Silva, "Problem of the Self in Buddhism and Christianity," 110.
10. De Silva, "Problem of the Self in Buddhism and Christianity," 234–37.

transcendence. Building mutual relationships require selflessness to avoid egocentric attachments. Selflessness should not be confused with individual detachment or sanctity, and should be accompanied by entering into mutual relationships to become socially relevant and engaged. A person who is rightly related and selfless has "a deep concern for social justice and the removal of those things that create divisiveness between human being and human being." "Anything that is done compassionately to remove alienation of human to human, whether by the so-called religious people or by the so-called secular people, is spiritual."[11] De Silva directed the Ecumenical Institute for Study and Dialogue in Colombo which created space for scholars and activists from diverse national groups to engage in dialogue.

The Jordan of Asian Religion and the Calvary of Asian Poverty

Aloysius Pieris is the first Christian in the country to obtain a doctorate under the supervision of Buddhist monks. His deep awareness of the Asian dual reality of religious plurality and poverty arose with his immersion into Buddhism, which he studied literally at the foot of erudite monks and his empathic listening to the cries and hopes of two generations of Sinhala youth who were massacred for demanding social justice.[12] His methodology is equipped with the tools of scriptural analysis (both biblical and other Asian religions) and socio-historical analysis; he maintains that there cannot be two liberating voices, one in the Scriptures and another in contemporary history.[13] His classic trilogy, *An Asian Theology of Liberation* (1988), *Love Meets Wisdom* (1988), and *Fire and Water* (1996), has become a landmark in the Asian liberation theology movement.

Christians are called to embrace the most authentic spirituality of Asia, just as Jesus went through the baptism of water, representing the prophetic tradition as opposed to a self-righteous spirituality of a religious elite. The Baptizer was the renouncer who lived a spirituality of total austerity. Similarly, the nontheistic/wisdom-based Buddhist doctrine of not-self/detachment is embodied socially in the monastic life of the monks by the adoption of voluntary poverty in Asia. It is this authentic spirituality that the church, which is preoccupied with protecting its identity, power, and wealth in Asia, should consider as its first baptism. "Does not the fear of losing its identity keep the local church from discovering it?"[14] However, voluntary poverty practiced amidst the masses who experience enforced poverty makes no sense without participation in their struggle for justice and liberation which is based on love. The Baptizer attracted "the religious poor" who sought justice based on a material spirituality, not the acquisitive materialism of the ruling classes. The Baptizer condemned the latter

11. De Silva, "Problem of the Self in Buddhism and Christianity," 246.
12. See chapter 1, Pieris, *Prophetic Humour in Buddhism and Christianity*.
13. Pieris, *Genesis of an Asian Theology of Liberation*, 55.
14. Pieris, *Asian Theology of Liberation*, 48.

but did not impose his lifestyle on the religious poor. Jesus comes to the River Jordan "not to baptize others, but to be baptized, thus identifying with the 'religious poor' of the countryside": but there is a distinction between the two:[15] "The Baptizer preached bad news about the coming judgment, but Jesus, who he baptized, had good news to give about imminent liberation" by forming "a community of love."[16]

On the cross, Jesus goes through the second baptism (of fire), which is the price he pays to build a community of love on earth that forms the basis of Christian discipleship. "Does not the fear of dying keep the [church] from living its true mission?"[17] For Pieris, Jesus Christ is both the cry of the poor to God seeking liberation, and God's promise of salvation to them embodied in one person. This is the true identity of Christian faith. Through Jesus Christ, God enters into a covenant with the poor against Mammon (power, prestige, and wealth). In this sense, whoever struggles for justice, regardless of their religious affiliation, follows the path of Christ; but they should be recognized in their own terms, for Christ is synonymous with "the plenitude of salvation and revelation"[18] who is joined by "many other providential co-mediators, including us."[19] Was not the official church a counter-witness to the Gospel in the uprisings of the Sinhala youth? Pieris critiques not only an affluent church which thrives on the power of the West, but also those Buddhist monasteries that do not engage in the struggle for justice. However, Pieris invites the religious other to tell the Christians who Jesus Christ is following the question "Who do you say I am?"

A Buddhist monk who practices voluntary poverty and engaged in the struggle for social justice in the 1980s painted a mural of the Last Supper at Pieris's Centre, portraying Jesus as one who stood against class, gender, and caste discrimination.[20] In response to the national question, Pieris challenges racialized relations and upholds a theology of multiethnic peoplehood based on "a Divine Being genuinely concerned with the plight of the 'slaves', as opposed to 'a racist god.'"[21] Pieris has founded Tulana, the Centre for Interreligious Dialogue and Research, and has engaged in cross-scriptural reading and social analysis with university students and social activists for over four decades. He is the editor of *Dialogue* and *Vāgdevi*.

The Bowels of Compassion of Jesus and the Melting Heart of the Buddha

In 1980, Michael Rodrigo, a theologian and scholar of Buddhism, left the ecclesiastical comfort of urban centers and adopted voluntary poverty by forming a small Christian

---

15. Pieris, *Asian Theology of Liberation*, 46.
16. Pieris, *Asian Theology of Liberation*. 48.
17. Pieris, *Asian Theology of Liberation*. 48.
18. Pieris, *Genesis of an Asian Theology of Liberation*, 29.
19. Pieris, *Genesis of an Asian Theology of Liberation*, 30.
20. Pieris, *Fire and Water*, 133–37.
21. Pieris, *Fire and Water*, 135.

community with two nuns and a layperson in the heart of Uva-Wellassa, one of the most poverty-stricken Buddhist regions of Sri Lanka. British colonial memory and its associated Christian identity continued to haunt the villagers. The neocolonial state had let a multinational company acquire vast tracks of land for agribusiness, reducing farmers to exploited wage laborers. Rodrigo's community never preached the gospel and baptized. Instead, it engaged for years with the struggle of peasants for land, water, livelihood, health care, and education, and were joined by the Buddhist *sangha* who invited the priest to preach the *dhamma* in the temple relating it to the context. Rodrigo's community openly identified with victims of state repression in the second youth uprising. Conscious of the ongoing war against Tamils in the north and east—and which was supported by a majority of Sinhalese and major global powers—Rodrigo, a Sinhala Christian, empathized with the oppressed Tamil people, recognizing their historical grievances in signaling the way to peace based on justice between the two distinct nations.

Rodrigo contextualizes the compassion of Jesus ("the Bowels of Compassion of Jesus") for the multitudes who were hungry and the Buddha's loving kindness, *mettā* ("the Melting Heart of the Buddha"), as the point of departure for blending liberation and dialogue. This kind of compassion is so powerful that it moves faith communities in dialogue to stand for the life and livelihood of peasants and victims of repression.[22] Such a mission necessitates *kenosis* (self-emptying) and *anattā* (not-self) for, "unless there is this basic human trait operative in religion and society there is nothing truly human."[23] At a time of heightened levels of state repression, Rodrigo and his community opted to leave the region for safety, but during a community eucharistic celebration (which was never public) they decided to stay. As this act of worship drew to a close, on November 10, 1987, Rodrigo was assassinated by "an unknown gunman" from the state security apparatus. His life embodies the dual Asian baptism that Pieris proposed to Christians in Asia. Rodrigo continues to inspire not only many Christians, but also people of other faiths, giving Lankan theology an unsurpassable vitality through his life and death.

The Eucharist as a Common Meal and Mary of the Magnificat

Tissa Balasuriya combines his dual academic training in social analysis and systematic theology, posing difficult questions to the church regarding social inequalities. His most known works include *Jesus Christ and Human Liberation* (1976), *The Eucharist and Human Liberation* (1979), *Planetary Theology* (1984), and *Mary and Human Liberation* (1990). "Why is it that persons and people who proclaim eucharistic love and sharing deprive the poor people of the world of food, capital, employment and even

---

22. Rodrigo, "Buddhism and Christianity," 58.
23. Rodrigo, "Buddhism and Christianity," 56.

land?"²⁴ The local church has followed the colonial ways of celebrating the Eucharist by the Portuguese, Dutch, and British, and a vernacular liturgy has not altered its formalism and ritualism. The dynamism of the Lord's Supper and his final sacrifice has been suffocated by a church that has compromised with the prevailing power structures. "The Eucharist is universalist; the world is racist . . . The eucharistic bread is a common meal for all; but bread in the world is a commodity for trade. In the eucharistic ideas, land is for common use; in the present system of nation-states, land is for the successful conquerors."²⁵

His *Mary and Human Liberation*, which led to his brief excommunication by the Roman Curia, resulted from his encounter with the feminist movement, and from the super-exploitation of women in new modes of labor in the free-trade zones and in domestic work in the Middle East that emerged in Sri Lanka after 1977. Balasuriya problematizes traditional ways in which Mary was presented by a male church hierarchy as someone totally different from ordinary women, attaching excessive importance to her virginity, immaculate conception, and assumption, with dogmas and devotions which accord her a range of extraordinary titles. Vernacular inculturation has been uncritical of such Mariology, which reinforces Christian supremacy over other religions, as salvation is made possible for those who follow one born of a woman without original sin.[26] "Is it better for Mary to be immaculate, or to be normally human as other women and men have been and act? . . . What is bad about being a mother in the normal way, as the Creator has made human nature?"[27] He highlights how Mary, as "a mature adult woman who was concerned about her people," extended her support to "the struggle of her son and the group that gathered around him in a search for integral human liberation."

Balasuriya reconstructs a Marian Way of the Cross as a journey of human liberation. At every station of the cross Jesus and Mary together share the same "unbending determination . . . to the end." They knew the "price of human liberation."[28] This story is not governed by original sin, with Jesus paying the price, but concerns "the brutal use of imperial power, with the local elite to kill a prophetic leader of the Jewish people."[29] Balasuriya names different ways in which women are oppressed in the country and sees the Mary of the Magnificat as a source of strength for these women in their yearning for humanity. Christian discipleship is "a call to determination, courage and endurance . . . to transform the evil system that makes so many fall under the weight of the daily cross."[30] Balasuriya pioneered many campaigns for social justice. He

24. Balasuriya, *Eucharist and Human Liberation*, xii.
25. Balasuriya, *Eucharist and Human Liberation*, 141–42.
26. Balasuriya, *Mary and Human Liberation*, 119–20.
27. Balasuriya, *Mary and Human Liberation*, 201.
28. Balasuriya, *Mary and Human Liberation*, 251.
29. Balasuriya, *Mary and Human Liberation*, 255.
30. Balasuriya, *Mary and Human Liberation*, 251.

was a founding member of the Ecumenical Association of Third World Theologians and the founder-director of the Centre for Society and Religion in Sri Lanka.

Interrelationship of Struggles and Oneness

In the early 1990s, state repression of the 1987–1989 youth uprising and the war against the Tamils moved a group of Christians in the Western Province to form a committed group of activists to publish the Sinhala monthly, *Kithusara*, by which name the group is also known. Although not formally trained scholars, their work is informed by the work of the theologians noted above, and, in particular, by the life and death of Rodrigo. They also published a Tamil quarterly, *Oliyai Nokki*. Both publications communicated to the two national groups each other's struggles for justice. The group adopted a simple lifestyle, conducted social awareness programs with marginalized sectors such as children, women, fishermen and women, the landless, Tamil refugees, and diverse communities of faiths. They were highly critical of the official church which constantly compromised with the state.

The group's theological reflections are shared through frequent public seminars, discussions, pamphlets, hymns, and books that express the extent of their engagements with local socio-political and ecological realities. Their theology has not yet been published in English, but there are commentarial references to the group in some articles on Lankan Christianity. They have reinterpreted a key biblical imperative, showing the interrelationship of the distinct struggles on the island. "Whatever you would not like to happen to yourself, do not let it happen to your brother and sister. As you do not wish to see your land destroyed then do not allow the land of your brother and sister to be destroyed . . . As you wish for your grievances and struggle to be understood, understand the grievance and the struggle of your brother and sister . . ."[31] It is an appeal for justice to a Sinhala political movement which does not recognise the Tamil liberation struggle. In a popular hymn, they contextualize the mystical body of Christ as present amongst the poor, those killed in war and in the dry land by awakening us to the oneness of eco-humanity.[32] The group is one of the most formidable grassroots movements engaging in Sinhala-Tamil and interfaith conversations, blending faiths and justice.

The God of Mullivaikkal

Rasika Pieris, an emerging feminist theologian, makes the experience of war widows her context of theologizing by gathering their stories of resistance and hope, particularly after the massacre of Tamils in 2009 in Mullivaikkal. Following the methodology

---

31. Fernando, *Religion, Conflict and Peace in Sri Lanka*, 310.
32. Fernando, "Realisation of Anattā and Witness to Resurrection," 292.

of first-generation liberation theologians, she identifies the cause of the widows' suffering in sinful socio-political structures, not in personal sin or *karma* as preached by both the male hierarchy of the church and the Buddhist *sangha*. However, by adopting a feminist theological critique, Pieris questions the glorification of redemptive suffering in the form of voluntary suffering and sacrificial love that some liberation theologians tend to promote. Instead, she emphasizes overcoming suffering through a liberative struggle (against national oppression, militarization, land grab, enforced disappearances, state brutality, patriarchy, etc.). The experience of war widows is only a hermeneutical lens, but the liberative struggle is the norm with which the experience has to be critically assessed.[33] She points out how widows, particularly Tamil, are engaged in such a struggle which embodies hope even after a mass atrocity of genocidal proportions. "Tamil war-widows expressed that the God who they encountered in 'Mullivaikkal' is a God who struggled with them against the oppressor who attempted to eliminate Tamils and their dream of living in a distinct nation. They reveal that their God did not want them to suffer; instead, God was with them in their struggle to affirm the dignity of Tamils, the oppressed in general and the women in particular."[34] Pieris continues to work on programs to empower women.

CONCLUSION

The above theologies emerged in different contexts not simply as individual articulations. They reflect a critically reflective space in society that has been formed through a range of struggles by the marginalized on the island. In this space, we find a recovery of Scriptures, not simply exegetically but hermeneutically, utilizing critique and recreation based on evolving diverse experiences and liberative struggles. New faces of the liberating God are revealed, opposing an imperial deity, dismantling the colonial portrayal of the divine *as above* and *we are below*. Instead this God is *with* us and *ahead* of us, participating in our historical struggles. God speaks as a secular/pluralist Tamil resisting racial oppression. God is Nirvana, the realization of *anattā*, who calls for right relationships through voluntary poverty and struggle for justice amongst the Sinhala peasants. The self-emptying God revealed in Christ embodies both the cry and hope of the marginalized youth. These are sources for postcolonial theologies which arise from distinct sites of struggles which are interrelated with one another. Yet the interrelationship among struggles is blurred, as there is no postcolonial critique of the ways in which "One Sri Lanka" has been constructed as a neocolonial geo-strategic imperial asset which racially bolsters the Sinhalese over the Tamils and Tamil-speaking Muslims. The geopolitics of an empire that promises peace under One Sri Lanka goes not only against Tamil demand for freedom in their homeland, but also heightens Islamophobia against the Tamil-speaking Muslims. This peace is bleeding.

33. Pieris, "Hope that Confronts Oppression and Suffering," 99–103.
34. Pieris, *Breaking the Barriers*, 403.

It keeps Tamils under subjugation and deprives the Sinhalese of their political and moral consciousness, making the entire island a neocolonial military complex. The God of Mullivaikkal encountered by the Tamil war widows resists the imperial peace that obstructs the vision of interrelationship of distinct struggles. Lankan theology has to be enhanced seeing this new face of God.

BIBLIOGRAPHY

Balasuriya, Tissa. *The Eucharist and Human Liberation*. New York: Orbis, 1979.

———. *Mary and Human Liberation*. Colombo: Centre for Society and Religion, 2014.

De Silva, Lynn Alton. "Emerging Theology in the Context of Buddhism." In *Pioneering Explorations in Interreligious Dialogue by Rev. Dr. Lynn Alton De Silva*, edited by Marshal Fernando, 229–250. Colombo: Ecumenical Institute for Study and Dialogue, 2013. .

———. "The Problem of Self in Buddhism and Christianity." In *Pioneering Explorations in Interreligious Dialogue by Rev. Dr. Lynn Alton De Silva*, edited by Marshal Fernando, 103–16. Colombo: Ecumenical Institute for Study and Dialogue, 2013

Fernando, Jude Lal. *Religion, Conflict and Peace in Sri Lanka: The Politics of Interpretation of Nationhoods*. Berlin: LIT, 2013.

Fernando, Jude Lal. "Realisation of Anattā and Witness to Resurrection: Socio-political Implications for a *Dhammadīpa*." In *A Visionary Approach: Lynn A. de Silva and the Prospects of Buddhist-Christian Encounter*, edited by Elizabeth J. Harris and Perry Schmidt-Leukel, 275–98. Munich: EOS, 2021.

Guruge, Ananda, ed. *Anagarika Dharmapala*. 3rd ed. Colombo: Ministry of Cultural Affairs and Information, 1991.

Pieris, Aloysius. *An Asian Theology of Liberation*. Edinburgh: T. & T. Clark, 1988.

———. *Fire and Water: Basic Issues in Asian Buddhism and Christianity*. New York: Orbis, 1996.

———. *The Genesis of an Asian Theology of Liberation: An Autobiographical Excurses on the Art of Theologizing in Asia*. Gonawala-Kelaniya: Tulana Research Centre, 2013.

———. *Prophetic Humour in Buddhism and Christianity: Doing Inter-Religious Dialogue in a Reverential Mode*. Colombo: Ecumenical Institute for Study and Dialogue, 2005.

Pieris, Rasika Sharmen. *Breaking the Barriers: A Reflection on Suffering in Buddhism and Christianity in the Perspectives of War-Widows in Sri Lanka*. Doctoral thesis, Radboud University Nijmegen, 2017.

———. "Hope that Confronts Oppression and Suffering: Faith and War-Affected Women in Sri Lanka." In *Faith in the Face of Militarization: Indigenous, Feminist and Interreligious Voices*, edited by Jude Lal Fernando, 89–111. Eugene, OR: Pickwick, 2021.

Pillai, Joachim. "The Grace of Experiencing Nature: One Way of Looking at Fr Thani Nayagam's Life." In *Rev. Dr. Thani Nayagam*, edited by Anton Sinnarasa Philip, 61–72. Toronto: Canacath Thoothan, 2013.

Rodrigo, Michael. "Beginnings of Suba Seth Gedara. " In *Harvest Dreams of Fr. Mike*, edited by Milburga Fernando, 36–43. Colombo: Centre for Society and Religion, 2010.

———. "Buddhism and Christianity: Towards the Human Future." In *Harvest Dreams of Fr. Mike*, edited by Milburga Fernando, 55–72. Colombo: Centre for Society and Religion, 2010.

SECTION 4 | Emerging Theologies from Asia

Thani Nayaga Adigalaar Centenary Celebration Committee, ed. *Complete Works of Thani Nayaga Adigalaar, Volume 1*. Chennai: Poompuhar Pathippagam, 2013.

Velupillai, Alvapillai. "Thani Nayagam Adikal: The Man and His Vision." In *Rev. Dr. Thani Nayagam*, edited by Anton Sinnarasa Philip, 54–60. Toronto: Canacath Thoothan, 2013.

Xavier, N. Maria. "Thani Nayagam: A Pioneer Secular Priest." In *Rev. Dr. Thani Nayagam*, edited by Anton Sinnarasa Philip, 111–22. Toronto: Canacath Thoothan, 2013.

CHAPTER 17

Korean Theologies

SEBASTIAN KIM

For over five thousand years, Koreans have maintained their unique identity as a people although a small nation surrounded by powerful nations: China, Russia, and Japan. The mid-twentieth-century Korean thinker Ham Sok Hon characterized the country as the "queen of suffering" because the country was the victim of aggression by its neighbors, and by the West, from the mid-nineteenth century until recently.[1] Catholic Christianity was introduced to the Korean peninsula by European missionaries via China in the late eighteenth century and Protestant missionaries arrived mainly from North America a century later. Christianity grew in the midst of national crisis, which included Japanese occupation, the Korean War, postwar poverty, military-backed governments, and the division between North and South.[2]

Korean theological discourse has developed as Christians struggled to survive and nation-build amid these geopolitical challenges. Religiously, it has incorporated Christian theologies brought from outside on the one hand, and on the other hand, it has responded to traditional religions such as Buddhism, Confucianism, and shamanism. In recent years, particularly after the achievement of democratization around 1990, South Korea has gained confidence through her rapid economic growth, prioritization of education, transition to democracy through civil movements, and cultural ascendency around the world. In the midst of these national developments, Korean Christianity has forged its own distinctive theologies to cope with dire situations, lead

---

1. Ham, *Queen of Suffering*.
2. See Kim and Kim, *History of Korean Christianity*.

the nation out of its suffering, and provide vision and hope for the nations. However, often the churches have failed to meet the expectations of the people.

In this chapter, I shall first briefly discuss what I see as four distinctively Korean theologies formulated by Protestant theologians after independence from Japan in 1945 to democratization in the 1990s.[3] I shall then examine the post-democratization era of Korea, which differs significantly from the previous period both politically and socio-economically. Like any theology, Korean theologies did not appear out of a vacuum, but they are the outcome of their interactions with missionaries and theologies from the West and with the local context. Although the elements may not be original, they have been formulated into distinctively Korean theologies as churches engaged with the problems presented to them.

KOREAN THEOLOGIES IN POST-INDEPENDENCE KOREA

The colonialization of the Korean peninsula for thirty-six years by Japan caused pain and humiliation in every aspect of national life. It also inflicted serious persecution of Christians since they were at the forefront of the independence movements, and later, suffered the imposition of Shinto rituals on their worship. The economy and human resources were exploited to the limit, especially to serve the Japanese military toward the end of the Pacific War. Soon after independence, the country was divided by the superpowers and along Korean ideological differences. The resulting Korean War caused immense destruction of people and property on the Korean peninsula, which reduced Korea to one of the poorest nations in the world.

After this devastation and turmoil, four distinctive Korean theologies emerged. First, the gospel of holistic blessing had become dominant in Korean Christianity through the Protestant revival meetings that started in the early twentieth century. This form of faith and worship became increasingly popular among Christians after independence, especially through the rise of Pentecostalism. The person who epitomizes this approach is David (or Paul) Yonggi Cho of the Full Gospel Church in Seoul. The harsh reality of extreme poverty during post war Korea caused Cho to see the gospel as having promise for material as well as spiritual life. He adopted the theology of "threefold blessing": "spiritual well-being, general well-being, and bodily health." The theology of holistic blessing was not limited to the Full Gospel Church but extended to most of the mainline Protestant churches because of their revivalist tradition. In prayer meetings, revival meetings, and small group meetings, various gifts of the Holy Spirit were encouraged as a sign of God's blessing. Healings, success in business, and material blessings were often proclaimed by church leaders and testified to by members of congregation. Although this may seem like a version of the prosperity gospel, in spite of its problems and shortcomings, the gospel of holistic blessing was one way

---

3. See Kim, "Word and the Spirit," 129–53.

for Koreans to express their desire to overcome poverty and despair by casting their burdens onto God who holds the authority not only over the spiritual realms but also over every area of human life.

Second, theological discourse was drawn out from the labor struggles in the context of the government drive towards economic growth that resulted in an increasing gap between rich and poor, and between employer and employees. While the majority of Christian leaders regarded the inequality and injustice as a necessary evil for achieving economic growth that would somehow be sorted out as the whole nation made enough progress, a group of theologians and activists took a theological stance against the injustice. *Minjung* theology played a key role during the 1960s and 1970s in challenging the military-backed governments and the exploitation of factory workers by *jaebeol*, or family-run mega-companies. Suh Nam-dong argued that Jesus identified with the poor, sick, and oppressed ordinary people, or *minjung*, and that the gospel of Jesus is one of salvation and liberation. For Suh, the struggle with the powers and liberation from evil is not individual or spiritual but rather communal and political. He systematized *minjung* theology in the following years, seeing the *minjung* as the subjects (or agents) of history and introducing *han*, or anguish and despair, as the key theme for theology in the Korean context. Ahn Byung-mu, another well-known *minjung* theologian, asserted that Jesus identified with the oppressed to the extent that "Jesus is minjung and minjung is Jesus," and the event of the cross is the climax of the suffering of the *minjung*. He also insisted that the *minjung* is the owner of the Jesus community and that it is fundamentally a community that shares food. *Minjung* theology captured people's imagination through poetry and art. It was instrumental in building the civil movement that toppled the military government and challenged both church and society to deal with problems of injustice in South Korea.

The third strand of post-independence Korean theology, which was much discussed in the 1960s, was "folk Christianity" that seeks the integration of Christianity with Korean religiosity and culture. The Korean people are known for their religiosity. Major world religions—Buddhism, Confucianism, and Christianity—were introduced into Korea in different periods and each favored by different dynasties. These interacted with one another while the prehistoric traditions like shamanism pervaded each of them. The two foremost theologians in this field were Ryu Dong-sik and Yun Sung-beom. In his thesis on "Tao and Logos," Ryu suggested that the use of eastern philosophy of the Way is necessary for conveying the message of the Christian gospel in Asia. He also described the dynamics of the development of Korean theology as the result of constant interaction between "paternal" and "maternal" movements of the Holy Spirit. The former approach reflects the Confucian tradition and explains the conservative and hierarchical aspects of Korean church life, while the latter represents a shamanistic approach to the faith and is closely related to the revival movements and Pentecostal churches in Korea. Yun believed that Korean theology would blossom through creative exploration of the religious meaning of the *Dangun* myth—the story of the origin of the Korean people from the union of the son of heaven and a female bear—in light of Christianity. He insisted that Confucianism provides the background for Korean thinking, and so is an indispensable tool for Korean theologizing. Furthermore, he argued that the Confucian concept of "sincerity" can integrate dichotomized concepts in traditional theology, such as law and gospel, sacred and secular.

The majority of Korean Protestants are deeply conservative and hold an attitude of ardent commitment to the Scripture, which is our fourth strand of Korean theologies. In the missionary period, the Bible was translated into Korean script, which was regarded as inferior to the scholarly Chinese characters, but which made it available to women and working men.[4] Bible study was characteristic of the early Korean church and its revivals. Christians tended to take the Bible literally, and it was an integral part of their daily lives, both individually and collectively. Still today, key aspects of faith for most Christians in Korea are occasional *sakyeunghoe* (Bible conferences), *buhoenghoe* (revival meetings), and weekly home group meetings, which include Bible study, sharing of testimony, and *tongsung kido* (the whole group praying aloud, separately but simultaneously). Such practices reveal a theology that inhabits the biblical story as Korean Christians make it their own and identify with the suffering and redeemed people of Israel.

KOREAN THEOLOGIES IN THE POST-DEMOCRATIZATION ERA

Although the problems of poverty, inequality, and injustice remain, South Korea's emergence as the world's tenth largest economy and the establishment of democracy have changed the context for theologizing. In this section, we discuss contemporary theological discourses: the public relevance of theology; the formation of a missional church; diaspora theology; and the hope and aspirations of unification theology. These theological articulations are the outcomes of genuine search for theological responses to meet the contemporary challenges.

The lack of credibility of Protestant churches and the rise of public theology

When the Protestant Christianity was first introduced to Korea, people were attracted not only by its religious aspects that offered answers to their spiritual quests, but also by its moral and ethical teachings in the midst of national crisis of being threatened by the neighboring nations. Many national leaders embraced Christianity because they saw its potential to catalyze socio-political and economic reform and independence, and the churches played a significant role in the struggle before and during the Japanese occupation. However, over the years, as churches grew, under the military-backed government that encouraged political quietism, most conservative and

---

4. Blair and Hunt, *Korean Pentecost*, 67.

Evangelical churches became inward looking and concentrated their effort on their own congregation and on the more spiritual aspects of Christian life, such as revival meetings, evangelism, and church growth. Now, in the post-democratization era, in the context of growing prosperity, high levels of education, and increasing secularism, the integrity and credibility of the popular Korean churches has been challenged. They are accused of a lack of authentic spirituality in church leadership, of a superior attitude to non-Christians, and of poor social and personal ethics in the context of rapidly changing and multicultural Korean society.

One of the most significant responses to this problem is the development of public theology in Korea, as shown, for example, by the establishment of the Institute of the Public Theology and Church (IPTC) at the Presbyterian University and Theological Seminary in Seoul. The purpose of the institute is "encouraging the Church to nurture a public responsibility so the Kingdom of the triune God may be anticipated." It acknowledges the significant contributions of the Protestant churches in the public sphere but also points out some of the shortcomings. It emphasizes that the "Church plays a role as a sign, foretaste, instrument, and anticipation of the coming Kingdom, in close cooperation with other partners of the world" and that the "Church should be concerned with participating in the movement of *missio trinitatis* by aligning itself with justice, peace, integrity of creation." It also mentions that the institute, as an interconfessional and interfaith community, will work with NGOs and engage in research on public issues such as politics, society, culture and ecology, by disseminating Christian values in response to alternative solutions to contemporary issues.[5]

IPTC's "milestone" statement expands further that its aim is to help the Korean church to take up its public responsibility in the contexts of the kingdom of God and God's mission in history. While acknowledging the public contributions of Protestant Christianity, such as the social uplifting of the people and leading the movements of independence, democratization, and peaceful unification, it also points out that there are various factors preventing Korean churches from carrying out their public responsibilities. These include: the theological separation between church and the world; prioritizing soul over body; a materialistic focus on church growth; a tendency to support those who are in power and authority; and the ghettoization of the church community due to its ideological stance. The statement emphasizes the importance of an integral approach to the kingdom of God, of the church and the world as a life community, and of the foundation of society on democracy and justice.[6]

The collective efforts of IPTC and others to develop public theology for Korea have caused stimulating interactions between scholars of different disciplines. A key protagonist is Rhee Hyung-ki, who sees the importance of the ecumenical movement as taking up a public role in God's world. In particular, he emphasizes the importance of the World Council of Churches' active engagement with global issues such as

---

5. Hyung et al., *Public Theology and Public Church*, 12–13.
6. Hyung et al., *Public Theology and Public Church*, 14–24.

poverty, inequality, and injustice. He seeks a "deep transformation of the relationship" between church and world, and advocates ecumenical partnership for the establishment of the kingdom of God.[7] By interacting with wide scholarship not only from the West but also from the Majority World, Jang Shin-geun identifies four different understandings of the publicness of theology: an apologetic approach; emphasizing social transformation; concern with the identity of Christianity itself; and contributing to civil society. He concludes that public theology is primarily dealing with public issues through a praxis-theory-praxis methodology. So public theology is witness and engagement, not only by interacting with public issues, but also by seeking dynamic conversation between Christian identity and public life, understanding the church's public role and acting it out by seeking a public church and a public faith, pursuing global-local and ecumenical collaboration, and facilitating interdisciplinary dialogue to seek the common good.[8]

From the perspective of Christian social involvement and social ethics, Yim Sung-bihn points out that an important area of the public engagement of theology is dealing with authority and encountering the powers of this world. His basis for the public engagement of the Korean churches is on the inseparability of the identity of the gospel and the social involvement, the integration of words and deeds, and the reflective nature of theological inquiry. He calls for those who are involved in public theology to be biblical, bilingual with respect Christian and secular discourse, interdisciplinary, critical, and inclusive.[9] From the point of view of systematic theology, Yoon Chul-ho challenges Korean Christians' understanding of the gospel, arguing that the complete gospel of the kingdom must be understood as an inseparable integral relationship between the salvation of individual souls and the reign of God's love and justice. In particular, the life of Jesus Christ emphasizes that, although the gospel is based on death and resurrection, it is perfectly aligned with the proclamation and practice of Christ's kingdom.[10] He defines public theology for the Korean context as "a theology that emphasizes the social responsibility of the church and Christians based on the gospel of the kingdom" and an "action theology" that has communicative-transformative characteristics for realizing the kingdom of God.[11] Jeong Jae-young presents many challenges through a keen sociological analysis of various topics that are sensitive issues for the Korean church, such as conversion, defectors from North Korea, believers who do not attend church, and church offerings. In particular, he strongly insists on the restoration of the public nature of the church community in secularized Korean society. He argues for a "community of practice morality" that excludes the idea that the church is an exclusive community, expresses responsibility

---

7. Rhee, "Nature and Public Responsibility of the Church," 83–136.
8. Jang, "What is Public Theology?," 27–79.
9. Yim, *Public Theology*, 15–32.
10. Yun, *Public Theology for the Korean Church*, 37–52.
11. Yun, *Public Theology for the Korean Church*, 13–17.

and duty toward those outside the community, and goes beyond pursuing the interests of individual or the group to which one belongs.[12]

Offering theological insights on contemporary issues in Korean society leads to lively debates and discussions both within and outside the church. The interests of public theologians in Korea are particularly focused on the public credibility of churches in a modern and pluralistic Korean society. They call the churches to engage in the wider society with genuine and humble attitudes to achieve the common good and justice for all sections of society rather than having a church-centered and missionary-minded approach towards their neighbors.

Church growth, the "Nevius principle," and the search for a model for mature church

The presence of megachurches is a commonly known feature of South Korean Protestantism. Their theology of growth and expectation of prosperity is characteristic of popular Korean Christianity. However, in the current secular and increasingly individualistic climate, the megachurches have received strident criticism from outside. Moreover, within the churches, there is uneasiness about the ethics of growth at all costs and renewed discussion about what constitutes a mature church.

During the second half of the last century, Korea witnessed remarkable church growth. Among other factors, the revival movements and the "Nevius principle" contributed significantly to this growth and to a theology of growth as the sign of a mature church. The "Nevius principle" was a version of the three-self method of church planting (self-propagation, self-governing, and self-supporting) that had been formulated for China by John L. Nevius.[13] It was adopted by the Presbyterian missions in Korea in 1891 to create self-sufficient local churches as part of a strong, independent native church that was missionary in its own right and not dependent on foreign missions. The Nevius method, and its theological principle of growth as the nature of the church, was not only successful in producing independent local congregations, it also informed the post-independence models of nation-building.

From the Korean Protestant point of view, the achievement of "Christian Korea" by numerical church growth was part of a deliberate strategy toward the wider goal of evangelizing the whole nation. A desire for numerical growth was strongly put forward by both church leaders and Christian politicians right after liberation from Japan in August 1945. In this political climate, there was a strong movement towards making South Korea a Christian nation, especially between 1945 and 1948. Christian clergy and politicians repeatedly emphasized the Christian spirit as the foundation of the new nation.[14] The aim of increasing the Christian population and the practice of

---

12. Jeong, *Sociological Understanding of Religion*, 319–38.
13. Nevius, *Planting and Development of Missionary Churches*; Clark, *Nevius Plan*, 86–96.
14. IKCHS, *History of Korean Church*, 44.

target-setting for numerical growth that had been well established since the missionary period and was echoed in government target-setting for economic growth in the new, modernizing South Korea. Revival and church growth were dominant concerns for church leadership and self-propagation became the chief interpretation of the mission of the church. Their method was to save individuals and they believed this would eventually lead to the salvation of the whole nation both in terms of its spiritual and political life. Evangelism was no longer left to revivalists and Bible women but church members were the main means of evangelization and were mobilized into a variety of activities toward this end.

The majority of Korean churches are small or medium-sized, and megachurches are not necessarily representative of the Korean churches. However, the influence of megachurches is significant, and it needs to be discussed in the historical and ecclesiological contexts of overall church growth in South Korea. Megachurches have grown as part and parcel of Korean revivalist movements and programs to make South Korea a majority Christian nation. They are largely a product of the zeal of Christians who have taken the three-self principle seriously and see church growth as a visual demonstration of success, which signifies the blessing of God. In addition to this theology, megachurches share other distinctive characteristics of the Korean Protestant churches: a conservative and Evangelical vision for a democratic and free society that upholds religious freedom in the face of the Communist threat from the North; an emphasis on the priority of local, self-governing self-propagating, and self-supporting churches; enthusiasm for evangelism with a competitive spirit; creating and maintaining various programs and groups within the church; and systematic evangelism among young people, students, and conscripted soldiers. Meg churches contribute to various aspects of the life of the Korean churches, chiefly to overseas mission, social activities, and Christian NGOs.

As the growth of megachurches is integral to Korean Protestant church growth, so the strong contemporary criticism of the megachurch in the post-democratization era needs to be examined in the context of the Protestant church in general. Although popular among their members, megachurches are resented by many others. Protestant, (and especially megachurch) dominance in Korean society was not received as a blessing for all. Kim Seong-geon criticizes the megachurches as having a gospel of success and cheap grace, and being a consumer community and not the community of sharing. He further argued that megachurches tend to not to seek a public faith for the common good for other congregations and wider society but rather seek self-expansion and self-interest regardless of the needs of others. These weaknesses, he suggests, are the result of growth without depth in conjunction with faith that seeks blessing, class distinctions, materialism, individual sectarianism, competition, lavish and selfish financial expenditure, and lack of Christian discipleship.[15] Kim Jin-ho is even more critical and accuses megachurches of worshiping power and having

---

15. Kim, "Pro-Americanism of Korean Protestant Church," 16, 23.

fundamentalist moral standards that cause more harm than good to Korean society as a whole.[16] Lee Won-kyu, a sociologist and an ardent critic of Korean Protestant churches, points out that, in spite of their very high social and material contributions to society, and also the low rate of criminal offenses by church members compared to the general public, the religiosity of Protestant Christians is deepening while their social credibility is low and worsening. He blames this on a lack of spirituality, morality, and communal identity among the Protestant Christians that is specially to do with the poor quality of church leadership.[17]

Korean Protestant churches have been earnestly self-governing and self-supporting to the extent that this method causes a stumbling block for ecumenism and sharing of resources. Many had a survival-of-the-fittest theology that celebrated the victory of Christianity over Communism and its political dominance. Numerical success led to triumphalism in Protestant rhetoric and claims that demographic growth and political power are blessings from God. Along with their optimistic and dynamic preaching styles, most leaders of megachurches tend to hold anti-communist, pro-American, right-wing political views, Evangelical and Charismatic theological perspectives, and conservative attitudes towards social and moral issues. Though the members of megachurches are sincere and dedicated in their ministry within their churches and towards wider society, they often tend to see themselves as holding a powerful position and are therefore resented by those outside these prestigious bodies. Perhaps the problem is not so much to do with the existence of megachurches—they are the result of God's grace and also of dedication of leaders and congregation. It is more to do with the problem of Protestant theology succumbing to a cultural environment in which numerical growth is the key sign of God's blessings.

Diaspora churches and the search for an authentic Korean mission theology

After the success of the Seoul Olympics in 1988 and the flowering of its democracy, South Korea's foreign relations became increasingly multilateral and South Koreans more freely explored the rest of the world through trade, travel, and mission activities. Korean Christianity largely embraced an international vision and worldwide Korean networks and activities began to have significant global impact. This resulted in the establishment of Korean populations in Latin America and Western Europe and the community in North America substantially increased. In the diaspora, the church functioned as a social center, offered welfare services, and also ran the Korean school. It often had dedicated personnel to do this since churches at home sent out pastors or chaplains to minister to diaspora communities. In 2009–2010 there were estimated to be over 5,500 Korean diaspora churches in 176 countries around the world. At the same time, factors such as the growth of the Korean economy and an aging population

16. Kim, "Pro-Americanism of Korean Protestant Church," 68.
17. Lee, *Crisis and Hope of Korean Church*, 7, 216–26.

led to increasing numbers of foreign visitors, migrant workers, and other immigration within South Korea.

The priorities of diaspora churches are to minister to the local Korean community and to serve its interest in that particular country or region. But diaspora churches may also have a missionary theology toward their context. They may see themselves as a chosen people exercising a leavening and even salvific effect on their surroundings.[18] The churches are a training ground for the second generation who may integrate into the wider society. In the US, those who drop out of the Korean-medium congregations of their parents often move to English-speaking congregations or set up new pan-Asian and multiethnic churches.[19] Many have developed a distinctive "hybrid" Christian expression of their own.[20] Korean Americans form the largest non-white group in American Evangelical seminaries and some are in leadership of national or international Evangelical organizations.[21] Whether conscious of it or not, diaspora churches are part of the wider Korean expansion, global exploration, and missionary movements. In the 1980s missionary work was seen as enhancing the national reputation by pioneering regions where Korea was unknown. The diaspora churches support Korean business ventures, overseas studies, and diplomatic and outreach activities. They are part of South Korea's soft power which had been greatly enhanced since the 1990s by the transformation of its image from war-torn, unstable dictatorship to stylish democracy.[22]

The Korean missionary movement was primarily an activist movement addressing the "unfinished" task of world evangelization. However, a distinctive Korean world mission theology can be discerned that has several features. The first is a desire to "repay the debt of the gospel." The grace received from Christ's suffering on the cross and the sacrifice made by the missionaries to Korea together represented a gift which demanded a generous response. Furthermore, to be able to "repay the debt" is a matter of national pride and a duty to the martyrs whose blood should be the seed of the church.[23] Second, Korean Christians regard the growth of the Korean church and the economic miracle of twentieth-century Korea as a unique blessing from God that gives them a particular responsibility, especially for the evangelization of Asia. They believe that their Christlike experience of suffering, and their transformation from depravity to prosperity, means they can identify with Asia's poor and gives them a burden to share what they have received.[24] A growing perception that the churches in Europe and North America, which had once led world mission, are dying or even

18. Lee, "Founding and Development of the Korean Diaspora Forum," 202–3.
19. Ecklund, *Korean American Evangelicals*, 39–44.
20. Kim, *Faith of Our Own*, 160–65.
21. Kim, *Faith of Our Own*, 5, 161.
22. Kim, *History of Korean Christianity*, 553–54.
23. CPCK, "Statement on the Mission of the Korean Churches."
24. Kim, "Word and the Spirit," 133.

"dead," encourages a belief that the torch of the gospel is now being passed on to Korea.[25] Third, Korean mission theology inherits the theology of church growth in the power of the Spirit and extends it on a global scale. The Great Commission to "go and make disciples" is interpreted to mean the conversion of as many as possible from all the different ethnicities to explicit faith in Christ and membership of the Christian community.[26]

As early as 1983, attempts at overseas mission were being criticized by some church leaders. They complained that churches and denominations were competing with each other to send more missionaries; that there was no consistent and comprehensive mission policy; and that leaders were too ambitious considering that few Koreans had cross-cultural experience. Missionary attitudes were also criticized as imperialistic and paternalistic, boastful of the Korean church, and replicating Korean Christianity without sensitivity to the local culture. Missions lacked coherent policies and failed to build up relationships with churches on the mission field. Missionaries were poorly qualified and trained. Only in the twenty-first century, as the missionary movement is contracting, have Korean churches and mission agencies begun to reflect on mission methods and theology.

In recent writings, mission theologians critically engage the traditional mission theology and practices of Korean churches, which emphasize evangelism, conversion, church planting, and church growth. Lee Hu-cheon identifies the key problems of Korean mission practice in Korea and worldwide are: the tension between Evangelical and ecumenical groups; individualism between the churches, inequality between large and prosperous churches and small and struggling churches; and the lack of sensitivity of churches to the wider society. He develops a Korean "missional church" theology that promotes more integral approach to mission. Lee proposes not to abandon the church growth project, but to complement it with the idea of a "healthy church" by prioritizing the local socio-cultural situation in mission, and encouraging the revitalization of small churches. In the same vein, Han Kook-il further defines his understanding of missional church as the Christian community being engaged "with the neighborhood, in the neighborhood, and for the neighborhood" to overcome church individualism and promoting growth together. He sees the problem of traditional Korean mission theology as placing too much emphasis on personal salvation. He proposes the reshaping of ecclesiology so that church takes an interest in every sphere, not just the spiritual and religious realms, and develops a congregation of missional Christians who practice a holistic understanding of mission. By way of implementing this concept of missional church, Kim Young-dong emphasizes the importance of friendship in the Korean context. Since God called us as friends and sent us as friends (John 15:12–15), he argues that friendship is the central element of God's mission and key to achieving God's mandate in relationship with humanity. Moreover, since God

---

25. Oh, "History of the Korean Diaspora Movement," 181.
26. See Kim and Kim, *History of Korean Christianity*, 299–315.

calls Abraham "friend" (2 Chr 20:7), mission is the restoration of friendship between God and his creation. So friendship mission presupposes indwelling the presence of God, sharing our whole being, and walking with God as a companion. From the writings above, we can see that mission theologians and others are making a conscious attempt to broaden the "church growth" model beyond numerical growth by employing a more integral approach to the mission practice of the Korean churches.

Towards a theology of unification

Nearly eighty years since the division of the peninsula, the achievement of peace and reconciliation between North and South is still the most urgent agenda item for the Korean churches. The division of the land is seen to lie behind some of the social woes of South Korea, such as polarized thinking, difficulty collaborating, and the divisions of its churches. So, articulating a relevant theological discourse that can be accepted by both liberal and conservative sections is an imperative.

Immediately after the Korean War of 1950–1953, the atrocities committed by the Communist armies during the Korean War, the persecution of Christians in the North and the destruction of churches there tended to produce Christian anti-communism and a desire to confront its evils. However, as South Korea moved toward democracy, progressive Christian leaders in the South interacted with their counterparts in the North through the mediation of the World Council of Churches. In February 1988 the Korea National Council of Churches (KNCC) issued a "Declaration of the Korean National Council of Churches toward the Unification and Peace of the Korean People" that made a significant impact both within the church and on the whole nation. The declaration started by affirming that Christ came to the earth as the servant of peace and proclaimed the kingdom of God, which represents peace, reconciliation, and liberation. It claims that, accordingly, the Korean church is trying to be with people who are suffering. In the main thesis, the declaration acknowledges and confesses the sins of mutual hatred, of justifying the division of Korea, and of accepting each ideology as absolute, which is contrary to God's absolute authority. The declaration then proclaimed the year 1995 as a Jubilee Year for peace and unification when Koreans could celebrate the fiftieth anniversary of the liberation from Japan together. Reflecting on the biblical pattern of restoration of a just community (Lev 25), it set down practical steps toward the Jubilee Year, including church renewal, so that the church becomes a faith community for peace and reconciliation, and working together with all the churches to employ all the necessary means toward peace and reconciliation. It was the proclamation of the liberation of the Korean people from the bondage of ideological hegemony, and from political systems that hinder the formation of a common community.[27]

---

27. See Park, "Theological and Political Task," 25–44.

The declaration exhibited the Korean Christians' insistence on the agenda of the reunification of the two Koreas as they trust God's sovereign power over the problem of division, the slavery of hatred, and the bondage of ideological conflict. Indeed, it was argued that the Jubilee movement should create a "people community" of justice, restoring a common identity of Koreans sharing the same struggles and pain.[28] The long separation of the Korean people into two very different socio-economic and political systems means that there are very few shared identities. The restoration of this concept of *koinonia* between the South and North is urgent, especially given the severe economic hardship and even starvation in the North. Sharing of resources is seen as a theological imperative for the churches in the South, who have been active in sending aid to the North.

In his "theology of reunification," David Kwang-sun Suh sees the Jubilee restoration as the creation of a sharing community of South and North, employing the concepts of *koinonia* (fellowship) and *oikumene* (the household of God). He writes metaphorically of the cross of division and expresses his resentment that, in spite of Korea being the victim of Japanese imperial aggression, Korea had to be divided again by the imperialistic policy of the Cold War superpowers, and in that sense, Koreans are bearing the cross of division. He then argues that, under this cross, Christians in the North and the South yearn for the resurrection which was demonstrated through Christ and promised to his disciples, and that this will be manifested through sharing at table together.[29] The Korean churches carry this cross of pain and suffering while they long for the hope of resurrection when the people of the peninsula will again be together.

CONCLUSION

As we consider the above contemporary Korean theologies, one of the most pressing challenges for the Korean society, and therefore for formulating a Korean theology, that emerges is the problem of polarization in so many areas of life. Some of the recurring concepts in contemporary theologies in Korea are integrity, wholeness, and reconciliation. Holding different views and opinions in any society is perfectly legitimate and should be encouraged as this is key aspect of democratic society. However, to avoid conflict, holding a view requires an attitude of self-critique of our own beliefs and conduct, rather than blind commitment to one's own group, political party, or community. A strength of the Korean people is that they value commitment and loyalty to persons, beliefs, organizations, and interest groups. However, this is also a weakness if people refuse to listen to the other side, oppose any other view, and even attack others on the basis of their differences rather than collaboratively seeking truth and justice. Koreans have witnessed deep and unreconcilable polarization in public

28. Min, *Peace, Unification and Jubilee*, 295–305.
29. Suh, *Korean Minjung in Christ*, 183.

life, especially in politics, the economy, and religions that is exacerbated by the continued division into North and South. The call for the churches to meet the challenge of contemporary Korean society is greater than ever, and there are current Korean theologies that aim to equip churches with critical and reflective capacities so that they can fulfil their prophetic and priestly roles for the people in the wider society and equip Christians to fulfill the requirement to "act justly and to love mercy and to walk humbly" with our God[30] and with our neighbors.

BIBLIOGRAPHY

Blair, William N., and Bruce Hunt. *The Korean Pentecost and The Sufferings Which Followed.* Edinburgh: The Banner of Truth Trust, 1977.

Clark, Charles Allen. *The Nevius Plan for Mission Work in Korea.* Seoul: CLS, 1937.

CPCK (Council of Presbyterian Churches in Korea). "Statement on the Mission of the Korean Churches in the New Millennium." *IRM* 89 (2000) 233–38.

Ecklund, Elaine Howard. *Korean American Evangelicals: New Models for Civic Life.* Oxford: Oxford University Press, 2006.

Ham, Sok Hon. *Queen of Suffering: A Spiritual History of Korea.* Translated by E. Sang Yu. London: Friends World Committee for Consultation, 1985.

Hyung, Gi Lee, et al., eds. *Public Theology and Public Church.* Seoul: Kingdom, 2010.

IKCHS (Institute of Korean Church History Studies). *A History of Korean Church I.* Seoul: Christian Literature, 1989.

Jang, Shin-Geun. "What is Public Theology?" In *Public Theology and Public Church*, edited by Hyung Gi Lee et al., 27–79. Seoul: Kingdom, 2010.

Jeong, Jae-Young. *The Sociological Understanding of Religion in the Korean Church.* Seoul: Open Publishing House, 2012.

Kim, Jin-ho. "Pro-Americanism of Korean Protestant Church: Its Colonial Unconsciousness." *Historical Critique* 70 (2005) 64–81.

Kim, Sebastian. "The Word and the Spirit: Overcoming Poverty, Injustice and Division in Korea." In *Christian Theology in Asia*, edited by Sebastian Kim, 129–53. Cambridge: Cambridge University Press, 2008.

Kim, Sebastian, and Kirsteen Kim. *A History of Korean Christianity.* Cambridge: Cambridge University Press, 2015.

Kim, Sharon. *A Faith of Our Own: Second-Generation Spirituality in Korean American Churches.* New Brunswick, NJ: Rutgers University Press, 2010.

Lee, Soon-keun. "The Founding and Development of the Korean Diaspora Forum." In *Korean Diaspora and Christian Mission*, edited by S. Hun Kim and Wonsuk Ma, 197–206. Oxford: Regnum, 2011.

Lee, Won-kyu. *The Crisis and Hope of Korean Church from the Socio-Religious Perspectives.* Seoul: KMC, 2010.

Min, Yong-Jin. *Peace, Unification and Jubilee.* Seoul: Korean Institute of Church History, 1995.

Nevius, John L. *The Planting and Development of Missionary Churches.* Shanghai: The Presbyterian, 1899.

---

30. Mic 6:8 (NIV).

Oh, Doug K. "History of the Korean Diaspora Movement." In *Korean Diaspora and Christian Mission,* edited by S. Hun Kim and Wonsuk Ma, 181–96. Oxford: Regnum, 2011.

Park, Jong Hwa. "Theological and Political Task for Jubilee in the Church and People in Korea." In *50th Anniversary of Liberation and Jubilee,* edited by Korean Association of Christian Studies, 25–44. Seoul: Korean Association of Christian Studies, 1995.

Rhee, Hyung-Ki. "The Nature and Public Responsibility of the Church." In *Public Theology and Public Church,* edited by Hyung Gi Lee et al., 83–136. Seoul: Kingdom, 2010.

Suh, David Kwang-sun. *The Korean Minjung in Christ.* Hong Kong: CCA, 1991.

Yim, Sung-Bihn. *Public Theology.* Seoul: Jeyoung Communications, 2009.

Yun, Cheol-Ho. *Public Theology for the Korean Church and the Kingdom of God.* Seoul: Saemulgyul Plus, 2019.

CHAPTER 18

Palestinian Contextual Theology

PETER LODBERG

Christianity is closely related to cities and places. Bethlehem, Jerusalem, and Nazareth are some of the Palestinian cities that have become known worldwide because they are the context of the life and history of Jesus, who was confessed as the Christ by people in the first congregations.

But the biblical cities are not only historical sites to commemorate past glory and biblical history. They—and many other places in Israel and Palestine—are still home to Christian worship, life, and theological reflection. If the Bible is regarded as the first example of Palestinian contextual theology, this tradition of interpreting the life and experiences of ordinary people in the light of the faith in God as creator, redeemer, and life-giver is kept alive by Christian laypeople, clergy, and theologians even today.

The context, however, is different from the context two thousand years ago, even though there are political, religious, and social structures of similarity. Also today, it is an important theological task to reflect on the content and meaning of Christian faith in relation to our human experiences as peoples living in a particular historical context. Thus, the resources of theology are beside the two classical resources Scripture and tradition also human experience and historical context.

In this chapter we show how Palestinian theology is being developed in constant dialogue with social, political, and religious experiences of injustice, occupation, humiliation, insecurity, and displacement. It is a theology that shall keep hope alive despite of war and colonial intervention and help to maintain a Christian identity and witness in the Palestinian territories with 0.82 percent of the population being Christians and in Israel with 2 percent Christians.[1]

GIVING A VOICE TO THE VOICELESS

Palestinian contextual theology as it is known today started in the early 1980s. One source of inspiration was several books that told the history of Palestinian Christians from a personal perspective. They represent a biographical theology, when they give voice to the experience of displacement after the Nakba ("catastrophe") in 1948, when more than seven hundred thousand Palestinians were forced to leave their homes by the Israeli military forces, and the war in 1967, after Israel occupied the West Bank, the Golan Heights, East Jerusalem, Gaza, and the Sinai Peninsula, the so-called Naksa ("setback").

Among the first Palestinian theologians to write his own personal story from a biblical perspective of the land is Elias Chacour (1939–). He served as the archbishop of Akko, Haifa, Nazareth, and All Galilee of the Melkite Greek Catholic Church from 2006 to 2014. In 1984 he published his memoirs entitled *Blood Brothers: The Dramatic Story of a Palestinian Christian Working for Peace in Israel*.[2] In his book, Chacour tells how his village of Kufr Baram was destroyed after the Nakba, and what it means to live his life as a refugee in his own country.

Also, Naim Stifan Ateek (1937–) uses a biographical theological approach to his theology. In his book *Justice and Only Justice: A Palestinian Theology of Liberation*, Ateek introduces his theology by telling how the Zionist troops, the Haganah, occupied his hometown of Beisan (Beth Shean) on Wednesday, May 12, 1948—two days before the State of Israel was proclaimed.[3] Two weeks later the Christians were taken on buses to Nazareth, and the Muslims from Beisan were sent to what is now Jordan.

A third example of a biographical approach to the formulation of a Palestinian contextual theology is found in the work of Mitri Raheb (1962–). One of his first books is called *I Am a Palestinian Christian*, and it elaborates a Lutheran theology from the perspective of being born in Bethlehem, the city of David and Jesus, and living in continuity with the history that is connected to the biblical figures and their landscape, culture, and environment after the Israeli occupation of the West Bank in 1967[4].

These personal perspectives can be enlarged to identify different historical periods as important to the process of Palestinian theology. The first period is from 1948-1967, when theological discussions concentrated on how to understand the establishment of the State of Israel theologically. Several European and American

---

1. Johnson and Zurlo, *World Christian Database*.
2. Chacour, *Blood Brothers*.
3. Ateek, *Justice and Only Justice*.
4. Raheb, *I Am a Palestinian Christian*.

theologians understood the creation of the Israeli state as an important step in fulfilling God's plan of salvation for the world. This understanding estranged Palestinian Christians from their fellow Christians in Europe and the US, as it linked the establishment of the State of Israel to the suffering, humiliation, and defeat of others, who also confess Jesus Christ as Lord and Savior.

The second period runs from 1967–1983 and is characterized by two questions: how can Israel's victory in June 1967 be understood theologically; and what does it mean for Christians to live with Muslim neighbors in the occupied West Bank, Gaza, and East Jerusalem? Especially, the challenge came from an intensified Jewish national-messianism, that interpreted the war victory as a God-willed confirmation of the State of Israel and its exclusively Jewish character. At the same time many initiatives were taken to colonize the West Bank by building Jewish settlements on land belonging to many Christian families.

The third period lasts from 1983–1987 and is characterized by a growing understanding of the importance of the historical dimension of the Christian church in Palestine. The church becomes more rooted in its own history and more aware of its links back to the early church in Jerusalem. It opens for more intensified ecumenical cooperation among the Christian churches. Instrumental for this development is the Al-Liqa' ("Encounter") Center for Religious and Heritage Studies in the Holy Land. It was established in 1982 as a response to the Iranian Revolution, that challenged the religious landscape.[5]

The center was established in Bethlehem under the leadership of Geries Khoury (1952–2016), who was a Melkite, and in cooperation with Christian and Muslim religious leaders, activists, and academics. The main idea behind the Al-Liqa' Center and its many conferences is that religion in the region is an important social and political force in public life and not only an expression of personal piety.[6] Thus, the Al-Liqa' Center has been instrumental in formulating a Palestinian contextual theology as a public theology. Its main theological publication is the document from 1987: *Theology and the Local Church in the Holy Land: Palestinian Contextualized Theology*. It is the result of a series of meetings at the Tantur Ecumenical Institute in Jerusalem that aimed at building the church and the serving of society.

The ecclesiology of the document belongs within the ecumenical tradition of communio-ecclesiology based on the work of Vatican II and the Faith and Order Commission of the World Council of Churches. The church is both local and universal, and the local church is both sign and instrument of the kingdom of God in communion with other local churches. The document also tries to balance what is called "general theology" and a "contextualized theology." The general theology refers to the long tradition of the church, and contextualized theology covers present theological challenges in culture and society. One of the theological challenges comes

5. Raheb, *Politics of Persecution*, 123.
6. Marteijn, "Revival of Palestinian Christianity," 257–77.

from national or cultural identity and includes the question: what does it mean to be a Christian in a minority situation living with Muslims in occupied territories? Here the issue of ecumenical cooperation among the churches is enlarged to encompass the interfaith relationship with Muslims, who share the same national identity as Christians. Dialogue of religion, thus, becomes an important religious and national issue in Palestinian contextual theology.

THE FIRST INTIFADA (UPRISING)

Twenty years after the beginning of the Israeli occupation of East Jerusalem, Gaza, the West Bank, the Sinai Peninsula, and the Golan Heights the political situation changed dramatically and introduced a new and fourth period in Palestinian contextual theology that is still pending. On December 8, 1987 a minibus carrying laborers coming back from Israel was hit by an Israeli military vehicle in Gaza. Four of the laborers in the minibus were killed, and seven others were injured.

The response from a population that had lost all confidence in the Israeli government and the Palestinian leadership came the next day. The incident was the match that lit the fire of the Intifada. The Palestinian people began to organize themselves from below and took the initiative by establishing new grassroots movements in order to shake off the occupation. The Intifada has been called "the earthshaking cry of a whole nation suffering from prolonged injustice. . . . It is a grassroots revolt against a policy of reducing a nation to a minority of second-class citizens or stateless refugees."[7]

The Intifada called for an answer from theology and the Palestinian churches. Part of the answer was formulated at the First International Symposium on Palestinian Liberation Theology at Tantur on March 10–17, 1990. The aim of the conference was to establish a conversation among all historical church traditions about their own theology, contextualized in their struggle for liberation. The task of theology was no longer only to interpret the world but help to change it. The inspiration came from Latin American liberation theology, and as in the case of liberation theology generally, Palestinian liberation theology is reflection on practice. It follows the method of *seeing, analyzing, and acting*. Therefore, theology must begin by describing and analyzing the situation of oppression and the struggle for liberation. According to the conference, for Palestinians this situation of oppression is Israeli occupation, and the struggle for liberation is the Intifada.[8] Thus, the task of theology is to serve not only the Palestinian churches, but the whole of the Palestinian nation to shake off the Israeli occupation.

Instrumental in organizing the conference and developing a Palestinian theology of liberation is Naim Stifan Ateek (1937–). He served as canon of the Anglican St. George Cathedral in East Jerusalem from 1985 until 1997 and founded in 1990

---

7. Abboushi, "Intifada and the Palestinian Churches," 57.
8. Ateek et al., *Faith and the Intifada*, xi.

an ecumenical liberation theology center called Sabeel ("the Way," "the Spring"). According to Ateek, Sabeel and Palestinian liberation theology have two interconnected tasks: to contribute to the liberation of the oppressed and to liberate theology from being absorbed into fossilized liturgies and a Zionist reading of the Bible, where God is understood as a nationalistic God instead of a God for all.[9]

Ateek is especially concerned about the role of Christian Zionism in the international political and theological debate on the Israeli occupation. He is aware on the one hand of the long history and tradition of Christian anti-Semitism in Europe and on the other hand of the European philosemitism. In its Protestant and Evangelical form philosemitism inspired theologians and politicians in England to a theology of dispensationalism that saw the return of the Jews to Israel as the beginning of the end times. This idea of the restoration of the Jews to Palestine received official British support with the Balfour Declaration of 1917, which was incorporated into the British Mandate for Palestine in 1922 and became part of the UN Partition Plan for Israel and Palestine in 1947.

According to Ateek and Sabeel the declaration represents a premillennial dispensationalism that takes on political importance, and after the establishment of the State of Israel in 1948 it helps to sacralize the Israeli state in a totally new way. Challenged by this sacralization of the Israeli state by Christians in Europe and North America as well, Ateek seeks to dezionize and desacralize the understanding of the State of Israel and the land of Israel.

His basic point based on biblical readings is that the land belongs to God as showed in Christ. The Old Testament contains a development in the understanding of God from a narrow and ethnic understanding of God to a universal God for all. The New Testament transfers the Old Testament perspective of God and land back to Christ—from place to person. The New Testament perspective helps us to read the Bible as a story about a loving, just, inclusive God of all people who invites everybody living in the Holy Land to share the land as its good stewards.

Sabeel Ecumenical Liberation Theology Center is currently located In Shu'afat in East Jerusalem, where the staff organizes many conferences with local and international participants as part of a global network of groups called Friends of Sabeel.

JERUSALEM SPEAKS

The establishment of theological centers as Al-Li'qa and Sabeel was not the only response to the dramatic situation in the last part of the 1980s. In the Roman Catholic Church Michel Sabbah (1933–) was consecrated on January 6, 1988, by Pope Paul II as Roman Catholic patriarch of Jerusalem. He was the first Palestinian-born person in

---

9. Ateek, *Palestinian Christian Cry*, 12.

that position, and the event highlights the indigenization of ecclesial leadership in the Palestinian churches during the 1970s and 1980s.

Sabbah became a leading person among the church leaders of the historical churches in Jerusalem. Just two weeks after his consecration on January 22, 1988, Sabbah signed with other heads of churches in Jerusalem the first joint statement. It represents a new stage of cooperation among the historical churches, and the occasion was the Intifada.[10] The church leaders understood the grievous suffering of "our people on the West Bank and in the Gaza Strip. They are also a visible expression of our people's aspirations to achieve their legal rights and the realizations of their hopes."[11]

It is a statement of solidarity with people who experience all forms of injustice and oppression:

> We stand with the suffering and the oppressed, we stand with the refugees and the deported, with the distressed and the victims of injustice, we stand with those who mourn and are bereaved, with the hungry and the poor. In accordance with the Word of God through the prophet Isaiah, chapter 1, verse 17: "Learn to do good; seek justice; correct oppression; defend the fatherless; plead for the widow.[12]

The statement is remarkable because for the first time in centuries the churches express their common faith and conviction. Theological differences and historical disagreements are put aside because the dramatic situation of the Intifada calls for a common response and leadership in a time of crises. The reaction of the heads of churches is to call for an end to the occupation and a just peace.

The heads of churches have established a common praxis of issuing statements about burning issues that are challenging the life of Palestinian Christians such as a projected mosque in Nazareth (November 28, 2001), the separation wall (August 26, 2003), or the Palestinian election (February 1, 2006). They also used the common statements to address political leaders at home and abroad to raise the concerns of the Christian churches in Palestine.

On August 22, the heads of churches issued a joint statement on Christian Zionism. It is considered as "a modern theological and political movement that embraces the most extreme ideological positions of Zionism, thereby becoming detrimental to a just peace within Palestine and Israel."[13] The statement rejects Christian Zionism doctrine as false teaching that corrupts the biblical message of love, justice, and reconciliation.

---

10. The Head of Churches represented the Greek Orthodox Patriarchate, the Latin Patriarchate, the Armenian Patriarchate, the Syrian Orthodox Bishopric, the Greek Catholic (Melkite) Bishopric, the Anglican Bishopric, the Lutheran Bishopric, the Syrian Catholic Church, and the Franciscan Custody of the Holy Land.

11. May, *Jerusalem Testament*, 20.

12. May, *Jerusalem Testament*, 20.

13. May, *Jerusalem Testament*, 123.

According to the heads of churches Christian Zionism supports and legitimizes a political system that establishes illegal settlements and constructs the separation wall on confiscated Palestinian land which undermines the viability of a Palestinian state and peace and security in the entire region.

Another important issue for the heads of churches is the status of Jerusalem. In 1994 they published a memorandum entitled "The Meaning of Jerusalem for Christians," and on September 29 it was followed up by a new statement on Jerusalem.[14] Again the construction of the separation wall is addressed. Many Christians are being excluded from the precincts of the Holy City, and the political authorities is unilaterally changing the status of Jerusalem so it will lose its character as an open city for three religions. The heads of churches call on all religious leaders in the Holy Land to work together in order to reach a common vision of the city that "might unite the hearts of all believers."[15]

THEOLOGY BEHIND THE SEPARATION WALL

As stated by the heads of churches, today, Jerusalem is separated from the West Bank by a wall, and behind the separation wall and its connected checkpoints and watchtowers the Palestinian people are living in cities like Bethlehem, Ramallah, Jericho, and Hebron as in a prison. Wendy Brown calls the separation wall "an architectural instrument of separation, of occupation, and of territorial expansion mandated by the twinning of state-sponsored and outlaw extensions of settler colonialism."[16]

The separation wall has become the context for doing theology, and behind it theologians, pastors, laypersons, and congregations are challenged to find their own way and formulate the importance of the Christian faith under very difficult political, cultural, financial, and religious circumstances. The separation wall has become the theological context for Palestinian theologians like Mitri Raheb and Isaac Munther (1985–)—both living in Bethlehem and working in the Evangelical Lutheran Church in Jordan and the Holy Land.[17] They are theologically trained pastors and they reflect theologically not only to understand the present context but also to change it through writing, researching, preaching, and educating people to keep hope alive in their daily life.

Raheb understands himself as a contextual theologian rather than a liberation theologian and stresses the importance of reconnecting to the old Palestinian culture that almost disappeared because of the uprooting of the Palestinians in 1948 and 1967. Thus, in 1995 he established the center Dar al-Nadwa in Bethlehem as a place for dialogue between faith and culture, and it was followed by the Dar al-Kalima

---

14. May, *Jerusalem Testament*, 125.
15. May, *Jerusalem Testament*, 128.
16. Brown, *Walled States*, 41.
17. Raheb has published more than twenty books in different languages; Isaac has published several books. See "Bibliography."

University College of Arts and Culture in 2006 and the Diyar publishing house in 2011. Dar al-Kalima is the first institution of higher education in Palestine to focus its educational objectives on the performing arts, visual arts, and cultural heritage.[18] The aim is through arts to raise the level of cultural and social awareness for the development of a vibrant and active civil society.

According to Raheb changes in church and society come from below and from young well-educated people who engage themselves in the life of civil society. If Raheb in his earlier writings dealt with issues of Palestinian Christian identity and the Bible in the Israeli-Palestinian context he has in his recent works analyzed the importance of what is called "the theology of the Empire." It understands the Bible from a Western perspective with severe consequences for people living in not only Palestine, but in the Middle East.[19] Also today, Palestine is occupied by an imperial state that uses the same mechanisms as the different empires in biblical times and must be challenged by the peoples of the land. Today, both liberal Western theology and conservative and fundamentalist theology are uncritical of the State of Israel according to Raheb. Despite their theological differences, they contain a pro-Israeli bias avoiding the present reality and suffering of the native Palestinian people. Just as empires through history has misused theology and religion to give themselves a nonhistorical and divine identity, this is done today by the American empire and its Israeli sound state.

Raheb's criticism against Western theology and politics towards the Middle East also involves the issue of Christian persecution. He rejects the widespread impression in the West that Palestinian Christians are a persecuted minority by the Muslims. His own experience is that Western journalists are not interested in reporting about the Israeli military occupation. Instead, they are interested in sound bites about Christian persecution which they can use, because they confirm an illusion that is widespread in the West.[20]

Just as in his book *Faith in the Face of Empire* Raheb uses in his book *The Politics of Persecution* a longue durée approach to examine the situation of Christians of the Middle East from the invasion of Napoleon Bonaparte in 1799 to the so-called Arab Spring of 2011. The aim is to discuss the issue of Christian persecution from a Middle Eastern perspective as an alternative approach to how Western media and diplomacy deal with Christian persecution today. For Raheb there is no doubt that the West has never shown a real interest in the life and opinions of Middle Eastern Christians. The West serves its own political, military, and economic interests, and the West is willing to sacrifice the Christians if necessary. Strong examples are the lack of real support for the Armenians in 1915 or the Iraqi Christians during the American-led invasion of Iraq in 2003. Also today, so Raheb, Middle Eastern Christians are being orientalized, victimized, and minoritized by people in the West who want to speak on their

---

18. https://www.daralkalima.edu.ps/
19. Raheb, *Faith in the Face of Empire*.
20. Raheb, *Politics of Persecution*, 2.

behalf. It is a position that serves the interests of primarily Evangelical Christians and Christian Zionists that claim an uncritical support of the policies of Israel and its occupation. Today, it is the Palestinian Christians who are sacrificed on the theological and political alter of the West.

TOWARDS KAIROS PALESTINE

If the 1980s saw the emergence of a robust Palestinian theology, then the first half of the 1990s were a period of optimism. The Oslo Peace Accord in 1993 brought international recognition of the Palestinians as a national people with the Palestinian Liberation Organization (PLO) as an organization that could negotiate on behalf of the Palestinian people. An independent Palestinian state became a real possibility, and a number of peace conferences were held, but without much success.

Dramatic political changes took place in Israel after a Jewish settler Yigal Amir in November 1995 killed prime minister Yitzhak Rabin during a big peace rally. Amir was a strong opponent to Rabin's signing of the Oslo Peace Accord, and the murder created a severe political crisis in Israel. Many Israelis felt that the settler movement had become too strong and was developing to become an internal threat to national security.

The Christians in Palestine welcomed by the turn of the millennium in March 2000 Pope John Paul II (1920–2005) who visited Palestine and Israel during his millennium pilgrimage to the Holy Land. The pope's visit came in relation to the signing of important agreements with the State of Israel in 1999 and the PLO in 2000. During his visit Pope John Paul II stressed that the suffering of the Palestinians must end and that the Palestinian people should have their own homeland.

The pope's position was in line with the policy of the Roman Catholic patriarch Michel Sabbah, and it was reiterated by Pope Francis (1936-) during his Holy Land pilgrimage on May 24–26, 2014 on the occasion of the fiftieth anniversary of the meeting between Pope Paul VI (1897–1978) and Patriarch Athenagoras (1886–1972) in Jerusalem. At the welcoming ceremony after landing at Ben Gurion Airport in Tel Aviv, Pope Francis said that the two-state solution must become a reality. The State of Israel has according to the pope the right to exist within international recognized borders, and there must also be recognition of the right of the Palestinian people to a sovereign homeland and their right to live with dignity and with freedom of movement.[21]

The position of the Roman Catholic Church globally and locally has been consistent during the years on the rights of Palestinians. There is a clear awareness of the Palestinian Christian suffering, the right of Palestinians to their own state, and free and open access to the holy places in the Holy Land for all three religions, Judaism, Christianity, and Islam. The special status of Jerusalem as a city for two peoples

---

21. Pope Francis Program, www.vatican.va.

(Israelis and Palestinians) and the three religions must be maintained, when the future of the Jerusalem is decided by common agreement through mutual collaboration and consultation.[22]

Between the visits of Pope John Paul II in March 2000 and Pope Francis in May 2014 the second Intifada happened, also known as the Al-Aqsa Intifada, because it started after Israeli opposition leader Ariel Sharon (1928–2014) together with a delegation from his Likud party forced their way onto the Temple Mount, the third holiest place for Muslims. On September 29, 2000—the day after Sharon's visit—and after Friday prayers, riots broke out in and around the Old City of Jerusalem. In the following days and months many violent clashes took place in the West Bank. Raheb has described how it was to live under the siege in Bethlehem after the Israeli military invasion in April 2002.[23]

The optimism of the 1990s came after the Al-Aqsa Intifada, followed by a period of crisis and uncertainty. Israel began the construction of the separation wall around the West Bank in 2002 and continued its building program of new settlements and plan to separate Israelis and Palestinians living in the West Bank through the physical infrastructure of building separate roads and bridges to colonize the Palestinians and squeeze them out of their land.

A MOMENT OF TRUTH

The crisis of the first decade of the new millennium called for a new step forward for contextual theology. In 2005 Rifat Odeh Kassis (1958–), a human rights activist from the YMCA and the Lutheran church in Bethlehem, took the initiative to gather an ecumenical group of fifteen Palestinian clergy and laypeople to write a Palestinian kairos document.[24] It is significant, that the theological inspiration in Palestine is now coming from South Africa, because the struggle against apartheid resonates with the experiences of being a Palestinian in a more and more fragmented society.

The Palestinian kairos document was presented on December 11, 2009 in Bethlehem as a word of faith, hope, and love from the heart of Palestinian suffering by among others Michel Sabbah, Mitri Raheb, and Naim Ateek.[25] The document was endorsed by the heads of churches in Jerusalem, and it represents the result of the last forty years of theological renewal in Palestinian contextual theology.

The purpose of the document is to tell the world about the consequences of the Israeli occupation from a theological point of view. The inspiration comes from the South African *Kairos Document* in 1985, and already in the introduction the authors relate to the South African situation during apartheid, when they challenge

22. Raheb, *Jerusalem*, 40–42.
23. Raheb, *Bethlehem Besieged*.
24. Kassis, *Kairos for Palestine*.
25. Kassis, *Kairos for Palestine*.

the international community to "stand by the Palestinian people who have faced oppression, displacement, suffering and clear apartheid for more than six decades" (Preface).[26]

The reality of separation as the core political and theological issue is repeated in relation to the building of the separation wall: "The separation wall erected on Palestinian territory, a large part of which has been confiscated for this purpose, has turned our towns and villages into prisons, separating them from one another, making them dispersed and divided cantons" (1.1.1).[27] This is most visible in relation to Gaza. The occupation, the building of settlements, and the Israeli control of Palestinian natural resources, including land and water, take place in the name of God and in the name of force.

Because of this reality, that also divides members of the same family, the occupation is called a "sin against God and humanity because it deprives the Palestinians of their basic human rights, bestowed by God" (2.5).[28] A theology that legitimizes separation of people as it happens in occupied Palestine is not in accordance with the biblical message of justice and reconciliation in Christian theology.

As a counter theology to the realized political theology of separation, the document *Kairos for Palestine* develops a trinitarian theology, formulated as a confession according to the articles of the creed. It says:

> We believe in God, one God, Creator of the universe and of humanity;
> We believe in God's eternal Word, his only Son, our Lord Jesus Christ, whom God sent as the Savior of the world;
> We believe in the Holy Spirit, who accompanies the Church and all humanity on its journey.

As it is clear from this brief overview, the Palestinian kairos document works with universal language. It speaks about universe, world, and all humanity. Creation, salvation, and sanctification involve everybody and everything. They replace theological language that divides and wants to differentiate between people as if creation, salvation, and sanctification are reserved for a special group of people.

An important theological concept in the document is the kingdom of God. It is stated that the church points to the kingdom, which cannot be tied to any earthly kingdom. A reference is made to John 18:36, where Jesus says before Pilate that my kingdom is not from this world. There is in Jesus's saying an eschatological reservation to identify any political system with the will of God. The kingdom of God on earth depends on God and not "on any political orientation, because it is greater and more inclusive that any particular system" (3.4.3.). The task of the church in light of the

---

26. Kassis, *Kairos for Palestine*, 79.
27. Kassis, *Kairos for Palestine*, 180.
28. Kassis, *Kairos for Palestine*, 186.

kingdom of God is instead to promote the values of the kingdom like justice, truth, and human dignity in any political system.

This understanding of eschatology and politics comes close to the theology of hope in the writings of the German theologian Jürgen Moltmann (1926–). In his book *Theology of Hope*, he carefully distinguishes between Christian eschatology and secular ideals.[29] Moltmann, who has always had a special focus on the future as an important part of eschatology, spells this out in his book *The Coming of God* thus: "The future is God's mode in history. The Power of the future is his power in time."[30] The central theological idea is that God's future is already now at hand in our world, and we must understand our lives in the light of what we can become in the future.

The Palestinian kairos document reflects this understanding in its section on hope. It is stated in 3.1 that "despite the lack of even a glimmer of positive expectation, our hope remains strong . . . because it is from God. God alone is good, almighty and loving and His goodness will one day be victorious over the evil in which we find ourselves."[31] Thus, hope is different from and stronger than optimism, because it comes from God who is already at work among people and in the world. The many signs of hope are strong examples of God's presence according to the document.

Palestinian contextual theology is a theology of resistance to Israeli occupation and a theology of hope. It is calling the occupation a sin, because it separates people against God's will. The global Christian church is called to resist theologies that legitimize a sinful politics of separation (apartheid). Under normal circumstances Christians have different opinions about politics, but *Kairos for Palestine* and Palestinian contextual theology call on the churches and their theologies to realize that they are involved in a conflict where the integrity of Christian faith is at stake. It is a confessional moment of truth, and it is not anymore enough to discuss and analyze. It is time (kairos) for action in the meaning of Dietrich Bonhoeffer, who said during the German church struggle that the deed is the first confession.

BIBLIOGRAPHY

Abboushi, Nadia. "The Intifada and the Palestinian Churches." *Faith and the Intifada. Palestinian Christian Voices,* edited by Naim S. Ateek et al., 57–61. Maryknoll, NY: Orbis, 1992.
Ateek, Naim Stifan. *Justice and Only Justice: A Palestinian Theology of Liberation*. Maryknoll, NY: Orbis, 1989.
———. *A Palestinian Christian Cry for Reconciliation*. Maryknoll, NY: Orbis, 2008.
Ateek, Naim, et al., eds. *The Bible and the Palestine Israel Conflict*. Jerusalem: Sabeel, 2014.
———, eds. *Faith and the Intifada: Palestinian Christian Voices*. Maryknoll, NY: Orbis, 1992.
Brown, Wendy. *Walled States, Waning Sovereignty*. New York: Zone, 2017.

29. Moltmann, *Theology of Hope*, 325.
30. Moltmann, *Coming of God*, 24.
31. Kassis, *Kairos for Palestine*, 186.

Chacour, Elias. *Blood Brothers: The Dramatic Story of a Palestinian Christian working for Peace in Israel*. Grand Rapids: Baker, 2003.

Chapman, Colin. *Christian Zionism and the Restoration of Israel: How Should We Interpret the Scriptures?* Eugene, OR: Cascade, 2021.

Duchrow, Hans G. Ulrich. *Religionen für Gerechtigkeit in Palästina-Israel. Jenseits von Luthers Feindbildern*. Otterstadt, Germany: Stiftung Hirschler, 2018.

Johnson, Todd M., and Gina A. Zurlo, eds. *World Christian Database*. Leiden: Brill, 2021.

Kassis, Rifat Odeh. *Kairos for Palestine*. Ramallah: Bailasan, 2009.

Kuruvilla, Samuel J. *Radical Christianity in Palestine and Israel: Liberation and Theology in the Middle East*. London: I. B. Tauris, 2013.

Löffler, Roland. *Protestanten in Palästina. Religionspolitik, Sozialer Protestantismus und Mission in den deutschen evangelischen und anglikanischen Institutionen des Heiligen Landes 1917–1939*. Stuttgart, Germany: Kohlhammer, 2008.

Mansour, Ruland Khoury. *Theology of Reconciliation in the Context of Church Relations: A Palestinian Christian Perspective in Dialogue with Miroslav Wolf*. Carlisle, UK: Longham, 2020.

Marteijn, Elizabeth S. "The Revival of Palestinian Christianity: Developments in Palestinian Theology." *Exchange* 49 (2020) 257–77.

May, Melanie A. *Jerusalem Testament: Palestinian Christians Speak, 1988–2008*. Grand Rapids: Eerdmans, 2010.

Moltmann, Jürgen. *The Coming of God*. Minneapolis: Fortress, 1996.

———. *Theology of Hope*. New York: Harper & Row, 1967.

Munther, Isaac. *Christ at the Checkpoint: Blessed Are the Peacemakers*, Bethlehem: Diyar, 2018.

———. *From Land to Lands, from Eden to the Renewed Earth. A Christ-Centered Biblical Theology of the Promised Land*. Carlisle, UK: Langham, 2015.

———. *The Other Side of the Wall: A Palestinian Christian Narrative of Lament and Hope*. Downers Grove, IL: InterVarsity, 2020.

Raheb, Mitri. *Bethlehem Besieged: Stories of Hope in Times of Trouble*. Minneapolis: Fortress, 2004.

———. *Faith in the Face of Empire: The Bible through Palestinian Eyes*. Maryknoll, NY: Orbis, 2014.

———. *I Am a Palestinian Christian*. Minneapolis: Fortress, 1995.

———, ed. *Jerusalem: Religious, National and International Dimensions*. Bethlehem: Diyar, 2019.

———. *The Politics of Persecution: Middle Eastern Christians in an Age of Empire*. Waco, TX: Baylor University Press, 2021.

CHAPTER 19

Middle Eastern Theologies

VIOLA RAHEB

CONTEXT

In addressing Middle Eastern[1] emerging theologies, one must first to start by analyzing the contexts in which these theologies are reflecting faith (with)in their specific context and time. This paper focuses on emerging theologies in the region within the last few decades and can in no way offer a historical analysis of the geo-political developments that have shaped and continue to shape the current contexts, nor can it address the socio-political developments in the very different respective countries. It therefore only scratches the surface by highlighting some of the crosscutting themes and trends in the region.

Unpacking the contexts in the Middle East in the last century requires a critical analysis of colonial histories, postcolonial state formation and decline, wars, conflicts, and resistance. The ongoing occupation of Palestinian land, the impact of the "war on terror" post 9/11 on the region including the American invasion of Iraq, the Arab Spring, the war in Syria and Libya, ongoing immigration, the rise of extremism and radicalism, especially in the context of "IS," and political and economic instability resulting in dire economic living conditions, are but a few of the present contextual realities surrounding political fragmentation of the region.

---

1. Allow me to problematize the term "Middle East" at the beginning of this paper, as this terminology in itself reflects a colonial perspective on the region. For more information see Proglio, *Decolonising*.

The lives of people in the region, Christians included, are conditioned by these realities and Middle Eastern theologies, just as all theologies are contextual and are accordingly shaped by these contextual realities.[2]

A NEW GENERATION OF THEOLOGIANS IN THE MIDDLE EAST

In addressing the expressions of faith through theology in the Middle East region we first have to acknowledge the following points of entry:

- The presence and witness of Christians in this region is endogenous and stretches back to the advancement of Christianity itself.[3]
- Christian theologies and expressions of faith have historically been and continue to be shaped by diverse cultural and linguistic traditions.[4]

Christian theologies and faith in the region have been proclaimed in a multireligious context from the outset, which has shaped its understanding of and interaction with other faith traditions.

Theological thought and production in the Middle East have covered a wide range of topics that stretch from theological and cultural to philosophical, intellectual, and political, covers a wide range of disciplines. Accordingly, categorizing theological thought from the Middle East into classical Western theological disciplines or aligning it with defined concepts, e.g., liberation theology, public theology, feminist theology is, in my view, less helpful.

For many decades theological studies have been perused abroad mostly in Europe and the United States. At the same time, even when perused in one of the theological institutions in the Middle East, the theologies taught were seldom rooted in the actual socio-cultural and religious context of the region or even the country itself. In the last few decades a new generation of Middle Eastern theologians has begun taking the lead in the theological field.

Meanwhile we are experiencing a shift on more than one level, on the one hand more and more Middle Eastern theologians are unpacking Orientalism as the prevailing approach in addressing Christian presence in the region. In this context the theological writings on Palestine from various Middle Eastern theologians since the 1960 have brought about a paradigm shift.[5] As an example, I would like to draw attention to the theological statement entitled "What is Required of the Christian Faith Concerning

---

2. For more details see the chapter on the story of Middle Eastern Christianity by country and in the world context, in Raheb and Lamport, *Christianity*, 449–559.

3. For more on Middle Eastern Christianity see Bader, *Christianity*; Raheb and Lamport, *Christianity*; Raheb, "Christianity in the Middle East," 375–95; Bailey and Bailey, *Who Are the Christians*, 12–27; Cragg, *Arab Christian*; Wessels, *Arab and Christian?*.

4. For more details see the chapter on contextual expressions on Christianity in the Middle East in Raheb and Lamport, *Christianity*, 223–331.

5. Khodr, "World Conference"; Khodr, "Theological Reflections"; Khodr, "Palestine Between."

the Palestinian Problem," which was published on June 18, 1967, and so during the 1967 war, by four theologians, Fr. Jean Corbon, Fr. George Khodr, Rev. Samir Kafeety, and Albert Laham.[6] With their text, the four theologians presented a contextual reading of the political developments with regard to Palestine, thus challenging many prevailing "Western" theological positions on Palestine. At the same time the authors call attention to the need to reconsider positions on Palestine, underlining the fact that events in Palestine present a challenge to the conscience of Christians of all churches. This challenge has been addressed extensively since the end of the eighties in various Palestinian contextual theological writings[7] and beyond.

The same applies to challenging Western theologies focusing on the persecution of Christians mainly by Islam and Muslims. Christian theological engagement with Islam in the Middle East has a long-standing history and a rich theological heritage[8] that is being rediscovered. Among the leading figures of the twentieth century in this field are Georges Khodr, metropolitan bishop of the archdiocese of Mount Lebanon of the Orthodox Antiochian Church,[9] the Egyptian Dominican priest George Anawati,[10] and the Egyptian Jesuit priest Samit Kahlil Samir.[11] Their contextual theological approach to Islam is a shift in theological writings from a rather apologetic approach towards a proactive contextual engagement. In her talk at the seminar "The Church Mission Today in the Middle East" in 2019, Dr. Bechealany, then the general secretary of the Middle East Council of Churches, eloquently underlined this proactive role stating:

> "Since our churches belong to the Antiochian heritage, they must imitate their Mother Church by adopting the culture of Arab societies, to become a local Church missionary to the Arab people." Arab culture comes from us and is ours; it is knitted into our heritage, our humanity, our concepts and beliefs, along with the Muslim heritage, humanity and beliefs. It is our common home, our common language and the cradle of our civilization. In this context, how can we not remember Youakim Moubarak, George Khodr, Jean Corbon, and all those who regarded Arabism as the mother of numerous children? It is the culture that overcomes the boundaries of nationality and faith, going beyond religious, social and political identities.[12]

---

6. A German translation is printed in Löffler, *Arabische Christen im Nahost-Konflikt*, 33–43.
7. For more see Khoury and Zimmer-Winkel, *Christian Theology in the Palestinian Context*.
8. For an extensive collection of this work consult Graf, *Geschichte*.
9. Khodr, *Ways*; Khodr, "Christianity"; Kattan, "Cross."
10. For Anawati's work on Islam consult Anawati, *Études de philosophie musulmane*; Anawati, "Assessment"; Anawati, "Christentum und Islam."
11. Samir, *Patriarch*.
12. Bechealany, "Dr. Bechealany in a Seminar," para. 5.

MIDDLE EASTERN WOMEN THEOLOGIANS

In the last decades the hitherto absent voices of women in theological knowledge production in the Middle East have experienced a boost. A new generation of theologically trained women has enriched the theological discourse while challenging both the patriarchal church and society contexts. Mary Mikhael, former president of the Near East School of Theology (NEST), Beirut, Lebanon, and the first woman seminary president in the Middle East (1994–2011) has contributed in various publications to bringing up women theological voices to be heard.[13] This voice had frequently been called to be silent in the name of more relevant issues or priorities as often declared:

> Women who try to bring up their own concerns and express their sense of call to the ministry are made to feel guilty, as if they are trying to create difficulties for the church, which is already struggling with "more important" issues such as security, violence, emigration of youth, finances, and others.[14]

One of the recent theological debates, especially in the evangelical churches in the Middle East, is the theme of ordaining women to ministry. Though many of these churches have been proclaiming that man and woman are created equally in the image of God the praxis reveals a different reality whereby women do not enjoy the same rights as those accorded to men. Especially in Evangelical churches in the region, where visiting female pastors from partner churches were often allowed to minister while the local women theologians were denied the same right. Debates on theological and/or cultural restrictions on and against the ordination of women have been underway for some decades. The National Evangelical Synod of Syria and Lebanon had opened up the opportunity for women to preach in 1993. The General Assembly of the Fellowship of the Middle East Evangelical Churches underlined in January 2010 that there are neither theological nor biblical reasons for denying the ordination of women.

However, it took almost seven years before the first female pastor, Rola Sleiman, was ordained in the National Evangelical Church in Tripoli on February 26, 2017. Rev. Sleiman pointed to the social challenge for ordaining women in a pluralistic religious and a patriarchal context. The debate was not a theological one, but rather on questions of reception in sister churches, e.g. Orthodox and Catholic churches, conservative Evangelical churches, and by Muslims and society at large. Nevertheless, Rev. Sleiman stresses that "Being an ordained minister is a true and live demonstration of God's love and equality."[15]

The late Fr. Georges Massouh, then head of the Center for Christian-Muslim Studies at the University of Balamand in Lebanon, as Rev. Sleiman regarded the absence of ordained women in the Evangelical Churches in the region was due to social customs.

---

13. Mikhael, "Women in Middle Eastern," 54–60; Mikhael, "Ordination," 153–62.
14. Mikhael, "Women in Middle Eastern," 60.
15. World Communion of Reformed Churches, "Profile Rola Suleiman."

And although such a tradition does not exist within the Orthodox Church: "There is no theological hindrance to ordaining female bishops in the Orthodox Church."[16]

Two months later Rev. Najla Kassab,[17] president of the World Communion of Reformed Churches (WCRC), was ordained. In his sermon Rev. Dr. George Sabra, president of the Near East School of Theology (NEST) underlined the importance of this ordination in the context of the rise of "religious extremism, intellectual rigidity, cultural reactionism and social isolationism" as a counter example to the prevailing "suppression of freedoms, especially the rights and freedoms of women."[18]

On April 3, 2022 Rev. Mathilde Sabbagh, the first female pastor in Syria, was ordained in the National Evangelical Synod of Syria and Lebanon. In 2018 Rima Nasrallah van Saane, assistant professor of practical theology at the Near East School of Theology[19] was the first female pastor to be ordained in the National Evangelical Church of Beirut (NECB).

In Egypt, the discussion about women's ordination in the Evangelical churches is already underway. Hence, Anne Zaki[20] is teaching practical theology at the Evangelical Theological Seminary in Cairo.

Among the diaspora Middle Eastern Evangelical communities, there were female pastors earlier on. Niveen Sarras was ordained in the Evangelical Lutheran Church in America and has published on feminist exegeses.[21] Gihan Farag is the first Egyptian ordained female pastor, although in Texas. She describes her motivation for ordination: "Priesthood is a call from God to men and women alike and not a privilege for men."[22]

The themes addressed by women theologians stretch over a variety of disciplines. However, we are still at a stage where these voices are mostly working on an individual level lacking joint exchange, cooperation, and networking that would lead to the development of a more systematic approach to engaging in and voicing women's theological thought in the region.

JOINT THEOLOGICAL DOCUMENTS AND THE PUBLIC SPHERE

On the other hand, we are experiencing a change in the way theology is thought about, taught, and practiced. Theologies that are grounded in the Middle East and that engage

---

16. Hanna, "Roula Sleiman."

17. See President of the World Communion of Reformed Churches (WCRC) (August 1, 2022): http://wcrc.ch/about-us/excom/president-najla-kassab.

18. *NEST Newsletter*, June 2017.

19. Nasrallah van Saane, "Itinerant Feasting," 319–42; Nasrallah van Saane, "Kinetics of Healing," 270–84; Nasrallah van Saane, "Rearranging Things," 74–95.

20. Zaki, "Women Ordination."

21. Sarras, "Prophet Amos"; Sarras, "Feminist Reading."

22. Hussein, "Will Egypt Ever Have Female Pastors?"

both with the local and global context are increasingly moving from the periphery to the public sphere. Central themes for local Christians in the region to name just some are land, war, resistance, nonviolence, forced migration, refugees and displacement, uprisings and revolutions, violence, and citizenship. This shift is reflected in the extensive number of publications, conferences, and debates. This paper cannot dwell on the individual writings of Middle Eastern theologians from the various countries, rather it tries to highlight a few of the Christian ecumenically formulated documents that help offer a more comprehensive view of the themes in question.

Kairos Palestine

In December 2009, an ecumenical group of Christian Palestinians published the kairos document, "A moment of truth: A word of faith, hope and love from the heart of Palestinian suffering."[23] This is a document developed by a group of theologians and laypeople from the various Christian denominations in Palestine, including three women.[24] Amidst a hopeless situation, the document is a "cry out from within the suffering in our country, under the Israeli occupation, with a cry of hope in the absence of all hope, a cry full of prayer and faith in a God ever vigilant, in God's divine providence for all the inhabitants of this land."[25] As a document of faith, it formulates a contextual narrative theology from the perspective of suffering, using contextual exegesis to address three central Christian theological concepts: faith, hope, and love. Hermeneutics of Lamentations is central for understanding both the document as well as the hope anchored in faith as an active hope that defies everything to work for peace, justice and creative resistance, and the need for transformation. The document, like the statement of 1967, calls Christians "to revisit fundamentalist theological positions that support certain unjust political options with regard to the Palestinian people."[26] In the statement of 1967 the theologians call upon all Christians to reject any nationalism based on religious or ethnic exclusivism, A call that is reinforced again in 2009, "We condemn all forms of racism, whether religious or ethnic, including anti-Semitism and Islamophobia, and we call on you to condemn it and oppose it in all its manifestations."[27]

---

23. Kairos Palestine, *Moment of Truth*.

24. The group members were Patriarch Michel Sabbah, Archbishop Atallah Hanna, Rev. Dr. Jamal Khader, Rev. Dr. Rafiq Khoury, Rev. Dr. Mitri Raheb, Rev. Dr. Naim Ateek, Rev. Dr. Yohana Katanacho, Rev. Fadi Diab, Dr. Geries Khoury, Ms. Cedar Duaybis, Ms. Nora Kort, Ms. Lucy Thaljieh, Mr. Nidal Abu Zuluf, Mr. Yusef Daher and Rifat Odeh Kassis as the coordinator.

25. Kairos Palestine, *Moment of Truth*.

26. Kairos Palestine, *Moment of Truth*, 6.3.

27. Kairos Palestine, *Moment of Truth*, 6.3.

Middle Eastern Theologies

From the Nile to the Euphrates: A Statement on Christian Responsibility and Citizenship Law

In 2014, upon the invitation of Diyar Consortium, a group of Christian academics and young scholars from the various countries of the Middle East issued the statement "From the Nile to the Euphrates: A Statement on Christian Responsibility and Citizenship Law"[28] addressing the future of the Christian population in this region. In its contextual analysis, the document summarizes the key challenges in the region in ten points: The relationship between religion and the state, constitutions and legal systems, the security of all citizens, management of human and natural resources, the status and contribution of women, hope, education, and equal opportunities in the labor market for youth, human dignity and quality of life, authentic spirituality, reason in the age of unreason, and a unifying vision for the future.

The second part of the document addresses the role of Christians both as individuals and as part of their societies. "We are also committed to guarding the dignity of all humankind, regardless of gender, ethnicity, religion or belief."[29]

In light of the changing context in the region, issues pertaining to religious freedom, religious, ethnic, or sectarian prejudice, and citizenship are increasingly debated. Citizenship is moving to become a central theme for a basis of a joint future in the region and is being increasingly addressed through various documents and positions. Tarek Mitri calls it the third path beyond "minority-centered activism or resignation" that

> . . . involves reinventing through political participation the pact of citizenship that binds Christians and Muslims together, and renewing the role that *nahda* (renaissance) played during the early 20th century. To be sure, a new political and social order is in the making. The pact of citizenship that was a determining factor in various independence movements is to be reclaimed and enacted in the present longing of Arab peoples for freedom, dignity, and democracy.[30]

Assaad Elias Kattan stresses the need for both Christians and Muslims in the region to rediscover "the value of genuine citizenship":

> Far from seeking to rehabilitate the nationalisms of the past, as though the experiences of more than a hundred years were insignificant and devoid of influence, Christians today are invited to rediscover, along with Muslims, the value of genuine citizenship as well as how indispensable it is for establishing modern and free Arab societies. Genuine citizenship not only collides with communitarianism and whatever social structures we have inherited from the

---

28. The Christian Academic Forum for Citizenship in the Arab World, *From the Nile*.
29. The Christian Academic Forum for Citizenship in the Arab World, *From the Nile*, 20.
30. Rāhib, *Ar-Rabīʿ al-ʿArabī wa Masīḥiyyū ash-Sharq al-Awsaṭ*, 48–49.

Middle Ages. It also wards off anxiety, fear and all kinds of protective mechanisms nourished by our current role syndromes.[31]

In light of the ongoing conflicts, wars, and fragmentation in the region, new publications following the "Arab Spring" are offering a contextual theological reading of the socio-political scene.[32] A leading question here is the position of Christians and churches towards and against power, repression, and the will to resist:

> The Christians are not invited to revolt against a regime of power. Autocratic, repressive, corrupt, political, secular or religious or against the people represent the system. They are, contrary to that, invited to revolt against tyranny, repression and corruption per se . . . .[33]

"We choose a life in abundance—Christians the Middle East: for a renewal of theological, social and political choices."

On September 28, 2021, a new ecumenical document, "We Choose Abundant Life—Christians in the Middle East: Towards Renewed Theological, Social, and Political Choices," was presented at St. Elias Church in Antelias, Beirut, Lebanon. Eleven personalities[34] from the region worked on the fifty-page document for nearly two years. The document uses contextual theological methods and is divided into three major chapters; the first chapter looks at the historical and current geo-political context, the second chapter analyzes the ecclesial and theological context, and the third chapter formulates possible strategies and choices to be made in light of the challenges addressed. The goal, it is argued, is: ". . . to move from an obsession with existence and survival to taking the risk of presence and witness."[35]

The document makes it clear from the outset that it intends to address issues that have previously been considered inappropriate in public discourse. Human rights, freedoms, justice, citizenship rights, and diversity are identified as among the most pressing issues for Christian presence and witness in the region and are critically examined from a Christian theological position.

The document calls for a liberated vision aiming at ". . . reinventing Arabism as a cultural space and an inclusive cultural concept, away from a forced, ideological

---

31. Kattan, "Christians in the Arab World," 53.

32. Rāhib, *Ar-Rabīʿ al-ʿArabīwa Masīḥiyyū ash-Sharq al-Awsaṭ*; Awad, *Freedom*; Zaki, "Al-Aqbāṭ"; Sabra, *Christian*.

33. Awad, "About Christ the Revolutionary and What Revolution Christianity Means," 25.

34. In alphabetical order—Prof. Souraya Bechealany, Fr. Kahlil Chalfoun, Fr. Gabriel Alfred Hachem, Rev. Najla Kassab, Prof. Assaad Elias Kattan, Rev. George Jabra Al-Kopti, Michel Nseir, Rev. Dr. Mitri Raheb, Ziad El Sayyeh, Sister Emilie Tannous, and Fr. Rouphael Zgheib.

35. We Choose Abundant Life Group, *We Choose Abundant Life*, 42.

Arabization that contradicts the spirit of cultural openness."[36] This vision can only be undertaken jointly with fellow Muslims.

For the future of Christians in the Middle East, the document expresses the vision of living together with believers of other religions especially Muslims ". . . as brothers and sisters and uphold human dignity and freedom."[37] Thus, the document later expands this vision to reach out to Jews where it states that "Christians are invited to develop a theological and intellectual approach that allows us to open a new page in relations with Jews, who have always been an integral part of the Middle Eastern tapestry and its pluralistic identity."[38]

The document takes a clear, unequivocal stand on justice and humanity, and thus testifies a living courageous faith, a strength of resistance, a will for reform, liberation and renewal, prophetic visions, and much hope. The churches are urged to take a clear and unambiguous position in favor of the above issues and are asked to commit to them.

3.4 Women and theological ecumenical liturgies

In their article on the history of the World Day of Prayer, Eileen King and Helga Hiller write about the new understanding of equality and solidarity among the Christian women who promoted the World Day of Prayer (WDP) and whose daughters and grandchildren have been holding the World Day of Prayer every first Friday in March since then:

> When North American women, in 1926, called for a World Day of Prayer and the first WDP was celebrated around the world in 1927, Christian women had understood: We are now equal partners in a worldwide sisterhood of prayer, sharing our sorrows and joys.[39]

National committees for the World Day of Prayer exist in the following Middle Eastern countries: Egypt, Jordan, Lebanon, Palestine, Tunisia, and Turkey.[40]

Since its establishment more than ninety-five years ago, Christian women from the Middle East have contributed to the development of six liturgies. The first Middle Eastern country to contribute with a liturgy was Egypt in 1959 and again in 1975. In 1994 the liturgy came from Palestine and in 2003 from Lebanon to be followed once again by Egypt in 2014. In 2024 the liturgy will once again come from Palestine.

In her work, Heidemarie Winkel underlines that the WDP ". . . has become one of the rare religious structures in Arab Christianity that enables women to act as

---

36. We Choose Abundant Life Group, *We Choose Abundant Life*, 34.
37. We Choose Abundant Life Group, *We Choose Abundant Life*, 34.
38. We Choose Abundant Life Group, *We Choose Abundant Life*, 45.
39. https://worlddayofprayer.net/wdpic-history.html.
40. https://worlddayofprayer.net/national-committees.html.

theological and spiritual leaders . . ."⁴¹ Yet, though this structure exists it is never the less sad to note that when a historical review of theological documents and statements on the Middle East are made, whether in the region or internationally, the WDP liturgies are rarely mentioned, if at all.

We Choose Abundant Life makes a promising stand in this regard, asking the churches "to develop its structures, teachings and practices to activate the participation of women in all fields, including ministry, leadership and decision-making."⁴²

BIBLIOGRAPHY

Anawati, Georges C. "An Assessment of the Christian-Islamic Dialogue." In *The Vatican, Islam and the Middle East*, edited by Kail C. Ellis, 51–68. New York: Syracuse University Press, 1987.

———. "Christentum und Islam. Ihr Verhältnis aus christlicher Sicht." In *Dialog aus der Mitte christlicher Theologie*, edited by A. Bsteh, 197–216. Farnum, UK: Ashgate, 1987.

———. *Études de philosophie musulmane, Études musulmanes*. Paris Librairie Philosophique 15. Paris: Vrin, 1974.

The Arab Working Group on Muslim-Christian Dialogue, Dialogue and Coexistence: An Arab Muslim-Christian Covenant. https://www.agmcd.org/files/covenant.htm.

Awad, Najib. "About Christ the Revolutionary and What Revolution Christianity Means." *Telos Magazine* 1 (2020) 22–25.

———. *And Freedom Became a Public-Square: Political, Sociological and Religious Overviews on the Arab Christians and the Arabic Spring*. Berlin: LIT, 2012.

———. *Orthodoxy in Arabic Terms: A Study of Theodore Abū Qurrah's Theology in Its Islamic Context*, Berlin: De Gruyter, 2015.

Bader, Habib, ed. *Christianity: A History in the Middle East*. Beirut: MECC, 2005.

Bailey, Betty Jane, and J. Martin Bailey. *Who Are the Christians in the Middle East?* Grand Rapids: Eerdmans, 2010.

Bechealany, Souraya. "Dr. Bechealany in a Seminar about the Church Mission Today in the Middle East at the Holy Spirit University—Kaslik." 2019. https://www.mecc.org/mecc/2019/2/27/dr-bechealany-in-a-seminar-about-the-church-mission-today-in-the-middle-east-at-the-holy-spirit-university-kaslik.

The Christian Academic Forum for Citizenship in the Arab World. *From the Nile to the Euphrates The Call of Faith and Citizenship: A Statement of The Christian Academic Forum for Citizenship in the Arab World*. Bethlehem: Diyar, 2014.

Cragg, Kenneth. *The Arab Christian: A History in the Middle East*. Louisville: Westminster John Knox, 1991.

"Die Vorreiterin." https://de.qantara.de/inhalt/libanons-erste-pastorin-die-vorreiterin.

Graf, Georg. *Geschichte der Christlichen Arabischen Literatur*. 4 vols. Studi e Testi 118, 133, 146, 147. Vatican City: Biblioteca apostolica vaticana, 1944–1951.

Hanna, Obaidah. "Roula Sleiman: The First Female Bishop in the Middle East." https://raseef22.net/article/1068898-roula-sleiman-first-female-bishop-middle-east.

---

41. Winkel, "Mobilizing Gender."
42. We Choose Abundant Life Group, *We Choose Abundant Life*, 44.

Hussein, N. A. "Will Egypt Ever Have Female Pastors?" www.al-monitor.com/originals/2019/09/egyptian-woman-ordained-in-texas-church.html.

Kairos Palestine. *A Moment of Truth: A Word of Faith, Hope And Love from the Heart Of Palestinian Suffering.* https://www.kairospalestine.ps/index.php/about-kairos/kairos-palestine-document.

Kassab, Najla. "A Middle Eastern Christian Approach to the Old Testament." *Theological Review* 1 (1992) 35–48.

Kattan, Assaad Elias. "Christians in the Arab World: Beyond Role Syndrome." *Ecumenical Review* 64 (2012) 50–53.

———. "The Cross as Islam: Georges Khodr's Approach to Islam as a Paradigm of Contextual Theology." *Journal of Eastern Christian Studies* 69 (2017) 69–78.

Khodr, Georges. "Christianity in a Pluralistic World—the Economy of the Spirit." *The Ecumenical Review* 23 (1971) 118–28.

———. "Palestine Between Biblical Texts and War." *Al Muntada* 5–6 (1967) 8–9.

———. "Theological Reflections of Eastern Christians on the Palestinian Problem." *Al Muntada* 55 (1972) 18–23.

———. *The Ways of Childhood.* Crestwood, NY: St. Vladimir's Seminary Press, 2016.

———. "World Conference of Christians for Palestine: Testimony of Bishop George Khodr." *Al Muntada* 38–39 (1970) 21–22.

Khoury, Rafiq, and Rainer Zimmer-Winkel, eds. *Christian Theology in the Palestinian Context* N.d.: AphorismA, 2019.

Löffler, Paul. *Arabische Christen im Nahost-Konflikt. Christen impolitischen.* Spannungsfeld, Frankfurt: Lembeck 1976.

Mikhael, Mary. "Ordination of Women and the Church in the Middle East." *Theological Review* 32 (2011) 153–62.

———. "Women in Middle Eastern Societies and Churches." *Theological Review* 64 (2012) 54–60.

Rāhib, Mitrī. *Ar-Rabīʿ al-ʿArabīwa Masīḥiyyū ash-Sharq al-Awsaṭ* ("he Arabic Spring and the Christians of the Middle East). Bethlehem: Diyar, 2012.

Nasrallah van Saane, Rima. "Itinerant Feasting: Eastern Christian Women Negotiating (Physical) Presence in the Celebration of Easter." *Exchange: A Journal for Missiological and Ecumenical Research* 42 (2013) 319–42.

———. "Kinetics of Healing: Protestant Women Pledging Baptism in Saydnaya Orthodox Monastery." *Studia Liturgica* 42 (2012) 270–84.

———. "Rearranging Things: How Protestant Attitudes Shake the Objects in the Piety of Eastern Christian Women." *Journal for Material Religion: The Journal of Objects, Art and Belief* 22 (2016) 74–95.

NEST Newsletter. June 2017. https://www.theonest.edu.lb/documents/fe_newsletter/Newsletter-June-2017.pdf.

Proglio, Gabriele, ed. *Decolonising the Mediterranean: European Colonial Heritages in North Africa and the Middle East.* Cambridge: Cambridge Scholars, 2016.

Raheb, Mitri. "Christianity in the Middle East, 1917–2017." In *History of Global Christianity*, edited by Jens Holger Schjørring et al., 3:375–95. Leiden: Brill, 2018.

Raheb, Mitri, and Mark A. Lamport, eds. *The Rowman & Littlefield Handbook of Christianity in the Middle East.* Washington, DC: Rowman & Littlefield, 2020.

Sabra, George. "Christian Mission in the Wake of the Arab Spring." *International Bulletin of Missionary Research* 38 (2014) 115–18.

Samir, Khalil Samir, ed. *The Patriarch and the Caliph: An Eighth-Century Dialogue between Timothy I and al-Mahdi*. Chicago: The University of Chicago Press, 2016.

Sarras, Niveen. "A Palestinian Feminist Reading of the Book of Jonah." *Journal of Lutheran Ethics* 15 (2015). https://www.elca.org/JLE/Articles/1112.

———. "The Prophet Amos and Palestinian Women." *Journal of Lutheran Ethics* 13 (2013). https://www.elca.org/jle/articles/13.

Tarek, Mitri. "Christians in the Arab World, Minority Attitudes and Citizenship." *Ecumenical Review* 64 (2012) 43–49.

———. "Who are the Christians of the Arab World?" *The Ecumenical Review* 89 (2000) 12–27.

We Choose Abundant Life Group. *We Choose Abundant Life: Christians in the Middle East: Towards Renewed Theological, Social, and Political Choices*. Beirut, 2021. https://online.anyflip.com/mijbx/mawd/mobile/index.html 2021.

Wessels, Antonie. *Arab and Christian?: Christians in the Middle East*. https://brill.com/view/journals/exch/27/1/article-p89_13.xml?language=en.

Winkel, Heidemarie. "Mobilizing Gender Around the Globe: The Ecumenical Movement as a Resource for Gender Equity in Arab Christianity." In *Religion on the Move!: New Dynamics of Religious Expansion in a Globalizing World*, edited by Afe Adogame and Shobana Shankar, 225–42. Leiden: Brill, 2013.

World Communion of Reformed Churches. "Profile Rola Sleiman." http://wcrc.ch/justice/ordination-of-women/profile-rola-sleiman.

Zaki, Andrea. "Al-Aqbāṭwa-l-thawra, Dār al-Thaqāfa" ("The Copts and the Uprising"). *Exchange* 49 (2020) 237–56.

———. "Women Ordination in Egypt." *Horizons* 22 (2010) 113–45.

———. "Women's Ordination as Pastors: A Middle Eastern Perspective." Speech, CBE: Becoming New: Man and Woman Together in Christ, Los Angeles conference, October 30, 2017. https://www.youtube.com/watch?v=A9GTJQjYA7M

SECTION 5

Emerging Theologies from Africa

CHAPTER 20

Theological Ethics in a Time of Crisis

AGBONKHIANMEGHE E. OROBATOR

THE NARRATIVE OF RELIGIOUS PROSPERITY IN AFRICA

Africa is a deeply religious continent and religion seems second nature to an African. This explains perhaps why—against the backdrop of Christianity's history—Pope Benedict XVI declared that the African continent "constitutes an immense spiritual 'lung' for a humanity that appears to be in a crisis of faith and hope."[1] This flattering designation expresses an explicit belief in the capability of the religious status of Africa to oxygenate a spiritually asphyxiated humanity. More importantly, the pope's nomenclature of "immense spiritual 'lung'" is symptomatic not only of the trajectory of development of religion in Africa, but also of the characteristic receptiveness of the continent to momentous change and new opportunities in the highly globalized and networked world of the twenty-first century.

Despite the challenges facing the continent, Africans have been receptive to the Christian faith. On this continent to be a Christian is not a badge of tradition and a cultural acquisition; it is a way of life that colors, shapes, influences, and conditions every aspect of life. To live is to believe. As I pointed out in my *Theology Brewed in an African Pot*, "Philosophers, sociologists, anthropologists, and theologians . . . never tire of reminding us that religion runs deep in the veins of Africans. They say Africans are notoriously and incurably religious."[2]

---

1. http://www.vatican.va/holy_father/benedict_xvi/homilies/2009/documents/hf_ben-xvi_hom_20091004_sinodo-africa_en.html.
2. Orobator, *Theology Brewed in an African Pot*, 14.

Several demographic studies corroborate this view. A nineteen-country scientific survey of Islam and Christianity in sub-Saharan Africa by The Pew Forum on Religion and Public Life notes:

> Indeed, sub-Saharan Africa is clearly among the most religious places in the world. In many countries across the continent, roughly nine-in-ten people or more say religion is *very important* in their lives. By this key measure, even the least religiously inclined nations in the region score higher than the United States, which is among the most religious of the advanced industrial countries.[3]

This finding bears significant implications for the fortunes of Christianity on the continent: "One-in-five of all the Christians in the world (21 percent) now lives in sub-Saharan Africa. Over a period of one hundred years Christianity in sub-Saharan Africa has recorded an astronomical 70-fold increase in membership, from 7 million to 470 million."[4]

As mentioned, the explanation or reason for the impressive growth of Christianity may lie in the African anthropological constitution. Reverence for transcendence and a sacramental view of reality are constitutive elements of African anthropology. The physical world is so profoundly sacralized that the boundary with the spiritual realm of ancestral spirits, divinities, and deities is either blurred or permeable. Consequently, in the African indigenous religious worldview nothing is considered lifeless in the natural environment.

For example, in this worldview, *ecology* means more than a physical environment of organisms and inanimate objects. At a much deeper level, ecology constitutes a universe of spiritual meaning and attendant ethical imperatives. Ecology is not simply cold and detached matter; one's sense of self is intimately tied to one's relationship with the natural environment. Hence the belief is strong that the natural universe is both origin and sustenance of life. Therefore, reverence for the environment or protection of ecology is not an optional task; it is a religious experience and a moral imperative. Such belief system creates a fertile substratum for the growth of religion—like Christianity or Islam—which integrates transcendence and sacramentality into its core architecture. More importantly, it serves as an invaluable source of material for theological reflection in the African context.[5]

Another equally important factor is that, demographically speaking, Africa is a growing continent; it is part of what Phillip Jenkins refers to as the "Southern boom."[6] Analysts project dramatic population growth across most of the Global

---

3. Pew Forum on Religion and Public Life, "Islam and Christianity in Sub-Saharan Africa."
4. Pew Forum on Religion and Public Life, "Islam and Christianity in Sub-Saharan Africa."
5. Although not directly addressed in this chapter, twin crises of climate change and global warming are the themes of emerging studies in African theological ethics. See Rwiza, *Environmental Ethics*, and Chu Ilo, *African Ecological Ethics*.
6. Jenkins, *Next Christendom*.

South, while decreasing across most of the Global North. This demographic boom has consequences for the fortunes of Christian communities. By 2050, for example, of the ten largest populations of French-speaking Catholics, it is estimated that five would be in African countries (Democratic Republic of Congo, Burundi, Madagascar, Rwanda, and Cameroon). The situation would be the same in Anglophone Catholicism (Uganda, Nigeria, Kenya, Tanzania, and Malawi).[7] The Christian churches are direct beneficiaries of Africa's demographic growth. In other words, the phenomenal growth and expansion of the continent's two largest religions is a direct consequence of a larger demographic expansion.

Given the foregoing and taking account of the fortunes of Islam and Christianity, the evidence affirms that religion is a prosperous phenomenon in Africa. Since 1900 Christianity has recorded a net increase of 57 percent; Islam recorded a net increase of 29 percent—both at the expense of indigenous African religions.[8]

THE REALITY OF CRISIS: FRAMING THEOLOGICAL ETHICS FOR AFRICA

There is, however, an unsavory flip side to the glowing narrative of religious prosperity in Africa. One of the disturbing facts of the growth of religious affiliation in Africa is that it is set in the context of multiple and complex dysfunctionalities. This fact prompted Ugandan theologian Emmanuel Katongole to make the poignant and controversial claim that "churches and coffins are perhaps the two most prevalent images associated with Africa today."[9] His observation vividly illustrates the troubling paradox of the phenomenal growth of Christianity in a context of escalating socio-economic and political crises. This situation casts a long shadow on theological scholarship on the continent.

There is a growing body of recent scholarly works that engage Africa's complex crises in theological terms. Several new voices are paying closer attention to the socio-economic, cultural, religious, political, and ecclesial context of the continent in order to discern and delineate pertinent and emerging theological issues and the potential for impacting the practice of Christianity. The focus, methodology, and outcomes of these approaches signal interesting vistas for theological ethics in Africa.

The way African theology engages with these issues diverges from the traditional moral theology of the West in at least two significant ways. First, although it recognizes the importance of the Bible and does not dispute it as a basis for moral thinking and ethical considerations, African theological ethicists appeal to a wide range of sources.[10] These sources primarily consists of principles and criteria derived from Catholic

---

7. Allen, *Future Church*, 144.
8. Pew Forum on Religion and Public Life, "Global Christianity."
9. Katongole, *Sacrifice of Africa*, 29.
10. See Istas, *Patterns of Morality in the Bible*, 34–49; and Bere, "Bible in Africa," 139–65.

social tradition or Catholic social teaching and African cultural norms, shared values, and religious beliefs.[11] Second, rather than concern itself with "confessing sins" and regulating moral patterns of individual behavior, theological ethics addresses critical issues that shape and affect not only behavior but more critically their effect on the lived realities of women and men in society.[12] An important subset of these issues relate primarily to crisis situations, which is the main focus of this essay.

THEOLOGY FORGED IN A CRUCIBLE OF CRISIS

During the First Special Assembly for Africa of the Synod of Bishops (1994), Cardinal Hyacinthe Thiandoum of Dakar, Senegal, posed a haunting and pivotal question: "In a Continent full of bad news, how is the Christian message 'Good News' for our people? In the midst of an all-pervading despair, where lie the hope and optimism which the Gospel brings?"[13] The quest to provide a credible and effective answer to this existential query is what shapes African theological ethics.

Africa is caught in the throes of multiple crises. An inventory of crises that have particular resonances in Africa presently include but is not limited to: violent conflict, civil war, and political instability (South Sudan, Cameroon, DRC, Somalia, Ethiopia, Libya), widespread lack of accountability and transparency in political and public office (Uganda, Congo, Chad, Zimbabwe), sectarian atrocities and violence orchestrated by terrorist groups (Nigeria, Mali, Somalia, Burkina Faso, Mozambique, Mali), poverty and hunger, and human mobility linked to migration and forced displacement.

Many broad articulations of a theological approach to these crises exist, the two most compelling illustrations of which are Emmanuel Katongole, *The Sacrifice of Africa: A Political Theology for Africa* (2011), and Cyril Orji, *Unmasking the African Ghost: Theology, Politics, and the Nightmare of Failed States* (2022). Between these two African theologians, it is possible to identify diverse themes, features, and characteristics of African theological ethics in the context of crisis.

Two important notes need to be made here. First, embedded in these articulations—as in several contemporary articulations of theology in Africa—is a strain of postcolonial criticism, given the continent's historical reality and enduring legacy of colonial domination. In many ways, colonialism is a malevolent ghost that Africa has never been able to exorcise. Thus, Africa remains a sacrificial lamb on the altar of "the colonial project [that] have had no qualms perpetuating the same wanton sacrificing of lives in pursuit of their political ambition and greed."[14] Without discounting its significance or undermining the catastrophic nature of colonialism, this strain

---

11. Magesa, *Anatomy of Inculturation*, 77.
12. See Mugambi and Nasimiyu-Wasike, *Moral and Ethical Issues in African Christianity*.
13. John Paul II, *Ecclesia in Africa*, no. 40.
14. Katongole, *Sacrifice of Africa*, 17.

constitutes too narrow a focus to provide sufficient entry into the diverse and complex issues of concern to African theological ethics in the twenty-first century.

Second, current articulations of theological ethics in the context of Africa's crises have benefitted from some aspects of African theology of reconstruction that gained prominence in the 1990s, albeit, so far, it has neither delivered on its strident promise nor realized its ambitious aspiration.[15]

African theological ethics engages critically and creatively with socioeconomic and political issues. It maintains an intent focus on contemporary African contextual realities and it is by necessity both interdisciplinary and cross-disciplinary. Furthermore, theological ethics in the time of crisis rests on the basic premise or assumption that "theology in Africa must take misery and oppression seriously as a context for its reflection on and reconstruction of the social order."[16] This theological task is not confined to the analysis of an individual theologian. Rather, it is considered an essential constituent of the mission of the Christian community and begins by considering the latter's sociological context. "Such a starting point, by drawing attention to the African context within which the church is located, will highlight the pressing social and existential challenges that confront millions of Africans on a daily basis."[17]

Drawing upon the resources of Christian Scripture, tradition, and theology, as well as authentic African cultures, traditions, and values, theological ethics in a time of crisis aims to achieve a new "social imagination of Africa" capable of propelling Africa's initiation into modernity and engendering progress and human flourishing.[18]

A PORTRAIT OF THEOLOGICAL ETHICS IN A TIME OF CRISIS

Rather than remain at the level of documentary analysis, it would be useful to consider a few concrete examples of how African theology engages and proposes remedies for multiple and complex situations of crisis that threaten human existence and the survival of African societies and communities.

A theological analysis of power, authority, and leadership

The theological approach to the exercise of power, authority, and leadership emerges in the context of a widespread vacancy of credible and competent political leadership capable of promoting integral development, social transformation, and human

---

15. See Getui and Obeng, *Theology of Reconstruction*; Mugambi, *Church and the Reconstruction of Africa*; Mugambi, *From Liberation to Reconstruction*; and Mana, *Théologie africaine pour temps de crise*. Proponents of the theology of reconstruction aimed to overcome the impasse created by the controversy between "inculturation" and "Black theology," both dominant components of African Christian theology. See Martey, *African Theology*.

16. Orji, *Unmasking the African Ghost*, 4–5; Uzukwu, *Listening Church*, 1–9.

17. Katongole, "Church of the Future," 164.

18. Katongole, *Sacrifice of Africa*, 20.

flourishing. It recognizes that the current predominant models of political engagement fall woefully short of politics at the service of humanity and society.

African theologians agree that leadership deficit or lack of governability counts as the greatest challenge to Africa's progress and development. A chronic leadership gap dovetails with weak institutions of governance to keep Africa perpetually underdeveloped. The ramifications of chronic leadership deficit or failure as a vector of underdevelopment and impoverishment in Africa are staggering. Poor leadership militates against key drivers of development and transformation, namely, strong institutions of state and policy-driven agenda for growth, ruled-based society, and civil and political institutions built on trust and cohesion. There are several contemporary scenarios that illustrate the widespread leadership crisis in Africa.[19]

The first scenario involves leadership tussles between Africa's "strongmen" or "big men" with devastating consequences for their populations, such as violence, killings, forced displacement, and violation of human and people's rights, such as have been witnessed in Zimbabwe, Ivory Coast, DRC, Congo-Brazzaville, Central African Republic, South Sudan, Madagascar, and Burundi.

A second scenario of leadership deficit is the self-perpetuation of autocratic leaders in office, also with brutal consequences for the people. Past and recent examples include: Robert Mugabe (Zimbabwe), Paul Biya (Cameroon), Idriss Déby (Chad), José Eduardo dos Santos (Angola), Teodoro Obiang Nguema Mbasogo (Equatorial Guinea), Yoweri Museveni (Uganda), Denis Sassou Nguesso (Congo-Brazzaville), Pierre Nkurunziza (Burundi), and Joseph Compaoré (Burkina Faso). This phenomenon has produced an embarrassing cast of inept "dinosaur leaders" that constitutes "part of the larger African ghost syndrome."[20]

The third scenario concerns predatory leadership that thrives on extensive practice of corruption, rent-seeking, and impunity. In this instance, not only does poor leadership hold back the progress of peoples, it actively undercuts any prospect of transformation. Examples are too numerous to mention.

In the fourth and final scenario, the breakdown of leadership has led to the emergence of failed or extremely vulnerable states. Examples include: Libya, Somalia, South Sudan, and Central African Republic.

How does theological ethics respond to this crisis of leadership? A common approach exhorts leaders to moral probity and personal integrity in the exercise of their political responsibilities. This seems to be the approach preferred by the Catholic Church. The African Synod (2009), for example, pleaded for the emergence of

> saints in high political office: saintly politicians who will clean the continent of corruption, work for the good of the people, and know how to galvanize other men and women of good will from outside the Church to join hands against

---

19. See Orji, *Unmasking the African Ghost*.
20. Orji, *Unmasking the African Ghost*, 7.

> the common evils that beset our nations. . . . Many Catholics in high office have fallen woefully short in their performance in office. The Synod calls on such people to repent, or quit the public arena and stop causing havoc to the people and giving the Catholic Church a bad name.[21]

In reality, Africa's political history shows that the continent has not lacked "devout" politicians. But their credibility as "saintly" or even "Christian" remains open to debate. The weakness of this exhortatory approach lies in the difficulty of exerting a direct influence on governance by religious communities. The latter faces the vexing challenge of how to translate rhetoric into effective political action that is not limited to pious exhortation and supplication.[22]

Attempting to overcome this impasse, the African synod opted for a greater pastoral engagement with political leaders through pastoral care and formation in the values and principles of Catholic social teaching:

> Therefore, the Synod Fathers call upon all Pastors to offer present and future leaders in political and economic life a fitting doctrinal, pastoral and practical formation as well as spiritual support (by setting up chaplaincies). They request Catholic universities to establish faculties of political science. Catholic Social Teaching is a valuable means which should be spread as much as possible.[23]

This approach of the second African Synod that emphasizes an active engagement with political leaders through formation and pastoral care offers a better chance of success.

The second approach of African theological ethics to the failure of leadership prioritizes the profiling of faith-based models of credible leadership as a counterpoise to the proliferation of inept leaders. These models or case studies serve as inspiration in the quest for "a unique and distinctive form of leadership that can at once interrupt and call into question the self-serving forms of 'big man' leadership in Africa."[24] Part analytical and part biographical, the theological studies are often seeking "great inspiration in the stories of leaders" to discern, distil, and translate Gospel-inspired leadership lessons and principles.[25] Each of the leadership profile that theologians single out represents a strand of the tapestry that forms the new social imagination and a radical ecclesiological identity for Africa. They "represent different aspects . . . of a fresh vision of the church [and society] in Africa, engaged in the very concrete

---

21. African Synod, "Message to the People of God," no. 23.
22. Egan, "Governance Beyond Rhetoric," 100.
23. African Synod, "Final Propositions," no. 25.
24. Katongole, "Church of the Future," 170.
25. Carney, *For God and My Country*, 129–36. See Orobator, *Pope and the Pandemic*; Orobator, "Unsung Icons of Liberation."

and dynamic ways in the mundane and everyday tasks of crafting the temporal, social, geographical, and practical implications of that story."[26]

Reconciliation, justice, and peace

In one sense Jesus's remark about the kingdom of heaven could serve as an apt metaphor for Africa's predicament: "the kingdom of heaven suffers violence, and the violent are taking it by force" (Matt 11:12). Outside of South Africa, there seems to be a dearth of scholarly theological literature on the scourge of political violence and conflict in Africa. Over the last two decades, the escalation of civil and political crises and violent conflicts in Africa has given rise to many academic institutions and programs that address the twin issues of peace and reconciliation from theological and ethical perspectives. Katongole frames the issue in the following striking terms:

> The widespread phenomenon of political violence on the continent, which often masquerades itself as "ethnic" violence, poses a major challenge to the Church's identity and mission as sacrament of God's peaceable kingdom. Recent examples, such as Rwanda, South Sudan, Congo, and CAR, confirm the extent to which violence has become a perpetual feature of social life in Africa, not because of recalcitrant or "age-old animosities," but as a very modern problem, where "ethnicity" is imagined, reproduced, and exploited to further the political project of Africa's modernity. The widespread participation of Christians in violence raises a major theological and social challenge for the African Church.[27]

His final point about the participation of Christians in this "very modern problem" of manipulation and exploitation of ethnicity to generate violence has spawned a subset of theological analyses focusing on reconciliation, justice, and peace, as critical components of African theological ethics in a time of crisis. As mentioned, this was the theme of the second African Synod in 2009.[28]

African theological ethics does not engage these themes in generalized terms. Rather, it focuses on specific and concrete instances. One such instance is the Rwandan genocide of 1994. Twenty-five years after this tragedy, new theological voices and discourses have emerged in response to challenge violence induced by distorted visions and ideologies of ethnicity, and the imperative of reconciliation, justice, and peace. Two leading voices worth considering are Elisée Rutagambwa and Marcel Uwineza, themselves survivors.[29]

---

26. Kantongole, *Sacrifice of Africa*, 196.
27. Katongole, "Church of the Future," 166–67.
28. The synod's theme of "Reconciliation, justice, and peace" inspired two edited volumes: Orobator, *Reconciliation, Justice, and Peace*; Orobator, *Practising Reconciliation, Doing Justice, Building Peace*.
29. Rutagambwa and Uwineza, *Reinventing Theology in Post-Genocide Rwanda*; Uwineza, *Reconciling Memories*. See also Rutagambwa, "Is Blood Thicker than Faith?"; O'Neill, "Never Again."

Three aspects of this analysis are particularly striking when viewed from the perspective of theological ethics in the context of crisis. The first is the humility, honesty, and courage required to engage in the task of "re-membering" an event as consequential as the genocide in Rwanda, especially because of the contemporaneous nature of the incident. The African scholars are either themselves survivors of the tragedy or closely related in time to it. Their theological consideration of the relevant issues doubles as an arduous theological pilgrimage that entails preserving, honoring, and healing the collective memory of victims and survivors. This theological analysis recognizes that memory serves a higher purpose—not a memory that has been instrumentalized to distort or repeat a past of violence; but, rather, memory as a hermeneutical tool for interrogating the past and a moral force for learning its lessons and shaping the future in fidelity to the living biographies of victims and survivors of historical violence.

The second feature of this approach is that theological ethics of this kind assumes the nature of a testimony. The scholars recount personal stories in order to bear witness to the power of the gospel to engender and sustain durable processes of reconciliation, justice, and peace. By this means, they demonstrate that reconciliation, justice, and peace are not reified notions or abstract concepts. They serve as principles and criteria for theological discernment and ethical engagement with pressing social issues. These elements are the foundations on which a new society and a new theology are to be constructed, while being nurtured with truth, accountability, and integrity.

The final dimension is an ecclesiological perspective. The community called church has an important and valid role in this process of rebirthing society from the ruins of violence and conflict, albeit it assumes this task only as a chastened co-worker and co-pilgrim with victims and survivors. Scholars in this field are keen to point out that to undertake this task with credibility and proclaim anew the good news of Jesus Christ, the church must travel the long road of repentance, contrition, and conversion.

Poverty and socio-economic and political disequilibrium and dysfunctionality

In his groundbreaking account of the emergence of poverty in Africa, historian John Iliffe incisively demonstrated that poverty was not a static reality, but that it evolved within human history.[30] More importantly, Iliffe's research also proved that poverty was neither a disembodied abstraction nor tasteless fodder for mere theoretical disquisition or statistical computation; it has been and always is connected to concrete human experiences, such as health, age, mobility, disability, land, labor, gender, and environment. Furthermore, poverty is shaped by religious traditions. Religion is deeply implicated in the reality of poverty in Africa.

---

30. Iliffe, *African Poor*.

In Africa, some Christian churches increasingly perceive their roles in distinctly economic terms. They exist to meet critical needs connected with socio-economic collapse or political dysfunctionality, since "Africans generally rank unemployment, crime and corruption as bigger problems than religious conflict."[31] Curiously, some Christian churches are founded, branded, and marketed specifically to tackle these challenges, thus creating a potent link between socio-economic malaise and the role of the churches in dealing with it.

As social services collapse and social crises, economic degradation, and political upheavals spread, religion offers—or claims to offer—a solution in the form of a widely diffused and extremely popular phenomenon known in general terms as "prosperity gospel." The kernel of this "gospel" is the idea that wealth and health can be guaranteed for adherents who possess the right amount of faith and sow seeds of their own prosperity and well-being by making substantial financial contribution.

In contrast to the foregoing, African theological ethics has advanced two rebuttals: First, the necessity to critique this facile and misleading interpretation of the Gospel and, second, the urgency to generate alternative analyses and narratives that are credible and empowering for ordinary Africans. Here the works of two pioneer African theologians, Engelbert Mveng (1935–1995) and Jean-Marc Ela (1936–2008), have been pivotal in the emergence of a theological ethics shaped in the context of the crisis of poverty.

Mveng, a Cameroonian Jesuit, artist, and poet, coined the term "anthropological poverty." This insidious phenomenon thrives "in despoiling human beings not only of what they have, but of everything that constitutes their being and essence—their identity, history, ethnic roots, language, culture, faith, creativity, dignity, pride, ambitions, right to speak."[32] In other words, this kind of poverty not only entails material deprivation, but also erodes the collective moral and cultural identity of a people.

Anthropological poverty happens "when persons are deprived not only of goods or possessions of material, spiritual, moral, intellectual, cultural, or sociological order, but of everything that makes up the foundation of their being-in-world and the specificity of their 'ipseity' as individual, society, and history."[33] The dignity of people who live in this kind of poverty have been extremely compromised to the extent that their existence loses its meaning, even if they possessed material goods. "It is a type of poverty, which no longer concerns only external or interior goods and possessions but strikes at the very being, essence and dignity of the human person."[34] For Mveng, this paralyzing form of poverty is a product of "slavery, colonialism, neocolonialism, racism, apartheid, and the universal derision that has always accompanied the

---

31. Pew Forum on Religion and Public Life, "Islam and Christianity in Sub-Saharan Africa."
32. Mveng, "Third World Theology–What Theology? What Third World?" 220.
33. Mveng, "Impoverishment and Liberation," 156.
34. Rwiza, "Laurenti Magesa, An African Liberation Theologian," 239.

'civilized' world's discourse upon and encounter with Africa—and still accompanies them today."[35]

The phenomenon that Mveng described in visceral terms has found an illuminating and compelling theological response in the analysis of his compatriot, Ela. He pioneered a theological ethics that bore resemblance to Latin American theology of liberation. His lasting legacy in contemporary African theological ethics stemmed from his ability to relocate the locus of theological discourses from the citadel of academia to the messy socio-economic, political, cultural, religious, and ecclesial context of the people. Two aspects this methodology are easily discernible in the methodology of theology of liberation, namely, doing theology from the periphery or the margins and the principle of preferential option for the poor.

Notably, Ela's theological analysis of the reality of impoverishment and marginalization was influenced and shaped by several years of voluntary immersion among and service to the socially disempowered, politically marginalized, and economically impoverished peasant Kirdi community of north Cameroon. "The misery, poverty, oppression, discrimination, intimidation and exploitation by the political authorities of the Kirdi people called him to commit himself to the struggle for social justice and to rethink his pastoral ministry and theological thought."[36] His firsthand experience of the "misfortune of poverty," which he depicted with the metaphor of "empty granary," and his radical commitment and preferential option for the poor led him to develop his sociology of development and an African "shade-tree" theology of the oppressed people that responds to the visceral "African cry" and is capable of liberating the church and the continent from their captivity to poverty.[37]

With this methodology, Ela "opened doors to a new wave of African theologians and to new ways of articulating African theological discourses" that "took into account new realities, new experiences, new audiences, and new signs of the times."[38] Not only does the methodology of taking account of—or paying attention to—social realities persist as the hallmark of African theological ethics, it also constitutes a lasting summons to and represents an ongoing aspiration of contemporary African theologians.

CONCLUSION

This chapter began on a buoyant note of the prosperity and pervasiveness of religiosity in Africa, with particular emphasis on the phenomenal growth of Christianity. Although it is generally assumed that such pervasiveness represents a beneficial trend, current social crises indicate the emergence and intensification of alarming

---

35. Mveng, "Third World Theology," 220.
36. Mayemba, "Reviving a Church of the Poor and for the Poor," 47.
37. Ela, *Ma foi d'Africain*, 117–32, 195–218.
38. Mayemba, "Promise of a New Generation of African Theologians," 157; Ela, *African Cry*; Ela, *Repenser la théologie africaine*.

pathologies associated with the pervasive religiosity on the continent. This phenomenon of prosperity needs further critical probing and analysis before being adduced as a constant of religious growth in the Global South. In this context, theological analysis entails an explicit and critical account of the phenomenon of growth in the midst of multiple and complex crises.

Theological ethics in a time of crisis is an evolving field of study. The brief sketch presented in this essay seeks to illustrate how it generates particular analyses and responses for specific contexts, while drawing on resources of Christian traditions, especially Catholic social teaching; the Scriptures; African cultural and religious norms and values; and a fresh infusion of innovations and insights from other disciplines. This essay provides a glimpse into the focal points and methodology of theological ethics in a time of crisis.

The methodological features of this theological ethics include multidisciplinary and cross-disciplinary approaches, ecumenical collaboration, and the necessity of personal engagement. Neither simply an academic exercise conducted in the comfort of the citadel nor the outcome of the theological acumen of individual theologians, the methodology of theological ethics in a time of crisis is challenged, influenced, and shaped by the collective "joys and the hopes, the griefs and the anxieties of the people of this age, especially those who are poor or in any way afflicted."[39]

BIBLIOGRAPHY

African Synod. "Final Propositions." *Missionalia: Southern African Journal of Mission Studies* 29 (2009) 1–17.

———. "Message to the People of God." *Missionalia: Southern African Journal of Mission Studies* 29 (2009) 18–29.

Allen, John L. *The Future Church: How Ten Trends are Revolutionizing the Catholic Church*. New York: Image, 2009.

Bere, Paul. "The Bible in Africa: Is the Exegesis of the Biblical Text the Soul of Theology and Life of the Church in Africa?" In *African Theology in the 21st Century: A Call to Baraza*, edited by Elias O. Opongo and Paul Bere, 411–42. Nairobi: Paulines, 2021.

Carney, J. J. *For God and My Country: Catholic Leadership in Modern Uganda*. Eugene, OR: Cascade, 2020.

Chu Ilo, Stan, ed. *African Ecological Ethics and Spirituality for Cosmic Flourishing: An African Commentary on* Laudato Si'. Nairobi: Paulines, 2022.

Egan, Anthony. "Governance Beyond Rhetoric: The South African Challenge to the African Synod." In *Reconciliation, Justice, and Peace: The Second African Synod*, edited by Agbonkhianmeghe E. Orobator, 95–104. Maryknoll, NY: Orbis, 2011.

Ela, Jean-Marc. *African Cry*. Eugene, OR: Wipf & Stock, 1986.

———. *Ma foi d'Africain*. Paris: Kathala, 1985.

———. *Repenser la théologie africaine. Le Dieu qui libère*. Paris: Karthala, 2003.

---

39. Vatican II, *Gaudium et Spes*, no. 1.

Getui, Mary N., and Emmanuel Obeng, eds. *Theology of Reconstruction: Exploratory Essays.* Nairobi: Acton, 1999.

Iliffe, John. *The African Poor: A History.* Cambridge: Cambridge University Press, 1987.

Istas, Michel. *Patterns of Morality in the Bible: Handbook of Fundamental Moral Theology.* Nairobi: Paulines, 2019.

John Paul II. *Ecclesia in Africa.* September 14, 1995. https://www.vatican.va/content/john-paul-ii/en/apost_exhortations/documents/hf_jp-ii_exh_14091995_ecclesia-in-africa.html.

Jenkins, Philip. *The Next Christendom: The Coming of Global Christianity.* Oxford: Oxford University Press, 2002.

Katongole, Emmanuel. "Church of the Future: Pressing Moral Issues from *Ecclesia in Africa.*" In *The Church We Want: African Catholics Look to Vatican III*, edited by Agbonkhianmeghe E. Orobator, 161–73. Maryknoll, NY: Orbis, 2016.

———. *The Sacrifice of Africa: A Political Theology for Africa.* Grand Rapids: Eerdmans, 2011.

Magesa, Laurenti. *Anatomy of Inculturation: Transforming the Church in Africa.* Nairobi: Paulines, 2005.

Mana, Kä. *Théologie africaine pour temps de crise: christianisme et reconstruction de l'Afrique.* Paris: Karthala, 1993.

Martey, Emmanuel. *African Theology: Inculturation and Liberation.* Maryknoll, NY: Orbis, 1993.

Mayemba, Bienvenu. "The Promise of a New Generation of African Theologians: Reimagining African Theology with Fidelity and Creativity." In *Theological Reimagination: Conversations on Church, Religion, and Society in Africa*, edited by Agbonkhianmeghe E. Orobator, 153–68. Maryknoll, NY: Orbis, 2016.

———. "Reviving a Church of the Poor and for the Poor, and Reclaiming Faith doing Justice and Seeking Liberation: Convergence between Pope Francis and Jean-Marc Ela." In *The Church We Want: African Catholics Look to Vatican III*, edited by Agbonkhianmeghe E. Orobator, 43–54. Maryknoll, NY: Orbis, 2016.

Mugambi, J. N. K., ed. *The Church and the Reconstruction of Africa: Theological Considerations.* Nairobi: All Africa Conference of Churches, 1997.

———. *From Liberation to Reconstruction: African Christian Theology after the Cold War* Nairobi: East African Educational, 1995.

Mugambi, J. N. K., and A. Nasimiyu-Wasike, eds. *Moral and Ethical Issues in African Christianity: Exploratory Essays in Moral Theology.* Nairobi: Initiatives, 1992.

Mveng, Engelbert. "Impoverishment and Liberation: A Theological Approach for Africa and the Third World." In *Paths of African Theology*, edited by Rosino Gibellini, 154–65. Maryknoll, NY: Orbis, 1994.

———. "Third World Theology—What Theology? What Third World? Evaluation by an African Delegate." In *Irruption of the Third World: Challenge to Theology*, edited by Virginia Fabella and Sergio Torres, 217–21. Maryknoll, NY: Orbis, 1983.

O'Neill, William. "Never Again: Moving Forward After the Genocide in Rwanda." *America*, December 11, 2019. https://www.americamagazine.org/faith/2019/12/11/never-again-moving-forward-after-genocide-rwanda.

Orji, Cyril. *Unmasking the African Ghost: Theology, Politics, and the Nightmare of Failed States.* Minneapolis: Fortress, 2022.

Orobator, Agbonkhianmeghe E., ed. *The Pope and the Pandemic: Lessons in Leadership in a Time of Crisis.* Maryknoll, NY: Orbis, 2021.

———. *Practising Reconciliation, Doing Justice, Building Peace: Conversations in Catholic Theological Ethics in Africa*. Nairobi: Paulines, 2013.

———, ed. *Reconciliation, Justice, and Peace: The Second African Synod*. Maryknoll, NY: Orbis, 2011.

———. *Theology Brewed in an African Pot*. Maryknoll, NY: Orbis, 2008.

———. "Unsung Icons of Liberation: Rediscovering the Ideals, Principles and Lessons of Liberation Theology through the Lives of Contemporary Exponents." *ISIT* 5 (2021) 73–85.

Pew Forum on Religion and Public Life. "Global Christianity: A Report on the Size and Distribution of the World's Christian Population." December 19, 2011. https://www.pewresearch.org/religion/2011/12/19/global-christianity-exec/

———. "Tolerance and Tension: Islam and Christianity in Sub-Saharan Africa." April 15, 2010. https://www.pewresearch.org/religion/2010/04/15/executive-summary-islam-and-christianity-in-sub-saharan-africa/

Rutagambwa, Elisée. "Is Blood Thicker than Faith: Ethnic Violence and Christian Identity in Rwanda." In *African Theology in the 21st Century: A Call to Baraza*, edited by Elias O. Opongo and Paul Bere, 411–42. Nairobi: Paulines, 2021.

Rutagambwa, Elisée, and Marcel Uwineza. *Reinventing Theology in Post-Genocide Rwanda*. Washington, DC: Georgetown University Press, 2022.

Rwiza, Richard N. *Environmental Ethics in the African Context*. Nairobi: CUEA, 2021.

———. "Laurenti Magesa, An African Liberation Theologian." In *African Theology: The Contribution of Pioneers*, edited by Bénézet Bujo and Juvénal Ilunga Muya, 2:231–57. Nairobi: Paulines, 2006.

Uwineza, Marcel. *Reconciling Memories: A Theology from Wounds*. Leiden: Brill, 2022.

Uzukwu, Elochukwu E. *A Listening Church: Autonomy and Communion in African Churches*. Maryknoll, NY: Orbis, 1996.

Vatican II. *Gaudium et Spes*. Pastoral Constitution on the Church in the Modern World. December 7, 1965. https://www.vatican.va/archive/hist_councils/ii_vatican_council/documents/vat-ii_const_19651207_gaudium-et-spes_en.html

CHAPTER 21

An Egyptian Theology

SAFWAT MARZOUK

"Blessed be my people Egypt" are some of the most well-known words of the prophet Isaiah among the Christian minority in Egypt. These words are very precious to a community that is strongly rooted in its Egyptian identity and that for a long time has been struggling with various forms of marginalization. These words of hope declare that the Egyptians are claimed by the God of the Bible, and thus they give this minority an unwavering faith in the face of political, economic, and social struggles. These words of blessing and inclusion, which counter the negative representation of Egypt that is pervasive in the Old Testament, bring together for the Egyptian Christian minority the two aspects that comprise who they are, namely, their political identity, that is being Egyptians, and their religious identity, that is, being Christians who read the Bible as Scripture. No wonder then that these words are engraved on the stony wall of the church of St. Simon, the Tanner, in Cairo. A Coptic Orthodox tradition understands the words of the prophet that there would be an altar to YHWH in the midst of Egypt to be a reference to the Coptic Orthodox Church of the Virgin Mary in Deir Al-Muharaq. The reception of Isaiah's words in the Christian Egyptian context has heightened in the last decade.

In the wake of the revolution of 2011, Isaiah's oracle concerning Egypt was revived in many Egyptian circles. In Midan al-Tahrir (the Square of Liberty), Christian Egyptians gathered with other revolutionaries singing *barek belady,* "bless my country," echoing the concluding words of Isa 19. Father Makary Yonan, a prominent Coptic Orthodox priest, made direct connections between the motifs of judgment and restoration found in Isa 19 and the events that ensued after the January 25 revolution.

According to this line of interpretation, the political unrest and the economic struggles that resulted from the revolution, the rise of the Muslim Brotherhood, reflect the words of judgment that are contained in Isa 19:1–15, while the toppling of the regime of the Muslim Brotherhood in 2013 was a divine response of liberation to the cries of the Egyptians who were oppressed. In Isa 19, the prophet speaks of a cruel ruler who will come to power, the Egyptians will cry out to the LORD, then God interferes and delivers them. The fear of an authoritarian religious regime, such as the Muslim Brotherhood, along with the longing for a republic that celebrates religious freedom, and that prospers economically, has shaped this interpretive approach.

It is important to take seriously these contextual factors and their hermeneutical results that sustain the faith of the Christian Egyptian community in the face of fear of the unknown and in a setting of marginalization. Yet, the aforementioned reception of Isa 19 is fraught with issues that obstruct a more nuanced appropriation of this complex chapter for the contemporary Christian Egyptian context. On the outset, this approach collapses the distance between the world of the text and the world of the readers. This collapse may result from a misunderstanding of the nature of the biblical prophetic traditions; similar to dispensationalist approaches to the Bible, some assume that the prophets in the Bible were predicting the very far future. The collapse in other cases results from a desire to find an orienting compass in the midst of economic and political instabilities, and the Bible quite often is appropriated uncritically to offer this hope. In addition to the collapse of time and space between the context of the text and the context of its readers, this interpretive approach described above, similar to many contextual hermeneutics, it is inconsistent in the way it deals with the Bible. For example, most of the Christian Egyptian minority do not identify with Egypt when they read the book of Exodus, but they enthusiastically identify with Egypt of Isa 19, for the obvious reason that Isa 19 has a happy ending. The end of the chapter reverberates with good news for the Egyptian minority.

The hermeneutics of trust that are applied by some Christian Egyptians as they read Isa 19 leave behind some critical issues about the place of this chapter in the consciousness of the community. For example, a positivistic reading does not reflect on the loss of the religious identity and heritage when the text speaks of the conversion of the Egyptians (and the Assyrians for that matter) into the religion of YHWH. Nor does this approach raise any suspicions about the political and economic subjugation of Egypt under the power of YHWH and Judah. Is the texting advocating for a Yahwistic empire and hegemony that seek to replace human empires? Furthermore, because this approach focuses solely on identifying with Egypt, it does not ask what this text may have meant to ancient Israelites, and what the implications would be for the contemporary Christian Egyptian minority if the text were to be read through the lens of its primary ancient audience, i.e., the people of Judah. What difference does it make to ask about the reason Isaiah speaks words of judgment against Egypt? And what would that say to the Christian Egyptians in their historical milieu? How did the words of inclusion of Egypt and Assyria into the religion of YHWH challenge some of the nationalistic tendencies within the context of the religious conversation in ancient Judah? What does this message say to the Christian Egyptian minority as it navigates its identity in a multireligious context?

Wrestling these questions will, I believe, yield more nuanced Christian Egyptian readings of Isa 19 that take seriously the world of the text as well as their world. I will argue that a hermeneutical approach that is dialectical produces more complex readings of texts and contexts than a typological or linear hermeneutical approach. By a dialectical approach I mean that one reads the text in multiple ways, from different perspectives, and the results of these readings would remain in tension. In a dialectical approach, different truths stand side by side demanding an answer from one another without settling the matter. In order to develop this thesis, I will begin with a detailed discussion of the literary and historical contexts of Isa 19. Then I will turn to the aspects of the hermeneutical dialectical and dialogic approach that will investigate what the text says about judgment, hope, inclusion, and religious and political identity and what these motifs may mean for the Christian Egyptian minority in light of the experiences of minoritization and in light of the longing to liberation, healing, and freedom.

A LITERARY AND A HISTORICAL STUDY OF ISAIAH 19[1]

The prophetic traditions concerning Egypt in Isa 19:1–25 can be divided into two major sections. The first section, 19:1–15, contains poetic oracles that declare YHWH's judgment against Egypt. The second section, 19:16–25, contains a series of prose oracles, which present a more hopeful announcement of the divine blessing, restoration, and healing of Egypt as well as a vision of a harmonious relations between Egypt, Israel, and Assyria.

Words of Judgment against Egypt

The oracle against Egypt in Isa 19:1–15 begins with a theophany,[2] in which YHWH, riding on a cloud, approaches Egypt with judgment in the form of a political chaos and oppression (Isa 19:1b–4).[3] The image of YHWH riding on a cloud animates YH-

---

1. The superscription in 19:1a characterize this section as an oracle concerning Egypt. The genre of Isa 19 can be categorized as "prophecy concerning a foreign nation." This type of prophecy usually presents YHWH's plan concerning the world nations. YHWH is presented as the primary actor of judgment and restoration. Unlike other oracles concerning Egypt in other prophetic literature (e.g. Jer 46; Ezek 29–32), the oracle in Isaiah ends with a profound word of hope for Egypt. As an oracle concerning a nation, Isa 19 is part of a collection of oracles against the nations found in Isa 13–23.

2. On the genre of theophany see Sweeney, *Isaiah 1–39*, 268.

3. The image of YHWH riding on a cloud, which parallels the portrayal of the Canaanite god Baal, is well known elsewhere in the Old Testament (Deut 33:26; 2 Sam 22:11; Ps 68:5). Wildberger, *Jesaja*

WH's freedom and sovereignty over nature and world history.[4] According to this text, YHWH destabilizes Egypt by causing a civil war (v. 2),[5] destroying Egypt's counsel (v. 3), and handing Egypt over to a harsh ruler (v. 4). These acts of YHWH are presented in three statements, each has a first-person-singular verb, which underlines YHWH's direct involvement in causing this political chaos. As YHWH approaches Egypt a civil disorder will erupt, Egypt's idols[6] will tremble, and the political wisdom will vanish. As a result, the spirit of the Egyptians shall be made void. Their confusion will turn into a state of helplessness. Yahwistic sovereignty is demonstrated in verse four as YHWH hands over the Egyptians to a harsh ruler. The identity of this cruel king is hard to determine. While some scholars believe it to be a reference to the Assyrian king Sargon,[7] other scholars argue that it is a reference to the Ethiopian king Shabako, who established the authority of the Nubian dynasty.[8] While it is hard to determine the identity of this harsh king, the description recalls the exodus narrative, albeit the reversal that this harsh king oppresses the Egyptians (Exod 1:14).[9]

The following unit, verses 5–10, shifts the language of judgment from the political crises to different manifestations of economic crises that will come upon Egypt as a result of drying up the Nile. Biblical traditions are well aware of the fact that the Nile is the source of life in Egypt.[10] Drying up of the Nile is a natural disaster that leads to economic crises and therefore to human suffering. The text uses a passive form to speak about drying up the Nile. Although the Nile went through natural cycles of inundation and low water levels, the use of the passive likely points beyond the natural cycle to speak of a drought caused by YHWH's judgment over Egypt. Egyptians believed that the rise of the water in the Nile was a gift from the gods.[11] Isaiah, however, continues his attack on the Egyptian belief system, by proclaiming that the Egyptian gods will not be able to control the flooding of the Nile. This natural disaster will harm farmers, fishers, and textile workers, no matter what the size of their economic asset is, they will all suffer and languish (Isa 19:8–10).

The oracle moves to target Egypt's political leadership represented in its king and his counselors (Isa 19:11–15). The text uses the style of taunt or mockery that seeks to highlight the foolishness of the counselors and the wise ones who surround Pharaoh.

13–39, 710.

4. Watts, *Isaiah 1–33*, 253.

5. Verse 2 presents a picture of the civil conditions of Egypt during the twenty-fifth dynasty. See Breasted, *History of Egypt*, 536.

6. The word used for idols *elilim* implies "that these gods are nothing beyond the images they represent" (Tull, *Isaiah 1–39*, 319).

7. Wildberger, *Jesaja 13–39*, 714.

8. Watts, *Isaiah 1–33*, 253. See Roberts, *First Isaiah*, 256.

9. Childs, *Isaiah*, 143.

10. The Nile figures prominently in many texts that relate to Egypt (e.g. Exod 7; Ezek 29–32). Blenkinsopp, *Isaiah 1–39*, 315.

11. Wildberger, *Jesaja 13–39*, 714.

Through a series of rhetorical questions that text seeks to underline the point that their ancient legacy of political wisdom will be shown to be incompetent to reveal YHWH's plans concerning Egypt. Pharaoh's counselors in Zoan (known also as Tanis), which is in the northern east of Delta and Noph (also known as Memphis), failed to identify YHWH's plan for Egypt.[12] The intelligence of the chiefs of Egypt is compared to that of animals, and they end up misleading Egypt because YHWH has unleashed a spirit of confusion. As a result, Egypt is doomed and no one, leader or follower, will be able to do anything about it.

Blessed Be My People Egypt

Isaiah 19:16–25 contains a sequence of prose oracles that proclaim words of hope, healing, and restoration for Egypt. The five oracles that are included in this section are introduced by the formula "on that day" (19:16, 18, 19, 23, 24). In these oracles, YHWH's plans for Egypt transition from words of judgment and fear, which dominated the content of the previous sections, and are summarized in verses 16–17, to manifestations of the inclusion of Egypt, along with Assyria and Israel, into the realm of YHWH's blessings. The vision of inclusion in these oracles include the following aspects: Egyptian cities will speak the tongue of Canaan (18), an altar and a stele will be built in Egypt for YHWH (19–20), Egyptians will acknowledge YHWH (21), when Egyptians cry out to YHWH because of oppression, YHWH will save them (22), a highway between Egypt and Assyria signifies economic collaboration, and a universal blessing for Egypt, Assyria, and Israel (23–25).

Thematically speaking, Isa 19:16–17 fits with the oracles of judgment that are found in Isa 19:1–15. Yet, these verses are connected with the oracles of hope in that they begin with the phrase "on that day." It is reasonable to think of verses 16–17 as transitional and connecting pericope between the motifs judgment and restoration.[13] As a summary of the previous oracles of judgment, verses 16–17 succinctly advance Isaiah's political perspective which underlines the weakness of Egypt and the condemnation of entering into political alliances with the Egyptians.

Unlike the majority of the oracles against the nations in general and most of the oracles against Egypt in particular, in other prophetic texts (e.g. Ezek 29–32; Jer 46), Isaiah's prophecy concerning Egypt ends with proclamations of restoration. Isa 19:18–25 declares that the final word concerning Egypt in YHWH's plan is not that of judgment. Five cities in Egypt will speak the tongue of Canaan, which is the Hebrew

---

12. The subject of YHWH's plan for the world (14:26), which is brought up in 19:12 and 17, was already presented in relation to YHWH bringing the Assyrians in chapters 7–10. See the discussion on this theme in Blenkinsopp, *Isaiah 1–39*, 315; Watts, *Isaiah 1–33*, 252; and Seitz, *Isaiah 1–39*, 155.

13. The theme of the Egyptian fear of Judah has been understood as a reference to Cambyses's conquest of Egypt in 525 BCE when the province of Yehud worked as the battleground for such an event. It has also been suggested that it is a reference to the defeat of the Ptolemies at the battle of Panias in 198 BCE. Blenkinsopp, *Isaiah 1–39*, 318.

language. This might be a reference to cities in Egypt, where a Jewish diaspora dwelt. Only one city's name is mentioned in Isaiah, the city of the sun, while the other four referenced in Jer 44:1. Even in the city that belongs to the sun god, the language of Canaan will be spoken, which might be referring to those who confess loyalty to YHWH.[14] Moreover, in 19:19, there is a reference to an altar that is built for YHWH in the midst of Egypt. This is thought to be a reference to the cult center of Leontopolis.[15] It is possible that this altar was set up in a Jewish military unit like Elephantine (opposes Deut 7:5; 12:3) in order to serve as a sign of divine presence.[16]

In Isa 19:20–22, the author presents a set of unique and astonishing reversals in the relationship between YHWH and the Egyptians. When the Egyptians cry out to YHWH because of their oppressors, YHWH will send them a savior, and YHWH will defend and deliver them. Many of the Hebrew words that are used in verse 20 echo two important traditions in the history of YHWH's relationship with Israel itself. For example, in the book of Judges, YHWH interfered in the life of the oppressed Israelites and delivered them from the hands of those who mistreated them (Judges 3:9, 18). Another, significant example is found in the book of Exodus, where the Israelites cry out because of the misery and suffering that the Egyptians are bringing upon them (Exod 3:1–10). Here, however, the Egyptians are not the oppressors but the oppressed. They are the ones who cry out to YHWH, and YHWH listens and liberates them. Furthermore, the claim that YHWH makes himself known to the Egyptians and the Egyptians know YHWH recall the covenantal language that is found in Exod 3, 6, and Ezek 20. Thus YHWH will be known not only to the Israelites, but also to the Egyptians. There is yet another important reversal here. For the most part the language of the knowledge of YHWH by the Egyptians is usually accompanied by manifestations of Yahwistic judgment over Egypt without a mention of healing or restoration (e.g. Exod 14 and Ezek 29–32). Here in Isa 19, YHWH will be known to the Egyptians not only as a judge, but also as a savior and a liberator. Even if YHWH will strike Egypt, a language known from the plague narratives in Exod 7–11, YHWH will heal them. In response to YHWH's saving act, the Egyptians will worship YHWH. They will serve YHWH with sacrifices and by fulfilling their vows.

YHWH's tent is big enough to include Egypt and Assyria along with Israel. The history of the relationships between Egypt, Israel, and Assyria has many incidents of enmity and violence. Yet, in this beautiful prophetic text, the prophet envisions an open and free movement between Egypt and Assyria, likely through Israel. This movement will not be marked by violence, invasion, or imperial subjugation. The highway will be a path for mutual commerce and mutual flourishing. These nations together will worship YHWH and fulfill YHWH's plans for the world. Together with Israel they will be a blessing in the midst of the earth. The curses of enmity, hatred,

---

14. Childs, *Isaiah*, 144.
15. Childs, *Isaiah*, 144; Clements, *Isaiah 1–39*, 171.
16. Blenkinsopp, *Isaiah 1–39*, 319.

violence, and subjugation will be put to an end. The blessings of peace, mutuality, cooperation, and harmony will reign. On that day, according to this visionary account, YHWH will bless Egypt by calling it "blessed be my people Egypt." On that day, according to this visionary account, YHWH will bless Assyria by calling it "Assyria, the work of my hands." On that day, according to this visionary account, YHWH will bless Israel by calling it "Israel, my heritage." The description "my people," which is applied to Egypt here is usually reserved for Israel (Ps 47:9–10). The description "the work of my hands," which is used to describe Assyria, usually refers to Israel (Isa 64:8). While the text includes those who have been alienated from a relationship with YHWH (i.e., Egypt and Assyria), this does not happen by way of excluding Israel. Israel remains YHWH's heritage (Deut 32:9). YHWH's tent has now expanded to include Israel's enemies. The three nations are blessed by YHWH as a fulfillment of the Abrahamic promise in Gen 12:3.

HERMENEUTICAL CONVERSATIONS

In this section I will address some of the hermeneutical dilemmas that appear in the process of reading Isa 19 in a contemporary Christian Egyptian context. The first part of the conversation will focus on the tension between historical critical reading of the text in relation to the history of reception of the text in the life of a faith community. The second part of the conversation will deal with the implications of reading the full message of Isa 19, the judgment as well as the hope. And finally, the last part of the conversation will explore the different meanings of the text that emerge as the readers enter the texts from different angles.

Beyond a Single Meaning

As I mentioned in the introduction to this chapter, many contemporary Christian Egyptian readers of Isa 19 have drawn connections between the chapter and current events that surrounded the revolution of 2011. These hermeneutical moves need to be reevaluated in light of the literary development of the text and in light of what we might be able to uncover about the historical contexts of these literary developments. As the following paragraphs will show, however, the literary developments of the text and the historical references within the text are disputed among scholars. Nonetheless, reading the text in its literary and historical contexts illumines our understanding of the text and it nuances how to appropriate these ancient texts into our contemporary contexts in healthy and ethical ways.

Scholars dispute the literary unity of Isa 19. The text of Isa 19 took a long time to write and likely went through a complex process to reach its final form. The two major sections of the chapter (1–15 and 16–25) differ in their literary style (poetry and prose), and in their message (judgment and hope).[17] Each of these sections shows signs of literary unity and also literary divergence. For example, verse 4 ends with the phrase "says the LORD," which usually marks the end of a unit. Furthermore, the economic disasters that result from drying up the Nile (vv. 5–10) interrupt the flow of the prophetic message about political chaos (vv. 1–4 and 11–15).[18] Despite these shifts in focus and signs of literary growth, verses 1–15 are unified in that they speak of different manifestations of the theophany report.

Based on the use of the formula "on that day," the reference to the five cities that speak Hebrew (see also Jer 42–44), and the shift from judgment to restoration, the unit of 19:16–25 is usually dated to the postexilic period.[19] Verses 16–17 are connected with the judgment motif of verses 1–15, but they are connected with the verses that follow since they also begin with the formula "on that day." These two verses, however, use singular verbs, whereas verses 18–25 employ verbs in the plural form. These verses use the name Judah, the following verses use the name Israel.[20] Thus, there seems to be divergence in style even amidst literary connections. The same observation can be made about verses 18–25. These verses have literary and theological continuity, but they also feature divergence in style and content. For example, the phrase "on that day" appears in the middle of verse 21 and not at the beginning as it does in every other small unit of the pericope.[21] Yet, there is a continuity in these smaller units in that they speak of the inclusion of Egypt and Assyria in the restorative plans of YHWH, which entail linguistic, economic, and religious aspects.

The complexity of Isa 19 is not only manifest in the literary development of the text, but it is also evident in the ambiguity of the historical references that shape the message of the text. The difficulty of dating the oracles of Isa 19, explains J. J. M. Roberts, stems from "the uncertainties involved in the Egyptian royal chronology of the late eighth century, and another difficulty is the ambiguously allusive quality of the historical referents in the text that leaves open multiple possibilities in the search for the most likely historical context or contexts for the material in Isaiah 19."[22] The

---

17. Sweeny, *Isaiah 1–39*, 268.

18. For different views on the composition of Isa 19 see Wildberger, *Jesaja 13–39*, 703–4, and Sweeney, *Isaiah 1–39*, 269.

19. For many scholars, Isa 19:16–25 is considered a later addition inserted to the text, and it presents a "universalist perspective" to the whole chapter. Furthermore, these scholars identify four or five successive editorial expansions within the unit based on the usage of the formula "on that day." Clements, *Isaiah 1–39*, 169–170; Kaiser, *Isaiah 13–39*, 105; Wildberger, *Jesaja 13–39*, 729–31.

20. Verses 16–17 relate to verses 1–15 not only by focusing on the coming judgment over Egypt, but also by emphasizing YHWH's purpose and counsel concerning Egypt, which opposes pharaoh and his counselors (v. 12). Moreover, verses 16–17 differ from verses 19–25 on a grammatical level. Verses 16–17 constantly utilize singular verbs and singular pronouns in reference to Egypt, while verses 19–25 employ plural verbs and pronouns. Sweeney, *Isaiah 1–39*, 270.

21. For a discussion on the relationship between verse 23 and verses 24–25, see Wildberger, *Jesaja 13–39*, 730; Clements, *Isaiah 1–39*, 170; and Sweeney, *Isaiah 1–39*, 269.

22. Roberts, *First Isaiah*, 252.

political chaos described in verses 1–4 reflects some of the political circumstances in Egypt during the late eighth BCE century, when there were struggles between different dynasties over power in Egypt down to 721 BCE or 716 BCE when the twenty-fifth dynasty was established under the rule of Pharaoh Shabako.[23] The reference to handing Egypt to a harsh ruler has been understood to either be a reference to kings from the Saite dynasty, the Nubian dynasty (see Isa 18:1–6) or a reference to the Assyrian imperial subjugation of Egypt.[24] The dating of Isa 19:18–25 ranges from the Assyrian period down to the Hellenistic period.[25] The rationale behind these attempts of dating the text would be that a development in the text reflects social or religious events that have taken place and that have shaped the theology of the text. For example, the cities that speak Hebrew would be Jewish colonies in Egypt, the altar would be used by a Jewish diaspora community, and the highway would reflect peaceful times between Egypt, Israel, and Assyria.[26] Connecting Isa 19:18–25 with the Jewish diaspora in Egypt happened as early as the Greek translation of the text, which changed the phrase "blessed be my people Egypt" to "blessed be my people *that is in* Egypt." While many scholars date the passage to the postexilic period, one wonders why mention Assyria, if the text was written during the Babylonian or the Persian period. Was Assyria used as a code for other powers that may enter conflict with Egypt and Israel? Or does the text come from a time in which the Assyrian Empire was still active? If that is the case, then what will one do with the fact that the five cities referred to at the beginning of the pericope are likely to be exilic?

The purpose of the previous discussion does not intend to undermine the importance of historical critical readings of the text. Quite the opposite. This brief survey seeks to show the complexity of the historical contexts that shaped the text. This complexity operates as a slowing-down mechanism to contemporary readers who tend to collapse the gap between the world of the text and their world, thinking that the prophet was predicting events that will take place in the very far future. Prophetic texts were engaged with immediate political and economic and social challenges, and

---

23. Hayes and Miller, *Israelite and Judean History*, 415–16. These dates essentially result from two different chronologies for the Egyptian dynasties of the eighth century BCE. See Kitchen, *Third Intermediate Period in Egypt*; and Kahn, "Inscription of Sargon II," 1–8.

24. See Seitz, *Isaiah 1–39*, 154. Roberts, *First Isaiah*, 253.

25. Shawn Zelig Aster and Csaba Balogh date some sections in the passage to different periods of the Neo-Assyrian empire. Balogh, *Stele of YHWH in Egypt*; Aster, "Isaiah 19," 453–70. Kaiser, for example dates the text to 118 BCE, *Isaiah 13–39*, 110. More recently Bernd Schipper argued that this vision of universalism comes from the Ptolemaic period. Schipper, "'City by the Sea will be a Drying Place,'" 25–56.

26. In 19:18 we are told about five cities in Egypt speaking the language of Canaan. These cities usually identified as the four Jewish colonies that Jeremiah mentions in 44:1, those of Memphis, Pathros, Tahpanhes-Daphnae, and Megdol, in addition to the city of the Sun. The Assyrians might have used "Judean auxiliaries" who were stationed in Egypt. Hence the reference to Hebrew being spoken in Egypt. Another possibility is that this verse is a later expansion that refers to the Jewish diaspora in Egypt. Roberts, *First Isaiah*, 263.

they were offering a theological perspective on these dynamics. Yet, this survey shows that historical critical scholarship does not have one view on the meaning of the text. This indetermination opens up the space to the history of reception and the history of the function of the text in the lives of the communities who read them. The text is a living organism. And so are the communities that read it. Thus, the reference to Egypt in these texts is received differently in a Christian Egyptian circle than to another audience with a different ethnic, religious, or cultural background. This hermeneutical move, reading the text from a Christian Egyptian perspective, is not seeking a typological identification between the text and the current world events, but it is seeking wisdom from the text that has spoken to faith communities and that continue to speak to them in diverse socio-political and religious contexts.

Listening to the Full Prophetic Word

The Christian Egyptian minority holds fast onto the words of hope, healing, blessings, and restorations promised in Isa 19. These words, taken as divine promises, are believed to name a different reality than the one that the community experiences. For some, this may mean that they find a refuge in the divine vision for Egypt, and become passive in working towards that reality, for others, these words are a source of inspiration to do what they can to overcome the gap between the reality and the hopes for a blessed future for the country they love. Some are, of course, skeptical if not cynical about the importance of these words in the midst of the realities of marginalization, poverty, oppression, and persecution. Indeed, the hermeneutical move of reading the text from a Christian Egyptian perspective is not merely about reading the words of hope as a magical spell that will transform the hardships that the minority is experiencing. Rather, these promises function as framework through which the Christian Egyptian minority sees itself in a new way. Not as rejected and vulnerable, but as beloved, embraced, and empowered.

Entering the text as Christian Egyptians and embracing the words of hope as source of inspiration in the midst of despair, chaos, and confusion should not ignore the other side of the text of Isa 19, namely, the words of judgment. Looking at the message of judgment is not meant to read contemporary chaos or challenges as fulfillment of divine judgement spoken centuries ago. Rather, looking into the discourse of judgment happens for the sake of gaining wisdom through understanding why the prophet declared these words to start with. Even though there is much uncertainty about the historical context of Isa 19, one of the intriguing and plausible suggestions is that the prophet proclaimed words of judgment over Egypt as a way of showing the people of Judah that Egypt is an unreliable political ally. In the period of 724–721 BCE, the northern kingdom Israel sought an Egyptian support in its rebellion against Assyria (2 Kgs 17:4), and about twenty years later, the kingdom of Judah sought an

Egyptian support also in its rebellion against Assyria.[27] For Isaiah, as well as for Jeremiah and Ezekiel after him, relying on Egypt meant lack of trust in YHWH, and these prophets tried to convince the kings of Judah not to rely on Egypt by capturing the political or the economic vulnerability of Egypt.[28] Thus, Isaiah 19, and other oracles against Egypt, are not predictions of what will happen, but rather they are oracles with rhetorical power that demand a response of faith and trust in YHWH. With this context in mind, as much as Isa 19:18–25 is offering a word of comfort to the minoritized community, the words of judgment in Isa 19:1–17 confront the Christian Egyptian community with a question about where they place their trust. Is their trust placed in political systems that promise them well-being with no regard to whether these systems follow the paths of justice and liberty, or do they put their trust in God by way of speaking truth to power exposing forms of oppression and exclusion?

Inclusion or Erosion

Christian Egyptian readers of Isa 19:18–25 celebrate the fact that Egypt is called "my people" by the God of the Bible. Egyptians in this pericope are presented as pious people. They worship YHWH with sacrifices. They fulfill their vows. When they cry out, God listens to their prayers and delivers them from oppression. They are blessed. This inclusion is a source of comfort and encouragement to those who experience alienation and marginalization. This vision of inclusion is marked by politics of harmony and peace between the three neighboring countries, Egypt, Israel, and Assyria.

As inspiring as this vision is, the rhetoric of inclusion in Isa 19:18–25 is nestled in a discourse that seem to advocate for the erosion of aspects of religious, linguistic, and cultural identity of the ancient Egyptian. The Egyptian gods are mocked and the Egyptians declare allegiance to YHWH. One of the main points that the judgment oracle is making is that YHWH is the true God who controls world events, while other deities of other nations, Egyptian gods in this case, are mere idols and are incapable of changing the course of events. The dominant view in this section is a polemical view in which Judah/Israel are set up over against Egypt, one the one hand, and YHWH is set up in opposition to the Egyptian gods, on the other hand.[29] Twice the prophet calls

27. The purpose of the oracle of Isa 19, therefore, was to undermine any alliance with Egypt. In this way, the oracle of Isa 19 functions as a persuasion in order to prove to Hezekiah "to stay out of the revolt since Egypt was unstable and unreliable ally that would fear even tiny Judah" (cf. 19:16; Sweeney, *Isaiah 1–39*, 271).

28. Roberts puts it this way "Here Egypt is the target of the oracle, though the real audience for the oracle is not Egyptians but the prophet's Judean contemporaries, especially the Judean royal court. The oracle against Egypt is a warning to the Judean court not to trust Egypt as a potential ally against the Assyrian threat, as the Philistines, Israel, Hamath, and other south Syrian states were repeatedly tempted to do in the last three decades of the eighth century BCE" (Roberts, *First Isaiah*, 255).

29. Early Christian interpreters saw a fulfillment to this prophecy at the time when Jesus took refuge in Egypt. The idols are shown to be nothing before YHWH, are destroyed upon Jesus's entry into Egypt. McKinion, *Isaiah 1–39*, 135–139. Cited in Tull, *Isaiah 1–39*, 319.

the Egyptian gods idols, in a clear misrepresentation of ancient Egyptian religious thought that did distinguish between the deity and the physical representation of the deity. At any rate, Isa 19 creates a "binary opposite" that, naturally, favors YHWH, the god of Israel. When Egyptians became Christians, the Hebrew Bible became their Scriptures and YHWH became their God, and as a result ancient Egyptian religious heritage became distanced from who they are. Many Christian Egyptians (and Muslim Egyptians for that matter) adopt the polemical perspectives of the Bible against ancient Egypt, and as a result, that layer of their Egyptian identity is alienated if not demonized. This is not an attempt to recover and restore an ancient religious heritage. This is a call to embrace an identity that is multilayered. This is a reminder to name what was lost. This is an invitation to stop demonizing our ancestors remembering that ancient Egyptian culture and heritage was included in the Bible in other ways that are marked by tolerance as we see the book of Proverbs, Song of Songs and the Psalms. And even beyond what was included in the Bible, Christian Egyptians should learn about their ancestors' worldview aside from how the Bible views it and as much as they know the Bible.

When one reads Isa 19:18–25 one wonders if by making the Egyptians and the Assyrians worship YHWH, pledge allegiance to YHWH, cry out to YHWH, the text is replacing human empires with a Yahwistic empire. In other words, is this a proclamation of inclusion or a religio-political propaganda that creates a Yahwistic hegemony? The answer to this question depends on what one compares Isa 19:18–25 with. For example, if one compares this passage to Deut 7, which excludes other nations from being in relation with YHWH, then Isa 19 is, indeed, an inclusive passage that expands the circle of Yahwism to include other nations. If one compares this passage with how Egypt is portrayed in the book of Exodus, in which Egypt is judged because of its oppression with no hope, and with other prophetic texts that include only judgment over Egypt, then Isa 19 is, indeed, an inclusive passage in that it extends the blessings of healing, salvation, and liberation to the Egyptians. But if one compares Isa 19:18–25 with Mic 4:5 which allows other nations to call upon their gods, then one might recognize a layer of imposition of Yahwism on these other nations beyond Israel. In other words, whether one determines that a passage is inclusive or exclusive is determined by what one compares it with.

That being said, Isa 19 is a text that written from the perspective of the powerless in the midst of an Assyrian imperial expansion and in the midst of the temptation to rely on Egypt as a political ally. Out of this place of powerlessness, Isaiah finds hope in YHWH's power and in YHWH's sovereignty. Thus, Isaiah's vision is not to create a Yahwistic empire, but rather to critique human empires. The real issue starts to appear in the history of interpretation, when contemporary empires and superpowers take the text of the powerless, which was meant to resist the empire, and make it their own and use it in order to justify their imperial expansions. Resistance to hegemony in Isa 19 is manifest in the following ways:

1. Egypt, Assyria, and Israel are included in a relationship with YHWH, but they are still distinct. Each nation is described in a different way and each nation still has its geo-political identity;

2. The ultimate point that the text envisions is that of blessing, healing, and liberation, in place of brokenness, violence, and curse.

3. God takes the side of the oppressed regardless of their ethnic background. The God who saved Israel from oppression in Exodus and in Judges is the God who delivers the Egyptians when they are oppressed.

Christian Egyptians identify with the Egypt of Isa 19:18–25 because Egypt is blessed by YHWH. What if Christian Egyptian readers of the text put themselves in place of the Judeans, who were the primary audience of Isa 19. After all, the prophet did not go to Egypt or Assyria to deliver these words. The prophet uttered these words to teach the people of Judah something about God's ways in the time of turmoil and instability. Thus, the prophet's words of inclusion that are embracing Egypt and Assyria in the folds of YHWH's people, creation, and blessings, were likely challenging to the fundamentalist and exclusionary political and theological streams of ancient Israel. It only makes sense, then, for Christian Egyptians, and other readers for that matter, who engage the text with an interest in what it means for their world here and now, to follow the prophet's lead who courageously spoke of Israel's archenemies as God's own people and who advocated for a posture of embrace in place of exclusion. In other words, Isa 19 is not only offering a blessing to the marginalized Christian Egyptians, but it is also calling on them to consider how they think about those who are different from them religiously and ethnically. As the text includes Egypt in God's blessings of healing and restoration, the text challenges those who were once outsiders and now consider themselves to be insiders not to close the door behind them, but to remember to extend the tent so that God's people would embody peace, harmony, and diversity that advocates on behalf of the oppressed and that celebrates difference within unity and harmony.

CONCLUSION

Isaiah 19 is an exceptional text in the theological contours of the Hebrew Bible and it is a text that holds a special place in the life of the Christian Egyptian minority. This essay highlighted some aspects of the recent history of reception of Isa 19 among those who read the text as Scripture within the Christian minority in Egypt. But at the same time, the discussion, leaning into biblical scholarship, offered ways to nuance the Christian Egyptian understanding of this passage. Thus, this essay is a continuation of the history of reception of this passage in the life of Christian Egyptians who are trying to make sense of their identity as they encounter how Egypt is constructed in the biblical traditions and as they fare in their socio-economic circumstances as a minoritized community.

To that end, the essay offered a study of Isa 19 that deals with the literary, historical, and theological elements that have shaped the content of the chapter. This was followed with reflections on the hermeneutical challenges and promises of creating an interpretive dialogue between the world of the text and the world of Christian Egyptian readers of the text as they seek to construct an identity and strategies of survival in the midst of persecution. I argued for a more dynamic hermeneutical engagement with the text and its context and with the realities of contemporary Christian Egyptians. I explored the ways the text offers words of hope and inclusion in its historical context, especially when compared with other texts in the Hebrew Bible in which Egypt receives no words of hope or restoration. Thus, the message of the text enables Christian Egyptians to see themselves embraced by the God of the Bible. I suggested that the text in its fullness calls the Christian Egyptian minority to discern a way to embrace this inclusion, but at the same time to name the erosion of identity that sometimes comes with it. The text in its fullness asks Christian Egyptians to reflect on where they put their trust, and whether they like the Judeans of Isaiah's time are putting their trust in the wrong power. Lastly, I suggested that as Christian Egyptians celebrate how the text blesses Egypt and includes Egyptians in God's plans of healing and restoration, they ought to ask themselves, how are they called to embody inclusion for those who are marginalized and oppressed?

BIBLIOGRAPHY

Aster, Shawn Zelig. "Isaiah 19: The 'Burden of Egypt' and Neo-Assyrian Imperial Policy." *JAOS* 135 (2015) 453–70.
Balogh, Csaba. *The Stele of YHWH in Egypt: The Prophecies of Isaiah 18–20 concerning Egypt and Kush*. Leiden: Brill, 2011.
Blenkinsopp, Joseph. *Isaiah 1–39: A New Translation with Introduction and Commentary*. New York: Doubleday, 2000.
Breasted, J. H. *History of Egypt*. New York: Scribner's, 1905.
Childs, Brevard. *Isaiah*. Louisville: Westminster John Knox, 2001.
Clements, R. E. *Isaiah 1–39*. Grand Rapids: Eerdmans, 1982.
Hayes, J. H., and J. M. Miller, eds. *Israelite and Judean History*. Philadelphia: Westminster, 1977.
Kahn, D. "The Inscription of Sargon II at Tang-I Var and the Chronology of the Dynasty 25." *Or* 70 (2001) 1–8.
Kaiser, Otto. *Isaiah 13–39: A Commentary*. London: SCM, 1974.
Kitchen, Kenneth. *The Third Intermediate Period in Egypt 1100–650 B.C*. Warminster: Aris & Phillips, 1986.
McKinion, Steven A. *Isaiah 1–39*. Downers Grove, IL: InterVarsity, 2004.
Roberts, J. J. M. *First Isaiah*. Minneapolis: Fortress, 2015.

Schipper, Bernd. "'The City by the Sea will be a Drying Place': Isaiah 19:1-25 in Light of Prophetic Texts from Ptolemaic Egypt." In *Monotheism in Late Prophetic and Early Apocalyptic Literature Studies of the Sofja Kovalevskaja Research Group on Early Jewish Monotheism*, edited by Nathan MacDonald and Ken Brown, 25-56. Tübingen: Mohr Siebeck, 2014.

Seitz, Christopher R. *Isaiah 1-39*. Louisville: John Knox, 1993.

Sweeney, Marvin A. *Isaiah 1-39: with an introduction to prophetic literature*. Grand Rapids: Eerdmans, 1996.

Tull, Patricia K. *Isaiah 1-39*. Macon, GA: Smyth & Helwys, 2010.

Watts, John D. W., *Isaiah 1-33*. Waco, TX: Word, 1985.

Wildberger, Hans. *Jesaja 13-39*. Neukirchen-Vluyn: Neukirchener Verlag des Erziehungsvereins, 1982.

CHAPTER 22

African Liberation Theology

DAVID TONGHOU NGONG

Like in other parts of the world, liberation theology has had a controversial presence in Africa and does not appear to have penetrated most churches.[1] The debate as to whether African theology should be liberation theology was carried out not only among theologians in the continent but also involved theologians in the African diaspora. This debate concluded that African Christian theology is characterized by liberation and inculturation. Today, however, it is acknowledged that such distinction may not be necessary because the theology of inculturation, which focuses on naturalizing the gospel in African contexts, participates in postcolonial discourse and is thus a dynamic of liberation.[2] In this case, liberation involves overcoming social, cultural, political, and economic forces that undermine the well-being and dignity of Africans. African liberation theology therefore sought to challenge dynamics of colonialism on the continent and this theology was mostly articulated in the 1970s and 1980s.

---

1. Given that the previous chapter dealt with Black liberation theology in Southern Africa, this chapter will address only what came to be described as liberation theology in Africa north of the Limpopo River and south of the Sahara. For a background to the development of liberation theology in Africa, see Parratt, *Reinventing Christianity*, 137–62.

2. Postcolonial discourse could be understood in many ways, but as used here, it is thinking and action that intend to free Africans from colonialism and its afterlives. Inasmuch as the theology of inculturation is a postcolonial discussion, it is a dynamic of liberation because it challenges oppressive thinking about Africans. For how the theology of inculturation participates in postcolonial discourse, see Antonio, "Introduction," 1–25. For the debate on African theology's connection to liberation theology, especially Black liberation theology, see Tutu, "Theology of Liberation in Africa," 162–68; Cone, "Black American Perspective on the Future of African Theology," 176–86.

African Liberation Theology

Two important moments seem to have attenuated the vigor of liberation theology on the continent. The first is the end of the so-called Cold War (which was a hot war in Africa) and the end of legal apartheid in South Africa. The second is the meteoric rise of Pentecostalism on the continent. First, the end of the Cold War and legal apartheid in South Africa seemed to give the impression that the moment of anticolonial struggle for liberation was over because the end of the Cold War was followed by the fall of the last colonial regime in Africa—the apartheid regime in South Africa. With the apparent end of anticolonial struggle, some theologians suggested that African theology needed to move from liberation to reconstruction.[3] With the end of legal apartheid in South Africa, it seemed that the continent had achieved the goal of liberation, understood as freedom from colonially derived oppressions, and should then move on to rebuilding its shattered countries. This argument, which was at the time described by some as hasty, played a part in weakening liberation theology on the continent.[4]

The second moment that appears to have attenuated the vigor of liberation theology in Africa is the rise of Pentecostalism around the world, including in Africa. As the adage has it, liberation theology chose the poor, but the poor chose Pentecostalism. While this adage was used in reference to how Pentecostalism seemed to have replaced liberation theology in Latin America, it is even more applicable in Africa where Pentecostalism is strongly challenging other forms of Christianity so much that there is now talk of the Pentecostalization of African Christianity. Pentecostal theology has stressed the empowerment of individuals through enabling them to overcome what are seen as demonic blockages that prevent them from experiencing fullness of life. Instead of providing the social, cultural, political, and economic analysis that liberation theology called for, Pentecostalism provides what may be described as supernaturalistic analysis that sees the problems that bedevil the continent as the work of malevolent spiritual forces.[5] Thus, while it could be argued that Pentecostalism is a spirituality for the marginalized, its analysis of the circumstances in which the marginalized suffer deprivation is quite different from what obtains in liberation theology. The supernatural explanation of what ails the continent seems to have undermined what may be said to be the rationalistic explanation of liberation theology. Like the end of the Cold War and the end of legal apartheid in South Africa, Pentecostalism has therefore contributed to undermining the power of liberation theology on the continent.

---

3. Two important texts made this argument at this time—Villa-Vicencio, *Theology of Reconstruction*, and Mugambi, *From Liberation to Reconstruction*.

4. For a recent recapitulation of the context in which the proposal of the shift from liberation to reconstruction was made, see Mugambi, "From Reconstruction to Reaffirmation," 151–57. Also see the Festschrift to Mugambi that focused on the question of reconstruction, Bongmba, *Religion and Social Reconstruction in Africa*.

5. Pentecostal politics in Nigeria could be seen as representative of this paradigm throughout the continent. See the recent analysis in Obadare, *Pentecostal Republic*.

In this chapter, I argue for the continued relevance of liberation theology in Africa, noting that African theology does not have to move from liberation to reconstruction; rather, liberation should be regarded as the very expression of reconstruction. In other words, liberation *is* reconstruction.[6] It is in the process of seeking liberation from all forces that seek to undermine our well-being that we achieve reconstruction. Liberation is here understood as achieving the freedom to live a dignified and flourishing life in a world that constantly undermines our humanity.[7] In this context, liberation is freedom that enables individuals, groups, and in fact, the whole planet to flourish. Because the ability to live flourishing lives constantly elude Africans because of their entrapment in multiple dynamics of oppression, the quest for liberation needs to be central to African Christian theology. At a time when the idea of liberation has been reduced only to certain pockets of African theology, such as in the context of sex and gender, I argue that liberation should be recaptured as the organizing principle of African theology. This is so because, for the most part, Africans have not been liberated from domination in a global cultural and political economy that is under the wiles of empire and racial capitalism. In fact, one of the problems with the theology of reconstruction was not that it announced the death of liberation too soon, as it was claimed at the time, but rather that it did not take seriously the dynamic of empire that still dominates much of Africa. That it did not take seriously the dynamic of empire that still dominates much of Africa could be seen in the fact that it took Nehemiah as its role model for reconstruction without a critical reading of Nehemiah as a tool of the empire. In that sense, Nehemiah was like many of the African ruling elite today who owe much to former colonizers, who still determine what they do, than to the people whose interests they are supposed to serve.

The first part of this chapter focuses on the work of Cameroonian sociologist and theologian Jean-Marc Éla, who saw liberation as central to African theology and showed how African life should be understood within the context of empire and racial capitalism. The next section argues that there are two important dynamics of liberation theology that need to be taken seriously going forward. These include theologies that address the issues of sex and gender and what might be termed post-nationalist liberation theology, a form of liberation theology which animates separatist movements in Africa. In all, African liberation theology needs to account for the question of empire, racial capitalism, sex and gender, and what has been termed post-nationalist nationalism, which is the rise of separatist movements in the continent. Such theology should not only be Pan-Africanist but also planetary in the sense that the salvation of Africa is inevitably tied to the salvation of the planet.

---

6. The idea that liberation is reconstruction is inspired by Amartya Sen's notion that development is freedom. See Sen, *Development as Freedom*. It is however not clear that we can say that reconstruction is freedom given that there are many unfree societies that are said to have undergone reconstruction.

7. For the idea of liberation as a process, see West, "African Liberation Theology," 131. For the idea of liberation as freedom, see Cochrane, "On Freedom," 226–42.

THEOLOGY, EMPIRE, AND RACIAL CAPITALISM

Few African theologians have captured Africa's predicament in the modern world like the Cameroonian sociologist and Roman Catholic theologian Jean-Marc Éla. He is among the first contemporary African theologians to focus his theology on the question of liberation, seeing liberation not just as political and economic, as seems to be the case in Latin American liberation theology that focused on the liberation of the poor, but also as including the cultural. Central to Éla's liberation theology is the question of how to enact the vision of the Eucharist as communion and sacrifice. For him, the Eucharist is an event that not only dramatizes the past but requires that the vision held in that past be made manifest in the present. "The celebration of the Eucharist," he writes, "is not an exhumation of the past, but rather a rendering present of an act and a reality that dominate all time."[8] It is an act that calls on its participants to give of themselves and share of themselves as the original enactment demonstrated. However, he noted the paradox that it is in this central celebration of the church, the Eucharist, that the African predicament is loudly encountered. The marginalization begins with the elements of the Eucharist themselves. The elements of the Eucharist are bread and wine, products that are not local to many African contexts. For many Africans to participate in the Eucharist, therefore, the elements must be imported from other countries, possibly from Europe and the United States. Here the Eucharist becomes the very locus in which the economic exploitation and cultural marginalization of Africans occur. Economically, Africans buy these products from regions of the world that do not necessarily buy from Africans, stimulating their economies while African economies decline. This situation could be ameliorated by using local foodstuff for the Eucharist, Éla suggests. But the suggestion that local foods be used in the Eucharist has been rejected by the ecclesial hierarchy.

As such, the Eucharist that is an enactment of a profound act of sharing becomes a locus for cultural marginalization and economic exploitation—African products are seen as not fit for use in the sacraments and Africans are forced to buy these products from abroad. This rejection of African food denigrates African cultural life and impoverishes African economies. It is only a microcosm for a global process which demonstrates the "domination of Africa by manifold forms of world imperialism."[9] This refusal to use African foods in the Eucharist may be connected to the insistence by colonizers and their postcolonial minions that Africans replace the growing of food crops with cash crops. Cash crops, such as cotton, groundnut, coffee, cocoa, rubber, and palm oil, among others, are destined for the international market and meant to raise profits for capitalists even as poor villagers suffer famine and malnutrition. This state of affairs situates Africans as people to be dominated rather than as those with whom the resources of the world should be shared. The Eucharist therefore raises

8. Éla, *African Cry*, 1.
9. Éla, *African Cry*, 6.

issues for how the church is implicated in racial capitalism and imperialism that specifically strangles Africans. An act that is meant to enact sharing and self-giving instead becomes the locus for exploitation.

Because of the emphasis on the Eucharist as an act of sharing and self-giving, questions of food and health care are central to Éla's theology. In fact, provision of food and health care are especially demonstrative of the reign of God Jesus Christ proclaimed and demonstrated. This is especially so in arid northern Cameroon where Éla worked and where most people continue to live in penury. While the replacement of food crops for cash crops was meant to oil the wheel of capital, health care in many African countries was also rooted in colonial exploitation. According to Éla, the modern health care systems in many African countries were not created to enhance the health of Africans for their own sakes. Rather, they was intended to enable them to be fit enough for capitalist exploitation. Given that sick people cannot work, the health care system that was created was intended to render the people just well enough for their labor to be exploited. This dynamic of exploitation was supported by a dominant theology that is the theology of the rich and powerful. It is a theology that portrays God as neutral in the world rather than as a God who takes side and who in Jesus Christ conspires with the poor and oppressed to overthrow systems of domination and install "fraternal communion." For Éla, therefore, the Eucharist enacts the vision of the reign of God that should be made manifest in our world. This is a vision in which the resurrection of Christ "becomes real and complete only when the poor pass from death to life."[10] The passing of the poor from death to life is not about a future resurrection but rather about the creation of "a different world right here, a world being gestated from the deeds of the everyday."[11] His goal is for theology to focus on the plight of the abandoned in Africa, especially those who reside in the rural areas and who suffer some of the most egregious exploitation and abandonment.

While Éla's idea about the exploitation of the poor appears rooted in the discourse of colonialism and the immediate postcolonial moment, much of what he addressed are still relevant today and, in some cases, even more so. His idea of the economic exploitation of Black Africans, especially as epitomized in the Eucharist, has become increasingly relevant, especially with the revitalization of the notion of racial capitalism. This idea captures the fact that the practices that oil the wheel of capitalism is rooted in the exploitation of Black people, including Black Africans.[12] African theology therefore needs to continuously wrestle with how global capitalism is organized in ways that are designed to facilitate the exploitation and early death of many Africans. While in the past the idea of the exploitation of Black people used to be connected to South Africa because of apartheid, that should not be the case today

---

10. Éla, *My Faith as an African*, 111.

11. Éla, *African Cry*, 53.

12. For more on the origin and development of the idea of racial capitalism, see Kelley, "Foreword," xiv–xvii.

as Black exploitation is a global phenomenon, as so many recent studies have pointed out. The internal components of this exploitation are due to rapacious African ruling classes and the external components are due to continued imperialistic dynamics from Western countries such as France and the United States and Asian countries such as China and Japan. The reconstruction of the continent is therefore dependent on the persistent naming and critiquing of the manifold internal and external dynamics of exploitation that continue to bedevil the continent. However, these are not the only issues that make African liberation theology continuously relevant. Issues of sex and gender continue to be more pressing.

SEX, GENDER, AND LIBERATION

The issue of sex and gender in African liberation theology deals mainly with the status of women in church and society and the question of sexuality, especially with reference to LGBTQ issues. Given that African women's theology is discussed in the next chapter, this section limits discussion of African women's quest for liberation to its connection to the LGBTQ question, which has recently become pressing in church and society in many African countries. It should however be noted in passing that the question of the status of women in church and society has mostly been raised by women rather than men. However, while women are concerned about the status of women in church and society, they are equally concerned about all the other issues African male theologians have been concerned about, such as the marginalization of the continent through the rapacity of the ruling elite and an imperialistic international order.[13] African women have been raising their voices to protest the marginal place women hold in church and society at least since the 1970s but their voices came to the fore especially after the formation of the Circle of Concerned African Women Theologians under the leadership of Mercy Amba Oduyoye in the 1990s.[14] It is especially with scholars such as Mercy Amba Oduyoye and Musa Dube that African women's struggle for liberation was intimately connected to the struggles of LGBTQ people. Two of Oduyoye's essays that focus on the question of marriage are especially relevant.[15] In these essays, Oduyoye laments how marriage in many African cultures seems designed to foster patriarchal purposes, even in African cultures that are ostensibly matrilineal, as in the case of the Akan.

Central to fostering this patriarchal tradition is the idea that a couple must procreate. The idea that procreation is central to married life had hardly been interrogated

---

13. See Dube, "To Pray the Lord's Prayer in the Global Economic Era (Matt. 6:9–13)," 611–30; Dube, "Divining Ruth for International Relations," 179–95.

14. See Zoé-Obianga, "Role of Women in Present-Day Africa," 145–49; Oduyoye, *Introducing African Women's Theology*, 9–10.

15. Oduyoye, "Feminist Theology in an African Perspective," 166–81; Oduyoye, "Coming Home to Myself" 105–20.

by African male theologians. They instead portrayed it as central to the African view of what it means to live a fulfilled life. As Oduyoye explains, the command to bear children is so central that marriages are ruined for lack of children. She uses herself as an example of a childless woman whose marriage underwent significant stress because she and her husband were unable to procreate. In the two essays noted above, she uses literary works that center procreation to narrate how the lives of women turn around their ability to fulfill the role of childbearer society assigns to them. This ability to procreate, she avers, should also been seen as the root of the negative attitudes many African cultures have towards LGBTQ people. "Included in the causes of homophobia, and this is particularly true in the case of lesbians," she writes, "are the insistence on marriage as the only legitimate sanction of childbirth and the 'highjacking' and appropriation of the mystery of birth on the part of the men."[16] Men hijack the mystery of birth because they see it as means to promote their memory after death. This is because, in many African traditions, it is mostly men who have children who could become ancestors. In fact, there are rituals performed for men who die without children to discourage such men from ever returning. This desire on the part of men to have children means that women are often blamed when a couple do not procreate, even if the fault is the man's. African male theologians had simply presented this need for procreation, and how a man would do anything to procreate, as a given. In fact, one of the reasons men often marry more than one wife is to secure offspring in case the first wife fails to give birth. Theologians such as John Mbibi and BénézetBujo had portrayed this state of affairs as simply an African philosophy of life. In the hands of African women, this philosophy of life became one that needed critique not only because it oppresses women but also because it oppresses LGBTQ people.

This intervention from African women theologians notwithstanding, LGBTQ liberation theology is still in its infancy in much of Africa. Two broad attitudes towards LGBTQ issues may be discerned in African Christian thought.[17] The first, embraced by most Christians, is strong opposition to LGBTQ people. In this regard, LGBTQ issues are regarded as not only unchristian but also un-African. Here, ideas against LGBTQ people are drawn from both indigenous cultures and the Bible to argue that LGBTQ people are foreign to both African and the Christian imagination. However, there is a minority view that argues that LGBTQ issues are *not* foreign to both indigenous and Christian imagination. This view holds that indigenous cultures are so diverse that while there may not be LGBTQ people in some cultures, they are present in many others. Thus, the argument is that there cannot be a blanket claim that these issues are foreign to the African imagination. From a Christian perspective, some have argued that Christianity is not averse to LGBTQ people. They draw from the Bible to argue that all people are made in the image of God and are thus endowed

---

16. Oduyoye, "Feminist Theology in African Perspective," 169.

17. For the delineation of different views of LGBTQ issues in African Christianity, see Gunda, "Contemporary African Christian Thought and Homosexuality," 208–14.

with dignity that must be respected, no matter their sexual orientation. An important leader in this regard is Desmond Tutu, the former Anglican archbishop of Cape Town, whose anti-apartheid crusade has been extended to LGBTQ issues. His aversion to the use of the Bible to denigrate others has led him to see the dehumanization of LGBTQ people as similar to the racist dehumanization of Black people under apartheid.[18] Another important voice in the struggle for the liberation of LGBTQ people is the Ugandan Anglican bishop Christopher Senyonjo. Against the backdrop of virulent anti-LGBTQ views in East Africa, his struggle for the rights of LGBTQ people has been quite noticeable so that several articles were dedicated to his work in a recent issue of the journal *Theology and Sexuality*.[19] While the majority voices that oppose LGBTQ rights in Africa may appear overwhelming, as demonstrated in the recent case of the anti-LGBTQ law being promoted by Christians in the Ghanaian parliament, minority voices that insist that being African and Christian are not incompatible with being LGBTQ are being loudly raised.[20]

Debates about the status of LGBTQ people in African liberation theology cannot be complete without engagement of the role of foreign influences in these debates. Engaging the role of foreign influences highlights the question of coloniality and the question of African agency that may be embedded in these debates. The debates on LGBTQ issues in Africa is seen as fueled by foreign agents, notably conservative and liberal Christians from America and Europe. Conservative Christians are said to be taking the anti-LGBTQ fight they seem to be losing at home to Africa, seeing Africa as the last bulwark against what is called the "homosexual agenda." In this regard, African churches have aligned with American churches that have rejected the idea that one can be Christian and defend the rights of LGBTQ people. Liberals, on the other hand, have also sent missionaries to some African countries to promote the fight for LGBTQ rights.[21] Considering the role of outside forces in this debate, one may wonder if African agency is eclipsed. What role are Africans themselves playing in this process? This question notwithstanding, Gunda is essentially right to state that LGBTQ debates in Africa must be placed within a global context in which African agency is not distinct from the action of foreign actors.[22] In this case, the struggle for LGBTQ liberation provides a lesson in liberation struggle all over the world, namely that liberation is often rooted in collective action rather than in the action of just a single people.

---

18. Gunda, "Contemporary African Christian Thought and Homosexuality," 212.

19. See *Theology and Sexuality* 26 no. 1 (2020).

20. For some of these voices, see van Klinken, *Kenyan, Christian, Queer*; van Klinken and Chitando, *Reimagining Christianity and Sexual Diversity in Africa*.

21. For more on the role of outside forces in the LGBTQ debates, see Gunda, "Contemporary African Christian Thought," 214–16; van Klinken, *Kenyan, Christian, Queer*.

22. Gunda, "Contemporary African Christian Thought," 216.

Section 5 | Emerging Theologies from Africa

LIBERATION THEOLOGY AND POST-NATIONALIST NATIONALISM

A recent phenomenon which has not been adequately accounted for in African liberation theology is what may be described as post-nationalist nationalism. Post-nationalist nationalism is the increasing identification with ethnic or certain colonial identities in the postcolonial nation-states, leading to the struggle for new, independent nation-states from the ashes of existing ones. In other words, groups in different African countries have become disillusioned with the existing arrangements and are fighting for new, independent nation-states. This is the case with countries like Nigeria, Cameroon, and especially Sudan, from which South Sudan, the newest African country, recently emerged. During the struggle for independence from European colonizers, the ethnic differences that existed among African peoples were largely put aside in order to confront the common enemy—the European colonizer. After independence, the hopes that the new countries would be inclusive of all those who are within its territories were dashed as many groups felt marginalized. The hope of flourishing new countries turned into a nightmare for many and different groups began to harbor the belief that a brighter future for them may be had only within a new country of their own. Thus, post-nationalist nationalism is situated within existing nation-states. In Nigeria, we have those who fought and continue to fight for an independent Biafra for the Biafra people. In Cameroon we have those who are fighting for an independent Anglophone state because they believe that there is no future for them in a unified Cameroon that includes the French-speaking region.[23] In Sudan, the South fought for independence from the North and gained its independence in 2011. Two things are remarkable about this new nationalism. The first is that it is directed against other groups that are Black rather than at white colonizers, as were post-World War II anti-colonial struggles for independence.[24] Dominant Black groups within the nation-state are described as colonizers from whom other Black people seek freedom. The second remarkable fact about this new nationalism is that it is sometimes underwritten by a theology of liberation, as ideas that derive from liberation theology are used in the struggle for a new nation. While African liberation theology was very vocal during the struggle for independence from European colonizers, contemporary African theology has been quite mute about this new post-nationalist liberation theology.

However, this post-nationalist liberation theology has recently been brought to the fore. A recent book called *Chosen Peoples* details how the people of South Sudan drew from the story of the Exodus, a story popular in liberation theology, to cast themselves as the oppressed Israelite whom God sought to free from the oppression of the North. Their narrative of oppression comes complete with a Moses in the person

23. Cameroon was colonized by Britain and France and the two parts—joined to form what came to be known as the federal Republic of Cameroon.

24. The exception may be Sudan where the North is said to be Arab even though the situation is more complex.

of the late John Garang who did not see the promised land (independence) and was replaced by Salva Kiir, their Joshua.[25] In Cameroon, there has arisen what is called a "theology of self-determination" which insists that it is God's will that the people of Anglophone Cameroon (also called Southern Cameroons) should become an independent country and rule themselves rather than being under the domination of Francophone Cameroon or East Cameroon. Dynamics of this theology justifies the use of violence, as was the case in Latin American liberation theology, in obtaining such a new nation-state.[26]

This theology, however, raises a profound problem from a Christian perspective. The problem is demonstrated in South Sudan where the new country descended into war immediately after independence from the North. A country that drew from the Christian mythos of a single people under oppression to seek independence immediately descended into a war that seems to be rooted in ethnic differences between the Dinka and the Nuer. Thus, after independence, the Christian identity from which they had drawn to fight for independence quickly gave way to ethnic identity. The question this descent into conflict raises is whether it is possible for the Christian faith to hold different ethnic identities together in a single country. In other words, in the African context where different ethnicities have been brought together to form independent countries, is it possible for the Christian faith to act as a glue that hold the people together or does ethnicity still override Christianity? Is it possible for Igbo Christians to live together with Yoruba Christians in Nigeria or for Anglophone Christians to live together with Francophone Christians in Cameroon or do the different "ethnic" identities override the Christian identity? With these questions liberation theology resolves into political theology as the question becomes how people of differing ethnic backgrounds may live together to ensure mutual flourishing.

Perhaps the question of how to live with the other to ensure mutual flourishing is a fitting question for the theology of liberation because it has been animated by contexts characterized by different ways of diminishing the well-being of the Other. In a world in which it has become increasingly difficult, if not impossible, to live in homogenous enclosures, the question of how to live with the Other to ensure mutual flourishing becomes even more pressing. The question challenges not only the post-nationalist spirit but also calls on Africans to imagine their living space as not only their local communities on nations but the entire continent and even the planet itself. In other words, African liberation theology ought to move beyond post-nationalist nationalism to a pan-Africanist and even planetary vision in which our well-being is rooted in the well-being of the Other, within the context of a healthy ecological system.

---

25. Tounsel, *Chosen Peoples*, 110–11. Also see Jok, *Sudan*.

26. For a summary of this new liberation theology in Cameroon, see Ngong, "African Political Theology and Post-nationalist Nationalism." Also see, Jumbam, *Independence or Nothing*, and Morris-Chapman, "Ambazonian Theology?"

CONCLUSION

This chapter has argued for the continued relevance of African liberation theology at a time when this form of African theology appears to be irrelevant. Here, liberation is seen to be the central organizing framework in which the well-being of Africans may be conceptualized. Such liberation should be framed from the standpoint of the struggle for mutual flourishing not only among Africans but also among Africans and peoples around the world. Such flourishing should be placed within the context of the care of creation on which human flourishing depends.

BIBLIOGRAPHY

Antonio, Edward P. "Introduction: Inculturation and Postcolonial Discourse." In *Inculturation and Postcolonial Discourse in African Theology*, edited by Edward P. Antonio, 1–25. New York: Peter Lang, 2006.

Bongmba, ed. *Religion and Social Reconstruction in Africa*. London: Routledge, 2018.

Cochrane, James, R. "On Freedom: Risking a (Faithful) Reinterpretation." In *Religion and Social Reconstruction in Africa* edited by Elias Kifon Bongmba, 226–42. London: Routledge, 2018.

Cone, James H. "A Black American Perspective on the Future of African Theology." In *African Theology en Route*, edited by Kofi Appiah-Kubi and Sergio Torres, 176–86. Maryknoll, NY: Orbis, 1979.

Dube, Musa W. "Divining Ruth for International Relations." In *Other Ways of Reading*, edited by Musa W. Dube, 179–95. Atlanta: Society of Biblical Literature, 2001.

———. "To Pray the Lord's Prayer in the Global Economic Era (Matt. 6:9–13)." In *The Bible in Africa*, edited by Gerald O. West and Musa W. Dube, 611–30. Leiden: Brill, 2000.

Éla, Jean-Marc. *African Cry*. Translated by Robert R. Barr. 1986. Repr. Eugene, OR: Wipf & Stock, 2005.

———. *My Faith as an African*. Translated by John Pairman Brown and Susan Perry. Repr. Eugene, OR: Wipf and Stock, 2009.

Gunda, Masiiwa R. "Contemporary African Christian Thought and Homosexuality." In *A New History of African Christian Thought: From Cape to Cairo*, edited by David Tonghou Ngong, 204–20. New York and London: Routledge, 2017.

Jok, Jok M. *Sudan: Race, Religion, and Violence*. 2nd ed. London: OneWorld, 2016.

Jumbam, Jerry. *Independence or Nothing: Theology of Self-Determination and the British Southern Cameroons*. Bloomington, IN: Arthur House, 2018.

Kelly, Robin D. G. "Foreword: Why Black Marxism? Why Now?" In *Black Marxism: The Making of the Black Radical Tradition* by Cedric J. Robinson, xi–xxxiii. Chapel Hill: The University of North Carolina Press, 2000.

Morris-Chapman, D. P. "An Ambazonian Theology? A Theological Approach to the Anglophone Crisis in Cameroon." *HTS* 75 (2019) 1–11.

Mugambi, J. N. K. *From Liberation to Reconstruction: African Christianity After the Cold War*. Nairobi: East African Educational, 1995.

———. "From Reconstruction to Reaffirmation: African Christian Theology in an Era of Hot Peace." In *The Routledge Handbook of African Theology*, edited by Elias Kifon Bongmba, 151–67. New York: Routledge, 2020.

Ngong, David. "African Political Theology and Post-nationalist Nationalism: The Case of the Cameroon Anglophone Crisis." *JPT* (May 2021) 1–17.

Obadare, Ebenezer. *Pentecostal Republic: Religion and the Struggle for State Power in Nigeria*. London: Zed, 2018.

Oduyoye, Mercy A. "A Coming Home to Myself: The Childless Woman in the West African Space." In *Liberating Eschatology: Essays in Honor of Letty M. Russell*, edited by Margaret A. Farley and Serene Jones, 105–20. Louisville: Westminster John Knox, 1999.

———. "Feminist Theology in an African Perspective." In *Paths of African Theology*, edited by Rosino Gibellini, 166–81. Maryknoll, NY: Orbis, 1994.

———. *Introducing African Women's Theology*. Sheffield: Sheffield Academic, 2001.

Parratt, John. *Reinventing Christianity: African Theology Today*. Grand Rapids: Eerdmans, 1995.

Sen, Amartya. *Development as Freedom*. Oxford: Oxford University Press, 1999.

Tounsel, Christopher. *Chosen Peoples: Christianity and Political Imagination in South Sudan*. Durham, NC: Duke University Press. 2021.

Tutu, Desmond. "The Theology of Liberation in Africa." In *African Theology en Route*, edited by Kofi Appiah-Kubi and Sergio Torres, 162–68. Maryknoll, NY: Orbis, 1979.

Van Klinken, Adriaan. *Kenyan, Christian, Queer: Religion, LGBT Activism, and Arts of Resistance*. University Park, PA: Penn State University Press, 2019.

Van Klinken, Adriaan, and Ezra Chitando, eds. *Reimagining Christianity and Sexual Diversity in Africa*. London: Hurst, 2021.

Villa-Vicencio, Charles. *A Theology of Reconstruction: Nation-Building and Human Rights*. Cambridge: Cambridge University Press, 1992.

West, Gerald. "African Liberation Theology." In *A New History of African Christian Thought: From Cape to Cairo*, edited by David Tonghou Ngong, 122–35. New York: Routledge, 2017.

Zoé-Obenga. Rose. "The Role of Women in Present-Day Africa." In *African Theology en Route*, edited by Kofi Appiah-Kubi and Sergio Torres, 145–49. Maryknoll, NY: Orbis, 1979.

CHAPTER 23

African Women's Theologies

LÉOCADIE LUSHOMBO

African women's theologies (AWT) is plural because these theologies refer to a vast continent and use different contexts and methods. AWT are an essential part of African political and liberation theology. They address colonial and postcolonial issues and the societal dynamics that undermine the flourishing of women within the contexts of specific socio-religious traditions and cultures. African women theologians share a premise that what undermines women does harm to the nation-state.[1] One essential common feature of AWT is the search to unmask the roots of oppression and powerlessness of African women. As Phiri[2] puts it:

> African women's theologies are a critical, academic study of the causes of women's oppression, particularly a struggle against societal, cultural, and religious patriarchy. They are committed to eradicating all forms of oppression against women through a critique of the social and religious dimensions both in African Culture and Christianity.[3]

Phiri suggests that oppression of African women takes roots in "patriarchy, colonialism, neo-colonialism, racism, capitalism, globalization and sexism." For Oduyoye,[4] among these root causes, patriarchization and other oppressive cultures are

---

1. Dube Shomanah, "Batswakwa."
2. She is from Malawi and has served with the World Council of Churches and a coordinator for the Circle of Concerned African Women Theologians (Circle).
3. Phiri, "Southern Africa," 156.
4. Born in Ghana, founded the Circle of Concerned African Women Theologians in 1989.

a severe disease that needs to be addressed. Thus, the need for a cultural hermeneutics to further a liberating theology of inculturation.

CULTURAL HERMENEUTICS TOWARDS A LIBERATION THEOLOGY OF INCULTURATION

African women have identified culture as a tool often used to further domination. A standard premise of African women's theologies is that Christian churches suffer from a cultural alienation that needs to be addressed to allow the flow of men and women's communication with God, as advocated by Oduyoye. In addition, African women theologians and feminist theologians claim that some oppressive cultures and practices have been long overlooked in Christian theology. Consequently, these oppressions are also ignored in African Christian theology.

The Circle of Concerned African Women Theologians (the Circle) was the promotor of AWT.[5] The Circle was launched at the Accra Conference in 1989, which was attended by seventy African women theologians. The issues that African women suffer and seek to redress were brought to the fore of this conference. Mercy Amba Oduyoye and Nyambura J. Njoroge[6] delivered their inaugural address urging African Christianity to do a "two-winged" theology through which both women and men could communicate with God.[7] Compared to those labeled feminist theologians, the Circle's distinctiveness is that it speaks to different and particular cultural contexts of Africa and Christianity in Africa. African women's theologies are an applied and contextual theology, "not satisfied with the mere announcing or denouncing of injustices"[8] of the African setting. To understand AWT, we need to consider these specific African settings.

African women theologians agree that this setting is marked by the historical events of slavery, colonization, and patriarchy that still affect the continent and women to date. Second, the African scene is shaped by a Christianity that was historically associated with colonizers and, in many ways, failed to affirm African cultures and religions as means by which the encounter with Jesus Christ could be met and fully lived. Besides, this association was characterized by imperialism and paternalism, and it still has its impacts on Christianity in modern Africa. Third, African women theologians also agree with the fact that African women historical figures play a grounding role for AWT. These figures provide grounds for theologizing. They marked the encounters of missionaries and European colonizers and the African

---

5. Nadar, "Feminist Theologies in Africa."

6. She is an ordained minister of the Presbyterian Church of East Africa in Kenya and the program executive for Ecumenical HIV and AIDS Initiatives and Advocacy at the World Council of Churches since 2007.

7. Oduyoye, *Transforming Power*, 77.

8. Hinga, *African, Christian, Feminist*, 15.

peoples' conversion to Christianity. These figures are pioneers of inculturation theology. Béatrice Kimpa Vita of the Congo pioneered what can be called decolonizing and inculturation theology today.

Kimpa Vita was born around 1682.[9] Her familial legacy is legitimately claimed by Gabon, Congo-Brazzaville, DR Congo, and Angola, each of which has a piece of the old kingdom of Kongo/Central Sub-Saharan Africa. She was a young woman whose conviction and need for an enculturated faith in God participated in affirming Kongolese women's *imago dei*. Her authority in AWT needs to be understood to grasp the emphasis of these theologies.

Kimpa Vita was a healer or prophetess in the African traditional religion, someone with a spiritual "knowledge" or "skill" that relates to religious matters or "spiritual mediators."[10] Her spiritual gifts were positively integrated within the scope of African traditional religion.[11] Kimpa Vita's message is seen by theologians, historians, and anthropologists as a call for a political and religious restoration of the kingdom and the building of a more humane society. For Dube, Kimpa Vita's message is the "typical example of a discourse of resistance, a decolonizing reading of the Bible, and a scramble to regain her land by re-reading the Text for decolonization."[12] She believed there was something wrong with a religion that could preach God's words in the context of slavery without condemning it.

In 1704, Kimpa Vita was convinced to have had a vision of Saint Anthony, who gave her the mission to restore the kingdom of Kongo.[13] From him, her movement took its name—the Antonian movement. She insisted that "Kongo needed black saints."[14] She began the Antonian movement that promoted the enculturation of the Christian message and liberation of the kingdom of Kongo. The movement witnessed several wars that enslaved millions of people.

Therefore, for Kimpa Vita, God speaks to people in their context. Sainthood could not be brought forth only by white Christians; it existed among the people wherever their intention was good and pure and there where the community had faith in the divine. She recognized that even the God preached by the missionaries in the fifteenth and sixteenth centuries revealed God-self to all, blacks and whites alike, and affirmed the sacredness of every human being. Kimpa Vita illustrated what Molefi Kete Asante calls "decolonizing" as a process of "launching of a revolutionary African consciousness to awake new responses to the human conditions."[15] She also

---

9. Nkosi, *Kimpa Vita*, 280.
10. Thornton, *Kongolese Saint Anthony*, 57.
11. Thornton, *Kongolese Saint Anthony*, 55–56.
12. Dube Shomanah, "Scramble for Africa as the Biblical Scramble for Africa" 6.
13. Wauthier, *Sectes et Prophètes d'Afrique Noire*, 23–24.
14. Thornton, *Kongolese Saint Anthony*, 160.
15. Asante and Ledbetter, *Contemporary Critical Thought in Africology and Africana Studies*, 4.

transgressed boundaries by claiming that divine revelation should not be secluded only for the privilege of white colonial missionaries.

The Circle of Concerned African Women Theologians (the Circle) builds upon Kimpa Vita's legacy and African inculturation theology. In addition, the Circle includes women from different Christian denominations and other religions such as Islam. Through the Circle, religious views and cultural dimensions of the life of African women are represented. Thus, African women theologians are concerned with African women's problems and the ways religion (African religion, Christian religion, and Islam) and culture, including African independent churches, affect their lives and participation in church and society. Thus, one of the tasks of the Circle is rewriting the stories of women. Furthermore, the Circle's theological agenda aims to uncover African women's moral agency and their contribution to liberation, enhancing, flourishing, and a liberating Christianity.

African women's theologies share the same concerns with feminist theologians as they struggle to make sense of Christianity and call on the consideration of oppression of women while putting "emphasis on praxis and action."[16] But, the emphasis on African women is more strongly put on the grassroots. The attention to grassroots actions of women as *locus theologicus* in AWT suggests that African women scholars cannot only engage in a "dialogical approach"[17] with other scholars. Considering the continent's challenges, they also need to engage communities and "situate their scholarship in the community for social transformation."[18]

The contributions of AWT can be grouped in three main points reflecting their theological claims:

1. African women's postcolonial biblical hermeneutics
2. African women's political theology
3. African women's christological thoughts: Which Christ for African women?

These claims are assessed through a shared cultural hermeneutics for a liberating theology of inculturation.

Cultural hermeneutics are how AWT bring women's experiences into their theological concerns. African women theologians speak cultural and social languages, not just academic ones. The hermeneutics culture affirms that cultures have been tainted by colonialism. For this reason, a critique of the colonial culture as it impacts women's lives is necessary. Furthermore, this critique enables African women theologians to appreciate and evaluate the resilient elements of the indigenous African cultures. As Kanyoro argues, "Culture is a double-edged sword. In some instances, culture is like the creed for the community identity. In other instances, culture is the main justification for

---

16. Hinga, *African, Christian, Feminist*, 6.
17. Hinga, *African, Christian, Feminist*, 7.
18. Dube Shomanah et al., *Postcolonial Perspectives in African Biblical Interpretations*, 22.

... oppression and injustice."[19] African women theologians uncover the empowering and disempowering cultural visions and practices of African or Christian traditions. Thus, AWT seek to retrieve a liberating culture from Christian and African traditions' perspectives.

Through cultural hermeneutics, AWT further elaborate the context of religion and culture, showing how they intermingle. Oduyoye suggests that this elaboration constitutes "the main arena of women's research and writings."[20] She characterizes AWT as bearing "the marks of creating a people whose human [dignity and] rights are trampled over"[21] retrieving a genderless concept of God, denouncing the colonial, imperial, and patriarchal patterns with which the Bible is shaped, and responding to the question of which model of Christ speaks the most to African women's experiences.

GENDERLESS CONCEPT OF GOD

African women's theologies demonstrate the ways Christianity negatively influenced the genderless features for God affirmed in African traditional religion. I focus here on two main elements: First, the suppression of God's female imageries and symbols and the local divine powers. This suppression was performed by the association of Western Christianity with colonial and patriarchal power. Second, the existence of priestesses who presided at sacred rites.

There is a need for a theology that embraces God as Mother to complement God as a Father for African women theologians. They suggest that African cultures and religion is resourceful in a genderless conception of God. African women theologians argue that the gender of God becomes an issue when it is used as a patriarchal tool to "dampen the spirits of the sisterhood or to draw boundaries around women's participation in the Church's ministry."[22]

The pioneering work here is that of Mercy Amba Oduyoye, who claims that "using male language to talk about God has made God male and, as a result, excluded women from their humanity."[23] By suppressing the genderless concept of God and local divine powers, Western Christianity and the colonial and patriarchal powers also suppressed African women's leadership in society. Besides, African men's androcentrism and patriarchy are reinforced by Christianity.

African women's theologies show the extent to which calling God "Father," or using the masculine pronoun for God, and even a Christomonism, or maleness of Christ-centered teaching of the Christian churches, negatively impact women's roles and leadership in church and society. Oduyoye uses some Nigerian cultures, such

19. Kanyoro, *Introduction to Feminist Cultural Hermeneutics*, 13.
20. Oduyoye, *Introducing African Women's Theology*, 24.
21. Oduyoye, *Introducing African Women's Theology*, 24.
22. Oduyoye, *Daughters of Anowa*, 194.
23. Oduyoye, *Daughters of Anowa*, 195.

as the Akan and Yoruba, who convey a gender-free language. For example, in Akan and Yoruba, God does not have a gender; God is the male-female one. She shows how female divinities are often wives and mothers in Yoruba representations. But then, she turns to Ghana, arguing that there are male and female deities, which are also associated with natural phenomena and who do not have male and female functions. Besides, "Gender plays little and often no part in who becomes an adherent of a particular deity."[24] Thus, AWT uncover the religious-cultural resources that are more neutral and inclusive, even regarding the gender of God.

Arabome also reinforces the idea of the imagery of God in African traditional religion as it challenges patriarchal structures and practices imposed by Christianity.[25] The conception of God as Mother or Father in African traditional religion accentuates the positive qualities of fatherhood or motherhood.[26] Arabome explains that "the African woman praises God who is neither male nor female but life, presence, and mystery."[27] Also, some cultures like the Zimbabwean had genderless divinity called "Mwari," who was referred to neither as male nor female and who could speak through women, men, or objects.[28] For African women theologians, texts on the gender of God need to be interrogated, deconstructed, and re-interpreted.

Christianity negatively influenced women's leadership in church and society because, among other features of African religion, Christianity declared some priestesses presiding at sacred rites as evil. Akossi-Mvongo illustrates this point by saying that "In African religion [women] play a prominent role and are considered in West Africa as the komians, or priestesses, who preside at sacred rites."[29] Orobator supports the same claim that in African traditional religion, there were women priestesses called *komians*,[30] but this practice has been repressed by Christianity as evil. So AWT takes the dialogical task of retrieving these roles to enable Christianity in Africa to consider the genuinely African and Christian.

Oduyoye, in turn, shows how African female ancestors participated in every sphere of life. Still, African women internalize a partial Christian view that has guided women as helpers or subordinates. Even the marginalization of African traditions has been sacralized by biblical interpretation and Christian theology. For African women biblical scholars, there is a need to retrieve the genderless concept of God and women's leadership roles from Scriptures. For this purpose, a decolonizing hermeneutic to reading the Bible is necessary.

---

24. Oduyoye, *Daughters of Anowa*, 113.
25. Arabome, "Dreams from My Mother, Prayers to My Father," 20.
26. Magesa, *African Religion*, 40–41.
27. Arabome, "Dreams from My Mother, Prayers to My Father," 21.
28. Dube Shomanah, "Introduction," 63.
29. Akossi-Mvongo, "Church We Want" 221.
30. Orobator, *Theology Brewed in an African Pot*, 142.

AFRICAN WOMEN BIBLICAL HERMENEUTICS

African women's biblical hermeneutics seeks to deconstruct any harmful understanding of Scriptures regarding women that contradicts Jesus's message.[31] This deconstruction uses *suspicion, liberation, hope, and healing lenses*. It seeks to respond to reading the Bible to help meet human flourishing on the continent. Nadar suggests that biblical narratives on women need to be retold through women's experiences to expose, interrogate, deconstruct, and re-interpret texts incoherent with Jesus's vision of love and liberation.[32]

In applying critical postcolonial hermeneutics to reading the Bible, Musa Dube shows how a specific use of texts can become annihilating to women and be supported by the African traditions themselves. To illustrate, she uses the example of the Pauline women's submission to their husbands' appeal as one of the common grounds for both African traditions and Scriptures that became annihilating to women. Dube suggests uncovering two realities in biblical texts: The reality of imperialism and that which justifies the oppressive patriarchal norms. For Dube, "Women in the colonized spaces not only suffer the yoke of colonial oppression but also endure the burden of two patriarchal systems imposed on them."[33] The Bible itself works to create colonial subjects and victims of patriarchy. She uses biblical narratives and proposes a more liberating interpretation for postcolonial African countries which challenge colonialism, racism, capitalism, and cultural chauvinism.

Okure traces the trajectory of African women theologians' reflection on women in the Bible in three significant features worth considering in African women's biblical hermeneutics. First, she suggests a "constitutive significance of Eve for a study of women in the Bible."[34] Several other African women biblical scholars study the significance of Mary, the mother of Jesus, as a model of womanhood as the church has long taught. Second, she agrees that the patriarchal components of the Bible invite women to apply new hermeneutical principles to reading the Bible. Third, AWT affirm that such patriarchal features have pastoral implications that should not be overlooked.[35]

Oduyoye, in turn, suggests that allying cultural to biblical hermeneutics is "a very fertile area for imaginative theological reflection."[36] The use of cultural hermeneutics in reading the Bible is liberating as they press us not to take biblical messages for granted, just as we do not have to take African traditions and rituals for the unchangeable. Whenever they undermine human dignity, they are to be called into question and changed.

---

31. Ayanga, "Religio-Cultural Challenges in Women's Fight against HIV/AIDS in Africa," 41.
32. Nadar, "'Texts of Terror,'" 78.
33. Dube Shomanah, *Postcolonial Feminist Interpretation of the Bible*, 20.
34. Okure, "Women in the Bible," 48.
35. Okure, "Women in the Bible," 48.
36. Oduyoye, *Daughters of Anowa*, 13.

Drawing on the fall in the book of Genesis (Gen 2:22), the text affirming that Eve was formed out of man's ribs, Paul's call to the submission of women to husbands, and on the fathers of the church who affirmed the view of women as the weaker sex, helpers, and cause of sin(s), AWT assess the impact of these texts on African women. They argue that women are consequently taken as inferior beings by nature compared to men. Okure shows that these readings are based on a misreading of the Genesis account.

Like many other feminist biblical scholars worldwide, African women biblical scholars take up the task of deconstructing this misreading, showing the solid sociocultural Jewish patriarchal drives behind them. For example, they show how Jewish culture left women without legal status, not allowed testifying in court, nor could they inherit property, nor were they expected to fulfill the precepts of the Torah as men. African women's biblical writings provide details of the many patriarchal Jewish oppressive elements towards women in the Bible, including the purity codes in Jewish society. However, they include the ways Jesus reverses these purity codes through his teaching and attitudes towards women. As Masena contends, "Jesus born as a man was best able to challenge male privilege and offer a more moving challenge to men to change their ways."[37] Their message of women's liberation is grounded in Jesus's liberation of all oppressed, including women.

Oduyoye strongly challenges the African churches "to work toward redeeming Christianity from" the image it conveys—that of "a force that coerces women into accepting roles that hamper the free and full expression of their humanity."[38] She calls on African women not to take the Bible for an absolute. She questions "any uncritical reading of biblical texts," reminding "the fluidity of their many translations."[39]

African women identify "cultural elements that are life-affirming for women in Africa whether they are validated by traditional Christian teaching or not."[40] They use narrative stories drawing from the African oral tradition, putting them side by side with the stories of women in the Bible. For Oduyoye, the retelling of stories was a traditional source of theology, but they seem to have been superseded by an analytical and deductive approach. Storytelling is another approach African women theologians take from feminist movements worldwide. The latter brought the stories back into academia, affirming their theological relevance.

An additional contribution of AWT is their articulation of how imperializing and patriarchal texts increase the anthropological poverty of women and, consequently, dampen their political participation. Lushombo borrows the concept of "anthropological poverty" from the African philosopher, theologian, and anthropologist Engelberg Mveng. He argues that this poverty is that of people who "sink into a kind

---

37. Maseno, "Gender and Christology in Africa for Social and Political Involvement," 58.

38. Oduyoye, *Daughters of Anowa*, 173.

39 Oduyoye, *Daughters of Anowa*, 174.

40. Oduyoye, *Introducing African Women's Theology*, 13.

of poverty which no longer concerns only the exterior or interior goods or possessions but [who are struck] at the very being, essence, and dignity of the human person."[41] Anthropologically impoverished people are bereft of their identity. Mveng considers anthropological poverty took root in the two main historical events of slavery and colonization. This poverty worsens by the many other patterns of destruction and pauperization that reinforce the enslaved and colonized's view of self as inferior.

Lushombo argues that what an imperialist and patriarchal reading of the Bible does to women, among other things, doubly impoverishes them anthropologically.[42] Dube's postcolonial reading of the Bible seeks to promote postcolonial subjects who do not perpetuate "a self-serving paradigm of constructing one group as superior to another."[43] For Lushombo, this paradigm is the endeavor of anthropological poverty.

Another contribution of AWT is the hermeneutics of Scriptures and cultures to re-read the legacy of resistance of African women historical figures as they do to re-read the stories of Kimpa Vita. Dube, Oduyoye, and Teresa Okure interpret the legacy of resistance using what they have called "*Talitha cum*" hermeneutics. African women's *Talitha cum* hermeneutics are ways to call on women to live and rise, even where she confronts oppressive powers that crush her at her very being.[44] Dube contends:

> *Talitha Cum* hermeneutics refers to the art of living in the resurrection space, the art of continually rising against the powers of death: the powers of patriarchy, the powers of colonial oppression and exploitation, the powers producing and perpetuating poverty, disease, and all forms of exclusion and dehumanization.[45]

It is a call to live as risen beings; this is a pressing call in African women's biblical hermeneutics and political theology.

AFRICAN WOMEN'S POLITICAL THEOLOGY

African women's political theology is pretty much in line with what Pui-lan defines as the task of postcolonial political theology. She argues "[P]olitical theologians must decolonize our minds and disengage from Eurocentrism and the colonial syndrome. A necessary first step is to rethink the history, scope, legacy, and concerns of political theology."[46]

African women's postcolonial political theology overall claims that to decolonize African minds, political governance needs to consider African values that favor

---

41. Mveng, "Impoverishment and Liberation," 157.
42. Lushombo, "Christological Foundations for Political Participation."
43. Dube Shomanah, *Postcolonial Feminist Interpretation of the Bible*, 15.
44. Dube Shomanah et al., *Postcolonial Perspectives in African Biblical Interpretations*, 34.
45. Dube Shomanah, "Talitha Cum Hermeneutics of Liberation," 138.
46. Pui-lan, "Postcolonial Intervention in Political Theology," 225.

democratic processes. These include respect for the sacredness of life and the African communal anthropology that promotes equal distribution of goods and solidarity—paying attention to new forms of politics that foster people's agency to address the challenges faced by their communities.

Oduyoye believes "men override culture when it does not suit them or are conservative when it suits them."[47] On the contrary, for the sake of the unit, African women themselves have internalized oppressive colonial patterns that make decolonizing minds more difficult. They tend to comply with the community's norms for the sake of the good of the same community. This internalization deepens their low self-esteem in the church and society, so they become accomplices in suppressing or disvaluing their participation.[48] This women's tendency makes the decolonizing task arduous in many parts of Sub-Saharan Africa. However, the decolonizing task is to be taken up not only by women themselves but also by the church as the body of Christ.

African women's political theology maintains that what hurts women in church and society hurts the entire body of Christ. Yet, for Oduyoye, "the Christian churches have not encouraged or even accommodated women who have raised their voices in protest."[49] African women theologians agree that women's beings, and all the factors doubly impoverishing them, seem not to be the church's concern. They remind that the church must take her task of empowering women to speak for themselves. The church must provide women spaces to access theological studies rather than obstruct their voices.

African women affirm women as political agents and continue to identify several postcolonial factors of the impoverishment of women in contemporary Africa. The first main factor is the many obstructions for women to influence the decisions that affect their own lives, and roles in church and society. The identification of these factors uses the cultural hermeneutic. Oduyoye suggests that the task of AWT is to question the criteria grounding these assigned and accepted roles and their efficiency for the flourishing of both church and society. In addition, the political theology of African women considers how the cultural taboos increase the culture of fear in women and impact their participation in politics.[50] AWT suggest that addressing these taboos is a task for both church and politics.

Oduyoye affirms that the seeds of marginalization of women at the socio-economic and political levels are found not only in the colonial policies but also within the African religious-cultural heritage. The latter simply helped the process of the former along. Likewise, both support the oppressive biblical gender norms onwards. The colonial policies that marginalized women succeeded to the extent that the African religious-cultural heritage favored African men to the detriment of women.

47. Oduyoye, "Feminist Theology in African Perspective," 175.
48. Oduyoye, *Introducing African Women's Theology*, 81.
49. Oduyoye, *Daughters of Anowa*, 183.
50. Oduyoye, "Feminist Theology in African Perspective," 172.

Oduyoye continues that the mothering ability of women gears them toward attention to life in general. Thus, they should be allowed to manage the community to whom they naturally give countlessly. She adds that the approach of African women is not a reactionary one to those of men; instead, it is that which thrives for good. This thriving drives their becoming subjects and agents in matters that affect their lives and their community. Oduyoye suggests it is only when the church will open the paths to women to become agents in decision-making affecting the church that the church "will become a home for both women and men."[51] A church that consistently and constantly overlooks women's voices, and the pastoral implications of the Gospel on their lives and theology, will be less likely to become an authentic voice of salvation—"Whatever is keeping subordination of women alive in the church cannot be the Spirit of God."[52] Nor can it be of Christ, whose teaching and attitudes have only been liberating to women.

AFRICAN WOMEN CHRISTOLOGICAL THOUGHTS

Considering that all Christologies are contextual,[53] African women theologians engage a christological question that Ela tried to respond to in his *African Cry*: Who is Jesus for the people who encounter him? Is the encounter with Jesus bringing about liberation and healing or "pain and tears"? How does the encounter with Jesus truly become good news?[54] Besides, African women theologians address several christological questions, including

1. What do African women say about Christ—who is Christ for African women?

2. Whether there is such a thing as women's Christology, and

3. Whether formal statements of Christology take into account women's experiences of life.

Although this paper's scope is not to respond to all of these questions, I will include a few insights shared in AWT.

Starting with Oduyoye and Amoah on the traditional christological claim that "Jesus is the Lord," they argue that this message affirmed the fact that the Christ hoped for by the Christian communities is the one whose lordship is expressed "in terms of a benevolent ruler."[55] A Christ who sacrifices himself to end human suffering and bring human beings into a new beginning is an eschatological one about the kingdom to come. This new beginning will come "*on the end of the age.*"

---

51. Oduyoye, *Daughters of Anowa*, 181.
52. Oduyoye, *Daughters of Anowa*, 182.
53. Maseno, "Gender and Christology in Africa for Social and Political Involvement," 58.
54. Éla, *African Cry*.
55. Okure, "Women in the Bible," 37.

African women's theologies include the African charismatic, independent churches in their approach to the lordship of Christ. These churches respond to future eschatology of the end of the age and the lordship of Christ by offering "*a Christus Victor.*" The churches see Christ the Healer as the center of Christology. The one who heals the wounds of women and turns the deaths of daily life into life. Christ heals now and today; he comes to comfort the people today. This consolation takes both the material and the spiritual dimensions. The many women involved in these churches embrace a Christ who affects their whole life. Nothing is outside the business of this Christ.

African women theologians also engage in dialogue with the Christology suggested by John Mbiti, who claims that, in African religious activities and beliefs, "No line is drawn between the spiritual and the physical."[56] Thus, African Christology affirms that Christ stands for spiritual-physical welfare. The people need a "Christ-Victor Christology" because they face the evil of any sort, the evil that denies them the sacredness of their humanity and abundant life. I argue that this vision of "Christ-Victor Christology" is one of the reasons why the prosperity gospel has grown on the African continent like mushrooms.

Women African theologians affirm the salvific christological function of the cross established by male theologians and go beyond what Christ means for the realities of their lives. The African woman's Christ is indeed the one who saves from the forces of death and gives a widow her child back when she is oppressed by any cultural norms that silence her and bend her over. It is the Christ that "transcends and transforms culture and has liberated [her] to do the same."[57] Christ for African women then becomes the liberator, companion, friend, teacher, and true Child supporting her mother, because as for the sacredness of all men and women, that of womanhood is also affirmed by Christ. For both Margaret Wanjiru and Anne Nasimiyu, the Christ for African women is "the anointed one who liberates from all oppression, the companion, friend, teacher and, caring compassionate nurturer of all."[58]

Christ is the Lord servant, teaching that the true sacrifice is freely and consciously made. He has broken down barriers of any sort. In him, the integrity of a woman caught up in a particularly oppressive culture is affirmed. In holding body and soul together, he has lifted any woman from the rituals and norms enslaving the body, whether grounded in patriarchal Christian thoughts or African traditions. He becomes a companion in performing mothering roles, bringing about life. African women's Christology seeks to formulate responses to the actual historical realities of each age and place. For this, it is more than the Christomonism male-centered approach; it is all-inclusive of women and their gifts and hardships.

---

56. Mbiti, *African Religions and Philosophy.*
57. Okure, "Women in the Bible," 43.
58. Maseno, "Gender and Christology in Africa for Social and Political Involvement," 67.

African women's political theology affirms that feminist liberation theology is not the panacea of Western Christianity, as some African male theologians tend to argue. It has roots in all cultures and histories, as the story of Kimpa Vita illustrates for the African setting. Oduyoye and Kanyoro, in *The Will to Arise,* draw essentially on historical African women's agency[59] to articulate their liberationist theologies.

To conclude, before 1989, African women's theologies were centered on retrieving the stories of the moral agency of women in history to confront the Christian message of liberation with the experiences of abuses and relegation of women at a lower level in church and society. Today, AWT continue to face dualistic anthropology when it comes to the views of women in cultural and socio-religious settings. In response to the Christian dualistic tendency, African women theologians bring up what Hinga calls the "theo-ethical challenges of gender binaries and disdain for the body"[60] in the scholarly theological debate. In this perspective of standing against such gender binaries and disdain of the body, African women theologians continually affirm a call to rise, the need for healing, and equal consideration of what endangers women's bodies and souls. They call all theologians and the church to coherent responses to allow men and women's empowering and liberating communication with God.

BIBLIOGRAPHY

Akossi-Mvongo, Marguerite. "The Church We Want: Ecclesia of Women in Africa?" In *The Church We Want: African Catholics Look to Vatican III*, edited by A. E. Orobator, 243–51. Maryknoll, NY: Orbis, 2016.

Arabome, Anne. "Dreams from My Mother, Prayers to My Father: Rethinking the Trinity of God, Woman, and Church." In *Feminist Catholic Theological Ethics: Conversations in the World Church*, edited by Linda Hogan and A. E. Orobator, 14–25. Maryknoll, NY: Orbis, 2014.

Ayanga, H. "Religio-Cultural Challenges in Women's Fight against HIV/AIDS in Africa." In *Women, Religion and HIV/AIDS in Africa: Responding to Ethical and Theological Challenges*, edited by Teresia M. Hinga, 34–48. Pietermaritzburg, South Africa: Cluster, 2008.

Dube Shomanah, Musa W. "Batswakwa: Which Traveller Are You?" In *The Bible in Africa: Transactions, Trajectories, and Trends*, edited by Gerald O. West and Musa W. Dube Shomanah, 150–62. Boston: Brill, 2000.

———. "Introduction." In *Other Ways of Reading: African Women and the Bible*, edited by Musa W. Dube Shomanah, 1–19. Atlanta: Society of Biblical Literature, 2001.

———, ed. *Other Ways of Reading: African Women and the Bible.* Atlanta: WCC, 2001.

———. *Postcolonial Feminist Interpretation of the Bible.* St. Louis: Chalice, 2000.

———. "The Scramble for Africa as the Biblical Scramble for Africa: Postcolonial Perspectives." In *Postcolonial Perspectives in African Biblical Interpretations*, edited by Musa W. Dube Shomanah et al., 1–26. Atlanta: Society of Biblical Literature, 2012.

---

59. Oduyoye and Kanyoro, *Will to Arise.*
60. Hinga, *African, Christian, Feminist,* xx.

———. "*Talitha Cum* Hermeneutics of Liberation: Some African Women's Ways of Reading the Bible." In *The Bible and the Hermeneutics of Liberation*, edited by Alejandro F. Botta and Pablo R. Andinach, 133–46. Atlanta: SBL, 2009.

Dube Shomanah, Musa W., et al., eds. *Postcolonial Perspectives in African Biblical Interpretations*. Atlanta: Society of Biblical Literature, 2012.

Éla, Jean-Marc. *African Cry*. Translated by Robert R. Barr. 1986. Repr. Eugene, OR: Wipf & Stock, 2005. Hinga, Teresia M. *African, Christian, Feminist: The Enduring Search for What Matters*. Maryknoll, NY: Orbis, 2017.

Kanyoro, Rachel Angogo. *Introduction to Feminist Cultural Hermeneutics: A Key to African Women's Liberation Theology*. London: Continuum, 2002.

Lushombo, Léocadie Wabo. "Christological Foundations for Political Participation: Women in the Global South Building Agency as Risen Beings." *Political Theology* (June 24, 2016) 1–24.

Magesa, Laurenti. *African Religion: The Moral Traditions of Abundant Life*. Maryknoll, NY: Orbis, 1997.

Maseno, Loreen. "Gender and Christology in Africa for Social and Political Involvement." Stellenbosch Theological Journal 6 (2020) 55–69.

Mbiti, John S. *African Religions and Philosophy*. 2nd rev. ed. Portsmouth, NH: Heinemann, 1990.

Mveng, Engelbert. "Impoverishment and Liberation: A Theological Approach for Africa and the Third World." In *Paths of African Theology*, edited by Rosino Gibellini, 154–65. Maryknoll, NY: Orbis, 1994.

Nadar, Sarojini. "Feminist Theologies in Africa." In *The Wiley-Blackwell Companion to African Religions*, edited by Elias Kifon Bongmba, 269–78. Malden, MA: Wiley-Blackwell, 2012.

———. "'Texts of Terror': The Conspiracy of Rape in the Bible, Church and Society: The Case of Esther 2:1–18." In *African Women, Religion, and Health: Essays in Honor of Mercy Amba Ewudziwa Oduyoye*, edited by Mercy Amba Oduyoye et al., 77–95. Maryknoll, NY: Orbis, 2006.

Odozor, Paulinus Ikechukwu. *Morality Truly Christian, Truly African: Foundational, Methodological, and Theological Considerations*. Notre Dame: University of Notre Dame, 2014.

Oduyoye, Mercy Amba. *Beads and Strands: Reflections of an African Woman on Christianity in Africa*. Maryknoll, NY: Orbis, 2004.

———. *Daughters of Anowa: African Women and Patriarchy*. Maryknoll, NY: Orbis, 1995.

———. "Feminist Theology in African Perspective." In *Paths of African Theology*, edited by Rosino Gibellini, 166–81. Maryknoll, NY: Orbis, 1994.

———. *Introducing African Women's Theology*. Sheffield: Sheffield Academic, 2001.

———, ed. *Transforming Power: Women in the Household of God: Proceedings of the Pan-African Conferences of the Circle of Concerned African Women Theologians*. Dansoman, Ghana: Sam Woode, 1997.

Oduyoye, Mercy Amba, and Rachel Angogo Kanyoro, eds. *The Will to Arise: Women, Tradition, and the Church in Africa*. Maryknoll, NY: Orbis, 1992.

Oduyoye, Mercy Amba, et al., eds. *African Women, Religion, and Health: Essays in Honor of Mercy Amba Ewudziwa Oduyoye*. Maryknoll, NY: Orbis, 2006.

Okure, Teresa. "Women in the Bible." In *With Passion and Compassion: Third World Women Doing Theology: Reflections from the Women's Commission of the Ecumenical Association of Third World Theologians*, edited by Virginia Fabella and Mercy Amba Oduyoye, 47–59. Eugene, OR: Wipf & Stock, 2006.

Orobator, A. E. *Theology Brewed in an African Pot*. Maryknoll, NY: Orbis, 2008.

Phiri, Isabel Apawo. "Southern Africa." In *An Introduction to Third World Theologies*, edited by John Parratt, 137–62. Cambridge: Cambridge University Press, 2004.

Phiri, Isabel Apawo, and Sarojini Nadar. "AWT." In *African Theology on the Way: Current Conversations*, edited by Diane B. Stinton, 90–100. London: SPCK, 2010.

Pui-lan, Kwok. "Postcolonial Intervention in Political Theology." *Political Theology* 17 (2016) 223–25.

Thornton, John K. *The Kongolese Saint Anthony: Dona Beatriz, Kimpa Vita and the Antonian Movement, 1684–1706*. Cambridge: Cambridge University Press, 1998.

SECTION 6

Emerging Theologies from Oceania

CHAPTER 24

Coconut Theology

SEFOROSA CARROLL

Coconut theology is an overarching umbrella term that describes both the emergence of contextual theologies in the Pacific as well as a reference to a particular Oceanic contextual theology. Coconut theology marks a watershed moment for Christianity in the Pacific, signifying the "liberation of the Pacific churches from the firm clutches of Western theology and Western culture which have been dominant and assumed superior for the last one hundred and fifty years."[1] In this sense coconut theology marked the beginning of two self-defining moments for Pacific theologies. The first was the affirmation that theology must indeed be contextual if it is to take seriously the concerns and issues of the local context. Secondly, the affirmation and recognition by Pacific theologians themselves that they possess the ability, skill, and knowledge to develop their own local theologies without having to depend on the received theologies of Christian missionaries or European theologians.

The term coconut theology is largely attributed to the Rev. Dr. Sione 'Amanaki Havea, the instigator of contextual theologies in the Pacific. Having not only perceived the need for contextualizing theology, he inspired and encouraged interest in its development[2] and most importantly "established a referent that other Oceanic contextual theologians could use to begin developing a discipline."[3] Havea had been challenged and inspired by a speech given by the then-governor general of Papua New Guinea, Sir John Guise, at the third Pacific Conference of Churches (PCC) Assembly in Port

---

1. Prior, "I Am the Coconut of Life," 37.
2. Forman, "Finding Our Own Voice," 116.
3. Tomlinson, *God is Samoan*, 66.

Moresby in 1976. Guise issued the challenge and question of when the Pacific would begin looking at a Pacific Christ instead of being content with a "Christ who was white faced, thin lipped and blue eyed."[4] Guise states:

> Reveal to us the Pacific Christ . . . Many thousands of Christians in the Pacific believe in the Christian faith, but they believe in Christ in an abstract form because Christ was not born in any of the Pacific countries; he may still be someone who does not belong to the soil of the Pacific.[5]

Guise's phrase "reveal to us the Pacific Christ" had struck a chord at the 1976 meeting. His challenge inspired the beginning of contextual theologies in the Pacific leading to several consultations on theological education and conferences on Pacific theology. Reflecting on Guise's challenge, Havea notes that it "perhaps was a starting point, which led our thoughts to go beyond the Pacific Christ as a picture to a Pacific Theology as a theme."[6]

"REVEAL TO US THE PACIFIC CHRIST"

Pacific Christologies and more broadly Pacific theologies are an attempt to earth Jesus in Pacific soil or in the Pacific context—a necessary need perceived out of the growing awareness that the Christianity inherited and later perpetuated by European or Western theologies was somewhat foreign or alien and served only as a lingering reminder of Christian missions and colonialism.[7] Leslie Boseto complained that

> when missionaries came to the mission fields they transplanted Western faith in a theological pod, and instead of taking out the "plant" and placing it in the local soil, they kept it in the pod and nurtured it with a Western environment and climate. This Christianity has been seen and taken as a foreign religion.[8]

Havea went a step further, asserting that the missionary endeavour packed more than the gospel or biblical text in their suitcases. Havea was troubled by the foreignness of the gospel and the notion that the Gospel had come to the Pacific as a secondhand message "relayed and handed over by the missionaries."[9] Havea claimed the good news was a simultaneous event, effective and available to all at the time of Christ. The gospel, therefore, did not arrive with the missionaries, the good news was already

---

4. Cited in Koria, "Moving Toward a Pacific Theology," 3.

5. From the speech by Sir John Guise delivered at the third General Assembly of the Pacific Conference of Churches in Port Moresby in 1976. Cited in Tuwere, "Agenda for the Theological Task of the Church in Oceania," 8.

6. Havea, "Foreword," 7.

7. For more on the development of Pacific Christologies in the Pacific and the Pacific diaspora, see Carroll, "Weaving New Spaces."

8. Cited in Havea, "Pacific Theology," 21.

9. Havea, "The Pacific and Theology in World Perspective," 63.

present. He argued that the missionaries' role was to make known the "Good News that was already here before they came!"[10] In this sense Jesus was introduced as a foreign figure in Pacific soil. He "embodied" less of the gospel and more of the culture and history of the missionizing and colonizing cultures.[11] The missionaries presented a Christ of their own image and culture; a fair-skinned Jesus with blond hair and blue eyes. The gospel values they espoused were entangled within their own cultural values. By the time Jesus was proclaimed and made known in the Pacific he had been cut off from his historical roots and Jewish history.

Alan Davidson describes the arrival of Christianity into the Pacific as an "exotic plant" and although "Christianity often retained many of its nineteenth-century European characteristics, it nevertheless penetrated deeply into people's culture, shaped their identity, and became a central part of village life."[12] In most if not all colonies Christian mission was inevitably linked with colonization. The missionary enterprise, which usually preceded colonization, was in most cases a civilizing mission. According to Neil Gunson, the missionary was the chief promoter of civilization, whereby colonization was regarded as the most efficient means of effecting Christian civilization. The idea that the role of the missionary was to introduce civilization together with the doctrine of the cross was developed into a principle missionary enterprise.[13]

This "redemptive process" wove its way through the process of education, the teaching of new methods of farming, trades, skills, building of proper houses, clothing, and through values and cultures of the native people. A remaining legacy of mission and colonial history is the continuing domination and influence of Western and European theologies on Pacific Christian identity, God, and church. It is against this history that the work of contextual Pacific theologies seek to address and redress. A common feature of Pacific theologies is their intent and effort to liberate Pacific theology from Western theology and Western culture.[14]

The 1985 theological education consultation in Suva followed by the first Evangelical Consultation on Pacific Theology held in Papua New Guinea in 1986 marked the beginning of the new era of Pacific theology. The purpose of the 1986 consultation was to provide the opportunity for Pacific Christians to discuss "what God's message

---

10. Havea, "Christianity in the Pacific Context," 12.

11. In a plenary discussion of the 1985 theological consultation in Fiji, the comment was made that the gospel came in a foreign package by Western missionaries. And although most of the South Pacific missionaries have been islanders since 1797, they too proclaimed a foreign message wherever they went. This, therefore, is an indication that the gospel was clothed in a foreign package and a foreign message proclaimed. See Havea, "Plenary Discussion," 25–28. In addition, the idea of foreign or foreigner embodied in the image/body of Jesus (fair-skinned, blonde, and blue-eyed) served to alienate the natives further. Jesus was introduced as a foreigner—Jesus was a foreigner. The notion of foreignness needs further interrogation.

12. Davidson, "Mapping Christianity Taking Root in Oceania," 21.

13. Gunson, *Messengers of Grace.*

14. Gibbs, "Emerging Indigenous Theologies in Oceania," 39.

means for Pacific peoples and how this message can be effectively communicated."[15] These consultations were significant as it was at both that Havea introduced a theological framework and basis for Pacific theology and his concept of coconut theology. Havea's work laid the initial groundwork and inspired interest in contextualizing Christian faith, theology, and earthing the gospel in Pacific soil. These consultations can be described as the defining moments for contextualizing and (re)locating Jesus in the Pacific. It also marked the era of the reinterpretation of Christianity by Pacific people themselves.[16]

Havea believed that in order for Pacific people to grasp the depth and meaning of God's salvific acts through the person and ministry of Jesus, the gospel needed to be understood within a Pacific worldview. He was of the firm view that theology is a gift from God describing it as "God's revelation to history and culture."[17] On this premise he believed an effort should be made to interpret the gospel from within "our history, culture and customs to illustrate in the light of the Good News, what God is like and is doing to us in his saving acts of revelation and salvation."[18] The gospel would cease being a foreign or a secondhand message to Pacific people, if it was experienced through Pacific eyes, heard and listened to with Pacific ears.

Havea described the task of Pacific theology as "an effort to put faith and the gospel in the local soil and context, so that they can exist in a local climate."[19] Theology, Havea maintained, "is a vehicle that could be used in discovering God in His hiddenness."[20] Theology is not something to be worshiped but rather to be used as "a torch to help us find our directions for knowing, worshipping and adoring our God of Creation and Salvation."[21] As a measure of theological accountability Havea identified "three yardsticks to test the strength of our thinking" and that which is "necessary for judging and approval of our theological thinking."[22] For Havea, the three criterion for Pacific contextual theologies are the Bible, what is proven throughout history, and relevancy in the current time.

In emphasizing the particularities of context, Havea equally stressed the importance of the universality of the gospel. Havea expressed this in several ways. In his seminal paper, "Christianity in the Pacific Context," Havea made a clear distinction between indigenization and contextuality, arguing that contextualization had to move beyond indigenization. He referred to indigenization as "the cultures, history and

---

15. Johnson, "Introduction," 9.
16. See Forman, "Finding Our Own Voice."
17. Havea, "Pacific Theology," 21.
18. Havea, "Christianity in the Pacific Context," 11.
19. Havea, "Christianity in the Pacific Context," 2.
20. Havea, "Pacific and Theology in World Perspective," 64.
21. Havea, "Pacific and Theology in World Perspective," 64.
22. Havea, "Pacific and Theology in World Perspective," 64.

customs of the people that grow out of the local soil."[23] Contextualization encompasses indigenization but moves beyond the local soil to consider the "sociological, political and environmental events of the past, present and even the future."[24] Havea, it seems was very aware of the risks of contextualization, mindful of how easy it would be to create a culturally and theologically myopic Christ shaped in the image of the Pacific Islander with no significant relevance beyond the region. Pacific theologies should engage and speak prophetically to the soteriological concerns and needs within and beyond the region.

Secondly, Havea asserts a Pacific theology should not only be regional but seek also to have universal relevance. Reflecting on the term Pacific theology, Havea contends that although the Pacific is limited to its region, theology, in general, refers to a wider range which must be viewed in its global and universal context. "We may reflect on the regional soil etc. for our understanding of what is relevant and near, but we must bear in mind that theology should relate and convey its meaning to benefit each individual in the community of faith in the global and universal context."[25] Drawing on the life and context of Jesus as an example, Havea noted that although Jesus's "parables were limited to his culture and environment, the meanings of and theological interpretations of the parables were universal; their catholicity relevant to the whole ecumenical community."[26] Therefore, theology, Havea contends, "must not be compartmentalized exclusively into one region but must be seen as a vehicle to convey to the believer the quality and richness of our quest to know God in His hiddenness. Theology is not an end in itself but a process and growth which opens the door of understanding to him who asks, seeks and knocks (Matthew 7:7)."[27]

Pacific theologies draw from within their cultures, using symbols, objects, culturally embedded concepts, myths, and legends to deepen, shape, and reconstruct their theologies. Havea began with the question—What if Jesus was a Pacific Islander? Havea insists that if Jesus had grown up and lived in the Pacific, he would have added another identification of himself—"I am the coconut of life." The coconut is chosen as it is fundamental to the existence of life in the Pacific Islands. Coconut trees are to be found on every island. It's significance for developing a Pacific contextual theology cannot be underscored. Havea's use of the coconut was an attempt to put faith and the gospel in the local soil and in the local context so it can exist in the local climate.

Havea's coconut theology comprises of three themes Christology, *kairos,* and communion. In terms of Christology, the coconut is "life" in two ways. The first is that the coconut supports and sustains the everyday life of the islanders. Coconuts are a life

---

23. Havea, "Christianity in the Pacific Context," 10.
24. Havea, "Christianity in the Pacific Context," 11.
25. Havea, "Christianity in the Pacific Context," 11.
26. Havea, "Christianity in the Pacific Context," 12.
27. Havea, "Christianity in the Pacific Context," 11.

source in the islands. Every part of the coconut tree is used in some way to sustain life on the islands by way of shelter, food, and everyday utensils and utilities.

Secondly, the life cycle of the coconut parallels or symbolizes the events of incarnation, death, resurrection, ascension, and Pentecost. The coconut fruit grows at the top of the coconut tree; when it ripens, it falls to the ground below. Given the nature of its shape it will roll to the lowest point of the ground where it will stop. If it is left on the ground, it will undergo a process whereby the coconut dies. In this way the fallen and disregarded coconut produces a new tree, which itself produces fruit to satisfy people's hunger and thirst. An image made more powerful by the fact that the coconut has "two eyes" and a "mouth"—the mouth being the part where the juice is consumed. Each coconut has a human face—it bears the image of the One who has given her/him life.[28]

The biblical parallels are obvious. Jesus was at first in the presence of the Father, equal with God on high—but he did not remain there. At the right time he came down to earth, descending to the lowest points of human life. In his life journey and ministry he was discarded and left to die. From his death and broken body came new life, a life which has produced "food and drink" to satisfy the hunger and thirst of the world.[29]

The second theme of coconut theology is *kairos*. Here Havea links the ripening of the coconut with both the Pacific notion of time (often referred to as "coconut time") and the biblical notion of the fullness of time both in the Old Testament (as in Eccl 3:1–8), and in the New Testament notion of *kairos* (Mark 1:15). The coconut ripens and falls to the ground when it is ready. The ripening of the coconut cannot be hurried or slowed and is thereby understood as a process beyond human control and "governed by forces beyond humanity."[30] In "coconut time" everything happens when it is meant to, be it yesterday, tomorrow, or today. In "coconut time," everything happens in good time. Havea maintains that in "coconut time" it is not whether one is late or early, what matters is the assigned task is completed and the mission fulfilled.[31] The Pacific understanding of "coconut time" is connected with the theological notion of time as "fulfilled time," or time as "opportunity," the "right time," "God's time," time as "grace."[32]

The third element of Havea's coconut theology is Communion. Havea argues that the coconut is more relevant than the bread and wine in the Pacific context. He makes the point that the use of unleavened bread and wine are contextual. In addition, unleavened bread and wine are very expensive to import into the Pacific. Havea makes the compelling argument that unlike the wheat and grape that are two separate elements, the coconut has both food and drink from the same fruit like the blood and

---

28. Prior, "I Am the Coconut of Life," 34.
29. Prior, "I Am the Coconut of Life," 33–34.
30. Prior, "I Am the Coconut of Life," 34.
31. Havea, "Pacific Theology," 24.
32. Prior, "I Am the Coconut of Life," 34.

flesh from the one and the same body of Christ.[33] Havea asserts "I am convinced that if Christ had grown up in the Pacific he would have used the coconut to represent the body which was bruised and crushed, and the juice for the blood as elements of the Holy Eucharist."[34] The development of communion liturgies and its practice has been used in some Pacific churches over the years but it has not been widely adopted as a common practice.

Mikaele Paunga observes that a limitation of coconut theology is its application to the Pacific migrant communities in the diaspora whereby the term "coconut" is a form of belittlement.[35] Describing the diasporic experience of Pacific migrants in New Zealand, Paunga notes the term "coconut people" has been applied to Pacific migrants as a label that marks them as "undisciplined, uneducated, uncivilized and unmannered."[36] Interestingly, in making sense of his experience as a second generation Samoan in New Zealand through reconstructing his Christology, Risatisone Ete adopts "the stupid coconut" as one of his titles for Jesus. Ete cleverly subverts and transforms the understanding of the "stupid coconut" by applying it to Jesus. Ete's point is that Jesus was seen as the stupid coconut because he would not conform to the structures of a supposedly pure society. He was branded "other," "different," someone who foolishly thought himself more enlightened than the rest. Ete maintains that it is "this image of Christ who encounters the New Zealand born Samoan experience, the Christ who stands with us as one who has been misunderstood, rejected, humiliated by a world that would not recognise him as one of its own."[37]

Alongside this image and based on the biblical image of the "foolishness of God," Ete contextualizes the image of Christ again by placing alongside it the Samoan image and notion of the vale. The vale is the village idiot, who has no social standing and is an outcast. Furthermore, Ete engages with Christian tradition and affirms the dual identity of Jesus—being fully human and fully divine. In addition, he employs the identities and roles common to the *fa'a* Samoa in his attempt to link the Gospel and culture—"an attempt to bring forth a Samoan articulation of Jesus which might resonate with the historical Jesus of the Gospels."[38] Jesus is therefore *matai*—his chief, a term which carries the connotation of being set apart or consecrated. To speak of Jesus as the *matai* is essentially to speak of him as one "set apart from us, a transcendent being, who is far removed from our life situations."[39] Therefore, to avoid a one-sided Christology and to balance the shortcomings of the *matai* image, Ete employs the image of the *vale*—the village idiot.

33. Havea, "Christianity in the Pacific Context," 14.
34. Havea, "Christianity in the Pacific Context," 5.
35. Paunga, "Contextual Theologies from Oceania," 73.
36. Paunga, "Contextual Theologies from Oceania," 73.
37. Ete, "Bridge in My Father's House," 21.
38. Ete, "Bridge in My Father's House," 24.
39. Ete, "Bridge in My Father's House," 24.

A recent and important development of coconut theology is that by I-Kiribati theologian Tioti Timon. In the context of climate change and the changing climate in the Pacific, Timon and Kaunda apply and expand the coconut theology developed by Havea to include and respond to issues of climate change using the medium of climate change songs in the I-Kiribati context. Timon and Kaunda are writing from within the context of "disappearing islands." Kiribati is currently one of five low-lying atoll islands in the Pacific at major risk and heavily impacted by climate change and in particular sea level rise.

Timon and Kaunda argue that coconut theology is inherent and "embedded within an indigenous knowledge thought-system and the daily cultural experiences of the Kiribati people."[40] They draw on the understanding of the coconut tree as critical and integral to Kiribati life. In the Kiribati context the coconut tree is understood as a divine source of all being and thereby critical to the existence of human life on the island. The coconut tree stands as both metaphor and faithful reminder of the God who sustains life in Kiribati. The coconut tree "provides food, shelter, and medicine and reminds the islanders of the life-giving God always available to them; and by growing along the coast, it protects the land from erosion." The coconut tree is not just a physical plant but a "spiritual statement symbolizing God's earthly presence. In the presence of the tree, the people are always reminded that they are living in full connection with the ultimate source of life—God."[41] As indigenous knowledge and theory, Timon and Kaunda assert "Coconut theology captures how Kiribati people define, construct, and make meaning of their experiences of God in part through their daily interactions with the coconut tree." In Kiribati cosmology and worldview, the coconut tree is "embedded within an ecological and relational understanding of God as the ultimate source of life."[42] This inherent knowledge is transmitted through songs. Timon and Kaunda explain coconut theology as "theory rooted within ecology and rationality uses song to connect the past with the present and the poor with the rich in order to improve the future."[43]

In their analysis of the I-Kiribati climate change songs, Timon and Kaunda demonstrate how coconut theology is expressed in three theological themes: resistance, lamentation and faith. In each of the three theological themes coconut theology is applied as a liberative and prophetic critique of context (local and global), culture and theology. As a theology of resistance, these songs speak out against the injustices of colonialism and globalization which has inevitably contributed to and caused Kiribati's current predicament. The church is also challenged to move beyond its "narrow focus on the theology of the salvation of the soul"[44] and "to stand against injustice in the lives

40. Timon and Kaunda, "'I Stand in the Middle of the Ocean,'" 1.
41. Timon and Kaunda, "'I Stand in the Middle of the Ocean,'" 1.
42. Timon and Kaunda, "'I Stand in the Middle of the Ocean,'" 1.
43. Timon and Kaunda, "'I Stand in the Middle of the Ocean,'" 2.
44. Timon and Kaunda, "'I Stand in the Middle of the Ocean,'" 4.

of the poor and voiceless"⁴⁵ especially those feeling the direct impact of climate change. As a theology of lamentation, these songs raise questions of what the future might be "as the sea level gradually creeps up and our islands are washed away?"⁴⁶

I-Kiribati songs of lamentation raise the challenge of the role and the ability of the church in providing effective theologies that are able to sustain people in their faith as they respond to and meet the bleak reality of their future as people, land, and culture. As a theology of faith, strong connections are drawn between the mission of the church in the context of climate change and environmental degradation alongside the promise of the fullness of life as advocated by Jesus in John 10:10. Here the faith in God the Creator is affirmed and simultaneously questions are raised about how faith in God affects perspectives on climate change. The church is challenged to be more eco-missional in its outreach and urged to be transformed through a deeper understanding of the interrelatedness and interconnectedness of humans and creation.

FUTURE TRAJECTORIES

Havea set the ball rolling by establishing a foundation and theological methodology that others could further add to and develop. I do not believe that he intended to carve anything in stone but rather to inspire, enable and begin the contextual theological project in the Pacific. His theological work marked a moment of permission giving as well as inspired the creative imagination of Pacific churches, leaders, and theologians to contextualize their theological thinking. I noted earlier that coconut theology is also an umbrella term used to describe the emerging contextual theologies in the Pacific. Many other Oceanic theologians have followed after Havea in developing their own expressions of "coconut theology" for their context. Themes such as land (*vanua*),⁴⁷ sea (*moana*),⁴⁸ community (*maneaba*),⁴⁹ and gender⁵⁰ are among the several explored since Havea's seminal paper on coconut theology.

One of the strongest critics of the Pacific contextual theologies in general is Tongan biblical theologian Ma'afu Palu. Palu believes that the Pacific contextual project has reduced theology into anthropology with its overemphasis on culture, context, and reflections on contemporary issues at the expense of Scripture.⁵¹ He is adamant that the Pacific Christ articulated by Pacific theologians is ontologically displaced from the Jesus Christ of the Bible indicting them for recreating Jesus in their own image

---

45. Timon and Kaunda, "'I Stand in the Middle of the Ocean,'" 5.
46. Timon and Kaunda, "'I Stand in the Middle of the Ocean,'" 7.
47. Tuwere, *Vanua*.
48. Halapua, *Waves of God's Embrace*.
49. See the following from Paunga, "Contextual Theologies from Oceania," 73–76; Boseto, "God as Community," 41–45.
50. Kanongata'a, "Pacific Women's Theology of Birthing and Liberation."
51. Palu, "Pacific Theology," 49.

as Pacific Islanders.⁵² Palu identifies that a major flaw these theological constructions share is that they are profoundly impractical at the grassroots level of the church.⁵³ Although I disagree with the basis of Palu's assertions against Pacific theologies, he has, however, highlighted some critical areas for ongoing theological reflection and development.

Palu brings to the fore the risks of contextuality if the theological methodology is not carried out well. As Gibbs has articulated "the 'What if' process provides an opportunity for creativity based on life experience but when done poorly it amounts to substituting a symbol for revelation."⁵⁴ The question of revelation, of the good news already being present in the Pacific before the missionaries came still needs further exploration, especially in relation to how revelation is or can be understood through indigenous epistemologies. This will be a critical and important area of work for the Pacific considering the economical, ecological, and development challenges it is facing. The second area of critical work is contextualizing faith and incarnating Jesus at the very local level. Palu is correct in his assessment, despite the contextual work undertaken since the 1980s, the majority of Pacific Islanders still hold an understanding of a mechanistic God who yields absolute power and control over everything.⁵⁵ Cecile Rubow and Cliff Bird in their survey on ecological responses to climate change in Oceania found many churches still hold a literalist view of the Bible and believe that God is in control of the weather.⁵⁶ Upolu Vaai asserts that in order for "churches to be dynamic and effective in addressing the new emerging social issues such as the climate crisis, they have to firstly critically address their faith and theological foundations to meet the challenges of such a crisis."⁵⁷

Jesus the "coconut of life" is still not fully earthed in Pacific soil, in many ways he is still a foreigner removed from the daily experiences of life in the Pacific in the sense that faith has no bearing on what we ought to be doing in the here and now in terms of discipleship. This leads to a third area of exploration which is that of enabling and strengthening connections between faith, and transformative action in the public sphere. The divide and understanding between faith as belonging to the private sphere and thereby having nothing to do with issues belonging to the public sphere still exists.

Ete, Timon and Kaunda, and Pacific feminist writers highlight in their theologies what coconut theology is often critiqued to be missing. Unlike contextual liberational theologies of Africa, Asia, and Latin America, Pacific contextual theologies did not arise from a response to economic and political struggle. The contextual project began and has been undertaken by intellectual elites. The earlier Pacific contextual theologies

52. Palu, "Pacific Theology," 40.
53. Palu, "Pacific Theology," 34.
54. Gibbs, "Emerging Indigenous Theologies in Oceania," 39.
55. Vaai, "'We Are Therefore We Live,'" 11.
56. Rubow and Bird, "Eco-Theological Responses to Climate Change in Oceania," 159.
57. Vaai, "'We Are Therefore We Live,'" 3.

tended to idealize culture offering little critique of it. But the Pacific theological landscape is changing as Pacific church leaders, communities, and theologians become more acutely aware of the need for pastoral, prophetic, and practical theologies.[58]

The challenge and future of any Pacific theology is threefold. On the one hand it must be able to be self-critical. It must be open and strong enough to critique our own cultural biases and oppressions within our own communities—some of these being the culturally traditional subservient place of women, which condones and perpetuates violence against women, the oppressive hierarchal relationship between people of different classes, the violence and marginalization of those of different sexual orientations, and the perpetuated violence and oppression between races. Secondly, Pacific theologies must continue to respond to and critique, even resist the place/space, image, and identity imposed by the Western world or host culture on us and compel us to appropriate action. Thirdly, Pacific theologies must respond to and address issues of development, ecology and climate change, and social justice that will invite and spur people into action. This third point is at present a pressing issue and one that the Pacific Conference of Churches is addressing through their mandate "Re-thinking the Household of God."[59] Perhaps in this phase of time we will experience more of the development of the public, prophetic, practical, and liberational aspects of Pacific "coconut" theologies and Christologies that compel just, compassionate, and liberating action.

BIBLIOGRAPHY

Boseto, Leslie. "God as Community—God in Meleanesian Community." *Pacific Journal of Theology* 2 (1993) 41–45.
Carroll, Seforosa. "Weaving New Spaces: Christological Perspectives from Oceania (Pacific) and the Oceanic Diaspora." *Studies in World Christianity* 10 (2004) 72–92.
Davidson, Allan K. "Mapping Christianity Taking Root in Oceania." In *Concilium*, edited by Dennis Gira et al., 13–22. London: SCM, 2010.
Ete, Risatisone Ben. "A Bridge in My Father's House: New Zealand Born Samoans Talk Theology." Bachelor of Theology diss., University of Otago, 1996.
Forman, Charles W. "Finding Our Own Voice: The Reinterpreting of Christianity by Oceanian Theologians." *International Bulletin of Missionary Research* 29 (2005) 115–52.
Gibbs, Philip. "Emerging Indigenous Theologies in Oceania." In *Concilium*, edited by Dennis Gira, Diego Irrarazaval, and Elaine Wainwright, 34–44. London: SCM, 2010.
Gunson, Neil. *Messengers of Grace: Evangelical Missionaries in the South Seas 1797–1860*. Oxford: Oxford University Press, 1978.
Halapua, Winston. *Waves of God's Embrace: Sacred Perspectives from the Ocean*. London: Canterbury, 2008.

---

58. The two following theses are demonstrative of the changing Pacific theological landscape and contextual methodology: Ropeti-Apisaloma, "Nafanua Theology," and Lusama, "Vaa Fesokotaki."

59. Pacific Conference of Churches, *Re-Thinking the Household of God*.

Havea, Sione 'Amanaki. "Christianity in the Pacific Context." In *South Pacific Theology: Papers from the Consultation on Pacific Theology, Papua New Guinea, January 1986*, 10–15. Parramatta, Australia: Pacific Conference of Churches, 1987.

———."Foreword." In *South Pacific Theology: Papers from the Consultation on Pacific Theology Papua New Guinea 1986*, 7. World Vision International South Pacific & Regnum, 1987.

———. "Is a Pacific Christ Possible?." In *Papauta 1978: South Pacific Consultation on Theological Education January 10–17, 1978*, 111–13. Suva, Fiji: Pacific Conference of Churches, 1980.

———. "The Pacific and Theology in World Perspective." In *Papauta 1978: South Pacific Consultation on Theological Education January 10–17, 1978*, 63–65. Suva, Fiji: Lotu Pasifika, 1980.

———."Pacific Theology." In *Towards a Relevant Pacific Theology: The Role of the Churches and Theological Education*, 21–24. Suva, Fiji: Lotu Pasifika Productions, 1986.

———. "Plenary Discussion." In *Papauta 1978: South Pacific Consultation on Theological Education January 10–17, 1978*, 25–28. Suva, Fiji: Pacific Conference of Churches, 1980.

Johnson, Lydia, and Joan Alleluia Filemoni-Tofaeono, eds. *Weavings: Women Doing Theology in Oceania*. Suva, Fiji: South Pacific of Association of Theological Schools & Institute for Pacific Studies, 2003.

Johnson, R. Boyd. "Introduction." In *South Pacific Theology: Papers from the Consultation on Pacific Theology, Papua New Guinea, January 1986*, 9. Parramatta: Regnum, 1987.

Kanongata'a, Keiti Ann. "A Pacific Women's Theology of Birthing and Liberation." *Pacific Journal of Theology* Series II, 7 (1992) 3–11.

Koria, Paulo. "Moving toward a Pacific Theology: Theologising with Concepts." *Pacific Journal of Theology* Series II, 22 (1999) 3–14.

Lusama, Tafue Molu. "Vaa Fesokotaki: A Mafulifuli Reconstruction of the Theology of Te Atua for a New Climate Change Story." PhD diss., Pacific Theological College, 2021.

Pacific Conference of Churches. *Re-Thinking the Household of God: Towards a Region of Sufficiency, Solidarity, Inclusiveness and Participation*. Suva, Fiji: Pacific Conference of Churches, 2010.

Palu, Ma'afu. "Pacific Theology: A Re-Consideration of Its Methodology." *Pacific Journal of Theology* Series II, 38 (2005) 30–58.

Paunga, Mikaele. "Contextual Theologies from Oceania." In *The Pacific Islands: Society, Culture, Religion*, edited by Manfred Ernst et al., 68–82. Suva: Pacific Theological College, 2009.

Prior, Randall. "I Am the Coconut of Life: An Evaluation of Coconut Theology." *Pacific Journal of Theology* Series II, 10 (1993) 31–40.

Ropeti-Apisaloma, Marie Penelope. "Nafanua Theology: A Samoan-Christian Argument for the Ordination of Women in the Congregational Christian Church of Samoa." PhD diss., Pacific Theological College, 2021.

Rubow, Cecilie, and Cliff Bird. "Eco-Theological Responses to Climate Change in Oceania." *WorldViews* 20 (2016) 150–68.

Timon, Tioti, and Chammah J. Kaunda. "'I Stand in the Middle of the Ocean': The Emerging Coconut Theology of Climate Change in Kiribati." *Pharos Journal of Theology* 100 (2019) 1–12.

Tomlinson, Matt. *God is Samoan: Dialogues between Culture and Theology in the Pacific*. Pacific Islands Monograph Series. Honolulu: University of Hawaii Press, 2020.

Tuwere, I. S. *Vanua: Towards a Fijian Theology of Place.* Suva, Fiji: Institute of Pacific Studies, University of South Pacific and College of St John the Evangelist, 2002.

Tuwere, Sevati. "An Agenda for the Theological Task of the Church in Oceania." *Pacific Journal of Theology* Series II, 13 (1995) 5–14.

Vaai, Upolu Lumā. "'We Are Therefore We Live': Pacific Eco-Relational Spirituality and Changing the Climate Change Story." *Toda Peace Institute Policy Brief* 56 (2019) 1–14.

CHAPTER 25

Oceania Theology

RANDALL PRIOR

The notion behind the term "Oceania theology" needs some explanation. At first it suggests the sort of theology, or theologies, that might be found within the geographical region of Oceania. This region includes the island nations of Micronesia, Polynesia, and Melanesia, together with the two nations more commonly aligned with the Western cultural world but each with their own indigenous or first peoples—Australia and New Zealand. The first peoples of each of these two nations share cultural similarities with the island peoples across the expanse of Oceania—the first peoples of Australia more closely connected to Melanesian cultures, those of New Zealand, Maori, having affinity with Polynesian cultures.

However, the term Oceania theology was adopted in the first instance, not as a geographical description, but rather in order to shape a theology that engages the fundamental worldview which is embedded within the many cultures located within the geographical region. In other words, Oceania theology was both geographical and cultural at one and the same time. Therefore, in order to understand this particular theology which, over the last three decades has become an increasingly significant theology, we need to understand certain core aspects of the cultural worldview that has inspired it. For those whose primary culture is the one shaped by the categories of a post-Enlightenment Western world, entering the Oceania worldview will seem like entering another planet. For that reason, the ideas and concepts that gave rise to Oceania theology are best introduced with a concrete case study, and one about the concept: *land*.

A CASE STUDY

"Land" among the small community of people in Kole Village on East Coast Santo in northern Vanuatu—a personal account from a member of the village church.[1]

This case study tells the story of the narrator's own tribal community and its families. For many generations past, they have lived as a harmonious community but in very recent times the situation has changed quite suddenly and dramatically. The people have found themselves in the unusual circumstance of open hostility and deep division which has had an impact on every facet of village life, including the narrator's own village church. The one source for this sudden change from harmony to hostility is land disputes.

The case study is narrated in two parts. The first part introduces the cultural importance of land; the second identifies how land has become the source of hostilities, and why that matters.[2]

Part One: The village story—the importance of land

Our ancestors all understood that the land they lived on was given to them by a superior being—a local god—known as *Ietaro*. Their understanding was that land was integral to their whole world; it was the basis upon which life was to be lived, the foundations of their customs and culture. Every clan within the tribe had its own inherited land area; the land belonged to the clan and the clan belonged to the land. We cultivated the land to produce food for daily survival, and for ritual occasions. All farming was subsistence farming so that what the people grew was for their own consumption. There was no such thing as individual land ownership; the land was a communal home: without the land the people could not exist, and without the people, the land was without purpose. Our whole life was lived on this land and was nurtured and sustained by this land.

The boundaries of land separating the clans were determined by distinctive geographical features—hills, valleys, creeks, volcanoes, stones, trees. Certain places on a clan's land were set aside for ritual purposes or were considered taboo for particular reasons of significance. Through the generations, a clan's land was passed down via a patrilineal system; it could never be bought or sold.

Our connection with the land was a deep spiritual connection. One of our chiefs (Chief Segion) described the land in this way: "The land is a mother to us; it provides all our human needs—it feeds us, gives us shelter, as well as a place of eternal rest when we die. The land defines the identity of our people."[3]

---

1. Paul, "Ownership," 202–16.
2. What follows is a summary of the full story.
3. Paul, "Ownership," 209–10.

The Bigger Story

This is a personal description arising from a tiny village in a remote part of Oceania, but it is recounted here because it is representative of a bigger story that embraces all the peoples of Vanuatu, indeed of Oceania.

Across the islands of Vanuatu, there are over one hundred distinct and different languages, which means over one hundred distinct and different cultural groups. Despite the diversity that spans these cultural entities, all the peoples hold in common a worldview that knows the intimate bond that connects the people and their land. At a 2002 national assembly workshop on "Gospel and Culture in Vanuatu," a group of eight men and women from the very southern island group reflected:

> In the past people considered land from two points of view. First, land was culturally the source of the whole of life. Land was treated with love and honor. Relationships among the people, and between people and the environment, depended on what the land produced. Even local names and characters were powerless without the land because names reflected people's association with the land.[4]

Stretching across the region of Oceania, including the first peoples of Australia and New Zealand, there are a vast number of cultures with diverse customs in terms of land ownership and usage, but there is one common thread that unites them all, namely that human life is nurtured and sustained within the profound intimacy between the people and the land. This intimacy defines human life as that which is lived within the life-giving "womb" of a motherly creation. A voice from Fiji:

> Indigenous Fijians have a strong sense of belonging to the land, and it is from this that they draw a definitive sense of what it means to be a human being. It is not so much a matter of *finding meaning* as belonging to the *vanua* (land or place), the basis of life on earth. A person does not own the land; rather, the *vanua* owns him or her.[5]

Another voice, this time from Maori in New Zealand:

> For Maori in New Zealand, human beings and everything in creation have a *wairua*, a divine sparkle that comes from the gods; respect for nature and creation is a natural consequence of this belief. Atua is the supreme God that is beyond any knowledge. Atua can also mean Rangi and Papa—the Sky Father and the Earth Mother—different forces of nature. A strong connection exists between the material world and the spiritual world. *Whakapapa* (genealogy) links animate and inanimate things, terrestrial and spiritual worlds, and is

---

4. Prior, *Gospel and Culture*, 3:22.
5. Tuidrakulu, "Fiji," 91.

what binds all things, interconnecting them. In Maori culture (therefore), land has a deep meaning.[6]

For those who live in cultures shaped by Western cultural categories perhaps one way of appreciating this Oceania concept is to recognize that every member of the community, from the moment of their birth through to their death, is gifted with three basic necessities for well-being: a home to live in, food to eat, and mutually supportive community life. A rich tapestry of rituals and festivities sustain these things. In striking contrast, those who live in a Western cultural world, with its very different worldview, may be deprived of any one or more of these three basic necessities, or have to spend much of their life attempting to acquire or preserve them. In Oceania cultures, they are part of everyone's birthright.

Part Two: The village story—land disputes—the narrator continues[7]

In recent modern times, the traditional system of using and owning land has been severely undermined and if we are not careful it will disappear for future generations. The change has come about as a result of the arrival of Europeans, starting from the mid-1800s. When they arrived, local people were persuaded to make land available to these visitors in exchange for goods which seemed attractive at first but were of little enduring value. Over the following years, European settlers slowly but surely took over much of our coastal land and began to develop it with plantations of coconut, cocoa, and coffee.

These foreigners had no insight into, or sensitivity to the traditional land system where the people and the land belong eternally to each other; land can be made available for any outsiders to use but they could never become the rightful owners of the land. Equally, the local people had no comprehension at all of the idea of buying and selling of land to foreign owners. When the foreign colonial government came to rule our islands at the end of the 1800s, they established a system for the registration of land purchase and land ownership, but this did not mean anything to the traditional village landowners.

As time went on, from the land that they had gained, the Europeans established large plantations for crops and raising animals, from which they made a lot of money. At the same time, the local people were being prohibited from entering the land or having access to its resources of food, including the resources of seafood in the adjoining coastal waters.

For the local people this experience began to undermine their way of village life, and it sowed the seeds of deep resentment and hostility towards foreigners. Their land was being taken away from them, and with the loss of their land, they were losing

---

6. Figueroa and Gibbs, "Catholics," 200.
7. Paul, "Ownership," 205–12, in summary form.

their human identity and well-being. But over time it also opened up new ideas about the potential use and material value of the land, and how the land could be used as a source of personal or family gain. Some opportunistic members of our community, for example, "sold" their land as a means of getting access to money or to items of value, often without thinking about the long-term consequences, and often without following the cultural rules about land, and in some cases against their own family rules. Others, equally opportunistic, obtained access to land upon which they began to establish their own sources of profit.

In more recent decades, since the independence of our country in 1980 determined that all land taken from us by the Europeans, be returned to the traditional landowners, the hostility between the local people and foreigners has now been transferred to hostility between our own people. The long period of European colonization had clouded the memory of clan ownership, leading to fights among local people about who is the traditional clan owner of certain pieces of land. Communities have become divided. In my case, my own clan left Kole Village because of an unresolved land dispute with other villagers, and we have formed a new village called Lorum.

Some families have also become divided, resulting in the severe breakdown of the traditional cultural practices that support and sustain marriage and family life. Even Christian churches have divided, leading to the creation of separated church communities in the one village, or to people leaving their own village and joining up with another church in a nearby village; both of these practices have cemented the divisions.

The overall outcome has been that the traditional ordered system of clan ownership of land that has endured for generations past, has been thrown into confusion, and the people have lost touch with their ancestral practices. Our human identity and well-being, built on the relational intimacy and interconnection between our people and our land, is now under threat.

The Bigger Story

In the case of the village people on East Santo, the burden of responsibility for the disruption of this intimate life-giving connection between the people and their land is laid at the feet of the nineteenth century European traders invading the community with their own very different worldview, fracturing the traditional life of the local people. Again the same story is duplicated across the island communities. At a 1999 workshop on gospel and culture in Vanuatu, held at the Talua Ministry Training Centre, a student group from the central islands reflected:

> There are a number of reasons why it is not clear who owns a particular piece of land.... it has become hard for people to determine the correct landowners ...and for individuals to prove that they are the custom owners, complicated even further by the changing attitude to land as a commodity to be exploited,

> driven by greed . . . leading to conflict between families, divisions in village communities, and even in the local church community.⁸

However, there is a further important observation to be made. While, in the particular case study of East Santo, the burden of disruption rests with European traders, others see the disruption also as an unintended consequence of the arrival of the early missionaries who introduced the Christian faith into the islands.

> Neither European settlers nor the early generation of missionaries was alert to the significance of land and environment for the human identity of Pacific Islanders. The impact of both was the dislocation of people from their land . . . Upon the arrival of missionaries, the people were urged to relocate off their land to the vicinity of the mission station, normally sited close to the coast because the missionaries much preferred the safety of travel by boat rather than walking inland. At the same time, the European settlers created their own impact—on the one hand by the unintentional importation of diseases over which local people had no immunity, and on the other, by establishing large plantations which effectively stole valuable local land, forcing many native peoples to relocate . . . So in different ways, both the Christian missions and the European settlers separated people from their traditional land.⁹

The joint impact of both European traders and colonial missionaries across the whole of Oceania is reflected in a more strident academic article titled "Faith and Culture" written by Samoan scholar Upolu Luma Vaai.¹⁰ Vaai considers that this joint arrival had such an impact on the cultural context of the peoples of Oceania that the peoples across the region have been severed from their ancestral heritage. What has happened is the breaking apart of the three fundamental cultural elements that lie at the heart of the cultures of the people, and that have always been understood as mutually interwoven and interdependent. These three elements, Vaai calls "the *oikos* triplets"—the three things that define the "*oikos*" or home of the people within their cultures: ecology, economy, and *oikoumene*. Following the arrival of Europeans, ecology was stolen and became a servant to a Eurocentric scientific household, where it was forcibly reduced to mere "nature" to be exploited. Economy was removed and became a servant to globalization, where its role of "managing a home" was modified to serve a neoliberal system that puts resources into the hands of just a few elites. And *oikoumene* was stolen by the church and made a servant to its human-centric theologies. This deliberate dismembering of the *oikos* triplets from their common roots forcibly altered the identities, roles, and purposes of each. "Economy without ecology

---

8. Prior, *Gospel and Culture*, 2:127.
9. Prior, *Gospel and Culture*, 2:126.
10. Vaai, "Faith and Culture," 236–46.

is aggressively capitalist. Oikoumene without ecology is brutally human-centric. And economy without oikoumene is cruelly secular."[11]

Aligned with the analysis of Vaai is a closer examination by Cliff Bird of the cultural disruption brought to the peoples of Oceania from missionary impact. Under the theme of "Integrity of Creation," Bird makes a forthright accusation that "the Christianity that intruded upon Oceania was bankrupt as far as creation theology was concerned."[12] The early missionary period, asserts Bird, was driven by the eighteenth-century spiritual awakenings across Europe, with its exclusive focus on the conversion of sinful individuals and the saving of lost souls. Accompanying this zeal for individual conversion was the assumption that the peoples of Oceania belonged to heathen cultures from which they needed to be delivered—from the darkness of their cultural world of idols and false gods into the light of the gospel and a belief in the Christian God. Thus, the Christian faith that was promoted across Oceania was insensitive to, and in direct conflict with local cultural practices and worldviews. Adding to this antagonism was the fact that the arrival of the Christian faith came at the same time as the arrival of a colonial empire with its interests in trade and financial profit, the outcome of which was a utilitarian and instrumentalist understanding of Christianity in relation to the created world, and an entrenched dualism between the material and the spiritual. In summary, the early missionary impact on the peoples and cultures of Oceania was to introduce a form of the Christian faith that took no account of, indeed stood over against, the intimacy of communal human life and the created world.[13]

With this picture of the historical background of the peoples of Oceania, we are now better able to understand the stimulus for, and the intent and significance of, "Oceania theology."

OCEANIA THEOLOGY: CONTEXTUAL PROTEST AND THE PIONEERING OF A NEW THEOLOGY

Oceania theology as a defined category of theology, came in the wake of a global movement known as "the contextualizing of theology."[14] This is a movement which has authorized peoples across all regions of the world to explore forms of theology that engage directly with the context within which they find themselves. The seeds of this global movement were sewn after the Second World War in areas of Asia where church leaders and theologians were faced on a daily basis with the challenges of political injustice and economic exploitation at the hands of foreign rulers, and for whom the content of inherited Western missionary theology, previously assumed to offer universal truth across every cultural context, provided no help and no hope. The

---

11. Vaai, "Faith and Culture," 236.
12. Bird, "Integrity," 337.
13. Bird, "Integrity," 329–40. This is a summary of Bird's analysis.
14. What follows is an overview of what is detailed chronologically in Prior, *Contextualizing*, 16–69.

church in these non-Western parts of the world needed to redefine the Christian faith so that it spoke into their local context in a meaningful and hopeful way. The "contextualizing" movement slowly gained momentum, spreading beyond Asia through the 1960s, taking more formal definition as "contextualization of theology" through the 1970s, and by the 1980s was beginning to make its mark in the global region of Oceania. For the island nations, this wave of contextualization coincided with the era when political movements across the Pacific, many of them pioneered by local church leaders, were guiding their own peoples towards political independence and cultural renaissance. Bird identifies this coming together of two distinct initiatives—contextualization and political independence—as a "kairos moment" that was to lead to "the reinterpretation of Christianity by theologians across Oceania."[15]

What evolved from the 1980s was a series of definable steps in the process of contextualization within and across Oceania, a development that for the first time, began to honor the traditional cultures of the people in a way that had not previously occurred. Local leaders and theologians began to articulate their own homegrown forms of theology. The earliest steps were tentative and superficial, but eventually were to lead more boldly and profoundly to that theology that was given the name "Oceania theology." It is possible to summarize these *steps* of contextualization as they occurred in Oceania:

- The adaptation, at first tentative and then more confidently, of Western theological content into language and symbols of Pacific cultures (most notably "coconut theology" pioneered by Sione 'Amanaki Havea)
- Giving focused attention to addressing issues affecting the lives of Pacific peoples—socially and culturally
- Engaging with socio-political struggles inherent in colonization, in search for liberation and political independence (Oceania's distinctive "liberation theology")
- A growing readiness to take up the task of shaping a theology which is embedded in Pacific cultures and experience ("gospel and culture" movements)
- Embracing personal and communal stories of suffering and oppression, particularly as represented by Pacific women ("women's theology")
- Reclaiming the Pacific worldview of the unity of human life with all creation into an "Oceania theology."[16]

What is unique about the call for an Oceania theology, is that it takes the process of contextualization into the very heart of the worldview of Pacific Islanders in a way that was unprecedented. None of the previous steps in the contextualizing process achieved what Oceania theology has achieved and is achieving. This theology constitutes a cry from the heart of the islander peoples, a protest against the threat to their

---

15. Bird, "Integrity," 333.
16. Prior, *Contextualizing,* 115–16.

very identity in the disintegration of the "oikos triplets," a call for the reintegration of what has been severed: the intimate connection between human life and creation, between each small village community and its land.

The pioneering of this particular theological development is commonly associated with the prominent Islander Illaitia Sevati Tuwere. Described in 1987 by his Indian colleague at the Pacific Theological College, Russell Chandran, as an "outstanding Fijian theologian,"[17] Tuwere held the positions of general secretary and president of the Methodist Church of Fiji, and was the second indigenous principal of the Pacific Theological College (1982–1988). His voice was one to be heard.

It was Tuwere who had been most prominent in first calling for the expression "Oceania" to replace the commonly used word "Pacific." He did so because the word "Pacific" was of colonial adoption while the word "Oceania" was a more authentic local way of defining the people in their ecological context, and of opening up ways of contextualizing theology among his own people.

Tuwere began by taking the unique Pacific understanding of land as represented in the word in his native Fiji, "vanua." While the theme of land was not entirely absent from earlier contributions to contextualization,[18] it formed the exclusive focus of Tuwere's disciplined research and subsequent doctoral thesis,[19] as a result of which he found himself being identified as the leading proponent of this theme.

For Tuwere, the Pacific notion of land was not simply one of many relevant features of Pacific cultures, but it lay at the very heart of the Pacific Islander's worldview. He speaks on behalf of cultures across the region in his assertion that for Fijians, the importance of land "cannot be overemphasized."[20] It has both literal and symbolic meaning, which are "inextricably tied together."[21] The literal meaning refers to specific location or place, including everything in it—house, garden, people in community, while the symbolic meaning refers to livelihood, identity, time, event, history, ancestors, and creation.[22] There is a profound sense in which the people and the land are soulless without each other.

Tuwere articulated these views first at the Weavers' conference in 1991, then persistently afterwards—at the inaugural meeting of the Ecumenical Association of Third World Theologians (EATWOT) in September 1994, and later at the programmatic four-year Pacific-wide forums on contextual theology.[23] Most notably, a regional workshop on "Pacific Indigenous Peoples' Struggle for Land and Identity" was held in Fiji to mark the beginning of the new millennium. The statement from participants

17. Chandran, *Cross*, v.
18. Kamu, *Samoan Culture*; Boseto, "Do Not Separate Us."
19. Tuwere, *Vanua*.
20. Tuwere, *Vanua*, 11.
21. Tuwere, *Vanua*, 33.
22. Tuwere, *Vanua*, 33–51.
23. Tuwere, "Emerging Themes"; Tuwere, "Agenda"; Tuwere, "What is Contextual Theology?"

at the end of the workshop declared, "To us as Pacific Indigenous Peoples, we say that the land as our mother, known as vanua, fenua, enua, hanua, fonua, whenna, te aba, etc., is life, our soul and identity: land is people, resources, cultures, beliefs, spirituality, languages, chiefly system and sea."[24] Recognizing that "land" includes also the surrounding seas and the land beneath it, the statement continues, "Our theological understanding of the land in the water is one of '"God's garden' . . . . There is a place for everyone in the garden and for every tool to be used. The purpose of the garden is to grow, to bloom, flower and to give fruit."[25] It then concludes, "The issue of land, history and identity is the main burning issue of the region . . . The theology of the land needs to be articulated as soon as possible."[26]

Given that what is at issue here is the very survival of Pacific Islanders, it is not surprising then that the topic of land, and with it the accompanying themes of creation, environment, ecology, and climate change, have now come to feature prominently in theological discussion and writings within the South Pacific. Again this is most clearly represented by Tuwere[27] who has set the agenda for others to pursue. At the 1994 meeting of EATWOT, he explained how, as principal of PTC, he had reshaped the curriculum of theology to be consistent with this Pacific worldview. He outlined a theology that uses the notion of "vanua" as indicating four things: "means of livelihood, making sense of time and event, place of traditions and ancestors, a reassuring of identity."[28] He then goes on to claim, "What is expected of us as theologians of the churches is to seek for the restoration of the presence of God within the created order . . . This view has always been an integral part of our belief and value system in Oceania and is essentially a Christian idea."[29]

Tuwere explains that this invites theologians from Oceania to "claim back parts of their cosmos that were rejected during the missionary and colonial period. This lost cosmos is experienced through our people who now find it difficult in many cases to remember their myths and legends, their dances and idioms, their thought categories and symbols."[30] For Tuwere, this has powerful connections with the heart and hope of the Christian gospel. Under "An Unfinished Agenda," Tuwere asks:

> Is there a vision of the future that we can all claim to feed our imagination and empower our zeal? Is there a dream that we can all dream together as we each seek to proclaim Christ and let his way be followed? . . . I believe there is. It is the eschatological vision of the reuniting of all things in Christ as found

---

24. "Pacific Indigenous Peoples' Struggle," 96.
25. "Pacific Indigenous Peoples' Struggle," 96–97.
26. "Pacific Indigenous Peoples' Struggle," 97.
27. But see also Boseto, "Do Not Separate Us"; Tofeano, "Eco-theology"; Everi, "Eco-theology"; Halapua, "HIV/AIDS."
28. Tuwere, "Agenda," 10.
29. Tuwere, "Agenda," 11.
30. Tuwere, "Agenda," 10.

in Ephesians 1:10: as a plan for the fullness of time, to gather up all things in Him, in heaven and things on earth.[31]

For Pacific Islanders, this transforms the heritage of Western missionary theology and its culturally captive focus on the action of God in human history and the conversion of individuals to the Christian faith. For the Pacific worldview, the saving work of God in history embraces the whole of creation, and the theological task is oriented to the renewal of creation. Over the last generation, this has become a normative feature of theology in Oceania. Its significance is the fact that it not only identifies land as a central feature of the context of Pacific peoples, but it establishes the Pacific worldview as the essential frame of reference for the contextualization of the content of theology within the Pacific.

For Bird, this development in theology constituted a "refashioned and reinterpreted Christianity," without precedent in Oceania Christianity. Under his preferred theme of "integrity of creation," this was not simply one of several elements of Oceania Christianity; it was nothing less than the totality, the interconnectedness—the relationality—of creation's every constituent and their places, purposes, and functions in relation the overall scheme of things.[32] In the context of Oceania cultures, it brings together every conceivable element that makes up the existence of life, articulated by Bird in these categories: the Oceanic peoples' view of the world, well-being, and wholeness, the primacy and interconnectedness of life, relationality, the sense of home, and belonging to Mother Earth, communal identity within and across families, and the notion of ultimate salvation as connected to the land-sea-atmosphere web of life.[33]

These interwoven categories that are embraced as Oceania theology, and their importance for Oceania peoples gave impetus to a new project initiated in 2017 titled "Reweaving the Ecological Mat" (REM). A partnership between the Pacific Theological College, the Pacific Conference of Churches, and the Oceania Centre for Arts in the University of the South Pacific, it was aimed at addressing the growing environmental crisis facing the region, a crisis threatening every interconnected reality of Oceanic life, still victim to the pervasive worldview categories of exploitation represented by Western cultural powers.

> The REM strategy is driven by the idea that the region can determine its own future, based on its religious and indigenous texts, its worldviews and the experiences and lessons of current realities . . . It is about the myriad intricate relationships of people, land, forest, rivers and sea, and the norms that govern, connect and link them into a web of sustaining life and meaning. It is a call

---

31. Tuwere, "Agenda," 12.
32. Bird, "Integrity," 333.
33. Bird, "Integrity," 334–37, in summary form.

for "the wombing of mission" in Oceania, that is, mission that responds to the cries of Mother Earth and her nurturing of human life.[34]

For Aiava, "If we neglect our ecological responsibilities, we also renounce our identity as peoples of Oceania."[35] Thus when the voice from Oceania cries out about the global climate crisis, and the plea for climate justice, it is a call that cries out about what it means to be human in a cosmically interconnected world.

CONCLUSION

The impact of Oceania theology since its pioneering appearance some three decades ago has been twofold: to determine that the most compelling theological focus in Oceania is to reclaim the intimate communion between the whole of the created world and human life, and secondly to embolden Islanders across Oceania to ground their theological pursuit from within their own unique cultural worldview.[36]

The outcome of REM has already stimulated two very publications of note: *Ecological Framework for Development*, and *From the Deep: Pacific Voices for a New Story*, both of them declarations of creation-based theology as a way of understanding the Christian faith in Oceania. This is the "truth for the future of interconnected and holistic life for people in Oceania. It must be lived out in the consciousness that humanity is but one strand in the land-sea-atmosphere web of interconnected life."[37]

Indeed it is a truth that may provide the most urgent agenda not only within Oceania but across all regions of the world. In a time when there seem to be such disintegrating forces impacting on our global environment, is it too much to claim that Oceania theology, understood in this Oceanic way, and arising as it has from this vast and dispersed region of Islander communities, offers a compelling evangelical agenda for us all?

BIBLIOGRAPHY

Aiava, Faafetai. "Mission and Evangelism." In *Christianity in Oceania*, edited by Kenneth R. Ross et al., 286–97. Edinburgh Companions to Global Christianity. Edinburgh: Edinburgh University Press, 2021.
Bird, Cliff. "Integrity of Creation." In *Christianity in Oceania*, edited by Kenneth R. Ross et al., 329–40. Edinburgh Companions to Global Christianity. Edinburgh: Edinburgh University Press, 2021.
Bhagwan, James, et al., eds. *From the Deep: Pasifiki Voices for a New Story*. Suva, Fiji: Pacific Theological College, 2020.

34. Aiava, "Mission and Evangelism," 286–87.
35. Aiava, "Mission and Evangelism," 294.
36. A very recent and vivid example of this is the 2021 collection of contributions found in Havea, *Theologies*.
37. Bird, "Integrity," 340.

Boseto, Lesley. "Do Not Separate Us from Our Land and Sea." *Pacific Journal of Theology* Series II, 13 (1995) 69–72.

Chandran, Russell. *The Cross and the Tanoa. Gospel and Culture in the Pacific: Report on the Consultation on Gospel and Culture held in Suva, Fiji, 27–29 July, 1987*. Suva, Fiji: South Pacific Association of Theological Schools, 1988.

Everi, Martin. "Eco-theology and Its Application to the Pacific Context." *Pacific Journal of Theology* Series II, 26 (2001) 69–94.

Figueroa, Rocío, and Philip Gibbs. "Catholics." In *Christianity in Oceania*, edited by Kenneth R. Ross et al., 190–204. Edinburgh Companions to Global Christianity. Edinburgh: Edinburgh University Press, 2021.

Halapua, Winston. "HIV/AIDS in the Pacific and the Injustice of Past and Current Theological Approaches." *Pacific Journal of Theology* Series II, 36 (2006) 46–55.

Havea, Jione, ed. *Theologies in the Pacific*. Cham, Switzerland: Palgrave Macmillan, 2021.

Kamu, Lalomilo. *The Samoan Culture and the Christian Gospel*. Suva, Fiji: Donna Lou Kamu, 1996.

"Pacific Indigenous Peoples' Struggle for Land and Identity: Statement from Participants of the Workshop held in Suva, Fiji, September 11–14, 2000." *Pacific Journal of Theology* Series II, 25 (2001) 96–98.

Paul, Gideon. "The Ownership of Land in East Santo: A Biblical Reflection." In *Gospel and Culture in Vanuatu 5: Women in Culture and Church and other Issues*, edited by Randall Prior, 202–16. Adelaide: ATF, 2006.

Prior, Randall, ed. *Gospel and Culture in Vanuatu 2: Contemporary Local Perspectives*. Melbourne: Gospel Vanuatu, 2001.

———, ed. *Gospel and Culture in Vanuatu 3: The Voice of the Local Church*. Melbourne: Gospel Vanuatu, 2003.

———. *Contextualizing Theology in the South Pacific: The Shape of Theology in Oral Cultures*. American Society of Missiology Monograph Series. Eugene, OR: Pickwick, 2020.

Tofaeono, Ama'amalele. *Eco-theology: AIGA. The Household of God: A Perspective from the Living Myths and Traditions of Samoa*. Erlangen, Germany: Erlangen Verlag fur Mission und Oikumene, 2000.

Tuidrakulu, Rusiate. "Fiji." In *Christianity in Oceania*, edited by Kenneth R. Ross et al., 91–99. Edinburgh Companions to Global Christianity. Edinburgh: Edinburgh University Press, 2021.

Tuwere, Illaitia Sevati. "An Agenda for the Theological Task of the Church in Oceania." *Pacific Journal of Theology* Series II, 13 (1995) 5–12.

———. "Emerging Themes for a Pacific Theology." *Pacific Journal of Theology* Series II, 7 (1992) 49–55.

———. *Vanua: Towards a Fijian Theology of Place*. Suva, Fiji: Institute of Pacific Studies, 2002.

———. "What is Contextual Theology?: A View from Oceania." *Pacific Journal of Theology* Series II, 27 (2002) 7–20.

Vaai, Upola Lumã. "Faith and Culture." In *Christianity in Oceania*, edited by Kenneth R. Ross et al., 235–46. Edinburgh Companions to Global Christianity. Edinburgh: Edinburgh University Press, 2021.

CHAPTER 26

Māori Theology

WAYNE TEKAAWA

Māori theology originates from the Māori people of Aotearoa New Zealand. The word "Māori" makes identity, knowledge, values, and the way that life is lived and understood as Māori central to theology. In a Christian context, this leads to a renegotiation of how a trinitarian God is understood and related to in the Māori world. In this chapter, I will give a broad indication of what Māori theology is and its contribution to Christian theology.

THEOLOGY AS GOD, LAND, AND PEOPLE

Māori people identify as tangata whenua, "people of the land" to Aotearoa New Zealand. This is the largest landmass in the "Sea of Islands"[1] known as Te Moananui-a-Kiwa, the Ocean of Kiwa. Aotearoa New Zealand consists of two large land masses—Te Ika-a-Māui (the North Island) and Te Waipounamu (the South Island)—and a number of smaller islands. The term tangata whenua denotes being born from the land as a matter of birthright, uniquely entitled to exercise a range of rights in all facets of life. Whenua has a double meaning; in one context it means the physical land, and in another context it refers to the placenta that develops during pregnancy. The placenta is a vital life-giving organ that delivers oxygen, nutrients, hormones, and antibodies from the mother to the baby in the womb, while also filtering out carbon dioxide and waste. As part of the birthing process, the placenta is expelled from the mother's womb. A

---

1. Epeli Hauʻofa called the Pacific, the "Sea of Islands." See Hauʻofa, *Our Sea of Islands*, 1–16.

custom still practiced today involves burying the placenta of a newborn baby in a special place that signifies the relationship between the land and the new person. Tangata whenua can mean both people born of the placenta and people born of the land. Tangata whenua thus entails belonging to the land rather than the land belonging to people. In Māori pūrākau (origin narratives), there are many stories that illustrates the relationship between the people and the land. These narratives provide a person with a number of birthrights: whakapapa (connections), tūrangawaewae (security, a pace to stand in the world), mana (unique status), and tapu (sacredness). These birthrights ground people with a sense of identity, belonging, and a secure foundation for life. The term "people of the land" is used in twelve of the Old Testament books. In Te Paipera Tapu, the Māori language Bible, tangata whenua is used to describe the Canaanites, who were the first inhabitants of the promised land.

Christianity arrived in Aotearoa New Zealand at the invitation of Māori leaders. The first invitation was extended in 1814 by Ruatara, a leader of the Ngā Puhi iwi.[2] Ruatara developed a special relationship with Samuel Marsden, a missionary based in Sydney, Australia, and invited his respected friend to bring Christianity to his people in the Bay of Islands in the northern North Island. Marsden arrived on Christmas Day with the words, "Behold, I bring you tidings of great joy."[3] The second invitation came in 1840 from the Kai Tahu iwi on the South Island. Despite the introduction of Christianity to Aotearoa New Zealand some twenty-six years earlier, Christianity had not yet spread to the lower regions of the South Island. Kai Tahu leaders, Taiaroa and Karetai, traveled to a Methodist mission board meeting in Sydney to present a request for a missionary to be sent to their people. A few months later, James Watkins arrived in Otago and established his mission station amongst the people of Taiaroa and Karetai. These select leaders saw something special in the biblical message as a way to improve the spiritual and physical quality of life for their people.

Māori theology has its origins in both the Māori and Christian worlds. From the Māori world it draws on traditions, spirituality, language, and mātauranga (knowledge). From the Christian world Māori theology draws on the four sources of Scripture, tradition, reason and experience. Māori theology emerges from a continuous conversation between both worlds with the outcome being to improve the quality of life for Māori and for everyone else. The following model crystallizes Māori theology:

Diagram 1:[4]

2. The Ngā Puhi iwi are a tribe of Māori and are numerically the large tribe in the country.

3. Ruatara meet CMS missionary Samuel Marsden in Sydney and became close friends. Ruatara invited Marsden to introduce his people to Christianity and Marsden arrive at Oihi in the Bay of Islands on Christmas Day 1814 conducting the first Christian worship service while Ruatara translated. This is recorded as the first Christian worship in the country and is acknowledged as the day that Christianity arrived in Aotearoa New Zealand.

4. Created by Wayne Te Kaawa, University of Otago, 2021.

	Māori:
	Spirituality MĀORI
	Language THEOLOGY
Theology: Scripture,	Traditions
Tradition, Reason, Experience	Knowledge

A proverb composed by Sir Apirana Ngata that has been applied to education also captures the essence of Māori theology.

E tipu e rea	*Grow tender one*
mō ngā ra o tou ao	*to meet the needs of your time*
Ko to ringa	*Turn your hands*
ki ngā rakau a te Pākehā	*to the tools of the Pākehā*
hei ora mo to tinana	*for your physical well-being*
Ko to ngakau	*Turn your heart*
ki ngā taonga a o tupuna Māori	*to the treasures of your ancestors*
hei tikitiki mo to mahuna	*as a crown for your head*
Ko to wairua	*Your soul to God*
ki te Atua, nana nei ngā mea katoa	*the author of all things*[5]

Māori theology is a combination of the best aspects of Māori and Christian life that is beneficial to the wholistic well-being of the people.

. . . people gathered together in elaborately decorated old church buildings in rural areas like Tikitiki, Motuti, or Hiruharema, surrounded by generations of people, both passed and living, together worshiping, reading the Bible, and singing songs of praise composed by their own people in their own language.

. . . people in the city who, due to COVID-19 restrictions, gathered together virtually through technology like Facebook or Zoom to hear and talk about issues of faith and life.

. . . people, be they young, old, Māori, Pākehā, or Pasifika, who, at Te Rautini in Hamilton, danced in rhythm to the beat of modern waiata composed by Cindy Ruakere and Luke Kaa-Morgan.

. . . people joined together before planting or harvesting kumara, just as they also gathered by the foreshore to give thanks for their bounty in a fusion of prayers of gratitude to their traditional and Christian Atua.

. . . people of all ethnicities coming together to commemorate and give thanks for special days and seasons in Aotearoa New Zealand's history like Waitangi Day

---

5. This proverb was composed by Sir Apirana Ngata in 1949 and written into the autography book of a schoolgirl Rangi Bennett to encourage her in her education. This proverb has inspired many generations of young Māori in pursing education achievement.

or Matariki, the time when the seven stars of Pleiades can be seen on the morning horizon signalling the beginning of a new year.

A proverb that best captures these images of Māori theology in action is:

He aha temeanui o teao	What is the most important thing in the world
Maku e kii atu	I will reply
He tangata, he tangata, he tangata	It is people, people, people

This proverb alongside the various images given illustrate what Māori theology is. It is, according to Rev. Māori Marsden, largely subjective, a taste of reality, a thing of the heart rather than the head. Abstract rational thought and empirical methods cannot, as Marsden says, grasp the concrete act of existing, which is fragmentary, paradoxical, and incomplete. The only way lies through a passionate, inward, and subjective approach.[6]

Among the many distinctive features of Māori theology Rev. Dr. Henare Tate highlights the following:

- theology as communal rather than individual.
- an orientation to the spatial rather than the temporal.
- land and water is central to culture, identity, and theology.
- the interrelatedness of the whole community of creation.
- theology emerges out of the culture, histories, and experiences of people.
- indigenous theology contains a strong element of resistance to colonization.
- theology is authentically Māori in its language and includes oral traditions and the arts.
- Recovery, critique, and reform.[7]

Māori theology is first and foremost an expression of theology done by, in, with, and for Māori who maintain ownership and sovereignty of the theology. As indigenous people, Māori have their own distinct values and knowledge systems that are located within their own cultural framework and embodied as living tradition. Māori read, interpret, understand, and faithfully strive to authentically live out the biblical teachings as Māori faith seeking Māori understanding.[8]

---

6. Marsden, *Woven Universe*, 23.
7. Tate, *He Puna iti i te Ao Marama*, 21.
8. Tate, *He Puna iti i te Ao Marama*, 21.

MĀTAURANGA MĀORI AS KNOWLEDGE AND WAYS OF KNOWING

One of the philosophical and educational foundations that informs Māori theology is mātauranga Māori which is the totality of knowledge gleaned from a uniquely Māori and holistic way of viewing the world. When Christianity arrived in the country, iwi and hapū began testing and adapting their traditional values, customs, ethics, beliefs, and practices against biblical teachings. As Dr. Hirini Kaa suggests, Christianity was as a place where mātauranga Māori could be renegotiated.[9] When Māori adopted Christianity, what resulted was not a linear progression or "conversion" from one worldview to another; rather, it involved a renegotiation of existing knowledge and understanding in the light of the new knowledge, understanding, and experiences ushered in through Christian faith. Graham Cameron, one of many Māori students completing doctoral research in theology, also supports this view, writing that mātauranga as Māori knowledge and understanding is not static but is an ever increasing phenomenon that, in a complex series of relational connections, informs and transforms older knowledge bases.[10] The utility and value of exiting knowledge can be challenged and renegotiated as new information, experiences, and ways of understanding the world emerge. Mātauranga Māori stands alongside Scripture, tradition, reason, and experience as a primary source of theology.

WOVEN WISDOM

The term "woven wisdom" was coined by professor Murray Rae, who co-teaches Māori theology with me at the University of Otago. It derives from the art of weaving, which is an important part of sustaining life throughout the Moananui.[11] This term and image is used often in theologies from the Moananui as a way of describing the interweaving links or connections between people, natural resources, creative efforts, God, and faith as life-giving relationships. The natural fiber that is used for weaving is native to the soil in which it grows and is nurtured by the elements. The weaver is a repository, linking the knowledge of the past with the future.[12] In Moananui, indigenous communities weave together items like baskets, kits, mats, or cloaks to celebrate a special occasion or achievement. These woven items are often reused and reworn, while the stories, history, and connections associated with and imbued in them are

---

9. See Kaa, *Te Hāhi Mihinare*, 9–17.

10. Cameron, "Te Ua Haumene," 9.

11. Moananui is the Māori name for the Pacific. In its fullness, it is Te Moananui a Kiwa, the great ocean of kiwa, the sperm whale. The ancestors of the Māori found their way around the Pacific ocean by following the migratory paths of the sperm whale. The word "moana" is a word that is used throughout the Pacific to describe the Pacific ocean. The term "Pacific" is a foreign word introduced by Spanish explorer Vasco Nunez de Balboa in the sixteenth century.

12. Puketapu-Hetet, *Māori Weaving*, 9.

celebrated, preserved, and passed onto to future generations. In much the same way, woven wisdom in Māori theology involves an intertextual reading of Scripture that incorporates sacred stories outside of the biblical Scriptures and accepts them as that: stories that are sacred. These stories give greater insight into biblical sacred stories, just as the biblical sacred stories offer a theological lens by which to understand and reinterpret traditional sacred stories.

The Rev. Māori Marsden is one of the earliest writers to apply a woven wisdom approach to examining Scripture and the traditions of Māori side by side. In doing so, he was able to give a more in-depth understanding of each. After comparing the traditions of his ancestors with the sacramental systems of his Christian faith, Marsden identified that certain spiritual principles that are universal in application. He compares, for example, the pure and tohi rites with baptism. Both rites contain water for blessing, naming, and dedication of a person to a certain Atua. Using Augustine's definition of a sacrament, Marsden highlights that both rites are an outward visible sign setting forth and pledging an inward spiritual grace that is transmitted to humans during the rite.[13] The reflections by Māori Marsden are a gift to us today, opening our eyes to see new possibilities when we engage with cultures other than our own.

Moeawa Callaghan is another exponent of woven wisdom who applies a theological lens to examine pūrakau (Māori origin narratives) in an article she wrote for the *First Peoples Theological Journal*.[14] In these origin stories, the physical world emerges out of a state of being known as Te Kore (the nothingness), which evolves into Te Po (the night), from which emerges Papatūānuku (earth) and Ranginui (sky). Various forms of creaturely life subsequently emerge and are regarded as the offspring of Papatūānuku and Ranginui. Among them are their children, who become "atua" when they complete the creation of the physical world. Atua has been loosely translated as "departmental god(s)" or "spiritual being(s) who are identified with some aspect of nature."

The successive stages of creation and the emergence of the elements from these stages accords with the importance of whakapapa (genealogy) to māturanga Māori. Indeed, whakapapa is widely considered the pinnacle of mātauranga Māori. One generation (Te Kore) gives birth to another generation (Te Po), and this cycle continues with each generation until they reach the ultimate goal of creation, humans. As the atua brought human life into the world, they overstepped their boundaries, which resulted in death becoming a permanent fixture in the life cycle. The notions of ultimate goal introduces eschatology into the story in the hope of joining the ancestors in Hawaiki after death.

In examining these pūrakau, Callaghan highlights an important difficulty in cross-cultural translation. Te Kore has been translated into English as "the nothingness," and Te Po as "the night or darkness," while the meaning of Atua has been equated to "God" or "gods." These translations were originally espoused by non-Māori

---

13. Marsden, *Woven Universe*, 2–23.
14. Callaghan, "Reflection on Creation Stories in Māori Tradition," 77–83.

researchers and writers.[15] As a platform for Māori theologians has begun to develop in academia, these pūrakau have been reinterpreted by Māori theologians in accordance with mātauranga Māori. This work has exposed and challenged the narrow and rigid Western view that informed early translations. Te Kore can, for example, also mean "potential" and Te Po can also mean "becoming." Within their own cultural context the epistemology Te Kore and Te Po are like different states or stages of gestation and birthing where the world emerges from the womb. In her intertextual reading of creation stories, Callaghan draws out several theological implications for today, noting that the way we view the world affects the way we live in the world. Ongoing theological debate is of critical importance since one's view of the world and consequently one's behavior in it is primarily affected by one's theological understandings.

Dr. Beverley Moana Hall-Smith is the first Māori person to earn a doctorate specializing in biblical studies from a Māori postcolonial feminist perspective. In her doctoral research, Hall-Smith applies a theoretical framework that favours kaupapa Māori bodies of knowledge that are applied as critical tools to Judg 19–21, one of the most disturbing and violent texts in the Bible. In doing so, she reveals how a Levite concubine who is unnamed and voiceless in the text is able to speak. Specifically, the Māori hermeneutical framework uses whakapapa (genealogy), a foundational concept of Māori life, as part of its interpretative method. Five further Māori concepts connected to whakapapa are also used to exegete the text. These are atuatanga (knowing of God), kaitiakitanga (stewardship), mauri (life principle), and tapu (sacred) and noa (ordinary/free from tapu). The metaphor of weaving is used throughout her research as she deconstructs the text. These Māori concepts are successfully used to interact with and explore the world of the implied author, the world of the text, and the world of the present reader. Biblical interpretation and hermeneutical tools drawn from the Māori world are more capable of speaking into the realities of inequality, oppression, assimilation, and exploitation experienced by indigenous people. The tools used to create these problems are ineffective in finding solutions and new tools are required. In her postcolonial reading of the text, Hall-Smith demonstrates that Māori theology possesses the critical tools to detect meaning and information in difficult texts that Western interpretative methods are unable to detect.

As tangata whenua in contemporary Aotearoa New Zealand, the flip side of connection with the land is a heightened sense of pain caused by alienation from the land. This reality has become a point of strength when reading and interpreting the Bible. The experiences of colonization and land loss sensitizes the Māori reader for words or actions in the Bible that dehumanize, be it through racism, stereotyping, racial profiling, prejudice, coercion, or discrimination. This reality also heightens the reader's sensitivity to power dynamics that create and maintain injustice and inequality. These assets are crucial to progressing the difficult conversations that theology must have in

---

15. For examples, see Best, *Some Aspects of Māori Myth and Religion*; Grey, *Polynesian Mythology and Ancient Traditional History*; and Alper, *Māori Myths and Tribal Legends*.

the context of gospel and treaty, a necessary thread in the woven wisdom tradition of Māori theology.

DIFFICULT CONVERSATIONS

As with all things in life, there is pushback. Māori theology seeks to responsibly contribute to pushback against colonization by responsibly engaging in difficult conversations concerning historical trauma and uncomfortable aspects of Aotearoa New Zealand's history. In response to colonization, land confiscations and the New Zealand Land Wars, a number of Māori prophetic movements emerged.[16] A commonality between Māori prophetic leaders like Te Ua Haumene, Te Whiti o Rongomai, Tohu Kākahi, TeKooti, and Rua Kenana is the state violence they and their followers were subject to, as well as their portrayal as villains, disloyal, rebels, fanatics, criminals, and murders. While they are studied as cultural, historical, and political figures from the perspective of the historian or anthropologist, few have engaged with these leaders as religious figures or theologians in their own right. Māori theology reclaims these people as prophetic Christian religious leaders, recasting them as biblically inspired and God-fearing visionaries who sought justice given their traumatic experience of colonization.

The Holy Scriptures provided much need inspiration to leaders like Te Whiti o Rongomai and Tohu Kākahi. Both these men were deeply moved by Jesus's Sermon on the Mount. Several verses were especially formative, including "Blessed are the peacemakers, for they will be called sons of God."[17] Another biblical verse that inspired them to think and act differently was from the prophet Isaiah to "turn their swords into ploughshares."[18] Two thousand years after Jesus spoke the beatitudes Te Whiti and Tohu applied the principles of the teachings and drew up plans to establish a community committed to peaceful passive resistant: Parihaka, at the base of Mount Taranaki. The specific role of the Māori prophets was to offer hope in a time and place where hope had been systematically destroyed. Māori theology has the responsibility to remind people that these stories of the Māori prophetic movements are Christian responses to injustice in this country and the pursuit of justice today still continues.

Another responsibility that Māori theology has is to address and correct theological amnesia. When the Christian story of Aotearoa New Zealand is told, it is often communicated from the perspective of the European missionary, who features at the center of the story either as a hero or a villain. Prevailing narratives around the arrival of Christianity often meld Māori into the background as nameless, faceless people,

---

16. The New Zealand Land Wars took place from 1843 beginning with the Wairau Affray and continued to 1916 and the Crown invasion of Maungapōhatu. Breeches of the Treaty of Waitangi fuelled by settler demand for land was the root cause of the Wars. In this timeframe much of the sixty-six million acres of land owned by Māori was taken by force or by confiscation. During the Land Wars and confiscations Māori prophetic movements sprang up in resistance.

17. Matt 5:9.

18. Isa 2:4.

and when they are brought into the fore, they are stereotyped as pagans and heathens who lived in darkness, prayed to their false gods, and participated in cannibalistic rituals. Also cast into the shadow of this story are the lesser-known kaiwhakaako, the Māori missionary teachers who are the real heroes of the Christian story. Māori theology gives preference to the stories of the kaiwhakaako, who are regarded as the key missionary agents responsible for the widespread acceptance of the Christian message amongst their own people, as well as the positive transformation of their tribal society.

Historian Hamiora Pio is adamant that 1814 was significant for the arrival of two things: Christianity and the musket. The musket was new technology used to settle conflicts, plunder the wealth of opponents, and capture slaves. The Bible was the liberating force that gained freedom for those taken into slavery. In response to the role that the missionaries and the Bible had in gaining their freedom, many of the liberated slaves became kaiwhakaako. In 1844, there were twelve European missionaries, whereas there were 295 kaiwhakaako. Ten years later, the number of European missionaries had almost doubled to twenty-three while the number of kaiwhakaako swelled to at least 558.[19] Piripi Taumata-a-kura was a well-known kaiwhakaako who introduced Christianity to his Ngāti Porou iwi.[20] The kaiwhakaako used Christianity and Te Paipera Tapu (the Māori language Bible) as an opportunity to expand their minds and worldviews while re-evaluating their own systems and knowledge. The end result was that there were able to renegotiate their religious and cultural orientation, beliefs, and practices as they developed a tribal based Christianity rather than an institutional church-based model. The pioneering work of Rev Dr. Hirini Kaa on renegotiation, iwi Christianity, and bringing the kaiwhakaako to the forefront must be acknowledged.

MĀORI THEOLOGY IN THE ACADEMY

In recent years, Māori theology has found its way into the academic world. Theological education and research within the context of gospel and treaty has lead various academic programs to reshape how they do theology as a Christian learning community. Woven into theology programs are distinctive and innovative approaches to incorporate learning styles and methodologies that are grounded in mātauranga Māori and indigenous epistemologies. Dr. Sandy Kerr speaking on her own institution, Carey Baptist College says:

> The curriculum has undergone a demonstrable transformation to include mātauranga Māori and epistemology (Māori knowledge and ways of knowing) woven throughout all Carey programmes of study. Where it was possible to train at Carey and not encounter mātauranga Māori in 2016, this is not possible in 2021.[21]

---

19. Kaa, *Te Hāhi Mihinare*, 12.
20. Ngāti Porou are a large iwi (tribe) from the East Coast of the North Island.
21. Kerr, "Forerunner to Change?"

This statement by Kerr has become standard in many theological programs in Aotearoa New Zealand with many papers and courses weaving Māori epistemologies and ways of knowing into the curriculum. Doing so has given new insights into reading and understanding Scripture, incorporating faith and life through the eyes of Māori in ways that weave a deeper understanding of being a follower of Jesus Christ.

Also changing are teaching styles. These are consciously moving away from a lecture theater-based monologue approach to a pedagogy where students and staff enter into total immersion marae-based learning. This offers student and staff an opportunity to enter into the Māori world and breathe, eat, talk, sleep, and live theology in a Māori context, further integrating their learning into their academic formation and faith practice. Comments from students who have completed their immersion papers include statements praising this unique approach:[22]

- The combination of marae-based learning and student interaction made this one of the very best courses I have taken. Breaks new ground when it goes off-campus.
- Truly a life-changing experience.
- The live-in block course is indispensable, priceless.
- I would do the block course again if I had a chance. There is so much goodness in it that one could attend every year, and still benefit every time. I cannot fault any aspect of this course.

As these exciting initiatives continue to emerge, the cloak of theological tradition is gradually recentered away from its colonial roots. They give better shape and meaning to the present and future as a theology of, with, and for Aotearoa New Zealand rather than a transplanted theology. Its point of uniqueness comes from the way it unapologetically challenges colonial notions of theology, instead amplifying the call that the message of Jesus Christ and its history of interpretation must be decolonized to give greater clarity to the truths of Scripture. Theology within the framework of gospel and treaty means that, according to Rev Dr. Benjamin Ong, pākehā cannot do theology in this country without Māori; when Pākehā ignore Māori in their theological endeavours, they ignore their responsibility as treaty partners. Māori must stand at the center of the hermeneutical relationship.[23] In order for this to happen, decolonization and re-indigenization of theology becomes *the* issue for theology in Aotearoa New Zealand.

DECOLONIZING AND RE-INDIGENIZING THEOLOGY

The taproot of churches in Aotearoa New Zealand comes from Great Britain (Anglican, Methodist, Presbyterian, Salvation Army, Baptist, Pentecostal), and from Rome

---

22. All comments taken from course analysis report 2020. CHTH217/317, University of Otago.
23. Ong, "Paakehaa-centred Interpretation," 8.

(Roman Catholic). In the last fifty years the influence of north American televangelism has also created the traveling Māori evangelists who represent everything that the traditional churches are not. The dominant ways of doing theology and expressions of Christian faith in this country are inherited from those places of origin. It is nigh impossible to exercise theological and liturgical sovereignty when the taproot of origin is from a foreign land. To be an authentic expression of the liberative message of God in Aotearoa New Zealand, Christianity as a whole, Christians as individuals, and churches as institutions must go through a process of decolonization and indigenize itself to the land of Aotearoa New Zealand. Until that happens, Christianity, Christians, and churches will continue to struggle to be secure in this land amongst its indigenous population and always be looked on with a great deal of suspicion and mistrust. This lack of trust arises from the baggage of a colonial past as Christians and churches held hands with the Crown in the New Zealand Land Wars becoming major benefactors in land confiscations. Even today some churches live on the financial and resource rich wealth of their dishonest past while those who were unjustly dispossessed of their lands, assets, and rights live in stark poverty today. In this context decolonization is a means of redemption for a sinful past.

From the 1980s on, decolonization became the priority of the Runanga Whakawhanaunga I Nga Hāhi o Aotearoa (Council of Māori Churches). Drawing from the prophet Daniel, the Runanga-based decolonization on the biblical verse, "E kore te uku e piri ki terino (clay will not stick to iron)."[24] This verse was partnered with *Pedagogy of the Oppressed* by Paolo Friere, which became the working text to understand the objectives and processes of decolonization. The member churches of the Runanga agreed and attempted to decolonize themselves as best they could, but despite their best efforts they remained as under-resourced silos of large churches who maintained their colonial links to foreign homelands. Even today, Māori in churches still mimic the structures and mannerisms of the sending "home churches."

Decolonizing the message of God and re-indigenizing it to the soil of Aotearoa New Zealand is the central contemporary challenge that Māori theology seeks to redress. A rereading of Luke 4:18–19 through a Māori lens highlights the place of decolonization in Jesus's message. In Luke's Gospel, Jesus attends the synagogue in his hometown of Nazareth and reads from the book of the prophet Isaiah. In this particular passage, the poor, the captive, the blind, and the oppressed are placed at the center of God's mission. Using this text, I would argue that Jesus's key focus can be understood as decolonizing the world in which he lived, making those in the margins the center of the good news. Jesus's ministry involved the reordering of the political, social, and religious world in which he lived. A definition of decolonization based on the statement read by Jesus in the synagogue is relocating the center of faith to the margins. In Aotearoa New Zealand those domiciled to the margins are predominantly Māori who are overrepresented in incarceration rates and negative health, education,

---

24. Dan 2:43.

and unemployment statistics, and shockingly in a global pandemic total half of the COVID-19 cases in Aotearoa New Zealand when they are only 14 percent of the population.

Māori theology openly challenges colonial notions of theology that normalize inequality and inequity in the patriarchal and hierarchical structures of the church. Decolonization of the church involves posing and responding to a series of questions concerning identity and ways of living:

- What does it mean to be both authentic to one's ethnicity and culture, be it Māori, Pākehā, Samoan, Cook Islander, or the like, while also being authentically Christian in the land of Aotearoa New Zealand?
- How do we indigenize Christianity to the soil of this land in ways that reflect God's love in, of, and for Aotearoa New Zealand?

These questions are consistent in the history of Aotearoa New Zealand. When Māori arrived in Whakatāne aboard the Mataatua vessel in the fourteenth century, the first question they asked was "how are we to live in this land?" Since then, all immigrants to this country at some stage must face this question of identity, being, and belonging. It is only when we openly engage with these questions that the kingdom of God will materialize in the land of Aotearoa New Zealand.

CONCLUSION

Māori theology has as its ultimate goal the wholistic well-being of the people. Whenever and wherever it is utilized, Māori theology brings positive benefits to the people. For both sacred story and the sacred biblical text, God, land, and people have been in constant relationship before day one of creation with the origin of land and people sourced in the creator God. Regardless if you use sacred story or sacred Scripture, people were created from the land, and the term tangata whenua (people of the land), while a self-descriptive term by Māori, is also a biblical term.

Māori knowledge, traditions, and spirituality, along with Scripture, tradition, reason, and experience are the primary sources that inform Māori theology as a theology in, with, and for the context of Aotearoa New Zealand. Indeed, I would argue that you can no longer do theology in this country without engaging with Māori theology. The contextual biblical interpretation and intercultural reading of Scripture that Māori biblical scholars have keenly participated in is just one example of this. Scholars have applied exegetical and hermeneutical tools developed in the Māori world with stunning success in ways that deepen and broaden understanding of the biblical text.

There are some difficult conversations that need to be had in both the religious and wider society in this country. Māori theology accepts its prophetic responsibility to hold theology, religion, churches, and Christians to account, ensuring that the injustices of the past are not repeated. These difficult conversations point to the reason why decolonizing theology and indigenizing theology to the soil of Aotearoa New Zealand is *the* mission for today.

BIBLIOGRAPHY

Alper, Anthony. *Māori Myths and Tribal Legends*. Auckland: Longman, 1996.

Best, Elsdon. *Some Aspects of Māori Myth and Religion*. Wellington: NZ Dominion Museum, 1922.

Cadigan, Tui. "How do Māori Speak About God Today?" In *The God Book: Talking About God Today*, edited by N. Darragh, 159–67. Auckland: Accent, 2008.

Callaghan, Moeawa. "A Reflection on Creation Stories in Māori Tradition." *First Peoples Theology Journal* 2 (2001) 77–83.

Cameron, Graham. "Te Ua Haumene: 'Beginnings' in an Historical Contextual Theology of Pai Mārire, the First Indigenous Christian Faith." PhD thesis, University of Otago, unpublished.

"Course analysis report 2020–2021." CHTH217/317: Introduction to Māori Theology and Religion. University of Otago.

Grey, George. *Polynesian Mythology and Ancient Traditional History of the New Zealand Race, as Furnished by Their Priests and Chiefs*. London: John Murray, 1855

Hall-Smith, Beverley Moana. "Whakapapa (genealogy), a Hermeneutical Framework for Reading Biblical Texts: A Māori Woman Encounters Rape and Violence in Judges 19–21." PhD diss., Flinders University, 2017.

Hau'ofa, E. "Our Sea of Islands." In *A New Oceania: Rediscovering Our Sea of Islands*, edited by V. Naidu et al., 1–16. Suva, Fiji: The University of the South Pacific & Beake House, 1993.

Kaa, Hirini. *Te Hāhi Mihinare, The Māori Anglican Church*. Wellington: Bridget Williams, 2020.

Kerr, S. Carey. "A Forerunner to Change?" https://www.carey.ac.nz/about-carey/carey-news/carey-a-forerunner-for-change/.

Marsden, Māori, ed. *The Woven Universe: Selected Writings of Rev Māori Marsden*. TeAhukaramu Charles Royal. Otaki, NZ: Estate of Rev Māori Marsden, 2003.

Ong, Benjamin. "Paakehaa-centred Interpretation in Aotearoa New Zealand: A Hermeneutic for Paakehaa in Partnership with Maaori." PhD diss., University of Otago, 2021.

Puketapu-Hetet, Erenora. *Māori Weaving with Erenora Puketapu-Hetet*. Auckland: Longman, 1999.

Rakena, Rua. "The Maori Response to the Gospel. Proceeding." Auckland: Wesley Historical Society, 1971.

Tate, Henare. *He Puna Iti i te Ao Marama, A Little Spring in the World of Light*. Auckland: Libro International, 2012.

Te Kaawa, Wayne. "Revisioning Christology through a Māori lens." PhD diss., University of Otago, 2020.

CHAPTER 27

Moana Theology

TE AROHA ROUNTREE

This chapter offers a glimpse into the complexities and nuances of *moana theology*. In a very moana way we look to the past, to move toward the future. An ideology captured in the Māori proverbial saying, *titiro whakamuri, kōkiri whakamua* (Look back and reflect to move forward). We must acknowledge where we have been, to help guide where we are going.

    We, as moana people have been romanticized and exoticized through histories of European encounter for centuries. From the Spanish and Portuguese in the sixteenth century who voyaged from the Americas, invaded, and occupied island nations including the Philippines, before navigating the Solomon Islands and the Marquesas Islands. To the Dutch, British, and French explorers of the early eighteenth century, who used their own *Pākehā/Pālagi* (European)[1] lens and first introduced to Europe the so-called savages and cannibals of Oceania. To the nineteenth-century sealers, whalers, and merchant traders, who came to plunder and exploit *Te Moananui a Kiwa* (The Great Ocean of Kiwa)[2] and beyond. To the ethnographers, anthropologists, and portrait artists, who reshaped our identities and images, and who often rewrote our traditions and stories for their own academic musings and for a high society English audience. To the missionary societies, who dismissed and demonized our values and

---

    1. The word Pākehā is used in te reo Māori to refer to people of European descent. The term Pālagi is commonly used in Samoan and Niuean or Papālangi in Tongan to refer to white people or people of European descent.

    2. Te Moananui a Kiwa is a Māori term for the Pacific Ocean and refers to the ocean of the ancestor Kiwa in Māori tradition.

belief systems, and who reinterpreted or worse stamped out our native wisdoms of both the natural and spiritual worlds.

We, as moana people have been colonized, missionized, and to some extent sanitized by Euro-Western missionary societies through the implementation of their language, traditions, and Christian faith, and the subsequent outlawing of our own. Is it any wonder that we have only in our more recent times found our prophetic voice to speak of our own theology? Rhetorical and yet answered with the development of this volume that attempts to gather, perhaps even elevate the "emerging theologies from the Global South."

We, as moana people have always been here, and we have encountered the Creator God generation after generation. We have transported those encounters, imbedded and entrenched in oral traditions of song and dance and story. We have shared those songs, dances, and stories amongst our island nations by word of mouth, by movement and gesture, and by narration. We have reframed and reshaped our song, dance, and story as we have journeyed across the moana, island after island. We have continually ferried our theology with us, to some extent reformed and refashioned by our distinctive cultural contexts from one island nation to another. However, our theology is yet still emerging.

We, as moana people are forced to acknowledge and speak to our colonization, our oppression, and our marginalization. We, as moana people are heavy-laden with a history of oppression and dispossession. We are forced to consider and discern the implications that colonized experience and historiography has had upon our somewhat displaced and dislocated theology. We are both burdened with, and compelled to, seek and reflect justice through the decolonizing of our theology and in the liberating and restoring of our native wisdoms. We continue to search for our place in the global theological discourse. We often find a place in contextual theology, indigenous theology, and perhaps as part of a kind of natural theology. All the while reimagining and reclaiming our faith and theology from the trappings of our colonial oppressors and their filtering and censoring of our cultural context.

To simply read, reflect, and analyze new material should not be the sole task of theological enquiry. Therefore, this piece of writing cannot simply be an exercise in gathering, collating, and disseminating information. Emergent theologies of Oceania are likely considered youthful in the broader history of theological discourse. When considering the exploration and examination of moana theology a slightly more moana style, a more nuanced approach may be required. It needs to be breathed, in and out. Theology of the moana is in the living out of our faith. It is in the storytelling of our people over generations. It is also in the traversing of our *vaka/waka/va'a* (canoe, vessel)[3] across Oceania. It is from all these things that our theology of the

---

3. In Rarotongan, Mangaian, and Marquesan the word *vaka* is commonly used to refer to a canoe. The Māori term for canoe or outrigger is *waka*. The word *va'a* is used in Samoan, Hawai'ian, and Tahitian for canoe, usually a double-hulled canoe.

moana emerges. The moana is one part of God's creation that can and does reveal a unique theology of depth and wisdom and complexity. This chapter attempts to navigate the waters of Oceania in search of insights, visions, and discourse of and with the Creator God. This chapter calls the readership to be submerged and engulfed in a moana theology!

This chapter attempts to evoke in the readers a movement and a rhythm of the moana, that engages and challenges them. Moana theology, like the ocean is often turbulent, and in contrast calming at other times. Moana theology is deliberately and intentionally confrontational and antagonistic because of our Oceania context. Moana theology is necessarily defiant and rebellious in order to bring about liberation and transformation. Moana theology is essentially a way of understanding God through creation, through the moana and its people.

QUESTIONS FOR DISCUSSION

1. *Why is it important to understand history and cultural context in Oceania?*
2. *What does colonization have to do with theology?*
3. *Can a colonized people find their prophetic voice?*
4. *What have you discerned about engaging with God through a moana lens?*
5. *How do we know something is moana theological discourse?*

MOANA GOD TALK—KŌRERO, 'ŌLELO, TALANOA, LAUGA[4]

How do we speak of moana and theology?

What language do we speak to enable understanding and comprehension?

The moana is where we come from, it is our home, our ancestor, our environment, our chartered territories, and our marine pathways. The moana is where our people derive all things. Therefore, it is only natural that we would look to the moana as a source of knowing and understanding our Creator God most intimately. How we speak of the moana is how we speak of our relationship with God, through an interweaving of creation and lived experiences.

As part of the Ka Wana series published by the University of Hawai'i, the Hawai'ian scholar, author, Anglican minister and healer Reverend Canon Malcolm Nāea Chun wrote a brief theological reflection as part of the introductory notes for the book *Kākā'olelo: Traditions of Oratory and Speech Making*. He began:

---

4. The term *kōrero* is Māori for discourse, discussion, conversation or to talk, to speak. In Hawai'ian the word for talk or discourse is *'ōlelo*. The Tongan term *talanoa* is used to refer to talking, speaking, or discourse. The word *lauga* in Samoan also means discourse or to engage in discourse.

> The Gospel according to John begins "In the beginning was the Word [. . .]." The missionary translators for this Gospel chose to use the original Greek *logos* instead of a Hawaiian word. Perhaps they thought the closet equivalent, 'ōlelo, did not express the depth of the word, although translators in Tahiti and Aotearoa (New Zealand) chose to use the native terms. It could be that the missionaries here did not learn from their Hawaiian assistants of the proverb "I ka 'ōleloke ola, i ka 'ōlelo ka make (In the word is life and in the word is death)," which emphasizes the care one needs to place upon what and how one says things and the reliance given to the spoken word."[5]

The Hawai'ian proverb of 'ōlelo expressed a deep affinity with the biblical text, in essence the word is life and death. The proverbial saying communicated a moana theology in the language and tradition of the native peoples. A theology that perhaps could not be articulated fully, or conceivably a theology that unfortunately could not be completely appreciated. A theology that was possibly inaudible and in comprehendible to the European missionary ear. The depth of meaning and power of 'ōlelo to an oral culture appeared lost in translation. The orality of Hawai'i, like many island nations, was subsequently silenced by the written world missionaries brought with them to Oceania. Our oral cultures became subject to the notions and impulses particularly of English missionary educators and translators of the day.

The oral cultures of Oceania speak in tradition, in narrative, and in story. We speak of our world, our people, and our faith in rhythm, in poetry, in metaphor, in imagery, and in memory. Much like the moana our theology is fluid not static and moves and shifts with each generation. As Jione Havea describes it, *talanoa* (talk, discuss) and fluidity are essential to a Pasifika or moana way of being: "Talanoa points to orality and oratory, a key vibe of which is fluidity. In Pasifika fluidity is not a concept or philosophy but a condition for and a characteristic of living. Pasifika islands are skirted by moana (deep sea), and fluidity shapes our mannerisms and cultures as well as links us from different and distant islands. We live in a saltwater world that shapes who we are."[6]

The moana for the peoples of Oceania is more than a vast body of water, it is a way of being and a source of life. The moana can serve as a guide to right relationship with God and creation. Theologian and scholar Winston Halapua, when reflecting upon moana and the interrelationship between land, sky, and humanity wrote, "A distinct contribution of the pioneering *moana* people to the whole movement of humanity over the ages is their knowledge of the ocean and the wisdom that sprang from their engagement with the experience of an interconnected source of life—the *moana*."[7]

The art of oratory in Oceania is respected if not revered, "Speaking or speech making, is still a very powerful, respected, and vital part of the Pacific Islands. In

5. Nāea Chun, *Kāka'olelo*, 1–2.
6. Havea, "Sea of Theologies," 5.
7. Halapua, *Waves of God's Embrace*, 11.

Western Polynesian islands of Sāmoa, Tonga and Fiji, orators are esteemed as messengers of wisdom, politics, and culture."[8] Traditionally, the orator's ability to attain knowledge and wisdoms of the ancestors and the Gods, provided opportunity to secure their social and political position in the village or tribal context. Nāea Chun described oratory in Polynesia in terms of both position and power: "While oratory shares this sense of status throughout the Pacific, in traditional times orators had both rank and status."[9] The Samoan tradition of the *tulafale* (orator) illustrates the importance of both lineage and oral competency. The Tahitian *'ōlelo* (orator) is recognized as a charismatic leader with mental agility, exceptional memory, and exercises social and political proficiency.

In Māori tradition great orators are remembered every time speakers recite the *whakatauki* (proverbial saying), *Ko te kai a te Rangatira, he kōrero (That which sustains the orators is speech)*. The proverb is derived from layer upon layer of lived experiences within a society that honors the gifts and graces of oratory. The proverb also conveys the importance of genealogical knowledge and native wisdom to a capable and skillful speaker. The orator is pertinent as a repository of knowledge and is vital to the dissemination of that knowledge particularly within an oral culture.

> A skilled orator will incorporate appropriate *whakataukī*, *pepeha* and *kupu-whakaari* (prophetic sayings of charismatic leaders) and references to important geographical and historical places of the *manuhiri* and *tangata whenua*; he will use metaphor and simile; recite appropriate *whakapapa*; make reference to things appropriate for the occasion; and have the skill of keeping the attention of the audience, including by the use of humour.[10]

Levesi Afutiti describes the importance of oral tradition and language in the Samoan context, "Considering Samoa's oral tradition, language has been the primary means of transmitting norms and values as 'word of life.' Through speaking and hearing, language helps give birth to one's self-understanding, chiefly because language molds one's worldview and disposition."[11] Afutiti's emphasis on the importance of language in the shaping of one's worldview speaks to the foundations of a moana perspective. Further Afutiti refers to the function of native texts and the incorporation of biblical texts in maintaining familial values such as parenting practices, "They use Samoan proverbs and wisdom sayings, together with biblical sayings, to stimulate the minds and hearts of children into deeper understanding."[12]

The tradition of storytelling and of storytellers, is synonymous with indigenous peoples the world over. The stories of our Oceanic roots uncover and expose a

---

8. Nāea Chun, *Kākā'olelo*, 2.
9. Nāea Chun, *Kākā'olelo*, 4.
10. Higgins and Moorfield, "Ngā tikanga o te marae," 80–81.
11. Afutiti, "Native Texts," 53.
12. Afutiti, "Native Texts," 53.

theology embedded in generations of oral tradition. The orality of Oceania cultures made memory and recitation important tools and mechanisms for the continuation of oral tradition within our societies. Revealing a distinctive way of speaking of moana theology, that brings to light the native wisdoms of both the ancestors and the *Atua* (Creator God).[13]

In many Oceanic traditions the orator of old has become the minister of the modern era. The ministers and pastors of today are often considered the new orators, with a new message and theology. In his *Pacific Prayer for the Moana*, Halapua gives thanks and praise for God's creation of the moana:

> Loving and embracing God, you are God of the universe and all creation. You create and give life and see that your creation is good. We praise you for your gift of the moana which covers most of the surface of your planet earth. We thank you for the oceans of the world. We thank you for the flowing of the oceans into one another and around the continents and islands. We thank you for the life giving of the oceans, for the oxygen, food, and resources they continually provide. We thank you that the ocean is home for most species small and great. We are people of the moana, our ancestors navigated by the stars and crossed the waves to find new homes. The voice of the waves breaking on the reef speaks of your constancy and your love, and your care for creation . . .[14]

Halapua, in his prayer celebrates the gift of the moana as a source of life and creation, essentially, he surmises that the moana is of the Creator God, and therefore an exemplar of the life-affirming grace of God. The haunting sounding of the conch and the beating of the drum from our Oceania *kainga* (home) call us to the Creator God. Halapua proclaims "We blow a conch calling for the worship of a life-giving God of immense goodness."[15] The conch echoes the voice of the moana, and the pounding of the waves are like the rhythmic heartbeat of the moana, a constant reminder and reflection of God's presence in the world. Halapua's prayer continues as he likens the waves breaking on the reef to God's constant love and care for creation, articulating the interwoven relationships of all creation.

This chapter is intended to introduce the readership to moana peoples and our theology. For the purposes of this introductory chapter, the term Oceania is utilized in a broad and inclusive manner. The term is used here to refer to the vast nations of Oceania, including Micronesia, Melanesia, and Polynesia recognizing our peoples' shared *whakapapa* (genealogy). Therefore, references to moana peoples are also inclusive of the many lands, seas, waterways, and communities of Oceania, while still maintaining our unique and diverse distinctions of language, culture, and tradition.

---

13. The Māori word Atua is used to refer to Gods (from native/indigenous traditions), however after colonization and missionary intervention, the word was also used to refer to the Christian God.
14. Halapua, "Pacific Prayer for the Moana (Ocean)."
15. Halapua, "Pacific Prayer for the Moana (Ocean)."

By way of a brief explanation of theology as it is applied in this chapter, it is *kōrero/talanoa* (discourse) concerning Creator God. Theology for the purposes of this chapter, considers the interrelationships between Creator and creation, God, and the universe. As a way of offering the most direct and simple definition, moana theology is a discourse concerning Atua/God from a moana worldview. Moana theology likely finds a comfortable place amongst the many Pasifika theologies that continue to emerge from the depths of Te Moananui a Kiwa.

QUESTIONS FOR DISCUSSION

1. *Why is orality important when trying to understand and articulate moana theology?*
2. *What does oral tradition have to do with moana theology?*
3. *Can a moana worldview express theology effectively for this modern era?*
4. *What is the moana saying to us of God's presence in Oceania?*
5. *How do we engage in moana theological discourse?*

MOANA SONG: WAIATAMAI!

How do we sing and chant of moana theology?

> "*Teararau o Tangaroa, e rere ki tepapaurunui*
> *Teararau o Tangaroa, e rere ki tepapaurunui*
> *Teararau o Tangaroa, e rere ki tepapaurunui*
> *Tahoranui ātea, te manawa o te moana*
> *Te mauri o Tangaroa*
> *Tangaroa whakamautai*
> *Tangaroa whakamautai*
> *Tūtara Kauika, he poutiriao*
> *Tewai o Tangaroa*
> *Tewai o Tangaroa*
> *Te tangi a tetohorā, he tohunōaitua*
> *Temau a Tangaroa*
> *Temau a Tangaroa*
> *Tangaroa whakamautai*
> *He kaitiaki, he taonga, he tipua*
> *He ariki, he taniwha, he tipua*
> *He kaitiaki, he taonga, he tipua*
> *Tangaroa whakamautai.*"[16]

16. Creative Talanoa, "Tangaroa Whakamautai by Maisey Rika."

This *waiata* (song) by Māori singer/songwriter Maisey Rika, sings of the story of Tangaroa (God/Ancestor of the ocean). In our Oceanic traditions, *Tangaroa/Tagaloa*[17] is the commander of tides, a guardian, an unexplainable phenomenon, an ancestor, and an ancient God. This song entitled *Tangaroa Whakamautai* (see Appendix 1 for an English translation) chants of the moana, the spiritual life force of Tangaroa. Maisey Rika gives this brief explanation for the inspiration behind the waiata, "Tangaroa Whakamautai theoretically speaks about looking after our natural resources in particular—the waterways. Who is the true guardian of the water and all its resources—it is Tangaroa."[18] According to Māori creation narratives Tangaroa, was one of the many sons of primordial parents *Ranginui* (sky father) and *Papatūānuku* (earth mother). Tangaroa is both the God of the moana and the progenitor of *ika* (fish). This song celebrates the life-giving waterways of Tangaroa and emphasizes the deep and intrinsic relationships between the many moana peoples.

The oral traditions of Tangaroa and of the moana feature in histories throughout Oceania, spoken from *marae* (gathering place) to *kainga* (village), carried on *vaka/waka/vaʻa* (canoe), and rooted in song and dance. Mosese Maʻilo wrote of our shared Oceanic traditions, "Stories drifted along the islands, and islands were connected by stories (of creation, of the tatau/tattoo, of Lata/Rata, of Tagaloa/Tagaroa, of the fine mat, of chiefly links, and so on) and histories (of navigation, of colonization and decolonization, of rival mission societies, and so on)."[19] The many creation narratives are a great example of how moana people speak of our theology. The Samoan traditions tell of Tagaloa-lagi who created the islands of Samoa who begat Papatu, who married Papaʻele. According to one Tongan account the gods are known as Papalimu and Papakele. The Tahitian stories speak of Ātea and Papatuʻoi, sky father and earth mother. The Hawaiʻian stories feature Wakea and Papa, and in the Rarotongan account Ātea marries the earth mother, Paparoaiteitinga.[20]

A common respect and veneration for the moana suggests an interconnectedness of moana peoples beyond language, culture, and tradition. The resounding call of the moana helps to give meaning, explanation, and understanding to the world and to creation. The moana speaks through a *whakapapa* (lineage) of oral tradition and gives volume to a uniquely moana-centered, prophetic voice.

But what does this all mean for moana theology? It means that our moana theology can be expressed in a multitude of ways and need not be confined to the classroom or to the pages of a textbook or even to the diaries of English missionaries. It means that we can find Creator God manifest in aspects of the moana and recall those accounts in song. It means that waiata is not just for singing, for entertainment, or

---

17. According to Māori tradition Tangaroa is the God/Ancestor of the ocean. The word Tagaloa is the Samoan term for God, creator, chief, and progenitor of the world/universe.

18. Maisey Rika, "My Driving Force Is My People."

19. Maʻilo, "Island Prodigals," 23.

20. Taonui, "Ranginui—the sky," 3.

for expressing emotion, it is also a tool or mechanism for theological discourse. Just like hymns, blessings, and praise and worship songs, these waiata tell a story of the interconnectedness of our Creator God and humanity as a part of creation. This is the basis for a moana theology that resonates and reverberates from within Oceania.

QUESTIONS FOR DISCUSSION

1. *Why is song a valid and intrinsic mechanism for theological discourse in Oceania?*
2. *What does Tangaroa have to do with theology in Oceania?*
3. *Why are moana/Oceania creation narratives considered to be theological tools?*
4. *What connections (if any) do you see between your own context and the moana/Oceania context?*
5. *What traditions or native wisdoms might be considered theological tools for reflection and discernment in your own context?*

MOANA DANCE: SACRED GESTURES

How might we interpret Ps 149?

How shall we dance in Oceania?

Shall we dance the Lakalaka, or the Tau'olunga, the Siva or the Sasa, the Haka or the Poi, the Meke or the Seasea, the Hula Kahiko or the Hula Auana?

Moana, a common term in Oceania for the ocean and a physical and spiritual paradigm of whakapapa, of identity, of home, of creation, and of God. Oceanic dance brings to life the world created for us. From the instruments we build, shape, and play that imitate natural bird songs and calls to the various movements, and steps we devise that mimic the rhythms and tempos of the natural world including animal and plant life, as well as the beats and cadences of the moana. Some moana peoples use dance to convey the stories of the ancestors and the Gods. Some of us attempt to impersonate or emulate the supernatural. While there are others of us that use dance to reflect or respond to contemporary issues, and to be an expression of prophetic voice.

Our ceremonial dance is often a visual and physical extension of the orator's speech and storytelling. We use our bodies and gestures to speak of our experiences of and interactions with creation and the Creator God. We might compare our gestures and mannerisms to the way in which Christians use hand gestures to engage in prayer or to indicate the blessing of the holy cross. We might find parallels with the traditional Christian practices of raising and clapping hands intimating veneration, or perhaps with the bowing or kneeling in prayer as an expression of humility.

Dance in Oceania brings to life the natural environment with what we as moana peoples would consider sacred gestures. The shimmering light reflected on the silver fern appears in the Māori dance practice of the *wiriwiri* (quivering of the hands). The sway of the trees in a gentle breeze or the waves upon the moana are expressed in the hand gestures and hip movements of the *hula kahiko* (traditional Hawai'ian dance). The quickening flight of the butterfly is often demonstrated in the swift hip movements and motions of the Tahitian *'ōte'a vahine* (traditional female dance).

Oceania dance is considered a religious or spiritual performance, as dances are often performed in honor of the Gods or in dedication to the Gods. Dance has been adapted and evolved as an expression of worship and prayer for many generations in Oceania. Indigenous peoples of the world have often used dance as part of their religious or spiritual practices and many have retained those practices despite colonization. Those who have taken on Christianity have in modern times, continued to modify, and alter traditional dance for Christian worship.

In the late 1990s the Vatican recognized the Hawai'ian hula as a sacred dance with "sacred gestures," allowing the Roman Catholic Church in Hawai'i to perform hula in official church celebrations and ceremonies. The Diocese of Honolulu in accordance with the directives from Rome, had previously banned any Native Hawai'ian sacred gestures during Mass or any other liturgical services. However, a formal dispensation sought by Bishop Francis DiLorenzo, was granted to the Honolulu church for hula to be engaged as a form of worship and prayer but not for entertainment.[21]

Moana theology has been captured and articulated through the many examples of dance across the traditions of Oceania. The metaphorical imagery of dance and movement lends itself well to moana theological expressions, including the mystery and enigma of God. There exists a sense of mystery and of the unknown in the moana. Halapua explained the expanse and mystery of the moana saying, "For Oceanic people the ocean is not a vast empty space. The moana holds mystery because of the depths of the ocean and its hidden life. Here is experienced the presence of gods of the ocean and the spirits of the ancestors."[22] What Halapua alludes to here is a recurring theme of interwoven relationships between humanity, and creation, each element a part of the other, interdependent and inter-reliant, each acting as a conduit to knowing God.

Pacific theologians have begun to explore the ways in which our people theologize, redefining how we think, talk, and write about our theology. The biblical scholar and theologian, Upolu Va'ai, describes the concept of relational theologizing as a theological dance:

> It allows us to rediscover God already dancing with us to the rhythms of life, expressed in little practices such as fishing, planting, oral stories, feasting, and birthing to name a few. A theological dance informed by the silent whispers of

---

21. *Honolulu Star Bulletin*, July 9, 1998.
22. Halapua, *Waves of God's Embrace*, 5.

the vanua (land) and the graceful movements of vaitafe (flowing rivers), transformed by the fluidity and unpredictability of the moana (ocean), animated by the mānava ola (breath of life) of the vaomatua (the elder forest), and dirtified by the rising dust from the malae, the ceremonial grounds of the Pacific dirt communities.[23]

Va'ai suggests that in the most mundane of daily activities we are constantly engaging in a theological dance with God, who is ever-present and who speaks to us through the lands, oceans, forests, and the dirt.

QUESTIONS FOR DISCUSSION

1. Why is dance considered to be sacred in Oceania?
2. What does dance have to do with theology in Oceania?
3. What parallels can be drawn between the moana and God?
4. What does dance tell us about God's rhythms and cadences in Oceania?
5. Why is the mystery of the moana considered an expression of God?

MOANA WAHINE: POETRY IN MOTION

Moana Wahine
Mysterious and engaging, yet somehow unattainable

Moana who sings, whose depths and breadths allude us all
Moana who dances, who moves and shifts with the ebbs and flows of the tides

Moana who cannot be brought to yield, by sand and rock
Moana who cannot be tamed, by winds and storms

Moana who cannot be conquered, by human or mammal
Moana the mauri (life essence, life force) of the sea

Moana synonymous with a wahine, sun-kissed brown skin, long wavy pitch-black hair, brown piercing eyes of suspicion and forth-right conviction
She is immersed and contented in her ancestors' wisdoms, as they speak to her of their people and their past

She is confident and comfortable in her cultural identity, and speaks the native tongue of her mother

23. Va'ai, "From Atutasi to Atulasi," 236–37.

She is fearless and foreboding
She is Moana Wahine

This poem personifies the moana and calls to mind the powerful image of a Pasifika woman. This poem speaks of the experiences and encounters between humanity and creation, as we interact and are intertwined with one another. This poem draws parallels between the moana and the Pasifika woman. The moana exemplifies strength and power, the Pasifika woman defines grace and wisdom, the nature of each is amplified in the recitation of the poem.

The name Moana is most often worn by women and the ocean, despite the many stories of Tangaroa/Tagaloa, is often attributed female traits and characteristics. Most recently the Disney animated movie of *Moana* (2016) endeavored to explore an inexplicable connection between a young Pasifika woman and the ocean. Despite what appeared to be a fumbled attempt to homogenize the cultures of Oceania, the depiction of Moana and her encounters with the ocean again give emphasis to the relationship between God and creation.

The place, status, and importance of women in Oceania as *whaea/fa'e* (mothers), as *ariki/ali'i* (chiefly leaders), as *matakite* (seers or oracles), and as *toa/malieto'a* (warriors and fighters) has been subverted by a colonial ideology of a native woman of little intelligence and diminished capacity. Like Oceania women, the place, status, and importance of Pasifika theologies, including moana theology in the global theological discourses has been largely dismissed or at the least disrupted. Moana theology has gone largely unnoticed and/or consigned to the backblocks of the discipline of theology in academia.

Theologians, clergy, and practitioners of native wisdoms of Oceania have for many years developed theologies derived from our worldviews. We acknowledge theological contributions that originated from the coconut, the *vanua* (land), and the moana. Other influential schools of thought have focused on the planting of theologies in Pacific soil. Much like the Māori Methodist theologian, Ruawai Rakena's example of "potted plant theology." Rakena suggested the need to break open the colonial pot, and to have the theology firmly rooted in the *whenua* (land). To the more recent contemporary exploration of a theology of *kapahaka* (Māori performance art/dance), that considers the medium of dance and music as theological tools. To Upolu Va'ai's Pacific dirt theology, that suggests a movement from what he describes as the "colonial digestive centers" to the dirt communities.

When our ancestors traveled across Oceania, they knew God. They understood God as well as they understood the oceans they traversed, the clouds and stars by which they navigated, and the migratory patterns of living creatures that helped guide their way. The wisdoms of our *tupuna/kupuna* (ancestors) are guides to help us make sense of the world, and it is from those same native wisdoms that we draw our theologies of the moana. Our moana theology is encapsulated in our stories, and in our song, and our dance.

Theology that emerges from Oceania endeavors to bring together our worldview and our God understandings. We understand God to be a part of all creation, from the dirt and the dust to the skies above and the deep oceans below. Moana theology provides us with a framework to understand creation and our place in it. Moana theology offers an alternative way of theologizing that is experiential and relational. Moana theology is not just an exercise in academic analysis or intellectual exploration. Moana theology is a way of being, a way of life, not separate from the people, the land, and the ocean but intimately related.

QUESTIONS FOR DISCUSSION

1. *How might you engage with or respond to this "Moana Wahine" poem?*
2. *What insider information is required to understand this native text?*
3. *How might you understand or interpret moana theology?*
4. *In what ways might you best express theology in your context?*
5. *How is your worldview reflected in your theology?*

BIBLIOGRAPHY

Afutiti, Levesi Laumau. "Native Texts: Samoan Proverbial and Wisdom Sayings." In *Sea of Readings: The Bible in the South Pacific,* edited by Jione Havea, 53–67. Atlanta: Society of Biblical Literature, 2018.

Creative Talanoa. "Tangaroa Whakamautai by Maisey Rika." https://creativetalanoa.com/2012/09/15/tangaroa-whakamautai-by-maisey-rika/.

Halapua, Winston. "A Pacific Prayer for the Moana (Ocean)." Posted by Rev. James Bhagwan, Secretary for Communication and Overseas Mission of the Methodist Church in Fiji and Chaplain/Trustee of the Traditional Voyaging Canoe the Uto Ni Yalo. June 7, 2016. https://www.youtube.com/watch?v=D82UUugxm4w.

———. *Waves of God's Embrace: Sacred Perspectives from the Ocean.* London: Canterbury, 2008.

Havea, Jione. "Sea of Theologies." In *Theologies from the Pacific,* edited by Jione Havea, 1–12. Switzerland: Nature Springer Palgrave Macmillan, 2021.

Higgins, Rawinia, and John C. Moorfield. "Ngā tikanga o te marae: Marae practices." In *Ki tewhaiao: An Introduction to Māori Culture and Society,* edited by Tania M. Ka'ai et al., 80–81. Auckland: Pearson Education NZ, 2004.

Honolulu Star Bulletin. July 9, 1998. http://archives.starbulletin.com/98/07/09/news/indext.html.

Ma'ilo, Mosese. "Island Prodigals: Encircling the Void in Luke 15:11–32 with Albert Wendt." In *Sea of Readings: The Bible in the South Pacific,* edited by Jione Havea, 23–36. Atlanta: Society of Biblical Literature, 2018.

Maisey Rika. "My Driving Force Is My People." April 02, 2015. https://pacificmusiczone.wordpress.com/tag/maisey-rika/.

Nāea Chun, Malcolm. *Kākāʻolelo: Traditions of Oratory and Speech Making*. Ka Wana 8. Honolulu: Curriculum Research and Development Group, 2006.

Taonui, Rāwiri. "Ranginui—the sky—Polynesian myths." *Te Ara—the Encyclopedia of New Zealand*. http://www.TeAra.govt.nz/en/ranginui-the-sky/page-3.

Te Punga Somerville, Alice. *Once Were Pacific: Māori Connections to Oceania*. Minneapolis: University of Minnesota Press, 2012.

Vaʻai, Upolu Lumā. "From Atutasi to Atulasi: Relational Theologizing and Why Pacific Islanders Think and Theologize Differently." In *Theologies from the Pacific*, edited by Jione Havea, 235–49. Switzerland: Nature Springer Palgrave Macmillan, 2021.

APPENDIX 1—TRANSLATION OF TANGAROA WHAKAMAUTAI BY MAISEY RIKA

The various waterways of Tangaroa
Flow back into its voluminous source
The vast expanse, the heart of the ocean
The life force of Tangaroa
Tangaroa commander of the tides
A pod of whales, a supernatural phenomenon
Evolving from the waters of Tangaroa
The waters of Tangaroa
The cry of the whale, signals a warning
The power of Tangaroa, The power of Tangaroa
Tangaroa commander of the tides
A guardian, a precious treasure
A strange/supernatural being
A god, Of the ancient prehistoric realm
A guardian, a precious treasure
A strange/supernatural being
Tangaroa commander of the tides.

Creative Talanoa. "Tangaroa Whakamautai by Maisey Rika." September 15, 2012. https://creativetalanoa.com/2012/09/15/tangaroa-whakamautai-by-maisey-rika/.

CHAPTER 28

Australia's First Nations Theology

ANNE PATTEL-GRAY

We begin the construction of Australia's First Nations theology by sharing about its culture, spirituality, and lifeways in the hope of gaining insight and understanding of our relationship to and with the Creator Spirit's; and the Creator's actions and interactions through our Ancestral Spirits in the creation of our world, humanity, customs, laws, ceremonies, songs, rituals, connection to land, water, and sea, language, cosmology, worldview, and philosophy. This is the basis of our First Nations identity, faith, and spirituality. Australia's First Nations peoples have a deep understanding of the Creator Spirit which has been nurtured over sixty thousand years and we give deep reverence to the secret/sacred ancestral narratives pertaining to the Creator Spirit as this holds great significance to our spiritual world.

Australia's First Nations people are considered to be the oldest living culture in the world. Through our theological method we took time to identify the Indigenous peoples in biblical narratives this has contributed to an informed our discourse and the focus of our exegetical and hermeneutical process in which we Australia's First Nations people take to explore this topic further. Especially through our collective experience this brings a different interpretation and reading through our First Nations lens which brings a new insight to our theology and grounds it within an Australian context.

To commence this process part of our methodology must include the process of decolonizing our minds, ideologies, and beliefs systems that have held us captive to a Western interpretation. As we believe the Creator Spirit was here in our beginning long before white colonizers invaded our land, therefore, we can now find the freedom to interpret our relationship with the Spirit Creator through our worldview. As we turn with a decolonized mind to biblical narratives.

PRECOLONIAL HERMENEUTICS

The ancient ancestral narratives speak of the Creator Spirit's actions and interaction with Australia's First Nations people which defines the Creator Spirit's relationship within our understanding and worldview before colonial invasion.

This method sets the foundation for a First Nations hermeneutical and exegetical process which allows us the freedom to reread the biblical narratives from our own precolonial perspective. In doing this we are challenged to decolonize our minds and to be open to the opportunity of reading the biblical texts through First Nations' eyes and understanding. Our approach in decolonizing the biblical narrative is not only to decolonize the interpretation of the Bible, but also to decolonize the biblical narrative itself.

In this context, colonialism can be understood as a mindset of individuals, communities or peoples that assume claim or activate the fundamental belief or worldview that they have the right to exercise dominion, control, or dispossession of other individuals, communities, or people.

This will enable us to examine our discourse and to consider how indoctrinated we are by Eurocentric colonial philosophy, values, and culture and show the forced domination of Western biblical interpretation that First Nations have been held in bondage to. This endeavor is to develop a truly Australian First Nations theology born out of and embedded in our land—Our Mother Earth.

SPIRITUALITY AND PHILOSOPHY OF LIFE

Australia First Nations people are profoundly religious in their character. The formalities of our life, the mode of our life and thought, and our every act have spiritual significance. Our most deliberate words and deeds revolve around religious considerations. We have a highly developed sense of the sacred, and our views of ourselves and of the world are preeminently religious.

We have always centered our lives in the spiritual-natural world. We are deeply committed to the Creator Spirit and to our Ancestral Spirits and to creation in consciousness and in instinct. Only though our spiritual connections to land and creation can we sustain our own cultural identity and life source. Therefore, we conceive of ourselves in the terms of the land. In our view the earth is sacred. It is a living entity in which other living entities have origin and destiny. It is where our identity comes from, where our spirituality begins, it is the connection to our ancestral narratives; it is where stewardship begins, and it is where life source is sustained. We are bound to the earth in our spirit. By means of our involvement in the natural world we can ensure our own well-being.

One of our greatest strengths is rooted in our ability to communicate with the spiritual world around us. This is manifested in our extensive use of symbolism, in our visionary experiences, in our spirituality, and in our use of language. These forms of communications and these symbols have clear expression in our ancestral narratives, the initiation ceremonies, the sacred sites, the healing rituals, and the rejuvenation ceremonies. They are evident in our oral traditions.[1]

To understand our worldview, non-indigenous people need to immerse themselves into our metaphysical world. This is not an easy task to undertake, because our perception of ourselves and our world—whether it is the physical, emotional, or spiritual—is not fragmented. Rather, these elements all co-exist together. The importance of this connection between ourselves and other living forms of creation is expressed through totemism. The ritual performance associated with this influences and ensures the reproduction of both the natural and the human continuation and the natural cycle of seasons. Through many thousands of years, we First Nations people have developed an intimate relationship between ourselves and our environment.

Through our spiritual interconnection with the natural world, we do not see ourselves as separate from it but as inextricably bound to it. Our place and survival in this world come as a direct result of this close relationship with our natural environment. Our relationship with our environment is not one of domination or manipulation. We do not erect huge religious cathedrals, churches, or synagogues to highlight the significance of sacred areas. Instead our sacred sites are natural land formations where our Ancestral Spirits interacted with creation and therefore based First Nations people's ownership of our spiritual identification and association with our lands, water, and sea.

Through the bestowal of land by the Creator Spirit to our ancestors, we Australia's First Nations people share in maintaining our interconnections, through shared responsibilities and obligations through our totemic relationships or as custodians of certain sacred site. This is done through rituals and ceremonies continually performed at the exact time each year. These cannot be done by just anyone, as they can only be done by those responsible as custodians of that particular site.

These may be done, however, by more than one language group. Those who share in these obligations may be custodians of a specific section of the ritual relating to a site through their totemic association and through shared ownership of sacred knowledge and so on. Cooperation or sharing is an important factor in any Australia First Nations society, not only between genders, but also between clan and tribal language groups. The division of labor is shared amongst the community as well as the responsibilities and obligation of sacred rituals and ceremonies shared between clans and tribes as each may have ownership of a certain section of a particular ritual.

1. Pattel-Gray, *Through Aboriginal Eyes*.

ANCESTRAL NARRATIVES

For Australia's First Nations people our ancestral narratives are the embodiment of truth as they detail the beginning of creation and the life of all living things. It is the basis on which First Nations' connection to land, water, and sea is associated and through which it is symbolized. Ancestral narratives are maintained in an oral tradition and told and retold by elders to the next generations and the ancestral narratives are recorded within the land, water, and sea of the Creator Spirit's actions and interactions with our Ancestral Spirits in the creation of our environment. The birth of our humanity, the essence of our religious beliefs, laws, ceremonies, and rituals are derived from our ancestral narratives. It holds time immemorial and is the eternal nexus to our Spirit Creator and Ancestral Spirits to the past, present, and future generations.

Our ancestral narratives are the embodiment of truth, and the authenticity is never questioned. They are not written in some book; the environment contains the stories, markings, and narratives of the Spirit Creator and Ancestral Beings found in our ancestral narratives.[2] Through our ceremonies and rituals First Nations sing and dance the ancestral narratives into life and they tell of the Creator's actions and interactions through our Ancestral Spirits which gives praise to the Creator Spirit and ensure the rejuvenation of the creation.

THE "DREAMING" CONCEPT

The ancestral narratives for First Nations people are both real and concrete and are the basis upon which our identity and relationships with the Creator Spirit, Ancestral Spirits, land, water and sea, environment and humanity are established. The "Dreaming" is a term constructed by white anthropologists to describe Australia's First Nations' ancestral narratives and religious life and here are First Nations scholars responding to some of this so-called Western scholarship. Cynthia Rowan highlights a time when "The Dreaming is a term that was pulled apart and psychoanalyzed by people like Freud in *Totem and Taboo* (1960), and Roheim in *Australian Totemism: A Psycho-Analytic Study in Anthropology* (1971) and *The Eternal Ones of Dream: A Psychoanalytic Interpretation of Australian Myth and Ritual* (1945). They attempted to define what was 'true' or 'real' in terms of their own cultural perception. They, Like many early scholars on different aspects of Aboriginal life, attempted to define the parameters of Aboriginal life; either the history the culture or the religion. These scholars interpreted what they saw and what they were told, and had it published in academic works which were then studied by other scholars and students at universities in Australia and around the world."[3]

---

2. Pattel-Gray, *Aboriginal Spirituality*.
3. Pattel-Gray, *Aboriginal Spirituality*.

These fundamental First Nations aspects differ greatly from Western concepts of dreaming; all Western preconceptions should be purged from the mind, in order to begin with openness and a willingness to view our First Nations religious and spiritual world with different eyes and understanding. "In Aboriginal societies such as the Arrente of Central Australia, the Dreaming was the time of 'power'. Arrente Dreaming stories are told, danced, and sung with the intention of re-creating, and I stress, re-creating the Dreaming or power. Every time the Dreaming is re-enacted it is re-created. Or, to put it another way, every time the Arrente women re-enact the Honeyant Dreaming they are creating the honeyants and the food supply associated with it."[4]

Even though historically we have seen many cases where the West has failed in such an attempt to have an open mind, however, we encourage the readers to try and open themselves to the unique spiritual and religious lifeways of the original peoples of Australia.

As Patrick Dodson writes:

> ... to offer some understanding of the deeply spiritual nature of Aboriginal people through an explanation of the Dreaming. An understanding of the concepts of the Dreaming is essential to any understanding of the Australia First Nations worldview. The English word "dreaming" can be misleading because the concepts which it translates are extremely complex, and largely are unrelated to the English meaning of the word. These concepts often are alternatively described as the "The Law'" They are a coherent and all-encapsulating body of truths which govern the whole of life. "The Dreaming" or "The Law" includes the past and ongoing activities of creative and life-giving forces which always retain a sense of immanence and transcendence, of the actual potential. Western understanding of time is beautifully confounded by these concepts.[5]

To provide a greater understanding of the historical development of the use of the word Dreaming, and where it came from, requires us to cover the early interactions of white anthropologists and Australia's First Nations. One of the biggest difficulties confronted by the anthropologist was the many First Nations languages. Spencer and Gillen were amongst the first to begin using the term Dreaming or Dreamtime, the term referred to by the Aranda people from Central Australia as Alchheringa or Altjiranga in describing the time in which the Creator through the Ancestral Spirits shaped the land and environment and handed down the law and lifeways, still being followed today by Australia First Nations. The Aranda term Altjirangangambakala means, "having originated out of one's own eternity," being immortal and it is this that forms the fundamental basis of the term Dreaming. Also, the Aranda "Altjirarama" means "to see or dream eternal things." Another First Nations language group, the

---

4. Pattel-Gray, *Aboriginal Spirituality*, 29.
5. Dodson, "Land Our Mother", 1.

Karadjiri people from the Kimberleys at the north of Western Australia, says Bugari.[6] In North West Australia the Ngarinyin people refer to the Dreaming as Ungud and the Yolngu people of North Eastern Arnhem Land speak of it as Wongar and the Pitjantjatjara people refer to it as Tjukurpa.

As a result of linguistic problems encountered by these anthropologists, it was easier for them to use this simple term Dreaming in describing this very spiritual and religiously complex aspect for Australia's First Nations tradition. Although the term Dreaming or Dreamtime was the English way to describe First Nations' understanding and belief, this reference is now used widely by First Nations people right across Australia when speaking to non-Aboriginal people. "For Aboriginal people the creative and life-giving forces are still very much alive. The land is full of the Ancestors of all human, plant and animal lives are represented in the landforms. This extends to celestial forms such as the planets and the stars, the moon and the sun. There are stories and songs throughout the land which relate these things. Sites where events of great significance occurred are holy places—sacred sites. Some places are so important that their story can only be told by the fully initiated people."[7]

It is important to note the decolonizing process calls for me to not use terminology that denigrates and disrespects my people's culture, spirituality, and religion. As you may have already noted, I use the term ancestral narratives to describe the ancient oral traditions of my people which embody truth, authority, and pride.

SPIRITUALITY

Australia First Nations' spirituality and religious beliefs are shared by many First Nations leaders and they have throughout the decades tried to convey their thoughts, beliefs, and culture with the Australian church and community. This however has been either ignored or met with contempt, leaving First Nations people with feelings of invisibility and rejection. Hence, I wish to highlight the views of a couple of very prominent First Nations Christian leaders and to share their views about our culture and spirituality.

Djiniyini Gondarra states:

> My understanding is that primal religions like ours depend on sacred stories . . . they are not made-up stories but are very real, sacred and holy. We do not need scripture or creeds to learn about the Spirit Powers. Our Aboriginal Spirituality is alive and everything we see in the God-given nature—the trees, bushes and creatures are all alive and not dead. Our culture is a living culture.

Australian Aborigines make no distinction between the religious and the secular, between the natural and the supernatural. Our religion can be seen as a particular

---

6. Pattel-Gray, *Aboriginal Spirituality*, 29
7. Dodson, "Warning to a Young Writer [Poem]," 806–7.

view of the universe and sets of relationships with it; relationships which include people, gods, Spirit, magical power, totems, the land, features of the landscape, living creatures, trees, plants, and all physical objects.

All of these are, in some sense, potential sources of power. Relationships with people and Ancestral Spirits are universally the most important, for at the center of life is the community of (people) and Spirits, all of whom are alive. This community, with membership of an extended family and links with a particular piece of land, gives a person identity and security, a reason for living, a sense of history, and an approach to the future. All the rituals of birth, initiation into adult life, marriage, and death are directed towards maintaining these links. Aboriginal spirituality aims at life, prosperity, harmony, control, and balance in all relationships particularly with (people) and Spirits; and "in this world rather than the next, although we believe in life after death."[8]

Australia First Nations leaders would speak boldly about our spiritual belief and faith and quite often be forcedly heard to state in no uncertain terms their understanding of the Creator God within our mist and that we had and continue to have a very strong relationship with our Creator Spirit. They would try and tell the missionaries and Western Christians and churches that they didn't bring God to this country as the Creator Spirit already existed in our land. Spirit and we have a deep understanding and reverence of the Creator Spirit.

A PROCESS OF INCULTURALTION[9]

A critical aspect involved in aiding the development of a First Nations theology is the process of inculturation. The importance I give to this process is not just limited to superficial cultural dressings, but rather a deeper process that has been described as incarnational. Pedro Arrupe first described this in 1981:

> Inculturaltion is the incarnation of the Christian life and of the Christian message in a particular cultural context, in such a way that this experience not only finds expression through elements proper to the culture in question, but becomes a principle that animates, directs and unifies the culture, transforming and remaking it so as to bring about "a new creation."[10]

While the phenomenon of secularization has brought about certain differentiation between social institutions like religion and culture, this has made us realize that inculturation is a continuing process and is never finished even among the so-called Christian community, but rather is an ongoing dialogue between gospel and culture. Even though the gospel has to be deeply involved in the culture and provide its basic meanings, insofar as culture has its own autonomy and develops in different ways, so

---

8. Pattel-Gray, *Aboriginal Spirituality*, 41–54.
9. Pattel-Gray, "Aboriginal Process of Inculturation," 13.
10. Arrupe, "Letter on Inculturaltion," 3.

too does the gospel also have to keep its own freedom to stand apart and challenge culture. The relationship between gospel and culture, therefore, becomes dialectical, although this dialectic remains incarnational in so far as it is the interior to any given culture. The interaction between human culture and Christianity is a natural process. Transformation of religious symbols and societal structures are either strengthened or weakened; there is not only a reinterpretation of symbols; there also may be the creation of new ones. This is made visible even in the Old Testament, where the word of God is spoken to a people who have a culture, worldview, rituals, and social structures of their own. This culture embodies already a first, founding and revelation of the word in creation both of the cosmos and of humanity as cited in John 1:1. This manifestation of the word remains the context in which further manifestations of the word acquire their significance as prophecy, referring back to the gift of God in all creation and pointing forward to the new creation to which God is calling us.

Inculturaltion is the process through which a particular community, in the context of its reality, culture, and life, responds to the word that is proclaimed. This involves two actions: first the message and second a response. The message proclaimed by Jesus is that the community of God is at hand; the idiosyncrasy associated with the rule of God is characterized through various biblical parables, which makes clear God's claim in the message and teachings of Jesus, and is therefore made visible though symbolically in the miracles accomplished by Jesus. This community of God is committed to, and works towards, establishing a community based on the values of freedom, justice, respect, and fellowship. God's message is a prophetic call to us, which requires conversion, and leads to a deeper commitment of building such a community. This proclamation does not come as a bolt of lightning, but rather, it alludes to the covenant made between God, humanity, and the whole of creation, in which Jesus came not to destroy, but rather to fulfill the promise made by the Creator Spirit, and therefore this promise is renewed at every age, in every situation, and to every people.

The original word was made flesh in the life of Jesus, in a particular time, place, and context, amongst a particular people, life situation, and culture, and has been recorded within biblical Scripture for us to read today. The task of First Nations Christians and theologians today is to incarnate the living Word not only into our cultural life and context, but also to enable the living Word to take shape in the blood, sweat, and tears of Australia's First Nations peoples and context.

So for me any endeavor towards the construction of a First Nations theology must encompass our cosmology, ontology, and epistemology. This begins with Creator's Spirit actions and interactions with creation through our Ancestral Spirits, bestowing land to our ancestors via language group to be custodians and stewards. This forms the basis of our identity and relationship with God, the Creator. Through the Creator Spirit, our Spirit Ancestors laid the foundation from which today we continue to show our reverence to the Creator Spirit. In order to know Jesus Christ, First Nations people must begin with our Aboriginal identity. The Creator Spirit gave birth to our humanity and informed our identity and we are affirmed that we are created in the image of the Creator. We are the people of the land, one tied body and soul with and to our Earth Mother. Only when we begin to see ourselves as one with the Creator Spirit, and through the Creator Spirit bound to our Earth Mother as a result of our Ancestral Spirits acts in and throughout creation, can we hope to find truth in the form of our identity which encompasses our cosmogony, ontology, and epistemology.

EXPERIENTIAL

As a First Nations theologian the development of my theology could not be done without setting the experiential context of the suffering, subjugation, and oppression of my people. Experience, both historical and current, therefore, defines the First Nations peoples' suffering and oppression of Western colonization and missionization in Australia, through the theft of land, genocidal acts, slavery, segregation of First Nations people from British settlements, the government and church process of the stolen generations, and Western environmental destruction of Aboriginal land and lifeways.[11]

Today, Australia's First Nations peoples continue to experience racial discrimination as the federal government suspends the Racial Discrimination Act that protect the human rights of Australia's First Nations people which see the continuing removal of our children from their families and community, which include governments taking control our peoples' income, high incarceration rates of First Nations children and young people, high suicide rates of our young people, and the dissemination of cultural heritage and cultural rights. These horrific acts that have been inflicted upon Australia's First Nations peoples have had a deep psychological impact on the lives of my people which has left them traumatized and the efforts of this trauma is still being felt today.

Sadly, the most frightening aspect of the church's complicity in the subjugation of First Nations peoples is the heartfelt sentiment usually expressed that it was done with the best of intentions. The forced imposition of the Christian missionaries and, in fact, those denominations that worked among Australia's First Nations communities, were partners with the government in the genocide. Unwittingly no doubt, and always with the best of intentions, but nevertheless, the missionaries were guilty of complicity in the destruction of First Nations cultures and tribal social structures—complicit in the devastating impoverishment and death of the people to whom they preached.

Other genocidal acts led to the crushing of Australia's First Nations people's identity and spiritual beliefs. The history of colonization is seen as the domination of the Western world, whether this is good or bad, it has impacted upon the physical, emotional, and psychological lives of First Nations people, resulting in intergenerational trauma through the vehicle of missionization.

---

11. Pattel-Gray, *Great White Flood*.

This, however, does not alleviate the enormous trauma inflicted upon my people. In defining the methodological process of the historical experiences and current experiences of continuing racism, discrimination, and marginalization is our lived reality.

One of the exceptional Native American Indian scholars, George Tinker expounds upon the destructive nature of colonization and that which has fused the Western minds is:

> The 'Western World' mythology that has come to dominate the entire globe's economics, politics, and academics, imposing itself as the national, unquestionable norm of human existence. This illusion of Western world superiority has functioned implicitly, and at times brutally explicitly, to facilitate the conquest and enslavement of native peoples, the exploitation of their labor and the natural resources, and genocidal destruction of whole cultures and peoples. The religious institutions of the 'West' have been consistently lent legitimacy to those acts. At some level the church has ultimately functioned to provide theological justification for acts of conquest, even when it has protested to the contrary or interceded at the surface level on behalf of the conquered.[12]

This invariably resulted in the missionary's culture, values, and social and political structures, not to say political hegemony and control, being imposed on tribal peoples, all in the name of the gospel. Tinker goes on to clarify more clearly his criticism of the West, by stating, "That is to say, the kerygmatic content of the missionary's Christian faith became entwined with the accoutrements of the missionary's cultural experience and behavior."[13]

Nevertheless this becomes a contribution to our understanding of why Australia's First Nations people have generally failed to enter the Australian mainstream and continue to live in poverty and oppression, marginalized on the periphery of white society, resulting in the fact that First Nations peoples have not found liberation in the gospel of Jesus Christ, but rather, continued bondage to Western culture that is racist, alien and alienating, and even genocidal against Aboriginal people. It is in this context that we begin to deconstruct the cultural oppression and historical lies of colonization and the hypocrisy of Christianity of the eighteenth and nineteenth centuries, and endeavor to reconstruct a history and theology based on truth.

CHRIST OUR ANCESTOR

Australia's First Nations peoples' spirituality and identities are given by the Creator Spirit and are the foundation of our faith. So, if we believe in Jesus Christ as incarnated of the Creator Spirit, then our Christology is a natural process in the development of our theology. Orthodox Christian theology holds that God is incarnated in Christ

---

12. Tinker, *Missionary Conquest*, 17.
13. Tinker, *Missionary Conquest*, 18.

Jesus, making the Word flesh and a living example for us to follow. Is it not possible, then, also to say that Christ is our Ancestor, since, as stated above, the Creator Spirit interacted in creation through our Spirit Ancestors in a living form? Christ is the divine link between the old lifeways. Just as we say that Christ is the new covenant of the Bible—and the old Covenant of Moses has been transcended through Christ—we can also say that, through our Ancestor Christ, we, the First Nations people, are embarking upon our new covenant, as Christ enables us to transcend our own cultural limitations, through the ability to critique our own culture and position in society.

My theological process therefore, begins with the nature of the Creator Spirit in our creation, spirituality, land, and identity. It is in this aspect that we can truly grapple with being made in the image of the Creator Spirit, and the implication that has for our humanity, laws, faith, and identity in our relationship with the Creator Spirit. It is only when we begin to reflect upon the ancestral narratives and the old cultural lifeways and the interaction of the Creator Spirit in the old traditional ways, that we can sustain and maintain our spirituality and the reflected divinity of the Creator Spirit, encompassed in our identity. This is where First Nations peoples find their strength and the affirmation of their identity and self-worth, through the acts of the Creator Spirit. From here we can struggle against the negative aspects of colonization, racism, and missionization and counteract the destructive impact and legacies rooted in the intergenerational trauma of both past and present realities. The Western missionaries and colonist said we were a godless and soulless—and therefore doomed—people, thus denying the very foundation of our humanity's being created in the image of the Creator Spirit. But, if we hold true Gen 1:26–27, that humanity is created in the image of God and that humanity is created good, then this is not only the basis of our self-worth through the Creator Spirit, but also the redeeming factor toward our salvation.

BIBLIOGRAPHY

Arrupe, Pedro. "Letter on Inculturation." In *Jesuit Apostolates Today*, edited by J. Aixala, 3–8. Gujarat Sahitya Prakash: Anand, 1981.

Dodson, Pat. "The Land Our Mother, The Church Our Mother." *Compass Theology Review* 22 (1988) 1–3.

———. "Warning to a Young Writer [Poem]." *The Sewanee Review* 81 (1973) 806–7.

Pattel-Gray, Anne. "The Aboriginal Process of Inculturation." Penny Magee Lecture 17 (2003) 13–19.

———, ed. *Aboriginal Spirituality, Past, Present, Future*. Melbourne: Harper Collins, 1996.

———. *The Great White Flood—Racism in Australia*. The American Academy of Religion 2. Atlanta: Scholars, 1998.

———. *Through Aboriginal Eyes—The Cry from the Wilderness*. Geneva: WCC, 1991.

Pattel-Gray, Anne, and Norman Habel. *Decolonizing the Biblical Narrative. Volume One: Ancestral Land Narratives of Genesis 1–11*. Adelaide: ATF, 2022.

Tinker, George E. *Missionary Conquest: The Gospel and Native American Cultural Genocide*. Minneapolis: Fortress, 1993.

SECTION 7

Emerging Theologies from Diasporic and Indigenous Voices

CHAPTER 29

North American Indigenous Theology

CARMEN LANSDOWNE

THEOLOGICAL REFLECTIONS ON INDIGENOUS WAYS OF KNOWING

Theology matters: what we do/think/say about God, the Spirit, and God incarnate matters. Our most profoundly held faith beliefs shape our thoughts and actions in ways that have real and tangible environmental and socio-political implications for the earth and the communities in which we live. Theology, as a discipline, has both value proposition and ethical responsibility to it. It requires us to think deeply and critically about life, the cosmos, and the land. It can also be poetic language that marries our actions and our faith.

George Tinker argues that all indigenous theology is political theology.[1] Specifically, that "any useful commentary by American Indians speaking to the Indian context today must reflect on the political state of Indian affairs and the political hopes and visions for recovering the health and well-being of Indian communities."[2] This is not to draw necessarily on the formal Western tradition of 'political theology' as begun by Metz and continued by Moltmann, Sölle, and others but rather to say that the political—laws, policies, and rights—must be considered as part of any theology that speaks to the indigenous context.

All narratives, all interpretations, all readings, and all contexts are not equal. In fact, this is the crux of what Gustavo Gutierrez argues in *A Theology of Liberation*:

---

1. Tinker, *American Indian Liberation*, 1–16.
2. Tinker, *American Indian Liberation*, 2.

History, Politics and Salvation. Saying that God has a preferential option for the poor does not mean that God *favors* the poor (read: oppressed, and therefore indigenous) over and above others. Gutierrez explained by saying, "In some ways, *option* is perhaps the weakest word in the sentence. In English, the word merely connotes a choice between two things. In Spanish, however, it evokes the sense of commitment. The option for the poor is not optional but is incumbent upon every Christian."[3]

Liberationist thought calls on Christianity to commit to addressing the systems of injustice that cause oppression and the marginalization of entire communities. It does not call us to choose life only for the poor (as some fear when they ask, "Does God not love the rich?"), but that while systems of injustice exist, neither marginalized nor dominant are free. In this way, I draw on a liberationist hope of freedom and attempt to open theology by employing indigenous epistemologies, and by privileging the indigenist philosophy and theology.

INDIGENOUS EPISTEMOLOGIES AS A METHOD FOR THEOLOGY

Indigenous epistemologies become interesting tools for a constructive theological enterprise in that they avoid the preoccupations of the discipline of Western epistemologies since Descartes—that is to say, traditional indigenous worldviews were not concerned with binary ways of thinking or how to decide what is "true." In general, indigenous epistemologies recognize multiple interpretations of truth and reality, and they do so for a pragmatic reason: teaching. While there are multiple approaches to Western epistemologies (Aristotle over Plato, to name an example), Western philosophies of knowledge have been attempts to theorize what defines knowledge.

In contrast, indigenist[4] perspectives take what is known and extrapolate meaning from that truth (rather than theorizing what defines truth and then measuring experience against that definition). To make a generalization, if Western perspectives have tended to be more deductive, indigenist perspectives would be more inductive. The privileging of indigenist interpretations becomes pedagogically important because if we are to seek liberation as global societies, the narratives of the oppressed must be exposed, lifted, and addressed and the oppressors corrected if the oppressed/oppressors are to be liberated at all.

First, a quick note as to why I use epistemology as opposed to "cultural difference." Epistemology seems less accessible as a focus of study than culture—and although the phrase "cultural difference" is often used to explain the gaps between

---

3. Gutierrez, in Harnett, "Remembering the Poor."

4. By *indigenist* I mean to include both indigenous perspectives and those perspectives of allies to indigenous thought. For example, Andrea Smith's indigenous heritage has been repeatedly called into question, but the spirit and content of her work superbly expresses indigenous concerns, and her work is therefore *indigenist*, if it cannot be securely claimed as indigenous. For more explanation of indigenist, see Waters, *American Indian Thought*.

indigenous and non-indigenous relationships, a dedicated study in epistemological difference is more focused in scope. If culture is a term used to express the interconnectedness of knowledge, language, belief, art, morals, customs, etc., epistemology is concerned primarily with ways of knowing.

The purpose of using indigenous epistemologies as a contrast to Western traditions may seem controversial when examined by a Western mindset. If you uphold the primacy of scientific method and philosophical reasoning, you could argue that there is *no* difference based on culture or history: epistemology is simply epistemology. However, epistemology as a discipline is one that has, for millennia, been most explicitly undertaken by Western thinkers, and with truly little questioning of whether their perspectives were limited at all by being positioned as Western. There is a particular heritage of European (and particularly Anglo-Saxon) thought that has been influential in the theological realm. This is particularly problematic and further complicated by the nature of epistemological inquiry itself. If the root question of this philosophical discipline centers on "what is justified true belief," then this question would be the same regardless of culture or background and therefore it would seem moot to offer alternative approaches to epistemology based on culture. Finally, the importance of the contrast rests in the fact that in the Western philosophical tradition, indigenous ways of knowing have traditionally been excluded.

My argument is that the question "what is justified true belief?" and its philosophical antecedents are useful as far as they give us an important perspective that represents the normative nature of Western hegemony. However, I do not believe that the hegemonic Western views of what constitute knowledge and belief are the *only* perspectives, and that the root questions of epistemological inquiry could be different if approached by distinct cultures.

There are just a handful of contemporary indigenous North American scholars writing in the field of philosophy who build on even more scant traditions of indigenous thought in the North American academy. As such, even though the individuals writing seek to represent, in most cases (and to varying degrees and by various methodologies) a pan-indigenous perspective, they are also still writing from uniquely individual perspectives. Indigenous communities have had their own discrete epistemological perspectives and systems of thought for as long as Western philosophers have been contemplating questions of truth and knowledge (if not before), but until the late twentieth century they have not been discussed as such. In the introduction to his book *Tsawalk: An Indigenous Worldview*, Nuu-chah-nulth theorist Richard Atleo highlights that his "theory of *Tsawalk* not only begins with these 'tales,' or origin stories, but also depends on these 'tales' both as the foundation of knowledge about the state of existence and as a guide for its interpretation."[5] In other words, truth and fiction cannot be so easily divided.

---

5. Atleo, *Tsawalk*, xi.

THE LIMITS OF QUESTIONING, NOT THE LIMITS OF REASONING

In his essay "What Coyote and Thales Can Teach Us," Brian Yazzie Burkhart outlines the differences in Western and indigenous epistemological bases. Burkhart uses the archetype of "coyote" as philosopher in Native American legends who often loses sense of himself and his place in the world because he is too busy wondering about things and about how they really work. Plato told the story of the Greek thinker Thales, unaware of what had been at his feet, was ridiculed for being so eager to know what was happening in the heavens that he fell down a well. The difference in the two approaches, Burkhart says, is that:

> Plato uses the story of Thales to make clear what philosophy *is*. He explains that '[the philosopher] is unaware what his next-door neighbor is doing, hardly knows, indeed, whether the creature is a man at all; he spends all his pains on the question, what man is, and what powers and properties distinguish such a nature from any other" (*Thaeaetetus* 174). The stories of Coyote, conversely, are meant to show Coyote's mistakes. Like Thales, Coyote has forgotten the simple things. He has forgotten his relations. He has forgotten what is behind him and at his feet. When Coyote behaves this way, he always finds trouble. He is mocked in these stories because he is behaving the wrong way. The stories are meant to show us how not to act; they show us what philosophy is not, and not, as in the case of Plato and Thales, what it is and ought to be.[6]

In indigenous epistemologies, according to the difference outlined here, there is less concern for metaphysical principles and more concern for the simple everyday things around us. Burkhart argues there is also an importance in the way in which questions are framed. Unlike Western epistemologies that "we can ask any question we desire and in any way we desire, and the answer will remain the same,"[7] indigenous epistemologies hold that "the way in which we ask questions (the way in which we act towards our relations) guides us . . . to the right answers, rather than the other way around."[8] Therefore, in indigenous philosophy, the thinker is guided by the limits of questioning rather than the limits of reason. This was true in my own learning from elders. I was told as a young adult that you could not learn with idle hands. Rather than sitting down to interview elders, it was more appropriate to be busy with them, and then you could talk. I learned some of my most important lessons about our culture and about our peoples' traditions while sewing, washing dishes, walking through the woods to gather traditional medicines. It is only when your hands are busy that you learn.

---

6. Burkhart, "What Coyote Can Teach," 15–16.
7. Burkhart, "What Coyote Can Teach," 16.
8. Burkhart, "What Coyote Can Teach," 16.

This is further nuanced in the way in which our indigenous statements about the state of things can imply a desired outcome or action; there are few situations where it is necessary to ask a question. This idea supports my experience of why we had to be busy to learn: asking questions was inappropriate. Spending time working with someone is an invitation to let them teach you something about life. Viola Cordova recounts the experience of raising her children and announcing: "your room is messy!" or "the garbage can is full!" to initiate the desired outcome: the room being cleaned, or garbage being taken out.[9] She explains:

> My value system is built around the concept of a human being that says that all humans are equal and therefore deserving of respect. Who am I to command another to do my bidding? . . . Just as one cannot tell another person what to do, one can also not ask for anything. To ask for something is to imply an inability to be independent. To ask for anything is to imply to the person asked that he or she has failed to be perceptive to the other's existence or needs. Telling another what to do implies a position of command that no human being, or *no real human being*, would presume to take upon him- or herself.[10]

Meaning is not shaped by inquiry into the human mind, but by participation in right action. The subtlety of human-to-human relationships is therefore much more focused on the other (and the needs and inherent rights to being of the other), and less so with the internal inquiry presented by the Western traditions of philosophy.

The difference is often evidenced when researchers are working with indigenous peoples. When a non-indigenous person asks an indigenous elder certain questions, "Native elders will respond by saying, 'We don't talk about those things,' or 'It is bad to talk about those things.'"[11] This cultural misstep is explored further by indigenous thinkers such as Linda Tuhiwai Smith in *Decolonizing Methodologies*.[12] Tuhiwai Smith's work, in general, represents a thorough examination of the Western bases of "research" and the implication of that research for indigenous peoples. In the opening of her book, Tuhiwai Smith writes, "the word itself, 'research,' is probably one of the dirtiest words in the world's vocabulary. When mentioned in many indigenous contexts, it stirs up silence, it conjures bad memories, it raises a smile that is knowing and distrustful."[13] As a response to the ways in which Western research of indigenous peoples has perpetrated colonialist agendas, Tuhiwai Smith puts forward a set of research protocols that are more reflective of the relationship-based epistemological positions of indigenous peoples. Specifically, she articulates a set of values that are prescribed for Maori researchers in their own cultural terms:

---

9. Cordova, *How It Is*, 25.
10. Cordova, *How It Is*, 25–26.
11. Burkhart, "What Coyote Can Teach," 17.
12. Smith, *Decolonizing Methodologies*.
13. Tuhiwai Smith, *Decolonizing Methodologies*, 1.

1. *Aroha ki te tangata* (a respect for people).
2. *Kanohi kitea* (the seen face, that is present for yourself to people face to face).
3. *Titiro, whakarongo . . . korero* (look, listen . . . speak).
4. *Manaaki ki te tangata* (share and host people, be generous).
5. *Kia tupato* (be cautious).
6. *Kaua e takahia te mana o te tangata* (do not trample over the mana of people).
7. *Kauakoe e whakahihi to matauranga* (don't flaunt your knowledge).

These sayings reflect just some of the values that are placed *on the way we behave* (emphasis mine).[14]

THE INDIGENOUS MORAL UNIVERSE

Burkhart outlines another indigenous principle: the moral universe. He writes, "The idea is simply that the universe is moral. Facts, truth, meaning, even our existence are normative. In this way, there is no difference between what is true and what is right . . . The guiding question for the entire philosophical enterprise is, then: what is the right road for humans to walk?"[15] This is perhaps one of the greatest points of contention between Western and indigenous worldviews. If right action is a priority over justified truth claims as the goal of rational inquiry, then dialogue cannot happen until the difference in limiting questions over reasoning is bridged.

The cultural difference as articulated by Burkhart, Cordova, and Tuhiwai Smith underscores the limits of Western questioning and the search for reason as experienced by indigenous communities. Without investing in intimate relationships where right actions become discernable because there is a relationship between two people (or groups of people), then there is a limit to true understanding. The Western reaction of "How can less knowledge be better?" is, "partly a result of Western philosophy's incapacity to grasp the idea that certain things *should* not be known."[16] This is not only true of indigenous/non-indigenous interactions, but within our own indigenous communities as well. There are powerful spiritual forces at work in some of our cultural practices, and (just like Western theological concepts) they can be used in ways that break down life rather than support life in abundance. For example, there was a particular healing song I was being taught by a hereditary chief from my hometown. I was under strict instruction not to teach it to a particular person who was not sober, because no good would come of it. It so happened that I ended up giving this person a ride in the chief's car one day, and the recording of the song was being played on the

---

14. Tuhiwai Smith, *Decolonizing Methodologies*, 119–20.
15. Burkhart, "What Coyote Can Teach," 17.
16. Burkhart, "What Coyote Can Teach," 17.

stereo. Not recognizing the song, the person asked, "What song is this?" I responded that it was a beautiful healing song, and proceeded to say "Oh listen to this part," over and over as I fast forwarded and rewound the song so as not to let them hear it start to finish, but also so I didn't have to create political issues by confessing the song was not intended for them—or rather that I was specifically forbidden to teach it to them.

These differences are not merely academic. They have guided failed interactions between indigenous and non-indigenous peoples in North America throughout the last five hundred-plus years. The dominance of Western approaches also continues to frame the way in which indigenous peoples are objectified in studies based on scientific empiricism that are disconnected from the moral relationality and limits on questioning that shape indigenous worldviews. Rather than viewing indigenous approaches as a limitation on knowledge, Burkhart offers that, "our knowledge is not limited since we have as much as we should."[17]

The difference lies in foundations of Western epistemologies that are grounded in propositional knowledge (truth and justification with the pinnacle being timeless truths), whereas indigenous epistemologies are grounded primarily in experiential knowledge, guided by a moral universe in which we are co-actors with the divine and creation. In dominant Western views, justification of truth is seen as evidence for a truth claim. Even Western perspectives that claim pragmatic or commonsense confirmation of a truth belief are first grounded in the science of logic (i.e., no one radically departs from Descartes, various criticisms of Descartes notwithstanding). This is counterintuitive from an indigenous point of view. Whether we call indigenous knowledge "experiential," "embodied," or "lived" knowledge, "this kind of knowledge is not improved by adding abstract propositional form and is not capable of being justified in the foundational sense and seems to need no justification."[18]

CIRCULAR RATHER THAN LINEAR CONCEPTS OF TIME

Another epistemological difference between indigenous and Western perspectives is the concept of a linear progression of time. Aside from the fact that indigenous oral traditions do not satisfy Western philosophical requirements of truth and justification, they are also uniquely epistemologically different in that their function is primarily pedagogical and ethical.[19]

Indigenous oral traditions are ways of explicating the moral universe. Indigenous oral traditions are pedagogical in that they teach communities central truths or values which are formative in right relationships for all of creation; indigenous oral traditions are also political in that they embody the consensus-based decision-making

17. Burkhart, "What Coyote Can Teach," 18.
18. Burkhart, "What Coyote Can Teach," 20.
19. For more one of the best explications of indigenous concepts of history and time are presented in Fixico's *American Indian Mind in a Linear World*.

model which native scholar Donald Fixico articulates in his understanding of "Indian thinking." He describes Indian thinking as:

> ... visual and circular in philosophy. Imbedded in an Indian traditional reality, this ethos is a combination of the physical reality and metaphysical reality. Listening and observing the natural environment is essential to the Indian mindset. Decision making is responsive in nature due to considering all of the physical and metaphysical factors affecting one's life. Coming to a consensus is coming to a balance of all factors so that the right decision is the best decision for all concerned.[20]

Fixico goes on to say that "The power of story through the oral tradition is also explained [in] how all of this[21] transcends time, thus making time less relevant to the power of oral narrative told effectively."[22] In addition, many indigenous cultures have strict ownership and protocols around use of stories, preserving the tradition (rather than accuracy) in a way that honors its origins and purpose. Unlike Hans Gadamer's valuation of history and authority, Fixico argues that indigenous perspectives value the principle of right action in meaning making. The purpose in telling a story is not to present knowledge *a priori* or the justification of *a priori* knowledge, but to define a right way of being in balance in the world and to synthesize a communal experience of what the right path of action should be.

Fixico's idea is supported by the arguments of Viola Cordova. She articulates a resulting difference between indigenous and Western worldviews in determining how to define or understand stability. For Western thinkers, stability is seen as a static, unchanging state. "'Stability' denotes, for the Native American, a balancing act,"[23] in a universe exhibiting many motions that will require different balances.

REJECTION OF WESTERN BINARY DUALISMS

Yet another epistemological difference lies in both the implicit and explicit foundations of (especially Cartesian) Western thought on binary dualisms. While the most prominent dualism in Western self-critiques (especially from feminist philosophers) is the mind/body dualism, Burkhart would argue for higher prioritization of the individual/collective dualism. He writes:

> ... the real Cartesian bias is the idea that knowledge can only be acquired and manifested individually, in or by the individual. The *cogito, ergo sum* tells us, "I think, therefore I am." But Native philosophy tells us, "We are, therefore I am." A Native philosophical understanding must include all experience, not simply

---

20. Fixico, *American Indian Mind*, xii.
21. Fixico refers here to truth, multiple purposes, and teaching people to learn.
22. Fixico, *American Indian Mind*, 13.
23. Cordova, *How It Is*, 71.

my own. If I am to gain a right understanding I must account for all that I see, but also all that you see and all that has been seen by others—all that has been passed down in stories. What place do I have to tell you that your experiences are invalid because I do not share them?[24]

This points to a significant difference in terms of binary dualisms between Western and indigenous thought; Western binary dualisms have been imposed on indigenous communities in north America. Our traditional communities are viewed as primitive and not developed or civilized, diminishing their traditional worldviews in profound ways. Philosopher Anne Waters argues:

> The maintenance of the rigid distinct boundaries of binary logic enables (through may not necessitate) an hierarchical value judgment to take place (e.g., mind over body, or male over female) precisely because of the sharp bifurcation. A nonbinary (complementary) dualism would place the two constructs together in such a way that one would remain itself, and also be part of the other. In this way, an hierarchical valuing of one being better, superior, or more valued than another cannot be, or rather is, excluded by the nonbinary logic.[25]

This is a final philosophical issue at stake: Western binary thinking can insist that indigenous epistemologies are a radical departure from Western epistemology. From a Western perspective this may be so, but from an indigenous perspective they can be complementary, adding up to the whole of human philosophical experience. While Waters would acknowledge that the domination of indigenous peoples in North America by successive generations of settlers has resulted in large gaps in the original ontologies and epistemologies of indigenous cultures, she argues that kernels of knowledge have remained. Just because many indigenous cultures have been actively eliminated or prevented from practice, it doesn't mean we don't understand them to be truth or have an intuitive critique of the culture imposed on us as the dominant alternative. She writes, "the importance of order and balance, as well as a proper (moral) behavior, are part of the cosmological understanding of our universe."[26] This perspective has often been dismissed because it is often presented in romanticized ways by indigenous and non-indigenous scholars outside of the field of philosophy. However, the work of the growing number of indigenous philosophers in the academy brings to light the ways in which this intuitive epistemological foil can show the academy a unique way of doing philosophy in a moral universe.

The recent work of an indigenous writer whose tertiary education was very much based in the traditional Western academy, Tsimshian lawyer Calvin Helin's *Dances with Dependency: Indigenous Success through Self-Reliance* is a strong example of the blend of two worldviews. In the introduction, Helin recounts a solemn oath taken

---

24. Burkhart, "What Coyote Can Teach," 25–26.
25. Waters, *American Indian Thought*, 98–99.
26. Waters, *American Indian Thought*, 103.

with his brothers in front of their dying father that they would "stick together."[27] The experience was formative, and while writing on indigenous self-reliance, the "self" is very much communal and based on the traditional values remaining in Tsimshian culture. He writes:

> Although it certainly might be helpful if more remnants of indigenous cultures were still in existence, we do not have to turn back the clock in order to find the still-pristine emotional legacy of our ancestors, stressing the importance of social interconnections and the necessary interdependence of families, Tribes or Nations. Or to recognize the value of self-reliance, high moral conduct, loyalty, self-sacrifice and leadership. This renewal must be done in a modern context in constructive partnership with the larger society.[28]

The non-discrete nonbinary thought bases of indigenous cultures is important regarding another aspect of cultural misunderstanding that happens between indigenous and non-indigenous scholars—namely, the question of the essence of indigeneity. So, for example, because the appearance of my "white" skin, because I am not "100 percent blood quantum" (or some acceptable percentage in US political discourse) or the right kind of "status" (meaning passed down by the father as defined in Canadian law), by Western standards, I might somehow be considered 'less' *Haíłzaqv* than someone whose percentage ranks higher or whose skin is darker. Yet I have been told by my elders that regardless of who my father is, and regardless of who my son's father is, we are *Haíłzaqv* (the correct spelling of what the government of Canada and Western scholarship has anglicized as "Heiltsuk").

Waters's reasoning for nondiscrete nonbinary dualisms in indigenous thought is based on transcultural studies of the surviving Native languages in North America. In outlining her own indigenous ontology and epistemology, she writes:

> I then thought about static bifurcations of the discrete binary (bounded) dualities of essentialisms in contemporary feminist thought and recent race theory: male/female, masculine/feminine, man/woman; black/white, Indian/non-Indian, Hispanic/not-Hispanic, Asian/non-Asian, etc. These discretely bifurcated and essentialized concepts suggested a way of being in the world that might run contrary to some Indigenist ontology we find remaining in American Indian languages. And the problem seemed to be not so much that "language has gone on a holiday," but rather, that deep structures of Indigenous thinking about ontological relations in the world conflicted with the discrete binary logic inherent in Euro-American reflection about relations in the world.[29]

---

27. Helin, *Dances with Dependency*, 14–15.
28. Helin, *Dances with Dependency*, 15.
29. Waters, *American Indian Thought*, 106.

She cites the cry of Caribbean women in race theory asking, "Why can't I be Black *and* Hispanic?" and Paula Gunn Allen (an indigenous literary critic) who asks, "Who are these people who want to control, through language use, who I am?"[30] I share this experience even in relation to my (late white, adopted) grandmother who objected, ever so politely, to me identifying as (solely) *Haítzaqv*. At the very least she would have preferred I self-identify as bicultural (it sounds so much more benign, doesn't it?). But my people have told me I am *Haítzaqv,* and "We are, therefore I am."

In her book *Reshaping the University*, Sami scholar Rauna Kuokkanen summarizes her experience in Vancouver, Canada when she attended a an academic talk. Excited by the plenary presentations, she was dismayed (although not surprised) at how the indigenous presentations were quickly quashed by hegemonic Canadian perspectives. The first response to the plenary she heard pointed to decolonizing Canadian history and the need to return to indigenous groundedness in land and questions of land ownership. Next, "a young woman want[ed] to know what defines First Nations identity in 2004 because for her, it seems unavoidably bicultural, both Canadian and Aboriginal at once."[31] Before the speakers could respond, another woman in the audience jumped in to point out the ways in which her First Nations friend is different from mainstream Canadians, which devolved into the need to provide adequate education for all and not to essentialize based on racial identity. Kuokkanen summarizes, "Then comes the grand finale, the classic hegemonic counter-narrative to anything indigenous: We're all Aboriginal! We just need to know our own heritage and cultural roots to find out that all traditions are the same. Once we have done that, the spaces for indigenous education automatically happen!"[32]

This type of cross-cultural miscommunication—that is when productive conversation about indigenous/non-indigenous relationships results in an elimination of difference—is evidence of the epistemological hegemony of dominant settler and arrivant societies that silence indigenous voices because they necessarily challenge the political history of North America. The point that, "it always goes back to a question of land" results in the hegemonic drive to eradicate difference, itself often a Christian theological impulse assumed from a reading of Gal 3: in other words, "there is neither/nor." Left unchecked, this hegemonic drive will continue to ensure that indigenous epistemologies remain disproven, discounted, fictional, anecdotal, and "inappropriately subjective" in an academy that is dominated by an unchallenged epistemology grounded on Cartesian thought.

Kuokkanen cites Gayatri Spivak's notion of "eurocentric arrogance of conscience" that is, "the simplistic assumption that as long as one has sufficient information, one can understand the other."[33] Based on some of the epistemological differences and the

---

30. Waters, *American Indian Thought*, 106.
31. Kuokkanen, *Reshaping the University*, 98.
32. Kuokkanen, *Reshaping the University*, 97–98.
33. Kuokkanen, *Reshaping the University*, 99.

ways they are often counterintuitive to each other, we can see why/how Spivak labels this Eurocentric perspective an "arrogance of conscience." But the question of "Can we know the 'other'?" is important because the future of indigenous/non-indigenous relationships depends on it. And indigenous epistemologies offer a gift in terms of how we approach knowing the other. We can avoid the discrete binary dualism of Us/Other. As Cordova reminds us, "We must, as philosophers, not lose sight of the fact that the reason for exploring alien ideas is to expand our understanding of the diversity of human thought and not to expand our own specific ways of thinking so that they encompass all others."[34]

The purpose of examining indigenous epistemologies alongside of Western approaches is to strive for nonbinary and complementary ways of knowledge. Assuming the purpose of creating this nonbinary complementary dualism is itself (consistent with indigenous epistemologies) both pedagogical and ethical in purpose, we might ask the question—to what end? Given the complete success of colonization's transformation of indigenous communities/cultures to cycles of paternalism and dependency, the identification of these social dynamics is imperative as a precursor to the much-desired healing and reconciliation sought by north Americans in the twenty-first century.

THE ORIGINS AND FUTURES OF INDIGENOUS EPISTEMOLOGIES

The remaining question relates to the origins of indigenous epistemologies. Are they about actually existing modes of thought among indigenous peoples, historic forms of thought that can be productively recovered? Or are they emerging modes of thought—in the process of dialogic and syncretic formation—that are both unprecedented and built upon "original instructions?" Yes. Indigenous epistemologies are strategically employed as the embodiment of actually existing, unprecedented *and* built upon "original instruction" forms of thought.

It is easy to articulate where the history of colonization has created the "gaps" in the traditional knowledge identified by Waters and others. Vine Deloria Jr. states:

> For American Indians the period of opportunity [to discuss historical/traditional/un-contaminated indigenous philosophy] probably ended for most tribes around 1900, when the last generation of people born free were in an elderly meditative stage of their lives.[35]

This would seem to intimate that it is not possible for discrete indigenous perspectives to exist outside historical interaction with and influence by Western modes of thought. But in my view that is not problematic since indigenous epistemologies are

---

34. Cordova, *How It Is*, 30.
35. Deloria, "Philosophy and the Tribal Peoples," 4.

nondiscrete in the first place. What exists, then, is a survivor spirit that persists in the face of genocide and continued colonialism, and this is not to be discounted.

I am not convinced that indigenous epistemologies represent a radical philosophical idea, nor that what some might perceive to be the relativization of epistemology—if, in fact, this is what happens in comparing epistemic foundations—is a bad thing. Since there is not a discipline of "indigenous epistemologies," in attempting to define some epistemological variance from Western epistemologies it is helpful to look at the two general categories in relation to each other. Indigenous epistemologies are built on original instructions in that contemporary indigenous thought builds on the remnants of what remains from the indigenous traditions and philosophies that *do* remain after intense efforts to assimilate native populations into the North American mainstream (to eliminate any challenge to the historic land claims of indigenous peoples on this continent). While it would not be possible, based on indigenous circular conceptions of history and an over-and-over-again returning to history, tradition, community, and groundedness in a particular *place*, to say that indigenous epistemologies are unprecedented, the *means* by which these epistemologies are being articulated (especially in the twenty-first-century academy) is certainly unprecedented.

BIBLIOGRAPHY

Atleo, Richard. *Tsawalk: An Indigenous Worldview*. Vancouver: UBC, 2004.
Burkhart, Brian Yazzie. "What Coyote and Thales Can Teach Us: An Outline of American Indian Epistemology." In *American Indian Thought: Philosophical Essays*, edited by Anne Waters, 15–26. Malden, MA: Blackwell, 2004.
Cordova, V. F. *How It Is: The Native American Philosophy of V. F. Cordova*, edited by Kathleen Dean Moore et al. Tuscon: University of Arizona Press, 2007.
Deloria, Vine, Jr. "Philosophy and the Tribal Peoples." In *American Indian Thought: Philosophical Essays*, edited by Anne Waters, 3–11. Malden, MA: Blackwell, 2004.
Descartes, René. *Meditations*. Translated by John Veitch. New York: Cosimo, 2008.
Fixico, Donald. *The American Indian Mind in a Linear World: American Indian Studies & Traditional Knowledge*. New York: Routledge, 2003.
Gadamer, Hans-Georg. *Truth and Method*. Translated by Joel Weinsheimer and Donald G. Marshall. New York: Continuum, 1994.
Harnett, Daniel. "Remembering the Poor: An Interview with Gustavo Gutierrez." *America: The National Catholic Review*, February 2003. http://americamagazine.org/issue/420/article/remembering-poor-interview-gustavo-gutirrez.
Helin, Calvin. *Dances with Dependency: Indigenous Success Through Self-Reliance*, Vancouver: Orca, 2006.
Hume, David. *An Enquiry Concerning Human Understanding*, edited by Stephen Buckle. Cambridge: Cambridge University Press, 2007.
———. *A Treatise of Human Nature*. Edited by L. A. Selby-Bigge. Revised by P. H. Nidditch. Oxford: Clarendon, 1975.
Kuokkanen, Rauna. *Reshaping the University: Responsibility, Indigenous Epistemes, and the Logic of the Gift*. UBC Press, 2008.

Malpas, Jeff. "Hans-Georg Gadamer." *The Stanford Encyclopedia of Philosophy (Summer 2009 Edition).* http://plato.stanford.edu/archives/sum2009/entries/gadamer/ 2009.

Smith, Linda Tuhiwai. *Decolonizing Methodologies: Research and Indigenous Peoples.* London: Zed, 1999.

Tinker, George "Tink." *American Indian Liberation: A Theology of Sovereignty.* Maryknoll, NY: Orbis, 2008.

Tuhiwai Smith, Linda. *Decolonizing Methodologies: Research and Indigenous Peoples.* London: Zed, 1999.

Waters, Anne, ed. *American Indian Thought: Philosophical Essays.* Malden, MA: Blackwell, 2004.

———. "Language Matters: Nondiscrete Nonbinary Dualism" In *American Indian Thought: Philosophical Essays,* edited by Anne Waters, 97–115. Malden, MA: Blackwell, 2004.

Wolterstorff, Nicholas. "Epistemology of Religion." In *The Blackwell Guide to Epistemology,* edited by John Greco and Ernest Sosa, 303–24. Malden, MA: Blackwell, 1999.

CHAPTER 30

African American Theology

FREDERICK L. WARE

African American theology is the study and interpretation of religious beliefs and practices that impact, positively or negatively, African Americans' existence and quality of life. There is great diversity in religion among African Americans. When specific to Christianity, African American theology represents an understanding of God's freedom and the good news of God's call for all humankind to enter life in genuine community established on justice. To be human is to live in freedom informed by an awareness of one's true identity in relation to God and moral responsibility to others in this universal community. African American theology crafts meanings of freedom, a central concept in both Christianity and American culture, essential for human flourishing. In the American context, racism intersects with various forms of injustice and thereby complicates the human condition with major obstacles to human community and flourishing. African American theology exposes the bondage of humanity and proclaims God's liberation, the transformation of persons and society, for the oppressed and their oppressors desirous of life in genuine and eternal community.

This chapter emphasizes African American theology's history and development in relation to theologies emerging in the Global South. African American theology is tied to these various theologies by the parallel social identities and historical experiences of peoples who are disentangling Christianity from the distortions resulting from colonial and imperial systems of oppression. Thus, African American theology is a development in Christian theology prioritizing contextualization, resistance to injustice, liberation, and the role of faith in human survival, community, and flourishing.

The chapter explores these connections in seven sections. Sections one and two describe the contexts from which African American theology emerged. Section one discusses chattel slavery and racial segregation as an existential crisis negating the humanity of Black people. Section two turns to the formation of law and sciences during the periods of slavery and segregation that codified racial thought and racism. Section three traces the origins of Black liberation thought to the rejection of body-soul dualism and emergence of Black spirituality and religious humanism. As illustrated in section four, the subsequent meanings of liberation and freedom were and continue to be influenced by interpretations of the Declaration of Independence and US Constitution, the nation's founding documents, and conceptions of egalitarianism and liberty in the Christian Bible. Section five discusses the theology embedded in basic cultural themes and social institutions, not only in the Black church but also other Black institutions. Sections six and seven turn to the contemporary Black theological movement. Section six examines the origins of Black and womanist theologies and paradigms for the construction of liberation theology from African American contexts. In the final section, the chapter ends with discussion of recent trends and further areas of development in African American theology.

EXISTENTIAL CRISIS OF SLAVERY AND SEGREGATION

With grandiose eloquence, the American Constitution reads:

> We the people of the United States, in order to form a more perfect union, establish justice, ensure domestic tranquility, provide for the common defense, promote the general welfare and secure the blessings of Liberty to ourselves and our posterity, do ordain and establish this Constitution for the United States of America.

These words are noble. They are expressive of the intent to create a government that will fulfill the needs of the people and disclosure of the moral norms that form the basis of the articles and subsequent amendments of the people's contract with their elected representatives.

Unfortunately, at the time the Constitution was drafted, it did not include Black people, enslaved or free, among "we the people." The colonies, which later became states, establish laws to maintain in perpetuity the economic, social, and political disadvantage of Black people. The Constitution's initial reference to Black people is that of three-fifths of a person to allow Southern whites, with large populations of Black people, to have representation comparable to that of Northern whites in the newly formed government. The status of Black people within the American nation would eventually be determined in the Supreme Court's decision in *Dred Scott v. Sanford* that Blacks are an inferior race, excluded from the terms "citizen" and "people" in founding documents, and have "no rights which the white man is bound to respect." Only after a great Civil War would Blacks' legal status under the Constitution begin to change through major amendments. Still, for many years thereafter, Blacks would engage in a protracted struggle climaxing in a civil rights movement in the 1960s to end *de jure* segregation.

Neither the Constitution nor the earlier Declaration of Independence recognized the full humanity of Black people, much less the possibility of their having citizenship in the new American nation. Prior to the effort to "form a more perfect union," the colonies' Declaration of Independence asserted that equality is self-evidently true. "We hold these truths to be self-evident, that all men are created equal, that they are endowed, by their Creator, with certain unalienable Rights, that among these are Life, Liberty, and the pursuit of Happiness."[1] The irony of the American Revolution fought in defense of freedom and equality is the restriction of these ethical ideals to whites only. In this flawed and fledgling democracy, the Christian church would divide along the line of race, nullify respect for human life (Black lives), limit the moral imperative of agape (love) toward all people, and make amoral the relations between Blacks and whites.[2]

CODIFICATION OF RACIAL THOUGHT AND RACISM

In the United States, racial thought and racism are reinforced by custom, law, religion, and science. The roots of this racialization in thought and practice began in the American colonies. Various colonial statues represent perspectives, at that time, slighting the humanity of enslaved Africans and their status in the new society being constructed in North America.[3] In 1662, forty-three years after the arrival of "20 or so Negroes" to the Jamestown settlement in the Virginia colony, slavery became hereditary. A child born to an enslaved Black woman inherited her slave status. Conversion to Christianity and baptism were expressly rejected as basis of equality with whites or emancipation from slavery. Across the colonies, a series of laws were enacted to prohibit enslaved persons from travel, assembly in groups, raising their own food, contracting for paid work, learning to read and write, or sexual relations or marriage with whites. Slavery became not only hereditary but also lifelong. Colonial laws carried with them fines and imprisonment for aiding or harboring a runaway slave.

Whereas chattel slavery would end at the conclusion of the Civil War between the Northern and Southern states, segregation by race would continue. Segregation, as a system of law, has to a considerable extent ended. The civil rights movement of the

1. The Virginia Declaration of Rights, from which Thomas Jefferson would craft the introduction to the Declaration of Independence, names the inalienable rights as "the enjoyment of life and liberty, with the means of acquiring and possessing property, and pursuing and obtaining happiness and safety." https://www.archives.gov/founding-docs/virginia-declaration-of-rights.

2. Thurman, *Luminous Darkness*, 3–5, 94.

3. For examples of these colonial and state statues, see Wright, *African-American Archive*, 5–7, 14–15, 38, 108.

1960s culminated in major federal legislation in public accommodations, voting, and housing that removed legal bases for racial discrimination. Still America is divided by race. Segregation is perpetuated through social and cultural practices with regard to sex and marriage, family and ancestry, child-rearing, residential location, and religious and voluntary associations that keep racial and ethnic groups somewhat separate.

ORIGINS OF LIBERATION THOUGHT

In response to the grave existential crisis and irony of deep-seated injustices in a nation aspiring to the ideals of freedom, equality, and democracy, African Americans have developed traditions of liberation thought. These traditions originate from a rejection of body-soul dualism, emergence of a distinct spirituality, and development of religious humanism. Defense and assertion of Black people's humanity begins with a holism, a view of body and soul, that affirms fully the human person. The value of the person is further defined in spiritual encounter with the Divine. Religious humanism emphasizes the inalienable freedom and therefore agency of the person even in the presence of the Divine.

Body-Soul Dualism

The Western dualism of body and soul has tragic consequences for oppressed persons. This dualism divides the human person into a combination of body and soul with no clear indication of how the two interact. The body is associated with that which is physical and therefore belongs to the material world. The soul belongs to another world by virtue of its association is with that which is spiritual and mental. In reconciling the two, the soul is valued over the body. Moreover, the combination of body and soul is made further bizarre by depiction of the person as either a "soulless body" or "bodiless soul," concepts described in Riggins Earl's *Dark Symbols, Obscure Signs*.[4]

As soulless bodies, the humanity of Blacks was denied altogether. Blacks were seen as bodies only, as physical machines for the production of wealth. Blacks were thought to be subhuman and on the level of beasts. Those whites who viewed Blacks in this way had no sense of moral responsibility toward them or even toward God for their mistreatment of Blacks. In *Narrative of the Life of Frederick Douglass* and *My Bondage and My Freedom*, Douglass describes Edward Covey, a "slave breaker," as a white person possessed of the worst cruelty born from this perspective of Blacks as soulless bodies.[5] Douglass suffered immense mental and physical abuse.

As bodiless souls, Blacks were, to a limited degree, regarded as human. Whites' acknowledgment of Blacks as having souls meant that whites recognized Blacks as

---

4. Earl, *Dark Symbols, Obscure Signs*, 5.

5. Douglass, *Narrative of the Life of Frederick Douglass*, 60–64; Douglass, *My Bondage and My Freedom*, 214–21.

possessing a valued aspect of personhood. However, the humanity recognized and affirmed in Blacks' souls was not affirmed in their bodily, physical existence. Regarding Blacks as bodiless souls, whites were compelled to make slavery more humane. For example, Charles Colock Jones, a Georgia plantation owner and Presbyterian minister, wrote and offered several lectures on *The Religious Instruction of the Negroes in the United States* (1842) where he admonished slave owners to assume responsibility for the spiritual welfare of their slaves. The human slave master was not only expected to provide religious instruction but also treat the slave well, providing food, clothes, medical care, periods of rest, tools, and so forth to facilitate their work.

According to Riggins Earl, liberation thought emerges from the desire of oppressed persons to be whole. The oppressed do not want to live as fragmented human persons. The wonderful aspects of their souls must be reconciled with the beauty in their bodies. The affirmation expressive of this desire of wholeness is "I am my body."[6] By this affirmation, the oppressed are saying: "The good and splendor in my soul is located in my physical body." Both the soul and the body must be equally valued.

Black Spirituality

Black spirituality is birthed from what Charles Long calls "soul-stuff."[7] This soul-stuff is a spirituality of freedom— a freedom to create and translate.[8] According to Long, this creativity sprang from African Americans' experience of God as radical otherness. In God's self-disclosure in the Black experience, Blacks are drawn into a new humanity, where they are fully human and transformed for life in God's reign. For the oppressed, God is a reality other than the harsh conditions of life to which they are exposed. This Black spirituality is characterized by Blacks' ability to "take the chaos and dross of human experience and to translate them spiritually and culturally into alternative modalities and symbols of black life that promote black identity, sanity and wholeness."[9]

In Christian churches, Black spirituality is decisively influenced by the concept of conversion.[10] Spirituality is not a retreat from this world but rather an engagement with it. The spiritual experience, using the language of conversion, became a new basis, power, and motivation for action. The personal conversion story may be told around the themes of "regeneration," being "born again," "getting religion," and "the Spirit falling or taking control." Through conversion, the person is delivered from the debilitating sickness of a false identity imposed by the system of oppression. The person attains a true self in relationship with God. Explained in various ways, persons describe an event when they discover their true identity and apprehend their purpose

---

6. Earl, *Dark Symbols, Obscure Signs*, 105, 174–75.
7. Long, "African American Religion in the United States of America," 21; Long, *Significations*, 9.
8. Stewart, *Black Spirituality and Black Consciousness*, 20–21.
9. Stewart, *Black Spirituality and Black Consciousness*, 18.
10. Lincoln and Mamiya, *Black Church in the African American Experience*, 6.

in life that often involves becoming more than or other than who they are prior to this moment of reckoning. Subsequent to conversion, there is the "shout," an affective response to the presence of the Divine which could be named as God, Jesus, or the Holy Spirit. The shout is an indication that conversion has taken place and that God is present in the Spirit to enable persons to experience a form of joy that is impossible in their normal experience.[11] In the encounter with God, within the context of worship, they realize the truth that God is liberating them from oppression, not to mention the other distresses in human existence.

Religious Humanism

Religious humanism may be, as African American philosopher Carol Wayne White suggests, a philosophical perspective rivaling Christian theism.[12] Indeed, there is early documentation of enslaved Africans' critique of Christianity. While there exists an anti-Christian rhetoric, humanistic thought is not reducible to critique of Christianity. According to White, religious humanism is simply a form of religiosity, in particular, an orientation towards life that affirms beauty and goodness in nature and the importance and value for human life without appeal to theism. Religious humanism also functions as a basis for rational argument and other uses of reason in the development of liberation thought. Essential to humanism is emphasis on the freedom of the person to think, feel, choose, interpret, and act in accordance with reason.

Though known mainly for his oratory and statesmanship, Frederick Douglass often expressed his opposition to racism and discrimination in humanistic terms. Douglass was a member and licensed preacher in the African Methodist Episcopal Zion Church, serving in roles such as sexton, steward, class leader, and clerk of his local congregation.[13] As a Methodist minister, a fact rarely noted about Douglass, he used Scripture and religious themes in his writings and speeches. However, he held in high regard reason and human agency.

In Frederick Douglass's *The Claims of the Negro, Ethnically Considered* (1854), he critiques racist scholarship and misuse of scientific method. Douglass claims human rights presuppose a basis in the notion of one humanity, a truth apprehended by reason as well as by biblical record of revelation. Douglass says:

> Human rights stand upon a common basis; and by all the reason that they are supported, maintained and defended, for one variety of the human family, they are supported, maintained and defended for all the human family; because all mankind have the same wants, arising out of a common nature. A diverse

---

11. Cone, *Speaking the Truth*, 21–22, 26–27.
12. White, *Black Lives and Sacred Humanity*, vii, 33, 119–20, 122, 126.
13. Dilbeck, *Frederick Douglass*, 51.

origin does not disprove a common nature, nor does it disprove a united destiny. The essential characteristics of humanity are everywhere the same.[14]

Douglass ended his own enslavement by his decision to escape and advocated the end of slavery by human action, not supernatural intervention. Believing physical resistance to evil is necessary, Douglass recruited Blacks for the Union army in the war to end slavery and save the Union. After the conclusion of the Civil War, during the era of Reconstruction and afterwards, Douglass's efforts came to focus on voting rights. He framed liberation thought and the struggle for freedom in terms of human and civil rights, both of which he believed are supported by the Declaration of Independence, US Constitution, the Christian Bible, and reason.

Meanings of Freedom

In African American theology, the concepts of liberation and freedom are basic elements in the structured language of sin and salvation.[15] In the linguistic and logical structure underlying sin and salvation, sin is a problem solved by salvation that leads to an improved outcome. When specific to liberation thought, the problem is bondage (oppression), the solution emancipation (liberation), and outcome freedom. Sin is the condition resulting from the misuse or denial of freedom, the individual's or someone else's, in context of universal community with God. Salvation is deliverance (relief or release) from situations that the individual (or group of persons) alone cannot escape and the subsequent achievement of an improved life. Both have personal and social dimensions.

Freedom is not only shaped by concepts of sin and salvation but also by the Constitution (e.g., the establishment and free exercise clauses of the First Amendment, and the Thirteenth, Fourteenth, and Fifteenth Amendments), Black protest movements, and Christian concepts of egalitarianism and liberty. These constitutional apparatus and Black protests appealing to them make for an interesting dynamic for the expression of Black spirituality in the public square. This context contributes to the shapes of a Black spirituality of freedom.

As an outcome that names salvation, freedom is also wedded to the concepts of self-actualization and self-realization. Freedom is distinguishable from liberation, that is, the means utilized for emancipating persons from bondage. James Cone defines freedom as the liberty for self-actualization, where the self is defined by the image of God (*imago Dei*).[16] To be free is to be Black in the manner in which God seeks to use one's Blackness in the fulfillment of that person's existence in the world. Anthony Pinn names this freedom "complex subjectivity," that is, Black existence in a variety

---

14. Douglass, *Claims of the Negro, Ethnologically Considered*, 34.
15. Ware, *African American Theology*, 147–48.
16. Cone, *Black Theology of Liberation*, 93–94, 101–3.

of modes.[17] For Pinn, freedom is African Americans' privilege to live as they wish, without a racial essentialism restricting individuals to a singular identity imposed on them or to one feature of any individual's personhood. As African Americans truly exist and seek to thrive in the various social spaces where they live, they are different in gender, sexual orientation, educational attainment, income status, religious beliefs, cultural traditions, and numerous other areas of life. To be free is to be human in all of the diversity that makes humanity what it is and has the capacity to become.

CULTURAL THEMES AND SOCIAL INSTITUTIONS

Liberation thought finds expression in prevalent cultural themes and social institutions. Cultural themes are concepts related to the ideals of liberation and freedom. When stated as propositions, these cultural themes function as foundational principles for constructing theological interpretations. Recurring cultural themes include the following four propositions:[18]

1. African American Christianity is an authentic expression of Christianity, in contrast to forms of "white religion" such as white Evangelicalism supporting racism.

2. African American people are distinct, having qualities not found in other peoples and claim to a glorious past and potential for great contribution to human civilization.

3. Community, expressed as Black solidarity, is vital for liberation, survival, and quality of life.

4. Education (literacy and knowledge) is a route to freedom.

Through the above themes, African American theology assigns priority to addressing the suffering of Black people, values and links freedom with equality and justice, and emphasizes the role of the church in the transformation of society.

The Black Church is an obvious expression of liberation thought in social institutions. The concept of "the Black Church" is a covering term to describe Christian congregations and denominations in the United States that are, in the composition of their membership, predominantly Black (with "Black" referring to African Americans and other groups of persons of African descent). Congregations and denominations of this type have long been the center of Black communities. Various Black colleges and universities, fraternities and sororities, businesses and professional associations, and civic and political organizations have patrons who hold membership in Black religious institutions. In some instances, Black religious institutions were instrumental in the establishment of other Black institutions and remain affiliated with them. Mutual aid societies, historical and literary societies, women's clubs, newspapers,and Colored

17. Pinn, *Terror and Triumph*, 157–59, 235n26.
18. Ware, *African American Theology*, 64–65.

Conventions also arose simultaneously and in association with Black religious institutions. Over the course of US history, the affiliation of African American Christians has remained consistent, ranging from 80 to 90 percent in Christian denominations and congregations that are predominantly Black and Protestant. Still a substantial number of Black Christians are affiliated with Roman Catholic and Orthodox churches and African- and Caribbean-based churches transplanted on American soil.

African American theology is transmitted orally and in print sources published by historic Black Christian denominations. These denominations are the African Methodist Episcopal Church (AME, est. 1816), African Methodist Episcopal Church Zion (AMEZ, est. 1821), Christian Methodist Episcopal Church (CME, est. 1870), National Baptist Convention, U.S.A., Incorporated (NBC, est. 1895), National Baptist Convention of America, Incorporated (NBCA, est. 1915), National Missionary Baptist Convention of America (NMBCA, est. 1988), Progressive National Baptist Convention (PNBC, est. 1961), Full Gospel Baptist Church Fellowship (FGBCF, est. 1994), Church of God in Christ (COGIC, est. 1907), and Pentecostal Assemblies of the World (PAW, est. 1914). *The Christian Recorder* (AME), which began in 1852, is the oldest continuous church periodical and theological journal fashioned as a major source for news, information, and exchange of ideas for African Americans. Other significant denominational publications for the dissemination of Black religious thought include *The Christian Index* (CME), 1867–present; *The Star of Zion* (AMEZ), 1876–present; *A.M.E. Zion Quarterly Review*, 1895–present; *National Baptist Voice* (NBC), 1915–present; and *The Whole Truth* (COGIC), 1907–present. In addition to these periodicals, Black Christian denominations regularly publish educational literature and manuals for their members and clergy. The educational literature, hymnals, discipline books, ministers' manuals, and convention proceedings and minutes are significant documentation of African American theology. Still, the theology in the churches remains mostly oral.[19]

In Gayraud Wilmore's *Black Religion and Black Radicalism*, he identifies radicalism as "the most distinctive, persistent, and valuable part of the religious heritage of African Americans in the United States."[20] This radicalism is the quest for economic, social, and political change. According to Wilmore, Black radicalism has undergone periods of waxing in waning in the history of the Black Church. The faith of the "Fathers and Mothers" in the initial stage of the Black Church, a collective the poor, was characterized by this radicalism. When Black denominations became "mainstream" and thoroughly middle-class, the Black Church became deradicalized and Black radicalism found refuge in secular organizations. In the civil rights and Black power movements, the Black once again became radicalized. When these protest movements waned, the Black Church would not lean again toward radicalism until the advent of the Black Lives Matter movement, which is independent not only of the Black Church

---

19. Ware, *Methodologies of Black Theology*, 19–20.
20. Wilmore, *Black Religion and Black Radicalism*, 147.

but also historic civil rights organizations. Still, as Leah Gunning Francis argues in *Ferguson and Faith*, young activists of the Black Lives Matter movement "created the space and impetus for the clergy . . . to live into their roles as leaders."[21]

CONTEMPORARY BLACK AND WOMANIST THEOLOGIES

According to James Cone, who is regarded as a pioneer in the contemporary Black theological movement, Black theology arose from three interrelated contexts.[22] Two of these contexts are the civil rights and Black power movements. The discussion and challenge surrounding Joseph Washington's *Black Religion* represents a third context. Martin Luther King Jr., interpreted the civil rights movement as the *zeitgeist*, God's Spirit working in the world to achieve beloved community, that is, justice in racially integrated society. At the emergence of the Black power movement, radical Black clergy of the National Conference of Black Churchmen (NCBC) interpreted Christianity in terms of the ideals of Black unity and cooperation in pursuit of amassing Black people's resources and development their institutions and culture. Black power was a check on the excesses of white power. When Washington's book, in spreading the claim of no theology in Black churches, gained recognition in white religious and academic circles, the NCBC, with support of Black seminary professors, took on the task of articulating and writing Black theology.

Frederick Ware's *Methodologies of Black Theology* delineates the paradigms functioning as models, perspectives, and frameworks for the construction of Black theology. He names the principal methodological approaches as the Black Hermeneutical School (BHS), the Black Philosophical School (BPS), and the Human Sciences School (HSS). These schools of thought have developed as a result of individual and collaborative work to define the theme of liberation in Black theology.

The BHS, which first emerged in clergy and seminary settings, is devoted to a quest for a "Black hermeneutic"—a method of biblical and theological interpretation that recovers and is accurate in representing the earliest expression of Christian faith and the struggles for liberation among African Americans in the United States. In the BHS, liberation is defined using biblical conceptions of God's liberating activity (e.g., the exodus) and various stories of freedom in African American experience (e.g., slave narratives). Regarding Black religion and Black experience as chief sources of Black theology, the BHS is guided by the idea of Black religious faith has an internal logic and requires no external justification, that is, the norm of non-foundationalist (i.e., biblical, communal, and personal) conceptions of Christian faith centered in Jesus Christ as the Black Messiah and Liberator of the Oppressed. Key thinkers in the development of the BHS include Katie Cannon, Albert Cleage, Cecil Cone, James Cone,

---

21. Francis, *Ferguson and Faith*, 5.
22. Cone, *For My People*, 6–11.

Kelly Brown Douglas, James Evans, Jacquelyn Grant, Dwight Hopkins, Major Jones, Olin Moyd, James Deotis Roberts, Delores Williams, and Gayraud Wilmore.

The BPS was formed by the entry of philosophers of religion into and the use of philosophy in the field of Black theology. In the BPS, liberation is defined by social and political philosophy, which may or may not be compatible with biblical story and Black story, such as in the case with Black humanism. For example, in Anthony Pinn's *Writing God's Obituary*, he argues that moral and ethical action in and for the sake of liberation does not necessarily come from religion or need religious justification. Liberation is valuable simply because oppressed people need and want it. Though Black religion is regarded as primary subject matter of Black theology, the BPS is guided by the norm, that is, foundationalist conceptions of Christian faith which can be explained and justified by various philosophical perspectives and academic canons of truth and rationality. Key thinkers in the development of the BPS include William R. Jones, Anthony Pinn, Cornel West, Alice Walker, and Henry Young. Though Alice Walker is not a religion scholar or theologian, several African theologians are influenced by Walker's brand of womanism which has leanings toward humanist philosophy.

The HSS encompasses the kinds of cultural studies of Black theology conducted by historians of religion, theologians of culture, sociologists of religion, religious studies scholars, and other intellectuals adhering to prevalent canons of scholarship in college and university settings. In the HHS, liberation is defined in terms of empowerment, a power to endure, revision, transform, and overcome various conditions of human life. With regard to the norm by which the HHS is guided, Black religion is treated phenomenologically, that is, as it is confirmed to exist, for example, by historical and sociological studies. Key thinkers in the development of the HSS include Cheryl Townsend Gilkes, C. Eric Lincoln, Charles Long, Henry Mitchell, Charles Shelby Rooks, and Theophus Smith.

Womanist theology arose as a corrective to Black theology which was and continues to be dominated by African American males. Still womanist theology has integrity and methodology apart from Black theology and white feminist theology. Key thinkers in the development of womanist theology include Karen Baker-Fletcher, Katie Cannon, Delores Carpenter, M. Shawn Copeland, Kelly Brown Douglas, Cheryl Townsend Gilkes, Jacquelyn Grant, Diana Hayes, Cheryl Kirk-Duggan, Clarice Martin, Jamie Phelps, Marcia Riggs, Cheryl Sanders, Linda Thomas, Emilie Townes, Renita Weems, and Delores Williams.

Womanist theology is characterized by a distinct methodology, an intentional holism that appreciates the insights and contributions of African American women regardless of their terms for self-identification, broadens the range of sources for theological reflection, and strives for a comprehensive analysis of oppression by race, class, and gender. Delores Williams claims that this kind of methodology is regulated by four emphases.[23] The first emphasis is what Williams calls womanist theology's multi-dialogical intent, which is Black women's involvement in dialogue and activism in social, political, and religious communities. The second emphasis is what Williams calls the liturgical intent of womanist theology as involving witness to and celebration of Christ's prophetic message. The third emphasis is what Williams calls the didactic intent of womanist theology, which involves teaching wisdom and sharing insights. The fourth emphasis is women's experience, namely the use of female imagery, women's stories, and gendered language in theology.

RECENT TRENDS AND FUTURE AREAS OF DEVELOPMENT

African American theology is well into the stage of academic discipline development that Williams R. Jones called "systematic construction."[24] This stage is characterized by an investigation of basic problems in African American theology, free of the subjective, confessional contexts that gave birth to the contemporary Black theological movement. African American theologians are today exploring topics and engaging systems of ideas beyond the range of issues debated by the pioneering Black and womanist theologians. Still, the moral overtones of freedom, equality, and justice remain.

Recent trends in African American theology worthy of note are Afro-pessimism, Afrofuturism, and Black transhumanism. Philip Butler's *Black Transhuman Liberation Theology: Technology and Spirituality* (2020) and Roger Sneed's *The Dreamer and the Dream: Afrofuturism and Black Religious Thought* (2021) are recent publications reflecting these trends. Each trend problematizes the Christian doctrine of eschatology and concept of hope that Olin Moyd identified early into the contemporary Black theological movement as the central category of Black liberation theology.[25] Eschatology addresses questions about hope and the future and authentic human identity in this imagined destiny. Afro-pessimism admits that, for many Blacks, life is a "living hell" but challenges assumptions that Black life is comprehensible only from a narrative of survival. African American theologians are now asking the questions: What is hope? How do persons move beyond merely hoping to thriving and flourishing? What does Blackness and Black life look like in this situation of thriving and flourishing when Blacks are accorded the freedom associated with complex identities? To answer these questions in Afrofuturism, Black theological reflection takes points of departure from science, technology, metaphysics, and science fiction in literature, music, and the arts. Afrofuturism explores conceptions of Black life and Blackness in a future shaped by science and technology. Black transhumanism similarly explores the possibilities of the sciences and technologies to improve human life and the human person, with particular focus on the Black life and Black personhood.

23. Williams, "Womanist Theology," 269–71.
24. Jones, "Toward an Interim Assessment of Black Theology," 515.
25. Moyd, *Redemption in Black Theology*, 32–33, 213.

In Eric Lewis Williams and Antonia Michelle Daymond's epilogue to the *T&T Clark Handbook of African American Theology*, they share a vision of new directions in African American theology.[26] According to Williams and Daymond, three areas warrant attention and development. The first area is the inclusion of Black women and their perspectives and deconstruction of the politics of gender and hegemonic Black masculinity in African American theology and churches. While Black women most certainly must be at the table for theological discourse, the discipline itself must address the problem of sexism and the ideologies and social practices that support this injustice. Considering the religious diversity of Black people, the second area is theological engagement with all religions, not just the Abrahamic traditions, in African American communities. The third area is the engagement of Black liberation theology in the United States with African theology, Afro-Caribbean theology, and other African diasporic theologies. Here *African American* theology would become *Africana* theology, the predicate "Africana" representing a broader term for the expanded scope of the field.

BIBLIOGRAPHY

Butler, Philip. *Black Transhuman Liberation Theology: Technology and Spirituality*. London: Bloomsbury, 2020.

Cone, James H. *A Black Theology of Liberation*. Twentieth Anniversary Edition. Maryknoll, NY: Orbis, 1990.

———.*For My People: Black Theology and the Black Church*. Maryknoll, NY: Orbis, 1984.

———. *Speaking the Truth: Ecumenism, Liberation, and Black Theology*. Grand Rapids: Eerdmans, 1986.

Cone, James H., and Gayraud S. Wilmore, eds. *Black Theology: A Documentary History, vol. 2, 1980–1992*. Maryknoll, NY: Orbis, 1993.

Daymond, Antonia Michelle, et al., eds. *T&T Clark Handbook of African American Theology*. London: Bloomsbury, 2019.

Dilbeck, D. H. *Frederick Douglass: America's Prophet*. Chapel Hill: University of North Carolina Press, 2018.

Douglass, Frederick. *The Claims of the Negro, Ethnologically Considered: An Address before the Literary Societies of Western Reserve College, at Commencement, July 12, 1854*. Rochester, NY: Lee, Mann & Company, 1854.

———.*My Bondage and My Freedom*. New York: Miller, Orton & Mulligan, 1855.

———.*Narrative of the Life of Frederick Douglass*. Boston: Anti-Slavery Office, 1845.

Earl, Riggins R. *Dark Symbols, Obscure Signs: God, Self, and Community in the Slave Mind*. Maryknoll, NY: Orbis, 1993.

Francis, Leah Gunning. *Ferguson and Faith: Sparking Leadership and Awakening Community*. St. Louis: Chalice, 2015.

Jones, William R. "Toward an Interim Assessment of Black Theology." *Christian Century* 89 (1972) 513–17.

---

26. "Epilogue" in Daymond et al., *T&T Clark Handbook of African American Theology*.

Lincoln, C. Eric, and Lawrence H. Mamiya. *The Black Church in the African American Experience*. Durham, NC: Duke University Press, 1990.

Long, Charles H. "African American Religion in the United States of America: An Interpretative Essay." *Nova Religio: The Journal of Alternative and Emergent Religions* 7 (2003) 11–27.

———. *Significations: Signs, Symbols, and Images in the Interpretation of Religion*. Aurora: Davies Group, 1999.

Moyd, Olin P. *Redemption in Black Theology*. Valley Forge: Judson, 1979.

Pinn, Anthony B. *Terror and Triumph: The Nature of Black Religion*. Minneapolis: Fortress, 2003.

———. *Writing God's Obituary: How a Good Methodist became a Better Atheist*. Amherst, NY: Prometheus, 2014.

Sneed, Roger A. *The Dreamer and the Dream: Afrofuturism and Black Religious Thought*. Columbus: Ohio University Press, 2021.

Stewart, Carlyle F. *Black Spirituality and Black Consciousness: Soul Force, Culture, and Freedom in the African-American Experience*. Trenton: Africa World, 1999.

Thurman, Howard. *The Luminous Darkness: A Personal Interpretation of the Anatomy of Segregation and the Ground of Hope*. Repr. Richmond, VA: Friends United, 1989.

Ware, Frederick L. *African American Theology: An Introduction*. Louisville: Westminster John Knox, 2016.

———. *Methodologies of Black Theology*. Repr. Eugene, OR: Wipf & Stock, 2008.

White, Carol Wayne. *Black Lives and Sacred Humanity: Toward an African American Religious Humanism*. New York: Fordham University Press, 2016.

Williams, Delores. "Womanist Theology: Black Women's Voices." In *Black Theology, A Documentary History, Volume 2: 1980–1992*, 269–71. Maryknoll, NY: Orbis, 1992.

Wilmore, Gayraud S. *Black Religion and Black Radicalism: An Interpretation of the Religious History of African Americans*. 3rd ed. Revised and enlarged. Maryknoll, NY: Orbis, 1998.

Wright, Kai, ed. *The African-American Archive: The History of the Black Experience through Documents*. New York: Black Dog & Leventhal, 2001.

CHAPTER 31

Latinx Theologies

RUDOLPH REYES II

There are a variety of ways people of Latin American descent identify themselves. Latina/o/x and Hispanic are pan-ethnic identities. Latinx uses *x* to represent the gender diversity within the community, rather than a gendered *o* (masculine/plural) or *a* (feminine) when referring to the comunidad.[1] Even when Latinxs use pan-ethnic labels, people prefer to use nationalities—Mexican or Salvadorian—or regional identities—Tejano or Nuyorican. As Latinx is an ethno-racial category rather than solely an ethnic or racial category, there are Asian Latinxs and Afro-Latinxs.[2] There is no one universal Latinx experience.

Latinx theologies are similar but distinct from Latin American liberation theologies. Latinx theologies are like Latin American theologies because of the shared connections between Latinxs and Latin America. These shared connections are the movement back and forth between the United States and Latin America of people and culture. Latinx theologies are distinct because they focus on Latinxs in the United States. While there are shared connections, there is a different context with unique histories and cultures. Latinx theologies emerge out of the movements for social justice like the Chicano movement and the Young Lords. While Latinx theologies predate the rise of these social movements, it was through this time of activism that Latinx theologies began to recognize themselves as Latinx theologies.

---

1. Spanish words are not italicized because Spanish is not a foreign language for Latinx theologies or a foreign language in the United States.

2. Access Alcoff, "Anti-Latino Racism," 107–26. I follow Jay Timothy Dolmage in using "access" rather than "see" when referring to sources for more information. Access Dolmage, *Academic Ableism*, 193n1.

There are a great variety of Latinx theologies. There are confessional Latinx theologies, written out of different Latinx faith communities: *From the Heart of Our People: Latino/a Explorations in Catholic Systematic Theology* edited by Orlando Espin and Miguel H. Díaz, *Teología En Conjunto: a Collaborative Hispanic-Protestant Theology* edited by Jose David Rodriguez and Loida I. Martell-Otero, and Samuel Solivan's *The Spirit, Pathos and Liberation: Toward an Hispanic Pentecostal Theology*. Other Latinx theologies take a particular Latinx social location as their point of departure, such as Andrés G. Guerrero's *Chicano Theology*, Michelle A. Gonzalez's *Afro-Cuban Theology*, or Teresa Delgado's *A Puerto Rican Decolonial Theology*. To learn more about Latina feminist theologies, read Michelle Maldonado's chapter in this volume. These Latinx theologies are not mutually exclusive, and the same theologian can write from many perspectives. While there is a great diversity of theologies, there is still need for more varieties to speak to the spectrum of Latinx experience.

Latinx theologies are collaborative, contextual, and liberative theologies. Latinx theologies are collaborative. Teologíaen conjunto is a collaborative way of doing Latinx theologies. Loida I. Martell-Otero defines this method as "a dialogical process that reminds us that genuine theology can only be done as a communal endeavor."[3] Martell-Otero, along with Zaida Maldonado and Elizabeth Conde-Frazier use this approach in *Latina Evangélicas: A Theological Survey from the Margins*. Martell-Otero, Maldonado, and Conde-Frazier wrote this book collaboratively. The final chapter is framed around a conversation between the authors on Latina Evangélicas. The book ends with an invitation. "Yet it is not a conclusion, but rather a beginning. We hope to continue the God-talk. Come and join us at the table. *Tenemos un cafecitolisto*."[4] Latinx theologies are open invitations to collaborate.

Latinx theologies are contextual, drawing upon epistemological, cultural, historical, and scriptural sources as contextual theology. Epistemology is a term for the ways we gain and validate knowledge. Nancy Pineda-Madrid argues for the importance of Chicana feminist epistemology for Latina theology. This way of knowing connects to the lived experience of Chicanas and their critical consciousness of class, gender, race, and oppression. "The very process," Pineda-Madrid writes, "of creating and validating 'knowledge' vitally contributes to the 'humanization' of subordinated populations like Latinas."[5] These ways of knowing can connect to artistic expression. Latinx cultural production like art, film, literature, poetry, and music is another site of theological reflection. Teresa Delgado engages Puerto Rican writers Esmeralda Santiago, Pedro Juan Soto, and Rosario Frerré. In these writers, Delgado identifies the themes of identity, suffering, and hope. As Delgado writes, these writers' prophecy "our Puerto Rican Identity, our ability to overcome suffering and the hope to which we aspire are linked

---

3. Martell-Otero, "Introduction," 5–6.
4. Martell-Otero, "Epilogue," 138. Italics in original.
5. Pineda-Madrid, "Chicana Feminist Epistemology," 241.

to our desire for self-determination and freedom from colonization."[6] It is artists who provide a means of telling the lived experience of people's desire for liberation.

Another site of reflection is Latinx histories. Elías Ortega-Aponte takes the activism of the Young Lords Party as a model of dissent to construct a Latinx religious ethic. The Young Lords were a Puerto Rican radical social movement in the seventies in the United States to fight against injustice. The recovering of the Young Lord's radical activism for Ortega-Aponte makes a needed intervention for Latinx ethics, which can tame dissent. Many Latinx histories need recovering and revisiting for theological reflection. Scripture provides another source. Justo González provides a Latinx interpretation of Moses as mestizo. Moses was Hebrew but raised as an Egyptian. After fleeing from Egypt, Mose connected with his Hebrew culture. This bicultural experience allowed him to advocate for his people because he could speak both languages and move between cultures.[7]

As a liberative theology, Latinx theologies make a preferential option for the poor, oppressed, and marginalized. Critical in the liberation struggle is to recognize the nature of oppression. Ada Maria Isasí-Diaz introduced feminist philosopher Iris Marion Young's five faces of oppression to Latinx theologies.[8] These modes of oppression are exploitation, marginalization, disempowerment, cultural imperialism, and violence. Young's five faces provide categories to distinguish different features of oppression.

The first three modes of oppression make up economic oppression. Exploitation is the transfer of resources from one group to another. Day laborers and domestic workers experience this exploitation when they are not paid for their labor because they are considered expendable. Marginalization is exclusion from social life. Latinxs experience marginalization when they are excluded from loans for affordable housing or offered housing in redlined zones. Disempowerment is exclusion from participating in the decision-making process.[9] Working-class Latinxs are disempowered when they are not given a say in their working conditions during a pandemic. Economic oppression impacts Latinxs in transferring resources outside of their communities, controlling where they can live, and putting them in unsafe working conditions.

Cultural imperialism is the imposition of the dominant culture's norms and values as natural and ideal. When Latinxs speak Spanish in public spaces, they are told to return to their home country. The norm and value of English as the only language that should be spoken is a form of cultural imperialism. These norms can lead to dehumanization and violence. Latinxs face multiple forms of violence. Latinxs are the

---

6. Delgado, *Puerto Rican Decolonial Theology*, 12.
7. This interpretation comes from González, *Santa Biblia*.
8. Access Maria Isasí-Diaz chapter 6 in *Mujerista Theology*.
9. I follow Claudia Card's use of disempowerment as an alternative term for powerlessness for this mode of oppression. As Card argues disempowerment describes an action done to a person. Access Card, "Injustice, Evil, and Oppression," 155.

target of hate crimes. In 2019, a white supremacist gunman, who targeted Latinxs, killed twenty-two people at an El Paso Walmart. The slow violence of pollution and poverty harms the Latinx body/mind. Police kill Latinxs in acts of police brutality. These forms of violence go unnamed and unnoticed. Latinx theologies fight for the liberation of Latinxs from these modes of oppression.

THEMES OF LATINX THEOLOGIES

Hybridity

Latinxs experience the blending of different cultures. This experience of in-betweenness and blending is called hybridity. For first- and second-generation Latinxs, this is between their parents' culture and American culture. Eldin Villafañe, building off Du Bois, calls this "triple consciousness."[10] This triple consciousness is seeing oneself from the eyes of white supremacy and the eyes of other Latinxs as inauthentic. This experience is expressed well in an often-quoted line from the movie *Selena*, a biopic of the short life of Mexican American singer Selena. Selena's father wants to teach his children about being Mexican American in the scene. He tells them: "We have to be more Mexican than the Mexicans and more American than the Americans, both at the same time! It's exhausting!"[11] This is one of the myriads of ways Latinxs experience hybridity. This sense of being caught between multiple cultures drives the creative engagement with hybridity within Latinx theological discourse.

In Latinx theology, the dominant metaphor for hybridity is mestizaje. Virgilio Elizondo introduced mestizaje into Latinx theology. Mestizaje for Elizondo is a term for hybridity as a universal phenomenon. For Elizondo, mestizaje acts as a *locus theologicus*—the place of theological reflection. As a *locus theologicus,* mestizaje becomes the key to reinterpreting Christian doctrine. There is a two-way reading of the Gospel and Mexican American experience. One direction is the "cultural rereading of the gospel" to demonstrate that Jesus' cultural identity as a Galilean was a mestizo one. This allows for a "gospel rereading of cultural life" where Mexican American experience connects with the gospel.[12] There are broader implications of this two-way reading. The church is called to gather all peoples of the world as a mestizo church. Mestizaje provides an identity with a vocation toward justice by which Christ and the church are understood.

Rubén Rosario Rodríguez in *Racism and God-Talk* puts forward mestizaje as a transcultural paradigm of mutual cultural exchange to dismantle racism from a Latinx perspective. Mestizaje for Rodríguez is a particular instance of hybridity. He recognizes that mestizaje is both potentially dangerous and liberatory. For Rodríguez,

---

10. Villafañe, *Liberating Spirit*, 23.
11. Gregory Nava, dir., *Selena*. Burbank, CA: Warner Bros, 2004.
12. Access Elizando, *Galilean Journey*.

mestizaje can contribute to problematic constructions of identity over and against other marginalized groups.[13] This troublesome nature of mestizaje has led to others seeking alternative metaphors for hybridity. A few of these alternative metaphors are ajiaco (Miguel De La Torre), mulataje, mulatizaje (Teresa Delgado), mezcolanza (Fernando F. Segovia), and spanglish (Edwin David Aponte). The liberatory potential is mestizaje as an affirmation of identity. Mestizaje as a metaphor is maintained because it permits pride in one's mixed identity and is flexible enough as a concept to enable reworking as mutual cultural exchange. Reframing mestizaje in this way allows for the metaphor to frame action for social change.

Edwin David Aponte in *¡Santo! Varieties of Latino/a Spirituality* explores the cultural blending in the diversity of Latinx religions and religious practices. Most Latinxs belong to forms of Christianity, mainly Catholicism, Protestantism, and Pentecostalism. Latinxs also belong to different religious traditions from Judaism, Isalm, Buddhism, Santeria, Cuanderismo, and Espiritualismo. In Latinx religions, there is a mixing of cultural traditions. Aponte uses Spanglish spirituality to describe these practices. Spanglish is a linguistic metaphor. Spanglish is the amalgam of Spanish and English words, sayings, and phrases. An example of a Spanglish spirituality is writer Sandra Cisneros who refers to her mix of Buddhism and devotion to Our Lady of Guadalupe as being a Buddhaloupist.[14] Spanglish spiritualities encompass the range of ways Latinx relate to the holy or santo.

Our Lady of Guadalupe is a multivalent symbol of Mexican and Mexican American culture and religion. Guadalupe's multivalence is the story, materiality of the physical symbol, and interpretations of Guadalupe. In the *Nicanmopohua* ("Here is recounted"), the recent Aztec convert Juan Diego encounters Our Lady of Guadalupe on the hill of Tepeyac in December of 1531. She instructs him to have a church built on the hill. After this encounter, he sought an audience with the incredulous Archbishop Juan de Zumárraga. Diego returns to the hill of Tepeyac, where Guadalupe instructs him to return the next day. The following day Diego meets with the archbishop, who believes Diego's sincerity, but tells him he cannot construct a church without a sign. Instead of meeting Guadalupe, Juan Diego takes care of his uncle Juan Bernardino, who is deathly ill. Later that night, his uncle asks him to get a priest to perform last rites. Diego travels an alternative route to avoid running into Guadalupe, but she appears to him anyway. Guadalupe tells him his uncle will be healed and then instructs him to pick up flowers in his cloak to take to the archbishop. These were gorgeous Castilian flowers, out of season and on the wrong continent. The sight of these flowers granted Diego another audience with the archbishop. When he meets the archbishop, Diego drops the flowers from his cloak revealing the image of Our Lady of Guadalupe. The archbishop repents of his unbelief, which leads to building a church on the hill of

---

13. For more on the problematic nature of mestizaje as theological metaphor access Medina, *Mestizaje*.
14. Cisneros, "Conversation."

Tepeyac. This is the narrative of the Marian apparitions housed in Basílica de Nuestra Señora de Guadalupe in Mexico City near Tepeyac.

The canonical account details the materiality of the cloak and the image of Guadalupe. The image appeared on "a maguey cloak that was rather thick and well woven, for at that time, the maguey cloak was the clothing and covering of all the humble commoners."[15] The materiality of the cloak is critical because it is a piece of clothing worn by the Nahua people. The cloak embodies the divine revealing itself through the materiality of Nahua clothing.

The first is the color of Guadalupe's face. Guadalupe is known as the "dark Virgin," or morena. The canonical narratives draw attention to the color of Guadalupe's skin. It is "courtly and somewhat dark" and "her color light brunette." Louise Burkhart speculates the artist of the image might have used the grayish pigment to reflect other "Black Madonnas," which allowed Guadalupe to appear as a morena.[16] This allowed the identification of Guadalupe to the Nahua people, for she looked like them and spoke in Nahuatl. Gloria Anzaldúa writes that for "Mexicans on both sides of the border, *Guadalupe* is the symbol of our rebellion against the rich, upper and middleclass; against their subjugation of the poor *indio*."[17] The divine image in a dark face allowed for resistance to oppression.

Second, the sun and the moon in the image of Guadalupe echo sixteenth-century depictions of the Immaculate Conception. Burkhart writes, "these elements derive from identification of the Immaculate Conception with the woman standing on the moon and dressed in the sun described in the Book of Revelations (12:1)."[18] Anzaldúa argues Guadalupe is the Nahua goddess, *Coatalopeuh,* and the Spanish mistook this name for the Spanish Guadalupe in Spain.[19] Either way, the Spanish saw a familiar image when they looked up Guadalupe.

The third is the floral design on Guadalupe's robe. "Nahuas conceived of the sacred in terms of a "flower world," Burkhart writes, "a sunny garden filled with flowers, brightly colored tropical birds, and precious stones like jade and turquoise."[20] This was not an otherworldly transcendent plane but was embedded in the material world and revealed through ritual transformation.[21] The flowers of Guadalupe's robe point towards this "flower world." The Nauha talk about philosophy in terms of flower and song. Virgil Elizondo writes that for the Nahua, the "beauty of the image (flowers) and the melodious sound (poetic word), the divine could be gradually experienced, and

---

15. Sousa et. al, *Story of Guadalupe*, 89.
16. Burkhart, "Cult of the Virgin of Guadalupe in Mexico," 206.
17. Anzaldúa, *Borderlands*, 52.
18. Burkhart, "Cult of the Virgin of Guadalupe in Mexico," 204–5.
19. Anzaldúa, *Borderlands*, 51.
20. Burkhart, "Cult of the Virgin of Guadalupe in Mexico," 210.
21. Burkhart, "Cult of the Virgin of Guadalupe in Mexico," 210.

one could gradually share in the divine wisdom."[22] Both Burkhart and Elizondo point to how the flower of Guadalupe's robe represented the flower world of paradise and the Nahua ways of knowing.

Guadalupe is a composite image, and Nahua, Spanish, and Mestizos see themselves in the image. While there is disagreement as to what extent Guadalupe is Coatlalopeuh or Mary of Spain, her brownness is woven together in the fibers of the cloak with an image of dark-skinned Immaculate Conception Mary that remembers the flower world.

Ethics

As a liberative theology, Latinx theologies are committed to emancipatory projects, and this commitment blends the traditional distinctions between theology and ethics. There is a rich Latinx ethics tradition. Accompimeñto, lo cotidiano, dignidad, liberating spirit, and trickster are concepts in Latinx ethics. Acompañamiento is the act of living in a relationship with others. God's preferential option for the poor, as Roberto S. Goizueta argues, require accompaniment with the poor. The people's response "caminemos con Jesús"—"let us walk with Jesus"—in the Holy Thursday procession demonstrates this accompaniment with Jesus in walking to the garden of Gethsemane. Acompañamiento is walking with the poor as friends in the struggle for justice. Interpersonal relationships are crucial for justice. As Goizueta writes, "[w]here the option for the poor is simply reduced to an option for social justice, the poor will inevitably be reduced to an abstract concept or a manipulable object."[23] The option for the poor is the "option for poor *persons*" in their particularities of space and place. To do otherwise treats the oppressed as objects and furthers dehumanization. Caminemos con Jesús is to walk with the poor in their everyday lives.

Lo cotidiano is the everyday lived experience of Latinxs. Ada Maria Isasí-Diaz grounded her mujerista theology in the lo cotidiano of Latinas. Lo cotidiano is a multifaceted concept for Isasí-Diaz with descriptive, hermeneutical, and epistemological elements. Lo cotidiano is the liberative experiences of Latinas and their struggle against sexual, ethnic, and economic oppression. From this experience, Latinas interpret the world around them and name themselves. In this way, lo cotidiano also emphasizes Latinas' way of knowing. As Isasí-Diaz argues, lo cotidiano provides both the critique and alternative vision.[24] Many los cotidianos offer different critiques and visions rooted in liberation for Latinx theologies.

Ismael Garcia argues that Latinx moral reasoning is ethics centered in community, where humanity's relational nature, corresponding to the relational nature of a personal God, aims to care for one another with the recognition of an individual's

---

22. Elizondo, *Guadalupe*, 35.
23. Goizueta, *Caminemos Con Jesús*, 195.
24. This account of "lo cotidiano" is taken from Isasí-Diaz, *Mujerista Theology*, 66–73.

dignity—given by God.²⁵ This emphasizes justice against the indignity of political, social, and cultural oppression and the recognition of diverse communities. Garcia's methodology is emancipatory ethics that aims to synthesize the moral reasoning of the Hispanic community and its theological commitments. The implications of Garcia's arguments are the importance of communities over abstract universal moral principles with the safeguards of dignity and recognition that allow for a diversity of ethical communities.

Eldin Villafañe centers the liberating Spirit in Latinx Pentecostal ethics.²⁶ This pneumatological ethic is best understood through Gal 5:25, "If we live in the Spirit, let us walk in the Spirit." One is empowered through Spirit baptism to take up the prophetic vocation and participate in Spirit's work. The Spirit's historical project is to bring about the reign of God and confront the "power and principalities" (social sin) with the Spirit's charismatic gifts. This work is Latinx Pentecostal church's awareness of themselves as a "barrio" church and a "community of the Spirit" for the world and in the world, but not of the world. In this way, to live in the Spirit is possible by the gifts of the Spirit to do the work of the Spirit.

Miguel De La Torre puts forward an ethics para joder in his trilogy on ethics: *Latino/a Social Ethics*, *The Politics of Jesús*, and *Embracing Hopelessness*. De La Torre critiques different facets of Eurocentric thinking which do not bring about the abundant life of Christ. An ethics para joder is a trickster ethic in screwing with the system as praxis—action and reflection. Christ as liberator is a trickster because he challenged systems of injustice. The embrace of hopelessness is an embrace of desperation—not despair—of the oppressed and rejecting salvation histories—secular and religious—that accepts oppression as part of progress and the middle-class hope that produces quietism. The spirit of liberative ethics moves from orthopraxis (right practice) to orthodoxy (right thought). The concepts of accompimeñto, lo cotidiano, dignidad, liberating spirit, and trickster guide social action against oppression.

Land

Land shapes the theological imagination of Latinx theologies. Carmen M. Nanko-Fernández maps three metaphors used by Latinx theologians: border, exile, and diaspora.²⁷ The choice of these metaphors is related to the experience of migration for Latinx theologians. These experiences of migration are connected to the land. Mexican, Mexican American, and Chicanx use border metaphors because of the US-Mexican border. Exile resonates with Cuban American theologians because many had to flee Cuba. In comparison, Puerto Ricans deploy diasporic metaphors. These metaphors provide another helpful heuristic theme of Latinx theologies.

25. Access García, *Dignidad*.
26. Access Villafañe, *Liberating Spirit*.
27. Nanko-Fernández, "Alternately Documented Theologies," 33–55.

In *Borderlands/La Frontera: The New Mestiza*, Gloria Anzaldúa argues for a new critical consciousness that embraces the contradictions and ambiguities as a means of healing and disrupting oppression. The borderlands—both physical and metaphorical—are places of intense struggle that lead to a new consciousness. These physical borderlands represent the US-Mexican border, as well as other borders. The metaphorical borderlands are between race, class, gender, and sexuality. The physical borderlands provide a metaphor to describe how the boundaries in society are policed. When one crosses the US-Mexican border, there is a militarized checkpoint to control who is allowed to cross. There are additional stops by the US Border Patrol in the Southwest to check for undocumented immigrants. This policing of borders happens along with race, class, sex, gender, and ability. Border crossing becomes an act of resistance to forms of oppression that, for Anzaldúa's borderlands, "are physically present wherever two or more cultures edge each other, where people of different races occupy the same territory, where under, lower, middle and upper classes touch, where the space between two individuals shrinks with intimacy."[28] These borderlands are where people meet and how these intersections meet within people.

The following two metaphors of exile and diaspora are related. Both metaphors relate to the diasporic experience but focus on two different aspects of that experience. As Nanko-Fernández points out, not all dispersal of peoples is exilic.[29] Justo L. González in *Santa Biblia: The Bible Through Hispanic Eyes* provides paradigmatic themes of how Latinxs read the Bible. One of these themes is exile. Cuban Americans connect the Hebrews' exile in Babylon with the exile of Cuban Americans from Cuba because of a communist government. Diaspora metaphor resonates with the experience of Puerto Ricans and the liminal status of Puerto Rico as US territory and Puerto Ricans as second-class citizens. It is this diaspora that Teresa Delgado wrestles with what it means to have a Puerto Rican theology. Borders, exile, and diaspora provide metaphors centered in Latinx social location. Latinx theologies are centered in the great varieties of Latinx experiences, giving rise to themes of hybridity, ethics, and land.

BIBLIOGRAPHY

Alcoff, Linda Martín. "Anti-Latino Racism." In *Decolonizing Epistemologies: Latina/o Theology and Philosophy*, edited by Ada María Isasi-Díaz and Eduardo Mendieta, 107–26. Transdisciplinary Theological Colloquia. New York: Fordham University Press, 2012.
Anzaldúa, Gloria. *Borderlands: The New Mestiza = La Frontera*. 3rd ed. San Francisco: Aunt Lute, 2007.
Aponte, Edwin David. *¡Santo! Varieties of Latino/a Spirituality*. Maryknoll, NY: Orbis, 2012.
Aponte, Edwin David, and Miguel A. De La Torre. *Introducing Latinx Theologies*. Rev. ed. Maryknoll, NY: Orbis, 2020.

---

28. Anzaldúa, *Borderlands*, 19.
29. Nanko-Fernández, "Alternately Documented Theologies," 43.

Burkhart, Louise M. "The Cult of the Virgin of Guadalupe in Mexico." In *South and Meso-American Native Spirituality: From the Cult of the Feathered Serpent to the Theology of Liberation*, edited by Gary H. Gossen, 198–227. New York: Crossroad, 1993.

Card, Claudia. "Injustice, Evil, and Oppression." In *Dancing with Iris: The Philosophy of Iris Marion Young*, edited by Ann Ferguson and Mechthild Nagel, 147–59. Oxford: Oxford University Press, 2009.

Cisneros, Sandra. "Conversation: Sandra Cisneros." Interview by Ray Suarez, PBS NewsHour, PBS, October 15, 2002. https://www.pbs.org/newshour/show/conversation-sandra-cisneros.

De La Torre, Miguel A. *Latina/o Social Ethics: Moving Beyond Eurocentric Moral Thinking*. Waco, TX: Baylor University Press, 2010.

Delgado, Teresa. *A Puerto Rican Decolonial Theology: Prophesy Freedom*. New York: Palgrave Macmillan, 2017.

Dolmage, Jay. *Academic Ableism: Disability and Higher Education*. Corporealities. Ann Arbor: University of Michigan Press, 2017.

Elizondo, Virgilio P. *Galilean Journey: The Mexican-American Promise*. 2nd rev. ex. ed. Maryknoll, NY: Orbis, 2005.

———. *Guadalupe: Mother of the New Creation*. Maryknoll, NY: Orbis, 1997.

Espin, Orlando O., and Miguel H. Díaz, eds. *From the Heart of Our People: Latino/a Explorations in Catholic Systematic Theology*. Maryknoll, NY: Orbis, 1999.

García, Ismael. *Dignidad: Ethics through Hispanic Eyes*. Nashville: Abingdon, 1997.

Goizueta, Roberto S. *Caminemos Con Jesús: Toward a Hispanic/Latino Theology of Accompaniment*. Maryknoll, NY: Orbis, 1995.

González, Justo L. *Santa Biblia: The Bible Through Hispanic Eyes*. Nashville: Abingdon, 1996.

Gonzalez, Michelle A. *Afro-Cuban Theology: Religion, Race, Culture, and Identity*. Gainesville: University Press of Florida, 2009.

Isasi-Diaz, Ada Maria. *Embracing Hopelessness*. Minneapolis: Fortress, 2017.

———. *En La Lucha/In the Struggle: Elaborating a Mujerista Theology*. 10th anv. ed. Minneapolis: Fortress, 2004.

———. *La Lucha Continues: Mujerista Theology*. Maryknoll, NY: Orbis, 2004.

———. *Mujerista Theology: A Theology for the Twenty-First Century*. Maryknoll, NY: Orbis, 1996.

———. *The Politics of Jesús: A Hispanic Political Theology*. Lanham, MD: Rowman & Littlefield, 2015.

Martell-Otero, Loida I. "Epilogue: Hablando Se Entiende La Gente." In *Latina Evangélicas: A Theological Survey from the Margins*, edited by Zaida Maldonado Pérez and Elizabeth Conde-Frazier, 127–38. Eugene, OR: Cascade, 2013.

———. "Introduction: Abuelita Theologies." In *Latina Evangélicas: A Theological Survey from the Margins*, edited by Zaida Maldonado Pérez and Elizabeth Conde-Frazier, 1–13. Eugene, OR: Cascade, 2013.

Martell-Otero, Loida I., et al., eds. *Latina Evangélicas: A Theological Survey from the Margins*. Eugene, OR: Cascade, 2013.

Medina, Néstor. *Mestizaje: (Re)Mapping Race, Culture, and Faith in Latina/o Catholicism*. Studies in Latino/a Catholicism. Maryknoll, NY: Orbis, 2009.

Nanko-Fernández, Carmen M. "Alternately Documented Theologies: Mapping Border, Exile and Diaspora." In *Religion and Politics in America's Borderlands*, edited by Sarah Azaransky, 33–55. Lanham, MD: Rowman & Littlefield, 2013.

Ortega-Aponte, Elias. "Raised Fists in the Church! Afro-Latino/a Practice among the Young Lords Party: A Humanistic Spirituality Model for Radical Latino/a Religious Ethics." N.p.: ProQuest Dissertations, 2011.

Pineda-Madrid, Nancy. "Notes Toward A Chicana Feminist Epistemology (And Why It Is Important for Latina Feminist Theologies)." In *A Reader in Latina Feminist Theology: Religion and Justice*, edited by María Pilar Aquino et al., 241–66. Austin: University of Texas Press, 2002.

Rodriguez, Jose David, and Loida I. Martell-Otero, eds. *Teologia En Conjunto: A Collaborative Hispanic Protestant Theology*. Louisville: Westminster John Knox, 1997.

Rodríguez, Rubén Rosario. *Racism and God-Talk: A Latino/a Perspective*. New York: New York University Press, 2008.

Solivan, Samuel. *The Spirit, Pathos and Liberation: Toward an Hispanic Pentecostal Theology*. Sheffield: Sheffield Academic Press, 1998.

Sousa, Lisa, Stafford Poole, and James Lockhart, eds. *The Story of Guadalupe: Luis Laso de La Vega's Huei Tlamahuiçoltica of 1649*. 1st ed. Stanford, CA: Los Angeles: Stanford University Press, 1998.

Valentín, Benjamín., ed. *In Our Own Voices: Latino/a Renditions of Theology*. Latino/a Renditions of Theology. Maryknoll, NY: Orbis, 2010.

Villafañe, Eldin. *The Liberating Spirit: Toward a Hispanic American Pentecostal Social Ethic*. Grand Rapids: Eerdmans, 1993.

Young, Iris Marion. *Justice and the Politics of Difference*. Princeton: Princeton University Press, 1990.

CHAPTER 32

Asian American Theologies

PETER C. PHAN

Of the two terms in the phrase "Asian American," the former has different connotations. Under "Asia," the United Nations refers to five regions: Western, Central, South, East, and Southeast Asia. However, in the US Census Bureau and US Office of Management and Budget, "Asians" refers to people of ethnic origins from East, Southeast, and South Asia and excludes Western and Central Asia. People from West Asia are categorized as Middle Eastern Americans and those from Central Asia as Central Asian Americans. This chapter adopts the US Census Bureau's and Office of Management and Budget's definition of "Asian" in speaking of "Asian American theologies." "American" refers exclusively to the United States of America, which is narrower than "North America."

THE ASIAN AMERICAN HISTORICAL CONTEXT

"Asian American"

In 1968, at the founding of the Asian American Political Alliance, the historian Yuji Ichioka coined the term "Asian American" to designate the "inter-ethnic-pan-Asian American" for political purposes. Of course, its meaning depends on what is meant by both "Asian" and "American," and this, in turn, depends on who is asking, who is defining, who is being defined, why, and in what context. A majority of Asian Americans feel ambivalent about its use as a self-defining term, both because "Asian" is used as a racial rather than ethnic marking (there is no such thing as the Asian race) and is too generic, obscuring the vast differences among different cultural and national groups (there are few physical, historical, and cultural commonalities between South Asians and East/Southeast Asians) and because "American" normally implies citizenship, which of course not all Asians in the US have.

Despite these valid criticisms, scholars of race and Asian American identity in the social sciences and the humanities point out that because Asians in the US have a "shared racial experience," that is, a common history of racial exploitation, discrimination, and oppression by the dominant white group, the term "Asian American" is a useful pan-ethnic category to create collective consciousness and group solidarity among diverse people who hail from different countries of Asia, even though "Asian" is imposed as a racial category by the dominant white class and is fictitious.

As for the nomenclature "Asian American theology," "Asian American" intimates the double components of this theology. On the one hand, as *Asian*, it is deeply rooted in Asian realities such as Asia's multiple and diverse histories, cultures, and religions that form the context and resources for Asian theology as well as the Asian theologies that have been elaborated by Asian theologians themselves in Asia. On the other hand, as *American* theology, it is elaborated in the United States and must take into account the distinctive challenges and opportunities of its new location.

I will begin with a brief overview of the history of Asian immigration in the US to explain the context of Asian American theologies. Next, I will systematically rather than chronologically expound on the various developments of Asian American theologies and their major themes. Lastly, I will indicate some of the areas in which Asian American theologies could be further developed to meet the diverse challenges facing Asian Christians in the US.

Asian Migrants in the US

Although migrants from Asia had been present in the US since the seventeenth century, large-scale immigration did not begin until the mid-nineteenth century. When the economy in the early second half of the nineteenth century was booming and the labor force was in short supply, foreign workers were welcome, but toward the end, when there was an economic downturn and job scarcity, they were seen as threats that needed to be eliminated. Like other foreign groups, Asians were welcome as a cheap labor force, but unlike white ethnic groups such as the Irish and the Italians, Asians were subjected to discrimination and exclusion not only because they were perceived as an economic threat depressing the white workers' wages, but also as a different *racial* group, the "Yellow Peril."

The first Asians who were victims of xenophobia were the Chinese and subsequently the Japanese. More than three hundred thousand Chinese landed in California during the gold rush (1848–1882) and by the 1850s they faced fierce competition from the white forty-niners. When the gold mines became exhausted in the 1860s, they found work in farming and the building of the Central Pacific Railroad until its completion in 1869. During the 1880s–1920s, various Chinese Exclusion Acts were passed in California and the US Congress to exclude Chinese immigration, the most notable of which were those enacted in 1822, 1892, and 1902.

The Japanese were the second largest group of Asians to immigrate into the continental US in the late nineteenth century, partly to fill the gap left by the Chinese. Emigration, especially of students, was promoted by the Meiji Restoration to acquire technological expertise in the West. Many Japanese farmers went to Hawai'i and California to look for jobs in agribusiness. Large-scale immigration of Koreans into the US occurred in 1903–1905, mostly to Hawai'i to work in the sugarcane plantations. After Japan annexed Korea in 1910, many Korean intellectuals, anti-Japanese activists, and political exiles came to the US. Like the Chinese, Japanese and Korean Americans encountered racial discrimination and exclusion in a series of legislative acts such as the Gentlemen's Agreement (1907), the Asiatic Barred Zone Act (1917), and the Johnson-Reed Act (1924). But the most outrageous act was Executive Order 9066, signed by President Franklin D. Roosevelt on February 19, 1942, after the Japanese bombing at Pearl Harbor, which brought about the incarceration of 120,000 Japanese, of whom 77,000 were American citizens, in concentration camps, as "enemy aliens" until the end of the Second World War.

A dramatic change in US immigration policy was brought about by the Hart-Celler Act, known as the Immigration and Nationality Act, which President Lyndon B. Johnson signed in 1965. It abolished the racially discriminatory national origins quota which favored European immigrants and opened the door wide for Asian immigration for family reunification, job opportunities, and education. Later, a large number of Indochinese, especially Vietnamese, Cambodians, Laotians, Hmongs, and Khmers came to the US as refugees after the end of the American political and military involvement in Indochina. South Asians, in particular Indians, migrated to the US and have distinguished themselves in information technology, medicine, and politics. (The current vice president of the US, Kamala Harris, is the daughter of an Indian mother, and there are several Indian American influential members of Congress.) In recent years, refugees came from Eastern Europe, the Middle East, Central Asia, and, most recently, Afghanistan as the result of military conflicts and religious persecution.

In 2020, according to the US Census Bureau, as reported by Pew Research Center, the Asian American population was 22.4 million, making up about 7 percent of the nation's overall population of 333 million, and their numbers are projected to surpass 46 million by 2060. Asian Americans trace their roots to more than twenty countries in East, Southeast, and South Asia. The largest group was the Chinese, making up 24 percent of the Asian American population, or 5.4 million people. The next two largest groups were Indians, who accounted for 21 percent of the total (4.6 million people), and Filipinos, who accounted for 19 percent (or 4.2 million people). They were followed by Vietnamese (2.2 million), Koreans (1.9 million), and Japanese (1.5

million). In 2017, Asians made up about 14 percent of the 10.5 million unauthorized immigrants in the US, mainly from India (525,000), China (375,000), the Philippines (160,000), and Korea (150,000).[1]

Asian American Christians

Asian American Christians are almost evenly divided between Protestants and Catholics. Roughly a fifth of all Asian Americans are Protestant (22 percent), and a slightly smaller percentage is Catholic (19 percent). Of Asian American Protestants, only Korean Americans have a majority Protestant population (61 percent). A third of the Japanese Americans surveyed (33 percent) and about a fifth of Chinese Americans (22 percent) and a fifth of Filipino Americans (21 percent) describe themselves as Protestant. The number of Protestant Indian Americans and Protestant Vietnamese Americans is much lower (11 percent and 6 percent, respectively.) Among Asian American Protestants, there is a higher proportion of born-again or Evangelical Protestants (58 percent) than mainline Protestants (42 percent). Nearly a third of Asian American Protestants (31 percent) describe themselves as Pentecostal Christians, Charismatic Christians, or both. The most common denominations among Asian American Protestants are Presbyterian (19 percent), Baptist (18 percent), Methodist (9 percent), and Pentecostal (7 percent). Nondenominational Christians make up 14 percent.

Of Asian American Christians, in 2020, 19 percent are Catholic, slightly less than Protestants (22 percent). About two-thirds of Filipino Americans (65 percent) are Catholic. Because most Filipinos are English-speaking they do not have separate ethnic parishes but are members of American parishes. Three-in-ten Vietnamese Americans (30 percent) are Catholic, with a large number of priests (about one thousand), seminarians, and religious sisters. Because older Vietnamese Catholics do not speak English, and where there are many of them, separate ethnic parishes have been set up for them. Where their number is not big enough to warrant a separate parish, a Mass in Vietnamese is made available to them on Sundays.

A total of 14 percent of Asian Americans are Buddhist. About four-in-ten Vietnamese Americans (43 percent), one-in-four Japanese Americans (25 percent), and one-in-six Chinese Americans (15 percent) are Buddhist. One in ten Asian Americans are Hindu, nearly all of whom trace their roots to India. Asian Americans also practice several other faiths, such as Islam, Judaism, Sikhism, and Jainism. A total of 4 percent of US Asians are Muslim.

---

1. See https://www.pewresearch.org/fact-tank/2021/04/29/.

ASIAN AMERICAN THEOLOGIES

Against this historical background, it is now possible to explicate Asian Christian theologies. It is in response to the existential condition of Asian Americans, Christian as well as non-Christian, that Asian American theologies are to be elaborated. As a preliminary for an adequate and appropriate Asian American theology, a careful analysis of this existential condition of Asian Americans must be done to highlight the issues which Asian American theologies must address.

Basic Trends of Asian American Theologies

Central to the existential condition of Asian Americans is first and foremost the experience of migration itself, the "being-a-migrant." Whether forced or free, economically or politically motivated, temporary or permanent, migration often presents overwhelming physical, psychological, economic, socio-political, familial, cultural, and religious challenges to people who have left their native countries to live in a foreign land. Migration and its multiple challenges are the humus from which Asian American theologies grow. Asian American theologies attempt to articulate the meaning of migration by exploring who God, Christ, and the Holy Spirit are for migrants; how the church can be a community of hope for migrants amid their sufferings and despair; how worship and prayer should embody their migratory experiences; and how spirituality can deepen the virtues required for living the Christian life as migrants in the US.

Second, one of the challenges for migrants, and a major concern especially for first-generation migrants, are how to preserve in the new country all the things known under the umbrella term of 'culture' that constitute their national, ethnic, and religious identities such as language, customs, festivals, literature, the arts, philosophical ideas, and religious practices. First-generation Asian American theologians undertook "inculturation" (Catholics) or "contextualization" (Protestants) as their primary task, attempting to articulate the Christian beliefs with the use of Asian philosophical and religious categories.

Third, Asian American theologies must be rooted in the daily life, what Latinx theologians call *lo quotidiano*, of migrants, especially the unskilled and the undocumented, who often are crushed by poverty, befuddled by strange languages and customs, cut off from their loved ones and deadened by loneliness, laboring at the so-called 3D jobs (dangerous, difficult, and dirty), working long and grinding hours at their family small businesses, and above all, marginalized and discriminated against, physically assaulted, and even killed by white supremacists simply because they are "Asian," perceived as racially different from them. Depending on their successes or failures, Asian Americans are viewed as "model minorities," "middle minorities," "forever foreigners," or "honorary whites."

While they must acknowledge the destructive effects of racialization on Asian Americans, Asian American theologies must not see Asians purely as victims of economic and political forces. On the contrary, as their histories in the US indicate, Asian Americans can be agents and masters of their destiny and have overcome all kinds of obstacles to achieve their full humanity and made significant contributions to American society and culture. Nevertheless, despite the undeniable successes of some Asian Americans, others are still unjustly deprived of opportunities for full human flourishing, and therefore Asian American theologies must be liberation theology advocating for their human rights and dignity.

In elaborating this liberationist theology, some Asian American theologians have framed it in terms of postcoloniality, which is thought to be highly appropriate for migrants who emigrate from countries formerly colonized by European and American empires and by Asian empires such as China and Japan. This postcolonial theology is built upon a postcolonial hermeneutics of the Bible and the sacred books of Asian religions.

Fourth, in addition to racism, Asian American women suffer from a type of oppression peculiar to them, namely, the patriarchal and androcentric system of both their native countries and the US. Whereas in the past only Asian men were allowed to migrate as laborers into the US, there has recently been the globalization of domestic work and the concomitant feminization of migration. As the birth rate in richer countries falls and as many women pursue careers outside the home, there is a need for migrant women to fill the "typically female" jobs, such as domestic work, child care, restaurant and hotel staff, entertainment (a euphemism for prostitution), assembly line work in clothing and electronics, and other low-paying menial work. Many female Asian American theologians have articulated a sophisticated feminist approach to theology.

Fifth, as the Christian faith is lived and celebrated in the community, Asian American theologians, especially those engaged in pastoral ministry and practical theology, have devoted special attention to elaborating a theology of the church appropriate for migrants and setting up ethnic parishes and congregations so that they can worship in their own languages and their rituals and their diverse spiritual needs can be adequately met.

Sixth, among Christian denominations and movements, Evangelicals/Pentecostals have been the fastest-growing groups in the US and around the world in the last few decades. As mentioned above, many Asian Americans self-identify as Evangelical and/or Pentecostal. In Asian American theologies Evangelicals/Pentecostals have recently emerged as important voices with distinctive accents.

Section 7 | Emerging Theologies from Diasporic and Indigenous Voices

Postcolonial Hermeneutics of the Bible

As noted above, a distinctive strand in biblical hermeneutics is postcolonial biblical interpretation, the foremost proponent of which is the Sri Lankan R. S. Sugirtharajah, who has been active not in the US but the UK. In a festschrift in honor of Sugirtharajah, the editor Tat-siong Benny Liew, a New Testament scholar, gathers other Asian American biblicists and theologians who share the postcolonial turn to reflect on Sugirtharajah's contributions on postcolonial hermeneutics and offer their own postcolonial interpretations on biblical texts. These include Kah-Jin Jeffrey Kuan, Mai-Anh Le Tran, Sathaianathan Clarke, Eleazar S. Fernandez, and J. Jayakiran Sebastian.[2] Liew argues that postcolonial hermeneutics needs not to choose between the margin and the diaspora nor between ethnic studies and area studies nor national and international boundaries as binary perspectives from which to interpret the Bible for Asian American migrants. This is so because the identity of Asian Americans is not something fixed, immutable, impenetrable, or inherent but "an invention of self that not only involves improvisation and the incorporation of others but also facilitates intervention."[3]

Another important collection of essays on Asian biblical interpretation is edited by Mary F. Foskett and Jeffrey Kah-Jin Kwan.[4] Space does not permit a summary of these essays but a survey of Asian American biblical scholarship cannot afford not to mention their names: Devadasan N. Premnath, John Yueh-Han Yieh, Samuel Cheon, Philip P. Chia, Andrew Yueking Lee, Lai Ling Elizabeth Ngan, Uriah Yong-Hwan Kim, Jean K. Kim, John Ahn, Mai Anh Le Tran (again), Sze-kar Wan, Gale A. Yee, Frank M. Yamada, Mary F. Foskett, and Henry W. Morisada Rietz.

Among those mentioned above, one who has authored a volume of her own on Asian American hermeneutics is Gale A. Yee, a third-generation Chinese American.[5] Yee recounts her journey as an Asian American Hebrew Scripture scholar trying to develop an Asian American biblical hermeneutics beyond the historical-critical method. She offers a feminist, postcolonial interpretation of the book of Ruth, 1 Kgs 21, Isa 56:1–8, and Ezek 16:44–63. Another scholar who has written extensively on Asian postcolonial hermeneutics is Kwok Pui-lan.[6] We will return to her work when speaking of Asian feminist theology.

---

2. Liew himself has authored a groundbreaking book on Asian American biblical hermeneutics, *What Is Asian American Biblical Hermeneutics?*

3. Liew, *Postcolonial Interventions*, 14.

4. Fosket and Kwan, *Ways of Being, Ways of Reading.*

5. Yee, *Towards An Asian American Biblical Hermeneutics.* In addition, she has edited *The Hebrew Bible: Feminist and Intersectional Perspectives* (Minneapolis: Fortress, 2018).

6. See especially Kwok, *Discovering the Bible in the Non-Biblical World* and *Postcolonial Imagination and Feminist Theology.*

Contextual Asian American Theologies: Theologizing between Two Cultures

The first generation of Asian American theologians focused their reflections on how the fundamental Christian beliefs can be expressed in the thought forms and categories of Asian cultures. Chief among these is the Korean Jung Young Lee. Drawing on the Daoist metaphysics of yin-yang and "both-and," Lee reinterprets the doctrine of the Trinity. Starting from the Son's dual nature of humanity and divinity understood as yin and yang, Lee argues that the Spirit represents the yin (feminine) and the Father the yang (masculine) of the Trinity. He further expounds on six patterns of intertrinitarian relationships which are obtained according to how the Father, the Son, and the Spirit are positioned first, second, and third in their mutual relationships. Lee considers these six relations Asian, patriarchal/Confucian, matriarchal/Daoist, contextual, new generation, and shamanic.[7] In addition to his Christian reading of the *I Ching*, Lee offers an interpretation of the Asian American experience in terms of marginality. Asian Americans are, he suggests, "in-between" and "in-both" the Asian and the American societies and cultures. Because of this existential predicament of marginality, Asian Americans can be "in-beyond" both Asian and American societies and cultures and can contribute new ways of being Asian and American.[8]

Another theologian that has contributed to the understanding of the marginality of Asian Americans is the Korean Sang Hyun Lee. Drawing on Victor Turner, Lee highlights three creative potentialities of marginality: openness to the new, the emergence of *communitas*, and the creative space for prophetic knowledge and action. However, according to Lee, the liminality of Asian Americans, especially the "dual liminality" of women, is turned into "coerced liminality" by racism and marginalization and as such it hinders the full development of the three potentialities mentioned above: "Asian Americans are in the predicament of 'coerced liminality'—a potentially creative in-betweenness that is suppressed, frustrated, and unfulfilled by barriers that are not in one's control."[9]

Another Korean theologian who has also made significant contributions to Asian American theology by drawing on the Korean culture is Andrew Sung Park. He focuses on the Korean reality of *han*, "the inexpressibly entangled experience of pain and bitterness imposed by the injustice of oppressors."[10] *Han* may be caused by social injustice, political oppression, economic exploitation, cultural marginalization, and violence, and if unresolved, it is passed down the generations and forms a collective unconscious of the people. For Korean Americans, *han* is caused by such things as racial prejudice, real estate redlining, transnational corporations, the "middle-agent minority" phenomenon, classism, and identity crisis. On the other hand, Park points

---

7. See Lee, *Trinity in Asian Perspective*.
8. See Lee, *Marginality*, especially 55–76.
9. Lee, *From a Liminal Place*, 33.
10. Park, *Racial Conflict and Healing*, 9.

out, Korean Americans are not only the sinned-against but also the sinning, and their sins consist of racism, sexism, and labor exploitation. As a way for Korean Americans to heal their *han*, Park shows how the three elements that according to him constitute "Koreanness"—*hahn* (paradoxical inclusiveness), *jung* (affectionate attachment), and *mut* (graceful gusto)—can be practiced in the US. This way consists in a quadruple way of "seeing well": "visual seeing" (hermeneutics of questioning), "intellectual seeing" (hermeneutics of construction), "spiritual seeing" (hermeneutics of affection), and "soul-seeing" (hermeneutics of celebration).[11] In a later work, Park makes a clear distinction between "hurt" or "wound" or *han* and "sin": what is needed for the former is healing which results in wholeness whereas what is needed for the latter is salvation which culminates in sanctification.[12]

Asian American Feminist Theology

Of all Asian theologies, feminist theology has arguably achieved a preeminent position. Its doyenne is undoubtedly Kwok Pui-lan, whom we have already met when speaking of postcolonial biblical hermeneutics. Kwok is a prolific author, editor, and activist. Trained at Harvard with a doctoral dissertation on the history of Chinese Christian women, Kwok subsequently turned her scholarly attention to Asian feminist theology, to which she wrote a comprehensive introduction.[13] Her feminist theology has five interrelated foci: Asian, Asian American, postcolonial, global, and pastoral. As an Asian and Asian American feminist theologian, Kwok is deeply committed to doing theology as an Asian woman, raising feminist theological consciousness, using Asian women's experiences and Asian religious traditions as sources and resources for theology, and interpreting the Bible with Asian women's oral retelling and performance of biblical stories. Kwok highlights the historical connection and mutual collusion among imperialism, patriarchy, androcentrism, religious exclusivism, and ecological destruction, against which she recommends postcolonial feminism as an adequate antidote. Furthermore, postcolonial feminism must not be confined to the proverbial ivory tower; rather, according to Kwok, it must inform the theological curriculum of seminaries and shape the pedagogical strategies in ministerial education and the different activities of pastoral ministry.

Along with Kwok is a large company of Asian American women theologians, most of whom are active in academic associations, especially the Pacific, Asian, and North American Asian Women in Theology and Ministry (PANAWTM), founded in 1984. Two commemorative collections of essays in celebration of this network's twentieth and thirtieth anniversaries, namely, *Off the Menu* (2007)[14] and *Leading Wisdom*

11. See Park, *Racial Conflict and Healing*, 145–59.
12. Park, *From Hurt to Healing*.
13. See Kwok, *Introducing Asian Feminist Theology*.
14. See Brock et al., *Off the Menu*.

2017),[15] feature the who's who of Asian American feminist theologians. Space does not permit naming all of them here but it is necessary to take a look at their names in the table of contents of both volumes to get a sense of the developments of Asian American feminist theology over the last three decades.

Among the early generation, the following should be mentioned: Nami Kim, Gale A. Yee, Jung Ha Kim, Rachel A. R. Bundang, Rita Nakashima Brock, Wonhee Anne Joh, Seung Ai Yang, and Boyung Lee. Among the younger generation, two should be mentioned: Grace Ji-Sun Kim and Choi Hee An, both Korean. Among the former's many works, two deserve mention: *Embracing the Other: The Transformative Spirit of Love* and *Invisible: Theology and the Experience of Asian American Women*. Kim singles out three oppressive systems that render Asian American women invisible, namely, racism, sexism, and xenophobia.[16] To overcome these social ills, Kim proposes a pneumatology in which the Spirit God, whom she associates with chi, empowers Asian American women to work for justice.[17]

Choi Hee An focuses more specifically on the lives of Korean women. In her *Korean Women and God*, Choi explores the reality of God as family, liberator, and friend and shows how this new understanding of God is a source of transformation and liberation for Korean women.[18] In *A Postcolonial Self*, Choi examines three "selves": The Korean ethnic self ("We"), the marginalized self ("I as the other versus We as the other"), and the postcolonial self ("I and We with others") and recommends the practice of radical hospitality and mutual sharing as a way to achieve the postcolonial self.[19] In *A Postcolonial Relationship*, Choi examines the dynamics of "racial triangulation" that places Asian immigrants between Black and white and between native and alien. This "double-in-betweenness" turns Asian immigrants into the "Third Other" characterized by "imperfect otherness." Choi analyzes how this "Third Other" lurks in the institutional practice of assimilation, in the coalition work of social justice practice, and in the belongingness of the psychological practice.[20]

Asian American Practical Theology and Spirituality

Another development of Asian American theology explores how Asian American churches can respond to the spiritual needs of their congregants. In the past recent decades, there has been a remarkable growth of parishes and congregations among Catholics, Protestants, and Evangelicals/Pentecostals. While this is something to

---

15. See Pak and Kim, *Leading Wisdom*.
16. See Kim, *Invisible*, especially chapters 2, 3, and 4.
17. See Kim, *Embracing the Other*, especially chapters 4 and 5.
18. See Choi, *Korean Women and God*, especially chapters 9–11.
19. See Choi, *Postcolonial Self*, especially chapter 3.
20. See Choi, *Postcolonial Relationship*, especially chapter 3.

rejoice at, it is no secret that these Asian American communities have experienced growing pains in establishing their identity and achieving their mission in the US.

These difficulties are exacerbated by insufficient financial and personnel resources, intergenerational differences, interracial marriages, multiethnic membership, gender discrimination, and laity-clergy power conflicts. Peter Cha, S. Steve Kang, and Helen Lee suggest that these conflicts are rooted in culture, gospel, and leadership. In these three areas, conflicts would occur if there is a discrepancy between what they call "explicit theology," that is, the "proclaimed faith" that is preached from the pulpit, taught in Sunday school, and affirmed in the churches' mission statements on the one hand, and "implicit theology," that is, the "practiced faith" that is embodied in a set of values and norms governing the relationship and action of the congregational leaders and members on the other hand. Using the metaphor of "household of God" for the congregation, Cha, Kang, Lee, and their associates offer a practical theology that would promote harmony between explicit and implicit theology and enable the congregations to grow into "healthy households of God."[21]

On Asian American spirituality, Young Lee Hertig's *The Tao of Asian American Belonging* is a groundbreaking work advancing what she terms "yinist spirituality." Rejecting the Western middle-class feminism that she considers reductionistic and dualistic, Hertig proposes a holistic spirituality based on the yin-yang philosophy of Daoism, one that is, she claims, akin to the African American womanist and the Latina women *mujerista* spirituality. Hertig shows how yinist spirituality is grounded in the Bible by offering a novel interpretation of the book of Esther, John 4, Acts 6, and 1 Cor 12. Finally, Hertig shows how yinist spirituality can help Asian American women overcome multiple marginalities in the family, at the workplace, and in the church.[22]

Asian American Pentecostal Theology

The most prominent Pentecostal Asian American theologian is Amos Yong, who describes himself as "a pneumatologian," that is, a theologian of the Spirit. Author and editor of more than fifty books so far, and that at a relatively young age, Yong (b. 1965) is the premier Asian American Pentecostal theologian, not only because of his extraordinary prolificity but also because his writings deal with almost all the *loci theologici* from the Pentecostal perspective. Central to Yong's theology are pneumatological ontology, which sees reality as relational and rational, and pneumatological imagination, which understands truth as pragmatic, correspondence, and coherence. Using both of these elements, Yong ranges over topics as diverse as theological method, the Trinity, love, theology of religion and interreligious dialogue, religion and science, disability, politics, and theological education.[23]

---

21. See Cha et al., *Growing Healthy Asian American Churches*, 9–17.
22. See Hertig, *Tao of Asian American Belonging*, especially xi–xxi.
23. A helpful collection of Yong's writings is Stephenson, *Amos Yong Reader*.

Asian American Catholic Theology

Compared with Asian American (especially Korean) Protestant and Pentecostal theologies, Asian American Catholic theology pales in both number and significance. Among the younger generation, the following deserve notice: Jonathan Y. Tan, Anh Tran, Stephanie Wong, Ruben Habito, Joseph Cheah, Antonio Sison, Julius-Kei Kato, David Kwon, Edmund Chia, Gemma Cruz, Carolyn Chau, Min-ah Cho, Sophia Park, Karen Enriquez, Susan Abraham, Linh Hoang, Erica Lee, Deepan Rajaratnam, Tracy Tiemeier, Catherine Punsalan-Manlimos, and Jaisy Joseph.

THE FUTURE OF ASIAN AMERICAN THEOLOGIES

Asian American theologies are unquestionably alive and well. At the same time, there are areas in which further work needs to be done. The first is the conversation and collaboration between the theologies that are being done in Asia and Asian American theologies. Despite encouraging exhortation and with very rare exceptions, these two theologies have developed almost on parallel tracks, learning from each other. Second, there should be more mutual fertilization among different Asian American theologies. No doubt currently Korean American and feminist theologies are the most developed, but there is little conversation between these two theologies and other ethnic, say Filipino and Vietnamese American, theologies. Third, there should be more dialogue between Asian American theologies and non-Christian religions. Except for a couple of theologians such as Jung Young Lee and Young Lee Hartig who have drawn on Daoism and its yin-yang philosophy and concept of *chi*, most others tend to be highly critical of Confucianism and have not carried out a sustained dialogue with Buddhism and Islam. Finally, there should be a constructive conversation between Asian American theologies on the one hand and Black, Latinx theologies, and the so-called mainline white theology on the other. Concerning white theology, the scholarly attitude has been more critical than serious listening. While Asian American feminist theologians such as Kwok Pui-lan, have initiated a dialogue with Black and Latinx theologies, Kwok's efforts are more the exception than the norm.

BIBLIOGRAPHY

Brock, Rita Nakashima, et al., eds. *Off the Menu: Asian and North American Women's Religion and Theology.* Louisville: Westminster John Knox, 2007.
Carnes, Tony, and Fenggang Yang, eds. *Asian American Religions: The Making and Remaking of Borders and Boundaries.* New York: New York University Press, 2004.
Cha, Peter, et al., eds. *Growing Healthy Asian American Churches: Ministry Insights from Groundbreaking Congregations.* Downers Grove, IL: InterVarsity, 2006.
Chan, Sucheng. *Asian Americans: An Interpretive History.* Boston: Twayne, 1991.
———, ed. *Remapping Asian American History.* Walnut Creek:, CA Altamira, 2003.

Cherry, Stephen M. *Faith, Family, and Filipino American Community Life*. New Brunswick, NJ: Rutgers University Press, 2014.

Choi, Hee An. *Korean Women and God: Experiencing God in a Multi-religious Colonial Context*. Maryknoll, NY: Orbis, 2005

———. *A Postcolonial Self: Korean Immigrant Theology and Church*. Albany: State University of New York Press, 2015.

———. *A Postcolonial Relationship: Challenges of Asian Immigrants as the Third Other*. Albany: University of New York Press, 2022.

Chung, Hyun Kyung. *Struggle to Be the Sun Again: Introducing Asian Women's Theology*. Maryknoll, NY: Orbis, 1990.

Espiritu, Yen Le. *Asian American Panethnicity: Bridging Institutions and Identities*. Philadelphia: Temple University, 1992.

Fernandez Eleazar S., and Fernando F. Segovia, eds. *A Dream Unfinished: Theological Reflections on America from the Margins*. Maryknoll, NY: Orbis, 2001.

Foskett, Mary F., and Jeffrey Kah-Jin Kuan, eds. *Ways of Being, Ways of Reading: Asian American Biblical Interpretation*. St. Louis: Chalice, 2006.

Hertig, Young Lee. *The Tao of Asian American Belonging: A Yinist Spirituality*. Maryknoll, NY: Orbis, 2019.

Jeung, Russell. *Faithful Generations: Race and New Asian American Churches*. New Brunswick, NJ: Rutgers University Press, 2005.

Joh, Anne Wonhee. *Heart of the Cross: A Postcolonial Christology*. Louisville: Westminster John Knox, 2006.

Kao, Grace Y., and Ilsup Ahn, eds. *Asian American Christian Ethics: Voices, Methods, Issue*. Waco, TX: Baylor University Press, 2015.

Kim, Grace Ji-Sun. *Embracing the Other: The Transformative Spirit of Love*. Grand Rapids: Eerdmans, 2015.

———. *The Holy Spirit, Chi, and the Other: A Model of Global and Intercultural Pneumatology*. New York: Palgrave Macmillan, 2011.

———. *Invisible: Theology and the Experience of Asian American Women*. Minneapolis: Fortress, 2021.

Kwok Pui-lan, ed. *Asian and Asian American Women in Theology and Religion: Embodying Knowledge*. New York: Palgrave, 2020.

———. *Discovering the Bible in the Non-Biblical World*. Maryknoll, NY: Orbis, 1995.

———. *Globalization, Gender, and Peacebuilding: The Future of Interfaith Dialogue*. New York: Paulist, 2012.

———, ed. *Hope Abundant: Third World and Indigenous Women's Theology*. Maryknoll, NY: Orbis, 2010.

———. *Introducing Asian Feminist Theology*. Cleveland: The Pilgrim, 2000.

———. *Postcolonial Imagination and Feminist Theology*. Louisville: Westminster John Knox, 2005.

———. *Postcolonial Politics and Theology: Unraveling Empire for a Global World*. Louisville: Westminster John Knox, 2021.

Kwok Pui-lan, and Stephen Burns, eds. *Postcolonial Practice of Ministry: Leadership, Liturgy, and Interfaith Engagement*. Lanham, MD: Lexington, 2016.

Kwok Pui-lan, Cecilia González-Andrieu, and Dwight N. Hopkins, eds. *Teaching Global Theologies: Power and Praxis*. Waco, TX: Baylor University Press, 2015.

Lee, Erika. *The Making of Asian America: A History*. New York: Simon & Schuster, 2015.

Lee, Jung Young. *Marginality: The Key to Multicultural Theology.* Minneapolis: Fortress, 1995.
———. *The Trinity in Asian Perspective.* Nashville: Abingdon, 1996.
Lee, Robert G. *Orientals: Asian Americans in Popular Culture.* Philadelphia: Temple University Press, 1999.
Lee, Sang Hyun. *From a Liminal Place: An Asian American Theology.* Minneapolis: Fortress, 2010.
Liew, Tat-siong Benny, ed. *Postcolonial Interventions: Essays in Honor of R. S. Sugirtharajah.* Sheffield: Sheffield Phoenix, 2009.
———. *What Is Asian American Biblical Hermeneutics? Reading the New Testament.* Honolulu: University of Hawai'i Press, 2008.
Lowe, Lisa. *Immigrants Acts: Asian American Cultural Politics.* Durham, NC: Duke University Press 1996.
Okihiro, Gary Y. *The Columbia Guide to Asian American History.* New York: Columbia University Press, 2001.
———. *Margins and Mainstream: Asians in American History and Culture.* Seattle: University of Washington Press, 1994.
Ono, Kent A. *A Companion to Asian American Studies.* Oxford: Blackwell, 2005.
Pak, Su Yon, and Jung Ha Kim, eds. *Leading Wisdom: Asian and North American Women Leaders.* Louisville: Westminster John Knox, 2017.
Park, Andrew Sung. *From Hurt to Healing: A Theology of the Wounded.* Nashville: Abingdon, 2004.
———. *Racial Conflict and Healing: An Asian-American Theological Perspective.* Maryknoll, NY: Orbis, 1996.
Stephenson, Christopher A., ed. *Amos Yong Reader: The Pentecostal Spirit.* Eugene, OR: Cascade, 2020.
Takaki, Ronald. *From Different Shores: Perspectives on Race and Ethnicity in America.* Oxford: Oxford University Press, 1994.
———, ed. *Strangers from a Different Shore: A History of Asian Americans.* Boston: Little, Brown, 1989.
Tan, Jonathan, Y. *Introducing Asian American Theologies.* Maryknoll, NY: Orbis, 2008.
Wu, Jean Yu-Wen Shen, and Thomas C. Chen, eds. *Asian American Studies Now: A Critical Reader.* New Brunswick, NJ: Rutgers University Press, 2010.
Yee, Gale A. *Towards An Asian American Biblical Hermeneutics: An Intersectional Anthology.* Eugene, OR: Cascade, 2021.
Yong, Amos. *Spirit-Word-Community: Theological Hermeneutics in Trinitarian Perspective.* Burlington, VT: Ashgate, 2002.
Yoo, David K., and Eiichiro Azuma. *The Oxford Handbook of Asian American History.* Oxford: Oxford University Press, 2016.

SECTION 8

Reflective Essays from the Global South

Stories of Struggle, Perspective, and the Future

CHAPTER 33

Latin American Reflective Essay

LUIS N. RIVERA-PAGÁN

LIBERATION THEOLOGY: HISTORICAL AND INTELLECTUAL ORIGINS

Liberation theology was the unforeseen *enfant terrible* in the academic and ecclesial realms of theological production during the last decades of the twentieth century. It brought to the conversation not only a new theme—liberation—but also a new perspective on doing theology and a novel way of referring to God's being and action in history. Its project to reconfigure the interplay between religious studies, history, and politics became a meaningful topic of analysis and dialogue in the general theological discourse. Many scholars perceive in its emergence a drastic epistemological rupture, a radical change in paradigm, and a significant shift in both the ecclesial and social role of theology.

Its origins are diverse, and not exclusive to theological and ecclesiastical horizons. One important source, neglected by some accounts, was the complex constellation of liberation struggles during the 1960s and early 1970s. It was a time of social turmoil, when many things seemed out of joint: a strong anti-war movement protest (directed against American military intervention in Vietnam and the global nuclear threat); a spread of decolonization movements all over the "Third World"; the feminist struggle against patriarchy and sexism; a robust challenge to racial bigotry; the Stonewall rebellion (June 1969) against homophobia and gay discrimination; student protests in Paris, Prague, Mexico, and New York in opposition to repressive states of all stripes; and guerilla insurgencies and social unrest in many Latin American nations. Many of these agents of social protest adopted the title of "liberation movement" as a means of public self-presentation, while "Fronts of national liberation" flourished all over the Third World.[1]

Another significant factor regarding the intellectual origins of liberation theology was the development of a nondogmatic Marxism that read Marx's texts as an ethical critique on human oppression and as a projection of a utopian non-oppressive future, something akin to a kingdom of freedom. This heterodox reading of Marx, by authors like the German philosopher Ernst Bloch, made possible something considered largely unthinkable, until then: a constructive and affirmative dialogue between theology and Marxism, located at the margins of church and party hierarchies with their rigid orthodoxies. Bloch's *Atheismusim Christentum*[2] set forth a hermeneutic that interpreted the biblical texts as a struggle between the voices of the oppressors and those of the oppressed, and provocatively asserted that whoever wants to be a good Marxist should constantly read the Bible (and vice versa, whoever wants to be a good Christian should have Marx as bedside reading).

Other iconoclastic authors like Herbert Marcuse and Franz Fanon were passionately read from Buenos Aires to Berlin, from Berkeley to Nairobi, with intellectual perspectives not limited exclusively to academia.[3] Exiled from Brazil, Paulo Freire delivered scathing critiques of traditional educational systems and promoted a pedagogy for the liberation of the oppressed.[4] Martin Luther King Jr. and Ernesto "Che" Guevara became emblematic icons and martyrs of those turbulent times. Paul Éluard's poem *Liberté*, recited and sung in many languages, became a poetic hymn that captured the passions and intentions of many:

> By the power of the word
> I regain my life
> I was born to know you
> And to name you
> LIBERTY[5]

Within the churches, important processes were also occurring. To the surprise of many, Pope John XXIII summoned the Second Vatican Council. Progressive Roman

---

1. The most famous of them, a model for many, were the Algerian Front of National Liberation, established in 1954, which led the revolt against French colonial domination (brilliantly depicted in Gillo Pontocorvo's 1966 film *Battle of Algiers*); the National Liberation Front for South Vietnam, created in 1960, which successfully fought against the division of Viet Nam and the military invasion of the United States; and the Palestine Liberation Organization, founded in 1964 to organize the struggle for Palestinian statehood. See Horne, *Savage War of Peace*; Fitzgerald, *Fire in the Lake*; and Cobban, *Palestinian Liberation Organization*.

2. Bloch, *Atheismus im Christentum*.

3. Marcuse, *Essay on Liberation*; Fanon, *Wretched of the Earth*.

4. Freire, *Educação como prática da liberdade*; Freire, *Pedagogía del oprimido*.

5. "Et par le pouvoir d'un mot/Je recommence ma vie/Je suis né pour te connaître/Pour te nommer/ Liberté."

Catholic theologians consider Vatican II an important turning point in the modern history of their church.[6] According to their interpretation, the council had three main objectives:

1. To change the attitude of the Roman Catholic Church towards the modern post-Enlightenment intellectual world, from censure and condemnation to openness and dialogue. The Italian word *aggiornamento* ("bringing up to date") became the watchword of those seeking to update the church.

2. To heal the fragmentation of Christianity by positioning the Roman Catholic Church within the emerging ecumenical movement. Delegates from Protestant and Orthodox churches were invited to observe the proceedings of the council.[7] A series of bilateral and multilateral dialogues began between Rome and other Christian denominations.

3. To face the plight of a world marked by suffering violence, oppression, and injustice with honesty and compassion. The council took place in a global context sundered by national liberation struggles, civil wars, and the painful gap between the haves and the have-nots of the globe. The quest for peace and justice was conceived as an essential dimension of the church's presence in the world.

John XXIII's 1963 encyclical *Pacem in terris*, published in the context of that conciliar process, seemed to be another sign of renewal, favoring a shift away from anathemization and hostility towards the modern world, and promoting a spirit of dialogue and solidarity. Such ecclesiastical openness was accompanied by several theological projects that seemed to shape an alternative way of looking at social conflicts.[8] An attempt was made to configure a "political theology" as a way to design a creative dialogue with Marxism and post-Enlightenment secular ideologies.[9]

LATIN AMERICAN LIBERATION THEOLOGY

Vatican II was followed by regional synods of bishops. The most famous of them was the general meeting of Latin American Roman Catholic bishops that took place from August 26 to September 6, 1968, in the Colombian city of Medellín. To the amazement of many observers, the Roman Catholic Church, which the radical intelligentsia in the continent had considered an ideological bulwark of prevailing social inequities, made a decisive pastoral shift, treating solidarity with the poor and destitute as a central concern.

---

6. See Flannery, *Vatican Council II*.
7. See Lindbeck, *Dialogue on the Way*.
8. See esp. Moltmann, *Theologie der Hoffnung* and Metz, *Zur Theologie der Welt*.
9. See Sölle, *Politische Theologie*.

If Vatican II opened the theological dialogue with modern rationality, Medellín was perceived as a prophetic convocation against poverty, inequality, and oppression. If Vatican II was mainly concerned with the gap between the church and secular modernity, Medellín was more concerned with the scandal of social injustice in a Christian continent. In a crucial section of their final resolutions, the Latin American bishops linked the Christian faith with historical and social liberation:

> The Latin American bishops cannot remain indifferent in the face of the tremendous social injustices existent in Latin America, which keep the majority of our peoples in dismal poverty that in many cases becomes inhuman wretchedness . . . A deafening cry pours from the throats of millions of men and women asking their pastors for a liberation that reaches them from nowhere else . . . Christ, our savior, not only loved the poor . . . he centered his mission in announcing liberation to the poor.[10]

Certainly, the Medellín conference was a meeting of bishops, not of theologians. But several Roman Catholic theologians were present and collaborated substantially in the drafting of the final documents. The general tone emerging from the conference allowed the possibility of rethinking the theological enterprise from the perspective of the liberation of the poor and the downtrodden.[11] Prior to the Medellín meeting, in July 1968, Gustavo Gutiérrez gave a lecture in Chimbote, Perú, significantly titled "Toward a Theology of Liberation,"[12] that established a close connection between spiritual redemption and human liberation. This lecture proved to be a pioneer text for Latin American liberation theology. It also inaugurated Gutiérrez's decades of fertile theological production (he was already eighty-two years old when, on July 17, 2010, he gave a lecture at Princeton Theological Seminary at the invitation of the Hispanic Theological Initiative).

In 1971, the first edition of Gutiérrez's most famous book, *Theology of Liberation*, was published, a landmark in Latin American theological writing. His triadic understanding of human liberation—liberation from social and economic oppression, history as a process of self-determined humanization, and redemption from sinfulness—became classic and a model to be universally reproduced.[13] Hugo Assmann's book *Opresión—Liberación: Desafío a loscristianos* was also published the same year. Assmann placed the emerging liberation theology in the wider context of the Third World: "The contextual starting point of a 'theology of liberation' is the historical situation of domination experienced by the peoples of the Third World."[14] Gutiérrez and Assmann were followed by a spate of several other theologians

---

10. Hennelly, *Liberation Theology*, 114 and 116; English translation slightly amended.
11. See Gutiérrez, "Meaning and Scope of Medellín," 59–101.
12. It is translated and reproduced in Hennelly, *Liberation Theology*, 62–76.
13. Gutiérrez, *Teología de la liberación*, 67–69.
14. Assmann, *Opresión—Liberación*, 50.

(Leonardo Boff, José Porfirio Miranda, Juan Luis Segundo, Jon Sobrino, Pablo Richard, Jorge Pixley, among others) whose writings were conceived as expressions of a new intellectual understanding of the faith: liberation theology.

Among the many texts that rocked the placid realm of theological production during those early years of Latin American liberation theology were José Porfirio Miranda's *Marx y la Biblia* (an important contribution to a liberationist hermeneutics and also sort of a theological companion to Bloch's *Atheismusim Christentum*), and Juan Luis Segundo's *Liberación de la teología*,[15] with its frontal challenge to traditional scholastic ways of doing theology.

What could be considered the main tenets of this theological movement? I would identify five:

1. *The retrieval of the "subversive memories,"* inscribed in sacred Scriptures, which are hidden below layers of cultic regulations and doctrinal orthodoxies but never totally effaced. This theological movement also gives hermeneutical and exegetical priority to the Exodus story, understood to be a paradigm of the liberating character of God's actions;[16] to the several prophetic denunciations of injustice and oppression;[17] and to the confrontations of the historical Jesus with Judean religious authorities and Roman political powers, alongside Jesus's solidarity with the "nobodies" of Judea and Galilee.[18]

2. *A historical understanding of Jesus's proclamation of God's kingdom.* The kingdom is conceived as referring not to some otherworldly postmortem realm, but rather to the unceasing hope of a social *configuration characterized by justice, solidarity, and freedom.* Leonardo Boff and Jon Sobrino identified Jesus as the Liberator, thereby recovering the semantic roots of the term redemption (the deliverance of a captive or a slave).[19] This Christology is one attuned to the plight of the indigents and, to use Frantz Fanon's term, to the "wretched of the earth."[20]

3. *The divine preferential option for the poor, the excluded, and the destitute of this world.* The church must become the church of the poor by sharing the poor's sorrows, hopes, and struggles. Initially the emphasis of the preferential option was socio-economic, but it was gradually widened to include other categories of social exclusion (indigenous communities, racial and ethnic minorities, women, and sexual orientation).[21]

---

15. Miranda, *Marx y la Biblia*; Segundo, *Liberación de la teología*.
16. See Croatto, *Exodus*; and Pixley, *Exodo, una lectura evangélica y popular*.
17. Houston, *Contending for Justice*.
18. Sobrino, *La fe en Jesucristo*.
19. Boff, *Jesus Cristo libertador*; Sobrino, *Jesucristo liberador*.
20. Cf. Martínez-Olivieri, *Visible Witness*.
21. Boff, *Igreja, carisma e poder*.

4. Theology cannot be reduced to an intellectual understanding of the faith; *it must also be a practical commitment for historical transformation.* The category of praxis, partly borrowed from Paulo Freire's pedagogy of liberation, partly an adaptation of Marx's eleventh thesis on Feuerbach ("philosophers have only interpreted the world in various ways; the point, however, is to change it"), acquired normative status.[22] History, therefore, understood as the realm of the perennial struggle against oppressions and exclusions, emerged as the locus for Christian praxis.[23]

5. God is reconceived not as an immutable and impassible entelechy but, in line with the biblical narratives, as a compassionate Eternal Spirit who hears and pays close attention to the cry of the oppressed and whose action in human history has the redemption of the downtrodden and excluded as its ultimate telos. Herein might be located liberation theology's main theoretical epistemological rupture and reconfiguration: a novel way of thinking about God's being and action in history.[24] Instead of contriving arcane scholastic definitions of the divine essence, God is named as Liberator.

Latin American liberation theology strove to forge a new way of being the church in the world: the base ecclesial communities were understood as seeds for reconfiguring the church as "the people of God." These congregations were considered expressions of the church's solidarity with the poor and oppressed in their aspirations for liberation and the promotion of human flourishing. They produced an impressive wealth of liturgical, musical, exegetical, homiletical, ethical, and literary resources in order to promote social and human emancipation. Their key theme was historical transformation. Leonardo Boff even advocated a new genesis of the church.[25]

ECCLESIASTICAL THEOLOGICAL DISPUTES

However, many in the hierarchical church, including some members of the Roman Curia, viewed these potential disruptions of episcopal authority with marked distrust and moved to restrict the autonomy of some Latin American theologians. Rome was also concerned about the consequences of this new theological perspective for dogmatic orthodoxy. A long-protracted confrontation emerged, one that still continues into the present.

Political power matters. Since their colonial inception, an official linkage between the state and the Roman Catholic Church has characterized Latin American nations. The royal patronage exercised by the Iberian crown entailed the acknowledgment by

---

22. Marx, "Theses on Feuerbach," 145.
23. Pixley and Bastian, *Praxis cristiana y producción teológica*.
24. Chacón, *Modelos de Dios en las teologías latinoamericanas*.
25. Boff, *Eclesiogênese*.

the church of the sovereignty and authority of the metropolitan state, but was paired with the state's recognition of the Roman Catholic Church's primacy in religious affairs. It was sometimes the source of acute conflict, whenever the ethical conscience of bishops, priests, missionaries, and theologians clashed with the severe exploitation of the native communities. Bartolomé de las Casas, to whose historical significance Gustavo Gutiérrez devoted a magnificent book, is perhaps the most astute theological analyst of such conflicts.[26] Yet it was a convenient arrangement for both partners, since it conferred a sacred aura upon metropolitan sovereignty and, conversely, provided the church with state protection.

The governments of the new states that emerged after the nineteenth century wars of independence promptly recognized the advantages of the papal patronage and tried to preserve it. This heritage forged a particular brand of Latin American Christendom closely linking the state and the Roman Catholic Church—a condition juridically inscribed in several national constitutions and Vatican concordats.

If the official connection of church and state was venerable, it was also vulnerable. The prophetic and evangelical subversive memories inscribed in the Christian Scriptures and traditions surfaced powerfully during the somber and violent times of Latin American military dictatorships (1964–1989), shaking the alliance between political powers and church authorities. The most famous of the ensuing conflicts took place in the midst of the violent civil war in El Salvador, a nation where nuns, priests, lay workers, and even the Primate of the Roman Catholic Church, archbishop Oscar Arnulfo Romero, were assassinated by the military or their right-wing allies.

Archbishop Romero tried to steer his church to become a defender of the poor and persecuted. He recognized that the forbearance of the ruling clans was as limited as their economic interests were great. Two weeks before his assassination, in an interview conducted by a Mexican newspaper, Archbishop Romero foreshadowed his death and gave a theological and pastoral interpretation of his personal destiny:

> I have frequently been threatened with death . . . If God accepts the sacrifice of my life, then may my blood be the seed of liberty, and a sign of the hope that will soon become a reality . . . May my death, if it is accepted by God, be for the liberation of my people, and as a witness of hope in what is to come.[27]

His assassination convinced many church authorities that liberation theology was seriously jeopardizing the social status of the Roman Catholic Church, and that a convenient, long-standing church-state covenant was endangered by the radical political interventions of some members of the clergy. Those church authorities thus moved decisively to suppress liberationist thought.

Ecclesiastical and social political considerations were not the only issues of concern for Vatican authorities. Doctrinal orthodoxy matters for the Roman Catholic

---

26. Gutiérrez, *Las Casas*.
27. Romero, *Voice of the Voiceless*, 50–51.

Church. Under the prefecture of Cardinal Joseph Ratzinger, the Sacred Congregation for the Doctrine of the Faith strongly criticized what it considered liberation theology's ominous doctrinal deviations. On August 6, 1984, with the approval of Pope John Paul II, it issued the admonishing "Instruction on Certain Aspects of the 'Theology of Liberation,'" followed by an admonition to Leonardo Boff, and another general critique, "Instruction on Christian Freedom and Liberation" (March 22, 1986). Liberation theology was accused of borrowing improperly from Marxist thought, emphasizing historical and social liberation to the detriment of spiritual salvation, promoting class struggle instead of reconciliation, disdaining the church's social doctrine, and politicizing biblical hermeneutics, Christology, and the church. The goal of the authoritative reprimands was

> to draw attention . . . to the deviations and risks of deviation, damaging to the faith and to Christian living, that are brought by certain forms of liberation theology . . . the "theologies of liberation" especially tend to misunderstand or to eliminate . . . the transcendence and gratuity of liberation in Jesus Christ, true God and true man . . . One needs to be on guard against the politicization of existence, which, misunderstanding the entire meaning of the kingdom of God and the transcendence of the person, begins to sacralize politics and betray the religion of the people in favor of the projects of revolution.[28]

Traditionally, indictments like these were able to silence the accused theologians. Not this time. Prompt reactions by Gustavo Gutiérrez, Leonardo Boff, and Juan Luis Segundo were evidence that Rome had lost the capability to repress this new theological movement.[29] On April 9, 1986, John Paul II sent a letter to the Brazilian bishops, which several scholars interpreted both as an attempt to quell the growing dispute, and thereby avoid a sharp rupture in the Latin American church and, also as a validation of the claim that the concept of social and political liberation is an important dimension of the church's pastoral mission.[30] Since then, several Roman Catholic theologians have sustained an effort to convince Rome that liberation theology is a valid and legitimate rethinking of the apostolic tradition, and to demonstrate that this new form of theology does not constitute a threat to the church's orthodoxy or integrity.[31] However, some influential sectors of the Roman Curia still look askance at liberation theology, as evidenced by the Sacred Congregation for the Doctrine of the Faith's scathing critique of Jon Sobrino's Christology.[32]

28. "Instruction on Certain Aspects of the 'Theology of Liberation,'" 394 and 411–12.
29. Cf. the strong response of Segundo, *Teología de la liberación*.
30. Pope John Paul II, "Letter to Brazilian Episcopal Conference"; see Hennelly, *Liberation Theology*, 498–506.
31. See Ellacuría and Sobrino, *Mysterium liberationis*. On November 16, 1989, Ellacuría (then rector of El Salvador's Central American University), five other Jesuits priests, and two domestic servants were assassinated by a group of soldiers.
32. See "Notification on the works of Father Jon Sobrino, SJ," http://www.vatican.va/roman_curia/

Many Roman Catholic narratives disregard other sources that contributed to the birth of liberation theology. In the 1960s, several Latin American Protestant churches were undergoing similar processes of rethinking the relationship between salvation, history as the sphere of divine-human encounter, and liberation.[33] In fact, the first extensive monograph that focused on historical and social liberation as the central hermeneutical key to conceptualize the Christian faith was the doctoral dissertation of Rubem Alves, a Brazilian Presbyterian. In May of 1968, Alves successfully defended his dissertation at Princeton Theological Seminary, which was titled *Towards a Theology of Liberation*.[34] Alves wrote it under the direction of Richard Shaull, who for a good number of years had been working in theological education in Latin America, first in Colombia and later in Brazil, and who was crucial for the development of a liberationist theology in Protestant Latin American circles.[35] Shaull had also been instrumental in the 1970 English publication of Paulo Freire's *Pedagogy of the Oppressed*, a key text in the development of Latin American liberation theology.[36]

Alves's dissertation is a powerful text, written in a splendid literary style. It was published as a book in 1969, two years before Gutiérrez's, but with a significant change in the title: *A Theology of Human Hope*. Apparently, the publishers believed that the concept of "hope," with its obvious connotations to the writings of Jürgen Moltmann, would be more commercially attractive or relevant than "liberation." Yet, despite the change of title, Alves conceptualizes the temporal dialectics proper to theological language in terms of a historical politics of liberation.

> The acts of remembering and hoping that determine the language of the community of faith, therefore, do not have any reality in themselves but in the engagement in the ongoing politics of liberation which is the situation and condition of theological intelligibility . . .[37]

BIBLIOGRAPHY

Alves, Rubem. *A Theology of Human Hope*. Washington: Corpus, 1969.
———. "Towards a Theology of Liberation: An Exploration of the Encounter Between the Languages of Humanistic Messianism and Messianic Humanism." PhD diss., Princeton Theological Seminary, 1968.

congregations/cfaith/documents/rc_con_cfaith_doc_20061126_notification-sobrino_en.html. Also noteworthy is the defense of Sobrino by almost forty theologians in Vigil, *Bajar de la Cruz a los Pobre*.

33. See Neely, *Protestant Antecedents of the Latin American Theology of Liberation*.
34. Alves, "Towards a Theology of Liberation."
35. Shaull, *Hombre, ideología y revolución en América Latina*. See also Neely, *Protestant Antecedents*, 253: "it is doubtful if any theologian has more consistently and directly contributed to the shaping of the contemporary Protestant theologians of liberation than Richard Shaull."
36. Freire, *Pedagogy of the Oppressed*.
37. Alves, *Theology of Human Hope*, 163. On the theological trajectory of Alves, see Cervantes-Ortiz, *Serie de sueños*.

Assmann, Hugo. *Opresión—Liberación: Desafío a los cristianos*. Montevideo: Tierra Nueva, 1971.

Bloch, Ernest. *Atheismusim Christentum*. Frankfurt am Main: Suhrkamp, 1968.

Boff, Leonardo. *Eclesiogênese: as comunidades eclesiais de base reinventam a Igreja*. Petrópolis: Editôra Vozes, 1977).

———. *Igreja, carisma e poder: ensaios de eclesiologia militante*. Petrópolis: Vozes, 1981.

———. *Jesus Cristo libertador; ensaio de cristologia crítica para o nosso tempo*. Petrópolis: Editôra Vozes, 1972.

Cervantes-Ortiz, Leopoldo. *Serie de sueños: la teología ludo-erótico-poética de Rubem Alves*. Quito, Ecuador: Consejo Latinoamericano de Iglesias, 2003.

Chacón, Jonathan Pimentel. *Modelos de Dios en las teologías latinoamericanas*. Heredia: Universidad Nacional de Costa Rica, 2008.

Cobban, Helena. *The Palestinian Liberation Organization: People, Power and Politics*. Cambridge: Cambridge University Press, 1984.

Croatto, José Severino. *Exodus, a Hermeneutics of Freedom*. Maryknoll, NY: Orbis, 1981.

Ellacuría, Ignacio, and Jon Sobrino, eds. *Mysterium liberationis: Conceptos fundamentales de la Teología de la Liberación*. Madrid: Editorial Trotta, 1990.

Fanon, Franz. *The Wretched of the Earth*. New York: Grove, 1965.

Fitzgerald, Frances. *Fire in the Lake: The Vietnamese and the Americans in Vietnam*. Boston: Little, Brown and Company, 1972.

Flannery, Austin P., ed. *Vatican Council II. The Basic Sixteen Documents: Constitutions, Decrees, Declarations*. Northport, NY: Costello, 1996.

Freire, Paulo. *Educação como prática da liberdade*. Rio de Janeiro: Paz e Terra, 1967.

———. *Pedagogía del oprimido*. Montevideo: Tierra Nueva, 1968.

———. *Pedagogy of the Oppressed*. Translated by Myra Bergman Ramos. London: Continuum, 2000.

Gutiérrez, Gustavo. *Las Casas: In Search of the Poor of Jesus Christ*. Maryknoll, NY: Orbis, 1993.

———. "The Meaning and Scope of Medellín." In *The Density of the Present: Selected Writings*, 59–101. Maryknoll, NY: Orbis, 1999.

———. *Teología de la liberación: perspectivas*. Salamanca: Sígueme, 1973.

Hennelly, Alfred T., ed. *Liberation Theology: A Documentary History*. Maryknoll, NY: Orbis, 1992.

Horne, Alistar. *A Savage War of Peace: Algeria 1954–1962*. New York: Penguin, 1987.

Houston, Walter J. *Contending for Justice: Ideologies and Theologies of Social Justice in the Old Testament*. London: T. & T. Clark, 2006.

"Instruction on Certain Aspects of the 'Theology of Liberation.'" Reproduced in *Liberation Theology: A Documentary History*, edited by Alfred T. Hennelly, 393–414. Maryknoll, NY: Orbis, 1992.

John Paul II (Pope). "Letter to Brazilian Episcopal Conference." In *Liberation Theology*, edited by Alfred T. Hennelly, 498–506. Maryknoll, NY: Orbis, 1992.

Lindbeck, George A., ed. *Dialogue on the Way: Protestants Report from Rome on the Vatican Council*. Minneapolis: Augsburg, 1965.

Marcuse, Herbert. *An Essay on Liberation*. Boston: Beacon, 1969.

Martín-Baró, Ignacio, and Jon Sobrino. Maryknoll, NY: Orbis, 1998.

Martínez-Olivieri, Jules. *A Visible Witness: Christology, Liberation, and Participation*. Minneapolis: Fortress, 2016.

Marx, Karl. "Theses on Feuerbach." In *The Marx-Engels Reader*, edited by Robert C. Tucker, 145. New York: W. W. Norton, 1978.
Metz, Johannes Baptist. *Zur Theologie der Welt*. Mainz: Matthias-Grúnewald, 1968.
Miranda, José Porfirio. *Marx y la Biblia*. Salamanca: Ediciones Sígueme, 1972.
Moltmann, Jürgen. *Theologie der Hoffnung*. München: Chr. Kaiser, 1966.
Neely, Alan P. *Protestant Antecedents of the Latin American Theology of Liberation*. PhD diss., American University, 1977.
Pixley, Jorge V. *Exodo, una lectura evangélica y popular*. México, DF: Casa Unida de Publicaciones, 1983.
Pixley, Jorge V., and Jean-Pierre Bastian, eds. *Praxis cristiana y producción teológica*. Salamanca: Ediciones Sígueme, 1979.
Romero, Oscar. *Voice of the Voiceless: The Four Pastoral Letters and other Statements*. Maryknoll, NY: Orbis, 1998.
Segundo, Juan Luis. *Liberación de la teología*. Buenos Aires: Ediciones Carlosd Lohlé, 1975.
———. *Teología de la liberación: Respuesta al Cardenal Ratzinger*. Madrid: Ediciones Cristiandad, 1985.
Shaull, Richard. *Hombre, ideología y revolución en América Latina*. Montevideo: ISAL, 1965.
Sobrino, Jon. *Jesucristo liberador: lectura histórico teológica de Jesús de Nazaret*. San Salvador: UCA, 1991.
———. *La fe en Jesucristo: ensayo desde las víctimas*. San Salvador: UCA, 1999.
Sölle, Dorothee. *Politische Theologie. Auseinandersetzungmit Rudolf Bultmann*. Stuttgart: Kreuz, 1971.
Vigil, José María, ed. *Bajar de la Cruz a los Pobres: Cristología de la Liberación*. México: Ediciones Dabar, 2007.

CHAPTER 34

Asian Reflective Essay

Pathways for Building God's Household in Asia

JOSE MARIO C. FRANCISCO

Contemporary geopolitical and technological developments generated much interest in all aspects of the Global South. Thus, multidisciplinary studies on religions include descriptive accounts and critical analysis of Asian Christianity. Researchers encounter countless journal essays, monographs, and handbooks from major publishing houses. Such great breadth is appropriately suggested by the title of the multiauthor anthology *Harvesting from Asian Soil*.[1]

Of greater import from these studies are the voices of Asian Christians past and present. No longer are their stories and reflections relegated to "mission encounters" within church history. Nor their national and ethnic identities considered diminished by their Christian faith. Their strong voices forge their own paths as Asian Christians, despite their common minority status and earlier colonial associations in some contexts.

Given such bountiful harvest and multiple voices, this essay cannot cover even most significant studies. It only sketches the continuing journey of Asian Christianity through the multifaceted theme of building God's household.

This widely current theme points to Asian Christian discussions from both Catholic and Protestant traditions. Originally derived from the biblical word *oikos* (to dwell), it opens up diverse religious approaches and theological themes. Not surprisingly, it has been extensively employed in the 1997 World Council of Churches document *Ecclesiology and Ethics*[2] and Pope Francis's recent encyclical *Laudato si*:

---

1. Tirimanna, *Harvesting from the Asian Soil*.
2. Best and Robra, *Ecclesiology and Ethics*.

On Care for Our Common Home.[3] It enables Christians to reinterpret central theological themes; for instance, African Conradie in relation to ecclesiology[4] and Filipino missiologist Recepcion for a theology of mission in our globalized world.[5]

Moreover, the theme reflects the present constructive moment in Asian theological enterprise. Earlier efforts focused on deconstructing traditional vocabulary forged within European contexts, such as the Christology of the 2000 post-synodal exhortation *Ecclesia in Asia*. With greater emphasis on Jesus's proclamation of God's reign, they instead sought to describe an Asian Jesus; for instance, Sugden's *Seeking the Asian Face of Jesus*[6] and Amaladoss's *The Asian Jesus*.[7]

Recent scholars focus on constructing theologies and articulating Christian practice on Asian terms. They draw primarily from what has been referred to as "lived religion"[8] of Asian Christians rather than from traditional texts and standard commentaries. Primary materials—stories and symbols, art and architecture, pilgrimages and festivals—shape theological reflection as well; for instance, Koyama's *Water Buffalo Theology*[9] or Song's *In the Beginning Were Stories, Not Texts: Story Theology*.[10] Without loss of critical rigor, Asian theological engagement becomes less a technical method and more a way of proceeding that is "holistic and integrated, experiencing reality as one and interdependent."[11] It has even reshaped scholarship in theological disciplines; for instance, Kwok Pui-lan and R. S. Sugirtharajah's work in biblical studies[12] and the anthology from Asian ethicists, *Doing Catholic Theological Ethics in a Cross Cultural and Interreligious Asian Context*.[13]

Within such horizon, this essay sketches the continuing journey of Asian Christianity with thematic pathways based on *oikos*: "the quests for economic justice (the *nomoi* or regulations within the household), ecological sustainability (the *logos* or underlying principles of the household) and ecumenical fellowship (*oikoumene*—participating as members of the whole household of God)."[14] These interrelated paths are discussed in the following sections; each situating their role in building God's *oikos* in Asia, but enfleshed through illustrative references.

---

3. Pope Francis, *Laudato Si*.
4. Conradie, "Whole Household of God (Oikos)," 1–28.
5. Recepcion, *God's Global Household*.
6. Sugden, *Seeking the Asian Face of Jesus*.
7. Amaladoss, *Asian Jesus*.
8. McGuire, *Lived Religion*, 12–17.
9. Koyama, *Water Buffalo Theology*.
10. Song, *In the Beginning Were Stories, Not Texts*.
11. Amaladoss, "Asian Theological Trends," 105.
12. Pui-lan, *Postcolonial Imagination and Feminist Theology*; and Sugirtharajah, *Asian Biblical Hermeneutics and Postcolonialisim*.
13. Chan and Kochuthara, *Doing Catholic Theological Ethics*.
14. Conradie, "Whole Household of God (Oikos)," 1–2.

Celebrating Diversity

God's household is characterized as *oikoumene*, the participation of all household members. Far from its usual denominational understanding, its wider meaning refers to "the unity of all peoples of the earth."[15] Thus Christian practice is inherently diverse.

From its beginnings, Christianity has faced diversity in Asia, arguably the most wide-ranging and multifaceted natural and cultural diversity because of its vast expanse and long history. Christianity could not ignore fundamental concerns whether such diversity has a place within God's household and what space those who are seen as "other" have in this household.

Contemporary Asian Christian response to this diversity is twofold. On the one hand, Christianity embraces Asian diversity in its many forms. Diversity is celebrated as Asia's gift to Christianity. On the other, Christianity validates Asian diversity by recognizing it as the epiphany of God's incarnate presence in all creation.

Asian Christianity, like other spiritual and religious traditions, is imbedded in personal and communal lives, encountering different social constituencies, interacting with all social forces and appropriating local material and cultural resources. This contextual character is reflected in what Asian Christians bring to God's household.

Asian Christians incarnate their faith through bodily movement and symbolic imagery: bowing in reverence, touching sacred representations, or sitting in lotus position for meditation and common worship. Christian celebrations tap into traditional practices. Contemporary Philippine liturgical music uses local musical idioms from the traditional *kundiman* love songs. In accordance with the long-standing Javanese *ziārah* pilgrimage tradition, Catholics process to major Marian shrines, like Muslims to tombs of prominent Islamic missionaries.[16] Through this inclusive tradition, both participate at each other's shrines without compromising their religious identity.

Artists and architects create Christian imagery and spaces using traditional idioms. Jesus is represented in Buddhist sitting position. Facial features of images resemble the natives', thus projecting them as their own. In the church altarpiece of the Philippine town Silang, archangel Gabriel's annunciation occurs in Mary's bedroom complete with mosquito net ubiquitous in ordinary Asian houses. Korean Christians depict the Holy Family in ordinary peasant's attire or elaborate royal robes.

Church architecture adapts to native topography and climate as well as local materials like red clay and volcanic tuff. Local motifs like lotus flowers or tropical fruits are used in European-designed churches. Vietnamese churches at home and in migrant diaspora have traditional roof designs. More striking is the Redemptorist Church in Pattaya, Thailand completely rendered in Buddhist tradition: the church itself looking like a temple, with Christ appearing Buddha-like.

---

15. Abiarajah, "Changing Paradigms of Asian Christian Attitude to Other Religions," 365.
16. Laksana, "Multiple Religious Belonging or Complex Identity," 493–509.

More than just ornamental, this celebration of diversity is profoundly expressed in Asian theologies. Theological reflections are languaged through local and often nonalphabetic scripts, influenced by world religions as well as diverse indigenous, spiritual, and wisdom traditions. For example, Philippine theologians have explored the rich nuances of the Tagalog word *loob* (interiority) and its equivalents in other languages to articulate God's faithfulness and human moral relations.[17]

But this is perhaps best illustrated in the centuries-old Christian reflection on traditional and Confucian ethos originating in China and enduring throughout present-day East and Southeast Asia. From the historic Rites controversy involving Mateo Ricci onward, Asian Christian theologians have appropriated symbolic and conceptual resources from this ethos. They have argued over the appropriate linguistic expressions for God and have employed the concepts of *yin* and *yang* to describe human and divine natures. According to Julia Ching, Confucianism provides "a dynamic discovery of the worth of the human person, of the possibilities of human greatness and even sagehood, of one's fundamental relationship to others in a society based on ethical values, of an interpretation of reality and a metaphysics of the self that remain open to the transcendent."[18] Thus these traditional and Confucian contexts have helped shape and deepen Christian theological reflection.

This celebration of diversity extends to wherever Asian Christians live. Their household is no longer restricted to local ghettos of Christendom in minority situations or the imaginary of a Christian nation in the Christian-majority Philippines. Whether in their localities or in global diaspora, they bring their practices and reflections to these new contexts, engendering further diversity.

OVERCOMING EXCLUSION

Notwithstanding its hospitality toward diversity, Asian Christianity contends with social forces that marginalize the greatest number of the world's poor. Despite emerging economic wealth in China, India and sectors in other regions, Asia's poor suffer from social discrimination, insufficient basic human resources and unjust structures. Moreover, Christian churches have at times contributed to and legitimized this exclusion. Hence, the imperative for economic justice, the *nomoi* or regulations within the Asian household.

Asian Christian responses to this imperative are shaped by diverse forms of the endemic poverty of specific sectors. Though initially based on social status, gender identity, and religious belonging, these forms often interact and become fundamentalist dispositions and structures; in some contexts for instance, to be considered an exemplary Christian woman requires being deferential to male authority in church

---

17. Mesa, *Jose M. de Mesa*; and Miranda, *Loob*.
18. Kung and Ching, *Christianity and Chinese Religions*, 90.

and family. Given this, these are best described in relation to four representative sectors of Asia's poor.

First among them are the Asian poor excluded by traditional and contemporary social structures; for instance, many rural agricultural and urban construction laborers. Catholic social institutes initially promoted papal social teaching during the Cold War against communism.

But greater openness to modern perspectives brought about deeper engagement with the indentured poor. This was first exemplified by Korean Christians' solidarity with those considered *minjung* (poor and oppressed) during the 1960s neoliberal economic growth. They bore witness to their plight and became involved in labor and student unions, providing material support and sanctuary for their safety.[19]

Out of this engagement came *minjung* theology influenced by ordinary symbols and literary concepts. Theological reflections focused on the word "han," meaning "*frustrated hope, the collapsed feeling of pain, letting go, resentful bitterness,* and *the wounded heart.*"[20] They articulated contextual theologies of sin and of psychosocial woundedness.

The second sector consists of countless indigenous peoples suffering from social discrimination. They have been subjects of Christian foreign missions, either legally attached to the sixteenth-century patronage agreement or closely associated with other powers in later Protestant evangelization. But even when "purified" of indigenous ways, they remained marginal in church and society.

In contrast, contemporary Asian Christianity works to overcome their cultural and structural exclusion. Not only has it incorporated indigenous material and cultural elements but also shaped a Christianity enriched by shamanistic rituals and other traditions: indigenous theology "seeks to reflect on the faith experience of Indigenous people on the one hand and to re-appropriate the Indigenous cultural values for theological reflection on the other."[21] According to Malaysian theologian Fung, this "paves the way for the Church to enter into a gradual understanding of alternative ways by which the shamans and the indigenous communities express their religious experience and how they articulate their understanding of God, their experienced of being possessed by the Spirit (spirit-possession), and the liberative-salvific mission of this God."[22] Thus Christ is described with indigenous symbols such as living house, elder brother, and even rooster.

The third sector of South Asian, dalit, constitutes a singular community of Asia's poor because of their inherent and total exclusion. Lowest in the centuries-old caste system shaped by social and religious forces, the dalit, also known as untouchable, suffer oppression in all realms, further reinforced by Hindu political fundamentalism.[23]

19. Suh, "Biographical Sketch."
20. Park, *Wounded Heart of God*, 31.
21. Vashum, *Christology in Context*, 132.
22. Fung, "Mystique of Dialogue," 272.
23. Amaladoss, *Call to Community*.

Despite dalit efforts at resistance and some government and civil society reforms, caste is so deeply ingrained that even Christianity's commitment to equality has not eradicated discrimination within the churches.

In response, dalit Christians have widely engaged in emancipating practice and theological reflection. They consider moving from Hinduism as "a liberating exodus experience" even though this results in discrimination as dalit and as Christian. Dalit theologian Nirmal thus appropriates the biblical figure of the wandering Aramean, which "recalls the status of the dalits as 'no people' who become God's people."[24] Moreover, some even describe God as a dalit God for the dalit people.

The sectoral exclusion of women is wide-ranging in Asian societies. Intertwined with the other three, it is the conjuncture of gender and sexuality with dominant forces in both traditional and contemporary cultures. They could be uncompensated mothers or daughters, workers in subsistence farming or overseas urban factories with unjust conditions as well as members of marginalized ethnic or caste populations. Their exclusion is greater, simply because they are women; hence, what is known as the feminization of poverty.

Asian Christian engagement with their sector emerged with awareness of and reflection on women's existential situations rather than a priori ideological grounds. While cognizant of feminisms elsewhere, this engagement is not, as some church leaders claim, "a western ideology."[25]

Moreover, Asian Christian women have claimed their rightful place. Though all Christian churches depend on their profound devotion and extensive service, they receive little recognition and participation in church life and governance. Cartagenas's assessment of clericalism in the Philippine Catholic Church applies to other contexts as well: "Their [clerics'] gender and ethnic provenance hold the key to understand the various forms of dysfunctions concerning sexuality and intimacy, sex and gender, power and authority to which they are socialized early on and in which they move and have their being for the rest of their lives."[26] Ignoring such dynamics marginalizes Asian Christian women and undermines inclusivity, transparency, and accountability within churches.

In response, Asian Christian women push churches toward greater participation in broader feminist movements and provide critical theological reflection. Though some teach at male-majority theological centers, Asian women theologians create independent spaces to tell stories of and about women, and to share these with one another. Early voices include Indonesian Katoppo, Filipina nun Mananzan, and Korean Hyun Kung Chung.[27] Then followed organizations of women theologians; for instance,

---

24. Nirmal, *Indigenous People*, 220–21.
25. Francisco, "Letting the Texts on RH Speak for Themselves," 223–46.
26. Cartagenas, "Terror of the Sexual Abuse," 371.
27. Pui-lan, *Introducing Asian Feminist Theology*, 25–33.

the 1983 Women's Commission of the Ecumenical Association of Third World Theologians, and the more recent Ecclesia of Women in Asia.

Their reflection begins with what is known as the hermeneutics of suspicion; it is "triggered by the painful experience of an unjust situation which leads sufferers to look closely at the traditional doctrines, symbols, rituals and structures and seek to reinterpret them in terms of the pre-cultural or counter-cultural religious experience."[28] Feminist theologians then interrogate prevailing cultural ethos, scriptural texts, and religious traditions to uncover resources to overcome exclusion and promote equality.

Perhaps the most substantive Asian feminist contributions lie in biblical studies. They shed light on many women characters often ignored in biblical exegesis, recover feminine images of the divine and develop more inclusive descriptions of church as God's people and Christ's body.

These mirror Christian responses to exclusion of the poor, indigenous peoples, and dalits. Though the particular contours of their exclusion vary, Asian Christian practices and reflections all promote inclusion in God's household. Indigenous theologian Vashum's claim that indigenous theology is "a theology of liberation"[29] applies to those of other sectors. Moreover, their theologies of liberation remain profoundly Asian, rooted as they are in diverse Asian contexts.

In practice, Asian Christians find common cause with other social actors and movements in their contexts. They partner with them and in some instances, join radical political movements against authoritarian and populist regimes.

EXTENDING BRIDGES

Given social and religious forces of exclusion, the need to extend bridges between and among peoples and sectors is both fundamental and comprehensive. Celebrating diversity and overcoming exclusion are but the embodiment of the *logos* or underlying principles for God's household to be continually life-giving. These principles emerge in Asian Christianity's involvement in interfaith dialogue and ecotheology: the first expresses the fundamental relationship of all humanity before God; the second, the comprehensive interdependence of all creation.

First, Asian Christianity values and participates in interfaith dialogue. Despite the enduring presence of world religions and multiple indigenous traditions, tension and conflict often arise in their relations. Deeply woven into social fabric, they are co-opted by ethnic, class, and political fundamentalisms and frequently operate with the religious majority dominating the minority.

Asian Christianity has contributed to disharmony, often through claims of religious superiority. But it now seeks to strengthen bridges through what has come to be known as the dialogues of life, spirituality, social concern, and belief. Asian Christians

---

28. Amaladoss, *Life in Freedom*, 54.
29. Vashum, *Christology in Context*, 132.

cooperate with other religious communities in strategic action for those suffering poverty and war.[30] Equally important are dialogues of life and spirituality. Everyday life connects people of various faiths as neighbors and helps them participate in their respective celebrations. Being present before the divine in spirituality centers like ashrams are analogous to Pope John Paul II and other religious leaders praying at Assisi.

These manifest the fundamental basis of Asian interfaith dialogue. Though differing views and contentious issues remain as in other contexts, Asian contexts for dialogue prove to be both singular in character and evocative of profound reflection. First, centuries-old de facto religious plurality rather than recent concepts ontological pluralism shape these contexts. Moreover, binary oppositions between proclamation and dialogue or between *missio ad gentes* (mission to peoples) and *missio cum gentibus* (mission with others) are inappropriate for these contexts; the Federation of Asian Bishops' Conferences views "this triple dialogue [with religions, cultures, and the poor] not as a means but as mode (attitude, way, stance) of proclaiming Christ in Asia."[31]

Asian theologians then stand on the common ground of *communicatio in sacris* (communion in the sacred): "when we start from pneumatological considerations we will be able to relate harmoniously our faith in Jesus Christ with the recognition of God's grace and the presence of the Spirit in other religious traditions."[32] Often borrowing patristic vocabulary like "seeds of the Word," they bear witness to the profound spiritual and wisdom traditions in their neighbors' lives.

Asian theologies engage in reinterpreting Christianity from other faith perspectives or in comparative descriptions of their different elements. Moreover, they challenge churches to strengthen bridges among them and within each. Such links undermine sectarianism and promote ecclesial unity among leaders and laity, men and women, and those of different ethnicities. All these are based on the recognition of divine presence in all and of their rightful place in God's household.

Second, Asian Christianity also needs to articulate its religious bond to the entire cosmos and its life-forms. Asia boasts of varied natural resources and great biodiversity. However, peoples' traditional harmony with their environments has been disrupted by neoliberal capitalist economics and technologies, leading to ecological destruction. Asia's poor suffer most from extreme climates and destroyed natural habitats.

Asian Christians contributed to this degradation because of distorted views of stewardship and collusion with economic interests. But their recent practice and reflection engage various environmental issues; for instance, they have supported indigenous peoples in many Asian contexts in resisting usurpation of traditional lands for industry and commerce.

---

30. Tabing-Reyes, *Weaving our Lives and Stories*.
31. Brazal, "Dialogue and Proclamation of Truth," 433.
32. Wilfred, "*Nostra Aetate* of Vatican II," 38.

Furthermore, Asian Christians use biblical and traditional resources for a comprehensive ecotheology based on the integrity of creation. This theological discourse stresses all creation's value, unity, and interdependence, thus undermining any anthropocentrism, and "highlights the whole household of God's creation, especially the world of nature, as an interrelated system."[33]

Other resources within Asian contexts, Wilfred insists, come from dialogue with other religious traditions.[34] Theologian Phan discusses Buddhist and Daoist resources for an Asian ecotheology: "the 'Great Sages of the Past' to whom *Laudato si* refers (no. 47) and from whom we can acquire 'true wisdom as the fruit of self-examination generous encounter between persons' (no. 47), include also the spiritual masters of Asian religions."[35]

This emerging Asian ecotheology then does not only promote action on particular environmental issues but also articulates the inherent bond encompassing all humanity and the material and natural world as creatures in God's household.

CONCLUSION

At such a critical moment in the contemporary world and global society, the journey of Asian Christianity brings its renewed commitment to build God's household. Asian Christians draw from the depths of their varied contexts and thus articulate Christian practice and reflection refracted through multiple lenses of ethnicity, gender, and other forces.

Asian Christianity treads through the interlocking pathways of celebrating diversity, overcoming exclusion, and strengthening bridges. Along the way, it highlights the welcome participation of people of great diversity within God's household, the social structures that promote equality and govern their relationships, and the all-encompassing foundation of equality before God and the integrity of all creation.

As it journeys to be inclusive, liberating, and integral, Asian Christianity shares with all Christians challenging theological insight and pastoral practice as well as spiritual wisdom harvested from Asian soil.

BIBLIOGRAPHY

Abiarajah, S. Wesley. "Changing Paradigms of Asian Christian Attitude to Other Religions." In *The Oxford Handbook of Christianity in Asia*, 347–67. Oxford: Oxford University Press, 2014.

Amaladoss, Michael. *The Asian Jesus*, Maryknoll, NY: Orbis, 2006.

---

33. Troster, "What is Eco-Theology?," 382.
34. Wilfred, *Theology for an Inclusive World*, 152–73.
35. Phan, *Asian Christianities*, 156.

———. "Asian Theological Trends." In *The Oxford Handbook of Christianity in Asia*, edited by Felix Wilfred. New York: Oxford University, 2014.

———. *A Call to Community: The Caste System and Christian Responsibility*. Anand: Gudyarat Suhitya, 1994.

———. *Life in Freedom: Liberation Theologies from Asia*. Gujarat: Gujarat Sahitya Prakasi, 1997.

Best, T. F., and M. Robra, eds. *Ecclesiology and Ethics: Ecumenical Ethical Engagement, Moral Formation and the Nature of the Church*. Geneva: World Council of Churches, 1997.

Brazal, Agnes M. "Dialogue and Proclamation of Truth: Reception of *Nostra Aetate* and *Ad Gentes* by the FABC." *Journal of Dharma* 42 (2016) 433.

Cartagenas, Aloysius Lopez. "The Terror of the Sexual Abuse by Roman Catholic Clergy and the Philippine Context." *Asian Horizons* 5 (2011) 371.

Chan, Yiu Sing Lúcás, and Shaji George Kochuthara, eds. *Doing Catholic Theological Ethics in a Cross Cultural and Interreligious Asian Context*. Bangalore: Dharmaram, 2016.

Conradie, Ernst. "The Whole Household of God (Oikos): Some Ecclesiological Perspectives." Parts 1 and 2. *Scriptura* 94 (2007) 1–28.

Francisco, Jose Mario C. "Letting the Texts on RH Speak for Themselves: (Dis)Continuity and (Counter)Point in CBCP Statements." *Philippine Studies* 63 (2015) 223–46.

Francis (Pope). *Laudato Si: On Care for Our Common Home*. With commentary by Sean McDonagh. Maryknoll, NY: Orbis, 2016.

Fung, Jojo M. "The Mystique of Dialogue: The Pathway to Spirit-Power for a Liberative Struggle." In *Spirituality through Interreligious Experience*, edited by Xavier Tharamel, 266–80. New Delhi: ISPCK, 2019.

Koyama, Kosuke. *Water Buffalo Theology*. Maryknoll, NY: Orbis, 1995.

Kung, Hans, and Julia Ching. *Christianity, and Chinese Religions*. New York: Doubleday, 1989.

Laksana, Albertus Bagus. "Multiple Religious Belonging or Complex Identity: An Asian Way of Being Religious." In *The Oxford Handbook of Christianity in Asia*, edited by Felix Wilfred, 493–509. Oxford: Oxford University Press, 2014.

McGuire, Meredith B. *Lived Religion: Faith and Practice in Everyday Life*. Oxford: Oxford University Press, 2008.

Mesa, Jose M. de. *Jose M. de Mesa: A Theological Reader*. Manila: De La Salle University Press, 2016.

Miranda, Dionisio M. *Loob: The Filipino Within*. Manila: Logos, 1988.

Nirmal, Arvind P. *Indigenous People: Dalits*. Edited by James Massey. Delhi: ISPCK, 1994.

Park, Andrew Sung. *The Wounded Heart of God: The Asian Concept of Han and the Christian Doctrine of Sin*. Nashville: Abingdon, 1993.

Phan, Peter C. *Asian Christianities: History, Theology, Practice*. Maryknoll, NY: Orbis, 2018.

Pui-lan, Kwok. *Introducing Asian Feminist Theology*. Cleveland: Pilgrim, 2000.

———. *Postcolonial Imagination and Feminist Theology*. Louisville: Westminster John Knox, 2005.

Recepcion, Andrew G. *God's Global Household: A Theology of Mission in the Context of Globalization*. Naga City: Agnus, 2007.

Song, C. S. *In the Beginning Were Stories, Not Texts: Story Theology*. Eugene OR: Wipf & Stock, 2011.

Sugden, Chris. *Seeking the Asian Face of Jesus*. Delhi: Regnum, 1997.

Sugirtharajah, R. S. *Asian Biblical Hermeneutics and Postcolonialism: Contesting the Interpretations*. Sheffield: Sheffield Academic, 1999.

Suh, David Kwang-sun. "A Biographical Sketch of an Asian Theological Consultation." In *Minjung Theology: People as the Subjects of History*, edited by Yong Bock Kim, 15–37. Maryknoll, NY: Orbis, 1983.

Tabing-Reyes, Corazon, et al. *Weaving our Lives and Stories: Women, Racism and Peace-building in Asia*. Hong Kong: Christian Conference of Asia, 2004.

Tirimanna, Vimal, ed. *Harvesting from the Asian Soil: Toward an Asian Theology*. Bangalore: Asian Trading Corporation, 2011.

Troster, Lawrence. "What is Eco-Theology?" *Cross Currents* 63 (2013) 382.

Vashum, Yangkahao. *Christology in Context: A Tribal-Indigenous Appraisal of North East India*. New Delhi: Christian World Imprints, 2017.

Wilfred, Felix. "*Nostra Aetate* of Vatican II, An Asian Re-reading after Fifty Years and the Way Forward." In *Spirituality through Interreligious Experience*, edited by Xavier Tharamel, 34–53. New Delhi: ISPCK, 2019.

Wilfred, Felix. *Theology for an Inclusive World*, Delhi: ISPCK, 2019.

CHAPTER 35

African Reflective Essay

Theology as Critical Discourse

ELIAS KIFONBONGMBA

In this essay offers a sketch of selected themes addressed by African theologians—a broad overview of classical and contemporary theology up to its postcolonial phase. African theology as critical discourse and practice which has evolved the colonial to the postcolonial period has inspired liberation, adaptation, reconstruction, gender discrimination, cultural and human dignity, economic and social justice and promoted with will to be church and community on African terms without diminishing critical collaboration and global partnerships. The theological mission which blossomed in late colonialism, accented its liberation priorities and later turned its castigating impulses to address the postcolonial despoliation.[1] Strands broadened during the revolutionary and liberation struggle for independence, moved out of its decolonial position into the postcolonial turn.[2] European incursion and colonial practice shaped theological imagination during the long deadly night of colonialism. Theologians reviewed and rejected aspects of missionary and colonial theology and responded with a theology of critical reaffirmation; drawing resources from African intellectual, spiritual, and cultural systems to critique and circumscribe dominant colonial motifs about African religiosity. The theology that has emerged is fascinating and engaging.

First African theology is a cultural and religious project. The historic publication *Des Prête Noirs s'Interrogent* grounded African theology in local religious roots

---

1. Bongmba, *Dialectics of Transformation in Africa*.
2. Heaney, *Post-Colonial Theology*. As with liberation theology, it is challenging to keep up with the literature on theology and the postcolonial era and theme.

and Christian history.³ Placide Temple's groundbreaking book *Bantu Philosophy*, invited an African response which promoted theological thinking and Alexis Kagame invited readers to discover categories of being in Rwanda. W. T. Harris and Harry Sawyerr, discussed belief in a Supreme Being among the Mande people offering a theological engagement from an African perspective.⁴ African theologians made it clear that biblical revelation should be understood in the light of African religiosity.⁵ Bolaji Idowu and John Mbiti who earned doctorates in theology in England, both made distinct contributions to theological imagination because they grounded the study of African Christian themes in the religious worldview of Africans. Alyward Shorter called for the adaptation of theology, emphasizing the staying power of African cultures and religions and called for adaptation of theology to African worldview.⁶ African religiosity as a background to Christianity and its theology received in my view a ringing endorsement in Bengt Sundkler's *Bantu Prophets in South Africa*.⁷ Kwesi Dickson stressed the importance of African culture to religion and the development of theology.⁸ Benezêt Bujo grounded his theology in the African social context, calling on theologians to take the cultures of Africa seriously in their theological reflection.⁹ Fabein Ebbousi Boulaga criticized missionary denigration of African culture which demanded Africans detach themselves from their pre-Christian world.¹⁰ Joseph Healey and Donald Sybertz have promoted a theology of enculturation grounded African proverbs.¹¹ Kwame Bediako has argued "theology is called to deal always with culturally rooted questions."¹² Laurenti Magesa has underscored the importance of the African religious background for understanding theology.¹³ Abongkhianmeghe E. Orobator in his brilliant book *Theology Brewed in an African Pot* has discussed theological ideas, drawing illustrations from local Nigerian ideas about God, highlighting the political and social disruption that took place with the coming of a new God.¹⁴ Orobator notes that curious idea that this God had no name

3. *Des Prête noirs s'Interogent*.

4. Harris and Sawyer, *Springs of Mende Belief and Conduct*. See also Dickson and Ellingworth, *Biblical Revelation and African Belief*; and Fashole-Luke, "African Christian Theologies," 172–73.

5. Dickson and Ellingworth, *Biblical Revelation and African Belief*.

6. Dickson and Ellingworth, *Biblical Revelation and African Belief*, 2.

7. Sundkler, *Bantu Prophets in South Africa*.

8. Dickson, *Theology in Africa*, 32. See South African critiques of the cultural approach in Tutu, "Black Theology/African Theology." See also, Boesak, *Farewell to Innocence*; Buthelezi, "Toward Indigenous Theology in South Africa," 7ff.

9. Bujo, *African Theology in its Social Context*; Ela, *My Faith as an Africa*, 33–34.

10. Boulaga, *Christianity without Fetishes*, 23.

11. Healey and Sybertz, *Towards an African Narrative Theology*.

12. Bediako, *Theology and Identity*, xv.

13. Idowu, *African Traditional Religions*; Mbiti, *Introduction to African Traditional Religion*; Magesa, *African Religions*.

14. Orobator, *Theology Brewed in an African Pot*.

but also had many names, and was proclaimed by a mad preacher who talked about three persons in one God.

Second, theologians have practiced political and public theology which goes back to the Bible and Saint Augustine's *City of God*.[15] Political theology was captivated in the long struggle for freedom in Southern Africa where theologians championed independence in Zimbabwe, Mozambique, Angola, and leading scholars at all universities and seminaries in South Africa challenged racism and apartheid, building a resistance movement grounded on the radical tradition of Karl Barth, Dietrich Bonhoeffer, and liberation and Black theologies. Theologians promoted Black consciousness and waged an untiring struggle against apartheid, drawing resources from religion, the arts, humanities, and social sciences. The end of racial discrimination and apartheid ushered in a theology of reconciliation at the end of apartheid.[16]

Political theology was advanced in the theology of reconstruction. Charles Villa Vicencio published on the subject, sketching the idea of reconstruction, but the full-blown argument was made by Jesse N. K. Mugambi in his book, *From Liberation to Reconstruction*.[17] Political theology expanded in the era of Afro-pessimism, building up to postcolonial theology. Paul Gifford's historical study, *Christianity in Africa: Its Public Role*, offered theologians a new anchorage for political theology because the book exposed the debilitating impact of "big man" politics that brought many African states to the brinks of financial collapse.[18] A number of theological monographs, including Elias K. Bongmba's *The Dialectics of Transformation in Africa*, spelled out the malaise of the state and called for practice of love.[19]

In a landscaping work Christianity and democracy John de Gruchy argued that the political revolutions of 1989 in Europe were a catalyst of the democratic change around the world. De Gruchy criticized the Western liberal democratic tradition for the battle between capitalism and communism. Nevertheless, he called for a just world order propelled by democratic practice grounded on the teachings of biblical prophets, Jesus Christ, and the communal life of the early Christian church. De Gruchy stressed the importance of ubuntu, arguing that "its contemporary reaffirmation is essential for the renewal of democracy in Africa and more universally."[20] Theologians have appreciated Mahmood Mamdani's *Citizen and Subject*, and Achille Mbembe's *On the Postcolony*, an excruciating autopsy of the postcolony, because both books have prosecuted the case against misrule in Africa, a devastation Mbembe has described as

---

15. Saint Augustine, *City of God*.

16. Allan Boesak, Ntumeleng Mosala, Manas Buthelezi, John W. de Gruchy, Charles Villa Vicencio, Steve Biko, James R. Cochrane, Gerald West, Tinyiko Maluleke.

17. Vicencio and Mugambi, *From Liberation to Reconstruction*; Vicencio, "Religion, Revolution and Reconstruction," 48–59.

18. Gifford, *African Christianity*. Gifford would publish other texts on the subject of church and state in other parts of the continent.

19. Bongmba, *Dialectics of Transformation in Africa*.

20. Bongmba, *Dialectics of Transformation in Africa*, 191.

necropolitics.[21] Necropolitics has diminished human dignity. In an earlier study James R. Cochrane called for ideas that promote the restoration of human dignity that has been crushed by political malpractice in the postcolony.[22]

Third, theology in Africa has emphasized women's right in feminist theology. African feminist theology was given a human face in the work of Mercy Amba Oduyoye's personal journey, intellectual interaction with Brigalia Bam and other scholars, notably Letty Russel prepared Oduyoye to start the Circle of Concerned African Women Theologians (the Circle) in 1989.[23] Oduyoye and members of the Circle resolved to write and live theology that would reject male domination of women, resist patriarchy, and promote gender equity, ecofeminism, and justice. Oduyoye and her colleagues called into question socio-cultural ideas and biblical texts that contributed to the subjugation of women, arguing that theology cannot ignore the liberation by African women. The work of the Circle has radically disrupted male-dominated theology by centering women's issues. *The Will to Arise* summoned African women to stand up, speak, and claim the will to be, thus launching a critical multidisciplinary theological engagement that questioned and rejected patriarchy and called for justice. Members of the Circle started a quiet revolution that would reverse the biased interpretation of sacred texts and Christian history and call on African women to rise up and speak.[24] A new generation of women scholars engaged in critical and culturally informed study of theology, church history, and a feminist reading of the Bible to promote gender equality. They rejected female genital cutting, and all forms of violence against women, including the economic and political marginalization of women.

One strategy of reading the Bible by Musa Dube involved retelling of biblical stories to awaken readers to see injustice and gender discrimination which fueled crises like the HIV/AIDS pandemic and gave HIV/AIDS in Africa a woman's face because women were victimized by culture, religion, and social conventions of subjugation, abuse, and promoted false sexual mythologies that rejected the use of condoms, most of the time blaming women for being vectors of the HIV/AIDS virus. The members of the Circle carried out and published research exposing injustices, called for action that would promote justice and equality, and published several studies that highlighted the discrimination that was victimizing women throughout the continent.

Fourth, African theology is an ethical project and theologians have employed interdisciplinary tools to understand the call for an ethical approach to social living that promotes communal responsibilities. Theologians have inquired on the status and fate of the Other, described by Jesus as the "least of these my brethren."[25] Wari-

---

21. Mamdani, *Citizen and Subject;* Mbembe, "Provisional Notes on the Postcolony"; Mbembe, *On the Postcolony,*

22. Cochrane, *Circles of Dignity.*

23. Fiedler, *Coming of Age*, 24.

24. Dube, *Other Ways of Reading.*

25. Benezêt Bujo; Paulinus Okechukwu Odozor; Samuel Waje Kunhiyop; Nimi Wariboko.

boko ethical discourse and praxis comes with a complexity that is as demanding as it is revealing and grounded in theological, intercultural, philosophical, and political analysis. Wariboko has called attention to what one could describe as the Calabari life ethic by discussing a cultural norm which motivates people to live lives worthy of remembrance.[26] One compelling theological expression for ethics is found in the eschatological discourse where Jesus told he would receive people into his reign because of what they did to the "least" of his brethren. Ethics is both individual and communal. Wariboko, whose philosophical theology has opened multiple conversations on ethics and theology, has given theologians new paths of inquiry for philosophical theology in Africa.[27]

In an earlier work, I argued that alleged practice of witchcraft could be understood by doing a theological and philosophical analysis using the philosophy of Emmanuel Levinas's philosophy and ethics of the other.[28] I am still convinced that otherness, framed in the ethical thought of Levinas that has defined ethics as an intersubjective engagement in a face-to-face relationship, offers a compelling argument for addressing witchcraft. African theologians have embraced otherness, grounding it in *ubuntu*, which means "humanity" or "humaneness." The concept embodies the best of human values; love, support, and respect for one another in the political community. In Southern Africa where the term has earned a greater currency with the expression "*umuntu ngumuntu ngabantu*," which means "a person is a person through persons." Bénézet Bujo has argued that *ubuntu* demonstrates that personhood is not defined strictly by *cogito* but also by *relatio* (relationship) and *cognation* (kinship).[29] Likewise, Augustine Shutte has argued that ubuntu reflects a genuine interaction of life forces with the self and others.[30] The debates on ethics and theology in Africa continues to invite a thoughtful balance between communalism and individuality.[31] The theology of ubuntu remains a viable construction because it reflects the ethos of ecclesial community as well as concretize African communal values. Theological ethics can fall into what Kwame Gyekye has decried as absolute communitarianism; he offered instead that moderate communitarianism individuality and community are part of African life.[32]

One theme that has emerged in ubuntu is the prioritization of another person, regardless of family of origin, gender, class, religion, sexual orientation, or politics. What stands out in this proposition is the view that the individual as an entity cannot and should not be submerged into the community and lose his or her freedom to make

---

26. Wariboko, *Depth and Destiny of Work*, 139–77. See Paris, "Similarities Between Nimi Wariboko and Aristotle" 46–52.
27. Falola, *Philosophy of Nimi Wariboko*.
28. Bongmba, *African Witchcraft and Otherness*.
29. Bujo, *African Theology in its Social Context*.
30. Shutte, *Ethic for a New South Africa*.
31. Bongmba, *African Witchcraft and Otherness*.
32. Gyekye, *Tradition and Modernity*.

decisions as an individual. The priority of the other does not displace the community. At best, it suggests that a strong and well-balanced view of individuals strengthens the community. Ubuntu opens the door for a theological and ethical praxis that balances individuality and community. Charles Villa Vicencio addressed politics and human rights in the work of nation-building.[33] Central to his argument is the notion that the rule of law offers possibilities to reconstruct human rights. Villa Vicencio argued that first-generation rights such as the Universal Declaration of Human Rights offer individual rights, liberties, and freedom of expression, movement, and association. Villa Vicencio employs legal philosophy to promote social values that contribute to reconstruction. Villa Vicencio's argument invites theologians to an interdisciplinary engagement with ethics. He argued that to achieve second generation rights, theologians ought to stand together with the poor, or what liberation theologians called a preferential option for the poor.[34]

Paulinus Ikechukwu's magisterial study, *Morality Truly Christian Truly African*, breaks new ground in theology and ethics. He grounds his analysis in *Gaudium et Spes* and the fact that humanity is crested in the image of God to live in community as men and women who must oppose inauthentic living and build solidarity that offers solutions to the dehumanization of others and creates conditions for human thriving.[35] Odozor affirms "basic freedom . . . that . . . pertains to the determination of the self with regard to the totality of existence, the fundamental choice between love for self and love for serving the Lord."[36] Odozor argues that an African communitarian emphasis does not undermine individuality and because the human being has value because of the redemptive work of Jesus.[37] He grounds this contextual approach in love taught by Jesus and rejects moral relativism.[38] The teachings of Jesus must rule in debates on abortion, same-sex relations, sex work, and divorce and remarriage. *Aru* in Igbo culture are considered abominations and include sexual relations between relatives. The debates on contraceptives preceded a contested history of same sex relations and revolutionized sexuality. Opponents of these lifestyles are now called "closed minded, homophobic, non-inclusive, and intolerant."[39] Odozor proposes a moral theology grounded in the faith community, the bearer of the gifts of Christ. The themes of the African Synod of 1994 and 2009, "Reconciliation, Justice, and Peace" offer guidelines.[40] The bishops argued that foreign perspectives on gender were being

---

33. Vicencio, *Theology of Reconstruction*.

34. I am indebted to Cochrane's discussion of Villa-Vicencio's book and his other writings on human dignity. See Cochrane, "Critical Review of Charles Villa-Vicencio," 85–95.

35. Odozor, *Morality Truly Christian, Truly African*, 222–23.

36. Odozor, *Morality Truly Christian, Truly African*, 225.

37. Odozor, *Morality Truly Christian, Truly African*, 228–29.

38. Odozor, *Morality Truly Christian, Truly African*, 252.

39. Odozor, *Morality Truly Christian, Truly African*, 265.

40. See Orobator, *Reconciliation, Justice, and Peace*.

pushed into Africa. Not all readers will agree that all controversial issues in Africa are imposed from outside. It is clear that the African quest for a local communitarian ethic is an ongoing negotiable project.

Health care remains a major theological problem for Africa today. First, sacred texts discuss disease and different forms of therapies in which medicines and miracles dominate. Second, Africans face medical challenges but miracles do not always work, and medicines are in short supply. Malaria has not been eradicated. Third, Africa and other parts of the world still live with HIV and AIDS. There is no evidence that the Ebola virus has been eradicated and now Africans also live with the SARS coronavirus 2, COVID-19, which has affected all people living with HIV/AIDS at greater risks. Theologian Lado Tonlieu Ludovic has argued that solving the AIDS pandemic by promoting only individual responsibility is not working well. Faith communities emphasized abstinence and that might have compromised the ABC approach (Abstain, Be Faithful, Use Condoms) that targeted different sectors of the sexually active population. The failure to promote a rigorous gender equity means that many women are at risk of infection with HIV/AIDS, due to structural inequities and weak economies have exacerbating the sexual vulnerabilities of many women and male sex workers. There is still a need for a robust theological engagement that will address the social, economic, cultural, and political conditions that drive the spread of HIV/AIDS.

Evelyn Namakula Mayangja has argued that fighting AIDS has been hampered by a deficit of political leadership. But the task for the church is to work for effective liberation of the people in the spirit of *Gaudium et Spes*. This invites faith leaders to criticize bad political policies. During the high noon of the battle to contain HIV/AIDS, South African theologians launched the African Religious Health Assets Program (ARHAP). James R. Cochrane and Steve de Gruchy and their colleagues at the University of Memphis in Tennessee highlighted the tangible and intangible assets which faith communities have that are deployed in fighting disease and creating conditions for promoting well-being.[41] Key findings from Zambia confirmed that faith communities have assets that are essential to health care. The assets include tangible (medical equipment and infrastructure, staff) and intangible assets, like the care and nurturing role members of the community play as they give comfort and support to people who are ill.

Another health challenge that has hit Africa is the Ebola virus, which the World Health Organization describes as a hemorrhagic fever believed to be transmitted to humans from animals such as "bats, porcupines, and non-human primates." First reported in 1976, the most severe outbreak that spread internationally occurred in 2014–2016. It is transmitted through contact with "blood, secretions, organs or other bodily fluids of infected people, with surfaces and materials . . . contaminated with these fluids." There have been twenty-five outbreaks of the disease in Africa and other parts of the world. Persons infected with the virus die quickly if they do not get

---

41. Cochrane et al., *When Religion and Health Align*, ARHAP Report, 2009.

immediate medical attention. The 2014 outbreak affected 28,500 persons and resulted in the deaths of eleven thousand people, mostly in West Africa. The WHO reports that a vaccine under development has been tested in Guinea and the Democratic Republic of the Congo. Since there are no known treatments, prevention of infections is the best way of controlling the spread, utilizing case monitoring and "contract tracing." Addressing it requires good laboratory services, and when someone dies, the burial should be handled by those trained to handle the bodies with care. Theological approaches that stress miracles ought to stress safe practices as well.[42]

COVID-19 demonstrates that the 1978 Alma Ata Declaration that projected health for all by the year 2000 did not happen. The science of the infection and prevention of further infections is clear and includes wearing a mask, staying away from crowds, and getting vaccinated. Given the danger posed by COVID-19 and uncertainties that loom in global health today, I am reminded of Stuart C. Bates's magisterial study *Inculturation and Healing*, a broad theological probe in which he returned to the question of inculturation and argued that inculturation was the key to what he called "theological judgement," which I read broadly as a claim that even in crucial things like health, African theology must pay attention to local cultural ideas and practices because culture involves the arts, thought, way of life, and a mode of being as local community of discourse that aims at humanizing each and the social fabric.[43] A Christian theology of health and healing will always walk the intercultural path to arrive at a holistic approach to health and healing.

Sixth, African theology is also a discourse on the environmental crisis. Theologians have recognized that with an estimated 25 percent of the surface area being desert and the forests and wetlands disappearing, Africa faces a growing environmental and ecological crisis. Theologians have called for action that could stem the environmental crises caused by climate change. M. L. Daneel initiated the African Earthkeeping project to awaken the church to do something about environmental degradation.[44] Ernst Conradie has argued that four main approaches to the environment has emerged over the years. The first appeals to the Bible and calls for responsible stewardship and conservation of the resources of the earth.[45] Second, researchers have called for the restoration of ancestral lands. Third, leaders have promoted sustainable development; and finally, the promotion of environmental justice. Conradie also argues that this also concerns other parts of Africa. Conradie has argued that theologians increasingly employ the term ecotheology to promote environmental awareness.[46]

---

42. https://www.who.int/health-topics/ebola#tab=tab_1. See also Elias Kifon Bongmba, "Notes on Health in Africa," unpublished reflection, 4.

43. Bate, *Inculturation and Healing*, see especially chapters 8, 9, and 10.

44. Daneel, *African Earthkeepers*.

45. Conradie, "Approaches to Religion and the Environment," 439 ff.

46. Conradie, "Some Hermeneutical Reflections on Ecotheology," 294–95.

Susan Rakoczy has argued that women have adopted ecofeminism as a compelling motif for ecological justice, given the massive evidence degradation, global warming, water shortages, the depletion of over 70 percent of fish stock, and deforestation shrinking the resources of the earth by 42 percent. Many species are vanishing and at the time of the publication of her book, it was estimated that 20 percent of all living species would vanish in 2029.[47] The environmental crisis affects women the most because in many communities they are the breadwinners. Due to the environmental crisis, "women in . . . Africa, Asia, and Latin America know from daily experience that patriarch/kyriachy and the domination of nature results in poverty . . . Their daily household responsibilities are made much more difficult."[48] Rakoczy rejects dualisms which associate women with nature and argues that an ecofeminist perspective rejects these dualisms which are grounded in effective and domineering male categories. She reviews feminist responses and initiatives, especially in the Global South, and offers a theological vision that is grounded in a holistic vision of intercommunion and ecofeminist understanding of the Spirit who gives life, heals the earth, and empowers and enables responsible stewardship. She also calls for Africa to raise questions about human habitat, water, and food sustainability. The focus on gender is *apropos* since the most well-known environmentalist on the continent was Wangari Mathai of Kenya who championed the planting of trees and was recognized and honored with the Nobel Peace Prize.

Food security remains a serious concern and calls for more theological analysis and training at a local level.[49] In his contribution Ernst Conradie called attention to drought that complicated life in South Africa in 2016. Conradie called on theologians to address the moral and spiritual roots of the crisis.[50] He pointed out the limitations of "ecclesial resolutions," arguing that Olav Fykes Tveit's "Ten Commandments" which he presented at the World Economic Forum called for examining food choices people make.[51] These ten commandments serve as an invitation for people to develop a certain disposition to everything in the created order to ensure that people practice sustainability. Nisbert Taisekwa Taringa, in an ethical study of the environment in Africa grounded in the social antienvironmental world of the Shona and Christian worldviews, has called for a complementarity and called for eco-spirituality, eco-justice, and stewardship.[52] Most African communities have some kind of perspective on ecology and spiritual. One hopes that faith leaders will continue to promote a spirituality that recognizes the precarity of the situation, especially in Africa, and motivate members of the faith community to take proactive stands to slow down desertification and climate change.

47. Rakoczy, *In Her Name,* 298 ff.
48. Rakoczy, *In Her Name,* 303.
49. See Werner and Jeglitzka, *Eco-Theology, Climate Justice and Food Security,* 45.
50. Conradie, "Climate Justice, Food Security and God," 109–14.
51. See https://www.oikoumene.org/news/tveit-on-the-ten-commandments-of-food.
52. Taringa, *Comparative Analysis of Shona and Christian Attitudes to Nature,* 88.

BIBLIOGRAPHY

Augustine (Saint). *The City of God*. London: Penguin, 2003.

Bate, Stewart C. *Inculturation and Healing: Coping-Healing in South African Christianity*. Pietermaritzburg: Cluster, 1997.

Bediako, Kwame. *Theology and Identity: The Impact of Culture upon Christian Thought in the Second Century and Modern Africa*. Oxford: Regnum, 1992.

Boesak, Allan. *A Farewell to Innocence*. Maryknoll, NY: Orbis, 1977.

Bongmba, Elias Kifon. *African Witchcraft and Otherness: A Philosophical and Theological Critique of Intersubjective Relations*. Albany: State University of New York Press, 2001.

———. *The Dialectics of Transformation in Africa*. New York: Palgrave MacMillan, 2006.

———. "Notes on Health in Africa." Unpublished reflection.

Boulaga, F. Ebbousi. *Christianity without Fetishes: An African Critique and Recapture of Christianity*. Maryknoll, NY: Orbis, 1984.

Bujo, Benezet. *African Theology in its Social Context*. Translated by John O'Donohue. Maryknoll, NY: Orbis, 2006.

Buthelezi, Manas. "Toward Indigenous Theology in South Africa." In *The Emergent Gospel*, edited by Sergio Torres and Virginia Fabella, 56–75. Maryknoll, NY: Orbis, 1978.

Cochrane, James R. *Circles of Dignity*. Minneapolis: Fortress, 2009.

———. "A Critical Review of Charles Villa-Vicencio's *A Theology of Reconstruction*." *Journal for the Study of Religion* 8 (1995) 85–95.

Cochrane, James R., Barbara Schmid, and Teresa Cutts, eds. *When Religion and Health Align: Mobilising Religious Health Assets for Transformation*. ARHAP Report, 2009. Piertermaritzburg: Cluster, 2011.

Conradie, Ernst M. "Approaches to Religion and the Environment." In *The Routledge Companion to Christianity in Africa*, edited by Elias Kifon Bongmba, 438–53. Oxford: Routledge, 2015.

———. "Climate Justice, Food Security and God: Some Reflections from the Perspective of Eco-Theology." In *Eco-Theology, Climate Justice and Food Security: Theological Education and Christian Leadership Development*, edited by Dietrich Werner and Elizabeth Jeglitzka, 438–53. Geneva: Globethics.net, 2016.

———. "Some Hermeneutical Reflections on Ecotheology." In *The Routledge Handbook on African Theology*, edited by Elias Kifon Bongmba, 122–40. New York: Routledge, 2020.

Daneel, M. *African Earthkeepers, Vol. 2. Environmental Mission and Liberation in Christian Perspective*. Pretoria: Unisa Press, 1999.

Dickson, Kwesi. *Theology in Africa*. Maryknoll, NY: Orbis, 1984.

Dickson, Kwesi, and Paul Ellingworth. *Biblical Revelation and African Belief*. Maryknoll, NY: Orbis, 1969.

Dube, Musa W. *Other Ways of Reading the Bible*. Atlanta: Society of Biblical Literature, 2001.

Ela, Jean Marc. *My Faith as an Africa*. Maryknoll, NY: Orbis, 1995.

Falola, Toyin, ed. *The Philosophy of Nimi Wariboko: Social Ethics, Economy and Religion*. Durham, NC: Carolina Academic, 2021.

Fashole-Luke, E. W. "African Christian Theologies." *Scottish Journal of Theology* 29 (1976) 172–73.

Fiedler, Rachel Nya Gondwe. *Coming of Age*. Luwinga/Lilongwe: Mzuni, 2017.

Gifford, Paul. *African Christianity: Its Public Role*. Bloomington: Indiana University Press, 1998.

Gyekye, Kwame. *Tradition and Modernity: Philosophical Reflections on the African Experience.* New York: Oxford University Press, 1997.

Harris, W. T., and Harry Sawyerr. *The Springs of Mende Belief and Conduct: A Discussion of the Influence of the Belief in the Supernatural among the Mende.* Freetown: Sierra Leone University Press, 1968.

Healey, Joseph, and Donald Sybertz. *Towards an African Narrative Theology.* Maryknoll, NY: Orbis, 1996.

Heaney, Robert S. *Post-Colonial Theology: Finding God and Each Other Amidst the Hate.* Eugene, OR: Cascade, 2019.

Idowu, E. Bolaji. *African Traditional Religions: A Definition.* London: CMS, 1973.

Magesa, Laurenti. *African Religions: The Moral Traditions of Abundant Life.* Maryknoll, NY: Orbis, 1997.

Mamdani, Mahmood. *Citizen and Subject.* Princeton: Princeton University, 2018.

Mbembe, Achille. *On the Postcolony.* Studies on the History of Society and Culture 41. Oakland, CA: University of California Press, 2001.

———. "Provisional Notes on the Postcolony." *Journal of the International African Institute* 62 (1992) 3–37.

Mbiti, John. *Introduction to African Traditional Religions.* 2nd ed. Oxford: Heinemann, 1991.

Odozor, Paulinus Ikechukwu. *Morality Truly Christian, Truly African: Foundational, Methodological, and Theological Considerations.* Notre Dame: University of Notre Dame Press, 2014.

Orobator, Agbonkhianmeghe, ed. *Reconciliation, Justice, and Peace: The Second African Synod.* Nairobi: Acton, 2011.

———. *Theology Brewed in an African Pot.* Maryknoll, NY: Orbis, 2008.

Paris, Peter. "Similarities Between Nimi Wariboko and Aristotle." In *The Philosophy of Nimi Wariboko* by Toyin Falola, 237–56. Durham: Carolina Academic Press, 2021.

Rakoczy, Susan. *In Her Name: Women Doing Theology.* Pietermaritzburg: Cluster, 2004.

Shutte, Augustine. *An Ethic for a New South Africa.* Pietermaritzburg: Cluster, 2001.

Sundkler, Bengt. *Bantu Prophets in South Africa.* London: Routledge, 1948.

Taringa, Nisbert Taisekwa. *A Comparative Analysis of Shona and Christian Attitudes to Nature.* Moldova: KS OmniScriptum, 2010.

Tutu, Desmond. "Black Theology/African Theology: Soul Mates or Antagonists." *The Journal of Religious Thought* 32 (1999) 25–33.

Vicencio, Charles Villa. "Religion, Revolution and Reconstruction: The Significance of the Cuban and Nicaraguan Revolutions for the Church in South Africa." *Journal of Theology for Southern Africa* 73 (1990) 48–59.

———. *A Theology of Reconstruction: Nation-Building and Human Rights.* Cambridge: Cambridge University Press, 1993.

Vicencio, Charles Villa, and Jesse N. K. Mugambi. *From Liberation to Reconstruction: African Christian Theology after the Cold War.* Nairobi: East African Educational, 1995.

Wariboko, Nimi. *The Depth and Destiny of Work: An African Theological Interpretation.* Trenton, NJ: Africa World, 2008.

Werner, Dietrich, and Elizabeth Jeglitzka, eds. *Eco-Theology, Climate Justice and Food Security: Theological Education and Christian Leadership Development.* Globethics.net Global 14. Geneva: Globethics.net, 2016.

CHAPTER 36

Oceania Reflective Essay

Theology of Prophetic Anger

KATALINA TAHAAFE-WILLIAMS

There is much excitement amongst contemporary historians and commentators about the theological implications of the demographic shift in world Christianity from the Global North to the Global South. Some suggest that the historical significance of this moment for world Christianity and for the world church is analogous to the transition of the early church from a persecuted faith to a state religion courtesy of Constantine, and to the unprecedented impact of the European Reformation sparked by Luther and his ninety-five theses.[1]

For many this stunning transformation in the landscape of world Christianity is an affirmation of its status as a world religion and of the diminishing hegemony of Western Christianity. It is a shift that has led to deeper explorations and analyses of Christian developments in the various regions of the Global South within the last half-century, from Africa to Asia, the Middle East to Latin America, and of course Oceania. These explorations have given the world direct access to the stories of the evolution of Global South Christianity as well as the possibility to assess commonalities and differences in regional and national experiences.

We learn that in most Global South contexts, the growth and expansion of Christianity was largely due to effective Indigenous agency independent of Western influences. We learn that the blurring of the line between church and state is normative in many places which could either be advantageous or detrimental to Christianity depending on the religious affiliation of the region or country. Where another world religion is dominant, Christianity is likely to be faced with some form of persecution

---

1. Bevans and Tahaafe-Williams, *Contextual Theology*, 16.

or suppression which may even be codified into law. On the other hand, where Christianity is the dominant religion the ambiguity in the faith-state relationship allows room for Christians to engage the public space and lead efforts for social justice.

We are reminded of the intense religious plurality in most of the Global South regions and the fact that in those places Christianity is not only a minority religion, it is also the religion of minorities. Nevertheless, Christian numerical presence and intergenerational vibrancy in these Global South contexts starkly contrast with the declining Christian presence in the more secularized Global North. And precisely because Global South Christianity's existence in such multireligious situations is a daily negotiation, it should be seen as a valuable resource for equipping world Christians in navigating the multireligious and multicultural world of the twenty-first century.

The Global North and Global South dichotomy continues to be a contested construction and of much concern is the question about the definition and composition of the latter. These are notable concerns given that a substantial part of the Asia region is geographically located in the Global North (including China, Taiwan, Japan, South Korea in the east, and India in the south), not to mention that major countries within this region are the economic equals or have even surpassed many of the so-called developed countries in the west.[2] An added complexity is the fact that colonial-settler societies in the Global South (such as Australia and New Zealand in Oceania) are not only populated by descendants of white European colonizers, they are also culturally, socio-economically, and politically Western. Some Asian scholars are proposing "the Global East" as a new and useful conceptual framework that would include East Asian countries with similarities in geographical location, economic development, cultural traditions, and colonial histories.[3]

The last three decades saw a remarkable growth in Indigenous theological presence and visibility. Apart from the usual systemic and systematic obstacles, Indigenous theological voices are often silenced by a deep and ongoing sense of ambivalence towards Christianity that sometimes requires being accompanied by an Indigenous Christian apologetic. Recognizing that these are part and parcel of the legacy of Christianity's colonial history, much of the Indigenous theological activities in the early twenty-first century have been focused on uncovering the ongoing impact colonization has had on Indigenous identity and on developing Indigenous theologies that engage with the dynamics of power, resistance, and land as central and foundational to Indigenous spirituality.

So yes, much has been made of the major shift in world Christian identity and numerical presence from the Northern to the Southern Hemisphere. Understandably, there is great interest in how theological thinking, setting, and education may have changed along with or because of this shift. Notwithstanding the theological implications, there are a growing number of scholars from both north and south who caution

2. Yang, "Afterword," 957.
3. Yang, "Afterword," 957.

against an overenthusiastic and premature claim of the dawn of a *post-imperial* world Christianity.[4] The point is made that it is not only *wistful* thinking given that economic and socio-political powers are still the domain of Global North Christianity, it is also risky thinking because it masks the historical and current power of the imperial west (with the US at the front lines) to shape global Christian practices.[5] In the meantime, Africa is gaining a great deal of attention as the new epicenter of global Christianity. Except that despite its numerical strength and youthful energy, Africa lacks the resources necessary for sustained impact in world Christianity.[6]

As the archbishop of Canterbury, Justin Welby, points out, the average twenty-first-century Anglican is a young Black woman with three children, earning an income of two dollars a day, has lost at least two close relatives to AIDS, and is likely to live in a place where there is extreme persecution or violent conflict. And this same woman will walk four miles each Sunday to a church service that lasts three hours.[7] This stark image is not the picture that comes to mind of the average Christian in a Global North context. It is a disturbing image that raises deep and mixed reactions in me, and begs the question as to why this should be the state of things.

I began this reflection by highlighting some key scenarios reflecting the richness of common experiences and concerns in Global South Christianity, including Oceania, which add credence to the claim that the center of Christianity has shifted to the south. Yet this sounds like an empty claim when we know that economic and political powers gained through colonial and imperial history are still in the possession of Global North Christianity. There is no denying the extensive influence Western Christianity wields on the world Christian landscape with its wealth, resources, publications, theological institutions, faith-influenced state policies, and grassroots mission activities.[8] Moreover, the US is still the largest provider of global Christian missionaries today and therefore still a major player on the world religious stage.

It could be said that the multidirectional flows of Christian influences including south-south and south-north exchanges may be a counter to the power imbalance between north and south. Attention is drawn to the fact that South Korea is the second largest provider of Christian missionaries around the globe after the United States, and that through migration the existence of diasporic, migrant, multicultural, and international churches are transforming the world Christian landscape generally, and the face of Western Christianity specifically.

My own ministry had put me on the front line, actively engaging Global North Christianity on how to receive the gifts of their Global South brothers and sisters. As the Assembly Secretary for Racial Justice, Multicultural Ministry, and Inter Faith Relations

4. Maxwell, "Afterword," 951.
5. Maxwell, "Afterword," 951.
6. Freston, "Afterword," 945.
7. Welby, "Afterword," 955.
8. Yang, "Afterword," 957.

with the United Reformed Church, UK in the early 2000s, I experienced firsthand the transforming effect minority ethnic Christians (mostly Black and Asian) had on the face of Christianity in the British Isles. Before I left Geneva just over two years ago, it was my experience through extensive travel around Europe that in every city whether Stockholm, Rome, or Paris, I would find worshipers and worship leaders of diverse backgrounds in every church service that I joined. I know from close participation and involvement with mainline churches and ecumenical bodies in North America that similar multicultural trends have been the case there as well, for the past three decades at least.

Closer to home, the impact of globalization in the Oceania region and the associated increase in migration have led to a strong presence of Pacific migrant churches in Western diasporas including in North America and the UK. New Zealand and Australia currently host the biggest Pacific Island communities and churches outside of the Pacific Islands. The presence of Pacific Island Christians in the membership and structures of historic mainline churches in the two nations have transformed the face of Christianity in those contexts.[9]

There is no disputing the impactful contribution of Global South Christians to the religious landscape of the Global North. But in terms of power dynamics and relationships, it is safe to say that the micro level of denominational ministry and relationships mirror the macro picture of world Christianity painted above. Put another way, it is one thing to be visibly diverse in denominational membership, it is another to determine the order and shape of the whole church. In the case of Oceania, New Zealand and Australia have quite different experiences. Whereas the New Zealand historical mainline churches have made structural changes to enable more equal power sharing with Pacific Islanders and to recognize the special primacy of the Indigenous Maori, the Australian churches are still some ways behind on both fronts.

The incredible and rapid rise of populist nationalism gaining unprecedented popularity as it spread throughout the west gives me reason for pause. Coupled with the re-emergence of white supremacist ideology and rhetoric in the public space, we are seeing an alarming transformation in the Western political landscape that permeates not just the traditional corridors of power, but local grassroots structures, networks, and social groups as well. These developments are especially potent and visible in the current political landscape of the US, though they are seen to a lesser degree in other Western contexts including Australia.

As former WCC Executive Staff for Mission and Evangelism, I collaborated with colleagues in the Vatican to organise the 2018 World Conference on Xenophobia, Racism and Populist Nationalism in Rome, which included a special audience with Pope Francis. That world conference brought together state, civil society, academic, and religious leaders from around the globe to seek cohesive and realistic responses to the alarming spread of populist nationalism and xenophobia throughout Europe and other parts of the world. It was a sobering lesson to learn that populism was likely to

---

9. Lamport, "Preface," xxiii.

be around for a while and that it was attracting quite a broad-based following ranging from middle-class to blue-collar workers to university graduates.

A fundamental claim of populist nationalism is that liberal democratic immigration policies allow too many migrant ethnics into the nation bringing with them changes that will make the country unrecognizable.[10] For many in the dominant culture, it is bad enough that *they* are reshaping the religious landscape, but changing the culture, politics, and indeed the whole fabric of the society will surely follow and that would be unbearable. Certainly, in Europe and the US there are deep anxieties amongst many members of the white dominant culture over the real possibility that in the not-too-distant future brown and Black people may become the numerical majority—2042 in the US according to some.[11] Not surprisingly, studies show that attitudes to race, cultural change, and gender, more than economic worries, are the major underlying issues of concern for supporters of populist nationalism.[12] White followers of populist political parties and leaders are convinced that their national identity and way of life will be destroyed by immigrants and that white people are subjected to more discrimination than Black people and other minority ethnic groups.[13]

As an Oceanian womanist theologian, I have tried to sketch the Christian landscape on which I am engaging theologically, both at macro and micro levels. The picture I see is not comforting. I am torn between derision and tears as I picture a white middle-class populist churchgoer who is outraged that she should be made to feel like a stranger in the invaded space she assumes is her country, and the image of the average Anglican painted by the archbishop of Canterbury. I articulated previously my mixed reactions to the latter image, but I can be forthcoming by confessing that anger is right there in the mix. Anger that the existential challenges this young Black Christian woman faces daily should be normative under any circumstances. Anger at the reminder of all those Native Americans, First Nations peoples, Aboriginals, Maoris, Samis, Polynesians, Melanesians, to name just a few of the world's Indigenous populations, who did have their identities and ways of life destroyed and who are constantly being imagined into invisibility in their own countries. Anger that the outraged populist mentioned seems oblivious to that reality, to her complicity in that reality, and worse still, that she probably does not care. Anger at the double standards and collective amnesia and the ignorance and the racist denials and the indifference. Anger that into the third decade of the twenty-first century I am still compelled to label myself an Oceanian womanist theologian as reminder that Pacific women theologians in Oceania are still some distance from recognition and equality. Anger that too often in their theological positioning and social justice posturing Pacific male theologians continue to overlook the double-whammy marginalization of their Pacific sisters.

10. Eatwell and Goodwin, *National Populism*, 270–72.
11. Eatwell and Goodwin, *National Populism*, 33.
12. Eatwell and Goodwin, *National Populism*, 4.
13. Eatwell and Goodwin, *National Populism*, 33.

Oceania Reflective Essay

I am angry that my anger is probably futile and won't make a difference! For after all is said and done, Global South Christianity will go back to navigating the extensive reach and influences of Global North Christianity for access to the shaping of world Christianity. And I will go back to negotiating marginal theological and ministry spaces in a so-called multicultural church where my capable but threatening colored presence is overlooked in favor of more pliable colored versions of the low-hanging-coconut kind. Yes, I am angry, and go ahead, caricature me as angry and hostile! I wish for my anger to be seen, to be recognized, not dismissed out of hand as just another angry colored woman with a chip on her shoulder!

Christianity is commonly perceived as a religion of peace. Time does not allow for this perception to be unpacked now but the point needs to be made that peace does not preclude anger, just as love does not preclude anger. It is possible that anger has motivated many actions for peace. Parents love their children but that does not make the children exempt from their parent's anger. Indeed, it is often the case that we get angry with something or someone precisely because we love and care. Indifference is the response we have for something we do not care about. Sometimes anger is the only thing that stands between us and giving up or surviving difficult situations.

Interestingly, the word *Pacific* etymologically comes from Latin meaning "peaceful." That implies calm, placid, gentle, and quiet, and it is easy to conjure up a scene of palm leaves, gentle breezes, calm lagoons, and beautiful sandy beaches. Add a typical south seas sunset and you have the perfect quintessential Oceania-Pacific scenery. Beautiful and peaceful. Anger has no place in that scenery. Yet, Pacific-Oceania is also prone to hurricanes and cyclones. And although the immediate image that comes to mind is of devastation and chaos, there is also the clearing away of clutter and waste, and there are also new beginnings and opportunities.

I suggest anger is a theologically under-explored and undervalued concept. Anger has been overly demonized in church circles and in Western civil society. Being nice, gentle, kind, and polite were some of the dominant values in my Christian upbringing. They are good solid Christian values, no one would dispute that. However, the culture of niceness in the church is so pervasive that often it gets in the way of doing what is right or in keeping and maintaining a high level of accountability. I witness the way this culture of niceness functions in the church quite frequently and have found myself calling it the "unbearable niceness of being"—a play on the title of Milan Kundera's 1984 book *The Unbearable Lightness of Being*. This culture of niceness may not have been out of place in the so-called polite society of the Jane Austen and the Brontë sisters' novels. Being nice sometimes compels one to be dishonest and/or lie, even for good reasons.

Of course, I am not so naïve as to promote anger as good under all circumstances. Yes, anger can be dangerous and needs careful handling and managing. I should know, I have been angry since the age of nine when I discovered I was a racialized *other*. I have spent a lifetime managing my anger and channelling it in ways that are constructive. Anger can also be a form of speaking truth to power, of being prophetic.

The prophets of the Hebrew Bible always speak in prophetic anger—sometimes their words are quite harsh that I often feel my anger pales in comparison.[14] But they are speaking tough words on behalf of a God who loves us enough to get angry with us. We cannot presuppose that a God who loves us never gets angry with us. However, Western liberal Christianity and theology have done a great job of excising a wrathful angry God from the Christian imagination, and of implanting a gentle meek and mild Jesus in our minds so that many Christians cannot imagine Jesus any other way. So much so that the Jesus who overturns the tables in the temple and throws out the money changers is seen as acting out of character, as an uncharacteristic Jesus, since the normal Jesus does not get angry.[15] Yet, the Gospels are riddled with incidents where Jesus rebukes the Pharisees, Scribes, and Sadducees, even his disciples get their fair share.[16] We are reminded too that Jesus had strong emotions, for he wept out of compassion for the crowd, and he lamented the fate of his beloved Jerusalem.[17]

British theologian Anthony Reddy suggests that Jesus has been held captive to a narrow reading of the Bible by Western Christianity because an angry God who chastises and rebukes cannot be reconciled with the neutral transcendent God who does not take sides or intervenes on the side of the marginalized.[18] For many Global South Christians God is understood as One who actively responds and intervenes in liberative ways so a God who does not intervene would be incomprehensible for them. James Cone insists that a God without wrath who does not condemn oppression is not a liberating God and is a God that the marginalized have no use for.[19] Some see Jesus's anger at the temple as Jesus being both prophetic as well as being Godly—that is, being like the angry God of the Old Testament.[20]

The exciting development in world Christianity is unfortunately marred by the underlying power imbalances that exist within Christianity at both macro and micro levels. The credibility and integrity of our faith is at stake if intentional proactive and multilevel efforts are not made to address these issues. In the very least our theological activities in the coming years should prioritize addressing these challenges head-on. I propose a *theology of (prophetic) anger* should be added to our efforts. We know anger can lead to changes for the better, for the common good. Imagine Luther nailing his ninety-five theses to the Wittenberg church door—could that have happened without some amount of anger involved? Of course not. And those who study Luther know about his anguish and frustrations. I think we need to all get angry for the needed change to come.

---

14. See Jer 16:1–4 for example.
15. John 2: 14–16.
16. See Matt 23:1–36 for example.
17. Matt 15:32; Luke 13:31–35.
18. Reddy, *Nobodies*, 154.
19. Cone, *Black Theology*, 70–73.
20. Reddy, *Nobodies*, 156.

A theology of prophetic anger will begin honest and open conversations about power and power dynamics in our relationships in the churches, in the north and south, and at grassroots and global forums. Vinoth Ramachandra, the Sri Lankan theologian and physicist reminds us that theology is more than doctrinal and systematic debates. It is a way ". . . of embodied seeing and doing that seeks to manifest the transformative power of God-in-Christ in the world."[21] The vision for a theology of prophetic anger cannot be more accurately articulated. Our theologizing must be concerned with public issues shaping our twenty-first-century world and which profoundly impact both the church and society. Critical theological approaches can also be foundational for a theology of prophetic anger given their commitment to prophetic discourse, liberatory action, community agency, and constant self-critique.[22] A theology of anger, which also prioritizes individual agency, demands that we keep ourselves honest about power dynamics and relations; that we keep one another accountable; and that we be aware of our own biases, social locations, privileges, and complicities. A theology of prophetic anger requires space and opportunities for open and honest conversations about what makes us angry, what riles us up. They will be safe, nonjudgmental spaces, outcome-oriented, with structured facilitating leadership.

The setting is ripe for a theology of anger in Oceania, especially with the issues of climate justice and economic exploitation being high on the social justice agenda. Pacific Island church leaders know about prophetic leadership, and a theology of prophetic anger approach will help rekindle the drive to utilize their religious influence and political power in the islands for the common good. In the case of New Zealand and Australia, the underlying issues of power dynamics and relationships are played out in the historical mainline churches' ministry with Indigenous and migrant communities. New Zealand is doing well in these areas primarily because both *Maori* and Pacific Island communities have prioritized equipping their own for high-competence bicultural leadership, with the strong support of ecclesial and state agencies at local and national levels. A theology of prophetic anger will enrich and enhance those efforts and will help in the Australian context to focus church and community energy in the same way.

Looking to the future, the unprecedented growth of the Christian faith in China within the last half-century, even under moments of extreme repression, means that in a few years, China will be home to the biggest Christian population in the world. China is well on the way to being the biggest economy in the world, and it is an indispensable player in world geopolitics. Are we ready for the real potential that China could become the new center of global Christianity given the possibilities that it presents spiritually, economically, and politically? A theology of prophetic anger conversations around power dynamics and relationships will help uncover some of the inherent biases and prejudices that get in the way of world Christians doing the work to be ready for this possibility. The racist arrogance I see in the way some Western

---

21. Ramachandra, *Subverting*, 13.
22. Schweitzer, "Intersecting," 331.

media and politicians relate to China is appalling and politically unwise. No one can pretend that there aren't issues of concern about China, but there is the gospel instruction that one should remove the beam from one's eye first.[23] A theology of prophetic anger will help Western Christians promote a more respectful prophetic approach in their respective public spaces. This is a legitimate concern given that parts of Oceania are caught up in the middle of the geopolitical tensions among global superpowers.

Malcolm X was reported as once saying: "Usually when people are sad, they don't do anything. They just cry over their condition. But when they get angry, they bring about a change." An underlying root cause for anger that makes a *theology of prophetic anger* critical is that far too often, in the way power dynamics work in our relationships, the one being dehumanized is blamed for the situation that dehumanizes them. This must stop!

BIBLIOGRAPHY

Bevans, Stephen B., and Katalina Tahaafe-Williams, eds. *Contextual Theology for the Twenty-First Century*. Eugene, OR: Pickwick, 2011.

Cone, James H. *A Black Theology of Liberation*. New York: Orbis, 1986.

De La Torre, Miguel, and Stacey M. Floyd-Thomas. *Beyond the Pale: Reading Theology form the Margins*. Louisville: Westminster John Knox, 2011.

Eatwell, Roger, and Matthew Goodwin. *National Populism: The Revolt Against Liberal Democracy*. Milton Keynes, UK: Pelican, 2018.

Fabella, Virginia, and R. S. Sugirtharajah, eds. *The SCM Dictionary of Third World Theologies*. London: SCM, 2003.

Freston, Paul. "Afterword." In *Encyclopedia of Christianity in the Global South*, edited by Mark A. Lamport, 945. 2 vols. Lanham, MD: Rowman & Littlefield, 2018.

Heinrichs, Steve, ed. *Unsettling the Word: Biblical Experiments in Decolonization*. Manitoba: Mennonite Church Canada, 2018.

Lamport, Mark A. "Preface." In *Encyclopedia of Christianity in the Global South*, . 2 vols. Lanham, MD: Rowman & Littlefield, 2018.

Maxwell, David. "Afterword." In *Encyclopedia of Christianity in the Global South*, edited by Mark A. Lamport, 951. 2 vols. Lanham, MD: Rowman & Littlefield, 2018.

Ramachandra, Vinoth. *Subverting Global Myths: Theology and the Public Issues Shaping our World*. Downers Grove, IL: IVP Academic, 2008.

Reddy, G. Anthony. *Nobodies to Somebodies: A Practical Theology for Education and Liberation*. Peterborough: Epworth, 2003.

Ross, Kenneth R., et al, eds. *Christianity in Oceania*. Edinburgh Companions to Global Christianity. Edinburgh: Edinburgh University, 2021.

Schweitzer, Don, and Derek Simon. *Intersecting Voices: Critical Theologies in a Land of Diversity*. Ottawa: Novalis, 2004.

Welby, Justin. "Afterword." In *Encyclopedia of Christianity in the Global South*, edited by Mark A. Lamport, 953. 2 vols. Lanham, MD: Rowman & Littlefield, 2018.

Yang, Fenggang. "Afterword." In *Encyclopedia of Christianity in the Global South*, edited by Mark A. Lamport, 957. 2 vols. Lanham, MD: Rowman & Littlefield, 2018.

---

23. Matt 7: 5.

CHAPTER 37

Diasporic Reflective Essay

A Theological Reflection on Diaspora Consciousness

KEUN-JOO CHRISTINE PAE

The term "diaspora" evokes unexplainable sorrow, antagonized feelings, and nostalgia for something lost or forgotten. Homelessness, uprootedness, and tragedies paint the images of people of diasporas when I think of them. Diaspora often indicates the forced "dispersion" of people from their homelands owing in part to war, violence, poverty, political corruption, and climate change. Since I was not dispersed from my homeland South Korea when I left there more than twenty years ago, it took me a long time to picture myself in the Asian diaspora. At that time, I was an international student who pursued an advanced degree in Christian theology and ethics at an Ivy League university. I chose to leave the country for a better opportunity. However, as my days in the United States turned to years, I was disillusioned by the "better" options that this country could offer for a person like me who is marginalized and invisible. My cultural, social, and racial marginalization stems from transpacific migration—geopolitical and metaphorical uprootedness.

Like many diasporic subjects, I have lived in between and betwixt spaces, negotiating multiple legal institutions, the political climate in various places, foreign policies, various cultures, inter- and intra-religious diversity, and racial politics "here" and "there." Here and there have been interchangeable in my life. Even if I physically live in the United States, central Ohio in particular, my home still seems to lie over "there" on the east coast of South Korea. For the past twenty years, I have never overcome feelings of alienation or not-belonging "here (the US)." Simultaneously, I do not belong there, either. Although I insist my spiritual, cultural, physical, and even political belonging to South Korea (there), Korean society pushes me to the margin. I am pejoratively called a black-haired foreigner in Korea who takes advantage of Korea's universal health care system and social welfare. A physical, social, and cultural distance between South Korea and me eventually woke me to diasporic consciousness. Discomfort from the discrepancy between a physical home and a spiritual/metaphoric/symbolic home is part of my everyday life. At the same time, I see a new world or horizon emerging from a mysterious space of transformation, in-between space—*nepantla* or the borderland, namely in-between space.[1]

How can a diasporic subject live without losing her sense of personhood or meaning of life? As a Christian social ethicist by academic training, I often ask this question because ethics is a series of questions about how one should live. In a diasporic context, I meditate on how diasporic subjects hold their integrity living in multiple institutions, cultures, and fragmented spaces. My meditation first begins with the typologies and biblical meanings of diasporas. Then, imaginatively traveling through different borders, historical moments, and spaces, I delineate border crossing, colonial and imperial diasporas, and home where a diasporic consciousness arises. This essay imaginatively, interreligiously, and interspiritually weaves diverse stories and images of diasporas from the US-Mexican border, Japan, and South Korea to search for a liberative diasporic consciousness.

FRAMING DIASPORA

Marin Bauman's short essay "Exile" differentiates exile from diaspora. While both terms of exile and diaspora have biblical origins of Jewish experiences of displacement, exile refers to forced geopolitical and physical displacement generally caused by a nation-state.[2] In addition, exile is seldom associated with "religious connotations or sentiments" such as soteriological imagination that God will call all of God's dispersed children on earth and save them.[3] Here, exile and diaspora, the two related concepts, suggest that a diaspora discourse moves beyond physical and political displacement. If "exile" throws critical light on people's lived experiences of displacement often by a nation-state, "diaspora" includes the spiritual, emotional, cultural, and symbolic interpretations of those experiences and their transnational and intergenerational impact.

Robin Cohen's now-classic text, *Global Diasporas*, introduces five categories of historic diasporas: victim, labor, trade, imperial, and cultural diasporas.[4] As the name suggests, a victim diaspora indicates "the catastrophic tradition of diaspora" caused by war, famine, genocide, and natural disaster.[5] Labor and trade diasporas signify political and economic power differentials among diasporic subjects as the latter describes

1. Anzaldúa, *Light in the Dark/Luz En Lo Oscuro*, 28.
2. Bauman, "Exile," 23.
3. Bauman, "Exile," 23.
4. Cohen, *Global Diasporas*, x.
5. Cohen, *Global Diasporas*, xi.

ethnic entrepreneurship, while the former usually represents indentured laborers' experiences. A cultural diaspora shows the formation of postcolonial, hybridized, and fragmented identities of diasporic subjects such as the Caribbean peoples. An individual and an ethnic group may experience multiple forms of diasporas simultaneously and change the characters of diasporas. Take, for example, Jews, who showed a victim diaspora. They were periodically successful in trade and commerce through their diasporic history (trade and labor diaspora) and now evince "a high degree of cosmopolitanism appropriate" to the global age (cultural diaspora).

Similarly, at the turn of the twentieth century, the first mass transpacific diasporas of East Asians, including my people Koreans, represent a labor and trade diaspora. However, Asian American studies scholars point out that transpacific migration is inseparable from the historical intimacy between the Japanese and US empires. For example, the indenture of Koreans in the Americas at the turn of the twentieth century is easily categorized as a labor diaspora. Still, they were victims of poverty and Japanese annexation of Korea, similar to the Irish diaspora during the potato famine in the nineteenth century (victim diaspora). Furthermore, as Korean American sociologist Grace M. Cho argues, the Korean diaspora has been haunted by the transpacific migration of Western princesses (*yanggongju*), who sexually catered to American soldiers stationed in Korea since World War II.[6] The collective memories of the Korean War (1950–1953) associated with shame, guilt, and trauma which Western princesses embody are deeply ingrained in the Korean diaspora, particularly in the transpacific space.[7] Thus, to trace a shared consciousness among diasporic subjects, Cohen's typology would be most helpful if the complexities and heterogeneity among diasporic subjects and their experiences were considered.

VULNERABILITY OF TRANSNATIONAL/TRANSBORDER MIGRATION

Maria Mesa, a thirty-nine-year-old Honduran mother of five, had walked for months to get to the US-Mexican border in Tijuana. Taking five children with her on the foot journey from Central America to North America, Mesa desired to reunite with her husband living in Louisiana in the US.[8] Mesa's family was part of the so-called Central American caravan, who fled political turmoil, armed conflict, and abject poverty in their home countries. Yet, the term "caravan," originated from a North African and Western Asian group of merchants traveling through deserts, and does not limn the

---

6. See Cho, *Haunting the Korean Diaspora*.

7. According to the records from the US Embassy in Korea in 1988, a statistical average of fifteen relatives followed every military bride to the United States. Most Korean GI wives from the 1950s to the 1980s were Western princesses. These women are the backbone of Korean American communities in major US cities. See Yuh, *Beyond the Shadow of Camptown*, 109.

8. Gutierrez and Siemaszko, "Photographer Reveals Story behind Iconic Image of Fleeing Migrants at Mexico Border."

dispersion of Central and South Americans whose survivability is precarious here and there. Indeed, they do not travel for trading goods.

Kyung-Hoon Kim is a South Korean based in Tokyo, Japan, photographing for Reuters. In 2018, he started journeying with caravans from Mexico City to the San Ysidro crossing linking Tijuana, Mexico, to San Diego, United States. Kim captured the photo of Mesa and her five-year-old twin daughters fleeing fanatically smoking tear gas fired by US border protection agents in November of 2018. They were among the peaceful protesters marching along the Mexican side of border walls. Kim's photo brought international attention to the Trump administration's brutal immigration policy, indiscriminately attacking border crossers, including Mesa's children, as if they were criminals, terrorists, and threats to US security.[9]

Border crossing does not simply signify physical movements but also legal movements from one sovereignty to another. While crossing borders, diasporic subjects, such as Mesa and her children, must pass through multiple geopolitical and legal institutions and successfully prove them harmless to the communities where they permanently or temporarily stay. Legal, political, and economic vulnerability is not equally distributed among diasporic subjects. Mesa's life-and-death situation at the US-Mexican border is incompatible with the experiences of tourists or trade diasporas. If prematurely developed, the notions of cosmopolitanism and global citizenship would romanticize transnational movements, excluding Central American caravans' experiences, and fail to interrogate the complexities of the victim and labor diasporas.

Mesa and her children in the smokey borderland visualize what Gloria Anzaldúa lamented, "The U.S.-Mexican border *es una herida abierta* where the Third World grates against the first and bleeds."[10] Transborder migration, particularly for poor Third World women, is dangerous—death and violence are ubiquitous. In part, the danger is caused by their non-belonging status: they do not belong to any sovereign nations. Mesa could not belong to Honduras because the Honduran government does not or cannot protect poor women and landless farmers. She belongs neither to Mexico nor to the US. Non-belonging means no systematic or institutional protection. Hence, non-belongers cannot prove their harmlessness to others. Their survival depends only on global citizens of conscience or good Samaritans on the road.

COLONIAL AND IMPERIAL DIASPORAS

To a certain extent, Kyung-hoon Kim is a diasporic subject. Since I do not have Kim's biographic information, I do not know whether he is a temporary resident or a *zainichi* Korean in Japan. Nonetheless, Kim's physical location in Tokyo reminds me of *zainichi* Koreans. Along with Korean Chinese (*Joseonjok*) and *Goryeoin* in Central Asia and Russia, *zainichi* Koreans embody a tragic chapter of Korean history. All these Korean

9. Specia and Gladstone, "Border Agents Shot Tear Gas into Mexico. Was It Legal?"
10. Anzaldúa, *Borderlands La Frontera*, 25.

diasporas, as well as those in the Americas, happened at the turn of the twentieth century when Euro-American empires colonized 90 percent of the world. At that time, imperial Japan arose as an Asian-Pacific superpower and prepared its annexation of Korea after it had won the Sino-Japanese War (1894–1895) and the Russo-Japanese War (1904–1905). Both wars were fought in the Korean peninsula. Korean diasporas during this period provoke in ethnic Koreans across the globe feelings of sorrow as we collectively remember Japanese colonialism followed by the Korean War. *Zainichi* Koreans illuminate the colonial and imperial impact on diasporas and thus, help us decolonize diasporas.

Zainichi Koreans are usually defined as Korean emigrants and their descendants from colonial Korea who remained in Japan after their country's liberation.[11] Over two million Koreans lived in Japan at the end of World War II, primarily representing labor and victim diasporas. Many of these Koreans were draftees by the Japanese colonial government and were forced to fill the labor shortage in Japan at the height of the Pacific War. After the country won independence in 1945, as many as 1.4 million Koreans were repatriated to Korea.[12] However, Koreans' journey back home was deadly. After a mysterious explosion, the Ukishima, the first Japanese ship carrying Korean laborers and their families to Korea, sank in the Maizuru Gulf near Kyoko.[13] Between five thousand and eight thousand Koreans died.[14] Survivors from the Ukishima and victims' families still demand that the Korean and Japanese governments thoroughly investigate the Ukishima incident.

Japanese Korean American scholar Sonia Ryang summarizes the multiple stages of *zainichi* Koreans' transformation: "first as colonial immigrants, then as stateless people, and more recently, as permanent residents with cultural and economic roots built in Japan and with little to no possibility of returning to their ancestral homes in Korea."[15] This transformation from living in "colonial metropolis to postcolonial temporary station" or from an unwelcoming place to an adopted home reflects *zainichi*

---

11. Jang, "Special Permanent Residents in Japan: Zainichi Korean," 1–2. The Japanese government does not distinguish post-World War II Korean immigrants from colonial immigrants.

12. Between 1939 and 1945 during the height of the Pacific War, imperial Japan sent roughly two million Korean civilians overseas: 200,000 soldiers, 200,000 civilian employees of the military, 720,000 forced laborers, 300,000 members of the volunteer labor corps, 80,000–200,000 comfort women, and 500,000 agricultural laborers in Manchuria. See Pae, "Factory Girls, Comfort Girls," 115.

13. Kim, "Underwater Monument to Be Set Up in Memory of Ukishima Victims."

14. Lee, "Survivors of the Ukishima." The Japanese government officially announced that 3,785 boarded on the Ukishima, but the survivors of the Ukishima claimed that more than 7,500 people sailed on the ship and more than 5,000 died. They also argue that it is unclear who exploded the ship. No official investigation of the Ukishima explosion has been conducted. In 1999, the underwater monument in remembrance of Ukishima victims was erected by the committee of Koreans who demanded truth about the Ukishima incident (See Kim, "Underwater Monument to Be Set Up in Memory of Ukishima Victims").

15. Ryang, "Space and Time," 522.

Koreans' life caught in between Japan and Korea.[16] To be sure, the *zainichi* Koreans are not a homogeneous group. Yet, their lives mirror Korea-Japan relations, South Korea's economic development, global sanctions on North Korea, and Japan's political economy. For instance, *zainichi* Koreans were stateless people until 1965, when South Korea and Japan reestablished the diplomatic relationship. In 1964, the total *zainichi* population was approximately 580,000, including eight thousand originally from northern Korea.[17] The 1965 Basic Treaties between Korea and Japan protected the legal status of *zainichi* Koreans by allowing them to get South Korean nationality to apply for permanent residency in Japan. However, most *zainichi* Koreans opted out of the opportunity mainly for two reasons. First, they saw the separation between North and South Koreas as temporary. Second, the oppressive American military authorities in Japan disillusioned *zainichi* Koreans about the American military-controlled South Korea. As a result, they supported nationalist socialism and favored the North Korean regime until the 1980s.[18] Today, approximately thirty thousand pro-North Korea *zainichi* Koreans remain stateless.[19] For the past thirty years, more and more *zainichi* Koreans, especially third- and fourth-generation Koreans, have pursued naturalization as they started critically reflecting on ethnicity separate from nationality.[20] These ethnic Koreans in Japan represent a cultural diaspora. At first, they did not belong to either Korea or Japan but now embrace both Korean and Japanese identities without splitting them over two national and political entities.

While most *zainichi* Koreans have been excluded from Japanese society living in impoverished ghettos for a century, many Japanese settlers in Korea made a fortune in Japan's newly acquired territory during the colonial period. By 1945, over 700,000 Japanese civilians had settled in Korea. They were "merchants, traders, prostitutes, journalists, teachers, and continental adventurers who, in remaking their lives on the peninsula, also helped to make their nation's empire."[21] Japanese in Korea were a mixture of the middle and lower class in their home country but did not experience racial/ethnic discrimination or lived in impoverished ghettos in Korea. Of course, some of them did not make a fortune in Korea. These Japanese expatriates could be considered victims of Japanese colonialism and war. When the Japanese empire collapsed, they were re-displaced in Japan, leaving their properties in Korea, and have lived in "self-imposed silence or kept their memories private, out of shame or fear of association with [their nation's] militarist past."[22]

---

16. Ryang, "Space and Time," 522.
17. Ryang, "Space and Time," 524.
18. Ryang, "Space and Time," 525.
19. Jang, "Special Permanent Residents in Japan," 4–5.
20. Jang, "Special Permanent Residents in Japan," 7–8.
21. Uchida, *Brokers of Empire*, 3.
22. Uchida, *Brokers of Empire*, 5.

My mind over Kyung-hoon Kim's photo of Mesa travels through the Pacific Ocean and moves beyond time and space. Particular experiences of varied diasporic subjects reflect the complex layers of domestic and international politics. These subjects reveal complex power relations among their (ancestral) homelands, and between host communities and expatriates. Yet, I wonder whether a diasporic consciousness as the spirit of solidarity can emerge among diasporas even in historical conflict (i.e., Japanese diaspora and Korean diaspora) just as Kim felt an instant connection to Mesa. I also wonder how Koreans felt during Japanese colonialism as they lived diasporic lives in their homeland, similar to Native Americans in North America and Palestinians in Palestine.

DIASPORIC CONSCIOUSNESS FROM HOME TO HOME

What is home? Where is home? A diaspora discourse raises questions about a home. Home is a heavily loaded word. On the one hand, it arouses feelings of nostalgia, warmth, comfort, and utopia. On the other hand, as feminist scholars point out, home is a dangerous space for many women and children where they experience domestic violence, patriarchal gender hierarchy, and exploitation. From a postcolonial perspective, feminist theologian Kwok Pui-lan reminds us that home is not simply a private sphere but intersects with "national identity, ethnicity, citizenship, law, and women's rights."[23] Kwok's critical point is especially true in the diasporic and postcolonial context filled with dangerous transborder migration, war, violence, hybridized culture and ethnicity, and so forth. A so-called homeland could have been full of miseries, deaths, violence, and discrimination. Many dangers of diasporas seen through Mesa and *zainichi* Koreans are the ongoing legacy of colonialism. So is the internal displacement of Native Americans, many Chicanas and Mexican Americans, and Palestinians. In the meantime, feminist scholars have warned of the danger of ethnocentric nationalist nostalgia for a precolonial society. Even when the postcolonial world does not seem to give homes back to diasporic subjects, how can they construct homes materially and metaphorically? How would they forge a diasporic consciousness accentuating liberation from fears and interdependence among all living beings? Concluding this essay, I meditate on the home as a way to search for a liberative diasporic consciousness.

Just as Gloria Anzaldúa compares herself to a turtle that carries home on its back, Kwok states that "home is not a fixed and stable location but a traveling adventure, which entails seeking refuge in strange lands, bargaining for survival, and negotiating for existence."[24] These feminist reflections on home revolve around how diasporic subjects hold their integrity while living in multiple institutions, cultures, fragmented spaces, or simply *nepantla*. In her posthumous book, *Light in the Dark*,

---

23. Kwok, *Postcolonial Imagination and Feminist Theology*, 101.
24. Anzaldua, *Borderlands*, 43, 102.

Gloria Anzaldúa notes that *nepantla* is the Nahuatl word for an in-between space similar to "liminal space" where the constant transformation of the self happens.[25] *Nepantla* is the connective tissue and bridge between the material and the immaterial and between ordinary and spirit realities.[26] Soul work, imagination, and creative work in *nepantla* cross over multiple times and spaces. Finally, we can see that the self is one of the many members and imaginal figures. For Anzaldúa, spirituality or soul work connects different forms of consciousness and realities—a different kind and way of knowing.[27] Anzaldúa's understanding of the self is possible only with in-depth empathy, as seen in Zen master Thich Nhat Hanh's poem, "Please, Call Me by My True Name." In the poem, "I" takes multiple forms: a bud on a Spring branch, a frog, a hungry boney boy in Uganda, a refugee girl who threw herself to the ocean after being raped by a sea pirate, and a sea pirate.[28] Radical empathy and deep compassion for all suffering beings are cultivated through Zen meditation and Mahayana Buddhist teachings of emptiness and interbeing/interdependence. The Mahayana Buddhist notion of emptiness does not mean nothingness or a nihilistic approach to life. Instead, emptiness illuminates the quintessence of beings beyond languages and perceptions, the necessity of being liberated from false selfhood to end suffering, and enlightenment to the realities of interbeings—all forms of lives are interconnected. In emptiness, all forms of lives radically embrace one another despite their conflicted relations, chaotic co-dependency, love, compassion, etc. For me, emptiness is where everything begins and where everything ends. Theologically speaking, a God incarnated through the form of Jesus can be compared to emptiness.

A diasporic consciousness emerges when the "I" consciously resides in between a physical sense of home (the materially concrete context) and an imagined, symbolic, and metaphorical home (emptiness and interconnectedness). Diasporic subjects' understanding of their integrity and personhood is formed in a healthy tension between a geopolitical home and a symbolic home. If a geopolitical home indicates where "I" am physically located, a symbolic home is to where "my" desires and longing for wholeness and liberation from fears will carry "me." Hence, one's inner transformation and spiritual work cannot be separated from the outer-worldly changes for justice. Prolonged turmoil at a physical home in the concrete geopolitical context would enable diasporic subjects to critically apprehend the meanings of home, security, peace, and justice. Although politically vulnerable subjects' epistemic privilege of knowing God's peace and justice should be recognized and respected, political economic crisis and turmoil should not be justified on a spiritual level. Injustice and oppression are generally harmful to diasporic subjects' livelihood and personhood.

---

25. Anzaldúa, *Light in the Dark/Luz En Lo Oscuro*, 28–29.
26. Anzaldúa, *Light in the Dark/Luz En Lo Oscuro*, 28.
27. Anzaldúa, *Light in the Dark/Luz En Lo Oscuro*, 38.
28. Thich Nhat Hanh, "Please, Call Me by My True Name."

Finally, let us consider how to build up a diasporic consciousness. If diasporas involve creative, cultural, and symbolic meanings of home, self-referentiality can be an entry point to diasporic discourse but cannot represent diasporas. Yet, diverse diasporas create multiple contact zones here and there with historical specificities and beyond particular times and spaces. My understanding of diasporic consciousness relies on Kwok's elaboration on diasporic imagination. To signify diasporic imagination, Kwok proposes the image of the storyteller:

> [W]ho selects pieces, fragments, and legends from her cultural and historical memory to weave together tales that are passed from generation to generation. These tales are refashioned and retold in each generation, with new materials added, to face new circumstances and to reinvent the identity of a people.[29]

As a diasporic subject, I am a storyteller. One's identity, the identity of a people, and desires for home and rootedness are shaped by stories—what stories are told and retold, how these stories are told, and who tells the stories. Telling stories requires me to be accountable to myself and multiple diasporic subjects. Telling diasporic stories involves creative nonfiction writing—I am telling certain truths about dispersion and painful displacement with accountability beyond my lived experience. As Kwok elaborates, a diasporic consciousness "finds similarities and differences in both familiar territories and unexpected corners; one catches glimpses of oneself in a fleeting moment or in a fragment in someone else's story."[30] I interweave my diasporic stories with the stories from the Ukishima, Western princesses, Central American caravans, and *zainichi* Koreans as I see myself in fleeting moments of their lives. These stories teach me how to live with integrity in fragmented spaces, telling me who I am and to whom I should be held accountable.

BIBLIOGRAPHY

Anzaldúa, Gloria. *Borderlands/La Frontera: The New Mestiza*. San Francisco: Aunt Lute, 2007.

———. *Light in the Dark/Luz En Lo Oscuro: Rewriting Identity, Spirituality, Reality*. Edited by Ana Louise Keating. Durham, NC: Duke University Press, 2015.

Bauman, Eric. "Exile." In *Diasporas: Concepts, Intersections, Identities*, edited by Kim Knott and Seán McLoughlin, 19–23. London: Zed, 2013.

Cho, Grace M. *Haunting the Korean Diaspora: Shame, Secrecy, and the Forgotten War*. Minneapolis: University of Minnesota Press, 2008.

Cohen, Robin. *Global Diasporas: Introduction*. Repr. London: Routledge, 2008.

Gutierrez, Gabe, and Corky Siemaszko. "Photographer Reveals Story behind Iconic Image of Fleeing Migrants at Mexico Border." *NBC News*, November 26, 2018. https://www.nbcnews.com/news/us-news/photographer-reveals-story-behind-iconic-photo-fleeing-migrants-mexico-border-n940271.

---

29. Kwok, *Postcolonial Imagination and Feminist Theology*, 46.
30. Kwok, *Postcolonial Imagination and Feminist Theology*, 50.

Jang, Hawon. "Special Permanent Residents in Japan: Zainichi Korean." *The Yale Review of International Studies*, 2019. http://yris.yira.org/comments/2873.

Kim, Min-hee. "Underwater Monument to Be Set Up in Memory of Ukishima Victims." *The Korea Herald,* August 12, 1999. https://advance-lexis-com.denison.idm.oclc.org/api/document?collection=news&id=urn:contentItem:3X62-9K60-007K-G16X-00000-00&context=1516831.

Kwok, Pui-lan. *Postcolonial Imagination and Feminist Theology*. Louisville: Westminster John Knox, 2005.

Lee, Jae-ho. "Survivors of the Ukishima: Find Truth before We All Die." *Hangyerei 21*, August 13, 2019. https://h21.hani.co.kr/arti/cover/cover_general/47457.html.

Pae, Keun-joo Christine. "Factory Girls, Comfort Girls: A Feminist Theo-Ethical Reflection on Korean Girl Soldiers in Japanese Empire." In *Female Child Soldiering, Gender Violence, and Feminist Theologies*, edited by Susan Willhauck, 109–22. New York: Palgrave Macmillan, 2019.

Ryang, Sonia. "Space and Time: The Experience of the 'Zainishi,' The Ethnic Korean Population of Japan." *Urban Anthropology and Studies of Cultural Systems and World Economic Development* 43 (2014) 519–50.

Specia, Megan, and Rick Gladstone. "Border Agents Shot Tear Gas into Mexico. Was It Legal?" *New York Times*, November 28, 2018. https://www.nytimes.com/2018/11/28/world/americas/tear-gas-border.html.

Thich Nhat Hanh. "Please, Call Me by My True Name." Plum Village, June 2020. https://plumvillage.org/articles/please-call-me-by-my-true-names-song-poem/.

Uchida, Jun. *Brokers of Empire: Japanese Settler Colonialism in Korea, 1876–1945*. Cambridge: Harvard University Press, 2014.

Yun, Ji-Yeon. *Beyond the Shadow of Camptown: Korean Military Brides in America*. New York: New York University Press, 2002.

AFTERWORD

CHLOË STARR

This important and long-awaited cornucopia of theologies presents a joyful abundance of ideas, truths, and visions of God. For those of us in the former Christian heartland of North America, it also offers a corrective and a challenge. Many of us who studied theology even in the twenty-first century followed an arc from Augustine through Anselm and Aquinas to Barth and Bultmann. Not only did we not proceed very far in the alphabet, but our readings, and so our theological visions, were heavily skewed by gender, country and language of origin, historical period, and a series of other trammels. This much we understood and applauded the classmates and predecessors who called for greater inclusion of voices, more women scholars, more non-European voices. But it has taken longer—and more recent student movements such as calls to "decolonize the syllabus"—for us to begin to grasp other limitations of our theological education, including its implicit epistemological hegemonies.

The exciting breadth and diversity of theological insights and methodologies in this volume invites an immediate expansion of our horizons, an awareness of some of the great riches of thinking and of perception in different languages, areas of the world, and ways of existence. It enables students and educators to deepen their grasp of God and extend or revitalize a syllabus. But it does more than open up a syllabus: it also prizes open cracks in our structures of theological education. These theologies offer an expansion not just of content, or of peoples and voices, of who is doing the theology, but of form also. *How* do we teach these multiple theologies set out in this volume? *What* do we do with the critique of our teaching and examination modes that some of these theologies bring, with their basis in oral or experiential modes? And *when* will the correctives that these essays demand be reflected in our seminaries and divinity schools, where these theologies are not always present in core systematics courses, but, if they exist at all, offered as electives in Asian-American theology or as part of a world Christianity course that might survey everything from Minjung to moana?

Some of these theologies are emergent. Some are long established, or part of churches that have existed for over a millennium in India or China. For the greater part, what is emergent is our (Western) awareness of their existence and understanding of their value and their claim on our attention. As the theologies are afforded more prominence, an appreciation grows of our complicity in our own North American centeredness—while often still believing that the teaching we provide or proclaim is universal in scope. These are truly global theologies. The term Global South may be convenient, but it is also deeply problematic as a marker of difference to signal to a (rich, northern) audience. It reflects neither a geographical nor economic reality—see for example, the inclusion of Sami, Korean or Chinese theologies—nor the self-designation of most of those writing. The "global south" is stretched by the inclusion of indigenous voices and diasporic writers from North America and elsewhere in the so-called first world, and evolves here from a metaphor for "the rest of the world" to a concept of under-representation, a methodological marker of minoritization, and of inequality.

One of the first gains of this volume for those of us in the "north" is a turn of the lens. While the history of Christianity and theology in many of the nations, peoples and cultures included here has been presented to us historically from a missionary perspective, or through the lens of mission history (an external, ethnographic view), here we listen to the voices of scholars and theologians from the lands and people groups they are representing. These are not just liberative voices, extricating their own thinking from Western or colonial frameworks or reappraising Western ideas for their own purposes. All theology is contextual (even if we have often thought of "contextual theology" as that done by others, outside Western canons). We do not merely each do our own theology for ourselves from within our contexts, but all theologies speak to each other and push back against mis-readings of God and humanity. The lens here is frequently focused back on the West, a corrective lens that sharpens our own vision. As Te Aroha Rountree writes, the moana people "have been romanticized and exoticized through histories of European encounter for centuries." This now is a period of corrective: a time to listen, to absorb, to change.

The first liberation that the theologies perform is therefore a release from other people's agendas. As postcolonial critiques have taught, the subject must shape the discourse, and be able to sense, and remove, the imposition of someone else's situatedness on scholarship. To take an example: histories of the bible in China have been histories of the work of missionary translation teams, not histories of the reception of the message or its transformation into story and song—or even of the Chinese co-workers on those teams, whose input was critical to the quality of language and expression of each Bible edition. Central to this volume is the liberation from the form and shape of inherited theologies. Several essays foreground epistemological dialogues, that de-center Western ways of knowing, in line with post- and decolonial understandings. The official church may catch up slowly. For cultures that use dance as a form of conveying narrative, a sacred dance may equate to the reading of a passage of Scripture. It was in the 1990s that the Hawai'ian hula dance was recognized as sacred, and Roman Catholic authorities authorized its use in church celebrations, as Rountree notes. Metaphors of life through which God is apprehended only make fuller sense to those who inhabit them, who grasp and draw out their meaning—so it is natural that when life is water-based, as for certain Pacific or South-East Asian communities, their theologies use waterways and oceanic imagery as a source for knowing God. Many essays in the volume recognise the reality that the church in various parts of the world has suffered for long periods of time from a lack of access to formal theological training, or even to priests and ministers, and yet the Spirit has continued to teach and inspire new theological developments.

Certain themes and readings recur across the different sections of the book. Biographical and narrative theologies abound in this global theology, from the Pacific to Taiwan to Ghana, as journeys from the self outwards deflect the long imposition of others' readings. Writers are also freed from a particular, or a unimodal identity. As Peter Lodberg's essay on Palestinian contextual theology shows, multiple and overlapping belongings may shape a theology, as the small Palestinian church engages ecumenically and in inter-faith relationships with the Muslim neighbors with whom it shares a national identity. As numerous recent studies, especially of Pentecostal Christianities, have shown, in cultures where Christianity is a minority faith or coexists with older religious expressions, religious identities may be accretive, and indigenous religions may shape Christian practices in different ways as the religion develops. Despite all too many nineteenth-century missionary attempts to stamp out cultural expressions that they did not recognize, or deemed pagan, the Christianity that is thriving in Korea, in East Africa, in Mongolia and elsewhere may draw elements of shamanist or animist practices into its own worship and prayer life or reflect local cosmologies and kinship patterns in its theological life.

The reclamation and recollection of pre-Christian ways emerges in various aspects of the theologies covered here, with one of the most important and critical for our moment being in the retrieval of ecological worldviews and spiritual practices. A core theme running throughout the essays this reclamation of older spiritualities that predate the Victorian mission heyday which coincided with industrialization and a mindset of dominating the land and extracting its goods. This move is both a recognition of the practical and deep wisdom of much indigenous teaching and lore, but also an affirmation of the theological claim that Christ was always present in lands and teachings before the missionary presence and proclamation. Theologies of the coconut tree of the I-Kiribati and other Pasifika peoples exemplify this, as Seforosa Carroll shows, with the tree a symbol of God's provision and presence, metaphor of incarnation and resurrection, and rallying point for a theology of resistance against destructive ways of living that fuel climate change. Agbonkhianmeghe Orobator's essay on theological ethics in a time of crisis likewise emphasizes the reverence for transcendence and sacramental reality in many sub-Saharan African worldviews, and the universe of spiritual meaning encapsulated in the term "ecology" that binds people into a relationship with the land. As the richer industrialized nations come to terms with the devastating effects of a lack of attachment to the land and the global legacy of their past expansionist greed, and the absence of a moral imperative towards nature that Orobator describes, along with and the concomitant impoverishment of spirituality, these theologies offer a resource and a truth-telling. The call to eco-missional living and understanding is a warning we must all heed, as we engage with the related theologies that emphasize corporate life and salvation over merely individual redemption.

If this volume represents a challenge to the imaginations of those of us in the old world, it also furnishes a chance to catch up with the realities of Christian growth and demographic change. As Harvey Kwiyani's essay discusses, in an age when only a third of Christians in the world are white Westerners, the task for mission and evangelism has been taken up by others Christian communities, many of whom regard Europe as in urgent need of re-evangelization. Brazil, South Korea, and India number among the top ten mission-sending countries in the world. The largest church in Europe is one in Kyiv led by a Nigerian pastor; the largest church in the United Kingdom is also led by a Nigerian pastor, a convert from Islam and the founder of a global television station that broadcasts into two hundred countries. Twenty-seven thousand missionaries from the Republic of Korea were serving abroad in 2020, almost always operating in second or third languages, attempting to leave a very light cultural footprint.

This volume presents a rich selection of essays, but it is only a selection, to invite further exploration and conversation. As Michelle Gonzalez's article on Latina feminist theology demonstrates, the diversity within groups and the contested nature of many of the labels attached to them cautions against overly simplified analyses. While many, for example, now take Latinx to be the standard term for Latino and Latina theologies, others denounce it as a linguistic aberration, or retain the term Hispanic, or reject any such pan-ethnic label in favor of a nation-of-origin appellation. For some, *mujerista* is a term to claim and celebrate, for others it erases the Latin American history of feminism. As Latin American theologians have developed theologies of *lo cotidiano* that connect the divine with the lived realities of daily and domestic life and foreground women's intellectual work in their construct, others have challenged their inclusivity with regard to queer communities. This volume presents a series of essays in a moment of time, but these underscore the dynamic nature of theologies. Whether in the description of the different stages of Palestinian theologies under occupation and displacement since the Nakba, or in the development of theological ethics as the Christian population of sub-Saharan Africa grew from 4 to 470 million over the last century, these theologies offer not just a corrective to the spatial concentrations of a "traditional" theological corpus, but to a temporal focus that has often privileged early church or medieval formulations and writings over the profusion of the present. As an anthology of living theologies, this selection gives a sense of the possibilities of the greater whole, and a starting point for the difficult work of discerning the connections and their implications for us.

One of the immediate gains of a global volume is the ready comparisons across regions and scholarships that are often pursued in isolation. There are evident connections between, for example, the Latin American diversity Gonzalez describes and issues of terminology in Asian American theologies. As Peter Phan notes, the designation "Asian" in the academic field uses a United States census bureau definition rather than, say, a United Nations one, thus excluding West and Central Asia. While "Asian" might be a useful term for creating solidarity and collective consciousness, it is a "fictitious" racial category (there is, as Phan notes, no Asian race) and its use as a race marker creates assumed commonalities between South and East Asian cultures, languages and peoples where none may exist. A shared experience of oppression or exploitation in the United States forms the basis for much theologizing among minoritized groups in America, but the work that is done employs very different cultural resources that might be alien to other linguistic groups within the same (hyphenated) group. Andrew Sung Park's work on *han*, for example, draws on a particular concept in Korean culture, while Jung Young Lee's writing on the Trinity in the light of Daoist metaphysics or Grace Ji-sun Kim's pneumatology that utilizes a framework of *qi* reference concepts with wider East Asian purchase. As Phan shows here and elsewhere in his work, there is much work still to be done within Asian American theologies, across the language and cultural barriers between Vietnamese, Filipino, and Chinese thinkers, in dialogues with Asia-based Asian theologies, as well as in broader inter multi-cultural theological work among difference racial and ethnic groups, especially the major streams of Latin American and African American thought. Frederick L. Ware's essay in the volume offers a starting point for naming common causes of justice and liberation for all minoritized groups in the United States from an African American perspective, and identifying parallel experiences among groups attempting to extricate themselves from distortions of Christianity brought through the systematic oppression of colonial systems and interest groups.

The book is a statement, and a starting point. The volume offers nothing less than a claim for a re-ordering of world theology. It offers the opportunity to augment our imagination, and as we listen to the stories, to hear the call to limit the claims of own cultural position. The emergence of multiple theologies across the world that are contending with the legacy of a Western heritage that has at times obscured the Christ it attempted to illuminate should not provoke a defensive response. As we celebrate an era of the truly global and the opening up and spectacular expansion of intellectual and spiritual horizons that the collection promises, we who operate from a position of privilege do need recognize the damage caused by the historic imposition of culturally inflected Western theologies on others as if they were the universal gospel itself, and reflect on our part in the continuance of any such harm. The haunting narratives of colonial dispossession and of "dislocated" theology, whether among Pacific Islanders or African Americans, witness to the terrible toll that our misunderstanding of God and God's word can cause. These witnesses help us to grasp the enormity of what has taken place in certain times and places, and to respond. We do so in a new era of relations between churches and academic institutions of theology across the globe, that the work of the scholarship showcased here has been foundational in bringing about. We can delight in the depths of insight that these global theologies bring to us all in the church worldwide, at the same time as acknowledging (and committing to?) the hard work that lies ahead.

About the Contributors

CONNIE AU (PhD, University of Birmingham, UK) is a part-time lecturer of the Ecclesial Theological Seminary in Hong Kong. She was one of the associate editors of *Brill's Encyclopedia of Global Pentecostalism* (2021).

RAIMUNDO C. BARRETO JR. (PhD, Princeton Theological Seminary) serves as associate professor of world Christianity at PTS and is general editor of the *World Christianity and Public Religion* series. His publications include *Evangélicos e Pobreza no Brasil: Encontros e Respostas* (2019) and the co-edited volume *Decolonial Christianities: Latin American and Latinx Perspectives* (2019).

ODJA BARROS (PhD, Escola Superior de Teologia) is Igreja Batista do Pinheiro in Maceió, Brazil and works at the Gender Research Center at Faculdades, Escola Superior de Teologia, São Leopoldo, Brazil.

ANA MARÍA BIDEGAIN (PhD, Catholic University, Leuven, Belgium) is a professor of Latin American religions at Florida International University. Her main research themes revolve around the history of Latin American Christianity and she has published in several languages.

ELIAS KIFON BONGMBA (PhD, University of Denver, The Iliff School of Theology), originally from Cameroon, holds the Harry and Hazel Chavanne Chair in Christian Theology and is professor and chair of the Department of Religion at Rice University, Houston. Bongmba is author of *African Witchcraft and Otherness: A Philosophical and Theological Analysis of Intersubjective Relations,* and editor of the *Routledge Handbook on African Theology.*

SEFOROSA CARROLL (PhD, Charles Sturt University, Australia) is programme executive for Mission from the Margins/Ecumenical Indigenous Peoples Network, World Council of Churches in Geneva. She is a contributor to *Christian Theology in an Age of Migration* (2020), *Contemporary Feminist Theologies: Power, Authority and Love* (2021), and *Afterlives: Jesus in Global Perspectives* (2022).

ALEXANDER CHOW—see biography in About Editors and Editorial Advisory Board on page xii.

GEMMA TULUD CRUZ (PhD, Radboud Universiteit, The Netherlands) and is senior lecturer in theology at Australian Catholic University. She is author of *Christianity Across Borders: Theology and Contemporary Issues in Global Migration* (2021), and editor of *Catholicism in Migration and Diaspora: Cross-Border Filipino Perspectives* (2022).

ELEAZAR S. FERNANDEZ (PhD, Vanderbilt University) is president of Union Theological Seminary, Philippines. Among his edited works are *Teaching in a World of Violent Extremism* (2021) and *Teaching in a Multifaith World* (2017).

JUDE LAL FERNANDO (PhD, Trinity College, Dublin) coordinates the MPhil in contextual theologies and interfaith relations programme in the School of Religion. He is the editor of *Faith in the Face of Militarization: Indigenous, Feminist and Interreligious Voices* (2021) and *Resistance to Empire and Militarization: Reclaiming the Sacred* (2020).

JOSÉ MARIO C. FRANCISCO, SJ (PhD, Graduate Theological Union, USA) is a professor at Ateneo de Manila University. His publications link Asian cultural and religious studies, the latest being *Between Celebration and Critique: Snapshots from 500 Years of Philippine Christianity* (2021).

MICHELLE A. GONZALEZ (MALDONADO) is dean of the College of Arts and Sciences at the University of Scranton and author of *A Critical Introduction to Religion in the Americas: Bridging the Liberation Theology and Religious Studies Divide* (2014).

SEBASTIAN KIM (PhD, University of Cambridge) is Robert Wiley Professor of Renewal in Public Life and academic dean for the Korean Studies Center at Fuller Theological Seminary, and is a fellow of the Royal Asiatic Society. His most recent books include *A History of Korean Christianity* (2015) and *Theology in the Public Sphere* (2011).

VOLKER KÜSTER (Dr. theol., Heidelberg; Dr. h.c., Lund) is professor of comparative religion and missiology at Johannes Gutenberg-Universität Mainz, Germany and author of *The Many Faces of Jesus Christ* (2001), *God/Terror* (2021), *A Protestant Theology of Passion* (2010), and *Zwischen Pancasila und Fundamentalismus* (2016).

HARVEY KWIYANI (PhD, Luther Seminary) is chief executive officer of Global Connections (formerly the Evangelical Mission Association) in England. He is also tutor in Pioneer Ministry at the Church Mission Society. He has published several books including *Sent Forth: African Missionary Work in the Wes* (2014) and *Multicultural Kingdom: Ethnic Diversity, Mission, and the Church* (2020).

CARMEN LANSDOWNE (PhD, Graduate Theological Union) is a Heiltsuk woman from the central coast of British Columbia and an ordained minister in the United Church of Canada. She is an adjunct professor in Indigenous and interreligious Studies at Vancouver School of Theology.

PETER LODBERG (PhD, dr. theol., Aarhus University) is professor in missiology and global theology at Aarhus University in Denmark. His main research topics focus on the relation of state and church, Christianity in the Middle East, ecumenical dialogue, and the importance of globalization for local churches.

LÉOCADIE LUSHOMBO, IT (PhD, Theological Ethics, Boston College) is assistant professor of theological ethics at the Jesuit School of Theology of Santa Clara University in Berkeley and the Catholic University in Congo. She recently published *The Politics of Forest Conservation: Ethical Dilemmas* and *Virtue-Based Just Peace Approach*.

SYLVIA MARCOS (Post-doctorate, Harvard Divinity School) is professor and chair of feminist theology at Universidad Iberoamericana, Mexico. Her recent publications include *Teología India: la Presencia de Dios en las Culturas. Entrevista con Don Samuel Ruiz*, 57 (2020) and "Reshaping Spirituality: Indigenous Decolonial Struggles for Justice in Mexico" in *CRL James Journal* (2021).

SAFWAT MARZOUK (PhD, Princeton Theological Seminary) is associate professor of Old Testament, Union Presbyterian Seminary, Richmond, Virginia. He is the author of *Egypt as a Monster in the Book of Ezekiel* and *Intercultural Church: A Biblical Vision for an Age of Migration*.

DAVID TONGHOU NGONG (PhD, Baylor University), from Cameroon, is professor and chair of the department of religion and theology at Stillman College in Tuscaloosa, Alabama. His research interest is in theology and African cultures and politics. He is editor of *A New History of African Christian Thought: From Cape to Cairo* (2017).

AGBONKHIANMEGHE E. OROBATOR, SJ (PhD, Theology, University of Leeds) is president of the Jesuit Conference of Africa and Madagascar. He is the author of *Religion and Faith in Africa: Confessions of an Animist* and *The Pope and the Pandemic: Lessons in Leadership in a Time of Crisis*.

KEUN-JOO CHRISTINE PAE (PhD, Union Theological Seminary, New York) is associate professor of religion/ethics and women's and gender studies (Denison University, Ohio) and has published on transnational feminist ethics of peace and spiritual activism, including "Spiritual Activism as Interfaith Dialogue: When Military Prostitution Matters" in *Journal of Feminist Studies in Religion* (2020).

About the Contributors

Anne Pattel-Gray (PhD, University of Sydney) is head of the School of Indigenous Studies at the University of Divinity, Melbourne Australia and spent over thirty years in senior management as a CEO in the NGO sector. Pattel-Gray is a descendant of the Bidjara/Kari Kari Nations in Queensland and an Aboriginal leader within Australia.

Peter C. Phan holds the Ignacio Ellacuría, SJ Chair of Catholic Social Thought at Georgetown University. He has earned three doctorates and received four honorary doctorates and is the first non-Anglo to be elected president of the Catholic Theological Society of America and of the American Theological Society. In 2020 he was given the John Courtney Murray Award, the highest honor of the Catholic Theological Society of America, in recognition for outstanding and distinguished achievement in theology.

Randall Prior (PhD, University of Divinity, Melbourne) has been a professor of mission studies at Pilgrim Theological College, and was previously on the faculty of United Theological Faculty (both in Australia). He is the author of *Contextualizing Theology in the South Pacific: The Shape of Theology in Oral Cultures*, published in the monograph series of the American Society of Missiology (2019).

Luis Rivera-Pagán (PhD, Yale University) is the Henry Winters Luce Professor of Ecumenics emeritus, Princeton Theological Seminary. Has published several books, among them are *Historia de la conquista de América: Evangelización y violencia* (2021) and *Essays from the Margins* (2014).

Viola Raheb (PhD, University of Vienna) is responsible for scientific communication and projects at Pro Oriente Foundation. She has published several books and articles, including "Conflict with the Old Testament about the Land" in *Christian Theology in the Palestinian Context* (2019), and is editor of *Latin Americans with Palestinian Roots* (2012).

Rudolph P. Reyes II (PhD, University of Denver/Iliff School of Theology) is instructor of Christian ethics and Latinx studies at Garrett Evangelical Theological Seminary. His most recent publication is "Beyond the Prophetic Temptation of Ecological Disgust" in *Gonna Trouble the Waters: Ecojustice, Water, and Environmental Racism* (2021).

Te Aroha Rountree (MA Hons, University of Auckland, New Zealand) is a descendant of the Ngai Tuteāuru and NgāPuhi tribes and senior lecturer in Māori/Moana studies at Trinity Theological College (Auckland), where she teaches mātauranga Māori and theological discourse. Her latest publication is "Jesus Does a Haka Boogie: Tangata Whenua Theology," in *Theologies from the Pacific* (2021).

Fernando F. Segovia—see biography in About Editors and Editorial Advisory Board on page xii.

About the Contributors

CHLOË STARR (DPhil, University of Oxford) is professor of Asian Christianity and theology at Yale Divinity School. Monographs include *Chinese Theology: Text and Context* (2016) and *Red-light Novels of the Late Qing* (2007).

MUTHURAJ SWAMY (PhD, University of Edinburgh) is director of the Cambridge Centre for Christianity Worldwide, and project manager for Theological Education for Mission in the Anglican Communion, London. He is author of *The Problem with Interreligious Dialogue: Plurality, Conflict and Elitism in Hindu-Christian-Muslim Relations* (2016) and *Reconciliation* (2019).

KATALINA TAHAAFE-WILLIAMS—see biography in About Editors and Editorial Advisory Board on page xii.

WAYNE TEKAAWA (PhD, University of Otago, New Zealand) is lecturer in Māori theology at University of Otago. His most recent publication is "A Gifted People: Māori and Pākehā Covenants within the Presbyterian Church" in *Mana Māori and Christianity* (2012).

FREDERICK. L. WARE (PhD, Vanderbilt University) is professor of theology and associate dean for academic affairs at Howard University School of Divinity in Washington, DC. He is author of *African American Theology: An Introduction* (2016) and co-editor of *T&T Clark Handbook of African American Theology* (2019).

Index of Names and Subjects

Aboriginal spirituality, 390
Accra Conference, 315
Achille Mbembe, *On the Postcolony*, 477
Adivasi theology, 185–86
Adviata, 179
aesthetics, 61
African Cry, 324
African Methodist Episcopal Zion Church, 416
African Synod, 278–80
African women's theology, 478
African-American, theology, 410ff.
    Africana theology, 423
    black hermeneutic, 420
    and Christianity, 418
Afro-Caribbean Christians, 100
Afrofuturism, 422
Afropessimism, 422
Afutiti, Levesi, 374
Ahn, John, 442
Akossi-Mvongo, Marguerite, 319
Aleaz, K. P., 182
Allen, Paula Gunn, 407
Alliance for Progress, 118
Al-Liqa' ("Encounter") Center for Religious and Heritage Studies in the Holy Land, 248
Alves, Rubem, 131–32
Amaladoss, 180, 182
Amaloorpavadoss, 180
Ambedkar, B. R., 184
Amir, Yigal, 254
Amoah, Elizabeth, 324
An Asian Theology of Liberation, 223
"An Unfinished Agenda," 353
anattā, 222
Anawati, George, 261
Anderson-Rajkumar, Evangeline, 187
anger, as theologically under-explored and undervalued concept, 491
    in Oceania, 493
    prophetic anger, 492
anthararyamin, 179
anthropological poverty, 282–83
Antonian movement, 316
Anzaldúa, Gloria, 433, 501–2
Aotearoa New Zealand, 357–58, 363, 367
    history of, 360
Appasamy, 179
Aquino, María Pilar, 140–42
Arabome, Anne, 319
Aranda people from Central Australia, 388
Arrupe, Pedro, 390
Asante, Molefi Kete, 316
ashram, 179
Asian,
    immigration, 437
    meanings of, 436
    migrants, 437, 440
Asian-American,
    basic trends in, 440ff.
    Catholic theology, 447
    Christianity, 439
    feminist theology, 444
    future of, 447
    han, 443, 468
    liminality, 443, 501
    Pentecostal theology, 446
    theologies, 436ff.
    women, 441, 469
Assmann, Hugo, 153, 456
Ateek, Naim Stifan, 247, 249, 255
Atheismusim Christentum, 454
Atleo, Richard, 399
Australia's First Nations Theology, 384
    "dreaming" concept, 387
    racial discrimination, 391
autocratic leadership (Africa), 278

Index of Names and Subjects

avatara, 179
Azariah, M., 185

Báez-Camargo, Gonzalo, 127
Bahkti marga, 179
Balasuriya, Tissa, 225–26
Balfour Declaration, 250
Bama, 185
Bandung: Journal of the Global South, 22
Banerjee, K. M., 178
Bates Stuart C., *Inculturation and Healing*, 482
Bechealany, Souraya, 261
Behind the Words, 156
Benedict XVI, Pope, 273
Bhabha, Homi, 42
"big men/strong men" scenario (Africa), 278
Bird, Cliff, 340, 350
Black Lives Matter movement, 419
black spirituality, 415, 417
black transhumanism, 422
Blood Brothers: The Dramatic Story of a Palestinian Christian working for Peace in Israel, 247
Bongmba, Elias K., 477
Bonhoeffer, Dietrich, 257
Bonino, José Miguez, 132
Bonn Center for Dependency and Slavery Studies, 20
Boseto, Lesli, 332
Bowels of Compassion of Jesus, 225
Braga, Erasmo, 126–27
Brahman, 179
Brahmanical traditions, 182
Brazilian Evangelical Confederation, 130
Brown, Wendy, 252
buhoenghoe (revival meetings), 234
Burkhart, Brian Yazzie, 400, 404

Callaghan, Moeawa, 362
Cameron, Graham, 361
Canaan Hymns (Jia'nan Shixuan), 210
Carey Baptist College, 365
Catholic Action, 113, 114
Catholic Patriotic Association (CPA), 207
Catholic Social Tradition/Catholic Social Teaching, 276, 278
CELAM, 121, 124
Center for Christian-Muslim Studies (Lebanon), 262
Centre for Interreligious Dialogue and Research, 224
Centre for Society and Religion in Sri Lanka, 226
Ceylon, 218

Chacour, Elias, 247
Chakkarai, 179
Chandran, Russell, 352
Chenchiah, 179
Cheon, Samuel, 442
Chia, Philip P., 442
Chiapas, Catholic Church in, 162–64, 167, 171–72
Chinafication/Sinicization (*zongjiao Zhongguohua*), 206
Chinese Christologies, 208
    Chalcedonian Christology, 211
    Cosmic Christ, 208, 210
Chinese Congress of World Evangelism, 214
Cho, David Yonggi (Paul), 232
Cho, Grace M., 497
Cho, Yonggi, 86–87, 89
Chosen Peoples, 310
Christ-for-All Evangelistic Ministries, 82–83
Christian Institute for the Study of Religion and Society (CISRS), 183
"Christian Korea," 237
    mega churches, 237
    three-self principle, 237
Christian scholars (*Jidutuxueren*), 207
Christian Zionism, 250–53
Christianity fever (*Jidujiao re*), 206
Christianity in the Pacific Context," 334
Christianity
    culture, and, 14
    dialogue, need for, 14–17
    growth of, 7
    movement to the south, 12
Chun, Malcolm Nāea, 372
Church and Society Movement, 124, 127
Church of North India, 182
Church of South India, 182
Church of the Poor, 116, 121, 123
Church, response to culture, 12–14,
Church's Sector of Social Responsibility, 130–31
Circle of Concerned African Women Theologians, 315, 317
Civil Rights Movement, 413
Clark, Sathianathan, 185
Clooney, Francis, 54
Coconut Theology and Sione 'Amanaki Havea, 351, 373
Cohen, Robin, 496
colonialism, 9; destructive nature of, 393, 475ff.
colonial-settler societies in the Global South, 487
Commission on Church and Society (ISAL—Iglesia y Sociedad), 124
Conde-Frazier, Elizabeth, 140–41

Cone, James, 417, 420
contextual theology. 2
contribution of Global South Christians, 489
Coptic Orthodox Church, 287
Corbon, Jean, 261
Costas, Orlando, 133
Couch, Beatriz Melano, 133
Cox, Harvey, 80
Cross-cultural, 52–53
cultural Christians (*wenhua Jidutu*), 207
cultural imperialism, 427

Dalit theology, 180, 182, 184–85
Dangun myth, 233–34
Dao theology, 210
Dar al-Kalima University College of Arts and Culture, 252
Davidson, Allen, 333
Dayam, Joseph Prabjakar, 185
de Alba, Klor, 169
De Gruchy, John, 477,
de Gruchy, Steve, 481
De La Torre, Miguel, 40–41, 432
de Silva, Lynn A., 222
Declaration of Independence, 413
"Declaration of the Korean National Council of Churches toward the Unification and Peace of the Korean People," 242–43
decolonizing/inculturation theology, 316
Delgado Teresa, 144, 426
Deloria Jr., Vine, 408
Devanandan, P. D., 180, 182, 183
Devasahayam, V., 185
Dhamma-dipa, 218
Dharmapala, Anagarika 218
diakonia, 1
Dialogue, 224
dialogue, need for. *See* Christianity
diaspora, 495
    categories of historic diasporas, 496
    colonial and imperial, 498
    diasporic consciousness, 496, 502–3
    exile differing from diaspora, 496
Díaz, Miguel H., 426
Dietrich, Gabriele, 187
DiLorenzo, Bishop Francis, 379
Diyar Consortium, 265
Diyar publishing house, 252
Dodson, Patrick, 388
Doing Catholic Theological Ethics in a Cross Cultural and Interreligious Asian Context, 465
Douglass, Frederick, 416
Dred Scott v. Sanford, 412

Dube, Musa, 307, 316, 320, 322, 478

Earl, Riggins, 415
Ebola Virus Disease, 481
ecclesiolastical theological disputes, 458
Ecological Framework for Development, 355
ecology (African), 274
eco-theology, 187
Ecumenical Association of Third World Theologians (EATWOT), 9–10, 57–58, 206, 226, 352–53
Ecumenical Institute for Study and Dialogue, 223
Ecumenical Institute Tantur (Jerusalem), 248
ecumenical movement, 59–60
Elizondo, Virgilio, 102
Ella, Jean-Marc, 282–83, 304–6, 324
epistemic. *See* global south
Espín, Orlando O., 136–37, 146–47, 426
Esther, Comandanta, 168–69
Ete, Risatisone, 337, 340
ethics, 61–62
Eurocentric
    arrogance of conscience, 407
    theologies, 9–10
    thinking, 432
Evangelical Consultation on Pacific Theology, 333
Evangelical Theological Seminary (Cairo), 263
ever-generating God (*shengsheng Shen*), 209
explicit theology, 446

Faith and Order Commission (WCC), 248
Faith in the Face of Empire, 253
Farag, Gihan, 263
feminist/womanist theology, 186–87
Fire and Water, 223
First International Symposium on Palestinian Liberation Theology, 249
First Special Assembly for Africa of the Synod of Bishops, 276
Fixico, Donald, 404
folk Christianity (Korea), 233
Foskett, Mary F., 442
Francis, Pope, 67, 69–70, 254, 255
Freire, Paulo, 156, 367, 458, 461
French Dominicans, 114
French-speaking Catholics, 275
Friedli, Richard, 53
From the Deep: Pacific Voices for a New Story, 355
"From the Nile to the Euphrates: A Statement on Christian Responsibility and Citizenship Law," 265
Full Gospel Church (Seoul), 232

Index of Names and Subjects

Ganadason, Aruna, 187
Gandhi, M. K., 178
Geertz, Clifford, 53
General Assembly of the Fellowship of the Middle East Evangelical Churches, 262
geographical. *See* global south
George, Samuel, 188
Gibbs, Philip, 340
Gideon, Rohan, 188
Global Ethics, 54
global south, 7–12, 20–33
    epistemic, 24
    flexible, 23–24
    geographical, 22
    and global north dichotomoy, 487
    structural, 22–23
    subaltern, 23
globalization, 62
    impact of in the Oceania region, 489
Gondarra, Djiniyini, 389
Gonzalez Michelle A., 426
González, Justo L., 433
Griffiths, Bede, 179
Guadalupe, 430–31
Guerrero, Andrés G., 426
Guise, John, 331–32
Gunson, Neil, 333
Gutiérrez, Gustavo, 119, 124–25, 397–98

Halapua, Winston, 375–76
Hall-Smith, Beverley Moana, 363
Ham Sok Hon, 231
Han, Kook-il, 241
Hart-Celler Act, known as the Immigration and Nationality Act, 438
Harvesting from Asian Soil, 464
Havea, Jione, 373
Havea, Sione Amanaki, 331–32, 334–38
Helin, Calvin, 405
hermeneutics,
    post-colonial, 442
    pre-colonial, 385
Hick, John, 54
Hiebert, Paul G., 81
Hiller, Helga, 267
Hinga, Teresia M., 326
Hio-Kee, Samuel, 81
Hnuni, L., 187
Hollenweger, Walter, 53
hospitality. *See* liberation theology
Hrangthan, Chungi, 186
Huggan, Graham, 38–39

I am a Palestinian Christian, 247

Iglesia y Sociedad en América Latina, 131
Ikechukwu, Paulinus, 480
Iliffe, John, 281
Imchen, Narola, 187
inculturation, 3
    theology, 2, 3
Indian-hyphenated-Christian, 178
Indigenous,
    binary dualisms, 405
    experiential/embodied/lived knowledge, 403
    moral universe, 402
    relationship-based, 401
    theological voices, 487
    theology/indigenization, 2
    ways of knowing/epistemologies, 397–98, 400, 408
Institute of the Public Theology and Church (IPTC), 235
missio trinitatis, 235
intercultural theology, 2
    definition, 54
    dialogical, 56–57
    hermeneutic, 54
    identicatory, 56
interfaith dialogue, 470
International Association of Tamil Research, 222
International Movement of Catholic Students—International Young Catholic Students. 117–18
interreligious dialogue, 57–58
Intifada, 249, 251, 255
Isaiah 19 prophecies concerning Egypt, 289–300
Isasi-Díaz, Ada María, 141–43, 427
Ishwar (God), 179

Jacobs, Cindy, 89
Jang, Shin-geun, 235
Jenkins, Phillip, 274
Jeong, Jae-young, 236
Jeremiah, Anderson, 185
Jesus Christ and Human Liberation, 225
jiatingjuhui (house church), 212
Jin Tianming, 213
Jin, Aloysius Luxian, 209, 212
Jingyi, Cheng, 211
John Paul II, Pope, 122, 254, 255, 460
John XXIII, Pope, 454–55
John, V. J., 188
Jones, Charles Colock, 415
Jones, Stanley, 179
Joy, Elizabeth, 187
Justice and Only Justice. A Palestinian Theology of Liberation, 247

Index of Names and Subjects

Kafeety, Samir, 261
Kairos Document, 255–57
    Palestinian, 255–57, 264
    South African, 255
Kaiwhakaako, 365
Kanyaro, Rachel Angogo, 317, 326
Kassab, Najla, 263
Kassis, Rifat Odeh, 255
Katongole, Emmanuel, 276, 280
Kattan, Elias, 265
Kaunda, Chammah J., 338, 340
kenosis, 225
Kerr, Sandy, 365
Khodr, George, 261
Khoury, Geries, 248
Kim, Jean K., 442
Kim, Jin-ho, 237
Kim, Seong-geon, 237
Kim, Uriah Yong-Hwan, 442
Kim, Young-dong, 241–42
Kimpa Vita, Beatrice, 316–17, 322, 326
King, Eileen, 267
King, Jr., Martin, 420, 454
Kingdom Culture On-line School, 84–85
kingdom of God, 83–84
Kirdi people, 283
Kiribati, 338
Kithusara, 227
Knitter, Paul, 54
Kole Village on East Coast Santo in northern Vanuatu, 345
Korea National Council of Churches (KNCC), 242
Korean diaspora churches. 239–40
Korean mission theology, 240–41
Kremer, Hendrik, 179
Kumari, Prasanna, 187
Küng, Hans, 54
Kwok, Pui-lan, 210, 211

Laham, Albert, 261
Lalitha, Jayachitra, 185
Lamb, Samuel (Lin Xiangao), 210
land, theology import of, 344, 360
    and Latinx theology, 432
language, 1–2
Lankan theology, 217
Las Abejas, 171
Lasetso, Razouselie, 186
Latina feminist theologies, 426
Latinx, 425
    ethics, 431–32
    hybridity, 428–29
    and Latin American liberation theologies, 425
    mestizaje, 428
    theological themes, 428ff.
    variety of Latinx theologies, 426
Laudatosi: On Care for Our Common Home (Pope Francis), 464–65
Lausanne Movement, 206
Le Saux, Henri (Abhishiktananda), 179
Lee, Andrew Yueking, 442
Lee, Hu-cheon, 241
Lee, Won-kyu, 238
Leonardo Boff, Leonardo, 460
LGBTQ liberation theology, 307–9
liberation theology, 19, 67–75
    dialogue, 183
    hospitality, 71–72
    Oceania's distinctive, 351, 453, 470
    solidarity, 72–75
lo cotidiano, 142–44
Longchar, Wati, 186
Longkumer, Limatulla, 186–87
López, Alfred J., 23
Love Meets Wisdom, 223
Lowi, Michel, 153
Löwy, Michael, 125
Lü, Ruth (Lü Xiaomin), 210
Ludovic, Lado Tonlieu, 481
Lushombo, Léocadie Wabo, 321–22

Mahmood Mamdani, *Citizen and Subject*, 477
Māori, culture, 347
    prophetic movements, 364
    theology, 357–58, 365–67
Māoripūrākau (origin narratives), 358–62
Marathi, 179
marginalization, 427
Margull, Hans Jochen, 53
Marsden, Māori, 362
Martell-Otero, Loida I., 140, 426
Marxism, 114–15
Mary and Human Liberation, 225
Masena, Loreen, 321
Massey, James, 185
Massouh, Georges, 262
Mātauranga Māori, 361
Matt 25:35, 71
Maurer, Eugenio, 168
Mayangja, Evelyn Namakula, 481
Mbiti, John, 325
meaning making, principle of right action in, 404
Medellín conference, 455–56
Mencian Confucianism, 208

Index of Names and Subjects

mestizaje/mulatez, 138–1391, 41–142
Midan Al-Tahrir (Square of Liberty), 287
Middle East Council of Churches, 261
Mignolo, Walter, 39
migration, 63–64, 104–5
Mikhael, Mary, 262
Millennium Pilgrimage to the Holy Land, 254
minjung theology, 233, 468; *han*, 233
Minz, Nirmal, 186
Miranda, José Porfirio, 457
missioadgentes [mission to peoples] and *missio cum gentibus* [mission with others], 471
Moana, people, 370–71
   theology, 370, 382
Moananui, 361
Modernity/Coloniality/Decoloniality project (MCD), 44
moksha, 179
Molina, Raúl Sánchez, 69
Moltmann, Jürgen, 256–57, 461
Mong, Ambrose, 183
Morisada Rietz, Henry W., 442
Mourbarak, Youakim, 261
Mugambi, Jesse N. K., 477
Mullivaikkal, 228
multi-cultural, 52
Munther, Isaac, 252
Muslim Brotherhood, 288
Mveng, Engelberg, 282, 321, 322
myths, 166

Nadar, Sarojini, 320
Nakba ("catastrophe" 1948), 247
Nalunakkal, George Matthew, 188
Nasimiyu, Anne, 325
National Conference of Black Churchmen (NCBC), 420
National Evangelical Synod of Syria and Lebanon, 262
Nayagam, Thani, 221
Nayar, Pramod K., 43
Near East School of Theology (NEST), 262–63
Neo-Calvinist theology, 207, 213
neo-colonialism, 217
Nevius principle, 237
New Zealand Land Wars, 364, 367
Ng, David, 214
Ngan, Lai Ling Elizabeth, 442
Nirmal, A. P., 185
Nirvana, 222
Njoroge, Nyambura J., 315
North American Congress of Chinese Evangelicals, 214

Oceania Centre for Arts in the University of the South Pacific, 354
Oceania,
   emergent theologies of, 371
   oral cultures of, 373
   peoples of, 373
   theology, 344, 354
Oduyoye, Mercy Amba, 59, 307–8, 314–15, 318–19, 321, 322, 323–24, 326, 478
Ojo, Matthew, 96–97
Okure, Teresa, 320–22
Oliyai Nokki, 227
Ong, Benjamin, 366
Onyinah, Opoku, 84, 89
Opium Wars, 211
Orientalism, 180, 260
Orientalist gaze, 218
Orji, Cyril, 276
Orobator, A. E., 319
Ortega-Aponte, Elías, 427
Oslo Peace Accord, 254
overcoming exclusion, 467

Pacific Conference of Churches (PCC) Assembly (1976), 331–32
Pacific Indigenous Peoples' Struggle for Land and Identity, 352
Pacific Island Christians, 489
Pacific Prayer for the Moana, 375
Pacific Theological College, 352
Palestinian Liberation Organization (PLO), 254
Pali texts, 218
Palu, Ma'afu, 339–40
pan-African vision, 310
Panama Conference of 1916, 126
pandemic, 63
Panikkar, 180, 182
Pathil, 182
Paul VI, Pope, 254
Paul, K. T., 183
Paulose, Paulose Mar, 183
Paunga, Mikaele, 337
peasantry, 218
Pentecostalization of African Christianity, 303
Pew Forum on Religion and Public Life, 274
Phan, Peter, 71
Pieris, Aloysius, 182, 223, 224
Pieris, Rasika, 227–28
Pineda-Madrid, Nancy, 140, 144–45, 426
Pinheiro Baptist Church, 149–51, 158, 160–61
Pio, Hamiora, 365
Planetary Theology, 225
Polak, Regina, 72–73
post-nationalist nationalism, 310

Index of Names and Subjects

Prabhkar, M. E., 185
Premnath, Devadasan N., 442
Presbyterian University and Theological Seminary (Seoul). 235
prophetic anger, 486ff.
prosperity gospel, 85–87
Protestant Three-Self Patriotic Movement (TSPM), 207
Pui-lan, Kwok, 322, 501

Rabin, Yitzhak, 254
racial discrimination and legislative acts:
    Gentlemen's Agreement (1907), 438
    Asiatic Barred Zone Act (1917), 438
    Johnson-Reed Act (1924), 438
racial triangulation, 445
racism, 413
Radhkrishnan, S., 178
Rae, Murray, 361
Raheb, Mitri, 247, 252–53, 255
Rajkumar, Peniel, 185
Rakena, Ruawai, 381
Rakoczy, Susan and eco-feminism, 483
Ralte, Lalrinawmi, 187
Ramakrishna, 178
Ramanuja, 179
Reddy, Anthony, 492
religion, definition, 164
reverse mission, 97–98
"Reweaving the Ecological Mat," 354
Rhee, Hyung-ki, 235
Richard, Pablo, 151–52, 154
Rika, Maisey, 377
Rivera, Mayra Rivera, 145
Roberts, J. J. M., 294
Rockefeller Report, 120
Rodrigo, Michael, 224–25, 227
Rodriguez, Jose David, 426
Rodríguez, Rubén Rosario, 428
Roman Catholic Patriarch of Jerusalem, 250
Romero, Archbishop Oscar Arnulfo, 477
Roy, Ram Mohan, 178
Ruatara, 358
Rubow, Cecil, 340
Ruiz, Don Samuel, 162–63, 165
Rutagambwa, Elisee, 280
Rwanda Genocide, 280
Ryu, Dong-sik, 233

Sabbagh, Mathilde, 262
Sabbah, Michel, 250–51, 255
Sabeel Ecumenical Liberation Theology Center, 249–50

Sacred Congregation for the Doctrine of the Faith, 460
Said, Edward, 42, 180
Saint Thomas, apostle, 177
sakyeunghoe (Bible conferences), 234
Samartha, Stanley, 180, 182
Samir, Samit Kahlil, 261
Samoan tradition, 374, 377
Samuel, Joshua, 185
Sanneh, Lamin, 54
Sanskritic captivity, 180
Sanskritization, 186
Sarras, Niveen, 263
Sastriar, Vedanayagam, 179
sat-chitananda (truth-conciousness-bliss), 179
Sattal Christian Ashram, 179
Schneider, Nina, 21, 23–26, 32
schools, theological, 8, 11
Schussler-Fiorenza, Elisabeth, 158–59
Second Conference of the Latin American Episcopate, 116–17
Second Vatican Council. See Vatican II
second world. See global south
Segovia, Fernando, 13, 15n59
Segundo, Juan Luis, 460
Selvanayagam, Israel, 182
seminaries. See schools, theological
Sen, K. C., 178, 179
Senyonjo, Christopher, 309
Seoul Olympics (1988), 239
Separation Wall, 252, 255–56
Shabako (Pharoah), 295
Shakti, 186
shared racial experience, 437
Sharon, Ariel, 255
Shaull, Richard, 129–30, 132
Shimray, S., 186
Shouwang Church (Beijing), 213
    third church/third way, 213
Singh, Sadhur Sundar, 178
Sinhala, 218–23; ethnic group, 218
Sino-Christian theology (*Hanyushenxue*), 207, 210, 212
Sleiman, Rola, 262
Smith, Linda Tuhiwai, 401
solidarity. See, liberation theology
Solivan, Samuel, 426
Song, C. S., 211
Sonia Ryang, stages of Koreans' transformation, 499ff.
South Korean missionaries, 100–101
South Sudan civil war, 310
Southern Boom, 274–75; Anglophone Catholics, 275

523

Index of Names and Subjects

spirit ancestors, 391–93
spirit world, 81–82
Spivak, Gayatri, 42–43
structural. *See* global south
Student Christian Movement, 128–30
Studies in the Intercultural History of Christianity, 53
subaltern. *See* global south
subversive memories, 457
Sugirtharajah, R. S., 39, 46–47, 180–81
Suh, David Kwang-sun, 243
Suh, Nam-dong, 233
Sundkler, Bengt, 476

Talitha cum hermeneutics, 322
Talua Ministry Training Centre in Vanutu, 348
Tamez, Elsa, 153
Tamil, 218–23
    culture, 222
    names of God, 221
    Tamil Eelam, 219
    theological features, 221
Tang, Edmond, 209
Tangaroa, 377
    oral traditions of, 377
Tao and Logos, 233
Taprobane (Sri Lanka), 217
Tarek, Mitri, 265
Taringa, Nisbert Taisekwa, 483
Taylor, Charles, 11
TePaiperaTapu (the Māori language Bible), 365
terrorism, 63
Thanzauva, 186
The Baptizer, 223–24
"The Church Mission Today in the Middle East," 261
The Coming of God, 257
The Eucharist and Human Liberation, 225
The Global South, 20–21
"The Meaning of Jerusalem for Christians," 252
The Myth of Christian Uniqueness, 54
The Politics of Persecution, 253
"The Religious Instruction of the Negroes in the United States (1842)," 415
The Sacrifice of Africa: A Political Theology for Africa, 276
The Will to Arise, 326
Theology and Sexuality (journal of), 309
Theology and the Local Church in the Holy land: Palestinian Contextualized Theology, 248
Theology Brewed in an African Pot, 273
Theology of Hope, 256
Theology of Liberation, 456
Theology of unification, 243

theology, contextualizing of, 350–51
    western, 9–10
TheresKloß, Sinah, 20–21, 24, 26–27, 31–32
Thiandoum, Hyacinthe, 276
third world. *See* global south
Thomas, M. M., 182, 183
three-fold blessing (Korean), 232
Tiananmen Square democracy movement, 207
Tilak, N. V., 179
time, circular concepts of, 403
Timon, Tioti, 338, 340
Ting, K. H., 208. 209, 210, 212
Tinker, George, 393, 397
Tombs, David, 133–34
tongseonggido (group prayer), 234
Torres, Sergio, 58–59
Tran, Mai Anh Le, 442
transcultural, 53
translation, 2
tribal theology, 185–86
Troeltsch, Ernst, 212–13
    church-type (*da jiaohui* or *Kirche*), 212
    mysticism (*shenmizhuyi* or *Mytik*), 212
    sect-type (*xiao jiaopai* or *Sekt*), 212
Tutu, Desmond, 309
Tuwere, Illaitia Sevati, 352

Universal Church of the Kingdom of God, 88, 90
Unmasking the African Ghost: Theology, Politics, and the Nightmare of Failed States, 276
Upadhyaya, Brahmabandhav, 178, 179
Uva-Wellassa, 224–25
Uwineza, Marcel, 280–81

Vaai, Upolu Luma, 349, 379–81
Vaai, Upolu, 340
Vāgdevi, 224
Vanutu, islands of, 346
Vashum, Yangkahao, 186
Vatican II, 2, 115–16, 123, 179, 182, 248, 454
Veeraraj, Anand, 188
Villa Vicencio, Charles, 480
Villafane, Eldin, 432
Vinayaraj, Y. T., 185
Vishishta Advaita, 179
Vivekananda, 178
Währisch-Oblau, Claudia, 82–83
Walsh and Mignolo, 43, 45, 47
Walsh, Sánchez, 146
Wan, Enoch, 95–96, 210
Wan, Sze-kar, 442
Wanjiru, Margaret, 325
Ware, Frederick, 420
Waters, Anne, 405

"We choose a life in abundance—Christians the Middle East," 266
We Choose Abundant Life, 268
Weifan, Wang, 209, 210
Welby, Justin, Archbishop of Canterbury, 488
Werner Ustorf, 53
western captivity of the gospel, 178
Whakawhanaungatangaingā Hāhi o Aotearoa (Council of Māori Churches), 367
"What is Required of the Christian Faith Concerning the Palestinian Problem," 260–61
white man's burden, 218
White, Carol Wayne, 416
Wilfred, Felix, 185
Wilmore, Gayraud, 419
Winkel, Heidemarie, 267
womanist theology, 421
Women's Commission of the Ecumenical Association of Third World Theologians, 470
World Communion of Reformed Churches (WCRC), 263
World Conference on Xenophobia Racism and Populist Nationalism (2018), 489
World Council of Churches, 182, 235, 242
World Day of Prayer (WDP), 267
World Mission Conference of Edinburgh in 1910, 2
World Missionary Conference (1938), 126, 179
Wright, Delora Jan, 13

Xi Jinping, 206
Xiaofeng, Liu, 212, 213
Xiaoping, Deng, 206
    reform and opening up policy, 205

Yamada, Frand M., 442
yangjiao (foreign religion), 211
Yee, Gale A., 442
Yellow Peril, 437
Yieh, ohn Yueh-Han J., 442
Yim, Sung-bihn, 236
Yonan, Makary, 287
Yong, Amos, 446
Yoon, Chul-ho, 236
youth revolt, 220
Yuan, Allen (Yuan Xiangchen), 210
Yun, Sung-beom, 233

Zachariah, George, 188
Zaki, Anne, 263
Zhuo Xinping, 210

Milton Keynes UK
Ingram Content Group UK Ltd.
UKHW051635050724
445232UK00015B/54